# PLANNING THE TWENTIETH-CENTURY CITY

To Tony Sutcliffe and the
memory of Gordon Cherry

# PLANNING THE TWENTIETH-CENTURY CITY

## THE ADVANCED CAPITALIST WORLD

Stephen V. Ward

JOHN WILEY & SONS, LTD

OTHER WILEY EDITORIAL OFFICES

John Wiley & Sons, Inc., 605 Third Avenue, New York, NY 10158-0012, USA

WILEY-VCH Verlag GmbH, Pappelallee 3, D-69469 Weinheim, Germany

John Wiley & Sons Australia Ltd, 33 Park Road, Milton, Queensland 4064, Australia

John Wiley & Sons (Asia) Pte Ltd, 2 Clementi Loop #02-01, Jin Xing Distripark, Singapore 129809

John Wiley & Sons (Canada) Ltd, 22 Worcester Road, Rexdale, Ontario M9W 1L1, Canada

**Photo credits**: Author's photographs: 2.2, 2.4, 2.7, 2.8, 3.2, 3.3, 3.5, 3.7, 3.8, 4.1, 4.3, 4.4, 4.5, 4.8, 5.4, 5.6, 6.1, 6.2, 6.5, 6.7, 7.2, 8.2, 8.4, 8.6, 8.8, 9.1, 9.2, 9.3, 9.6, 9.7, 9.8, 10.1, 10.3, 10.4, 10.5, 10.6, 10.7, 10.8, 10.9, 11.1, 11.2, 11.3, 11.4, 11.5, 11.7, 11.8. Author's collection: 3.1, 3.4, 3.6, 4.2, 4.6, 4.7, 4.9, 5.2, 5.3, 5.5, 5.7, 6.3, 6.9, 7.1, 7.3, 7.4, 7.6, 7.7, 8.1, 8.5, 8.7, 9.4. Her Majesty's Stationery Office: 6.4, 8.3. Princeton University Press: 2.1. Fundació Catalana per a la Recerca: 2.3. Phaidon Press: 2.5. Bournville Village Trust: 2.6. Netherlands Architecture Institute: 5.1. Maggie Ward: 6.6. National Building Museum: 6.8. Courtesy of Thomas Hall: 7.5. Courtesy of K. Bosma and H. Hellinga: 9.5. Struthers Advertising (Mr Happy copyright Mrs Roger Hargreaves): 10.2. Greater Vancouver Regional District: 11.6.

**Cover**: World Centre of Communication, proposed in 1913 by Hendrik Christian Andersen and Ernest Hébrard.

ISBN 0-471-49098-9

Typeset in 9/11pt Caslon 224 from the author's disks by Mayhew Typesetting, Rhayader, Powys
Printed and bound in Great Britain by TJ International Ltd, Padstow, Cornwall

This book is printed on acid-free paper responsibly manufactured from sustainable forestry, in which at least two trees are planted for each one used for paper production.

# CONTENTS

# THE AUTHOR

Stephen V Ward is Professor of Planning History at Oxford Brookes University. He is President of the International Planning History Society (1996–2002), a former editor of the society's magazine, *Planning History*, and has recently become editor of the associated journal *Planning Perspectives*. He has written widely on planning history and related topics. His previous books include *The Geography of Interwar Britain* (1988), *The Garden City* (editor, 1992), *Planning and Urban Change* (1994) and *Selling Places* (1998). He is married with three children and lives in Grandpont, Oxford.

# ACKNOWLEDGEMENTS

I must begin by thanking the council of the International Planning History Society who in 1996, following the premature death of the society's founding president, Gordon Cherry, chose me as his successor. When I discovered exactly what the role involved, I realised that I needed to know far more about the evolution of planning throughout the world than I did at the time. To fill in the many gaps in my knowledge, I decided to undertake a crash course of personal education. I read everything I could find on planning history throughout the world. I must here thank the School of Planning and the library at Oxford Brookes University for allowing me to buy or gain easy access to so much of the relevant material. Presidential duties and other opportunities also allowed me to visit more countries and to see more of their planning efforts at first hand. Again I express my gratitude to the School of Planning at Brookes, for funding some of these research trips and further enabling me to explore several cities as part of student field visits. I must also thank those who gave funded invitations to speak in other countries, another important facilitator for my own cross-national learning. In addition, the Canadian High Commission generously funded a very formative summer of research in Vancouver in 1996.

Gradually, I realised that it might be useful to put all this work to some wider use. The idea of a book coalesced during 1997 and Wiley duly issued a contract, little knowing quite how much time would elapse before it would be fulfilled. Maggie Toy, Abigail Grater and their predecessor, Tristan Palmer, at Wiley showed unwavering faith in the project; patience when it failed to materialise by several promised deadlines; flexibility at various changes in the scope and form of the book; and, not least, efficiency in putting together the final product. It is appropriate here also to thank Rob Woodward of Brookes for his assistance with preparing the illustrations.

For their help in understanding the subject matter of this book, deep thanks are owed to fellow planning-historians or others who gave their time in various ways. Such have been the number of encounters, personal and electronic, which have helped to enlarge and focus my thinking that it is simply not possible to list them all. The following, however, have rendered special assistance in a variety of ways and should be thanked individually: Genie Birch, Jeff Cody, Friedhelm Fischer, Robert Freestone, Christine Garnaut, David Hedgcock, Thomas Hall, Carola Hein, Alan Hutchings, Liisa Knuuti, Laura Kolbe, Michael Lang, Barrie Melotte, Javier Monclús, Joe Nasr, the late Kermit (KC) Parsons, Ursula von Petz, Johan Rådberg, Pierre-Yves Saunier, Dirk Schubert, David Schuyler, Mercedes Volait, and David Wood. Naturally, none of them bear any responsibility for the ways I have used the material I gleaned as a result of their efforts.

The biggest debts, which I leave until the end, are of two kinds. First are those to my family. The emotional and practical support provided, once again, by my much-loved wife, Maggie, has been fundamental. Without her, I could never have done this. Our children Tom, Rosamund and Alice, despite the many pressures on their own lives as they go through the transition to adulthood, have also given me the personal space and support to allow this book to be written.

My final debt is, though, an academic one. Uniquely, I think, I was taught at the University of Birmingham in the late 1960s and 1970s by both Tony Sutcliffe and the late Gordon Cherry. The experience was doubly formative and was reinforced by subsequent regular contacts with both of them as they became the founding fathers of the international planning history network. It is no exaggeration to say that they have directly and indirectly shaped my academic interests and career. As a young student, I would never have believed how closely I would subsequently follow in their footsteps, tragically so in Gordon's case. The debt to them both will be obvious in the pages that follow. It is, therefore, both fitting and a pleasure to dedicate this book to them.

Stephen V Ward
Oxford, July 2001

## A NOTE ON TERMINOLOGY

A book such as this, dealing with both specific and national experiences and the formation of an international discourse of urban planning, raises important issues of terminology. Although some terms, most notably 'urban planning', are generic, so far as possible I have tried to use the specific planning terms coined or adopted in each country. In discussing non-Anglophone countries, however, it has obviously been necessary to give and use English translations of these terms. In such cases, I have also tried to show how close or distant the underlying concept is to that conveyed by the English words.

A specific problem arises in dealing with Anglophone countries, particularly the United States and Britain, well known for being 'divided by a common language'. In general, I have followed the preferred planning terminology of each country without 'translating' it into a standard version of English. This means that some things which are the same actually have different names, and some things which are different have the same names. For example, American 'row housing' = English 'terraced housing'; 'public transit' = 'public transport'; and 'transportation = 'transport'. However, the American 'greenbelt' towns are not the same as British 'green belts' and even 'city planning' differs slightly from 'town planning'. Reader beware!

# CHAPTER 1

# INTRODUCTION

The 20th century was the most brutal and destructive hundred-year period in human history. More people were killed in its wars, large and small, than in any other century. At times, the will to destruction was so immensely overpowering that the very future of human life seemed to be threatened. Yet, at the same time, it was also the most civilising and creative of centuries. Many of the very technological advances that facilitated destruction also fed world economic growth on a scale never before seen. Huge improvements in agricultural efficiency and medical knowledge meanwhile allowed an unprecedented increase in world population, from perhaps 1.6 billion in 1900 to about 6.1 billion in 2000. By then over 3 billion people lived in cities, compared to perhaps 250 million in 1900. Cities everywhere have been the engines and the symbols of economic growth, intensifying production, distribution and consumption. Too often, however, large parts of them were, and remain, deeply unsatisfactory settings for human life.

Generally speaking, though, the richest nations of the world have also been those with the biggest proportions of their populations living in urban areas. It is not surprising therefore that, during the 20th century, the affluent nations devoted so much attention to ameliorating and, indeed, trying to perfect the city. The underlying aim was to reconcile its economic dynamism with its other roles as a social, cultural and political entity. By 1914, these efforts were sufficiently developed in most advanced capitalist countries to warrant being given a specific name, such as *Städtebau*, town planning, *urbanisme*, city planning, *stedebouw*, *toshi keikatu* or *urbanismo*. Despite this proliferation of nomenclature, however, each nation did not autonomously evolve the ideas which lay behind the various labels. Almost from the outset there was a vigorous cross-national interchange of ideas and practice. No single international label ever emerged but we use the generic term 'urban planning' when signifying this growing international body of thought and practice. Of course, the notion of consciously shaping the physical form and disposition of the urban environment was not itself without historical precedent. What was new to the late 19th and, more especially, the 20th centuries, was the idea of making urban planning an integral part of capitalist urban development within broadly liberal and democratic societies.

The story of how this happened forms the central concern of this book. It is, in other words, a wide and long survey of the development of urban planning in the advanced capitalist world during the 20th century. Its main concern is to explain how, where and why urban planning thought and practice developed and spread throughout western Europe, North America, Australia and Japan.

## NARRATIVES, GRAND AND OTHERWISE

The ambition of this aim is self-evident. An earlier generation of urban-planning historians and commentators, such as Mumford (1961), Korn (1953) and Benevolo

(1980), were not afraid of such grand sweeps of historical writing. Yet despite (or perhaps, in part, because of) the recent expansion of scholarship in planning history, few other individual scholars have initiated comparable international syntheses or overviews in recent years. Conspicuous and important exceptions have been Anthony Sutcliffe (1981), Thomas Hall (1986; 1997), Tony King (1990), Gerd Albers (1997) and Donatello Calabi (2000). Much the boldest, and deservedly the best known, of this recent crop of 'grand narrators' is Peter Hall (1988; 1998), whose outstanding research and writing skills (and sheer energy) put him in a class by himself. Even he, though, like all the others, is obliged to insert limitations of period, subject focus and geographical area. There are limits as to what any individual, however remarkable, can encompass. It seems only to be collective works, most relevantly here Arnold Whittick's *Encyclopaedia of Urban Planning* (1980), that are able to come close to transcending such constraints.

## LIMITS OF THE BOOK

The present work certainly cannot avoid such narrowing. Considerations of coherence, length and manageability require that some bounds be set. Limitations of personal knowledge, understanding and linguistic range impose further constraints of a more arbitrary nature. The result is that the following pages focus on the countries of the advanced capitalist world. With occasional exceptions, the story is principally that of the large and, in planning terms, more innovative countries of northern and western Europe, together with the United States, Japan, Canada and Australia. It was in these countries, certainly, that what have been the world's most pervasive forms of 20th-century urban planning were developed and most fully elaborated.

Yet the gaps are large, and important. Absent, apart from faint echoes in the last two countries named and occasional passing comment, are the colonial and developing worlds. Also absent are the Communist or former Communist worlds. Even in western Europe, certain gaps are apparent. Spread across the periodised chapter structure, the reader will find the 20th-century planning histories of Germany, France and Britain recounted in some detail, along with that of the United States. Those of the Netherlands, the Nordic countries and Spain are also told continuously, but in lesser detail, as are those of Japan, Canada and Australia. Italy, Belgium and Austria appear rather more intermittently, reflecting their shorter periods in the international 'limelight'. Other countries feature only fleetingly, despite the fact that some, for example Switzerland, hold more interest than this brevity of treatment would suggest.

## THE TROUBLE WITH GRAND NARRATIVES

Even with omissions, however, the geographical spread is wide and the chronological coverage ambitious. The mere act of putting many different national (and local) experiences together between book covers does not itself give coherence. For the sanity of the author and convenience of the reader, there have to be some unifying elements that give a cohesive structure or, more simply, a plot line to the narrative. In some respects, the stronger this plot line, or the grander the narrative which is attempted, the better. It is always tempting in such circumstances to smooth out the bumps, moulding the presentation of detail to tell a clear and vivid story that will, perhaps, appeal to some half-formed sentiment in the minds of readers. Vividness and clarity have a price, however, because in varying degrees they deny the detail and variety of specific national and local experiences, the messy reality of how things actually happened. Not infrequently they also betray a desire to construct the story in simple moral terms, with heroes to be cheered and villains to be hissed. In writing about urban planning, we need look no further than Lewis Mumford (1961) and Peter Hall (1988) to find the garden city's inventor Ebenezer Howard and the arch-modernist Le Corbusier cast in these respective roles. (With admirable fairness, Jane Jacobs (1964) sees both of them, and indeed virtually all other planners, as villains.)

The more perceptive grand narrators are usually well aware of what they are doing, seeing the definition of a larger truth as more important than the many lesser ones that are thereby pushed into the background. Perhaps they are right. Yet, to their less informed readers and followers, there is too much of a subsequent temptation not to let the 'facts' stand in the way of a good story. The narrative, in other words, becomes mistaken for reality rather than simply being one interpretation of it. The starting point for this book is, therefore, a desire to pursue a slightly different course. Its plot line lies closer to the lesser truths and is less reverential towards what have come to be seen as the bigger ones. It derives from the author's value stance as an empirical historian of planning who is profoundly sceptical of generalisations and who values the smaller truths. It also reflects an extended immersion in the work of the many scholars throughout the world whose labours have uncovered many of these smaller truths of the history of urban planning.

## THE MAIN THEMES

But if there is to be no conscious grand narrative, what prevents the story being a mere accumulation of facts? The first part of the answer lies in two related themes which are pursued throughout. These are *innovation*, meaning the creation and adoption of new ideas and practices; and *diffusion*, their spread across international boundaries. It follows that the story is skewed towards those innovations which have had an international resonance. There is also a dynamic quality, emphasising cross-national learning and the points of contact between the urban planning repertoires of different countries. As such, the story omits much that is routine or very specific in national planning experience. Nor does it formally describe or compare the planning systems of different countries. The reader will certainly find ample material to feed such interests. But its main concerns are with the formation, development and international spread of western urban planning ideas and practice.

## INNOVATION AND DIFFUSION

### INNOVATION THEORY AND URBAN PLANNING

In what has become the classic theory of innovation, the first of the key themes, the economic historian Joseph Schumpeter defined it as having two key dimensions

—

(Schumpeter, 1939). The first, and most fundamental, is *invention*, meaning the discovery of new ideas with far-reaching potential. This is only loosely linked to business activity. The second is *innovation* proper, whereby new ideas are adapted, packaged and applied in practical ways. Schumpeter was, of course, interested in innovation in relation to the development of business. He saw innovation proper as the key process, directly integrated into business development and triggered by a restless entrepreneurial pursuit of profit. An obvious question, therefore, is how far this thinking can be applied to urban planning, which is normally organised by the state, ostensibly in the public interest. Profit rates are not, in other words, the central concern (though they may be a constituent factor). Perceptions of the long-term functional requirements of business as a whole have taken precedence over short-term market fluctuations or the priorities of an individual firm. Moreover, other interests beyond business have also influenced innovation to varying degrees. Movements within civil society, sometimes directly informed or inspired by the original inventors, have usually steered or prodded the innovation process.

## THE NATURE OF INNOVATION IN URBAN PLANNING

Relatedly, though in a more practical sense, it is also difficult in the field of urban planning to draw a clear distinction between invention and innovation. (Apart from anything else, no urban planning inventions or innovations ever appear to have been patented.) Yet there have been some fundamental urban planning ideas which could be said to have been 'invented'. These are the creative leaps in advance of any practice, often taking the form of large conceptual visions of what might be. But the reality of innovation has more often been that fundamental ideas have grown empirically from experimental or reflective practice, rather than occurring in advance of practical expression. Innovation, in the sense of application, has usually preceded invention.

## SIMILARITIES BETWEEN INNOVATION IN BUSINESS AND PLANNING

None of this, however, prevents us drawing on Schumpeter and subsequent work on economic innovation (P Hall, 1998). There are, after all, many features which are common to innovation in business and urban planning. In both, the practical application involved in innovation proper obviously requires the commitment of resources, so both will be subject to a more searching assessment than is strictly necessary for pure invention. We will, in some cases, find the profit motive applied just as directly in urban planning as in business where profit-seeking developers were the implementing agents of planning innovations. And there have been many similarities in the evolution of invention/innovation. From amateur beginnings, there has been greater institutionalisation and professionalisation of the process. Lone inventors, making their fortunes/reputations by creating and applying great new discoveries, have given way to specialist teams, often buried anonymously in large organisations. (Schumpeter himself scarcely foresaw, or wanted to foresee, the bureaucratisation of innovation.)

To anticipate, we will also find many parallels with the business world in the marked tendency to temporal and spatial clustering of urban planning innovations. In classic Schumpeterian theory, it was these clusters that stimulated and provided the main content of major long-term cycles of economic development. Many economists have, however, questioned whether the relationship really could be so simple. And clearly the fit of this part of the theory to urban planning history is less than convincing. Waves of urban planning activity were obviously triggered by much more than clusters of ideas and practices, even though they certainly shaped the content of what was actually done. On balance though, and despite some obvious mismatches, the various insights of classic innovation theory provide a useful set of prompts to help provide a loose structure for this historical account.

## DIFFUSION OF INNOVATIONS

Classic innovation theory conceives of diffusion as the inevitable corollary of successful innovation. But it sees diffusion as a dilution of the competitive advantage and profitability of the original innovator. It is therefore a spur to further innovation in order for entrepreneurs and capitalists to seek new ways of restoring profits. This line of thinking is obviously much less applicable to our area of concern. Certainly the development of urban planning has at times reflected insecurities about the competitive or strategic advantage of one city or nation compared to others. There has, in other words, been a good deal of learning from rivals. But the sense of rivalry never seems to have been an obstacle to the international flow of planning information, in part, perhaps, because commercial secrecy has only rarely been an issue. Even then, the essentially public nature of cities has meant that rivals can easily observe many of the physical aspects of planning innovations.

Nor has there ever been any real desire, at least amongst the advanced capitalist countries, to inhibit the spread of knowledge about planning innovations. Quite the opposite in fact, because innovative countries have normally been eager to broadcast their achievements to anyone interested, especially their greatest rivals. Some have certainly seen this as one way of demonstrating their international superiority. Yet, almost from the outset, modern urban planning has shown a strong internationalist spirit. This has been the case despite obvious problems produced by language differences and distance. Often the internationalism was reinforced by direct personal contacts between planners in different countries. The huge improvements in international communications during the 20th century have, of course, helped intensify these contacts. Even the major international ruptures represented by wars did not for very long restrict the flows of planning knowledge amongst the countries considered in this book.

## OTHER INSIGHTS ON URBAN PLANNING DIFFUSION

Classic innovation diffusion theory thus offers only a few insights that can be applied to urban planning. What, then, can we glean from other sources? Diffusion has certainly featured in previous historical writing on planning, but rarely as a major theme.

Typically, studies have examined diffusion as an integral part of wider or deeper inquiries. Their concern has been to show how a particular city, country or group of countries encountered key planning ideas or practices from elsewhere or how their own planning inventions and innovations spread. In other cases, diffusion has featured in the story of a particular planning tradition, such as the garden city or modern movements. What these studies have shown is that diffusion has occurred quite rapidly, and by a variety of means. They have also shown that it cannot be seen as a simple process of spreading fixed notions of planning from their original heartland.

A major concern has been the extent to which ideas and practices are changed during their diffusion. In other words, diffusion has often been closely interrelated with innovation (and even invention) as ideas and practices are reformulated in different places. Against this, there are also examples where what is adopted in one country directly mimics a model in another. Often, though, a distinction must be made between the original aspiration and the realities of implementation. The intention may well be to create a direct copy of an externally admired original, yet its realisation involves a much wider range of conscious and unconscious influences. Climatic, economic, legal, political, social and cultural factors may all play a part. It is highly unlikely, therefore, that the final outcome will show as close a resemblance to an external model as the original planning vision may have intended. Much depends, though, on who controls the diffusion process, and how tight that control is. There is a huge difference between planners in one country choosing to borrow a planning idea or model from another, and one where the idea or model is externally imposed with little or no discretion exercised within the receiving country. Many studies of colonial planning, for example, show external control of the diffusion process. Even within colonial settings, however, there have been many variations in the degree and form of that control.

## HOW AND WHY

### THREE ALTERNATIVE EXPLANATIONS

All this begins to shift the emphasis from the broad themes for investigation to the main areas in which we will search for understanding as to how and why innovations happened and diffusions occurred. This focus forms the other major element which gives the book coherence. Again, however, and in keeping with the author's general approach, it is not a single rigid or overarching framework of explanation. That would simply be yet another grand narrative, albeit one graced by pretensions to scientific method. Instead, three broad alternative ways of attributing causation in innovation and diffusion, derived from previous work about 20th-century planning and its history, are sketched out. These conjectures about the driving forces will certainly not be tested in the explicit or formal fashion demanded by formal scientific inquiry. To do this on such a broad canvas would require a book several times longer than this one. Rather, these alternative hypotheses will inform the narrative. This means that they will act as an implicit guide as to what aspects of the many individual episodes of innovation and diffusion will be discussed, and what surrounding information is presented and probed. From time to time the reader will be reminded of their importance but, in general, they will be applied with a light touch. These disclaimers duly made, we can identify the three principal areas in which historians and theorists of planning have looked to explain innovation, diffusion and other facets of their subject.

## STRUCTURAL EXPLANATIONS

At one extreme are what may be termed the structural explanations, which seek to understand what has happened in planning in terms of larger forces. The exact nature of the larger forces cited have varied. One general line of argument, more popular amongst theorists than historians, has stressed the primacy of the economic cycle with its tendency to generate periodic crises of capitalism that have 'required' some form of collective state response at the urban level to facilitate the resumption of successful capital accumulation (eg Castells, 1977). Often these responses have involved interventions which have a social as well as a directly economic significance. The assumption has been, broadly, that cities need both to keep their workforces healthy and well disposed towards their employers and to be efficient places in which to undertake production and distribution.

This kind of all-purpose economic structural explanation has often been refined. A few planning historians have, for example, identified what amounts to a functional imperative for planners, of reconciling the best interests of the various forms of capital at the urban level (eg McDougall, 1979). The needs of industrialists will obviously not be exactly the same as those of landowners and developers. High rents and high profits for developers may mean higher wages and lower profits for industrialists. Another important refinement of structural explanations has been to consider the geopolitical dimension alongside the purely economic. Many authors have seen international rivalries and tensions as important triggers of urban planning innovations and diffusions. This kind of argument has been most highly developed in writing about imperialism and urban planning (cg King, 1980). The argument here is that the political and governmental realities of colonialism are the overarching reality from which all else derives.

We could go on to suggest further elaborations and refinements, but the essential point is made. It cannot merely be assumed that explanation in urban planning history is confined solely to the activity itself. The potential structuring roles of economic and geopolitical forces (and, indeed, other broad parameters) need to be carefully considered. Context may not explain everything, as most planning historians would readily acknowledge. But this certainly does not mean that it is irrelevant to the 'text' of urban planning history.

## KEY INDIVIDUALS

At the opposite end of the spectrum, many planning historians have preferred to give explanatory primacy to key individuals. While, to varying degrees, this kind of explanation has recognised the importance of context, it is not credited with any precise role in determining what happens. Context, in this view, creates challenges and provides opportunities, nothing more. The 'text' of the urban planning response is seen as being altogether more autonomous, not inevitable or preordained but shaped by many random or chance circumstances. These involve, to a very large extent, the actions of creative and committed individuals, which in turn reflect the formative influences, experiences and encounters of those individuals. The existence of prominent individuals as innovators or diffusion intermediaries in planning is not, of course, a matter of dispute. The central question, however, is whether they can be seen as autonomous actors, literally making a difference by their actions, or whether they are really bearers of structural 'messages'. The latter involves considering whether, had the specific individuals who made a difference not existed, others would have come forward to fulfil the same role. In other words, if x innovator or y diffuser had not existed, would it have been necessary to invent them?

Just as few would claim that context is everything, so few would assert the absolute explanatory primacy of individuals. Several prominent historians of urban planning, such as Peter Hall (1988) and Gordon Cherry (ed, 1981) have, though, at times portrayed them as the principal active agents of historical change, rising to the challenges and seizing the opportunities thrown up by larger forces and events. This alone means that the individuals who 'made' planning's history must be carefully examined and treated, so far as possible, as historical subjects. Again, though, the wider evolution of ideas and practice is also important. For example, were alternative inventors of key planning ideas waiting in the wings if x (whose name we remember) had died from tuberculosis before articulating the key concept? What would have happened if y had known German and therefore read z's book in the original rather than a defective translation?

## REFORMIST AND TECHNICAL MILIEUS

Between these two extremes lies a distinctive midrange approach to explanation. It acknowledges both structural context and key individuals but cedes explanatory primacy to the milieus within which new ideas and practices were formed, debated, refined and publicised. In other words, the research focus is the reformist, technical and, to some extent, institutional networks within which new ideas are fashioned into relevant practices (eg Sutcliffe, 1981; Cherry, 1974). In relation to diffusion, these networks are also the settings into which imported ideas and practices are received and in which they are adapted. They may also be active agents in promoting international diffusion of ideas. The exact nature of these networks and the extent to which they focus on urban planning has varied. Some may be informal, loose or occasional networks, perhaps finding their expression in international gatherings such as conferences or exhibitions. Urban planning might only be one of many other concerns. Others may be much more formal and focused organisations. These would include reformist bodies, pressure groups, professional bodies formed around the new technical expertise of urban planning, or educational and research institutions. Sometimes, formal agencies of national or city government may also come to fill this role, though not usually as a matter of routine.

In explanatory terms, the focus on milieus offers a way of directly linking the structural and the individual. In such settings, the isolated musings of a lone visionary might well receive their first tentative airings. Here their ideas can be rehearsed and made into something altogether more practical and relevant to the 'real world'. Idealism, in other words, acquires a practical edge so that it can be more effectively promoted to politicians, business interests and civil society. The quantitative and qualitative 'density' of such networks within a particular country can also be taken as an important indicator of the strength of its urban planning discourse and technical capacity. Generally, we will find that the western countries which were most innovative in their urban planning were also those with the strongest networks. Conversely, those which were slower to adopt urban planning ideas were much weaker in this respect. Obviously, though, this correlation does not itself imply a causal relationship, but it highlights the need to probe this dimension.

## THE STRUCTURE OF THE BOOK

### CARVING UP THE CENTURY

The reader should now have a broad impression of the book's main areas of inquiry, the possible lines of explanation that will be pursued and, therefore, the kind of information that is needed. The templates in this chapter will give some shape to the narrative flow. But, as mentioned earlier, they will not be applied with so heavy a hand as to obscure the many peculiarities and paradoxes in the history of 20th-century planning. It only remains therefore to outline the structure of the book. This is broadly chronological, adopting what is, in some ways, an arbitrary periodisation. Undoubtedly a better chronological fit could be found if fewer countries were in the frame. But compromises have been necessary, particularly in the second half of the century, where the historian does not have the obvious international staging posts of major wars. Even these, though, are less clear-cut than they might seem. For a European focus, 1914 and 1939 are obvious watershed dates. For the United States, though, the equivalent dates are 1917 and 1941. The most arbitrary dates of all, however, are those at the very beginning and end of the century, significant for no other reason than the way we choose to measure time.

### THE CHAPTER STRUCTURE

The problem of beginning in 1900 is confirmed in the next chapter, which outlines the important 19th-century prelude. Largely, this is a story of invention and the beginning of innovation, with the first signs of cross-national learning. Chapter 3 then shows how these early initiatives blossomed in the new century into self-conscious national urban planning movements, with a mounting international dimension. There were further inventions but increasingly the emphasis was now on developing practical applications, which began to spread rapidly. The two chapters following cover another very creative period, namely 1914 to 1939, when the visionary inventors finally gave way to the practical innovators. Despite the disruptive effects of the First World War, rapid diffusion meant that virtually every advanced capitalist country encountered planning ideas and practices during these years. The scale of planning activity therefore requires us to handle this period in two chapters rather than one. These distinguish between the major formative planning traditions (in Germany, Britain, France and the United States) in Chapter 4 and the smaller countries and more derivative traditions in Chapter 5.

This geographical division in the chapters is repeated for each of the subsequent periods. Thus Chapters 6 and 7 deal with the Second World War and the period of reconstruction that followed. Everywhere the political saliency of planning rose to new heights. Major metropolitan strategic plans also appeared in many countries during the war or in the immediately following years. These built on earlier thinking but many also showed some novelty and reflected a complex international interplay of thought. Chapters 8 and 9 then show how the immediate concerns of postwar reconstruction gave way to a more full-blooded commitment to urban modernisation throughout the advanced capitalist world in the 1960s and 1970s. The common problems were now those of planning for mass affluence and especially motorisation. Everywhere the solutions revealed an almost boundless optimism about growth and technology. Yet the long international boom on which this optimism rested itself gave way to economic uncertainty during the 1970s, coinciding with widespread popular reactions against urban modernisation. The 1980s and 1990s, explored in Chapters 10 and 11, saw a dramatic recasting of the planning agenda. As a globalised market system emerged, planners were obliged to make cities into more competitive places, particularly where older industries had withered. The harder edge this gave to planning was meanwhile softened by the new mantra of sustainability, which asserted the need to make present growth respect longer term environmental and other values. To many planners, at least, this became the new guiding philosophy for their activity in the 21st century.

Finally, Chapter 12 draws together the main strands of the book, reviewing the relevance of the broad explanatory approaches we have spelled out in this chapter. There will, of course, be no big answer, but particular variables which have significantly affected the creation and global spread of urban planning will be specified. There will also be some final speculations about the directions urban planning is likely to take in the new century. Whether, in the event, these will prove as big a quantum leap as those of the later 19th and early 20th centuries may be doubted. It is with these earlier and fundamental changes that we begin.

## CHAPTER 2

# NINETEENTH-CENTURY ANTECEDENTS

The most fundamental problem facing the historian of planning is knowing when, and therefore where, to begin. When urban planning was newly established as an aspect of policy and professional activity, in the early 20th century, its history was conceived as stretching back to the earliest urban civilisations. Such a grand overview legitimised the new practice of urban planning, revealing its deep historical roots. Yet the long march from Mohenjo-Daro certainly did not uncover any self-conscious tradition of planning that was continuous from ancient times. It showed simply that many past civilisations had been obliged to order the physical arrangement of their towns and cities, especially when they formed new settlements.

Exactly why they did this is not always clear, especially when causation has to be inferred from archaeological evidence. Yet we know enough to be fairly certain that military and religious considerations were often extremely important. So too was power. Thus the urban planning that we know from surviving physical evidence, in other words the planning that was actually implemented, bears faithful testimony to a concentration of authority. Much of the planning we recognise today in ancient, classical, medieval or renaissance cities was the work of kings, princes, prelates, aristocrats or oligarchies, each powerful enough to define the urban order.

From the late 18th century, however, all this began to change quite rapidly (Sutcliffe, 1981; T Hall, 1997). In western Europe and North America, the combined effects of rapid economic growth and a dramatic increase in the number and size of cities created the broad preconditions for modern urban planning to develop and spread. 'Modern' planning embraced the new realities of the city as a dynamic and capitalistic centre of production, distribution, consumption and reproduction. It had to seek ways of allowing cities to function effectively as economic and social entities. Crucially important to this was the growing political ascendancy of liberalism. This challenged the traditional bases of power and promoted reform of government institutions by giving them greater popular legitimacy. Modern planning thus brought a shift from the laying out of fortifications or grand urban places that buttressed the temporal power of kings, princes and aristocrats. Instead it expressed newer functional priorities of land use, infrastructure, efficient circulation and, increasingly, social welfare.

These changes did not occur all at once or even proceed in precisely coordinated steps. Nor did the very broad changes in economy, urbanisation and government lead, in crude deterministic fashion, to the emergence of modern urban planning. Rather, they provided the broad context for the more immediate developments which actually spawned modern planning movements. The developments were closely associated with the marked increase in new ideas about the shaping of urban space from roughly the mid-19th century, and reached a peak in the last decade of the century. Some ideas were, from the first, practically expressed in specific actions or proposals. Others appeared in theoretical or speculative books, pamphlets, articles or lectures.

Both then became the subject of wider reformist endeavour and the object of technical expertise. A recognisable and self-conscious discourse of what eventually came to be recognised as urban planning grew, stimulating further innovations and refinements.

## HAUSSMANN AND THE REMODELLING OF PARIS 1853–70

Whether it is realistic to look for a single starting point in time and place for modern urban planning is debatable. This has not, however, stopped historians and other commentators trying. One of the favourite candidates has been Napoleon III's Paris, remodelled at the emperor's bidding by Georges-Eugène Haussmann during the years 1853 to 1870 (Pinkney, 1958; Sutcliffe, 1970; des Cars and Pinon (eds), 1991). Haussmann was an administrator, appointed prefect of the department of the Seine (which included Paris) in July 1853. Louis Napoleon, the newly proclaimed emperor, wanted a capital that would be a showpiece. The population of the city had grown from 581,000 in 1800 to just over a million in 1850. Yet Paris scarcely befitted its role. It was an overgrown medieval city, congested, filthy and politically unstable, its citizens feared by most French rulers. It was also experiencing inexorable economic pressures for change. These reflected the growth of capitalism, especially the coming of the railways and emergence of an increasingly dynamic land market. Given the enormity of the task, the new emperor's executive instrument had to be chosen with care. Loyalty to Bonapartism was the first requirement, of course, but the ability to overcome, even to harness, the multiple sources of potential opposition amongst the powerful Parisian middle classes was paramount. Haussmann, already an accomplished prefect in provincial Bordeaux, possessed the necessary qualities of forcefulness, subtlety, intelligence and cynicism.

## IMPACTS ON PARIS

It is said that on Haussmann's appointment Louis Napoleon handed him a plan of the Paris he wished him to create. The emperor wanted (and in large measure, got) a new network of great boulevards, with circulation places where they came together. Central to the overall concept was what Haussmann called *la grande croisée* (the great cross) of Paris, which improved north–south and east–west communications. In addition, there was extensive redevelopment in the very oldest parts. Haussmann's proposals, largely fulfilled after his time as prefect, included major road improvements in the southern part of the city and diagonal streets in the central zone.

All this was superimposed on the old arrangement of land plots, streets and alleyways. It was hugely disruptive to the historic environment and to existing interests, involving expensive and complex appropriations of land. Yet the approach had, in theory at least, the great advantage that the new *percées* (piercing streets) created new frontages that had much higher values. Haussmann was also able to exert careful facade controls on the rebuilding in relation to materials, height and architectural treatment (Sutcliffe, 1993). These gave great unity to the new thoroughfares that were created. Yet the restructuring of the street circulation system was only part of

Haussmann's overall achievement. Beneath the new streets a new drainage system was installed. Haussmann can also claim credit, along with the emperor, for several major new parks including the Bois du Boulogne, Bois de Vincennes and the Buttes Chaumont.

## HAUSSMANN'S METHODS

In practice, the Haussmann approach to forming new thoroughfares did not work quite as well as had been hoped. Acquisition costs increased, mainly because the colossal scale and rapid success of the whole undertaking encouraged speculation. (Between 1853 and 1869 roughly 2.5 billion francs was spent on urban improvements, an amount 45 times the *total* Paris city budget in 1851.) Nor did Haussmann's appropriation and disposal powers give him as much freedom as they initially

**Figure 2.1** *Many new thoroughfares were formed in Paris during the Second Empire, mainly under Haussmann's direction.*

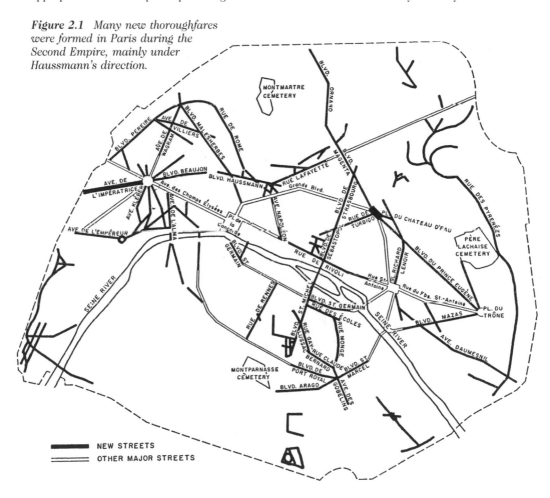

appeared to. In any case, the payback time was inevitably long term, while costs were incurred short term. The remodelling therefore had to be financed by massive amounts of credit, on a scale that was previously unknown (P Hall, 1998). Such was the pace of street improvement that Haussmann handed over large projects to entrepreneurs who implemented the whole process including appropriation.

These private agents were not paid until the scheme was complete and in order to bridge their funding gap Haussmann entered, without wider sanction, into extremely

**Figure 2.2** *The Avenue de l'Opéra is one of the streets most evocative of the Paris of the Second Empire. In fact, it had barely begun by 1870, but was completed in accordance with Haussmann's intentions.*

dubious loan and payment arrangements. By 1868 he had personally authorised loans raised against the credit of the state equivalent to about a quarter of the French national budget. Until this point few knew about, still less understood, these unorthodox practices, and revelations about them precipitated his downfall. Paradoxically, however, the discrediting of Haussmann did not bring his schemes to an end. Falling land values after the empire itself fell actually made them easier to bring to fruition.

## The first modern planner?

Can we then see Haussmann as the originator of modern urban planning (Sutcliffe, 1981; T Hall, 1997; P Hall, 1998)? In one sense, Louis Napoleon was quite deliberately echoing a premodern tradition of regal and princely planning. Yet, even more, he was addressing urban forces that were unmistakably modern and functional. The city that Haussmann fashioned was much more bourgeois and business-oriented than it was aristocratic and courtly. This is only half the point, however. Although Paris might be a modern city, Haussmannism must be judged as being only partly a forerunner of modern planning.

There are several reasons for this assessment. Most importantly, Haussmann was primarily undertaking a public works programme. And public works, though undeniably a part of modern urban planning in advanced capitalist countries, are rather less than the whole. They have, in fact, tended to be seen as one of the 20th-century planner's bluntest and most expensive instruments. Planning has, more typically, aspired to a more comprehensive coordination of public and private investment in the urban fabric. It has also involved a wider regulation of the use of private land, something which was entirely absent from Haussmannism.

A related point is that, despite Louis Napoleon's original map (which has not survived), there was evidently no overall master plan. Individual schemes were conceived incrementally within a very general conceptual one. Haussmann improvised street lines even while schemes were under way. In part, this avoidance of any very clear statement of intentions may have been a deliberate tactic to thwart the speculators. Yet it underlined the essentially opportunistic nature of Haussmannism. Nowhere in his work can we detect any theorisation of a comprehensive approach. The city's problems were always being addressed in a rather partial way.

## The wider impact of Haussmannism

These limitations did not, however, prevent knowledge of Haussmannism from spreading rapidly, and becoming one element of modern planning as it took shape over the following decades (des Cars and Pinon (eds), 1991; Pinon, 1995). There were similar schemes in many French provincial cities, most notably Lyons and Marseilles. During the 1860s, especially in the wake of the 1867 Universelle Exposition held in Paris, the model became international (Sutcliffe, 1981). Amongst its first, and closest, imitators was Jules Anspach (1829-79), mayor of Brussels from 1863 (Leblicq, 1995; T Hall, 1997). Anspach (significantly referred to as Ansmann in some reviews) directly sought Haussmann's advice about his own projects for the Belgian capital. There were also many echoes of Haussmannism in cities as diverse as Stockholm, Birmingham and Rome during the later decades of the 19th century (T Hall, 1997). More followed in the early 20th century, often far outside Europe (Werquin and Demangeon, 1995).

Yet these references never produced anything on the same scale as the original, and often differed in quite important aspects of detail. In most cities the main problem was not the already built core. Rather, it was to ensure that urban growth occurred on well conceived lines. This leads to the conclusion that Haussmannism was a breathtaking demonstration of the possibility of changing cities on a grand scale. Except on a rather modest scale, it was not itself a transferable model of exactly how they would be changed.

## CERDÀ, BARCELONA AND PLANNING THEORY 1859–67

Another powerful contender for the title of first modern urban planner is Ildefons Cerdà y Sunyer (the last part is usually omitted). A Spanish (more exactly, a Catalan) engineer, Cerdà produced the highly distinctive plan for Barcelona's Eixample (extension) beyond the former city walls in 1859 (Magrinyà and Tarragó (eds), 1996). He also published, in 1867, the *Teoría General de la Urbanización* (General Theory of Urbanisation), the first modern attempt to theorise urban planning. Despite this, and very unlike Haussmann, Cerdà has been a rather neglected figure. Recently, however, his reputation has been restored and he is now far better known internationally than ever he was during his lifetime.

Cerdà exhibited many qualities that are associated with the values of the modern urban planning movements of the early 20th century. A trained engineer, he possessed high technical skills, yet he combined these with a visionary quality that transcended specific physical settings. He understood the transforming effects of economic and technological change – above all the new railways – on urban living. (It is important to appreciate that in the 1840s Spanish cities, like many in continental Europe, were still by 1850 very tightly packed within defensive walls.) Finally, he combined his technical training and far-sightedness with genuine political idealism, founded on liberalism but with elements of utopian socialism.

## PLANNING BARCELONA'S EIXAMPLE

After 1849 Cerdà, having unexpectedly inherited the family fortune, was able to devote increasing attention to what he called *urbanización*, meaning the development of cities (Margarit, 1996; Estapé, 1996). But things did not exactly run smoothly. The 1850s were years of considerable unrest in Barcelona and because Cerdà actively identified himself with radical causes he was briefly imprisoned in 1856, and shortly after fled to Paris. When he returned towards the end of the year, however, events moved quickly. The Ministry of War had dropped Barcelona from their list of strategic cities, and as a result finally allowed its walls to be demolished and the extension to proceed. Then followed a struggle between the national Ministry of Development, which commissioned Cerdà to prepare the extension plan, and the Barcelona city council, which announced a competition (Gimeno, 1996). In 1859 the competition jury selected another entry but in 1860 they were overruled in Cerdà's favour by the national government.

## BUILDING THE EIXAMPLE

For the first few years after the plan was finally adopted, Cerdà controlled the detail of implementation (Gimeno and Magrinyà, 1996). He was also involved in other ways as he was, at various times, a city councillor and development promoter. These multiple roles helped to ensure that his plan formed a real basis for growth. Yet the process was a contested one. The bad feeling generated by the manner in which his plan had been adopted brought opposition to its actual provisions. However, after a short period of investor uncertainty the plan became the setting for a development boom. This reflected the rapid growth of the Catalonian economy. In addition, Spain's disastrous colonial wars in the 1890s, which culminated in the Spanish–American War, triggered a massive repatriation of capital, much of which was invested in urban development. Overall, between 1860 and 1900, Barcelona's population doubled to 533,000.

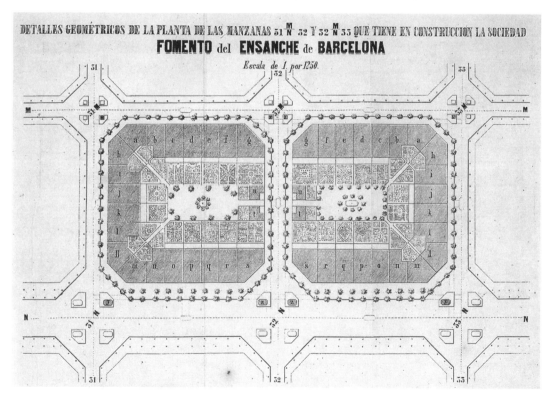

**Figure 2.3** *The most characteristic physical feature of Cerdà's plan for Barcelona's* Eixample *(in Castilian Spanish* Ensanche*) was the block, with its chamfered corners. Cerdà envisaged a quite low density of development, allowing much green space.*

The plan for the Eixample gave the city one of the most distinctive morphological structures in the world. Essentially it was a grid plan, but with chamfered rather than simple rectilinear blocks, allowing more generous treatment of road junctions. Major cross and diagonal highways were also planned within the grid to handle the heavier traffic flows. Except in the east of the city, the planned and actual grid and major highways are almost identical, covering a very wide area. Cerdà also made Haussmann-like proposals for a limited number of *percées* in the tightly packed Ciutat Vella (old city). One, the Via Laietana, was implemented in 1908. The major dilution of the plan arose, however, because of relaxations in the building regulations. Cerdà had envisaged buildings with a maximum height of only four floors (16 metres), with extensive open space in each block. In 1891, in the midst of a development boom, these regulations were relaxed to allow seven floors plus an attic (23 metres), increasing the maximum cover from half to nearly three-quarters of the block. These and later relaxations changed Cerdà's more open pattern to one of continuous building along street frontages, and extensive internal courtyard development.

*Figure 2.4* *The increasing pace of development in the later nineteenth and early twentieth centuries soon produced multi-storey development, covering much more of the blocks than Cerdà had wanted.*

## Cerdà as a Theorist

As well as the specific characteristics of Cerdà's Barcelona plan, the theory that underpinned them and his scientific methods were immensely important (Soria y Puig, 1995). Every aspect of the plan was supported by detailed research and could be rationally justified. As well as the actual plan itself, Cerdà authored detailed treatises on matters such as the social and economic conditions of the working population and the land-value implications of removing the city walls. The approach formed part of Cerdà's overall conception of *urbanización*, which he defined thus in the *Teoría General de la Urbanización*:

> . . . the series of measures aimed at arranging buildings and regulating their functions, as
> well as the body of principles, doctrines and rules to be applied so that the buildings and
> their arrangements, instead of oppressing, weakening and corrupting the physical, moral
> and intellectual capacities of man in society, promote their development as well as his
> individual wellbeing, and contribute to increasing collective happiness. (Lampugnagi,
> 1996: 63–5)

These words confirm how astonishingly close was Cerdà's 1867 definition of *urbanización* to notions of urban planning which became widespread throughout Europe and the United States in the early 20th century. They reveal a conceptual dimension that was absent from Haussmann's work.

## Why did Cerdà's ideas not spread?

Despite this, the wider impact of Cerdà's ideas was negligible (T Hall, 1997). Almost all of those who, a few decades later, formed the first self-conscious generation of urban planners did so in ignorance of his pioneering work. There were probably several reasons for this. The extent of local jealousies certainly prevented any acclamation within Barcelona itself (Margarit, 1996). This may be contrasted, for example, with the position of several local architects who worked in the Eixample, most prominently Antoni Gaudí who was treated with reverence. Yet there were also wider reasons. The Paris of Haussmann and Louis Napoleon was quite consciously being remodelled as a city to show to the world. This was not true of Barcelona. Cerdà was certainly aware of city improvements in other countries, and particularly Haussmann's work in Paris. Yet he does not seem to have taken any significant steps to publicise his own work, possibly because he was distracted by local tensions. It would, in any case, have been difficult because his work obviously predated the emergence anywhere of an urban planning literature. Cerdà's own deliberate actions may, though, have contributed to his wider obscurity. It has, for example, been reported that Haussmann admired Cerdà's work sufficiently to seek to buy his plans and studies (Estapé, 1996). Cerdà apparently rebuffed these approaches, however, saying he had made his plans for Catalonia.

We might also surmise that the increasing building density of the Eixample from the 1890s onwards discouraged the interest of the new urban planners who were then appearing in other countries. As we will see, most of them were by then interested in lower-density approaches. In their view, the Eixample would not have appeared particularly remarkable. Finally, we can note that other countries were not at this time predisposed to look to Spain for innovation (Sutcliffe (ed), 1980; 1981). In 19th-century terms, its political thought was scarcely advanced. The collapse of its overseas empire at the end of the century meant that it was in terminal decline as a world power. In addition, Spain's industrialisation was occurring late, not just after Britain's but also after that in Belgium, France, Germany and America (Wynn, 1984a). Moreover, unlike English, French or German, Spanish was not widely known in Europe and Cerdà's publications were not translated until much later. But, whatever the reasons, the key point remains that knowledge of Cerdà's work did not spread. Even in Spain *urbanización*, the term he coined to embrace the new activity of urban planning, did not retain this meaning. Despite the work of this relatively isolated innovator, other later figures became more widely recognised as the pioneers of a planning movement.

## OTHER MOVES TOWARDS URBAN PLANNING IN CONTINENTAL EUROPE 1850–75

### URBAN EXTENSIONS

Haussmann and Cerdà stand out in the third quarter of the 19th century because of the scale or theoretical sophistication of their work. Yet there were others, individually less significant, who also formed part of the immediate antecedents of modern urban planning practice and theory.

Though none showed anything approaching the conceptual sophistication of Cerdà's Eixample, planned urban extensions became quite common in continental Europe during this period (Sutcliffe, 1981; T Hall, 1997). The main pretext for their preparation varied. As in Barcelona, the removal or downgrading of urban fortifications was often important, for example in the extensions for Copenhagen (from 1857), Vienna (from 1859) and Amsterdam (from 1862). In other cases, urban areas which retained strategic importance were refortified around an enlarged area, for example Lille (from 1858). The more general pressures of economic and population growth were also important. These were the main concerns of the well-known 1862 Berlin extension plan prepared by James Hobrecht. The proposals for Stockholm, produced initially by the Lindhagen Committee (1866), were similarly inspired.

### NATURE OF EARLY EXTENSION PLANS

The nature of these plans varied but essentially they were road and street layouts, typically revealing some thought about major and minor thoroughfares. Most gave priority to formal aesthetic rather than functional criteria (T Hall, 1997). The extension plans were also underpinned by building regulations of varying sophistication. Though certain functional demarcations of space were typical (for example between

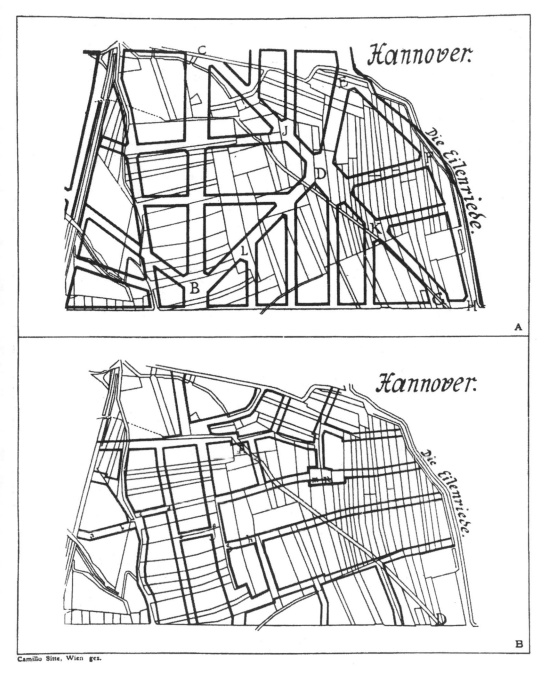

Camillo Sitte, Wien gez.

**Figure 2.5** *From the first German planning great attention was given to street alignments in new urban districts. Designs were initially very formal, but, from the 1890s, the ideas of the Austrian, Camillo Sitte, proposed a new approach that respected traditional features (see pp 28–29). The contrast is shown here in a district of Hannover.*

the street and the area for building, or areas for public parks), full land use and density zoning was not yet present. There were variations in patterns of landowner-ship, though it is clear that private implementation of these extensions predominated.

The extent of regulatory control over private interests also varied. Fairly rudi-mentary powers of wider control, rather closer to modern planning, began to appear in legislation. Several of the German states were earliest in this respect, particularly Prussia from 1855 (Sutcliffe, 1981). The equivalent date for Italy was 1865 and, for Sweden 1874 (Calabi, 1980; 1984; T Hall, 1991a). The last-named legislation was the most significant and was widely applied. It effectively updated the Swedish state's historic responsibilities for town development, applying them to new priorities of the industrial era. Under it, all towns were obliged to prepare a *stadsplan* (town plan). This label itself is significant because it shows an early formal use of a term that, a few decades later, became the most basic component of the new international planning discourse.

## DIFFUSION OF EXTENSION PLANNING IDEAS AND PRACTICE

More generally, it is not clear how far there was an inter- or intranational diffusion of ideas and practices associated with these extension plans. The general impression is that, as we might expect, projects in the biggest cities of the most powerful countries were best known and even then usually within their own linguistic realms. As noted for Cerdà, innovations in less important countries might well go almost unnoticed elsewhere (T Hall, 1997). Albert Lindhagen, for example, articulated some principles of extension planning to underpin Sweden's 1874 legislation, using Finnish (and, indirectly, Russian) precedents of town design and theoretical examples (T Hall, 1991a). Yet Lindhagen was no more successful in establishing a wider basis for planning thought than Cerdà had been in the previous decade. His ideas attracted little international attention. Significantly too, the early Swedish linking of town – ie, *stads* – and *plan* was not picked up elsewhere before it had appeared, much later, in English.

## BRITISH INNOVATIONS BEFORE 1875

### DIFFERENCES IN THE ENGLISH-SPEAKING WORLD

As we have shown, planned extensions were usually of urban centres that were dismantling or, in a few cases, rebuilding their fortifications. This was no simple matter. After the development of gunpowder urban defence works had become very extensive. With a surrounding zone where building was usually prohibited (often called the glacis), they were major spatial features of many continental cities. Their removal (or reconstruction) dramatically changed urban development possibilities. It is not therefore surprising that such occasions stimulated important public action to determine how extension would occur. Yet this link with fortifications also limited the international spread of ideas about urban extension. They did not at this stage cross the English Channel, still less the Atlantic. However, this is not to say that there were not important developments in Britain and the United States that deserve a place amongst the antecedents of modern planning.

## Urban innovation in Britain

Up to about the mid-19th century Britain was, in most respects, the most innovatory country in the world. For much of the rest of the century it continued to be in the forefront of all kinds of new developments. Although much of this dynamic creativity was associated directly with Britain's formidable industrial and trading prowess, it also extended into many other fields, including the government and management of cities (Briggs, 1963). The pressures for this innovation were indeed great. London, with almost 2.7 million people at mid-century, had lately overtaken Edo (the present Tokyo) to become the world's largest city (Sutcliffe, 1981; T Hall, 1997). At the time of the Great Exhibition of 1851 it was roughly five times the size of New York and two and a half times the size of Paris. Several of Britain's regional cities, notably Liverpool, Manchester, Glasgow and Birmingham, had built-up areas with populations greater than those of most European capital cities.

It was then a combination of necessity and inventiveness that made British cities into world leaders in improving the quality of urban life. Particularly notable were the innovations in urban public health from the 1840s onwards, especially in public water supply and the development of waterborne sewerage (RA Lewis, 1952; Wohl, 1974; 1983). Important, too, were the provision of parks and public amenities and, from the 1860s, the removal of slum housing. All these innovations began to receive attention from other countries (Sutcliffe, 1981). German and American cities, for example, borrowed British public health innovations, especially in water supply and sewerage, and often drew directly on British expertise.

## An absence of coherence

There was an important gap in this inventory of innovation, however. Hugely impressive though it was, it lacked any conscious notion of comprehensively shaping the city – in other words of planning (Ashworth, 1954; Cherry, 1988). The 1840s debates about public health in Britain's growing towns encouraged a few tentative suggestions in this direction, but they were not widely favoured. Peripheral expansion thus continued in an essentially incremental fashion, but with building standards that compared favourably to those in many other European countries. Perhaps it was the absence of huge fortification works that allowed a less comprehensive approach to land development issues to seem sufficient in Britain. Or perhaps the scale of growth discouraged any overarching public attempts to guide the process. Individual land-owners and developers quite often imposed their own controls, usually attempting to create higher-class suburban districts, but these were exercises in disjointed private action rather than comprehensive public planning.

The same was broadly true in the urban cores. Thus in the 1860s and 1870s municipal moves in London, Liverpool, Glasgow, Edinburgh and other cities to create new streets and remove slums became discreet public works projects. As in Haussmann's Paris (which influenced the formation of some of the new streets) these heralded no immediate shift to more comprehensive thinking. This key transition in Britain still lay some way off, and was to require a greater awareness of continental initiatives than had yet developed.

## URBAN PARKS IN THE UNITED STATES 1858–76

### A NEW URBAN SOCIETY

In the United States meanwhile, there were faint glimmerings by the 1870s of a comprehensive approach. In one sense, of course, the scale of town formation in the 19th century required a rudimentary form of urban planning (Reps, 1965). This essentially followed earlier approaches to colonial planning and, initially at least, was largely devoid of any of the distinctive features of modern planning. In almost all cases the plans were little more than crude physical templates, intended to attract population and capital to a newly commodified landscape. An exception was the nation's capital, Washington, planned by the French military engineer, artist and architect Major Pierre Charles L'Enfant, in 1791 (Reps, 1991). His plan showed a direct connection with European *ancien régime* planning, reinterpreted to reflect democratic rather than autocratic government. Yet the city's slow growth before the Civil War scarcely made it a model for wide emulation. Instead, it was in ·the big trading and industrial cities that the main North American moves towards modern planning occurred.

### OLMSTED AND CENTRAL PARK

The most important single figure in this immediate prehistory of American urban planning was Frederick Law Olmsted (DA White, 1988; Fisher, 1994; Olmsted, 1997). Yet it might well not have been so. Before he found his enduring niche as a landscape architect, Olmsted tried many things. Thanks to the indulgence of long-suffering and wealthy parents, he was at various times farmer, travel writer, distinguished social commentator on slavery in the old South (quoted by Karl Marx in *Das Kapital*), publisher, Sanitary Commission director and mining estate manager. Another role, from 1857, was as park superintendent of the yet to be laid out Central Park in New York.

Already the largest city in the United States, New York had topped half a million by mid-century (and was to exceed 800,000 only 10 years later). It is easy therefore to appreciate its civic leaders' desire to preserve a substantial oasis of green on what was then the edge of the city. Olmsted was ideally placed when the competition to design the park was announced in 1858. An architect friend, Calvert Vaux, approached him and the two prepared what became the winning design. Vaux's late partner, Andrew Jackson Downing, had been the most renowned American landscape gardener of his day before his premature death in a river accident. It seems almost certain that, had he lived, Downing and Vaux would have won the competition. As it was, Olmsted was propelled to the forefront of American park design.

## THE ENGLISH CONNECTION

Like Downing, Olmsted drew inspiration from the English concept of the countryside after his first visit to Britain in the early 1850s (Garvin, 1996). While in Britain he also encountered the then novel concept of the public park, at Birkenhead across the River Mersey from Liverpool. Designed by Joseph Paxton and opened in 1847, Birkenhead Park stands as the prime (though not strictly the first) exemplar of the public park movement that so quickly gained momentum in urban Britain from the 1840s. Olmsted was immediately attracted to the concept of a people's (as opposed to an aristocratic) park and saw it as an ideal transplant to his own, democratic, homeland.

## PARKS AS A BASIS FOR CITY-WIDE PLANNING

What was important, however, was that the Americans soon took the concept of the park in new directions. Far more than in Europe, in the United States citywide approaches to park provision and design became a crucial stepping stone to city planning (Sutcliffe, 1981; Fogelsong, 1986). Olmsted was central to this transition. After Central Park, Olmsted and Vaux's second main commission, for Prospect Park in Brooklyn from 1866, moved beyond the park itself to include the park approaches in the design. Concurrently, in 1868/9, he was also commissioned to design Riverside, a high-class suburb of Chicago, where residential environment and park were merged.

By 1870, Olmsted had effectively elaborated a parks-based concept of city planning (Olmsted, 1870; 1997). He theorised all of this in a paper read before the American Social Science Association in Boston in that year. Called 'Public Parks and the Enlargement of Towns', his address implicitly linked the park, the parkway and the planned residential community. He never fully realised this conjunction of elements in practice. However, in his work in Buffalo (1868–76) he showed much of its potential, creating a city park system linked by park-like roads called parkways. (Even more extensive was Boston's 'Emerald Necklace' created largely by the Olmsted firm in the 1880s and 1890s.)

## ASSESSMENT

Olmsted was responsible for many other commissions and had a tremendous influence on the prehistory of American city planning (Fogelsong, 1986). Other park planners followed his lead. Yet their work fell short of urban planning as it came to be understood in the early 20th century. Missing, or at least undeveloped, was the functional dimension of the city as a place to make and distribute goods and services. Nor was there within the park vision any very great measure of social reformism. Parks certainly could be seen as a contribution to the health and wellbeing of the urban masses but it was very much the 'carriage set' that derived most of the benefit. The parks were invariably created in the better-off districts, enhancing their amenities and property values. Nevertheless, the conservative reformism of the parks movement left an enduring legacy to American city planning. Indeed, an unusually strong emphasis on parks formed perhaps its most distinctive early characteristic compared to equivalent European movements.

## German and Austrian innovations 1876–1900

The last quarter of the 19th century marked a critical phase in the development of modern urban planning. As we have seen, Cerdà's extraordinarily comprehensive approach failed to gain wider recognition. Later in the century, however, there grew to be a critical mass of thought and practice on urban planning. Everywhere, but particularly in western Europe and North America, there was a noticeable growth of interest in the nature of the city, its problems and how they might be remedied. The pace of innovation in urban reformist thought quickened correspondingly. Knowledge of these innovations was also spread more rapidly than ever before, from city to city and, increasingly, from nation to nation. Specific events such as exhibitions or competitions played important roles in this diffusion. So, too, did the increasingly organised character of urban reformist movements and relevant professional groupings. Together they made possible the coalescence of ideas and practices which we can finally recognise as modern urban planning.

### The background to German innovation

In contrast to the pre-1875 period, most of the key innovations occurred in the newly united nation-state of Germany or, at least, in the German-speaking world. In a general sense, they form part of the story of Germany's extraordinary rise to world economic and strategic prominence in the later 19th century. Echoing British trends, German urban growth went hand in hand with industrial expansion.

By 1900 more than half Germany's population was urbanised (a position that had been reached in Britain 50 years earlier) (Ladd, 1990). Though it remained well short of London's, Berlin's population had increased at a spectacular rate (Matzerath, 1984). It had more than doubled from the mid-century to reach a million by 1875 and about 1.9 million (2.7 million with adjoining districts) by 1900, making it Europe's third largest city. Berlin was unique in Germany. Hamburg, Munich, Leipzig and Breslau (the present Wrocław in Poland) were more like Britain's large provincial cities, all with populations in the range of 400,000 to 750,000 by 1900. It was, though, the slightly smaller regional cities, such as Frankfurt or Cologne, fast growing but never entirely losing their modest scale, which were the most typical manifestations of German urbanisation. More unusual was the Ruhr, a multicentred urban industrial region which experienced spectacular growth in a rural setting during the later 19th century, passing two million by about 1900 (Reulecke, 1984; Hötker, 1988). Set against the general backdrop of German dynamism, these varying urban characteristics together proved to be quite encouraging to specific innovation in urban planning. On the one hand, they produced acute urban problems to fuel reformist rhetoric. This was especially so in Berlin, widely seen as Europe's most congested city by 1900, with health problems to match. On the other hand, the more limited scale of the regional cities, which enjoyed considerable autonomy, provided a setting that was more conducive to fruitful innovations. The unusual spatial characteristics of the Ruhr also stimulated new planning ideas in the late 19th and early 20th centuries.

## NEW LEGISLATION AND TOWN EXTENSIONS

As we have seen, town extension had been growing in significance since the mid-19th century. In Germany a somewhat crude pattern had been usual. Increasing criticisms of this approach, and a crisis in the development industry in the early 1870s, triggered important reforms (Sutcliffe, 1981; Ladd, 1990). Following slightly earlier moves in some other states, the Prussian state parliament, the most important in Germany, passed a new law on street lines (*Fluchtliniengesetz*) in 1875. The other states adopted these same measures within a few years. The effect was to make town extension plans almost universal for all urban expansions. Municipalities had automatic compulsory purchase rights for the new streets in the extension plans, and permitted the costs of building, draining and lighting the new streets to be passed to the frontage owners.

Most municipalities initially prepared extension plans on the pattern of the 1862 Hobrecht plan for Berlin and permitted very high-density development. There were mounting criticisms from reformers and the professionals most involved in the process, chiefly the Verband Deutscher Architekten-und Ingenieurvereine (the Confederation of German Associations of Architects and Engineers). This respected body epitomised the wider rise of technical expertise that was so important to German ascendancy at this time. In 1874 the Verband produced a model approach to town extension that was to be very influential over the immediately following years.

## BAUMEISTER AND *STADTERWEITERUNGEN*

Two years later the main author of this approach published an important work on the subject that became modern urban planning's first textbook (Baumeister, 1876). It was called *Stadterweiterungen in technischer, baupoliseilicher und Wirtschaftlicher Beziehung* (Town extensions: their links with technical and economic concerns and with building regulations). Its author, Reinhard Baumeister, was a professor of civil engineering at the college of technology at Karlsruhe. With previous experience in railway construction, he entered the emergent practice of planning in 1872 when he won a competition to prepare the town extension for Mannheim. Subsequently he prepared many other extension plans, mainly in Baden.

The book defined two principal tasks for *Stadterweiterungen*: 'to produce new housing and to expedite circulation' (cited Ladd, 1990: p 85). This actually went further than the Verband which, two years earlier, had deleted the housing references from Baumeister's draft guidelines. Yet, as will be shown, German planning remained weak on the housing front and the subject did not form a major part of Baumeister's book. Generally his approach was prosaic and practical. In the light of later developments, it also seems extremely cautious. Theorisation of ideal solutions, in the manner of Cerdà's work of a few years earlier, was absent. Yet there was a scientific and functional basis offered to guide urban development. This was especially evident in matters such as streets and major roads, but is apparent too in the treatment of housing and the organisation of business and industrial districts. Here, then, was a straightforward guide for the burgeoning number of practitioners. And, as planning education began, in 1880, at the college of technology in Aachen (another German first), it had its first textbook (Imbert, 1990).

## LATER TOWN EXTENSIONS

Baumeister stopped short of advocating zoning but his proposals were clearly moving in that general direction. Zoning did not actually appear as a single step, however. It gradually evolved out of town-extension practice during the 1880s and 1890s. A key point came in 1891 when Frankfurt introduced spatially differentiated building regulations – the *Zonenbauordnung* – (Sutcliffe, 1981). These marked the beginning of effective density zoning and intensified the trend towards functional zoning. However, the emergence of zoning was not the only change in town-extension practice. Another important trend was locating town extensions within a citywide approach. The more perceptive practitioners had quickly realised that large extensions could not be considered solely on their own terms. The likelihood was that their development would have important implications for the rest of the city. The man who grasped this first and elaborated the need to move beyond town extension was Josef Stübben (Stübben, 1885; GR Collins and CC Collins, 1965).

## BEYOND TOWN EXTENSION: JOSEF STÜBBEN

Josef Stübben was an architect who had worked briefly in railway management before becoming, in 1876, director of works at the western border city of Aachen (Ladd, 1990). In 1880 Stübben and another architect from the same city produced the winning entry for the extension of Cologne. In its recognition of the need to reconsider the structure and functioning of the city as a whole this extension plan stood out from previous schemes. It was on the strength of this that Stübben was invited, in 1881, to direct the implementation of the Cologne extension plan. He went on to plan extensions for over 30 towns and cities.

He was a prolific writer and in 1890 he published a prodigious volume entitled *Der Städtebau* (Town building). It formed part of a much larger multi-authored work called the *Handbuch der Architektur*, though alone it ran to 30 chapters with 23 appendices and 900 illustrations. It quickly superseded Baumeister's book as the standard German text, and definitively marked the broadening of the concept of German urban planning from *Stadterweiterungen* to the more comprehensive *Städtebau*. Eventually three editions were published.

## BEYOND TOWN EXTENSION: CAMILLO SITTE

In fact, it was not only Stübben who was responsible for this conceptual broadening. In 1889 a Viennese architect, Camillo Sitte, had published a work called *Der Städte-Bau nach seinen künstlerischen Grundsätzen* – Town building according to artistic principles – (Sitte, 1965; GR Collins and CC Collins, 1965). Compared to Stübben's textbook, it was more selective and more committed in tone. Sitte himself was not a planning practitioner in the manner of Baumeister or Stübben. He had barely practised even as an architect but from 1875 had directed schools of applied arts, first in Salzburg and then, from 1883, in Vienna. He was, however, a prolific writer and critic on the arts generally, and well known within Viennese artistic circles. His book needs to be understood against this background. Once it was published, however, he rapidly attained a central position in Germanic planning thought at this most formative period. At a stroke he widened its horizons, creating a new movement that challenged formal and mechanistic assumptions about town extension. The book was an instant success in Germany and, as we will see, soon became known elsewhere.

Sitte's essential argument was for a more organic approach to urban planning. He was inspired by the morphological qualities of historic towns in Europe, mainly those formed in the medieval period. His ideas can be seen as the antithesis of highly formalised layouts with grand avenues and vistas. Even more, they made him a scourge of the unthinking, universal application of street-line regulations. As he showed, the qualities of organic historic towns arose precisely because of subtle variations around common features. As we might expect, these concerns moderated the growing emphasis on functional questions such as traffic circulation. The full wording of the title itself can be seen as a challenge to the scientific, engineering focus which hitherto had set the pace in German planning.

## THE LIMITS OF GERMAN URBAN PLANNING

Despite Sitte's own Austrian origins, the book's success showed the extent to which it reflected a growing current of thought in Germany. A group of planners quickly aligned themselves with Sitte's ideas. All this was further evidence that German planning thought was acquiring maturity and breadth. It showed, for example, that planning practice was more than a simple set of rules, rather it was something that demanded judgment and discernment. In effect, it confirmed the advanced development of urban planning in the German-speaking world.

Yet there was certainly no room for complacency in German planning. Many Germans, especially the liberal elite, continued to feel uneasy about the way their cities were developing. Housing, in particular the growing reliance on very high density tenement forms of working-class housing (known as *Mietskasernen*), remained a matter of serious concern, not least in Berlin (Bollerey and Hartmann, 1980; Bullock and Read, 1985; Bullock, 1999). Aware of the acute problems of the capital, the leaders of smaller and medium-sized cities viewed these same trends appearing elsewhere with alarm. The concerns of metropolitan and regional cities together fuelled an emergent housing reform movement in the 1890s.

## GERMAN IDEAS FOR HOUSING REFORM

The solutions were, however, rather less indigenous creations than those evident in the emergence of *Stadterweiterungen* and the wider concept of *Städtebau*. Some original German thinking on the living environment was evident. Especially notable was Theodor Fritsch's *Die Stadt der Zukunst* (The Town of the Future) published in 1896 (P Hall, 1988). It offered a Germanic vision of a low-density city that minimised the detrimental social and environmental effects of industry and urban life.

It was, however, in the Ruhr, where industrialisation occurred in a rural setting, that some of the best German practice in enlightened working-class housing design before 1900 was to be found (Bullock and Read, 1985). The need to attract labour forced industrialists to build relatively good housing, often with community facilities. Since many of the workers came from rural areas, small houses or cottage flats with gardens close by were common. High tenement buildings were in any case ruled out because of the risk of mining subsidence. The most enlightened of the Ruhr capitalists were the Krupp armaments makers. Under the leadership of Alfred Krupp, the family firm had provided 6,800 dwellings (von Petz, 1990a) by 1892. After an early phase of temporary wooden housing, permanent structures began to be built from the 1870s. Typical examples, both in Essen, were the cottage flats at Baumhof and the four-storey tenements at Kronenberg. The latter, at 1,500 dwellings, was the largest of the early schemes. Further expansion followed in the 1890s as Alfred's son Wilhelm embarked on further settlements at Altenhof, Alfredshof and Friedrichshof, setting even higher standards.

*Figure 2.6*  British cities were slow to develop a wide concept of urban planning. Instead of preparing ambitious extension plans on the continental pattern, they adopted building bylaws to ensure minimum standards. The results are shown here in Birmingham.

The inspiration for industrial urbanisation based on small houses with gardens came largely from the west. Early four-in-a-block house types had largely originated in Mulhouse in Alsace (in German hands from 1871, though previously part of France). The semi-urban industrialisation of Belgium was also viewed with interest. But it was Britain that became the major object of universal admiration by German housing reformers during the 1890s (Bollerey and Hartmann, 1980). Alfred Krupp had spent time studying British industrial methods in the early 1870s and some of his housing ideas came from that source. And, as British thinking about housing reform and planned community development progressed further in the 1890s, German reformers looked on with eager interest.

## BRITISH INNOVATIONS 1875–1900

### URBAN GROWTH AND LIMITED CONTROL

The interest was not yet reciprocated in Britain. Certain aspects of policy that seemed to underpin German economic success, such as technical education, had already

*Figure 2.7* *By the end of the century, industrial philanthropists such as George Cadbury at Bournville, also in Birmingham, were offering a more attractive living environment for factory workers.*

attracted British attention. But urban planning was not one of them, partly because there was still no British equivalent of *Stadterweiterungen* or *Städtebau*. This was despite a rate of urban growth that, though falling in percentage terms, was still very high. London's population, for example, increased from 4.8 million in 1881 to 6.6 million 20 years later, and the city was still the biggest in the world. The biggest provincial cities – Glasgow, Liverpool, Manchester and Birmingham – had populations within quite tightly drawn city boundaries that were in the range of 500,000 to 800,000 by 1901. Moreover, they all formed parts of coalescing metropolitan areas, each with a population of over a million population (in Manchester's case more than two million).

Remarkably, at least by German standards, this growth continued with only the most piecemeal public regulation. There was still no perceived need for an overall approach. The nearest British cities came to controlling or shaping their growth continued to be via their public health responsibilities, now being strengthened with widening housing powers (Wohl, 1974). Measures such as building bylaws, reinforced under the 1875 Public Health Act, did not, however, assume the wider planning significance of their German counterparts. Yet developments in housing were beginning to be much more important than previously in reforming the living environments of cities.

**Figure 2.8** *Along with Bournville, Port Sunlight, developed by William Lever, put Britain in the forefront of international thinking about housing reform and provided a practical expression of the garden city idea.*

## THE EMERGENCE OF MUNICIPAL HOUSING

Following earlier schemes, especially in Scotland, the Artisans and Labourers Dwellings Improvement Act of 1875 gave powers to municipalities to clear and rebuild slum areas (Gauldie, 1974; Yelling, 1986). The effects of the new legislation were modest and usually had little impact on housing conditions beyond the removal of slums. The most ambitious scheme was in Birmingham from 1876, where new commercial frontages were created. The problems of providing low cost, decent housing did not go away, however. Increased political agitation in the early 1880s led to working-class housing becoming the subject of a Royal Commission, which reported in 1885. The Housing of the Working Classes Act which eventually followed in 1890 was a landmark. It did not grant important new powers, but signalled a more active phase in municipal housing action. In many cities, particularly London and Liverpool, municipal tenement flats were built in inner city, usually slum-cleared, locations (Beattie, 1980). Foremost amongst the early schemes was the London County Council's Boundary Street estate in the East End, where over a thousand dwellings were built around a central public garden from 1893.

## THE COTTAGE AS A NEW MODEL

Already though, the main arena of urban housing reform was shifting outwards, reflecting the pattern of urban growth itself. As industry began to move to urban fringe locations, and as urban transport improved, the suburbs seemed to hold new promise. In 1888, William Lever started a model village for workers at his new soapworks near Birkenhead (Hubbard and Shippobottom, 1988). Called Port Sunlight, it set new standards for working-class housing, with low-density cottages in vernacular styles, small private gardens, allotments, extensive public open space and an impressive range of community facilities. From 1894 George Cadbury, a Birmingham cocoa manufacturer, developed Bournville (M Harrison, 1999). Though similar in many ways to Port Sunlight, it differed by not being a pure company housing scheme. Its greater emphasis on private gardens contiguous with the cottage housing made it an even more influential model. In 1898 the London County Council also began to reflect the new thinking, with the decision to build municipal housing in the suburbs. However, no such housing was built before 1900.

## HOWARD'S GARDEN CITY

The year 1898 also saw the publication of a hugely important book, *To-morrow: A Peaceful Path to Real Reform*, that within a few years propelled Britain into the forefront of international thinking about urban planning (Howard, 1898). Its author was Ebenezer Howard, an obscure shorthand writer and failed inventor with an interest in social reform. His idea, largely perfected in the early 1890s, was to replace the giant city with what he called the social city. This consisted of a network of small garden cities, most with a population of 30,000, carefully planned and built on communally owned land at relatively low densities. Since the land had been bought at agricultural values and would remain in collective ownership, the whole community would benefit from the increases in land value that would arise from urbanisation. The absence of a private land market would also allow growth to be strictly controlled. There was to be an agricultural belt around each garden city, preventing coalescence. There would, however, be good communications between the different settlements of the social city.

## ORIGINS OF THE GARDEN CITY

Unlike the previous writers to whom we have referred, Howard had no relevant professional experience. His influences lay more in social reformism (Beevers, 1988; Aalen, 1992). The approach was broadly socialistic with a voluntary, cooperative and pragmatic emphasis that contrasted with the growing mainstream socialist reliance on the state. Howard drew on earlier English utopian ideas, including Benjamin Ward Richardson's 1876 book *Hygeia or the City of Health* (Richardson, 1876). He was also influenced by colonisation of the world's 'empty lands', particularly by the ideas of Edward Gibbon Wakefield, the main promoter of South Australia. Despite never having visited Australia, Howard also particularly admired Adelaide, the capital of this colony. Its parkland belt, which prevented continuous urban development, clearly influenced his concept of the social city.

As a young man Howard had spent time in the United States, where he became familiar with American social thought. He was especially influenced by transcendentalism, the literary movement led by Ralph Waldo Emerson and Henry Thoreau, which emphasised the human relationship with nature. Later, after his return to England, he often seized on new American thinking. Thus the land-taxing ideas of Henry George (1880), which asserted public ownership of unearned and especially speculative increases in land value, and the socialistic visions of Edward Bellamy (1888), had a very direct bearing on the development of his own thinking. Some commentators have gone further with his American connections, inferring a very direct connection between Olmsted's Riverside plan and Howard's garden city (eg P Hall, 1988; Garvin, 1996). Both men were undoubtedly influenced by transcendentalism but, although Howard lived in Chicago during the suburb's early years, there is no evidence of a direct connection. In a book characterised by prolific 'name dropping', Howard makes no reference to Olmsted or Riverside. (He did, though, propose the notion of a large central park, adopting this actual name and possibly thereby alluding to Olmsted's New York efforts.)

We are on much safer ground in noting the land reformist associations of the garden city, especially with the British-based Land Nationalisation Society founded by the biologist Alfred Russel Wallace in 1882. It was this society that provided Howard with his first adherents in the Garden City Association, founded in 1899 (Hardy, 1991a). However, this was soon to change in the new century as the whole basis of the garden city movement widened.

# The city beautiful in the United States

## American urbanisation

Meanwhile, in the United States there were important further developments in thinking about urban planning. As in Germany, one of the main spurs to action was the sheer scale of urban growth (McKelvey, 1963). The population of New York City grew from 942,000 in 1870 to 3.4 million by 1900, though that of the metropolitan area was over five million (KT Jackson, 1984). Next, in 1870, was Philadelphia which passed a million in the 1880s. Boston had also passed the million mark by 1900. Both, however, were rapidly overtaken by the fastest growing big city, Chicago, which reached 1.7 million by 1900, a fourfold increase since the mid-1870s. This upstart metropolis became the principal setting for several key innovations in American urban planning in the late 19th and early 20th centuries.

This rapid growth, echoed in all American cities, had created an urban landscape that was crude by European standards. This was despite American urban wages being the highest in the world – they had to be sufficient to attract immigrants from Europe and to counterbalance the free or cheap land that was still being opened up for agricultural settlement elsewhere on the North American continent. They allowed American workers to aspire to housing that was generally better than that of their European counterparts. Given the strength of demand, it could readily be provided through the private market. Yet the public infrastructure and amenities of the cities remained poor. The parks movement had begun to have some effect, in stirring the expectations of the urban elites, but practical fulfilment was still limited. Meanwhile many cities, especially in the Midwest, continued with largely unpaved, dirt streets, polluted air and watercourses, bad public cleansing and shabby, unimpressive central areas.

## The city beautiful movement

The city beautiful movement, as it was widely being termed by 1900, came together during the 1890s to address these varied ills (Scott, 1969; Wilson, 1989). The movement was important as much for what it left out as for what it included (Fogelsong, 1986). Despite localised housing conditions that could be every bit as bad as in the great cities of Europe, especially in New York (Plunz, 1990), housing did not feature on the American route to urban planning (Marcuse, 1980). Nor, at this stage, did the pursuit of urban efficiency. The city beautiful certainly asserted a concept of urban order but, compared to German thinking, that order was expressed symbolically in buildings, civic art and landscaping. Any systematic regulation or coordination of speculative capitalist urbanisation was not yet on the agenda.

## Municipal improvement associations

The parks movement was one element in the city beautiful and also encompassed the municipal improvement associations which spread rapidly throughout the country in the 1890s (Wilson, 1980; Peterson, 1983a). Typically these associations, which were important arenas for local political activism by middle- and upper-class women, sought (and often achieved) modest improvements. Their staples were tree planting, billboard controls, drinking fountains, removal of eyesores and improved street cleansing. Yet their thinking, which spread outwards from the 'womanly' concerns for a well-ordered home, also led to more ambitious visions for the city.

## GRAND CIVIC DESIGN

The third major element in the city beautiful was the growing American interest in grand civic design (Scott, 1969). The inspiration was classical European and, more specifically, the approach associated with the École des Beaux Arts in Paris. Here was an architectural language that would reinforce the message of an American urban civilisation to equal or surpass those of Europe. It was this which the upstart American cities used as they tried to reform their corrupt city governments and build the new libraries, art galleries and concert halls. Although certainly not the first expression of this approach, the so-called 'White City' at the World's Columbian Exposition in Chicago in 1893 marked its definitive arrival and, more widely, that of the city beautiful movement as a whole. As part of the exposition, many temporary buildings were created in the grand classical style and in a landscaped setting. Many found in it a vision of a city very different to the one outside the exposition grounds.

## DANIEL BURNHAM AND THE 1893 COLUMBIAN EXPOSITION

Within a few years, the main elements of the city beautiful began to be transferred into plans for real cities. Public or semipublic buildings were grouped together into civic centres. Axial or symmetrical road layouts linked these into the existing city fabric. There were vistas along tree-lined boulevards, statues, ornamental public lighting and the grand parks that were already in vogue. The doyen of this new approach was Daniel Burnham, a highly successful Chicago architect who, with his partner John Root, had planned and orchestrated the success of the White City. In fact, it fell to Charles Mulford Robinson, a journalist, to give literary expression to the movement at the turn of the century. Nevertheless Burnham must be seen as its principal innovator and promoter.

## LIMITATIONS OF THE CITY BEAUTIFUL

The city beautiful had a rather limited impact, however, at least in its original form. The lack of emphasis on the functional elements of the city restricted its potential. Like the parks movement, it was essentially conservative reformism, an expensive way of meeting the needs of the urban elites that offered very little for the urban masses. But it was its failure to address the functional needs of urban capitalism that was most seriously to limit its potential as a movement within urban planning (Fogelsong, 1986). Already though, Americans were beginning to learn about the newer models of European urban planning that were emerging (Sutcliffe, 1981; Reps, 1997). Significantly, one visitor to the 1893 exposition was Josef Stübben who informed American engineers about the latest German developments in *Städtebau*. Such early connections with the emergent mainstream of international urban planning discourse grew much stronger over the following years.

## DEVELOPMENTS IN OTHER COUNTRIES

### FRENCH STAGNATION

The most important innovations in urban planning in the last decades of the 19th century were, then, those in Germany/Austria, Britain and the United States. In comparison with these, notions of urban planning reform stagnated in France. In large measure, this reflected a slowing of urban growth compared to that in the other countries and even to earlier French experience (Sutcliffe, 1981; G Wright, 1991). Yet a legacy of older problems, such as congested and unhealthy districts or poor traffic circulation remained, so this cannot explain everything. Haussmannism continued, albeit less frenetically than under the Second Empire and without further innovation. There was, though, some interest in housing reform which led in 1894 to legislation (Bullock and Read, 1985). This permitted the formation of housing societies (known as Sociétés des habitations à bon marché, after the key pressure group which had been formed five years earlier) that, with the advantage of tax exemptions and low-interest loans from the state, were intended to provide low-cost housing. Actual achievements were very limited, however, particularly compared to what was happening in Britain. And following France's defeat in the Franco-Prussian War of 1870–1 national pride did not allow any overt attention to be given to the important German innovations.

### CHARLES BULS AND DEVELOPMENTS IN BELGIUM

In fact, the most important urban planning developments in the French-speaking world in the late 19th century occurred in Belgium. There were several reasons for this. In part it reflected the particularly intense and early industrialisation of Belgium (even though there was less urbanisation than in neighbouring countries because many Belgian industrial workers maintained a link with the land). Also, this still relatively new state was particularly conscious of the need to learn from external examples. Compared to France, it was altogether more open to British and German ideas about aspects of urban management such as sanitary engineering and housing reform (Claude, 1989). Stübben himself was particularly interested in Belgium (which was, of course, far closer than the largest German cities to his bases in Aachen and Cologne). He also exchanged ideas with the key Belgian innovator in urban planning, Charles Buls (Smets, 1995).

Buls was the mayor of Brussels during the 1890s and became embroiled in the controversy over Leopold II's desire to monumentalise the Belgian capital. Putting his arguments together in a short work entitled *Esthetique des Villes* (Aesthetic of

Towns), he accepted the necessity for urban change but argued that its physical effects should be minimised to retain historic qualities. It was an argument very similar to Camillo Sitte's, though Buls claimed not to know this slightly earlier work (GR Collins and CC Collins, 1965). Like Sitte's work, however, Buls's book proved timely and popular and soon became widely known in urban reform circles in Francophone countries. In 1899, his ideas were translated into English by an American magazine. In Brussels, however, he met with little practical success and resigned as mayor, also in 1899.

## ARTURO SORIA AND *CIUDAD LINEAL*

In Spain, meanwhile, another important innovator, a Madrid engineer called Arturo Soria y Mata (the last part often omitted) had come up with a remarkably potent vision of urban development (Soria y Mata, 1996). In 1882 he first outlined his notion of a low-density *ciudad lineal* (linear city), along the route of a tramway or rail system. In theory, at least, his project was intended to be a true city with offices, shops, factories, schools and public buildings as well as housing. In practice, however, the few kilometres of linear city that were developed as a real estate venture in the northeastern suburbs of Madrid from 1894 comprised only villa residences (Wynn, 1984a).

Despite the modest scale of this venture Soria did not lack ambition, and tried to promote the notion of vast linear cities that would cross international boundaries. Despite the extreme modesty of his actual attainment, his ideas have survived and reappeared in various (often unrecognisable) guises in the 20th century (P Hall, 1988). It is ironic, though, that Soria stands out as Spain's major planning innovator, compared to Cerdà whose proposals left a far more definite imprint on his city of Barcelona. Both certainly suffered from Spain's comparative isolation from the most advanced parts of Europe. But Soria was able to create a linear cities movement rather than being a lone innovator. A journal to promote the linear city appeared in 1897, and thereby became the first serial publication in urban planning (GR Collins and CC Collins, 1965). Soria was also active at a more auspicious time than Cerdà. His efforts coincided with innovations in other countries, so his work was reported in their emergent planning literature in the early 20th century.

## OTHER PARTS OF EUROPE

Elsewhere in Europe, activity was mainly continuing along the same broad lines that had been apparent in 1875. Some of the new currents of thinking about urban planning had begun to spread, even beyond their original linguistic realms. By the 1890s, for example, the key German and Austrian works were becoming known in the Netherlands and Scandinavia as well as Switzerland. Thus Hendrik P Berlage, the greatest architect and urban planner in the Netherlands in the early 20th century, authored an appreciative summary in Dutch of Sitte's ideas in 1892 (Stieber, 1998). Haussmannism remained a continuing model to which many European (and non-European) countries referred.

Apart from the innovations in Spain, southern Europe remained almost wholly untouched by any of the newer ideas until after 1900. In part, this reflected the slower pace of southern European industrialisation and urbanisation (Wynn (ed), 1984a). Even Italy, an apparent legislative innovator in the full flush of its Risorgimento (the period of its unification – literally resurgence), could show little, by 1900, that had been done with its 1865 extension legislation (Calabi, 1980).

## JAPANESE INTEREST IN URBAN REFORM

Outside the principal European innovators and the United States, much the most interesting pre-1900 developments in planning came in Japan (Ishizuka and Ishida, 1988). The Meiji restoration of 1868 unleashed a strong Japanese desire to westernise, first in order to avoid western colonisation but increasingly to make Japan itself into a world power. At the same time, the imperial capital was moved from Kyoto to the largest city, Edo, which was renamed Tokyo (Watanabe, 1984). Western ideas about urban management and reform played a significant part in this process, which initially relied on imported expertise. The rebuilding of the Ginza district in Tokyo after a fire in 1872 was the first example of this westernisation (Noguchi, 1988; Fujimori, 1988; TMG, 1994). Traditional flimsy Japanese houses were replaced by brick buildings in western-style streets lined with pine, cherry and maple trees. The development's appearance was similar to those found in larger British colonial cities. An English engineer, Thomas J Waters, supervised the rebuilding which, although never completed, continued until 1877.

Meanwhile a Japanese delegation visiting Paris, also in 1872, returned full of admiration for Haussmannism. Another important early encounter, in 1886, was with the emergent German planning expertise (Watanabe, 1984; Hein and Ishida, 1998). However, ambitious proposals prepared by two German architects, Bockmann and Ende, to form a government building district at Hibiya in Tokyo did not materialise. As in Germany, the pressures to think coherently about Tokyo's future development derived from functional and health matters rather than the desire to create grand administrative districts.

## URBAN IMPROVEMENT IN TOKYO

The most important actual changes in urban policies came a few years later (Ishizuka and Ishida, 1988). After some controversy the government forced through the Tokyo Urban Improvement Ordinance in 1888 (Ishida, 1988b; TMG, 1994). It is a measure of the extent of the problems in Tokyo that ministers, assailed by growing pressures for military spending, took this step. Yet it involved much more than architectural statements. Edo's lanes and alleyways were not adequate in a city whose population had passed one million in 1883 and was continuing to grow very rapidly, to about 1.8 million in 1900. A serious cholera outbreak in 1886 highlighted many other problems.

The following year a major plan for the capital's urban improvement appeared. It was, essentially, a massive scheme of public works in the manner of Haussmann.

Included were proposals for some 317 new roads, 49 parks, many river and canal works and much else. It differed from Haussmann's approach, however, by being explicitly and comprehensively planned from the outset, with a detailed map showing all proposals. Yet this was not modern urban planning in the 20th-century sense because it lacked any controls over land use and density in private property. Inevitably for such an ambitious programme, implementation was delayed and incomplete. The costs of Japanese militarisation competed with major public works spending. Nevertheless, the 1889 improvement plan laid the infrastructural basis for the rapid industrialisation and growth of Tokyo in the late 19th and early 20th centuries.

## Australia and Canada

### European settlement in 'empty lands'

The two most autonomous and economically developed parts of the British Empire were the Dominion of Canada, created in 1867, and the Australian colonies, shortly to be federated to form the Commonwealth of Australia (in 1901) with similar self-governing status to Canada. Both were settler countries, largely peopled by European stock, mainly from the British Isles. The rights of the indigenous peoples of these countries were very substantially overridden by this process, especially so in Australia which was legally regarded as an empty land before white settlement. Populations were small – Canada with 4.83 million in 1891, the Australian colonies with 3.77 million – but immigration was continuing. Both countries had substantial cities, though Australia, with nearly half its people urbanised in 1891, greatly exceeded Canada which (on a slightly more generous definition of urban) had not quite 30 per cent (Forster, 1995; McCann and Smith, 1991). This was borne out in the size of cities. Australia's two largest metropolitan areas, Sydney and Melbourne, were both not far short of half a million people in 1900. Montreal, by contrast, was a little over half this figure, and Toronto well below half. Not surprisingly, therefore, it was in Australia that the most significant moves towards modern urban planning had occurred.

### Colonial and modern urban planning

Like the United States, Canada and other parts of the British Empire, Australia had a strong tradition of laying out entirely new settlements for colonisation (Home, 1997; Proudfoot, 2000). In a sense, therefore, the colonial land surveyors were the first planners, though their efforts differed from the modern forms of urban planning that were emerging in the late 19th century. In particular, they lacked the broad conceptual development that was the hallmark of the newer movements. Nor was there any continuing process of regulation once a private land market emerged in the new settlement. Moreover, it was in the biggest cities, long after the colonial surveyors had departed the scene, and not in the planted settlements of the frontier that the demands for the new urban planning appeared. Yet, just as aspects of princely planning persisted in Europe, so memories of colonial planning survived and influenced the emergent modern forms. The most obvious example is in Howard's citing of Adelaide's green belt in *To-morrow* (Howard, 1898; 1902). (Another, earlier, example was Cerdà's interest in the colonial plans of the cities of Latin America.) In the colonial societies, themselves, the connections were easier to make.

## John Sulman and the Laying Out of Towns

In part, perhaps, it was an awareness of this colonial tradition that brought about the first clearly documented use of the term 'town planning'. This, the usual British label for modern urban planning, was actually an Australian coinage (Freestone, 1996a). Its first use came in 1890, some 15 years before its adoption, apparently coined independently, in Britain itself (Adams, 1929).

The Australian inventor of the term was John Sulman. British-born and, like many Australians at that time, stubbornly British in outlook, he was already a successful architect in London before emigrating in 1885 and took with him a particular appreciation of European civilisation, especially of Italy and France. What he encountered was a rapidly growing urban society in a young country, rich with possibilities for those with ambitions to shape a new civilisation. This was certainly the tenor of a paper he read in Melbourne in 1890 on the laying out of towns. In it, he criticised Australia's relentless grid patterns, calling instead for a radial 'spider's web' approach with major diagonal streets. He also called for park reserves between suburban areas (on the Adelaide model). There were even hints of functional zoning, though there is no evidence that he was yet aware of evolving German practice. Nevertheless, Sulman was almost certainly the first person in the British world to articulate a comprehensive approach to shaping cities.

We should not, though, build too much on this paper. Sulman's use of the term 'town-planning' (hyphenated) was incidental (Freestone, 1983). It occurred only once in the paper and was certainly not being promoted as the key label. Nor did it mark the beginning of a continuous usage. Still less did it give rise to any real practical expression. Sulman himself did not apparently use the term with any regularity until after 1900. But as an international discourse of urban planning grew in the new century, confirming his prophetic musings, he won some recognition as an Australian 'St John the Baptist crying in the wilderness' (cited Freestone, 1996a: 47).

## Canadian developments

There was no equivalent figure in 19th century Canada, perhaps because there did not need to be. Although rather less of the country's territory was as hospitable for settlement as was that of the United States, many parts of its vast interior were capable of sustaining European-style farming settlements or more primitive rural economies. This allowed Canada to maintain a more rural character than was ever possible in Australia. Most Australian settlers remained relatively close to the first points of landing and the first settlements quickly became the biggest cities. In

Canada, there was more of a rural and small-town alternative to the big city, so we should not be surprised that efforts to tame or perfect the city were more muted than in Australia.

In the last decades of the 19th century Canada's city leaders had similar concerns to their counterparts in other countries settled by European immigrants, and all big cities in western Europe (Hodge, 1991; Wolfe, 1994). Disease and public health, slum housing and its elimination, public parks and public utilities preoccupied the leaders of cities such as Montreal, Toronto, Quebec, Ottawa, Hamilton and Winnipeg. More so than in most other countries, however, the risks of urban fire remained a particular Canadian preoccupation, a reflection of timber construction and poor water supplies. But none of these concerns, nor the continuing laying out of new settlements in the west of the country – especially along the new Canadian Pacific Railway – sparked any indigenous moves to bring them all together into a coherent discipline or policy. That had to wait until after 1900, when such ideas were imported from the United States and Britain.

## CONCLUSIONS: INNOVATION AND DIFFUSION

### THE SOURCES OF INNOVATION

By 1900 therefore, there had been a noticeable quickening of interest in urban problems and their solution in many parts of the world. In a general sense the forces that were driving this growing interest were industrialisation, urban growth and the ascendancy of liberal political ideology. The main innovatory countries were those that had the most dynamic economies, the largest and fastest growing cities and the most effective governmental institutions.

Yet the emergence of new thinking about urban planning did not coincide exactly with these general forces. Britain, for example, though it was the world's most heavily industrialised and urbanised country (and believed itself, at least, to be the most liberal), was rather slow to come to the idea of an overall approach to urban development. France, after the burst of imperial inventiveness represented by Haussmannism, proceeded even more slowly. Even in Germany, where the model apparently fits reality more closely, the actual centres of innovation were not always those where problems of urban and economic growth were most acute.

Then there were the occasional examples of remarkable inventiveness in less industrialised and less 'advanced' countries. Cerdà and Soria stand out particularly here. Yet the fate of their ideas, especially Cerdà's, tends also to confirm part of the general model. Almost certainly their thoughts had less influence than if they had originated nearer the main centres of economic and urban dynamism. The advanced thinking in parts of Scandinavia also received less attention for related reasons. The linguistic origins of the new ideas were also of some significance. It seems fairly certain that the Spanish or Swedish innovators would have had a bigger impact if their ideas had been originated in German, English or even French. Language was not everything, however. As Sulman showed in Australia, ideas generated on the periphery of the English-speaking world could equally be overlooked.

## THE ROLE OF DIFFUSION

These last points highlight the importance not just of innovation, but also of diffusion of new thinking. One of the main sources of Germany's lead in urban planning was its tremendous efficiency in this respect. Well-developed professional organisations and a highly efficient system of technical training ensured that knowledge spread far more rapidly within the German-speaking world than elsewhere. Competitions for town extensions also quickened this diffusion, forcing entrants to consider different approaches (Breitling, 1980).

Meanwhile growing numbers of major exhibitions were beginning to facilitate the spread of all kinds of ideas (Meller, 1995). These exhibitions could have an important domestic role, showing off the latest thinking in Paris, Berlin, Tokyo or Chicago to visitors from other places. Yet they also had a growing international role. Domestic innovations were opened up to foreign eyes. Domestic practitioners and reformers were able to make or personalise contacts with foreign counterparts. Increasingly, too, these exhibitions became occasions for drawing attention to new thinking from all countries. They thus began to play a key part in the formation of an international discourse.

However, we should not exaggerate what had happened by 1900 in this respect. Though the pace of innovation had quickened in many places during the 1890s much thinking was still relatively disconnected, especially from ideas in other countries. The absence of a significant body of literature, especially works that had been translated into other languages, was noticeable. Specialist international gatherings of those interested in urban planning lay largely in the future. Relatively few individuals had yet made personal international contacts.

## THE NEW CENTURY

All this was to change in the years immediately following. Innovations continued to occur with greater intensity than even in the 1890s. Yet improved mechanisms for diffusion allowed them to become more joined up than they had ever been in the old century. It was these that allowed a truly international urban planning discourse to emerge in the early years of the 20th century, as we will see in the next chapter.

# Chapter 3

# The Emergence of Modern Planning

For planning, the years from the opening of the 20th century to the outbreak of the First World War were extraordinarily creative. From being a self-conscious body of theory and practice only in the German world in the 1890s, modern urban planning now became known almost everywhere. The actual word 'planning', which had appeared only fleetingly before 1900, was widely adopted in the English-speaking world and beyond. Equivalent new names were adopted elsewhere, most notably the French term *urbanisme*. Whatever the national label, however, further conceptual innovation and practical demonstrations of earlier thinking were now firmly part of a common international discourse.

Germanic leadership in urban planning matters was no longer unchallenged after 1900. The tremendous conceptual potency of the English garden city idea was refined and extended in its practical elaboration. It rapidly became the most important single element of early 20th-century international planning thought, widely (if partially) emulated. The American city-planning movement, meanwhile, was shifting from the city beautiful to the far more practical model of the city efficient. In doing this, it set new standards in large-scale master planning and in planning techniques. In France public actions continued to lag behind Germany, Britain and the United States, yet it too became the source of important ideas. Even more, it was the artistic and technical virtuosity of the first generation of *urbanistes*, frustrated at the lack of domestic outlets for their expertise, that marked the main French contribution.

Yet to concentrate only on the exchange of urban planning ideas within the four main innovatory traditions is misleading. Throughout much of the rest of Europe modern urban planning, under its various names, was being energetically promoted as an enlightened and progressive response to the various problems of the city. Predictably, perhaps, its acceptance was greatest in countries such as Belgium, the Netherlands and Sweden which were closest to the major innovators. Yet the new ideas were spreading to the fringes of western Europe and beyond. There were also important developments outside Europe. Within the British Empire, Canada and Australia witnessed important planning initiatives in these years. Meanwhile Japan's unique project of westernisation saw the beginnings of an indigenous emulation of urban planning ideas from the west.

In this chapter, then, diffusion assumes a more central place in the story, alongside innovation.

## Britain

### Implementing the Garden City

The most outstanding example of rapid diffusion in these years was that of the garden city. There had been little sign of this in 1899, when Ebenezer Howard and a small

46
—

group of land reformers had founded the Garden City Association. The new century, however, coincided with a shift in the social basis of the association, drawing in leading businessmen, professionals and progressive landowners (Beevers, 1988; Hardy, 1991a). The result was that the garden city moved into the mainstream of liberal reformism as the association became a much more effective lobbying organisation. Alongside this, Howard's original prime interest in reforming society by local collective landownership and governance was subordinated to a reform of the physical arrangement of urban industrial life. Social reform, in other words, became narrowed into urban planning.

Howard had, of course, written about the physical form of his garden city but only as part of the larger project. The second edition of his book, entitled *Garden Cities of*

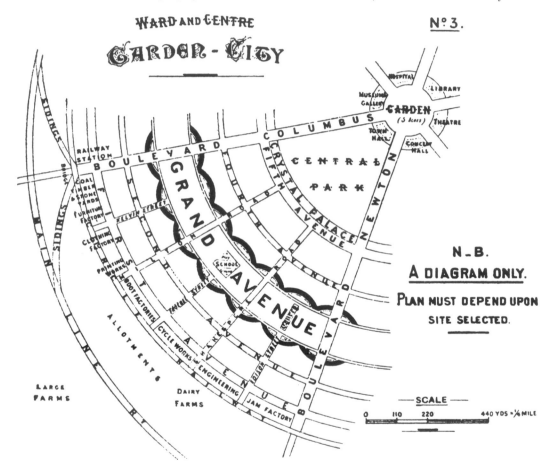

*Figure 3.1 The garden city quickly became the central focus of the new British town planning movement. Howard's emphasis on creating community and protecting nature were lasting endowments which attracted intense interest throughout the world.*

*To-morrow*, marked a noticeable shift (Howard, 1902). Though the text remained very similar to the original, subtle changes in the diagrams (and the title) diminished the overall vision of the social city and concentrated attention on the garden city as a physical entity. Even the establishment of Letchworth, the first garden city, in 1903, though it remained the purest practical expression of Howard's hopes, compromised his original ideals on land and governance (Miller, 1989). Its planners, Barry Parker and Raymond Unwin, also created a residential environment that was so attractive that it soon became synonymous with the garden city, partly obscuring Howard's original social reformism (Miller, 1992).

## THE GARDEN CITY AS A PHYSICAL IDEAL

The garden city was an ideal based on the English vernacular cottage tradition, already popular at Bournville and Port Sunlight (Hubbard and Shippobottom, 1988; M Harrison, 1999). Unwin and Parker subscribed to the Arts and Crafts tradition and the ideas of William Morris, and this same aesthetic quickly became synonymous with the garden city (Miller, 1992). Housing densities, at 12 per acre even for the cheapest

**Figure 3.2**  *One of the most admired achievements of the British garden city movement was Hampstead Garden Suburb. Planned by Raymond Unwin and Barry Parker, it benefited also from the architecture of the well known Edwardian architect, Sir Edwin Lutyens, shown here.*

cottages, were about a third lower than Howard had indicated, allowing more generous gardens. Instead of the longer terraces of housing which Howard had envisaged in his diagrams, shorter groups and more detached and semidetached forms became possible. It was an approach that proved to be very attractive both in England and, very soon, elsewhere.

## THE GARDEN SUBURB

Yet development at Letchworth proceeded very slowly. Despite Howard's own utopian desires to set up more garden cities, the practical reformers who dominated the movement as a whole looked instead to existing cities. In 1901, the association had held a major conference at Bournville which was henceforth understood as an application of garden city principles to existing cities. This train of thought soon led to the concept of the garden suburb which supplanted that of the garden city. Parker and Unwin had already produced a garden-village plan for New Earswick near York in 1902. Unwin also applied the same principles to Brentham, an existing suburb, in west London (Reid, 2000). But it was the Unwin-Parker plan for the new Hampstead Garden Suburb (originally 1905 but revised in 1906–7) in north London that had the biggest impact (Miller and Gray, 1992).

The suburb (actually in Golders Green) was promoted by Dame Henrietta Barnett, a wealthy philanthropist who had been active with the housing reformer Octavia Hill in late Victorian charitable works. In the mid-1880s Henrietta's husband, the Reverend Samuel Barnett, had pioneered the settlement house movement at Toynbee Hall in east London. This idea involved the creation or adaptation of buildings in slum districts where the charitable instincts of young and socially concerned middle-class people could be directly focused on the poor. The main interest was adult education, but other reformist impulses were also nurtured by such direct contacts. This proved especially so in the United States where the settlement house movement was adopted with rather wider impacts for urban reform than in Britain. Certainly, by 1902 the Barnetts' concerns had shifted to northwest London, to protecting the fringes of Hampstead Heath from ill-considered development triggered by the new tube railway then being built. From 1903, Dame Henrietta broadened her objective to include a garden suburb for all social classes. Parker and Unwin's plan, together with the more formal treatment of the suburb's central area by the leading architect Sir Edwin Lutyens, were hugely influential in Britain and elsewhere. By 1914, other examples had appeared in most larger English cities.

## THOMAS HORSFALL AND THE EXAMPLE OF GERMANY

The garden suburb, especially in its more elaborate manifestations such as Hampstead, represented the first serious British equivalents to town extension. The density and built form were radically different to the usual form of extension practised in Germany. Yet a real synthesis of German and English ideas was taking place. A Manchester reformer, Thomas Coghlan Horsfall, became the principal carrier of German planning ideas into Edwardian Britain (Reynolds, 1952; M Harrison, 1991).

He had become aware of German *Stadterweiterungen* in the 1890s, but it was not until the early years of the new century that he studied it in detail. A book reporting his investigations appeared in 1904, the supplement to a larger work. It was called *The Improvement of the Dwellings and Surroundings of the People: The Example of Germany* and it had a truly dramatic effect on urban reformist thinking in Britain (Horsfall, 1904).

The main reason for this lay not so much in the book's intrinsic qualities as in its timing (Sutcliffe, 1981; Cherry, 1974; Ward, 1994). The British elite were now far less complacent than they had been even 10 years earlier. The Boer War had revealed the poor physique of army recruits from the big cities – and the subject of physical deterioration had become the subject of a Royal Commission in 1903. There was a growing sense of international insecurity as Germany challenged British trade and strategic dominance. Combined with mounting domestic social unrest, this created circumstances conducive to international lesson-drawing. Horsfall's book was an extensive, admiring and somewhat repetitive description of German planning thought and practice. Yet, even in his admiration, he recognised that British urban housing was generally better than that in Germany. The real lesson was that the general urban environment outside the home could be greatly improved by following the German example. Infrastructure, transport, land use and layout could all be coordinated to good effect.

## JOHN NETTLEFOLD AND 'TOWN PLANNING'

This was certainly the message that was adopted, nowhere more so than in Birmingham. A local councillor and nephew of Joseph Chamberlain, John S Nettlefold, another avid drawer of lessons from Germany, led in following the German model (Cherry, 1975). Already in 1905 he was beginning to advocate planned municipal town extensions, if possible on municipally owned land (Nettlefold, 1908). Instead of council housing, there would be low-density cottage developments by limited-profit co-partnership housing societies (Skilleter, 1993; Birchall, 1995). With his city's medical officer of health, and quite unaware of Sulman's earlier use of it, he coined a new term to describe this concept – 'town planning' (Adams, 1929). This time, however, the term stuck and was quickly taken up in British discussions. By 1909 it had acquired legal status in Britain's first planning legislation, which itself owed direct allegiance to Nettlefold's hybrid concept (Sutcliffe, 1988). Its provisions permitted the preparation of town planning schemes (Nettlefold, 1914). These included reservations of new road lines, and adopted land use and density zoning to shape the extension of towns and cities, invariably at something close to garden suburb densities. The widespread municipal landownership that Nettlefold advocated was not encouraged, however.

## THE INFLUENCE OF CAMILLO SITTE

Although Birmingham was the main example, Horsfall's book fostered other synthetic borrowings from Germanic planning in Britain. His accounts of Camillo Sitte stimulated the interest of Raymond Unwin (Miller, 1992). In 1904/5 Unwin became familiar with Sitte's book through a French translation which had appeared in 1902. At about the same time he also visited historic German hill towns, and was not only influenced but also deeply moved by what he saw. His plans and sketches for Hampstead clearly show this in their Germanic touches. The connections are even clearer in his textbook, *Town Planning in Practice: An Introduction to the Art of Designing Towns and Suburbs* (Unwin, 1909), much the most authoritative of early British writings about the emergent practice.

## BRITISH PLANNING LITERATURE

There was, in fact, a growing volume of literature appearing in Britain at this time (Cherry, 1974). The periodical of the Garden City Association, called simply *The Garden City*, appeared in 1904 (Hardy, 1991a). This was joined in 1910 by Britain's first academic planning journal, *Town Planning Review*, produced at the School of Civic Design at the University of Liverpool. This was Britain's first planning school, albeit with a rather American title (M Wright, 1982). Both journals, but especially *TPR*, were important in introducing the British planning movement to foreign examples. The third main British periodical appeared in 1914 when the Town Planning Institute was formed. Called initially *Papers and Discussions*, and later the *Journal of the Town Planning Institute*, it included some international references though it usually focused more on evolving British practice.

## THE 1910 CONFERENCE

However, a one-off event was of more immediate importance in giving an international dimension to planning in Britain. This was the major international conference on town planning organised by the Royal Institute of British Architects in 1910 (Sutcliffe, 1981). Gatherings of the garden city movement had brought some personal contacts but against the background of an idea that was essentially British. The RIBA conference was altogether more widely conceived. The associated exhibition, for example, largely comprised non-British material and opened the eyes of early British practitioners to what was already under way in European countries other than Germany, and in the United States. Personal contacts also eased continuing communication. The participation of leading British planners in other international conferences began to increase noticeably.

## THOMAS ADAMS AND THE TOWN PLANNING INSTITUTE

Coming in the wake of the 1909 legislation, all these various developments coincided with the formation of a professional practice of planning. In 1914 this went a stage further with the creation of the Town Planning Institute, a professional body that catered for those involved in town planning practice (Cherry, 1974). The driving force behind the new body was Thomas Adams, who occupied a key place in the formation of the British planning movement (Simpson, 1985). A surveyor, in quick succession he worked for the Garden City Association and Letchworth Garden City, and became one of Britain's first planning consultants and the first government town planning inspector under the 1909 legislation. Though his work did not approach the conceptual significance of Howard or Unwin, Adams had one hugely important invention to his credit: the idea of a planning profession, distinct from architecture, engineering or surveying. As we will see, it was one that had important effects throughout the English-speaking world. Adams himself became Britain's foremost transatlantic planner, a theme to be developed more fully below.

## A SCOTTISH CONNECTION?

Another facet of Adams is also worth mentioning: he was a Scot. Despite Glasgow's important role in developing urban management in the 19th century, the crystallisation of the idea of town planning in early 20th-century Britain took place overwhelmingly in England. The garden city aesthetic derived from the vernacular architecture of the southern English countryside. The tenement form of housing that was dominant in Scottish cities, giving them much in common with many continental cities (and indeed New York), was increasingly marginalised by this thinking. Adams' own background was, in fact, agricultural and it was Howard's ideas about rural land that first excited his interest, touching a potent aspect of late 19th-century Celtic reformism (Aalen, 1992). Yet Adams' 'Scottishness' did not long survive his move south. At least within the context of British town planning, his career confirmed rather than challenged the movement's 'Englishness'.

## PATRICK GEDDES

The case of the other prominent Scot in the early British planning movement, Patrick Geddes, was quite different (Kitchen, 1975; Meller, 1990). A biologist and pioneer sociologist, Geddes was based first in Dundee and then in Edinburgh. Despite extensive international links, especially with French social thought, he remained peripheral to the main trajectory of London-based thought about urban reform. In various practical initiatives such as the famous Outlook Tower in Edinburgh, and in often obscure theoretical writings, Geddes contributed a wider social and cultural perspective on the new activity of planning. His was a distinctive, if often exceptionally confusing, voice. Essentially he asserted the importance of looking at the city and its region on a wide geographical scale, surveying all aspects of its evolution and development before attempting to plan. His ideas in the field of urban planning were elaborated most fully in *Cities in Evolution*, completed in 1912 but denied publication until 1915. It is notable for introducing a new word, 'conurbation', to the vocabulary of urban planning in Britain. As with many of Geddes' ideas, however, his focus on the new spatial scale of the metropolitan region had little immediate impact.

## GERMANY

Essentially then, British town planning in the early 20th century grew from a mixture of indigenous and imported ideas, the latter largely from Germany but with a few nods in the direction of Haussmannism. Yet the diffusional flows were certainly not just one way. If British reformers and politicians felt insecure enough to borrow and adapt ideas from their main rival, so too did their German counterparts whose insecurity was, in many ways, far greater. The still young German national and imperial state was faced on two fronts by fearsome potential enemies: France and Russia. Strategic rivalry with an even more feared enemy, Britain, was growing during the early years of the century. Germany also faced the new experience of a population mainly raised in what, by English standards, were extremely overcrowded cities: there were real fears about whether the kaiser's imperial army would be fit enough to maintain the Prussian reputation for invincibility. In a wider cultural sense, too, the new Germany felt that it was not respected in the world, that its art and architecture were widely seen as vulgar.

## THE EXAMPLE OF ENGLAND

All these factors made Germans, despite their own impressive achievements, look anxiously abroad (Sutcliffe, 1981). There was also a growing disillusion amongst reformers about the way extension plans had often been subverted by land specu-lators. The grid and barrack-like tenements seemed as entrenched as ever. Envy of English housing traditions, seemingly the most potent alternative to Germany's urban tenements, grew rapidly (Bollerey and Hartmann, 1980). Already by 1900, a German architect, Hermann Muthesius, had been despatched to the embassy in London with instructions to study English housing and draw lessons for Germany. By the time his report appeared in 1904, in a massive three-volume work entitled *Das Englische Haus* (The English House), German opinion was already absorbing the example of England. Thus the first garden city association outside Britain was established in Germany in 1902 (Bullock and Read, 1985). Howard's book appeared in German in 1907.

## A GERMAN GARDEN CITY MOVEMENT

The German garden city movement began as a utopian project. Almost immediately, however, it also became a home for other kinds of thinking. These included the sort of practical, middle-class, liberal reformism that was apparent in Britain. But more than in the London-based movement, strong conservative reformist tendencies were also apparent from the outset. In 1913, for example, a leading medical expert, anxious to secure his country's position as a world power, urged that, 'Germany needs garden cities more urgently than England does!' (Bollerey and Hartmann, 1980: 160). Theodor Fritsch also repackaged his ideas into the new thinking. Thus the second edition of his *Die Stadt der Zukunst*, which appeared in 1912, borrowed the Howardian term *gartenstadt* (P Hall, 1988). Fritsch's main platform, the conservative reformist journal *Der Hammer*, continued to push this broad message.

## HELLERAU

These different currents also began to be evident in actual developments associated with the German movement. The example regarded as being closest to the Howardian ideal was Hellerau, on the outskirts of Dresden (Bollerey and Hartmann, 1980). Begun in 1908, it was quickly labelled the 'German Letchworth'. It was actually more suburb than freestanding community, and its target population of 15,000 was well below the 30,000 favoured by Howard. Yet it had local employment and community facilities as well as low-density cottage-style housing. Its cooperative mode of development and control, and the prevailing utopian desire to educate its inhabitants into a new kind of society, also echoed Howard's wider reformism. The aesthetic was very traditional, however, more so even than in English examples. Its architecture and design conception (by architect Richard Riemerschmid) were directly drawn from German historic towns.

*Figure 3.3*  *There had been growing German interest in British housing reform for many years, nowhere more so than in the Ruhr, where the Krupp family had admired the efforts of British industrial philanthropists. Their own Margarethenhöhe, in Essen, was a German equivalent of Port Sunlight or Bournville.*

## MARGARETHENHÖHE AND FALKENBERG

The same was true of other products of the garden city movement in Germany at this time. Best known was Margarethenhöhe, a garden suburb in Essen, the chief town of the Ruhr (Bullock and Read, 1985; von Petz, 1990a; Böll, 1997). Begun in 1908, it was a creation of the Krupp industrial dynasty and was named after Alfred's widow who played a key role in its early development. Like Bournville (or New Earswick), it went beyond company housing. Only about half its residents (and it was much the biggest Krupp settlement) were actually company employees. Ultimately it housed some 5,000 largely white-collar families in one- or two-family garden dwellings. Its design, by Georg Metzendorf, was an impressive synthesis of Sitte and German Arts and Crafts. Approached by a bridge across a wooded valley, and surrounded by a wooded belt, its design strongly evoked the ideal of the small medieval town accessible through an archway. At its heart was a fine town square with impressive community facilities.

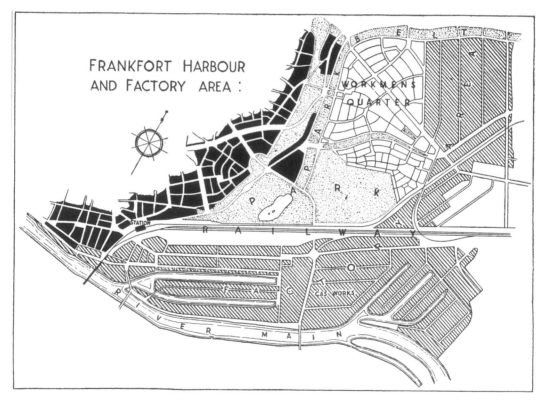

**Figure 3.4** *German planning led the world in the sophistication of its approach to land use and density zoning. Since 1890, Frankfurt had set the pace and was widely admired, here in an English planning text.*

However, there were signs of a new aesthetic emerging in at least one scheme – at Falkenberg-in-Grunau, near Berlin, begun in 1912 (Bollerey and Hartmann, 1980). The architect-planner here was Bruno Taut, who became a leading German modernist in the 1920s. His design emphasised starker, simpler housing forms, avoiding the historicist detail of contemporary schemes. In fact, the scheme was only partially implemented because of the First World War. Yet it marked the start of an important transformation in the German garden city that flowered after the war in the more progressive intellectual climate of the Weimar Republic.

## THE DEVELOPMENT OF PLANNING DISCOURSE

Germany was, then, profoundly affected by British planning thought. Despite having coined two umbrella terms for urban planning in the 19th century (*Stadterweiterungen* and *Städtebau*), from 1910 Germans still felt it necessary to adopt *planung*, directly borrowed from the new English term, as a suffix (Albers, 1980). Yet this surprising deference was not uncritical. Like the British, the Germans adapted what they borrowed to create something distinctive. Such was the level of planning discourse in Germany that new ideas would be closely debated, at professional gatherings and in a rapidly growing and more critical literature. Especially important was the new planning journal *Der Städtebau* which appeared in 1904 (GR Collins and CC Collins, 1965). In these circumstances, adaptations were inevitable. Yet German urban planning did not now evolve only by synthesising imported elements with its own pre-1900 innovations. This occurred, of course, but there were also notable examples of purely indigenous innovation.

## FRANZ ADICKES AND LAND POOLING

An important and influential innovation came in 1902, though admittedly it reflected many years of urging the adoption of a proposal to consolidate land holdings before development occurred, suggested in very vague terms by Baumeister. The Prussian parliament finally passed the so-called Lex Adickes (Law Adickes), named after its sponsor Franz Adickes, the mayor of Frankfurt. Since 1893, Adickes had been seeking powers to readjust land in order to ensure that the layout of new districts was not constrained by the small peasant strips that were typical of Frankfurt (Sutcliffe, 1981; Bullock and Read, 1985). The essence of the scheme was to pool land compulsorily and regroup the plots. This often took place voluntarily but landowners normally forced up prices. Adickes' proposals therefore became a symbol of a wider struggle between planners and landowners. Germany had very high costs for land development, reflecting the extent to which town extension planning had worked in the interests of landowners. Although several state parliaments had begun to enact readjustment powers during the 1890s, the main state parliament, in Prussia, had refused. In the event, its members accepted only a watered-down scheme, that applied only to Frankfurt, and limited the scale on which readjustment could be applied. The original concept was not forgotten, however, and continued to influence thinking in Germany and elsewhere, especially Japan (Hein and Ishida, 1998).

## Planning Greater Berlin

More firmly a product of the early 20th century were the important moves towards regional planning (Matzerath, 1984). The outward spread of Berlin, Germany's capital, had by the early 20th century moved the built-up area beyond the existing city boundaries. There was, though, opposition to enlargement of the city by the Prussian government and the more affluent suburbs. Their reluctance was politically and financially motivated. Like many large cities, Berlin was more radical than the surrounding rural and affluent suburban districts and its local taxes were higher.

A compromise solution seemed to lie in promoting the idea of regional planning. In 1908–9, a semi-official competition was launched for a plan covering the Greater Berlin area which (by 1910) had a population of some 3.7 million, compared to two million in the city (Kündiger, 1997b). The competition was won by Hermann Jansen and his associates. This and the subsequent exhibition in 1910–11 sparked a lively debate, both about the future of the Berlin region and about approaches to planning on a metropolitan scale. Meanwhile, in 1911 the Prussian government set up an inter-urban board for the Greater Berlin area which extended between 20 and 40 kilometres from the centre. In common with many voluntary associations whose members have different interests, it failed to work very satisfactorily. But, with the exception of the 1909 Chicago plan, it was in advance of anything comparable that was happening elsewhere.

## Planning the Ruhr

Another German metropolitan area quickly followed these initiatives and, after initial setbacks, met with rather more success than Berlin. This was the multicentred urban region of the Ruhr (Reulecke, 1984). The Berlin exhibition and a smaller one in Düsseldorf in 1910 were important in focusing minds (Ladd, 1990). The latter, especially, encouraged thinking about the Ruhr's development in a unified fashion. The driving force in this was Robert Schmidt, the deputy mayor of Essen, who had special responsibility for urban planning (von Petz, 1997a; 1999). He undertook an investigation in 1911–12 which, in the short term, failed to gain unanimous approval. Submitted as a doctoral thesis at Aachen, however, it remained an important contri-bution to a debate which resurfaced, rather more successfully, after 1918.

## France

In the new century France slowly started to justify again its reputation as a trendsetter in urban matters (Sutcliffe, 1981; Rabinow, 1995; G Wright, 1991). This slowness continued to reflect the less urgent pressures of French urban growth

*Figure 3.5* Tony Garnier *finally began to move French thinking about wider urban design beyond Haussmann. Recently an urban museum dedicated to his* Cité Industrielle *has been opened in Lyons in a housing scheme designed by him in the 1920s.*

compared to that in Germany and Britain. Surprisingly though, the strategic and economic insecurities which underpinned British and German moves were less acutely felt in France. Much still rested on the continuing Haussmann legacy and complacent assumptions about the superiority of French urban culture. Yet many reformers began to feel that French national pride was being dented by a failure to engage in the new innovations and artistic developments concerned with the development of cities. Unfavourable comparisons were made with the municipal achievements of many countries in northwest and central Europe, and the United States. As we have seen, such insecurities were elsewhere a spur to new indigenous initiatives, and there was also the desire to see and understand, however imperfectly, the developing ideas and practice of urban planning in other countries. Such trends were also apparent to some degree in France, and the new planning thinking of Britain and the United States became increasingly known. Swiss and Belgian developments (the latter now to a lesser extent) also allowed some second-hand exposure to German experience.

Direct Franco-German interchange was rare. The most obvious meeting point for the two traditions, Alsace-Lorraine, was in German hands at this time, evoking feelings far too painful to promote easy contact. Despite this, developments on this Franco-German interface continued to be important. The new border capital, Nancy, energised by the influx of Alsatian wealth and innovation after 1871, became a shop window for French creativity and progressive ideas. The city led in the pressure, for the moment ineffective, for French planning legislation. And it was Nancy that hosted France's first town planning exhibitions, in 1909 and 1913. Nancy was not France, however, and its progressive reformism was not typical. In many ways, the most remarkable progress of these years was in the technical development of urban planning, which ran well ahead of any wider commitment to urban reform.

## TONY GARNIER AND THE *CITÉ INDUSTRIELLE*

Chronologically the first important French innovator of the 20th century was the architect Tony Garnier, who proposed an idealised city (Pawlowski, 1993; Wiebenson, 1970; van der Kruit, 1997). Called the *cité industrielle* (industrial city), it appeared definitively in print only in 1917, when he was city architect of Lyons. Yet the idea had surfaced much earlier, originally in 1899–1900. At the time Garnier was a student at the École des Beaux Arts in Paris, France's premier school of architecture, and won the prestigious Prix de Rome.

While in Rome Garnier flouted custom and submitted not the expected study in the classical tradition, but a project for a frankly modernist *cité industrielle* (G Wright, 1991). It was not as fully elaborated as the later version, but many essentials were already apparent. Here was a utopian socialist settlement of 35,000 people,

*Figure 3.6  The garden city idea also had a big impact on French thinking. Here the French garden city society sets out its philosophy, showing how Howard's humanity and concern for nature had struck international chords.*

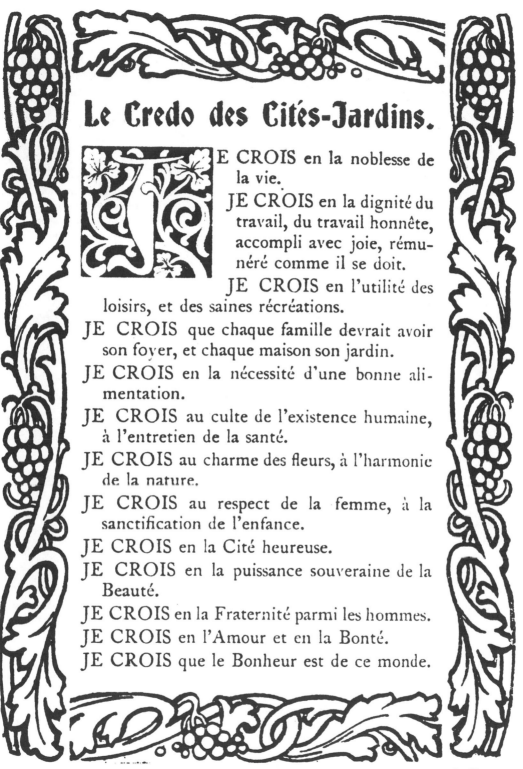

# Le Credo des Cités-Jardins.

JE CROIS en la noblesse de la vie.

JE CROIS en la dignité du travail, du travail honnête, accompli avec joie, rémunéré comme il se doit.

JE CROIS en l'utilité des loisirs, et des saines récréations.

JE CROIS que chaque famille devrait avoir son foyer, et chaque maison son jardin.

JE CROIS en la nécessité d'une bonne alimentation.

JE CROIS au culte de l'existence humaine, à l'entretien de la santé.

JE CROIS au charme des fleurs, à l'harmonie de la nature.

JE CROIS au respect de la femme, à la sanctification de l'enfance.

JE CROIS en la Cité heureuse.

JE CROIS en la puissance souveraine de la Beauté.

JE CROIS en la Fraternité parmi les hommes.

JE CROIS en l'Amour et en la Bonté.

JE CROIS que le Bonheur est de ce monde.

inspired by the writings of Émile Zola, without coercive state apparatus (such as police, law courts or prisons). Its wealth and main source of employment derived from heavy industry. Its buildings, formed in concrete, were flat-roofed, simple and unadorned, without ornament or decoration. All aspects of the *cité* showed careful planning in housing standards, hygiene, zoning and circulation. Garnier justified his project with an impassioned statement about its social philosophy.

The reaction was predictable. The scheme was rejected and, despite student riots against the decision, was not exhibited until 1904. Nevertheless, it galvanised the thinking of several of Garnier's contemporaries and had a powerful long-term influence, most notably on Le Corbusier. Garnier himself became the chief architect of his home city and was never a major international planning figure. Yet several of his associates, particularly Henri Prost, Leon Jaussely and Ernest Hébrard, soon became outstanding French practitioners of urban planning in Europe and beyond.

## THE MUSÉE SOCIAL

Whether Garnier knew of Howard's garden city, with which the *cité industrielle* showed important similarities, is unclear but is thought to have been unlikely. It is clear though that he and his contemporaries showed a growing interest in the emergence of urban planning in neighbouring countries. A growing number of French reformers began to share similar concerns (Sutcliffe, 1981; Gaudin, 1992). The most important focus lay in the Musée Social (literally, Social Museum), a progressive reformist body established in 1894. Its founder and leader was Jules Siegfried, whose background typified the roots of much French reformism. He was a Protestant businessman from Alsace – again the crucial interface between France and Germany – who became an admired and reforming mayor of Le Havre following the German annexation of his native province in 1870. The Musée Social was an attempt to develop the idea of reform and spread it more widely. In the early 1900s, Siegfried's creation began to show strong interest in aspects of social hygiene and established an urban and rural hygiene section in 1908.

## FRENCH KNOWLEDGE OF FOREIGN INNOVATIONS

These growing interests encouraged (and were encouraged by) French knowledge of foreign innovations. Under the auspices of the Musée Social there were visits to Germany, in 1902, and to Britain and the United States in 1904. Yet the findings of the individual observers were often idiosyncratic and never as systematic as the Anglo-German diffusions of the same period. Also, noticeably fewer French than Germans, British or, indeed, other nationalities, took part in international planning discourse during these years. It was entirely characteristic that when Camillo Sitte's book appeared in French, in 1902, it was translated by a Swiss architect, Camille Martin. Moreover, the major diffusional impact of this turned out to be that Sitte was rendered more accessible, not to the French, but to the burgeoning British planning tradition via Raymond Unwin (Miller, 1992). Despite these kinds of limitation, some limited understanding of German municipal policies, the English garden city and American parks policies began to influence French thinking.

## THE FRENCH GARDEN CITY MOVEMENT

The main figure who brought knowledge from the English-speaking world to the Musée Social was Georges Benoît-Levy (Read, 1978; Gaudin, 1992). This young Parisian reformer authored several books, mainly on garden cities which he defined in rather a vague and elastic manner. This was not merely the confusion between garden cities proper and garden suburbs that was widespread, even in Britain. Benoît-Levy managed to extend the garden city to include American parks planning and city beautiful ideas. He entirely omitted Howard's emphasis on land reform and left the impression that Bournville and Port Sunlight were more typical garden city products than Letchworth. Despite this, Benoît-Levy played an important role, with two other reformers Charles Gide and Charles Rist, in the formation of the Association des Cités-Jardins Françaises (French Garden City Association) in 1903 (Buder, 1990). Soria's ideas on linear cities also came to his attention shortly afterwards and in 1913 he formed a society for their promotion, later merged with the French garden city association.

## FRENCH GARDEN CITY DEVELOPMENTS

As everywhere, practical achievements were few. Given Benoît-Levy's emphasis on industrialist initiatives, it is not surprising that the scheme that was claimed as France's first garden city was employer-provided (Read, 1978; Bullock and Read, 1985). This was a very small scheme of 74 houses provided by the mining company at Dourges, adjoining a more typical Mulhouse-style employer village. Others followed and by 1914 there were a growing number of private or cooperative suburban ventures which claimed allegiance to the garden city idea. One notable example was Petit Groslay, a speculative low-density development on a 90-hectare site in the north-eastern suburbs of Paris, begun in 1912. Others of the same period developed on more cooperative principles. These included Draveil, which provided 350 individual plots on the 60-hectare grounds of a chateau in the southern suburbs of Paris. These, and others, were developed at densities well below those in British or German examples, with large plot sizes and much landscaped parkland. The cooperative settlements claimed to cater more for the working, rather than the middle, classes but this was probably even less true in France than it was in Britain and Germany. At best they reached only the lower middle classes. Yet the French understanding of the garden city had certainly become the preferred model for low-cost housing by 1914. There were some abortive moves to create a working-class garden city close to Paris shortly before war broke out. But, despite this failure and the many other disappointments of the French housing reform movement in the early 20th century, some important changes had already occurred. Although tangible achievement only came after the war, it was the creation of a national framework for housing organisations in 1912 that had laid the essential basis for the widespread creation of *cités-jardins*.

## EUGÈNE HÉNARD AND TRAFFIC CIRCULATION

More even than Benoît-Levy, the only French urban planner of this period to become widely known to his British and German counterparts was Eugène Hénard (Hénard, 1910; Rabinow, 1995; Sutcliffe, 1981). This was largely because he regularly attended the growing number of international conferences on urban planning. An architect and engineer, he worked at the Paris public works office until his retirement in 1913 (Landau, 1995). He achieved little of note in his actual work but was something of a visionary. Between 1903 and 1909 he authored a series of brochures on the future of Paris (Evenson, 1979). Their most interesting proposals concerned traffic circulation, then a brand-new subject. Hénard wanted extensive street widening but he also proposed multilevel movement systems that would separate different transport modes. He is also widely regarded as the inventor of the *carrefour à giration* (traffic roundabout). In fact, the idea of one-way gyratory circulation at intersections was probably first applied at Columbia Circle, New York, in 1905 (Todd, 1988). However, the concept took firmer root in Europe where it revolutionised the older concept of the circus, following its use at the Place d'Étoile in Paris in 1907.

## SOCIÉTÉ FRANÇAISE DES ARCHITECTES-URBANISTES

In 1910 a specific French word, *urbanisme*, first appeared in print to describe the emergent field of urban planning (*Urbanisme*, 1999). Over time, terms with this common linguistic root became favoured in all the Latin languages (*urbanismo* in Spanish, *urbanistica* in Italian). The French coinage, evidently the first, may have owed something to Cerdà's earlier term, *urbanización*, which had appeared in French in the 1870s. Of particular importance in fixing the newer term in planning discourse was the creation, in 1911, of a French organisation of professional urban planners (www.urbanistes.com). Its founders were a group of relatively young professionals, mainly architects (among them Hébrard, Jaussely and Prost), but included a few from other fields (engineering and landscape architecture). They had been active in the debates of the Musée Social and were anxious to open up opportunities for their talents in France. In 1914 the organisation was put on a more formal basis with the elder statesman, Hénard, as its first president. A few years later its title was simplified to Société Française des Urbanistes (SFU).

This was not a Gallic version of the British Town Planning Institute (Sutcliffe, 1981). From the outset, the TPI sought to organise and control technical expertise in a new area of statutory activity which cut across existing professional demarcation lines. The SFU, by contrast, was born out of the sheer frustration of a small group of reform-minded and exceptionally talented professionals. Throughout its history, membership of the organisation has remained the prerogative of a small, though influential, elite. Actually, the breakthrough that this first generation of French *urbanistes* looked for took a long time coming. Their pressures for a planning law in France were not successful until after the war. Yet they found compensations abroad, in other parts of Europe, Latin America and the French colonies. Despite their domestic frustrations, they were important because they formed the first cohort of international planning consultants.

## OTHER PARTS OF EUROPE

### SPAIN

Leon Jaussely was the first of the *urbanistes* to win acclaim outside France. In 1904 he won a competition in Barcelona to link newly annexed outlying areas with Cerdà's Eixample (de Torres i Capell, 1992). His plan (which, it has been suggested, incorporated some features of Garnier's *cité industrielle*) was notable for its road proposals in the outlying areas. These elements were eventually adopted, and shaped the city's outer development in the early 20th century. Yet Jaussely's proposals for the *Eixample* itself, modifying Cerdà's chamfered grid with Beaux Arts-style grand diagonal avenues, had little impact. Nevertheless, he had laid the foundations of France's international reputation in planning the 20th-century city. A few years later he confirmed his international credentials by entering the Greater Berlin planning competition, transcending the usually unbridgeable Franco-German cultural gulf (Bosma and Hellinga, 1997c).

Overall though, Jaussely's Barcelona triumph was not only significant for French *urbanisme* (Monclús, 1996). It was also a sign that the early Spanish innovation in modern urban planning was giving way to a growing deference to developments elsewhere. The home-grown linear city project continued to be promoted with some energy, but there was still little by way of real achievement. As elsewhere, the garden city idea quickly entered the debate, reinforcing a growing tendency to suburban development around the big cities. The best-known effort was that promoted from about 1900 by a prominent Barcelona industrialist, Eusebi Guëll. Planned from 1906 by the city's greatest architect, Antoni Gaudí, it showed some reference to Howard's ideas. There was to be no local employment but this low-density, middle-class garden suburb would have its own community facilities and overall control of long-term development. However, its elevation and remoteness from the city's tramways proved its downfall. Only three houses were built and eventually the failed suburb became the Park Guëll, one of Barcelona's greatest architectural sites. Guëll was also instrumental, through his son, in establishing the Spanish garden city society in Barcelona in 1912. As elsewhere in Europe, there was an intermingling of the imported model with other, already current, ideas. In this case, however, the latter were dominated by the home-grown linear city and the resultant synthesis was particularly distinctive.

### BELGIUM

Another country where *urbanisme* achieved early prominence was Belgium. The 1910 competition to plan the extension of Antwerp, following the removal of its fortifications, became a very French affair (Rabinow, 1995; G Wright, 1991). Hénard was on the judging panel. Prost and Marcel Auburtin (another founder of the SFU) were the winners. The Belgian encounter with the English garden city idea was also at this stage largely dependent on the somewhat wayward early French understanding of the concept (Smets, 1977; Uyttenhove, 1990c). A short-lived Belgian garden city association appeared in 1903, aiming to promote a garden city for the new Campine coalfield, but it fell apart only a year later. There were, however, several small developments along garden city lines by industrialists in this region. From about 1910 a few Belgian architects and reformers also began to gain a more complete understanding of the original British concept, independently of the French. Thus the most complete prewar Belgian example was a *cité-jardin* for coal miners at Winterslag, which dated from 1912 and showed evidence of these more direct encounters.

Yet Belgium was not entirely dependent on French developments. Belgian housing reforms were, in some ways, well ahead of those in France. More importantly, the country's bicultural character, Walloon and Flemish, gave it a unique quality amongst the nation-states of western Europe. This, along with its history and geographical position as the 'cockpit of Europe', encouraged strong internationalist sentiments amongst its reformers, the most prominent of whom was Paul Otlet, a Brussels lawyer (Meller, 1995). Otlet had many links with the emergent urban planning movement in several countries. He was especially keen to create an international world city (*cité mondiale*) in Belgium and spoke forcefully on the subject at a major international planning conference held in Ghent in 1913.

## THE WORLD CENTRE OF COMMUNICATION

Otlet was not alone. Also in 1913, a Norwegian-American sculptor, Hendrik Christian Andersen, published a detailed proposal for a city devoted to internationalism (Edwards, 1914; K Bosma, 1997b). The project, financed by an American business-woman, was dedicated to peace, international justice and harmony. Amongst many other features it would include a permanent home for the Olympic Games, themselves only lately revived in 1896. Andersen's collaborator on the detailed design was another of the pioneer French *urbanistes*, Ernest Hébrard. The plan itself was a remarkable blend of highly formal French Beaux Arts, American city beautiful, garden city and more general functional planning principles. The architecture and civic art were lavish in scale, crowned by a vast 'Tower of Progress'. Two immense nude male and female figures, inspired by the ancient Greek Colossus and evidently larger than New York's Statue of Liberty, formed a maritime gateway.

Proposed sites included Brussels, Bern, Constantinople (Istanbul), Rome and several others. Not surprisingly, the project was never implemented. Criticised at the time for its grandiose utopianism, it was nonetheless acknowledged, even by critics, for the exemplary completeness of its planning approach. It was also expressive of the real sense of internationalism that pervaded much of the emergent urban planning movement at the time. And, not least, it established the international reputation of yet another French *urbaniste*.

## THE NETHERLANDS

The Hague was among the sites mentioned as a possible location for the world centre. In fact, important synthesising developments in urban planning were already occurring in the Netherlands. With the introduction of their important Housing Act in 1901, the Dutch combined elements of both German planning thinking and British housing reform ideas (van der Heiden, 1988; Casciato, 1996; Stieber, 1998). The legislation, which came into operation in 1902, made the preparation of extension plans for towns with populations of more than 10,000 compulsory, and promoted the provision of social housing. Its extension planning provisions were immediately brought to prominence by developments in the largest Dutch city, Amsterdam, which had a population of 511,000 in 1900 (DRO, 1994).

## BERLAGE AND AMSTERDAM SOUTH

As noted in the previous chapter, Hendrik Berlage had begun to introduce planning ideas from the German-speaking world during the 1890s. The first Dutch word for urban planning, *stedebouw*, adopted around the turn of the century, was the exact linguistic equivalent of the German term. And there was already some wider acceptance of its principles. Thus in 1900 Amsterdam's city council, having rejected its own engineer's proposals on aesthetic grounds, commissioned Berlage to prepare a plan for the southern extension of the city (Stieber, 1998). The result appeared in 1904, to a mixed reception. While there was some praise for its aesthetic qualities, there were also criticisms that it was too 'German'. Other voices, more tellingly, argued that it would cost too much to implement it. In the event, this did not happen until it had been extensively revised (by its author) in 1915. Proposals for an extension plan for Amsterdam North also appeared during 1901–3, with a far more utilitarian character. Berlage himself also designed an extension for The Hague in 1908.

## DUTCH HOUSING REFORM AND THE BRITISH CONNECTION

The housing side, and with it the British connection, developed a little more slowly (Stieber, 1998). The sections on land appropriation in the 1901 legislation followed the English housing legislation of 1890. Little use was made of these provisions until the growing social democratic representation on Amsterdam's city council began to promote social housing provision more actively from 1913. Yet the initial development of institutions and ideas about housing reform betrayed a growing awareness of Britain. Its influence was palpable in the naming of the city's first housing society, in 1903. By calling it the Coöperatieve Woningbouwvereeningen Rochdale (Rochdale Cooperative Housing Society), its trades union founders paid homage to the Lancashire industrial town where the cooperative movement had formed. (The name also showed, incidentally, that physical and design ideas were not the only ones to spread.)

The latest British thinking about housing design also entered the Netherlands from 1906 as Dutch publications on the garden city (*tuinsteden*) appeared. Yet the full effects of this mixture of external influences with the remarkable and unique Dutch architectural movement known as the Amsterdam School, discussed in Chapter 5, only became apparent after 1914 (Casciato, 1996). Before then, it was Dutch developments in extension planning that began to attract international interest.

## SWEDEN

The relatively small size of Nordic cities limited their impact on the emergent international planning movement (T Hall (ed), 1991). In 1900 Copenhagen, with a population of just over 400,000, was the biggest. Stockholm, the capital of the largest Nordic country, had only 300,000, while Christiania (now Oslo) had under 250,000 and Helsinki a mere 91,000. Despite this, the Nordic cities were at least as advanced in urban planning matters as those in countries which saw themselves as leaders in the field.

It was, in fact, the remarkable far-sightedness of Sweden's 1874 legislation that finally caught the attention of foreign observers (T Hall, 1991a). In 1910, for example, Thomas Horsfall, the influential British commentator on German planning, gave it fulsome praise at the London international planning conference. However, Sweden had already strengthened the law in 1907, giving it, for the first time, real powers to regulate the form of buildings as well as street and plot layouts. As to the detailed ideas which informed the exercise of these impressive powers, Sweden showed the familiar interest in German *Städtebau* and the English garden city. Garden suburbs that combined the design principles of Unwin and Sitte appeared at Enskede in Stockholm, from 1908, and Landala in Göteborg, from 1911 (K Åström, 1967; Rådberg, 1994; Andersson, 1998). They were designed, respectively, by the two most prominent Swedish planners of the early 20th century: Per Olof Hallmann and Albert Lilienberg.

## OTHER NORDIC COUNTRIES

Elsewhere in Scandinavia Norway, newly and painlessly separated from Sweden in 1905, sought some expression of distinct national identity. From a traditional deference to Swedish trends, Norwegians began to seek their own understanding of emergent ideas from other countries (Lorange and Myhre, 1991). In fact, the sources of these ideas were the same as in Sweden – Germany and Britain – although the balance of influence was weighted a little more in favour of Britain. The consequences of the closer Norwegian interest in the garden city did not become apparent to any extent until after 1914 when indigenous planners began to wield greater influence.

In Finland, too, nationalist sentiments played their part, though in a different way, in the formation of the new planning discourse (L Kolbe, 1990; Sundman, 1991). Here the engagement with international planning ideas reflected the growing disenchantment with the country's position as an autonomous grand duchy within the Russian Empire. Liberal reformers, many of them Swedish-speaking, supported more cosmopolitan contacts to assert their cultural independence. Accordingly German and British approaches to urban planning, mainly received via Sweden, were embraced enthusiastically by early Finnish planners. Most prominent among these were Lars Sonck, who planned garden suburbs at Eira and Kulosaari on the fringes of Helsinki, and Eliel Saarinen, the first Finnish planner to establish an international reputation outside Finland.

By comparison with Norway and Finland, developments in Denmark were less shaped by larger nationalist aspirations (Knudsen, 1988; Larsson and Thomassen,

1991). Despite Danish friction with emergent German nationalism in the 19th century, Germanic planning ideas dominated the shaping of the country's planning. The principles of town extension and the ideas of Sitte were well known from an early stage. The concept of the garden city and the ideas of Unwin, himself so appreciative of the lessons of Sitte, were also known in Denmark from about 1902 as Danish enthusiasts became familiar with British developments. Despite such awareness of British planning, however, it was symptomatic of the general tenor of early modern Danish urban planning that in 1909 a competition to plan Copenhagen's development was won by a German, Carl Strintz, from Bonn.

## AUSTRIA

The impact of the Austrian Camillo Sitte's ideas on the emergent thinking about urban planning in western and northern Europe was not mirrored in his own country (GR Collins and CC Collins, 1965). Sitte himself died in 1903, and the last years of the Austro-Hungarian Empire saw a quite different approach to city planning becoming dominant (Banik-Schweitzer, 1999). It can be seen in the context of the great creative upsurge that preceded the imperial collapse in 1918. Its champion was Otto Wagner and it was played out in the imperial capital, Vienna (LO Larsson, 1984). Wagner published an important and influential book in 1911 called *Die Grossstadt* (The Great City). This adopted a line contrary to the dominant western trend by assuming an unrestricted and highly formal expansion of the big city. The book offered immaculately drawn images of an infinitely expanding Vienna, with no attempt to moderate its big city character. Densities would be high; gardens would be formal; streets would be urban and, in complete contrast to Sitte, rectilinear – they should be straight because busy people preferred straight lines.

Wagner was a highly influential figure in the development of Vienna at this time. Following his winning of the 1892–3 competition for the expansion of the city, he had been placed in charge of architectural design for the city's metropolitan railway. His scheme for the *grossstadt* gave particular emphasis to transport in the perfection of the great city, anticipating some aspects of modernist design thinking in the interwar years. Its immediate impact in western Europe was, however, more limited, than that of Sitte's contrasting philosophy. It was, though, received with slightly more interest in the United States, where Sitte's work was virtually unknown at this time, and where the pursuit of ways of asserting urban greatness was a stronger theme.

## ITALY

Of the larger countries of west and central Europe, Italy was certainly the slowest to embrace the ideas of modern urban planning (Calabi, 1980; 1984). This was doubly ironic, in view of its premodern urban design traditions and its early adoption of planning legislation in 1865. But slow urban growth and the undeveloped state of land markets in most Italian cities meant there was little pressure to use the legal instruments that were available. Many cities adopted regulatory plans, but these involved little more than planning street alignments, with none of the growing international interest in land use and density zoning. More importantly, this lack of enthusiasm was mirrored in the failure to develop a significant discourse of modern urban planning. Though there was awareness of developments in the German- and English-speaking worlds, active engagement with new ideas and practices was very limited before 1914.

A few examples of Italian practice stand out, such as the reconstruction of Messina following a massive earthquake in 1908 which killed 120,000 people. But even here, reconstruction began without a master plan. A royal decree of 1910 partially rectified this, though there was no provision for separating land for industry from areas for other activities until 1914. A small programme of housing provision, partly influenced by garden city ideas, began in the rapidly growing industrial city of Turin in 1907. A small garden suburb, Milanino, was begun in Milan in 1910 (Sutcliffe, 1981).

Milan also witnessed the most remarkable and internationally significant Italian conceptual development of this period (LO Larsson, 1984; Cohen, 1995). The Futurist group had been founded in 1909 by the poet Filippo Marinetti as an artistic movement concerned with the aesthetics of contemporary life, especially the machine and motion (Tisdall and Bozzolla, 1977). A later adherent was the young architect Antonio Sant'Elia who, in 1914, exhibited a Futurist vision of the Città Nuova (New City). No full city plan of the Futurist city was ever elaborated. Yet the massive high-rise architecture constructed in concrete, steel and glass, the vast transport arteries and multilevel circulation systems shown in Sant'Elia's drawings made a fundamental contribution to the emergent imagery of the modern city.

## THE UNITED STATES

The only buildings anywhere in the world that remotely resembled those in Sant'Elia's drawings were in the United States (Cohen, 1995). In turn, Sant'Elia's musings were one sign of a growing European fascination with the American urban aesthetic. This fascination was not, however, widely reproduced in the most fully elaborated theories of urban planning in Europe. (There is, for example, little evidence that Wagner's grossstadt took much account of American experiences.) In fact, the only European planning model that seemed to reflect the experiences of the United States, and other lands in the process of settlement, was Howard's garden city. Yet in the United States itself the movement for urban planning actually proved less accepting of Howard's ideas in their uncompromised form than he might have hoped. In part, this was because the great period of new settlement formation in the West was by now over. The urbanisation of the country was already a fact as the new century opened, with over a quarter of its population living in cities or their suburbs.

It is not surprising, then, that Americans shared the primary concern of European planners, namely to improve and enhance the burgeoning big cities. Nor is it surprising that, in view of the strong transatlantic flows of people and information that already existed, they also shared in many of the body of ideas and practices of their European counterparts (Rodgers, 1998). Although, at this stage, the flow was more westward than eastward, American city planning (as it was definitively labelled during these years) very rapidly synthesised the new notions it received from all the major emergent European planning traditions. And by the time war broke out in Europe, important new innovations had begun to flow in the opposite direction.

## CITY BEAUTIFUL PLANNING

As shown in the previous chapter, the main focus of American thinking by 1900 was the ideal of the city beautiful. This continued for some years to be the dominant paradigm, spread more widely within the country by the many, often rather contradictory, writings of Charles Mulford Robinson (Scott, 1969; Peterson, 1983a). The first two plans that seemed to fulfil the promise Robinson wrote about appeared in 1901 and 1902. One of these could hardly fail to be noticed. This was the plan endorsed by the McMillan Committee for Washington, the federal capital (Reps, 1991). Several leading exponents of the city beautiful, amongst them Daniel Burnham and Frederick Law Olmsted Jr, had produced the proposals which came after an arduous five-week European tour that said much about the aesthetic roots of their whole approach. Their report was peppered with illustrations of what had most impressed them – the gardens at Versailles, Fontainebleau, Compiègne and Vaux-le-Vicomte, the quays at Venice, Budapest and Paris, the memorial walk in the Thiergarten in Berlin and the great mall in Chichester. The proposals themselves also showed the paradoxical but, at that time, entirely characteristic deference of democratic Americans to the European, mainly French, classical urban grandeur created by thoroughly undemocratic

*Figure 3.7   The park had formed the major focus of American moves towards urban planning in the nineteenth century. It remained the central feature of the city beautiful movement, and was nowhere more apparent than in the plan for the National Mall in Washington DC.*

rulers. Yet this was combined with what was rapidly becoming a more distinctively American approach to urban landscape.

The other pioneering city beautiful plan, for Harrisburg, the small state capital of Pennsylvania, was on rather a smaller scale (Peterson, 1983a; Wilson, 1980). Now largely forgotten, it attracted contemporary attention as a model capable of wide-spread emulation. Soon many cities were taking action (Wilson, 1989). By 1908, city beautiful planning reports had been prepared, usually by private or semi-official organisations, for the large cities of New York, San Francisco and St Louis and a host of smaller cities (eg Brechin, 1990). Even Manila, the capital of the Philippines and in American hands following the Spanish-American war, had been subjected to a colonial version of the city beautiful formula.

The visions usually fell well short of what was actually achieved. Yet the movement did have a significant impact on the actions of city governments. Philadelphia, for example, began from 1908 to create what eventually became one of the most impressive realisations of the city beautiful approach outside the federal capital (Scott, 1969). The proposal was for a grand new parkway street that diagonally pierced, Haussmann-style, through the densely built-up rectilinear grid of streets near the city hall, connecting it with Fairmount Park, Philadelphia's outstanding public open space (RPFPTD, 1932). Everywhere there was also concern to reduce the visible sources of urban ugliness and squalor. This involved more prosaic proposals, for example to remove eyesores and reduce the advertising hoardings that disfigured many parts of American cities.

## LIMITATIONS OF THE CITY BEAUTIFUL

Such objectives implied direct regulation of private business activity, highlighting an important contradiction in the city beautiful approach (Fogelsong, 1986; Wilson, 1980). The previous chapter discussed some of the origins of the movement, within progressive urban elites. Wider support grew as part of the competitive civic booster-ism that was a characteristic feature of the American urban scene at this time. The city beautiful became a means by which cities could assert themselves as places for people of substance to live and invest in. This appeal was, however, riddled with contradictions, particularly when it required control of capitalist activity. Significantly, many critics noted that grandiose complexes of civic and cultural buildings approached by grand landscaped avenues coexisted with wider squalor and ugliness. (This contradiction had much in common with the Vienna of Otto Wagner.) Another strand of criticism was the scale of public spending necessary to implement the proposals. Other critics, including some more socially concerned business people, worried about the lack of attention to the living conditions of the urban masses.

## SOCIAL REFORMERS AND URBAN CONGESTION

Such concerns led some less conservative reformers to consider other approaches (Wirka, 1996; Simkhovitch, 1994). The main background was the settlement house movement, imported to New York from London in 1886 and publicised mainly by the work of Jane Addams in Chicago's Hull House from 1889. The settlement houses, based on the model of the Reverend Samuel Barnett's Toynbee Hall in the East End of London, were located in poorer neighbourhoods where they provided a setting for middle-class reformers, many of them young female graduates, to do good works. In fact, the concept became far more highly developed in American cities, especially New York, Chicago, Boston and Pittsburgh, than ever it did in Britain. Its initial potential for wider reform was, however, quite limited. Yet it laid an important basis for some of those who worked in the settlement houses to understand urban problems. Thus by the early years of the new century several figures associated with the movement, notably Florence Kelley, Mary K Simkhovitch and Lillian Wald, came to see the need for a wider approach. The result was the Committee on Congestion of Population (CCP), formed in New York in 1907.

## BENJAMIN MARSH AND CITY PLANNING

The CCP appointed Benjamin C Marsh, an energetic young man well versed in urban social problems, as its executive secretary (Kantor, 1994a). One of his first actions was to organise a large exhibition to raise consciousness about urban social problems and report on the solutions being adopted in other countries. In preparation, he visited Germany, France and Britain and was impressed, especially with Frankfurt's use of zoning and controls on private land. Though Marsh and the CCP were criticised as antibusiness for their enthusiasm for controls on the use of land (and for Henry George's land taxation ideas), they played a pivotal role in establishing a comprehensive American concept of urban planning, termed *city planning*, from about 1909. In that year Marsh published an important book, *An Introduction to City Planning: Democracy's Challenge and the American City*, which stressed previously unvoiced social arguments for planning. The CCP also organised the first national conference on city planning (1909), in Washington, and prompted New York to create a city commission on urban congestion (1910).

## THE AMERICAN GARDEN CITY MOVEMENT

Another, rather less important, strand in the mix of ideas that comprised American city planning was the garden city (Buder, 1990). There had been early contacts with the British movement in 1904–5 and a short-lived American association was founded in 1907. There were, however, important differences of intention between the two. There was no equivalent of Letchworth in the United States. Instead, the American movement encouraged the private creation of garden-city-type settlements, particularly by industrialists and public-minded developers. Howard's central concern for the communal ownership of land was ignored and there was less emphasis on reforming housing for the less well off, so that the garden city was understood almost entirely in design terms. The most important early triumph of this emasculated conception of the garden city was Forest Hills Gardens in New York, a nonprofit project of the Russell Sage Foundation, planned by Frederick Law Olmsted Jr from 1910.

## Burnham and the Chicago plan

Meanwhile the city beautiful tradition, exposed to reality and to increasing knowledge about recent European developments, was being changed into something that was both more comprehensive and more practical. The landmark in this transition was Daniel Burnham and Edward H Bennett's great plan for Chicago, published in 1909 (Hines, 1974; Wrigley, 1983; Scott, 1969). Privately sponsored by the Commercial Club of Chicago, the major business organisation of the city, it was notable for several reasons. Its scale alone, covering the whole metropolitan area, was unparalleled. It was also comprehensive in its coverage of functional as well as aesthetic aspects, innovative in its technical aspects and stunning in its presentation. All the familiar references to the great cities of Europe were present, with Haussmann's Paris well to the fore. A French illustrator brilliantly evoked what was intended; in one historian's words, 'a past that America never knew.' (Scott, 1969: 108)

The plan itself incorporated many features directly borrowed from Paris, particularly new diagonal streets that pierced the built-up grid (Werquin and Demangeon, 1995). Yet this search for legitimation by European historical reference was not the whole story. Thus the proposals to empark the entire lake front gave Chicago its most distinctive quality when they were implemented. And, even where European references were present, they were not always to beaux-arts classical grandeur. The calls to plan the suburbs, for example, were informed by German (and, lately, British) moves in the same direction. More importantly, the plan also had a very strong functional agenda, evident in topics such as transportation. It was certainly in these terms that it was promoted, to the Chicago business community and the population at large (Schlereth, 1994). The plan also had a wider international significance as the first modern plan from the United States to be admired in Europe (Sutcliffe, 1981). Since the 1890s, Europeans had begun to emulate American innovations in urban electric transit and to marvel at the scale and functional organisation of American buildings. Now, for the first time, American thinking about how cities should be organised began to be taken seriously.

## Towards the city functional

By 1909 the emergent American planning scene seemed set for a merger of the more practical turn city beautiful planning was now taking and the more radical and socially aware movement represented by Marsh and the CCP. In fact, this did not occur (Marcuse, 1980; Fogelsong, 1986). Almost from the outset, housing reform began to move in a different direction to city planning. This split reflected tensions between the various reform movements that were more difficult to bridge in America than they were in Britain. Many business people who were otherwise sympathetic to the idea of planning shied away from proposals for land-value taxes and anything but the most timid interventions in the urban land market. For their part, the 'housers' were increasingly frustrated with the way city planning ignored housing or treated it in a shallow and ineffective fashion.

This decoupling shifted city planning towards a more conservative concept. By 1910, it was widely accepted that the city beautiful alone was an inadequate, potentially bankrupting recipe. The ideology which now filled the vacuum left by the 'housers' was that of the city functional, a more practical and scientific approach that treated the city in businesslike terms. The new approach, spelled out overtly from 1911, stressed urban efficiency so there was great emphasis on transportation and orderly development (Scott, 1969). It also increasingly embraced an idea that Marsh had actually promoted: zoning.

## THE ORIGINS OF AMERICAN ZONING

Many of the arguments for zoning came, of course, from German cities. American knowledge of developments in Germany had increased greatly (Phillips, 1996). A key intermediary figure in this diffusion of knowledge was Werner Hegemann, a young German planner who spent long periods in the United States (CC Collins, 1996). Through his lectures and contacts with many key figures in the emergent movement, including Marsh, Olmsted Jr and Robinson, he elaborated on many of the lessons of German planning. On zoning, however, as on other aspects, the story was not a simple case of borrowing. A more primitive version of zoning had begun to evolve in American cities in the 19th century. This used the legal concept of police power to restrict, without compensation, activities seen as nuisances (JB Cullingworth, 1993; B Cullingworth 1997). In 1885, for example, the Californian city of Modesto had used this approach to limit steam laundries (run by Chinese) to certain parts of the city. As this rather suggests, American civic (and usually, therefore, business) leaders were already beginning to see advantages in protecting real-estate values by regulation, even before they learnt about German zoning. The latter can, then, be seen as a confirmation and sophistication of an indigenous approach that was already forming. The first American move towards more comprehensive zoning came in 1909/10 when Los Angeles made a distinction between industrial and residential zones (Scott, 1969). In 1913 the states of New York, Minnesota and Wisconsin adopted laws permitting cities to designate residential areas closed to industries. Yet, by the time war broke out in Europe in 1914, American use of this new approach was still quite limited.

## OTHER PARTS OF THE WORLD

### CANADA: THE WIDER CONTEXT

The citizens of the United States lived at peace with and spoke the same language as (most of) the people in its immediate and less populated neighbour, Canada. Canadian cities were small. In 1901 Montreal and Toronto were the only metropolitan cities with populations of over 100,000: 268,000 and 208,000 respectively (McCann and Smith, 1991). Most cities also lay very close to the American border, and were often closer to large American cities than to any comparable Canadian centre. In these circumstances, it was scarcely surprising that American innovations in planning quickly influenced the Canadian scene. Yet there was a powerful countervailing influence at work. Canada remained a self-governing dominion within the British Empire, the major element in the wider concept of British North America. In the early

20th century it remained heavily dependent on British trade, investment and immigration to sustain its growth. It is unsurprising, therefore, that British innovations in town planning had an equally important impact (Ward, 1999).

## THE CITY BEAUTIFUL IN CANADA

The early years of the development of Canadian urban planning show a tendency to seesaw between American and British influences. Initially there was great interest in the city beautiful paradigm, for example in proposals made for Toronto in 1906, and Calgary and Berlin (now Kitchener) in 1914 (Hodge, 1991). Also in 1914, the Federal Plan Commission appointed Edward Bennett, Burnham's associate on the 1909 Chicago plan, to prepare a plan for the Canadian capital, Ottawa, and Hull, its twin city (Gordon, 1998; DeGrace, 1985). Not all these planning efforts should be seen simply as being 'American', however. The one for Calgary was prepared by a British planner and landscape architect, Thomas Mawson, whose enthusiasm for the city beautiful knew no bounds in these years (Perks, 1985). Moreover, Bennett himself was actually British-born (though this fact was only ever mentioned in a Canadian context, where there was resistance to giving key professional roles to American consultants).

## BRITISH TOWN PLANNING IN CANADA

From 1909, however, British developments in town planning had provided an alternative model (Simpson, 1985). The strength of pro-British sentiment in Canada was, alone, sufficient to guarantee at least a hearing for them. Successive governor-generals (invariably British at that time) sponsored lecture tours by several British planners, including Thomas Mawson, Raymond Unwin and, of greatest long-term significance, Thomas Adams. British town planning also gained a powerful ally in the Canadian Commission of Conservation. This body was established in 1909 on the pattern of similar initiatives in the United States (Artibise and Stelter, 1981). Yet it was by no means a promotional agency for American ideas. Its medical officer of health detested the city beautiful model and looked to Britain for a more practical, relevant and less expensive alternative. 'Town planning' rather than 'city planning' became the favoured term and the provinces of New Brunswick, Nova Scotia and Alberta adopted town planning legislation modelled on the British pattern in 1912 and 1913. (Simpson, 1985) Most importantly, in 1914 the commission head-hunted Thomas Adams from his post with the Local Government Board in London to lead Canada's push toward town planning.

## AUSTRALIA: THE WIDER CONTEXT

As noted in the previous chapter, Australia was a surprisingly urbanised country, more so than Canada. It was essentially this which had drawn some Australians, particularly John Sulman, into the emergent field of planning at a very early stage (Freestone,

1996a). Governmentally, however, Australia did not acquire a self-governing status equivalent to Canada's until 1901 (Clark, 1995). The new century, therefore, opened at a critical moment in the transition to national self-determination. Yet the frame of cultural reference, echoing the dominant flows of trade, investment, immigration and geopolitical realities remained overwhelmingly British. Although many Australians looked, to some extent, to the United States as a model of what Australia might become – a predominantly Anglo-Celtic and European civilisation in a new land – sheer distance meant the continuous identification with American developments that occurred in Canada was impossible. It did the same in relation to developments in Britain and Europe. Everything was time-lagged. But there was an underlying cultural identification with Britain that partly transcended even the tyranny of distance (Freestone, 1997). All these contextual factors helped, in the longer term, to shape the evolution of early 20th-century Australian urban planning. In the short term, however, chance factors also played a critical role.

## PLANNING THE NEW CAPITAL

Nowhere was this more apparent than in the proposals for an entirely new federal capital, Canberra (Reps, 1997). Ambitious moves to engage the world's leading planners by means of an international planning competition in 1911–12 were marred by a boycott, orchestrated by Australian and British architects unhappy about the prize money offered and some of the conditions. The upshot was that, with the increasing volume of work available to the (still very few) planners in the world who had real international reputations, the general standard of entries was disappointing. No really well-known British or American planners participated. There were no Germans and only two French *urbanistes*, Donat Alfred Agache and the less well-known André Bérard. The only other European planner of international distinction to enter was the Finn, Eliel Saarinen. Despite these inauspicious beginnings the winning entry, by a little-known American planner from Chicago, Walter Burley Griffin, was a masterly exercise in the city beautiful, superbly presented (and strongly influenced) by Griffin's partner Marion Mahony (Freestone, 2000a). Having got a masterpiece that, in truth, they did not deserve, those responsible for the new capital then made many efforts to change the plan. Griffin, who moved to Australia in 1913 as planning consultant on the new capital, was able to fend off many of these early moves. Much dissension still lay in the future, however.

## THE EMERGENCE OF AN AUSTRALIAN TOWN PLANNING MOVEMENT

Though planning the new capital held the greatest symbolic significance, moves already occurring elsewhere in Australia's existing cities were reflecting altogether more pressing concerns (P Ashton, 1993; Freestone, 2000a). The new century also brought bubonic plague to Australia's largest city, Sydney, which intensified interest in British public health and housing reforms and led inexorably to the wider question of overall urban development. Eventually, in 1908, this reformist momentum led to a

New South Wales State Royal Commission on the improvement of Sydney and its suburbs. Sulman and an even more ardent Sydney advocate of town planning, John Fitzgerald, used the opportunity to draw attention to what they understood of the latest thinking from Europe and the United States.

Gradually the quality of first-hand information improved, a little later than it had in Canada (Freestone, 1989; Ward, 1997). State town planning associations began to be formed to raise awareness, beginning with New South Wales in 1913. A few Australians began to make extensive tours and attend international conferences. In 1914, for example, William Bold, the town clerk of Perth, was sent to London to attend the Imperial Health and Town Planning Conference, followed by an extensive tour of Britain, the continental Europe and, when his plans to visit Germany were thwarted by the outbreak of war, the United States (Webb, 1979). At about the same time, after some early postponements, British town planners began to visit Australia on lecture tours. Much the most energetic was Charles Reade, a New Zealander and key organiser in the London garden city movement, who was later to play a critical role in the embryonic Australian planning movement (Home, 1997; Garnaut, 2000).

## EARLY GARDEN SUBURBS IN AUSTRALIA

By 1914 the garden city, modified in familiar fashion to give emphasis to the garden suburb, had become the dominant planning model being received in Australia (Freestone, 1989). In part, this reflected a growing propagandist effort. Yet it also matched an already manifest Australian anti-urbanism and aspiration to low-density suburban living, to escape, in the expressive words of the new country's greatest balladeer 'Banjo' Paterson, the 'foetid air and gritty of the dusty, dirty city' (Paterson, 1995). Thus, even before any real knowledge of Howard's or Unwin's work arrived in Australia, private garden suburbs of bungalows, developed for profit in the very characteristic 'federation' style, had begun to appear. The earliest was Haberfield in Sydney, begun in 1901 (Freestone, 1989). Its originator Richard Stanton (later a stalwart of the Australian garden city movement) admitted knowing nothing of British schemes, though he had apparently visited Chicago. The first suburb with a direct connection to the garden city movement came in 1912 at Daceyville, also in Sydney. Planned initially (and somewhat crudely by the standards of Parker and Unwin) by Sulman and Fitzgerald, it was part of a state housing initiative and was intended to serve as a model for working-class housing. Again, however, this was only the start of a very prolonged engagement with garden city ideas.

## JAPAN: THE CONTEXT

Meanwhile, the most significant developments in planning outside the Atlantic world were taking place in the rapidly modernising nation of Japan. The extraordinary speed

**Figure 3.8** *The winning entry in the Canberra competition, by the American, Walter Burley Griffin, was a classic exercise in city beautiful thinking. It was to be many years, however, before its features were realised.*

of the change there became apparent to the world during the Russo-Japanese War of 1904–5. Spectacular Japanese successes confirmed the country's prowess as a military and colonial power. The war also intensified industrialisation in Japan and, of course, the urbanisation that was necessary to sustain it. Industrial cities, particularly Osaka, grew very rapidly, as did the Tokyo metropolitan area where the population rose from 1.5 million in 1900 to 2.76 million in 1915 (Ishizuka and Ishida, 1988). In turn, the wider pressures of this scale of urban change combined with Japanese interest in all western innovations to produce early encounters with the ideas of modern urban planning. As had been apparent in the 19th century, however, the borrowing was never simply from one source.

## DEN-EN TOSHI: THE GARDEN CITY IDEA IN JAPAN

The first significant borrowing came from garden city ideas (though not immediately from Howard's book) in 1905 (Watanabe, 1992). Japanese officials, so far as they understood the ideas, produced their own, somewhat wayward, account in 1907, introducing *den-en toshi* as the Japanese translation of garden city, a term which actually conveys a far more rural, agricultural aspect than its western meaning. Howard's notions of social and land reform and of providing good quality, low-cost housing in his garden cities were entirely ignored. Gradually Japanese understanding of the concept improved through direct encounters with Howard, and visits to Letchworth and other key British sites. Yet the misleading translation and skewed understanding persisted and began to acquire a wider salience. The appeal of the image evoked by the term was particularly strong in the booming industrial smoke-stack city of Osaka. It was here, from 1911, that the first Japanese moves came to create actual *den-en toshi* (which were essentially high-class garden suburbs) for commuters at Sakurai and three other locations on the new electric rail system. Similar moves began in Tokyo in 1913 (Watanabe, 1980), though it was Osaka that set the pace in these early years.

## TOSHI KEIKATU: THE EMERGENCE OF JAPANESE CITY PLANNING

By 1910, Japanese reformers and professionals were learning about the wider western concept of urban planning (Watanabe, 1984). In that year, members of the professional body of Japanese architects had been invited to attend the RIBA town planning conference in London (Watanabe, 1988). Through this they discovered the extent of activity in the west and, naturally enough, initially used a direct translation of the British term town planning (*taun puranningu*) to describe it. Soon, however, there were attempts to find a genuinely Japanese term. In 1913 an Osaka architect and reformer, Seki Hajime, theorised the emergent activity far more convincingly than any of his contemporaries. He showed how specific ideas such as the garden city and its variants fitted into a wider notion of planning. Significantly, he also introduced the term *toshi keikatu* (city planning) which soon became accepted. This reflected a growing familiarity with American literature and terminology. In fact, the most influential foreign planning model was from Germany. Japanese modernisers had borrowed much else from the Germans, including, very significantly, the Prussian constitution. This led them, in turn, to find many of the German planning tools and legal instruments on building lines, zoning and land readjustment particularly relevant (Hein and Ishida, 1998). Over the following years that influence, while never exclusive, was to become even more significant.

## CONCLUSIONS

### AN INTERNATIONAL AGE

The era which closed with the outbreak of war in 1914 was remarkably conducive to the international flow of ideas. Technological and organisational innovations had, within a single life span, immeasurably increased the possibilities of international communications, slow though they may appear to be by early 21st-century standards. Although the heyday of free trade was already past, goods, capital, people and information flowed freely around the world with, in some respects, fewer restrictions than exist today. Most of the pioneer planners who travelled by steamship and railway to international planning conferences, on lecture tours or to undertake planning commissions could do so without the need for passports or visas. There were, certainly, language difficulties but French, English and, to a lesser extent, German tended to be spoken, or at least understood, by some members of the professional middle classes in other linguistic realms. The nascent planning movements were also more than averagely endowed with individuals with an international outlook (Sutcliffe, 1981). Some planners, at least, were familiar with the recently developed artificial international language of Esperanto. Agache, for example (who was fluent in several languages) had learnt of the Canberra competition via an Australian Esperanto magazine (Reps, 1997: 75). Still more important was the visual dimension of planning. The lantern slides, plans and perspective drawings that were the stock in trade of the cosmopolitan planner as lecturer, competition entrant or exhibitor partly transcended language as a means of communication.

### THE MOTIVATIONS FOR INTERNATIONAL DIFFUSION

If these were some of the means by which planning ideas diffused, the wider motivations for innovation and diffusion lay deeper. They did not always echo the internationalist sentiments of those individuals who were the most active agents of diffusion. Amongst the principal national innovators of Europe and the United States, the driving force was the desire of middle-class reformers, of various types, to improve and order the cities which, as centres of economic production and social reproduction, underpinned national growth, wealth, power and prestige. These underlying concerns were variously tinged with nationalistic emotions such as envy, jealousy, fear or pride. In smaller, less powerful countries particularly, there was also a deference, not always admitted, to ideas that originated in others which were seen as models. There might also be more specific factors – for example, a search for a symbolic expression of otherwise frustrated desires for national self-determination, or the celebration of new-found independence by embracing wider planning possibilities than were formerly possible.

## THE WORLD TO COME

The outbreak of a war that was more intense, more pervasive and more devastating than any previously known could not but change this pattern. Some previously fruitful interchanges were disrupted, others were intensified. Against this, however, war also strengthened the political demands on governments everywhere to adopt urban planning and deliver the improvements it promised. Yet for all the impressive, if ultimately disappointing, practical elaborations and developments that were shortly to follow, the urban planning movements of the world never again quite recaptured the extraordinary and definitive creativity of the quarter century that ended in 1914. Whether we see the impacts of modern urban planning as good or bad, or (as most of us do) somewhere between these two, we cannot deny the importance of those few men, and even fewer women, who together defined its theory and practice.

# CHAPTER 4

# WAR, RECONSTRUCTION AND DEPRESSION I: THE MAJOR TRADITIONS

The active flow of planning ideas between the German- and English-speaking worlds, the most productive aspect of innovation and diffusion in early 20th-century urban planning, was all but suspended in 1914 with the outbreak of the First World War. The near-universal French mistrust of anything Germanic (and similar, if less extreme, sentiments in Britain) was confirmed. Some limited interchange was possible between Germany and the United States, which did not enter the war until 1917. The same was true in other countries which remained neutral for all or part of the war. Yet the broader mechanisms which had created an international planning discourse – the conferences, exhibitions, competitions and, in a more general sense, the unrestricted international travel and flows of information – now went into abeyance. The peace-time pattern was, however, replaced by more intense linkages on each side, especially amongst the western allies.

Physical destruction and population displacements, though limited compared with later wars, created totally new problems for urban planners. In turn, these encouraged international transfers of thinking and expertise, especially in relation to France and Belgium. Yet the war's capacity to force change and create new demands for urban planning did not stem solely from physical destruction. A war conducted on such a scale tested every aspect of the economies, governmental and social systems of the combatant nations, creating an impetus for reform and change when it ended. But compared to the obvious creativity in urban planning during the first two decades of the century, and the widespread political triumphs of the planning idea after 1945, the 1920s and 1930s are often viewed very negatively. Such perceptions reflect wider realities: the Great Depression; the rise of totalitarianism; the apparent failures of democracy; and, above all, the lost peace. In fact, these negative experiences were extraordinarily important in shaping prevalent western attitudes for much of the rest of the century. In a more positive sense, too, many of the ideas that actively shaped the world after 1945 were invented, or at least refined and rehearsed, in the two interwar decades.

So it was in urban planning. In this and the next chapter we examine these critical years, showing how important they were in the emergence of new visions of the city and, even more, in the further refinement and cross-fertilisation of older ideas with these new currents of thought. This chapter focuses on the four main planning traditions that had emerged before 1914, and which continued to be the most dominant. Much more so than before, however, their innovative efforts were now being supplemented, even challenged, by emergent traditions. The latter feature will be examined in the next chapter, along with some of the more completely derivative traditions that remained dependent on external models.

The general backcloth to these developments was the re-emergence and strengthening of international linkages. Even old enmities were partially overcome. Thus, with

German militarism temporarily neutered under the Weimar Republic and French pride restored, a fruitful Franco-German interchange of ideas about cities became possible in the 1920s. It was largely within these two linguistic realms and their close relatives that a self-conscious modern movement in architecture emerged, with important implications for urban planning. This movement sought universal, functional and rational design solutions. Consistent with this approach, it was, from the first, a powerful promoter of international connections, mainly within Europe. There was, however, a growing European admiration for the American vision of the urban future. During these years the United States assumed its dominant 20th-century role as the main source of economic, technological and cultural trends that, sooner or later, shaped the way everyone on the planet would either want, or be obliged, to live. When European modernists tried to envision the world of the future, 1920s America seemed, almost without trying, to be already creating it. There was not always an equal admiration for the conscious American planned response to these trends, though even here Europeans and others found much to learn from the United States, especially by the 1930s.

Alongside the new, self-conscious modernism, there developed a combination of rivalry and cross-fertilisation with earlier traditions of thought about designing cities, particularly the garden city and beaux-arts *urbanisme*. In many parts of the world these last two came increasingly to signify more ideologically conservative alternatives to modernism. It was these approaches, along with the more technical and 'neutral' activities of zoning and regulation, that remained, almost everywhere, the mainstream of urban planning thought and practice during the interwar years. Larger political events dramatically reinforced this general trend in the 1930s. The advance of modernism was checked in Germany as Nazism replaced the progressive spirit of Weimar. The new regime favoured an approach that combined variants of older urban planning models with more selective adoption of modernist principles. One consequence was that the geographical centre of gravity in European modernist thinking also shifted. In turn, this shift encouraged a more profound engagement by the English-speaking world with modernist thinking, setting the scene for important new developments during and after the Second World War.

## GERMANY

The final wartime years of imperial Germany produced little that was immediately significant in urban planning. In part, however, this was simply because few outside the German world were able, or prepared any longer, to listen. Even during the war years Germans remained fascinated by the garden city idea, which seemingly reconciled the contradiction of how to be a great industrial power while avoiding the problems of urban overcrowding (Bollerey and Hartmann, 1980). A notable wartime example was the garden suburb of Staaken at Spandau in Greater Berlin, built for munitions workers (TH Elkins and Hofmeister, 1988). New currents of architectural and planning thinking were also beginning to stir, but the authoritarian nature of late Wilhelmine Germany severely limited the opportunities for their expression. Agitation on the acute housing and overcrowding problems of German cities was treated harshly. Werner Hegemann, for example, had been under threat of imprisonment for organising just such a campaign when he left Berlin for the United States in 1913 (CC Collins, 1996).

By 1917/18, however, the political context was changing dramatically. In quick succession came strikes, mutinies in the armed forces, national defeat and attempted communist revolution. Together with the abdication of the kaiser, the granting of universal suffrage and the creation of the Weimar Republic in 1919, these events created a political climate in which urban social questions had to be taken very seriously (Kolb, 1988). Except in East Prussia (today a detached part of Russia), Germany had escaped serious war damage. As everywhere, however, the war had worsened the housing shortage and created a more aggressive social mood.

The years immediately following the First World War witnessed extraordinary achievements in urban planning. This was especially so between 1924 and 1929. The acute political instability of the early Weimar years, the crippling financial burden of postwar reparations and the great inflation of 1922 and 1923 prevented large-scale expressions of the new spirit in this early period. Yet there was no shortage of ideas. Around figures such as Bruno Taut and Walter Gropius, young architects who had begun to make their mark before 1914, a new movement for modern design now took shape (LO Larsson, 1984). An important arena for the development of its ideas was the new Bauhaus school for modern art and design. Formed by Gropius in Weimar in 1919, it was moved to Dessau in 1925.

## EARLY WEIMAR INNOVATIONS IN RESIDENTIAL PLANNING

There were some early signs of innovation in the design of housing schemes (*siedlungen*). One of the earliest, which first appeared in 1919 in Theodor Fischer's plan for the Alte Heide garden suburb in Munich, was the *zeilenbau* layout (Gold, 1997). This involved providing housing in rows aligned at right angles to the street, rather than as a traditional frontage development. By the later 1920s the layout was being widely deployed in German social housing and was subsequently emulated elsewhere. There were other interesting proposals, most notably by Hermann Jansen, the winner of the 1910 Greater Berlin competition, to separate pedestrian and traffic movements in residential layouts (Hass-Klau, 1990). The earliest of these date from 1921/2, before similar moves had begun in the United States.

## COMPREHENSIVE URBAN PLANNING

The early postwar years also brought important innovations in citywide development planning. A key figure was Fritz Schumacher (JM Diefendorf, 1993b; Meller, 2001) who, since 1909, had made his mark as the director of urban planning at Hamburg. He had there overseen several important developments, including the Stadtpark from 1910–14. At the very end of the war, he planned a garden suburb for some 800 dwellings, now called the Fritz-Schumacher-Siedlung, at Langenhorn in north Hamburg (Harms and Schubert, 1989). At about the same time he also planned a scheme at Dulsberg of over 5,000 flats in a green setting on the edge of the city.

In fact, though, his most important contribution to overall city planning lay elsewhere, in Cologne. That city's mayor, Konrad Adenauer, a future leader of West Germany after 1945, had launched a competition for a city expansion plan in 1919

(Mulder, 1997). Adenauer wanted to take the city's population from 700,000 to beyond a million. Cologne's physical development, however, had continued to be impeded by military considerations. The decision finally to dismantle its two rings of fortifications in 1918 created dramatic opportunities. Schumacher, who worked on the plan on secondment from Hamburg until 1923, took full advantage of these. What he produced was a plan for the entire city, with several innovative features. Most important was the proposal to transform the fortification rings into inner and outer green belts where scenic and recreational green spaces blended into farms and meadows. This offered a unique verdant framework for the city's growth, unparalleled in contemporary proposals. Parts of the plan were implemented in the 1930s and continued to provide a basis for planning until the 1960s.

Though Schumacher's proposals obviously had unique features, they were also a benchmark in the development of comprehensive urban planning. Other planners moved in different ways to solutions that offered some articulation of the expanding city. In 1921, for example, Ernst May, an important figure who blended garden city and modernist influences, produced a competition entry for satellite development around Breslau, now Wrocław in Poland (Bullock, 1978; Fehl, 1983). May had worked closely with Raymond Unwin before 1914 and resumed contact with him after 1918. He came to his scheme from knowledge of the English planner's theoretical suggestion (in 1912) for the satellite town. May's satellites, following Unwin, were to be physically separate from the parent city with their own community facilities. They lacked the employment base of the true garden city, however, and therefore relied on good public transport links. In the event, May had little influence on Breslau's development though, within a few years, his ideas were famously implemented at Frankfurt.

## DAS NEUE FRANKFURT

By the mid-1920s the more stable financial climate finally allowed large-scale implementation of the new ideas on residential planning and design in many cities. Frankfurt's efforts drew the most international attention (Lane, 1968; Bullock, 1978). The city already had, of course, a strong reputation for innovation in planning matters. Although it was gradually moving up the urban hierarchy, it was still exceeded in size by many of Germany's other key regional cities. With a population of 556,000 in 1930, it remained significantly smaller than Hamburg (1.12 million), Cologne (757,000), Munich (735,000) and a few others, including Essen (654,000) and Dresden (642,000). Yet its tradition of strong mayoral leadership and its relatively broad city limits (not hedged in by jealous neighbours and further enlarged in 1928) allowed it to achieve a disproportionate importance. Under May, appointed to the powerful role of *Stadtbaurat* (city architect and planner) in 1925, the city became a byword for the new approach.

## THE NIDDA SATELLITE TOWN PROJECT

In some respects, though, the approach was not so new. We have seen how May had proposed such a solution for Breslau in 1921. Now, in his native city, he finally had the chance to begin to implement his ideas. In fact, he favoured something closer to the garden city ideal: freestanding satellites 20–30 kilometres from the parent city centre. However, even in Frankfurt this was not possible for such locations lay well beyond municipal control. May's great project for a satellite town in the Nidda valley, immediately to the northwest of the city's central core, together with several smaller housing schemes, was a compromise (Fehl, 1983; Henderson, 1995). In the Nidda valley, where large areas of land were already in city ownership, May adapted and (in some ways) reversed the original concept of the satellite. Instead of an encircling green belt, the valley was to become a green centre with allotment-leisure gardens and parkland. Four component housing areas (*siedlungen*) were then built on the valley terraces, at Praunheim, Römerstadt, Höhenblick and Westhausen, as on the rim of a saucer. Local shopping and other community facilities were to be provided, but tram links to the centre meant that this would not be a self-contained settlement.

Both here and in the other *siedlungen*, May's team designed housing in terraced forms with small individual gardens or as low-rise flats with nearby leisure gardens. All buildings were flat-roofed, and showed many other features of the new modernist aesthetic (Lane, 1968; Bullock, 1978). Thus there were plain, rendered finishes with much use of concrete, standardisation of many components and some prefabrication. In many cases the new *zeilenbau* layouts were adopted with rows of dwellings arranged for maximum sunlight, fronting footpaths rather than streets. Throughout, there was great emphasis on rational design, most notably in the fitted 'Frankfurt kitchen'. Overall *das neue Frankfurt* soon won rhapsodies of approval from foreign observers. Yet the greatest project, the Nidda satellite town, was never completed as a unified concept. It never even received a name to give it identity as a single place. The leisure and community facilities were curtailed as economic problems resurfaced after 1929. By 1931, when the project effectively came to an end, less than 5,000 dwellings had been completed, a modest total compared to much else that was happening elsewhere around the larger cities of Europe.

## BERLIN *SIEDLUNGEN*

Although no other single housing project of the Weimar years was as significant in urban planning terms as that for the Nidda valley, there were certainly other important schemes (Lane, 1968; JM Diefendorf, 1993b). Many were designed by architects who were members of the 'Ring', a small group of avant-garde modernists. In Berlin, May's equivalent was Martin Wagner, who presided over what was, quantitatively, a far more impressive social housing programme than Frankfurt's. During the late 1920s, Wagner oversaw several seminal modernist schemes, designed by a host of luminaries of the modern movement including Bruno Taut, Walter Gropius, Hans Scharoun and Mies van der Rohe. Especially notable were the scheme at Britz, with its distinctive central horseshoe apartment block, and the Onkel-Tom-Siedlung (LO Larsson, 1984; Bullock, 1999). Another key *siedlung* was at Siemenstadt (1929–31), where the Siemens electrical company built a large workers' housing complex that used all the latest modernist ideas about planning and design.

## WEISSENHOF AND INTERNATIONAL CONTACTS

By this time the thinking of German modernists was actively influencing, and was in turn influenced by, their counterparts in neighbouring countries (Mumford, 2000; Gold, 1997). A key stage in this internationalisation was the famous Weissenhof exhibition in Stuttgart in 1927 (Lane, 1968). Organised by Mies van der Rohe, it brought together Germans (and other German-speakers) and leading modernists from the Netherlands and the French-speaking world. The following year the CIAM (Congrès Internationaux d'Architecture Moderne) was formed as a more enduring, if not always very efficient, means of promoting international modernist discourse. Its first conference (CIAM I) was held near Lausanne in Switzerland, still one of the major interfaces between the German and French worlds. However the Germans soon assumed a leading role and at May's invitation CIAM II, in 1929, was held in Frankfurt.

## INNOVATION OUTSIDE THE 'RING'

The modernist purists of the 'Ring', though they set the pace and became better known internationally than their contemporaries in German planning, certainly did not dominate everywhere. In Hamburg Fritz Schumacher, returning in 1923 to a strengthened municipal position after his triumphs in Cologne, oversaw further important flatted housing schemes at Barmsbek, 1926–31, and Jarrestadt, 1928–30 (Harms and Schubert, 1989). Less obviously innovative than contemporary developments in Frankfurt or Berlin, they were symptomatic of the more cautious modernisation of mainstream German planning. The basic formula remained similar to that of the earlier Dulsberg, with four- or five-storey flatted developments finished in local purple-brown brick (Denby, 1938). Flat roofs were now common, however, as modernist theory demanded. Site planning relied mainly on perimeter blocks but with some use of *zeilenbau* layout. Within each scheme there was usually a school, meticulously designed by the workaholic Schumacher himself. Always the entire schemes were interpenetrated by greenery and fringed by allotment-leisure gardens. These were a remarkable testament to Schumacher's insistence on open space and recreational opportunities for working-class tenants, even in a city acutely short of building land where the solutions available to May would have been quite impractical.

## METROPOLITAN PLANNING IN THE 1920s

These specific housing developments should be seen within a changing wider framework for planning. The early postwar years had seen some notable regional initiatives. In the Ruhr, the creation of a regional planning body in 1920, the first in Europe, revived prewar moves (Reulecke, 1984; Hötker, 1988). Comprising local authority, employer and, in a move which would only have been possible after 1918, worker representatives, this body quickly set to work on a regional plan (von Petz, 1997b; 1999). Robert Schmidt, who had pressed for the prewar moves, now gave dynamic leadership. By 1922 measures were in place to preserve existing green space and trees. A simplification of local government boundaries in 1929 further strengthened the capacity for collaborative action.

This had already happened in Greater Berlin, the other important arena of pre-1914 regional activity. In 1920, the Prussian state government authorised the merging of local authorities to form an enlarged city of Berlin (Matzerath, 1984). A new zoning plan was introduced for the capital in 1925. This outlawed the much-criticised barrack forms of tenement building (*mietskasernen*) and laid the basis for the modernist, lower density schemes that followed. In similar fashion, the zoning instruments of other cities came to reflect the new social content of planning. Elsewhere, however, achievements were more limited. Schumacher struggled vainly to find a framework for regional planning for the free city of Hamburg's wider metropolitan area (Pahl-Weber and Schubert, 1991). Hamburg's immediate neighbours, including the cities of Altona and Wandsbek, lay in Prussia which severely constrained the planning options. But this was an extreme case. In other areas, wider planning initiatives met with more success. Around Düsseldorf, Cologne and Frankfurt, for example, regional planning associations appeared in 1928 and 1929.

## PLANNING FOR THE MOTOR VEHICLE

Meanwhile, important developments were taking shape in another facet of planning to which Germany has made a major international contribution. Immediately after 1918, and despite very low car ownership, a powerful lobby for modern interurban motor roads began to take shape (Hass-Klau, 1990). The pressure came from a wide spectrum of business and local authorities as well as oil companies and motoring associations. The roads they wanted would be high speed, limited access routes without frontage development or intersections which required stopping the traffic flow. The first demonstration stretch of such a road was built privately in Berlin in 1921 (P Hall, 1988). From 1926, however, an organisation called HAFRABA (referring to the Hanseatic cities – principally Hamburg, Frankfurt, and Basle in Switzerland) pressed very effectively for such roads, especially on the north–south route which linked the cities that gave it its name. Shortly before Hitler took power in 1933, HAFRABA managed to create the first stretch, between Cologne and Bonn. Despite the inherent difficulties involved in building such major roads without a strong national (or at least regional) policy, some local authorities, working cooperatively, also managed to take important actions. In the Ruhr, for example, an east–west high speed road was built between Dortmund and Duisburg in the late 1920s under the auspices of the regional planning association.

Alongside these moves to promote motor vehicles (in a country where most road traffic remained horse-drawn in the 1920s) came measures to restrict their use in residential areas. Thus Hermann Jansen continued developing his road-safety residential layouts during the 1920s, with increasing awareness of the important American developments at this time (Hass-Klau, 1990). Meanwhile, the various innovations in residential-site planning that were apparent in the 1920s schemes in Berlin, Hamburg, Frankfurt and elsewhere, though usually introduced to improve sunlighting and reduce development costs, also offered new possibilities for separating pedestrians and traffic.

# The Nazi regime and urban planning

As the economic position worsened from 1929, the National Socialist (Nazi) Party began to have increasing influence in German public policy. After major electoral success in the early 1930s, Adolf Hitler established a Nazi dictatorship in 1933 (Frei, 1993). Henceforth, every aspect of German life was permeated by Nazi ideology. This was often confused, and even contradictory, a tendency that was particularly evident in urban planning, where certain trends associated with the previous period were strengthened, and others were weakened or reversed (JM Diefendorf, 1993b). On the whole, however, the powers of planners – at least of those who were able or prepared to work within the new regime – were greatly strengthened, a reflection of Hitler's great personal interest in urban planning. Partly because of this, important planning developments took place under the Nazis, some of which were admired internationally. Yet there were also very serious damaging effects to the international linkages and influence of German planning.

## The exodus of planners

The Nazi dislike of modern architecture with its somewhat left-wing and internationalist image and emphatic denial of national and historical style brought a marginalisation of many of the innovators of the 1920s (Lane, 1968). Some modernists were already beyond the pale. The most prominent of these was Hannes Meyer, the Swiss communist who headed the Bauhaus after Gropius (Schnaidt, 1965). In 1930 the right-wing local council in Dessau secured his dismissal and he moved to the Soviet Union to work as a planner. Several others followed suit. After the Frankfurt housing programme dried up, Ernst May took a team of planners to Soviet Russia (Bullock, 1978; Kopp, 1970). A moderate social democrat rather than a communist, May had no wish to remain in Russia but found himself unable to return to Germany. He lived in exile in Kenya for many years, only returning in 1954. Others who had genuine communist sympathies stayed longer in Russia. One such was Meyer, who moved to Mexico in 1939. In Germany prominent modernist planners, most notably Martin Wagner, were speedily removed from office (JM Diefendorf, 1993b). Wagner's friend Walter Gropius initially tried to work under the new regime but soon emigrated to Britain, before moving to the United States in 1937 (Gold, 1997). Wagner meanwhile had taken a job in Turkey but was brought to the United States by Gropius in 1938.

Nor was it merely the modernist purists who lost influence. Even Fritz Schumacher, a much less controversial figure, left office in 1933. (It is unclear whether he was dismissed or simply retired.) At least Schumacher remained in Germany. Much talent was simply lost, never to return. As well as the prominent names others, some of them very junior or not yet trained as planners and many of them Jewish, left for good (eg Blumenfeld, 1987). In later years, some of these exiles made distinguished contributions to urban planning, especially in the English-speaking world and, of course, in the future Jewish homeland of Israel.

## INTERNATIONAL CONNECTIONS IN THE NAZI YEARS

In one sense, of course, these exiles were spreading the Weimar planning experience to other countries. For the many planners who were able and willing to work under the Nazi regime, there were undoubtedly possibilities for decisive interventions that would have been harder to achieve elsewhere. This made possible some remarkable achievements which their counterparts in other countries found difficult to ignore (eg Barlow, 1940). Despite their liberal reformist traditions, there lurked in the hearts of planners everywhere an admiration for decisive, even authoritarian, action. This was especially so in the 1930s when the response of parliamentary democracies to the many problems of cities, and of the world more generally, appeared so dilatory and ineffectual. Nevertheless under the Nazis the international salience of German planning declined. To some extent, of course, this decline was a longer term phenomenon: events after 1939 ensured this would be the case. Yet, even before the Second World War, Germany's planners did not participate as easily as their immediate predecessors in international planning discourse. They continued to attend some major international events, such as those of the International Federation of Housing and Town Planning (IFHTP), successor to the International Garden Cities Association (Fischer, 1990). CIAM was, however, definitely forbidden.

Despite links with the mainstream of international planning, there was a growing ideological 'edge' to German contributions after 1933 that inhibited genuine engagement (Fehl, 1992). The close contacts that many architects and planners in other countries had formed with some of the exiles obviously made them suspicious of the new leaders of German planning. Actually, there were many similarities in the technical content of what was being planned elsewhere, especially in the English-speaking world. Yet leading planners working under the Nazis tended to draw overt ideological distinctions, asserting a superiority over other models which became a barrier. However, even if the wider international standing of their work was damaged, planners under the Nazis continued to be very well informed about developments outside their own ideological ghetto. This was a tendency which, surprisingly, remained true even after 1939.

## THE *AUTOBAHNEN*

Some aspects of Nazi urban planning, particularly those which could be seen as purely technical achievements, were admired and became widely known. Much the most important were the new *Reichautobahnen* (national motorways), extensively reported in the United States, Britain and elsewhere (Hass-Klau, 1990; RPA, 1936; Barlow, 1940). Despite early opposition by the Nazis to the proposals of HAFRABA, the organisation began to lobby Hitler as his power increased. By 1933 he favoured a very pro-car policy and uniquely ambitious plans for a national road system were soon being implemented. The first major section, connecting Frankfurt and Mannheim, opened in 1935. By the end of 1938, 3,000 kilometres had already been built. The young Colin Buchanan, later Britain's most internationally influential transport planner, saw them in 1937 and, like everyone else, was 'enormously impressed' (Hass-Klau, 1990: 116).

## THE NAZIS AND THE BIG CITIES

The Nazi attitude to big cities was particularly confused (Lane, 1968; Pahl-Weber and Schubert, 1991; Fehl, 1992; JM Diefendorf, 1993b). At one level, they were unnatural, unhealthy places, breeding grounds for disease, crime, degenerate cosmopolitan culture and Bolshevism. At another level, though, they were important to sustain industrial production, a prerequisite for world-power status. Finally, cities also had a major symbolic importance, both within Germany and more widely. They would represent national characteristics and provide opportunities for major displays of the power and achievements of the Nazi regime. These contradictory attitudes were never properly reconciled, with different facets dominating at different times and in different places. In the huge Ruhr conurbation, for example, the powers of the existing regional planning association were greatly strengthened. Its objectives were subtly changed, however, encouraging industrial workers to adopt more traditional peasant values by increasing opportunities for cultivation (Reulecke, 1984). There were also concerns to rebuild the region's racial purity after earlier waves of Polish immigration.

## THE 'REPRESENTATIVE CITIES' PROGRAMME

A particularly important Nazi initiative for the glorification of some of the most important cities was launched by Hitler in 1937 (Lane, 1968; JM Diefendorf, 1993b). New legal powers gave authoritarian powers that allowed land to be appropriated to implement dramatic changes. The property of Jews could already be seized without compensation, but non-Jews also found that their property rights were severely curtailed. Each chosen city was assigned a functional and symbolic role. Thus Berlin was to be the great capital of the Reich, and ultimately of the world; Hamburg would be the world's greatest port city; Munich the party headquarters and city of art; and Nuremburg the rallying point for the Nazi party. Following the *anschluss* (union) with Austria in 1938, Linz was added to the list – another centre for art and culture. Other cities including Cologne and Stuttgart were added subsequently. The motivations for this initiative lay in Hitler's desire for world domination, so plans had to give full expression to Germanic superiority. Within the extreme nationalism of this position lay another contradiction. The powerful imperative that Germany's great cities must outdo all others required its planners to be fully aware of planning developments in other parts of the world. Yet any internationalism had to be covert; they could not copy or borrow in any obvious fashion.

## SPEER'S BERLIN

Though the planners employed to implement this programme had obviously to be loyal Nazis, they were not without talent (JM Diefendorf, 1993b). In Berlin, for

*Figure 4.1 Frankfurt, under Ernst May's leadership, won international acclaim during the late 1920s. Römerstadt, shown here, was a modernist interpretation of the garden city, its apartment housing abutting directly on individual leisure gardens in the Nidda Valley (see pp 84–5).*

example, Hitler appointed Albert Speer, an urbane and shrewd young architect. In Hamburg, the replanning was headed by an exceptionally able planner, Konstanty Gutschow. Unlike Speer, Gutschow was not a particular favourite of the Führer, though Hitler acknowledged his skill. The briefs given to Speer and Gutschow reflected much of Hitler's own thinking, of course. For Berlin, where the plan was elaborated between 1937 and 1940, the underlying intention was that its population would rise from about 4.3 million people (in 1939) to about 10 million (Helmer, 1985; Düwel, 1997b). At the heart of the city there would be an immense new north–south ceremonial axis, along which major public buildings would be located. Closing the axis would be a vast domed Hall of the People, the biggest building in the world. This whole approach was, in effect, an inflated variant of the classical Beaux Arts-city beautiful tradition already favoured in many capital cities. However, more Functionalist approaches, reminiscent of modernism, were apparent elsewhere in the plan. A large new satellite settlement was to be built to the south, for example. Overall though, the plan was largely conceived in architectural terms.

## GUTSCHOW'S HAMBURG

Gutschow was charged with shifting Hamburg's centre of gravity from the Alster (the lake at the heart of the city) to create a more linear development along the River Elbe that would signify the great outward-looking seaport (Pahl-Weber and Schubert, 1991; JM Diefendorf, 1993b). The affected area was initially outside the city limits, though 1937 and 1938 also brought the long overdue creation of Greater Hamburg. On the Altona waterfront, Hitler wanted a single immense skyscraper and a vast suspension bridge. These features clearly reflected his desire to outdo New York, despite his disdain for its undisciplined capitalist development and its large and influential Jewish population. With typical thoroughness, Gutschow travelled to America to study the planning of skyscrapers. Yet he also considered Hamburg's overall functional and social development with great care, estimating that its population would grow from nearly 1.7 million in 1939 to at least 2.2 million. He had a somewhat different style of working to Speer. Despite having powers that would have allowed a very authoritarian approach, he never entirely succumbed to Hitler's desires. More importantly, he involved the wider local community of architects and planners, including the revered elder statesman of Hamburg planning, Schumacher. This helped to create a professional consensus which meant that many of his proposals survived the Nazi period and his own fall from grace after 1945.

## HOUSING UNDER THE NAZIS

This general theme of variety, high technical competence and a sometimes surprising subtlety characterised other facets of urban planning under the Third Reich. For example, there were some important developments after an initial reaction against the social housing schemes associated with the Weimar period. Slum clearance and redevelopments were undertaken in several cities. In Hamburg, for example, flatted blocks, similar in many ways to those built before 1933 were constructed (Harms and

Schubert, 1989). The main differences were that they had pitched, rather than flat, roofs. Their elevations were also less severely functional, with external decoration that reflected officially approved artistic ideals. Elsewhere, approaches to renewal were less comprehensive and more original buildings were kept (von Petz, 1990b).

The Nazis also favoured the original garden city model, a reflection of the concept's enduring appeal to conservative sentiments in Germany (Hass-Klau, 1990; JM Diefendorf, 1993b). At an early stage, they sanctioned several small model settlements which reflected many of the physical ideals of the garden city. These included Ramersdorf in Munich (for the unemployed), the Kameradschaftsiedlung at Zehlendorf in Berlin (for the SS elite) and Schwarzwald in Hamburg (for armaments workers). Yet there were also other examples which showed a stronger connection to the 1920s. The most important was the Frank'sch Siedlung in Hamburg developed by the Frank brothers, who had played a key role, alongside Schumacher, in Hamburg's social housing before 1933 (Harms and Schubert, 1989).

## THE NAZI NEW TOWNS

The most ambitious planning projects within the garden city tradition were two entirely freestanding new towns, now known as Wolfsburg and Salzgitter, near Braunschweig (Hass-Klau, 1990; JM Diefendorf, 1993b). The second, planned from 1938, has certain features in common with the later Corby new town in Britain, in that it was developed around an integrated steelworks. The first holds more interest from the urban planning viewpoint, although its Nazi origins have ensured that it rarely rates a mention in the international history of new-town planning. Planned from 1937, Wolfsburg was originally called the Stadt des Kraft durch Freude (Kdf) Wagens (literally, the town of the strength through joy cars). It was developed to build Hitler's proposed Nazi people's car, the Kdf Wagen (later renamed as the Volkswagen). The plan itself was a compromise between the kind of functional and social approach to planning that appeared in many post-1945 new settlements and the Nazi desire for urban grandeur and display (Omura, 1988a). These two tendencies were evident in the approaches of the two main planners, Peter Koller who was nominally in charge, and the more exalted figure of Albert Speer who pressed a small-scale version of the Berlin grand axis on his reluctant associate.

The latter (who in 1931 had prepared an important plan for Zagreb, then in Yugoslavia) gave most attention to the planning of residential areas. It was in this respect that urban planning generally was at its most impressive under the Nazis. There was the familiar emphasis on traditional architectural styles, undoubtedly very popular with many Germans. Also characteristic was the extensive use of woodland to interpenetrate and define the boundaries of distinct residential areas. In addition, the early sections of Wolfsburg, most notably the more affluent district of Steimkerberg, showed careful planning of community facilities. There were also interesting attempts to separate motor vehicle movements from housing. We have noted how this was a subject of growing importance in interwar Germany and Koller was clearly aware of both Jansen's work and that of American planners in the 1920s. At the time, however, he belittled the Radburn layout, the key American innovation (in part, we may suspect, because one of its principal originators, Clarence Stein, was Jewish).

## 94 THE INTERNATIONAL STANDING OF GERMAN PLANNING IN 1939

After 1939 many of the most authoritarian aspects of Nazi urban planning intensified, especially in relation to the territories that came under Hitler's direct control. This briefly promised the Nazis a way of imposing over a wider area their approach to urban planning. As we have seen, they had by 1939 limited the scope of German planners in the free international exchange of planning ideas that had been typical before 1933. There was still widespread knowledge of foreign developments amongst German planners. Yet, despite some interesting developments in planning after 1933, the *autobahnen* were the only German planning achievement under the Third Reich that were admired sufficiently to influence the content of planning discourse elsewhere.

**Figure 4.2** *The autobahns were the most admired aspect of German planning under the Nazis. Despite very low car ownership, a network of limited access high speed roads was rapidly created.*

# France

Nowhere was suspicion of Germany greater than in its neighbour and historic enemy, France, one of only two western countries to suffer extensive damage in the First World War. Although there was little aerial bombing, high-explosive shells (many fired from artillery made in the Krupp factories) had a devastating effect on settlements close to the western front (Bédarida, 1991; Couedelo, 1991). Some 450,000 dwellings were destroyed, principally in the north and east of the country. Most were in the countryside, but damage was severe in some small and middle-sized towns, such as Arras, Lens, Armentière and Soissons. The larger centres of Lille and Amiens were partially affected but the only city of over 100,000 population to be continuously bombarded was the historic city of Reims. The destruction strengthened the French movement for urban planning and led first to powers to assist rebuilding and finally, in March 1919, to the Cornudet law, France's first urban planning legislation.

## La Renaissance des Cités and American influence

An important initiative was La Renaissance des Cités formed in 1916 (Bédarida, 1991; Gournay, 1999). This was both a research bureau and a 'think-tank' which brought together a host of experts and personalities. Its work covered all aspects of reconstruction, though the specific proposals for the replanning of Reims are particularly notable. The initiative also shows something of the extent of American influence, as an early example of financial aid and technical assistance from the United States (G Wright, 1991). The principal intermediary was an American planner, George B Ford. A key figure in the coalescence of the city planning movement in the United States, Ford had been partly trained in France. In 1917 he returned there with the special housing service of the American Red Cross. Two years later he joined La Renaissance des Cités, itself funded partly by the Red Cross and other donors in the United States (amongst them, thanks to Ford's efforts, a prominent Boston businessman and planning enthusiast, Edward Filene).

The invitation to Ford, in 1920, to prepare a plan for Reims was thus a natural progression. The resultant plan incorporated many American elements, including zoning, parkways and civic centre proposals. It soon became the first plan approved under the Cornudet law. By this time, other intermediaries were also promoting French knowledge of American planning. An important figure in this interchange was the *urbaniste*, Jacques Gréber whose wartime experience planning the Fairmount Parkway in Philadelphia, further strengthened by American lecture tours to promote awareness of French urban devastation, made his a key voice (Cohen, 1995). He also wrote influentially on planning in the United States in a 1920 book, *L'Architecture des États-Unis: Preuve de la force d'expansion du génie français*, on American architecture and planning (Gournay, 2001). Interestingly, he saw this largely as, to quote the book's subtitle, 'evidence for the dynamic expansion of the French genius' (Cohen, 1995: 51). In contrast to Ford's direct understanding of recent trends, therefore, it is clear that Gréber was failing to appreciate the shifts of American planning away from the city beautiful paradigm.

## CITÉS-JARDINS AND THE DEVASTATED REGIONS

Both Ford's plan and Gréber's book referred to *cités-jardins* (meaning garden suburbs). As in other parts of Europe, French housing problems in the immediate aftermath of war were severe, especially in the devastated regions. The acute shortage of dwellings, combined with the more industrial character of northeastern France and its proximity to Britain (and, to some extent, Belgium), certainly intensified early postwar interest in garden city ideas. The social housing offices in the war-damaged departments were very active promoters of *cités-jardins*, sometimes using well-known *urbanistes*. Marcel Auburtin, for example, planned the 600-dwelling Chemin Vert scheme in Reims, built from 1920 (G Wright, 1991). Another important agency that built *cités-jardins* in this part of France was the Nord railway company (Gaudin, 1992). Ultimately 36 such schemes were built for its employees from 1919 (Baudouï, 1991). The first and largest, with over 1,100 dwellings, was at Tergnier. Planned by a very able Nord company engineer, Raoul Dautry (who became the minister responsible for planning after 1944), its distinctive street layout uniquely evoked the driving wheels, pistons and connecting rods of a locomotive. Other notable early postwar Nord schemes were at Lille-Déliverance and Longueau, near Amiens.

*Figure 4.3* *The French initially followed the English cottage ideal of the garden city very closely. This shows an early 1920's HBM scheme at Drancy in north eastern Paris.*

## CITÉS-JARDINS IN THE PARIS REGION

For different reasons, housing problems were also acute in the Paris region (Evenson, 1979). In 1916, a housing office was created for the Seine department which covered the Paris suburbs. It was led by Henri Sellier, a trades unionist and moderate socialist politician, who already favoured the garden city idea as it was understood in France (Read, 1978). He arranged wartime visits to the key British sites for his staff to underline his office's commitment to this solution. In contrast to the earliest French garden city enthusiasts, Sellier fully understood the differences between Howard's ideal and the French *cité-jardin*. Equally, he was well aware that, if the original concept had scarcely succeeded in Britain, it would be unlikely to do so in the Paris area where there was no widespread aspiration for low-density living. Instead Sellier's office, the main builder of social housing in the Paris region, launched a programme of suburban *cités-jardins* in the early postwar years (Swenarton, 1985).

The first six were small cottage schemes, the largest with populations of only about 1,000 (Evenson, 1979). They were effectively French versions of the design and site planning approach used at Letchworth and Hampstead Garden Suburb. The best known were at Drancy and Les Lilas on very low-cost sites in the working-class northern and eastern suburbs (Gaudin, 1992). Almost immediately, however, higher density developments were planned for more expensive sites. These efforts took the *cité-jardin* from attempted emulation to something truly distinctive. The first, and the one most closely associated with Sellier, was at Suresnes, in the western suburbs (Cornu, 1990). This *cité-jardin*, ultimately with nearly 2,800 dwellings, was conceived as a mixed development of five-storey apartment blocks and cottages. It had a superlative range of community facilities (including, eventually, a fine theatre). Yet, despite an overall density more than twice that of the British garden city ideal, there were also generous amounts of public space, far more than was usual for modest-cost Parisian housing.

## WIDER PLANNING PROPOSALS

These housing developments were much the most tangible evidence of the impact of planning ideas. Yet, in the climate of heightened early postwar interest in planning, there was a more general debate about the future development of the French capital (Evenson, 1979). In 1919, under the terms of the Cornudet law, an ideas competition was launched by the department of the Seine and the city of Paris to make proposals for the expansion of the whole metropolitan area. There were four categories, covering regional issues, the use of the fortifications and glacis (which, although no longer of military significance, were not finally removed until 1932), the city of Paris itself and various local projects.

For the first time, the competition gave the pioneer *urbanistes* a major outlet for their expertise in France itself. Thus Jaussely and Agache were placed first and second in the regional section. Both plans envisaged major growth, underpinned by heavy investment in the transport infrastructure and making extensive use of the *cité-jardin* concept in the areas of expansion. Other submissions went even further in this direction. Meanwhile, Gréber took the honours in the fortifications section with a

scheme that reflected his experience in Philadelphia, linking major highway provision, parks, recreation and housing (Cohen and Lortie, 1991). Overall, the
competition confirmed that, by 1920, France had finally acquired a multifaceted body
of modern urban planning ideas, no longer drawn only from its own Haussmannic
traditions but incorporating many features from the Anglophone world.

## LE CORBUSIER AND URBAN PLANNING

As in Germany, however, a new approach to planning and urban design began to
appear in the early 1920s. Much the most important figure in French modernism
between the wars was Charles-Edouard Jeanneret, who styled himself, rather
bizarrely, as Le Corbusier ('the crow-like one'). Although he primarily designed individual buildings, he authored several very influential works on urban planning which
articulated his evolving vision of the future city (Fishman, 1977). In contrast to most
of the visionaries at the turn of the century, he argued that modern design would
make it possible to live a good life in big cities. His first attempts had been in the early

*Figure 4.4* *Increasingly, however, community was sought in higher density
schemes, with an increasing recourse to very high residential blocks. This
example, the Gratte-Ciel, at Villeurbanne, adjoining Lyons, was one of the
most ambitious of these later schemes (see p. 101).*

1920s. In 1922 he exhibited the Ville Contemporaine (contemporary city), a vision of a modern city for three million inhabitants (Le Corbusier, 1922). Elaborated more fully in his book *Urbanisme*, published in 1925, the city would have a central area of 60-storey office towers, superhighways, a green belt and peripheral satellite towns and industrial areas. It was criticised because it appeared to accept the inequalities of capitalist society by segregating its inhabitants according to whether they were working or middle class.

This feature was also present in his attempt to apply his design principles to Paris, in the Plan Voisin, exhibited in 1925 (Le Corbusier, 1925). Since this proposed demolishing large parts of an internationally known historic city the criticisms grew even stronger. (All of this ensured that Le Corbusier became very well known.) By the end of the decade, he was moving toward a more egalitarian (and authoritarian) vision (P Hall, 1988; Ibelings, 1997). This shift reflected his growing involvement with Moscow's planning, as an adviser on competing plans which had been prepared for the Soviet capital. Without any specific references to Moscow, he exhibited his ideas at the 1930 CIAM in Brussels. They were finally published in 1935 as the Ville Radieuse (radiant city). While maintaining many of the basic features of his original in relation to highway arteries and green space, there were important changes in the spatial arrangements. Thus residential areas were now moved to the centre with dwellings (no longer segregated by class) in vast high-rise towers.

## Le Corbusier and CIAM

These visions had limited impacts on French cities between the wars. A few modernist housing schemes and advanced traffic engineering features such as underpasses were appearing by the 1930s. But this was as far as it went. The truth was that Le Corbusier was not at all typical of French *urbanisme* at that time. Though based in Paris, he was actually Swiss and thus well placed, at least in theory, to establish contacts with German modernists. (For their part, most *urbanistes*, like the majority of their fellow countrymen and women, continued to view anything German with great caution, at least before the later 1920s.) But Le Corbusier crossed the great divide at the 1927 Weissenhof Exhibition, to become a central figure in CIAM (Mumford, 2000). In fact, his profound sense of his own greatness rather inhibited the effectiveness of the contacts he made with other planners. Thus, it is clear that the German and Dutch members of CIAM resented his propensity to propose his own overarching approaches in a field where their practical achievements were far greater.

However, as the influence of the Germans declined after 1933 Le Corbusier's influence on CIAM increased. This was most blatantly apparent in the promulgation of the so-called Athens Charter, a series of principles on which modern urban planning should be conducted (Gold, 1997). The charter was supposedly a collective outcome of CIAM IV, largely held on board a cruise ship between Marseilles and Athens in 1933. In fact, no such collective charter was actually drawn up. The version that finally appeared in print in 1943, under Le Corbusier's name, owed as much to his own thinking (and the changed times) as it did to the seaborne congress a decade earlier. Nevertheless, his account has become the authorised version. History was effectively rewritten, giving Le Corbusier a more central place in CIAM than he deserved. The broad point, though, is that he garnered a disproportionate amount of the credit (or blame) for inventing the overtly modernist vision of the planned city. In doing this, he helped put Paris again at the very centre of international planning discourse.

## FRENCH PLANNING LITERATURE AND EDUCATION

Other developments were having the same effect. In the 1920s French was still the most widely understood language for the study of the humanities, social sciences, arts and culture. The growing volume of planning literature appearing in France between the wars, including two journals, *La Vie Urbaine* (founded in 1919) and *Urbanisme* (1932), could expect a wide readership, especially in southern Europe (GR Collins and CC Collins, 1965; *Urbanisme*, 1999). Another key factor was the emergence of French planning education. The Paris École des Beaux Arts had provided training for the first generation of French *urbanistes* and had exerted a powerful international influence. But urban planning was not its primary interest.

In 1919, the École des Hautes Études Urbaines (school of high urban studies) was founded at the instigation of Henri Sellier (Baudouï, 1990b). It offered a multi-disciplinary programme as a preparation for urban planning work. In 1924, it became the Institut d'Urbanisme at the University of Paris (IUUP). Building on the high reputation of Parisian learning, it quickly drew students from other countries. The combination of the Sorbonne's formidable legal and public administrative expertise and the practical experience of leading *urbanistes* of international standing enhanced and spread French planning thought. The dominating presence (amongst many other impressive names) was the historian, Marcel Poëte, a figure with an outlook and breadth of thought and knowledge similar to that of his friend Patrick Geddes (Calabi, 1996). Through his writings and extraordinary lucidity as a teacher, Poëte contributed greatly to the reputation of French *urbanisme*.

## FOREIGN EXAMPLES IN FRENCH PLANNING

Alongside the growing international status of French *urbanisme*, its practitioners received planning information from elsewhere more freely than before 1914. Despite Le Corbusier's anxiety to promote his own projects at CIAM, French reception of developments in Germany, the Netherlands and elsewhere was not entirely blocked. In the mainstream of planning, leading figures such as Sellier met regularly with their counterparts from outside the French-speaking world at conferences such as those of the IFHTP and International Union of Local Authorities (Saunier, 1999). Until the bases of this internationalism again began to erode in the later 1930s, this permitted French knowledge of important international, mainly European, developments. The latest thinking on housing, regional planning and roads, for example, was quickly received and discussed. Jacques Gréber's direct American experience was also apparent in a 1933 plan, widely known in France, for Marseilles (Meller, 2001). Against this, however, something of the traditional insularity of the general run of urban official-dom continued, especially in provincial France.

## SOCIAL HOUSING

The outcome of this synthesis of indigenous innovation and knowledge of external developments was several developments that commanded wide interest. Though their overall numerical quantitative significance fell well below equivalent developments in Britain, Germany or the Netherlands, the *cités-jardins* continued to evolve (Denby, 1938). This took them away from the English cottage ideal towards frankly modernist and innovative flatted developments. A notable scheme was the Quartier des États-Unis in Lyons, designed in the early 1920s but built from 1929 to 1934 (Pawlowski, 1993). Designed by Tony Garnier and reminiscent of his idealised *cité industrielle*, it comprised 1,568 flats in six-storey blocks of nontraditional design. From the later 1920s, the Seine department around Paris also adopted designs for large flatted schemes, such as Plessis-Robinson with 5,500 flats in modernist blocks (Evenson, 1979; Gaudin, 1992). Other schemes, particularly at Le Blanc Mesnil in the northeast Paris suburbs near Saint-Denis, were directly inspired by 1920s social housing in Vienna (Toulier, 1999).

Later developments, particularly Châtenay-Malabry (1,573 dwellings) and, above all, Drancy-La Muette (1,060) were more uncompromisingly modernist. The latter, designed by Eugène Beaudouin and Marcel Lods from 1932, included five 16-storey towers (Whitham, 1994). Despite a history that embraced farce (in that the towers remained unoccupied) and tragedy (it was used as a wartime deportation camp), the Cité de la Muette became an international modernist icon. A contemporary scheme even more radical in concept, though less known internationally, was Les Gratte Ciel ('the sky scrapers') at Villeurbanne, an industrial suburb of Lyons (Rabinow, 1995; Vollerin, 1999; Meller, 2001). With its 11- and 19-storey blocks designed by Môrice Leroux in a style reminiscent of New York, Villeurbanne along with Drancy-La Muette suggested that visionary thinking was becoming reality. Along with other high-rise social housing schemes of this period, especially those in Rotterdam and Stockholm, they were a portent of things to come.

## THE ORIGINS OF REGIONAL PLANNING

In the later 1920s, and with knowledge of developments in Germany and Britain, the need to consider the planning of the sprawling Parisian metropolitan area as a whole came to the fore (Couedelo, 1991). The Cornudet law rested on the same basic principles as German and British town extension. One of several weaknesses was that this approach had limited value when urbanisation spilled over local municipal and department boundaries. In 1928, the national government began to see the need for a regional approach to the planning of Paris, allegedly when the prime minister, Raymond Poincaré, was forced to take an unexpected detour through a wide section of the outer sprawl (Evenson, 1979) – much development, especially in working-class suburbs, was completely uncoordinated, lacking even basic infrastructures, and some areas were barely above the level of shantytowns. Poincaré immediately set up a committee to examine the planning of the whole Paris region within a 35-kilometre radius of the centre. In 1932, somewhat later than equivalent moves in Germany, the United States and Britain, new legislation provided a legal basis for a Paris regional plan to be prepared (extended in 1935 to the whole of the country).

## THE PROST PLAN

France's most prestigious *urbaniste*, Henri Prost, led the team that produced the Plan d'Aménagement de la Région Parisienne (PARP) of 1934 (Steenhuis, 1997; Evenson, 1979; *Urbanisme*, 1999). This was an important document. One key proposal was for a regional autoroute system, reflecting German, Italian and, increasingly, American developments. There were also proposals for extensions to the metro and the creation of a regional metro system. Broad zoning principles were introduced, involving broad land use and building density and height. Development would only be allowed if municipalities were able to guarantee proper servicing. There was also to be extensive protection of open spaces, enhancement of the settings of historic buildings and designation of areas for only agricultural buildings.

A key limitation was that the historic city of Paris resisted, and was excluded from, the Prost plan. Nevertheless, Prost was able to secure the final removal of the muddled collection of inadequate temporary dwellings from the glacis beyond the old fortifications. Predictably, in the face of many vested interests and broader political divisions the impact of this ambitious plan was limited. It was not finally approved (and then with reservations) until 1939, though it was not then superseded until 1960. There were some limited impacts in road developments, and the plan helped provide broad planning guidance for reconstruction in war-damaged municipalities after the Second World War. But PARP's key importance was in establishing the *idea* of a Paris region and planting certain longer term ideas that came to fruition under later rounds of planning. The belated extension of regional planning to other areas did not meet with any greater success (Couedelo, 1991). By 1940 only 14 regional associations had appeared, covering small areas that were inconsistent with viable regional planning.

## BRITAIN

In contrast to France (and Belgium) Britain suffered no significant physical destruction during the First World War. Yet the political salience of town planning and, even more, housing was greatly advanced (Ward, 1994). The serious prewar housing shortage, the needs of war production, the cessation of building and, above all, the political need to promise a better world after the war all fuelled the housing debate (Swenarton, 1981). Reformers used the changed circumstances of war to press their cause with energy. The wartime housing schemes associated with war production, especially at Well Hall in southeast London and at Gretna and Rosyth in Scotland, set important precedents, signifying government endorsement of garden-city housing standards.

### THE TUDOR-WALTERS REPORT AND MUNICIPAL HOUSING

Following the recommendations of the influential Tudor-Walters Committee of 1918, largely written by Raymond Unwin, and new housing and planning legislation in 1919, garden city standards were enforced for practically all assisted housing schemes (Miller, 1992). These 'homes for heroes', built in the first few years after the war, were of a standard that matched the very best of the prewar lower rent housing in Letchworth and the garden suburbs. Hopes that government would take the opportunity to sponsor the creation of freestanding garden cities did not materialise, despite strong pressure (Hardy, 1991a). The municipal garden suburb, built on a scale unparalleled anywhere else in the world, became the most typical manifestation of publicly shaped urban growth in Britain between the wars. The most astonishing of all these efforts was the London County Council's great township at Becontree, in east London (LCC, 1937). This was planned in outline, and begun, in 1920. Over 25,000 dwellings had been built by the time it was completed, in 1934. It had its own community facilities, including shops, schools, churches, parks and playing fields. Major local industry followed, though more fortuitously, so Becontree did not entirely deserve the label of garden city that it was sometimes accorded.

No other single scheme even came close in size to Becontree which, by 1934, had a population of about 115,000. Throughout the country, however, towns and cities, large and small, embarked on state-assisted cottage housing schemes in these early postwar years (Ward, 1994). At one level, they implemented much of what the pre-1914 town planning movement had wanted. At another, though, they were a denial of

*Figure 4.5* *Despite many misgivings on the part of Howard's supporters, a second garden city was created at Welwyn from 1919. More than Letchworth, it became a model of what a well-planned small town could offer to address metropolitan problems.*

wider town planning principles. Unwin had wanted to see these housing developments properly integrated with town planning schemes. The original concept of the 1919 legislation had been that municipal housing developments would be set within compulsory town planning schemes which shaped the overall development for the suburban fringes. This intention was rapidly diluted.

## A SECOND GARDEN CITY

Yet, if dilution was to be the dominant story of British urban planning in the early postwar years, there were also important initiatives outside the policy mainstream which kept more ambitious visions alive. Most important was the establishment of a second freestanding garden city, at Welwyn in 1919 (Beevers, 1988; Filler, 1986; de Soissons, 1988). Mistrustful of government intentions and weary of his associates' caution, Howard took an extraordinary personal step, bidding at auction for a large rural estate without having the money to pay for it. Though horrified, his associates were obliged to make the development work; failure would have seriously damaged the movement. From 1920, therefore, a second, and more carefully executed, example of the garden city took shape.

The young planner of Welwyn, Louis de Soissons, was, like Charles Reade, an early example of a planner who moved from the periphery of empire to its heart. A French Canadian, de Soissons brought a beaux-arts training to the original Arts and Crafts traditions of the movement, an influence which was palpable in the very form of his plan. He was also able to control its implementation to a much greater extent than was ever even attempted at Letchworth. And, if the microscale was carefully planned, Welwyn's promoters were also careful to locate it within a wider strategy for planned metropolitan decentralisation from London. In truth, such a positioning was more image than reality since there were no mechanisms to achieve it. Yet this conceptual refinement of the garden city was to prove extremely important in the longer term.

## OTHER PLANNING MOVES

British planning was still distinguished, however, by a preoccupation with the urban fringe and, although the efforts of the garden city movement partly obscured this, an absence of any serious official consideration of the city as whole. There were concerns about the large areas of slum housing built during the early phases of industrialisation in the late 18th and early 19th centuries, before effective building regulation was introduced (Yelling, 1992). But for the moment, the scale of the general shortage of housing was so great as to inhibit large-scale moves to redevelop slum districts. The idea of such a response was, however, already beginning to take shape in the early postwar years.

Another new initiative was in regional planning, where the prewar ideas of Geddes began to be applied, albeit to a very limited extent (Cherry, 1974). The first example was the officially sponsored South Wales Regional Planning Survey, published in 1921. This made proposals for the remodelling of settlements in a major coalfield, with garden cities instead of the existing pithead villages. The new coalfields at Doncaster in south Yorkshire and in East Kent also prompted early regional plans. By the early 1920s central government was encouraging similar initiatives throughout the country though, because these were advisory, actual achievements were invariably very limited.

## THE GROWING CITIES

More generally, the idealism and energy of the early postwar years soon gave way to caution (Ashworth, 1954; Cherry, 1988; Ward, 1994). By international standards, most parts of urban Britain survived the many economic and political threats of the interwar years very well. The country's economic structure, with its exceptionally low

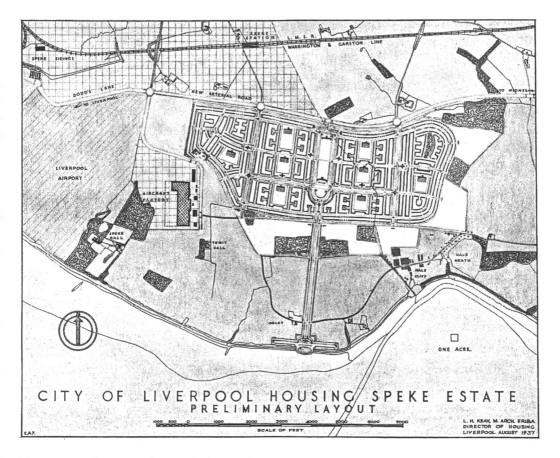

**Figure 4.6** *Reflecting garden city thinking and international examples, some cities tried to create peripheral satellite towns, offering employment and community facilities rather than just housing. An ambitious attempt was this one at Speke in Liverpool.*

reliance on agriculture, and its position as the hub of the largest global empire cushioned it against the world depression. Despite a sharp fall in the birth rate urban growth continued, though at a noticeably slower overall pace than before 1914. The big cities were still growing, but more slowly, and their core areas now began to show unmistakable signs of decline as large-scale suburbanisation finally became a mass phenomenon (AA Jackson, 1991). London overall added 1.2 million population between the wars (mainly by 1930), to reach 8.7 million by 1939. But outer London had actually gained nearly 1.8 million. In provincial Britain the pattern was the same (eg BVT, 1941). Within their increasingly tight limits, Birmingham grew from 922,000 to just over one million, Glasgow by just 100,000 to 1.1 million and Manchester actually declined a little to 728,000. Everywhere, though, there was dramatic growth in the suburban areas.

## THE GARDEN SUBURB ASCENDANT

Britain's dominant planning tradition remained the garden city 'revisionism' represented by the garden suburb (Ward, 1994). Though government commitments to subsidised housing never matched the generosity of the early postwar period they remained high. Local councils built 1.3 million dwellings, mainly in the cottage form officially recommended by Unwin in 1918. Some private building, broadly corresponding with these standards, was also subsidised. And by the 1930s private developers were, unaided, building on an immense scale at similar or even lower densities. Local planning schemes, where they existed, largely encouraged the garden suburb model. In fact, the cost and availability of land and the general expectations of house buyers meant that no such encouragement was needed.

The detailed planning of suburban areas varied considerably. Some of the council estates, including many of those of the London County Council, Liverpool, Birmingham and Nottingham and other cities, were of good quality. The best examples showed good design and site planning, retention of pre-existing features, some thought about provision of communal facilities and good communication links to city centres. Many more were adequate but dreary. Everywhere, the tendency to provide standard house types for similar income groups created a social homogeneity and visual monotony. The quality of planning of the private estates varied. There was usually less concern for community facilities. Yet, although planners in the 1930s often complained about unplanned private suburban development, the results were far better than, for example, the self-built unserviced areas that grew around Paris in the same period.

## SATELLITE TOWNS

Nevertheless, there was a growing tendency by the 1930s to see an infinite garden suburbia as part of the problem, rather than part of the solution to planning big cities. Within the garden city tradition, this led to a search for alternatives (Ward, 1992; Hardy, 1991a). The promoters of Welwyn Garden City, of course, lost no opportunity to trumpet it as an answer. Yet its growth was too slow and uncertain to win many converts. More promising were the directions in which the Frankfurt satellite towns pointed. These were widely discussed at international gatherings, although Britain's leading planner, Raymond Unwin, also maintained close links with May. The term 'satellite town' entered British planning discourse in the 1920s, even if often used rather ambiguously. During the 1930s, however, British examples that actually deserved the name appeared at Speke in Liverpool and Wythenshawe in south Manchester.

The latter was better known (Deakin (ed), 1989). After many delays, due largely to its being outside Manchester, its planning and development began in the 1930s. The overall plan, drawn up in 1931 by Barry Parker, was for a satellite town separated from the main city by a narrow green belt. There were to be local shopping and other communal facilities consistent with a settlement that would ultimately grow (though not until after 1945) to over 100,000 inhabitants (four times the target for Speke). These would live mainly in municipal cottages but there would be sizable amounts of private housing. There would also be local industrial employment so that some of the population would be able to work close to their homes. Parker also adapted some of the latest American thinking about residential neighbourhoods and parkway roads. Such ideas very soon became known in Britain, reflecting the two countries' common use of English, and the active intermediary roles of frequent Atlantic crossers such as Thomas Adams and Raymond Unwin (Simpson, 1985; Miller, 1992).

## Planning Greater London

From 1929 Parker's former partner, Raymond Unwin, had been further elaborating a planned approach to metropolitan decentralisation in his work for the Greater London Regional Planning Committee (Miller, 1992). Like many comparable initiatives at this time, the committee was established (in 1927) to give coherence to planning in an area that spanned many individual local authorities. Unlike most others in provincial Britain, however, it had the added authority that came from being a central government initiative. Unwin's reports, issued from 1929 to 1931, therefore attracted a great deal of interest. Like the slightly later Prost plan for Paris, they planted the idea of metropolitan planning. In 1929 Unwin introduced the notion of a 'green girdle' that would form a barrier to continuous suburban development. Beyond that, as outlined in a 1931 report, would be satellite towns and industrial garden cities within which metropolitan growth would henceforth be accommodated. Howard's social city had thus been reworked into a complete model for metropolitan decentralisation.

## Green belts

The last two, more ambitious, parts of this model recurred in inconclusive official discussions in the 1930s but brought no action. However, important moves were taken to implement Unwin's idea of the green girdle (Elson, 1986; Ward, 1994). From 1935 the newly Labour-controlled London County Council initiated moves to buy, or sterilise from development, land in the urban periphery. This marked the first important stage in the formulation of one of the key concepts of post-1945 British planning: the green belt. This term was, in fact, preferred to Unwin's frank allusion to an urban corset though the intent, to contain the city, was very similar. Comparable moves were also under way around other cities, notably Birmingham and Sheffield.

## REGIONAL PLANNING

The wider idea of regional planning also grew during the 1920s and early 1930s. By 1931 there were 104 town planning bodies involving multiple local authorities, though many covered only very small areas, in some cases nesting within larger organisations (Cherry, 1974; Ward, 1994). Many bodies provided an opportunity for counties to become active in town planning. A smaller number covered very large metropolitan regions, such as those for Manchester (1922) and the Midlands (1927). The leading proponent of the movement was Patrick Abercrombie, an architect-planner who had been strongly influenced by Patrick Geddes' ideas (Dix, 1981). With local assistance, Abercrombie and other planners produced a string of attractive advisory plans for regional committees. Invariably, his elegant prose and fine sense of illustration evoked a far more inspirational vision of the destiny of places than was ever possible in statutory town planning schemes.

## REGIONAL PROBLEMS

As some regions began to suffer in the Depression, however, the value of such advisory visions seemed dubious (Ward, 1986). Without the money to implement proposals, there seemed little point in zoning land for growth, or identifying major road routes, bridging points or sites for satellite towns. There was growing political pressure for a major public works programme and the regional advisory plans offered a shopping list of projects. Yet the government resisted this option. Despite the admiration British engineer-planners and some politicians had for the *Reichauto-bahnen* (Hass-Klau, 1990), there was no British equivalent of these. Nor did President Franklin D Roosevelt's even more widely admired New Deal in the United States inspire any British equivalent. Instead, from 1934 there was a cautious policy of targeting limited aid on the worst affected areas (Ward, 1988). From 1936, however, this acquired an altogether more significant dimension with the creation of large planned industrial estates, initially at Team Valley on Tyneside. The intention was to attract new industries to older, depressed regions, and the principle of giving financial and other assistance was increasingly accepted. Outside these central government initiatives, Wythenshawe and Speke satellite towns showed the potential of this as part of a comprehensive planning approach.

## SLUM CLEARANCE AND URBAN REDEVELOPMENT

More ambitious was the drive to clear the slums from the older parts of cities (Yelling, 1992). There had been intermittent interest in this since 1919 but relatively little sustained action until the 1930s, and especially from 1933. By this time, all the key interest groups were agreed that wholesale clearance and redevelopment was the only viable way to deal with the large areas of obsolescent housing that dated from the early industrial period. Earlier experiments with gradual renewal were now dismissed as mere 'slum patching'. The creation of this consensus on urban redevelopment brought further challenges to the garden suburb as a universal model. Such were inner city land values that higher density flatted forms were now widely accepted as essential on redeveloped and replacement housing sites. Since British architects and planners had little experience of such forms, these new policy directions led them to seek relevant foreign examples (Ravetz, 1974b).

## THE RISE OF BRITISH MODERNISM

These specific concerns became part of a broader shift. There had been only extremely limited British interest in the new modernist thinking of the 1920s. However, the 1930s moves towards urban redevelopment coincided with the first serious British engagement with international modernism. In 1933 a group of younger architects formed the Modern Architectural Research (MARS) Group, very much as a British chapter of CIAM (Gold, 1997). Their interest was further reinforced (though it was certainly not caused) by the appearance in Britain from about this time of modernists from continental Europe. Many, as already noted, were leaving Hitler's Germany because they were Jewish or had political associations which put them at risk, or simply because they found it difficult to secure work. Others came, for a variety of motives, from other parts of central and eastern Europe. For these others, although political shifts had often played a part in their emigration, there were also important 'pull' factors. Britain, being relatively prosperous at this time, had the advantage of offering more work than most other parts of Europe.

## MODERNISM AND PLANNING

The British modern movement, though it exerted only limited influence at this time, became what it was elsewhere: an avant-garde, introducing, and elaborating on, the new thinking (Gold, 1997). It was partly by this means that German, Dutch and French ideas began to become better known. There were also other, less obvious, connections. For example, the MARS Group showed a strengthening interest in linear-city forms, partly derived from Soviet examples, during the late 1930s. Refugees with direct experience of the Soviet scene, such as Eugen Kaufmann, a veteran of Ernst May's Frankfurt and Russian planning teams, found an eager reception for their accounts of Communist approaches to the planning of residential areas (Tetlow, 1959). These supplemented the main source (America) of new ideas about neighbourhood planning which derived from the garden city mainstream. Scandinavia, particularly Sweden, also became another important source of influence during the later 1930s. In part this was because the social democratic Nordic countries were seen, after 1933, as continuing the progressive modernist spirit of Weimar. Yet it also reflected a wider reorientation of Scandinavia towards the English-speaking world. At the often confusingly multilingual CIAM meetings, for example, the British and

Scandinavian contingents were often grouped together for discussions, separate from the French and German speakers.

Through its individual members, MARS was also directly involved in some of the most notable 1930s exercises in creating new planned living environments. One scheme directly intended as a model for slum cleared areas was Kensal House in London. Designed in 1936/37 by Maxwell Fry, the scheme could almost have been from one of the much-admired Berlin or Frankfurt *siedlungen* of a few years earlier. It made a sharp contrast to the more traditional neo-Georgian flat blocks that were then typical of London's slum-clearance replacement schemes. Another important development that showed a more overtly Corbusian influence was Highpoint I, a development in the Highgate district of London, designed for affluent residents by a Russian exile, Berthold Lubetkin and his associates, from 1933.

## OTHER SOURCES OF INFLUENCE

Though the MARS network was important, it was not the only means by which knowledge of external ideas was introduced. The IFHTP and IULA conferences continued to provide a steady drip feed of urban information from other countries. From about 1930, some bigger local authorities and other agencies sent delegations to inspect continental developments which seemed to have something to offer (Ravetz, 1974b). Not surprisingly, Germany, the Netherlands, France and Scandinavia were much visited. Also significant was Czecho-Slovakia (as it was then styled). Above all others, however, it was the Austrian capital, Vienna, that caught the British municipal imagination. Nowhere had flatted housing been built on such an immense scale. Several of the most important British redevelopment schemes of the later 1930s, particularly Gerard Gardens in Liverpool and the highly innovative Quarry Hill estate in Leeds, showed clear deference to Vienna (Ravetz, 1974a). The latter, with over 900 flats, was the only British scheme to approach in size the largest Viennese schemes. Even here, however, the borrowing was not simply from one source. The building technology and waste-disposal system were French while the external design showed some Germanic influence.

## TOWARDS A NATIONAL PLANNING POLICY

The British engagement with modernism mirrored the generally cautious attitude to all kinds of state intervention (Ward, 1994). Despite the strong commitments to municipal housing, the political hegemony of Conservatism throughout the interwar years spelled an underlying belief in market forces, especially on economic matters. The relatively timid British responses to the economic problems of the 1930s certainly disappointed many. But, alone, that disenchantment was never strong enough to force dramatic change. By 1937, however, there were the first glimmerings of more far-reaching changes. Government was not just perturbed at the various problems of slums, depressed areas and sprawling suburbs. It was also, after the Spanish and Abyssinian wars, increasingly fearful of the bombing risks inherent in unrestricted urban expansion. War with Germany and, very probably, Italy now seemed only a matter of time. Rather than take radical action, however, the prime minister, Neville Chamberlain, established an important Royal Commission to investigate these varied, but related issues which raised important questions about the future of planning policies. Known as the Barlow Commission after its chairman, Sir Montague Barlow, its report was published in 1940 in the more highly charged atmosphere of war (Barlow, 1940). It was to play an important part in establishing the idea of comprehensive, nationally based planning that was embraced immediately after the Second World War.

## BRITISH LESSON-DRAWING IN THE LATE 1930S

The report had another, more immediate, interest. In a lengthy appendix it reviewed the planning actions of other countries, showing how they were seen by the British official mind at this rather momentous time. It revealed how, as before the First World War, wider international insecurities could structure external lesson-drawing. Not that this was the only trend that it reflected. Above all, it showed the striking growth of the United States as a model: almost a third of the appendix was devoted to American planning. Only slightly less space, however, went to the once and future enemy, Germany. And no less than 15 per cent of the total coverage went on Italy. These two allocations were certainly far greater than could be justified by intrinsic professional interest. The remaining sections, in descending order, dealt with the Netherlands, India, France, Sweden, Japan, Singapore and Poland.

The most significant omission from this list was the Soviet Union, possibly because large sections of influential opinion still disliked communism far more than fascism. Yet, as we have seen, Russia held a particular fascination for modernists in the 1930s, even though (or perhaps because) hardly any of them actually went there. One influential visitor from the mainstream of British planning was Sir Ernest Simon, a Manchester Liberal (and great supporter of Wythenshawe). His account, though certainly not uncritical, revealed clearly why totalitarian states were warranting such attention from the British planning movement (Simon, 1937). There was, simply, a widespread fear that the democracies had lost their way and were falling behind Russia and the other dictatorships. Increasingly the message was that, unless the democracies learnt how to plan, totalitarianism would triumph.

## THE UNITED STATES

The main comfort for those whose thinking went in this direction was the United States. Under the presidency of Franklin Delano Roosevelt, the world's largest democracy had (rather to its own surprise) become a beacon for democratic planning in the 1930s, a counterblast to Hitler, Mussolini and Stalin. However, the growing fascination of European urban planners with the United States reflected much more than Roosevelt's New Deal or, indeed, America's rehearsals in the 1920s of many of the planning ideas that were later adopted by the New Dealers. There was a more fundamental sense of wonder at the dynamism of American cities, their size and number, the vastness of their buildings and the continual innovations in their functioning (Cohen, 1995). None of this was new, of course, but it certainly intensi-fied as the mass media, especially the new film industry, spread beguiling images of the American way of life.

Alone among the major innovatory nations, the United States had initially been little affected by the war in Europe. Developments of city planning thus initially continued along lines already apparent in 1914 (Scott, 1969). By that time annual meetings of city planners were taking place (though there was still no exact definition of what a city planner might actually be). The literature of city planning was also increasing, including a quarterly journal, *The City Plan*, which appeared in 1915.

## INTERNATIONAL INFLUENCES DURING WARTIME

Knowledge of European developments in urban planning also continued to grow. It was, of course, still possible for Americans to discuss the lessons of German planning objectively without the rancour which now attended any Germanic references in Britain. Thus, despite being required to register as an enemy alien when the United States entered the war, Werner Hegemann, an American resident from early 1916 to 1921, was still able to practise and speak widely, exerting a significant influence (CC Collins, 1996). This culminated in 1922 with the publication of *American Vitruvius: An Architect's Handbook of Civic Art*, co-authored with the American architect Elbert Peets (Hegemann and Peets, 1922). For the first time American city planners had a comprehensive source book for city design which, very importantly, allowed them to see European and American approaches as part of a common tradition

Another influential figure at this time was Thomas Adams, the prominent British planner, whose government post in neighbouring Canada made it quite easy for him to speak regularly at American planning conferences (Simpson, 1985). The United States' continuing love affair with the city beautiful also ensured contacts with French thinking. In 1917, for example, it was a young *urbaniste*, Jacques Gréber, who produced the detailed plan for the Fairmount Parkway in Philadelphia that was finally accepted (Scott, 1969).

## ZONING ASCENDANT

Yet although the American city planning movement was extending and refining its conceptual base, there were as yet few opportunities for applying it. A growing number of cities were creating planning commissions and sponsoring planning activity but often only in a token fashion (Scott, 1969). Certainly, there was nothing at this time on the grand scale, comparable to the Burnham and Bennett plan for Chicago. The really significant practical development in these years was the increasing sophistication of zoning techniques to a level that began to bear comparison with German practice. The landmark here was the 1916 zoning ordinance for New York City (JB Cullingworth, 1993). This reflected several active concerns including the impact of skyscrapers and, more immediately, the conflicts between industry and retailing in Manhattan. For the first time under United States law, the measure showed that it was possible to introduce a legally watertight zoning scheme for a large and complex city. The 1916 zoning plan survived the critical legal test: was zoning an appropriation of land rights, liable therefore for compensation payments, or was it a justified use of ordinary police power, whereby individual rights could be curbed for the common good without compensation? The latter view prevailed, though the legality of zoning was not finally settled until the 1920s.

Amongst city planners, however, there were increasing concerns that zoning was being adopted in isolation from any comprehensive notion of planning. Though it undoubtedly had the potential to be a useful instrument of planning, its early application promised no more than a formalisation of the status quo. Thus the New York zoning scheme resolved some immediate problems but offered much scope for massive overbuilding to continue. Recognising these limitations, planners wanted to prevent cities seizing on zoning as an apparently simple, painless panacea that, in reality, stored up long-term problems. Despite a few successes in the following years, these hopes remained largely unfulfilled.

## THE AMERICAN CITY PLANNING INSTITUTE

The early pattern of annual meetings, aimed partly at practitioners and partly at a wider public, led to the formation of the American City Planning Institute (ACPI) in 1917. (Scott, 1969). Like the London-based Town Planning Institute (though unlike the Paris-based Société Française des Urbanistes) the ACPI was intended as a fully integrative professional body. Thomas Adams was, in fact, one of its charter members, though it was Olmsted Jr and a young attorney, Flavel Shurtleff, who took the lead in its formation. Its composition differed from both the British and French bodies, indicating clearly how city planning differed from town planning and *urbanisme*. The TPI and, even more, the SFU were dominated by architects. In the TPI, though not the SFU, their influence was carefully balanced against engineers, surveyors and, to a lesser extent, lawyers. The ACPI was, by contrast, dominated by landscape architects (a profession then barely recognised in Britain) and engineers. The balance of its membership also embraced a far more diverse range of expertise than either the TPI or SFU. It was the heterogeneity of the ACPI that was, indeed, its most striking feature.

## WARTIME HOUSING

By the time the ACPI was formed the United States had entered the First World War and the industrialisation involved in producing military equipment provided new opportunities for the city planners. Already John Nolen, one of the foremost of this first generation of city planners, was employing garden city principles to plan a new industrial city being promoted by a group of New York businessmen at Kingsport, Tennessee (Crawford, 1994; 1997)). By the end of the year, the federal government had become directly involved as part of general moves to intensify war production. As new centres were developed, housing for workers became a priority (Comstock (ed), 1919). The newly formed United States Housing Corporation (USHC) and Emergency Fleet Corporation (EFC) sponsored the creation of several new housing schemes. The largest (with some 1,500 dwellings) and most famous was the EFC's scheme at Yorkship Village (now called Fairview) at Camden, New Jersey (Lang, 1996). Its planning, by Electus Litchfield, an architect who had worked at Kingsport, leant heavily on British garden city designs, especially the wartime schemes of the British government at Well Hall and Gretna (discussed above). The EFC's head of design, Frederick L Ackerman, one of the more progressive housing reformers in the United States at that time, had recently visited these and reported back in glowing terms. Yorkship and the smaller wartime schemes (though the war had actually finished before they were) thus showed closer reference to the garden city than anything which had yet appeared in the United States. However, they were expensive and their failure to cover their costs led to a political backlash. They were auctioned off immediately the war ended and, unlike in Britain, did not set a precedent for a wider social housing programme.

## INTERWAR URBAN GROWTH

The United States became the world's most dynamic capitalist economy during the 1920s. The principal object of wonder was New York which overtook London to become the world's largest city in the same decade (KT Jackson, 1984). By 1940 New York City alone had nearly 7.5 million inhabitants and its metropolitan area approached 11.7 million – and other American metropolitan cities also stood high in the world table (McKelvey, 1968). The second, Chicago, had a metropolitan population of 4.5 million, bigger than Berlin or Moscow. Exceptionally rapid growth in Los Angeles (2.9 million) meant that it was just overtaking Philadelphia (2.9 million). Other very large metropolitan areas, bigger than most European capitals, were Boston (2.4 million) and Detroit (2.3 million). The figures for the cities alone were far less impressive (New York was exceptional in this respect). To a greater extent than was yet true for almost all European cities, a growing proportion of growth had begun to spill over fairly static city boundaries into adjoining suburban districts (KT Jackson, 1985).The latter accounted for under 9 per cent of the national population in 1920 and grew to over 15 per cent (20 million people) in 1940.

Overall the proportion of Americans living in cities and suburbs grew from 34 per cent in 1920 to 48 per cent (63 million) in 1940. However, despite the absolute size of the population figure, the latter proportion was still only roughly equivalent to that in France, the most rural of the major European countries, and much lower than in Britain or Germany. In Europe urban population growth had been fuelled by migration from the continent's rural areas. In America the net migrational flow, traditionally from Europe, was to both the cities and the rural areas. However, mass immigration was legally restricted from 1924 and the Depression (which affected rural areas especially severely) brought further reductions in the number of people living outside cities. Increasingly, therefore, urban areas in the United States grew at the expense of rural ones.

## PLANNING IN THE AGE OF BUSINESS

The scale of metropolitan growth, and the confident 1920s expectation that it would continue, stimulated a great deal of planning action (Scott, 1969). As we have seen, the form of city planning that became dominant early in the decade focused very much on urban efficiency. Its principal underlying rationale for most cities was to sustain the inward flows of investment and population that were needed for growth. Broadly, this involved providing the necessary physical infrastructure, offering a degree of certainty for real-estate developers, investors and residents and promoting some visible symbols of urban civilisation. The main practical concerns of city planners were roads and transportation, land use and density zoning, parks and civic centres. The greater social concerns of interwar European planning, notably in the field of housing, were scarcely apparent, certainly in the everyday practicalities of the 1920s mainstream.

## HARLAND BARTHOLOMEW AND THE COMPREHENSIVE CITY PLAN

Thus the most typical products of American city planning at this time were comprehensive plans (as understood in the American sense of emphasising zoning, infrastructure and parks, with little attention paid to social housing). These were prepared for city planning commissions by consultants such as John Nolen or Harland Bartholomew (Hancock, 1994; Johnston, 1994; Lovelace, 1993). The latter especially, based in St Louis, was the very epitome of a city planner in the age of business, the profession's nearest equivalent to Henry Ford. Between 1920 and 1926 his firm undertook 20 of the 87 comprehensive city plans prepared in the United States by consultants. Nolen came next with 12 (Johnston, 1994; Krueckeberg, 1994). By 1930 Bartholomew's tally, going back to 1911, had grown to 50. What he gave to medium and smaller sized cities across the continent (including, in the 1920s alone, Memphis, Wichita, Des Moines, Knoxville and Louisville) was a technically impressive product which they could adopt immediately in a zoning ordinance to guide future development. There would always be a few projects to inspire, but the general tenor was predominantly practical and businesslike, avoiding the utopian or extravagant. Though his plans were never exactly identical, their content was formulaic, even using exactly the same diagrams for different cities. For their part, the city planning commissions who hired his firm were aware of this. They wanted something honed from experience, carefully costed and delivered to schedule that would advertise them as being progressive but firmly practical.

## METROPOLITAN REGIONAL PLANNING

There were, of course, many limitations to such an approach. One issue was that it tended to address the city, rather than the whole metropolitan area (Scott, 1969). Another, and more fundamental, issue was that it offered precious little to the huddled masses of the biggest cities, yearning to be free of the dingy overcrowded slums. There was a good deal of activity on the first issue during the 1920s. The combination of progressive business, professional and civic opinion that accepted the advantages of city planning frequently also saw the value of transcending city government and, in some cases, state lines. The early 1920s saw regional planning organisations, covering large areas, set up for Los Angeles (1920), New York (1921),

Chicago (1923) and Philadelphia (1924). By the early 1930s, 20 such bodies existed in the northeastern states alone (RPFPTD, 1932). Their actual form varied. Some, like the Los Angeles county body, were municipal initiatives. Others, including those for New York, Chicago and Philadelphia, were private agencies sponsored by business or philanthropic interests. On the whole, it was easier for the second type to transcend local jealousies. Partly for that reason (and partly because they were usually more lavishly funded) their plans were more impressive.

## THE REGIONAL PLAN OF NEW YORK

Much the most important was the Regional Plan of New York and its Environs, RPNY (Johnson, 1988, 1996; Kantor, 1994b). Funded by the Russell Sage Foundation (the developers of Forest Hills), it had a $500,000 budget. As befitted the world's biggest city, it also became the most lavish planning operation yet seen. When published, from 1927 to 1931, the plan and contributory surveys ran to 10 large volumes, excluding maps. It was also an impressive collaborative operation, involving leading American practitioners including Olmsted Jr, Nolen, Bartholomew, Ford, Bennett and Shurtleff. Most of the detailed work was undertaken by permanent staff members of the New York Regional Planning Association. Directing the whole operation was the British planner and recent adviser to the Canadian government, Thomas Adams (Simpson, 1985). In 1922 Charles Norton, the main promoter of the plan, had visited London and Paris seeking advice from both Unwin and Adams. Both men had learnt their craft in the garden city movement. Both also saw the need to compromise Howard's ideal, sacrificing the utopian ideal for the achievable good, but Adams had certainly gone further in this respect. Norton was impressed with Unwin's vision but it was the hard-headed practicality of Adams (which partly reflected a better understanding of the American scene) that impressed him more.

Something of Adams' understanding of the art of the practical pervades the plan itself. Much of the RPNY was designed to appeal to the progressive business sentiments that shaped much of American planning in this era. The technical and survey material was invariably impressive. In particular, the analyses of the metropolitan area's economy laid foundations of later work on economic base theory. In common with many other plans of the 1920s, however, the major emphasis was on transportation. The plan made ambitious proposals for rail transit which were not implemented. By contrast, the very ambitious proposals for highway construction were broadly followed and, moreover, with remarkable speed (a theme to which we will return). This imbalance had a decisive effect, making development of the New York region disproportionately reliant on the automobile. Other major proposals were for extensive park and recreational developments on the metropolitan fringes, which were implemented to a very large extent.

## DECENTRALISATION AND THE NEIGHBOURHOOD UNIT

There were some obvious omissions in the plan. Decentralisation to planned new communities, such as Unwin favoured for London, was promoted in only a very half-hearted fashion. Nolen and staff member Clarence Perry were its most enthusiastic proponents but other, more influential, voices were cautious. Adams recognised that the operation could easily be discredited if its aims seemed too utopian, so the final plan avoided specific suggestions. More generally, housing for lower to middle income groups was neglected. Despite these disappointments, however, the plan made one hugely influential conceptual contribution in relation to housing development: the neighbourhood unit (Perry, 1929; 1939). Drawing on observations over several years as a resident of Forest Hills, in 1926 Perry suggested a physical basis for planning socially cohesive residential communities in relation to schools, shops and other facilities. His work pointed to neighbourhoods in the range of 5,000 to 10,000 residents, a little larger than Howard's original concept of the ward, a term the latter used to describe the six residential districts of his imaginary garden city, but did not elaborate on.

## THE REGIONAL PLANNING ASSOCIATION OF AMERICA

The main criticisms of the social and spatial conservatism of the RPNY came from the Regional Planning Association of America, RPAA (Lubove, 1963; Spann, 1996). Founded in 1923, it was provisionally called the Garden City and Regional Planning Association, which better describes its outlook. It was a small group of left-inclined professionals and propagandists, several of whom had profound impacts on American and, in some cases, international planning. The best known internationally was the writer Lewis Mumford (Wojtowicz, 1996), but others included Frederick Ackerman, the former leader of the wartime EFC housing programme (Lang, 2001), the younger architect-planners Clarence Stein (KC Parsons, (ed), 1998) and Henry Wright, the ecologist Benton McKaye (Thomas, 1994), and housing reformers Edith Elmer Wood and Catherine Bauer (Bauer, 1934; Radford, 1996; Birch, 1994a).

The RPAA saw itself as an alternative voice to the RPNY, and developed more socially progressive planning ideas than those of the American mainstream (Scott, 1996). As befitted its New York centre of gravity, its outlook was cosmopolitan, looking to Europe as well as America. Its main international connections were initially with Howard, still a transatlantic figure even in his final years, Unwin and Geddes (P Hall, 1988). Its members wanted to undermine the RPNY's more compromised interpretations of garden city and regionalist ideas and show themselves as the true believers (which they were). Increasingly the RPAA showed strong interest in the new planning developments of continental Europe (Rodgers, 1998). Thus Bauer, Mumford, Wright and Stein were amongst the first Americans to see the German, Dutch and other European modernist housing and played an important intermediary role by introducing their ideas to the United States. They also viewed the new Soviet Union with considerable sympathy. (Stein himself worked very briefly on a plan for the north Caucasus region in 1927).

## STEIN, WRIGHT AND RADBURN

The most important tangible planning innovation associated with the RPAA was the Radburn layout which updated the garden city for the motor age (Stein, 1958; Buder,

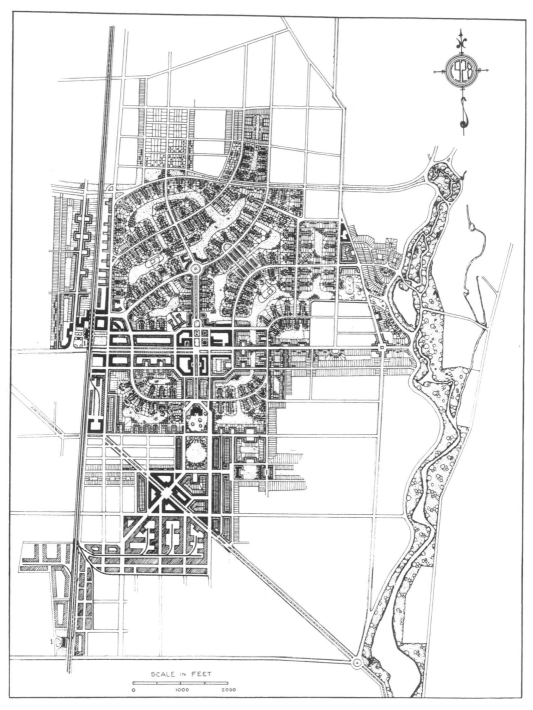

SCALE IN FEET

0    1000    2000

**Figure 4.7** *Radburn was an intended garden city, of which only one part was built. It gave its name to a distinctive and highly influential residential layout which offered complete segregation of pedestrian and vehicle movements, updating the garden city for the motor age.*

1990; KC Parsons (ed), 1998). The name refers to an abortive garden city in New Jersey, planned by Stein and Wright. Its developer was the City Housing Corporation (CHC), a limited dividend company set up by Alexander Bing in 1924 to build an American garden city. Bing was a member of both the RPAA and the RPNY committee. Work eventually began on Radburn in 1928 but the Depression restricted development to one neighbourhood, albeit of very distinctive layout. Its key provision is the complete separation of pedestrian and vehicle movements. Conceived within a 'superblock', much larger than was then typical of American cities, the housing turns its back on the street to face an inner park that is accessible only to pedestrians and from which all communal facilities may be reached without needing to cross roads.

Though they did not work closely with Perry, Stein and Wright were well aware of his neighbourhood unit idea, which was subsumed within their new layout. More intriguing were the similarities with the road-safety layouts being developed in Germany during the 1920s by Hermann Jansen (Hass-Klau, 1990). Yet, although they were increasingly familiar with the work of the German modernists, Stein and Wright did not directly know of Jansen's work. Nevertheless, they were certainly the first to secure a complete separation of vehicles and pedestrians in a residential layout. An earlier CHC project developed from 1924 at Sunnyside Gardens in Queens, New York, had laid much of the basis for Radburn. It was actually a CHC administrator, Herbert Emmerich, who in late 1927 had stimulated Stein and Wright to take the final step in achieving complete separation of pedestrians and motor traffic, after drafting a purely imaginary residential ideal called 'Safetyhurst' (Stein, 1958).

## PLANNING FOR THE AUTOMOBILE

By the mid-1930s, the United States had nearly 25 million automobiles (McKelvey, 1968; Scott, 1969). In relation to population, this was roughly 6 times the level in Britain and 12 times the German level. Although Germany (and Italy) showed an interwar interest in planning for the car that went far beyond its existing use, American concerns stemmed from pressures that were already manifest. Many innovations in motorised city life appeared between the wars. Thus the first suburban shopping mall designed for automobile access appeared in Kansas City, at the Country Club Plaza, in 1922 (Garvin, 1996). The first clover-leaf intersection was built on the Lincoln Highway near Jersey City in metropolitan New York, in 1930 (McKelvey, 1968). The first extended stretch of fully divided highway was in Detroit, in 1932. In 1935 came the first use of parking meters in Oklahoma City.

## PARKWAYS

Major road developments comparable with (and with some knowledge of) those in Germany and Italy were also well under way. New York, along with Los Angeles and Detroit, were the main innovators. In New York, the example noted by most Europeans, the important shifts initially seemed to be more about parks than roads. Parks, it will be recalled, had reflected the most salient theme in the early emergence of American city planning. The elder Olmsted, and others, had promoted the notion of the landscaped parkway that combined characteristics of park and highway. As motor traffic grew this idea gradually transmuted so that the highway aspect assumed precedence. The great functional advantage of the park connection was that road frontages would be publicly owned and could therefore remain undeveloped, which would also allow access to the road to be limited (P Hall, 1988). Even before 1914 the Long Island Motor Parkway had been built in this way. By the early 1920s others, such as the Bronx River Parkway were being completed.

The moves in this direction were strongly encouraged by the RPNY and, even more, by the powerful figure of Robert Moses, the Long Island State parks commissioner (Caro, 1975). As we have seen, the RPNY proposals included a comprehensive system of major highways and large parks around the fringes of the metropolitan area. Moses' ruthlessness and political clout meant they were built at extraordinary speed. Large state parks were created, most notably one at Jones Beach which opened in 1929, and were served by impressive new parkways and private toll roads which allowed rapid access for automobile traffic from the city.

## TOWARDS THE FREEWAY

As Moses consolidated his hold on public works – most especially the new Triborough Bridge project – throughout the New York region in the 1930s, he built many more, ever bigger, roads (RPA, 1937; 1938). Although most were still, in legal terms, park access roads this was increasingly a fiction. New York's Henry Hudson Parkway, opened in 1937, is better understood as the world's first urban freeway (Caro, 1975). It was a multilane divided highway with limited access and without frontage development. The new term 'freeway' had been coined to describe such roads in 1928, by Edward Bassett, legal adviser to the RPNY (RPA, 1936). Admittedly, there was still a park connection in that the scheme also created the vast Riverside Park. Yet its strategic position facilitated automobile commuting into the very heart of New York City. By the late 1930s freeways, both within and between cities, were widely seen as the way forward (Ellis, 1996). Across the country several states, led by New York and Rhode Island in 1937, were introducing legislation to allow their creation without legal ambiguity.

## BROADACRE CITY

The potential urban impacts of these emerging superhighways did not go unnoticed. In 1935 one of the United States' most famous architects, Frank Lloyd Wright, exhibited an urban vision for a technologically advanced society based on the automobile and electricity (Fishman, 1977; P Hall, 1988). He had been working on it since 1924, but his ideas did not become widely known until they were shown at New York's Rockefeller Center. Broadacre City, as it was called, was an ultra-low-density city (Wilson, 1983). Interspersed with dwellings built on acre lots (2.5 dwellings per hectare) were small farms, schools and factories. Wright's vision blurred the distinction between urban and nonurban more completely than any previous contribution to planning discourse. It accurately foresaw the potential for an affluent, technologically advanced society to withdraw completely from traditional urban communities and create a land of independent house-owners living private lives. City planners were wary of its apparent abandonment of the urban community – a theme that also seriously limited its export potential. Yet Wright undoubtedly expressed a growing social aspiration shared by many Americans, that has increasingly been fulfilled over the decades.

## THE NEW DEAL

In the mid-1930s, however, this still seemed a very remote dream for many millions of Americans (Scott, 1969; Hancock, 1988). In 1933 one in four workers had been unemployed, a worse rate even than in Germany. Many normal processes of life ground to a halt as banks reclaimed homes, businesses and farms. In both urban and rural communities many governmental projects, including planning, were curtailed by funding problems. Only the federal government could break this paralysis which reinforced the direct effects of economic depression. The new president, Franklin Delano Roosevelt, formerly state governor of New York, launched an imaginative and unprecedented programme of federally funded public works to put more money back into the wider economy. In doing this, he embraced the idea of planning in all its senses – economic, social and spatial.

The New Deal was the first large-scale demonstration of what would later be called Keynesian policies, after the British economist John Maynard Keynes. (It was also the exact democratic equivalent of Hitler's public works policies). Roosevelt's own understanding of Keynesian theory never moved beyond the intuitive stage. This was enough, however. The main obstacles to implementing the New Deal were political and legal, rather than theoretical. Roosevelt faced many challenges from business interests who were afraid of its implications for market capitalism. These attitudes restricted the extent of its impact, especially for planning.

## THE NEW DEAL AND CITY PLANNING

Within a few years Roosevelt launched many programmes that impinged on urban planning. None properly fulfilled initial hopes but they temporarily shifted the dominant climate of opinion. At the heart of government, for example, the president created a National Planning Board to advise on planning matters. Its chairman, Frederic Delano, was also chair of the RPNY committee (and Roosevelt's uncle and close ally). For the first time, the planning of American cities and regions became a matter of federal concern. City planners, particularly those with a social vision that transcended the familiar, city efficient nostrums of the mainstream, now saw a real opportunity to implement some of their ideals, at least in the early years. Thus the RPAA and their sympathisers, though to the left of Roosevelt, found themselves with increasing influence. American city planning also seemed to be finding the social conscience that had not quite managed to be present at its birth.

## The Tennessee Valley Authority

The Tennessee Valley Authority (TVA), the Resettlement Administration (RA) and the United States Housing Authority (USHA) were the most impressive initiatives (Scott, 1969; Hancock, 1988; Radford, 1996). The first, created in 1933, was the most universally admired spatial planning achievement of the New Deal (Barlow, 1940; J Huxley, 1943). It was an attempt to regenerate and comprehensively plan a huge poverty-stricken and ecologically degraded area in the valley of the Tennessee river. Covering an area 70 per cent of the size of England and Wales, it was truly a project to equal those of Stalin, Hitler or Mussolini, with federal powers to purchase land and undertake major projects, and (possibly reflecting RPAA lobbying) for comprehensive planning. Its largest projects were dams and hydroelectric generating stations, though a small new town, Norris, was planned on garden city lines. One of the earliest 'freeways' linked it with Knoxville. There were also many social and economic development programmes, though these, along with much of the planning, were soon marginalised. By 1937, the TVA was primarily a generating authority.

*Figure 4.8* *Part of President Roosevelt's New Deal involved the creation of several small new communities, the best known of which was Greenbelt, Maryland. Their planning reflected strong transatlantic influences, from both the British garden city and progressive housing efforts in cities such as Frankfurt.*

GREENBELT TOWNS

Yet the TVA survived. The RA appeared in 1935 and had only a short, if creative, life (Hancock, 1988). It was led by Rexford Tugwell, an ardent socialist and fervent believer in the garden city ideal. The RA took over existing programmes for the creation of small rural communities. Its most remarkable achievement was, however, the creation of small new towns (Stein, 1958). Though Tugwell wanted 25, only 4 were authorised and 3 built. These were at Greenbelt in Maryland, Greenhills in Ohio and Greendale in Wisconsin (which Tugwell tactlessly proclaimed as 'the first Communist town in America' (Hancock, 1988: 221)). The fourth, Greenbrook, New Jersey, fell foul of local jealousies, causing Tugwell's resignation and the demise of the RA as a separate agency in late 1936.

A total of only about 2,000 dwellings had been built in all three towns when the programme was curtailed. They fell well short of the garden city ideal, in that there was no local employment and the populations were too small to sustain self-contained communities. Yet they embraced neighbourhood-unit and Radburn principles, Greenbelt most authentically so because of Stein's direct involvement (Birch, 1983; Williamson (ed) 1997; KC Parsons (ed) 1998). They also showed how democratic capitalist societies could mobilise the power of the national state to create well-planned communities for those of modest income. These were important lessons for

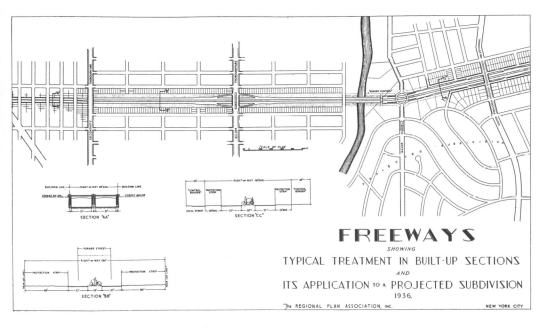

*Figure 4.9* New York was a world leader in the creation of urban freeways in the later 1930s. Conceived by the influential Regional Plan Association and implemented by Robert Moses, the city set an important precedent for cities throughout the west (see p. 120).

America and for Europe. By the time the programme finally disintegrated at the end of the 1930s (along with the New Deal's remaining social idealism) Europe was pre-occupied with war. The three new towns had already fulfilled their role as models.

## PUBLIC HOUSING

The other New Deal initiative of note was the acceptance of a federal financial responsibility for housing (Radford, 1996). In international terms this reflected a lesson from Europe more than one to it. More pertinently, in political terms it also reflected an already bad housing situation made dire by the Depression. In 1933, the federal government accepted that 38 per cent of the national housing stock was substandard. Nevertheless, intervention grew only incrementally, first under the public works programmes that facilitated other urban improvements (including parks and many of the new highway schemes). In 1934, however, the Federal Emergency Housing Corporation was created to undertake demonstration and slum clearance projects throughout the country. By 1937, some 79,000 dwellings had been built. In that year the first enduring housing legislation in the United States created USHA. Reflecting political and private-developer jealousies, the programme was now firmly set in a residual mode, focused on slum clearance and replacement housing for very low-income families. By 1941, some 130,000 dwellings had been built and 79,000 slums demolished. The planning of these schemes reflected the European-informed thinking of RPAA members such as Wood, Stein, Bauer and Wright. Typical examples were low-rise apartments and mixed developments of houses and apartments in landscaped settings, combining the design precepts of garden city and modernism. Stein's Hillside Homes, which provided over 1,000 apartment homes in the Bronx in New York, was an unusually good example, but the general run bore comparison with most European efforts (Stein, 1958; Plunz, 1990).

## AMERICAN PLANNING IN ITS INTERNATIONAL CONTEXT

By 1939, the traditional trading imbalance between American and European planning was beginning to be repaid as some achievements in the United States began to win world attention. This was especially so in Britain and the English-speaking world, but even totalitarian states, despite their ostensible disdain, took notice (Barlow, 1940; Cohen, 1995). American planning-thought itself remained fairly international in outlook, particularly so amongst the leaders of the New Deal initiatives. Yet the ideological partitioning of Europe into democratic and totalitarian states was having an effect across the Atlantic. Despite obvious parallels, there was little active cross-national learning between those who planned the *autobahnen*, *autostrada* and freeways. There was, for example, nothing to match the easy transatlantic linkages within the garden city movement, which had been built on a shared commitment to social progressivism (Rodgers, 1998). The most influential continental European figures encountered by American planners in the 1930s were more likely to have fled from totalitarianism, especially fascism, than be its supporters (McKelvey, 1968). Along with prominent earlier immigrants such as Eliel Saarinen, the 1930s arrivals in the United States played an important long-term role in strengthening the American engagement with modernism. As well as Gropius and Wagner, they included Oskar Stonorov from Russia, Hans Blumenfeld (from both Germany and Russia) and José Luis Sert from Spain. Despite the end of mass immigration, such cosmopolitan figures could move easily into an America that was still actively aware of its own European roots and whose biggest cities were still very open to outside influences and ideas.

## INTERIM CONCLUSIONS

Full conclusions on these critically important years must wait until we have reviewed the other planning traditions which, as we hinted, assumed much greater significance. For the moment, some reflections on the relative standing of the different major traditions are appropriate.

Once again, Germany occupied centre stage in international planning history by virtue of the energy, breadth and depth of its urban planning thought and action. Yet the rise of Nazism saw it move on to a more national path, increasingly remote from international planning discourse. Its planning remained interesting internationally but was observed now from a perspective more of fear than admiration. Although other countries gained from the Nazi squandering of the Weimar legacy, international planning discourse as a whole was diminished. None of the other main traditions were able to replace Germany's central contribution. France continued to excel (and, indeed, rise higher) in planning thought and technical accomplishment but remained underdeveloped in practical achievement. Nowhere else in the major planning traditions was the mismatch between professional capacity and political will quite so great.

Britain's traditional ownership of the garden city idea had assured it of a central place in the international mainstream. Yet the weakness of its initial engagement with modernism prevented it being at the cutting edge of planning thought until the very end of the interwar period. In many ways, it was the United States that had the greatest potential to assume the vacant central position. Yet its planning movement suffered from its more patchy start, its continuing lacunae regarding planning's social dimension and its sheer distance from newer movements. Many of these limitations were increasingly overcome in the 1930s, so America's international standing as a source of planning lessons was rising. By that stage, though, several other countries had also begun to receive greater attention from planners, as we will see in the next chapter.

# CHAPTER 5

# WAR, RECONSTRUCTION AND DEPRESSION II: THE OTHER TRADITIONS

By the 1930s, planners could draw ideas and models from a much wider range of countries than they had done in 1914. What, in effect, happened was that as planning ideas spread from their original heartlands they became the basis for further innovations. Mainly this occurred in European countries, including many that were smaller or less influential than the ones in which the major traditions developed. As we suggested in the previous chapter, some new ideas were able to emerge partly because they filled the vacuum left by Germany after 1933. The growing international interest in the Netherlands and Scandinavia, especially Sweden, reflects this. In a different way, larger events also played a role in the belated recognition, in the 1930s, of the Viennese model. Yet the widening range of planning innovations also reflected the genuine growth of internationalist and modernist sentiments, and the widening interest in urban planning during the 1920s. Even the Fascist regime in Italy was viewed in generally positive terms by other western countries, at least until the mid-1930s.

As occurred before 1914, the most avid consumers of the ideas gleaned from this widening range of innovators were planners in other innovatory countries. Within these external models they found echoes of their own endeavours, or spurs to further action. Elsewhere the patterns of borrowing gradually became more wide ranging. But on the fringes of Europe the contacts were more limited and planners were often clearly deferential to fewer influences. This was also broadly true in advanced capitalist countries outside Europe (apart, of course, from the United States) where uncritical borrowing remained typical. The only important exception to this pattern was Japan, where traditional deference to western planning thought and practice was being moderated by a growing indigenous technical capacity that went largely unnoticed elsewhere. Cultural affinities, proximity and, in some cases, sympathetic reactions to larger events meant that most urban planners confined their area of search for external lessons to Europe.

## BELGIUM

As we saw in the previous chapter, the experiences of the First World War helped to forge new, or strengthen existing, international connections. Much the most dramatic example of this was Belgium which, for a short time, took a central position in western thinking about urban planning. The war had a devastating impact on Belgium (Smets (ed), 1985). The greater part of the country was quickly overrun by the German army. As in France, there was serious destruction of historic towns, such as Ypres or Louvain. Almost 80,000 dwellings were rendered uninhabitable, roughly the same proportion as in France, though with a bigger impact on smaller towns rather than the countryside. Combined with the effects of a wartime cessation of building, Belgium returned to peace with, on some estimates, a shortage of 200,000 dwellings (Gobyn, 1985). However, the war had an even more dramatic effect on thinking about the nature of the solutions to be adopted than it had in France. The German occupation had caused a flood of Belgian refugees to neighbouring countries. In all, about 8 per cent of the population moved to France (where a Belgian government in exile was established), Britain or the neutral Netherlands (Uyttenhove, 1985; 1990b). Amongst the refugees were many figures who were politically or professionally interested in reconstruction. As such, this forced migration of the Belgians became an opportunity for learning more about housing and urban planning elsewhere.

## Belgium and the British garden city movement

Nowhere was this more so than in Britain (Uyttenhove, 1990a; Hardy, 1991a). The British had largely entered the war because of the violation of Belgian neutrality. There was intense sympathy for the Belgian refugees, fuelled by horrific wartime stories of atrocities by the occupying Germans. For British planners, the destruction of historic towns was atrocity enough. Belgium became an important wartime cause, especially for the London garden city movement. Large numbers of refugees actually moved to Letchworth to work at a Belgian-owned munitions factory (Miller, 1989). More consciously, an effective propaganda campaign targeted hundreds of Belgian architects and planners. The intensity of this actually prompted complaints from no less a figure than Josef Stübben in Berlin. The Germans, meanwhile, sought to promote their own schemes for housing as part of town extensions within the occupied country. Yet it was the British garden city lobby, building on strong prewar sympathies, that won the battle for the hearts and minds of Belgian urban planners.

## Belgium as a garden city

The Belgians were not simply passive recipients of British ideas about the garden city, however (Smets, 1987). As well as developing them into their own plans for reconstruction, they became important intermediaries in the flow of planning ideas between Britain, France and the Netherlands. Leading Belgian figures, particularly Raphael Verwilghen and Louis van der Swaelman, moved between the three countries during the war years, actively working with their leading planning figures as well as other Belgians (Uyttenhove, 1990a; 1990c). The most interesting conceptual innovation to arise from the intense wartime engagement with British planning was an enduring notion of the entire country of Belgium as a garden city (K Bosma and Hellinga, 1997a). This was first voiced publicly by Raymond Unwin at the London conference on Belgian reconstruction in 1915. It reflected the decentralised nature of much urbanisation in Belgium and the very fragmented pattern of landownership. Many industrial workers had rural homes with a garden plot and relied on light rail links, which were unusually highly developed, to reach their place of work. The prospects of creating pure garden cities were therefore remote. Yet there were certain echoes of Howard's overarching concept of the social city, where small settlements in close proximity to the countryside were linked by rapid means of communication.

## EARLY POSTWAR *CITÉS-JARDINS*

Although the idea of the garden city persisted, it did not form a basis for any immediate action. It was the familiar notion of the *cité-jardin* or garden suburb that seemed to offer an immediate solution to postwar housing problems. As in France (and, even more, Britain), the early 1920s brought a spate of housing schemes added on to existing small towns (Smets, 1977; Maes, 1985). The earliest showed close sympathy for the Arts and Crafts aesthetic favoured in Britain, for example at the Batavia garden village at Roulers planned by Verwilghen, or Le Logis-Floréal at Boisfort designed by van der Swaelman. More explicitly modernist designs in concrete and with flat roofs soon followed. Early schemes were Klein Rusland ('Little Russia') at Selzaete, and Victor Bourgeois' Cité Moderne at Berchem-Sainte-Agathe near Brussels, planned from 1921.

## WIDER MOVES TOWARDS PLANNING

This more limited concept of the garden city took its place within wider moves towards development and reconstruction planning in Belgium. From 1915, when a law for reconstruction was passed by the government in exile, Verwilghen and others began to develop new instruments for urban planning and prepare plans for the reconstruction of the devastated towns (Smets, 1987). They were hampered by inadequate knowledge of the actual destruction and imbued, in their exile, with a strong sense of the need to restore Belgium's historic identity. Ultimately this concern with external appearance, especially of the centres of the devastated towns, took priority over all other replanning considerations (Stynen, 1985). This was similar to the reality of what happened in most destroyed French historic towns, especially Arras. Yet there was in France, as we have seen in Reims, for example, a theoretical recognition at least that planning implied something more comprehensive. In Belgium the basis of this recognition was altogether narrower. Verwilghen's efforts to establish a more comprehensive approach to land use and development planning had by 1919 become diluted to street alignment plans and facade restoration.

The result was that significant international interest in Belgian developments in urban planning soon faded. This is not, in itself, surprising. All other things being equal, smaller countries have tended to be less important internationally than larger ones as sources of planning ideas, models and practices. There have, though, been some important exceptions, one of the most conspicious being Belgium's northern neighbour.

## THE NETHERLANDS

Since at least the First World War, the planning movement in the Netherlands has increasingly 'punched above its weight'. With a population of about 8.5 million in

1936, it was still only about one-fifth the size of Britain, France and Italy, and an eighth the size of Germany.

The early years after 1914 did not suggest a long-term ascendancy. The Dutch remained neutral throughout the war, though they did not escape its wider effects on economic activity. But their country suffered neither physical destruction nor the complete cessation of urban development that were typical amongst its neighbours. Unlike Belgium's sudden (and unsought) move into the international limelight, this was for the Netherlands a period of quiet achievement. The intense engagement with other combatant nations was absent. But the commitment to social housing, which had been gathering momentum before 1914, continued to grow, nowhere more so than in Amsterdam.

## Social housing

By 1923, over 16,000 social housing units had been built by housing associations and the city of Amsterdam itself, mainly from 1913 (Stieben, 1998). Extension plans, which continued to be prepared for different sections of the city, integrated the individual housing developments into the wider fabric of urban growth. The later war years and the early 1920s also saw the architectural movement known as the 'Amsterdam School' come to full flower in these same schemes, producing environments of unique quality (Casciato, 1996). Apartment buildings were usual, designed and planned to combine a respect for the individual dwelling with a strong sense of the collective environment of the street. In sharp contrast to trends almost everywhere else in neighbouring

*Figure 5.1 Amsterdam pioneered a distinct approach to urban planning and housing design in the years after 1914. Though influenced by garden city ideas, the approach was very firmly extending the city, in an overtly urban fashion. A good example is the Mercatorplein district, developed in the 1920s and recently very sensitively restored.*

countries during these years, Dutch housing layouts invariably preferred frontage development and building lines on, or very close to, public streets. Nowhere else in the Netherlands followed the architecture of Amsterdam exactly, but these broader characteristics were common.

Without ever abandoning these principles, garden city design ideas were applied in some areas. This was especially so in north Amsterdam where land was cheaper, and several small garden villages (*tuindorpen*) were built at Buiksloterham and Oostzaan. Similar schemes were planned at Vreewijk in south Rotterdam (1916) and at Daal en Berg in The Hague (1918) but more ambitious plans for a proper garden city, at het Gooi near Amsterdam, came to nothing (van der Wal, 1997; K Bosma and Hellinga, 1997b). Early Dutch moves towards regional planning also drew on the same tradition, notably in the First Rotterdam Garden City company's 1921 plan for IJsselmonde, the island where Vreewijk was located.

## INTERNATIONAL INFLUENCES ON DUTCH PLANNING

Through the earlier work of leading figures such as Berlage, Dutch planning had initially leant on Germanic thought and action. This was, though, increasingly diluted by admiration for British developments in housing and, especially, the garden city (Stieber, 1998). This mirrored a longer term shift in the outlook of many Dutch people in the 20th century, who sought stronger connections with the Anglophone world and relied less on the obvious linguistic affinities with Germany. In the 1920s, however, the new spirit of Weimar closely paralleled design and artistic movements in the Netherlands, so the German connection was re-energised, for a while at least (Molema, 1996). Several Dutch planners and architects developed strong associations with their German counterparts at this time. There were, for example, several Dutch members of May's team in Frankfurt (and later in the Soviet Union) and prominent Dutch representation at the Weissenhof Exhibition in 1927 (Lane, 1968; Bullock, 1978). Yet the country's adherents of modernism faced a powerful challenge. A traditional alternative was also strongly promoted. Its leader was MJ Granpré Molière who, from 1927, was the chief planning adviser to the Wieringenmeer, the first of the IJsselmeer polders to be reclaimed (van der Wal, 1997; K Bosma, 1990; K Bosma and Hellinga, 1997b).

## MODERNISM AND SOCIAL HOUSING

Despite such important domestic outlets for traditionalist approaches, the modernists were better known internationally. As well as the Dutch contributions to Frankfurt, 1920s developments in the Netherlands also attracted attention in their own right (Molema, 1996). Several important social housing schemes, especially those designed by JPP Oud, at the Hook of Holland and Kiefhoek in Rotterdam during the mid-1920s, ranked fully alongside the Frankfurt and Berlin schemes. In the Netherlands, however, highly innovative modern housing scheme designs continued into the 1930s. Outstanding in this respect was the nine-storey Bergpolder project in Rotterdam.

Designed by Willem van Tijen and others in 1934, this was the prototype of the high-rise slab block, a social housing form widely used after 1945.

## URBAN PLANNING

The International Garden Cities and Town Planning Federation (IGCTPF) conference held at Amsterdam in 1924 had decisively connected the Netherlands to the mainstream of international planning thought (JE Bosma, 1990). Reflecting both this widening knowledge and strong national pressures for urban growth, Dutch planning practice rapidly became far more sophisticated during the 1920s. Thus Willem Witteveen's 1928 extension plan for Rotterdam, intended to make the case for a massive boundary extension, drew on American parkway ideas which had been discussed at the IGCTPF (Mens, 1997). In the event, the boundaries were not extended, a solution that was partly justified by reference to the collective regional planning efforts of existing local authorities in the Ruhr, also highlighted at the Amsterdam conference. Yet it was not only the knowledge of external models that was important. The striking thing was how rapidly this knowledge was synthesised to create the basis for real innovation.

## DE CASSERES AND PLANOLOGIE

One of the most conceptually important Dutch plans of the interwar years was the 1930 expansion plan for Eindhoven (Dosker, 1997). The town was facing strong growth pressures, mainly because of the Philips electrical company. To cope with this in the absence of clear municipal policies, Philips had provided housing in and around Eindhoven for its workers. By the later 1920s, however, the need to provide for orderly and integrated development was widely recognised. A remarkable young man, Joel M de Casseres, who had studied planning in London and Paris, was hired by the Eindhoven public works department (K Bosma, 1990). In 1926, at the age of only 24, he had published a book, *Stedebouw*, which argued that urban planning should be conceived and undertaken not primarily as a work of architectural design but on a social scientific basis.

In 1929, the year he began work at Eindhoven, he coined a new word, *planologie*, to describe this approach. By 1939 it was being widely adopted in the Netherlands and, although it has not generally been taken up elsewhere, its essential principles have (though nowhere as early as they were in the Netherlands). To some extent, Patrick Geddes and others had already begun to move along this road. But de Casseres brought a much more rigorous social science approach. It led him to conceive and represent the Eindhoven plan not as a precise demarcation of space, but in far more indicative terms. It was a broad structure plan rather than a typical blueprint extension one. Nor was it to be seen as an ideal end state; it would need continuous review and have to be flexible. It was, almost certainly, the first plan that consciously embraced the dynamic nature of urbanisation, rather than simply imposing a static physical order upon it.

## THE AMSTERDAM GENERAL EXTENSION PLAN 1935

The most famous Dutch urban plan of the interwar years was, however, the Amsterdam general extension plan (DRO, 1994; Hellinga, 1997). Its importance was reflected in its scale which allowed for the city to grow, by peripheral expansion to the west and south, from a population of about 752,000 in 1930 to nearly a million by the end of the century. Accompanying it was one of the most highly sophisticated research and technical operations ever attempted. The plan laid the basis for the creation of the so-called western garden towns (*tuinsteden*) such as Slotermeer. After 1945 it was overtaken by much faster than predicted growth, but it should be counted as one of the most successful interwar efforts for a European big city.

### THE PLANNING PROCESS

The Amsterdam plan also marked an interesting trend in the professional evolution of planning as it was the first really important European one to be consciously prepared and presented as the work of a team (Hellinga, 1997). At an early stage the chief physical planner, Cornelis van Eesteren, had sought direction of the whole project in order to become its sole named author. Trained in Germany and France, van Eesteren was also a key figure in CIAM (he was its president for many years). This meant that many modernists have seen the Amsterdam plan as 'his' (Mumford, 2000). In fact, the research work of Theo van Lohuizen and the planning work of van Eesteren's deputy, and eventual successor, Jacoba (Ko) Mulder, were also of key importance. (We should also note that Mulder was one of the first women anywhere in the world to have a leading professional role in planning.) All worked under the overall direction of LSP Scheffer, the actual head of urban development. Thus, although van Eesteren was certainly one of the 'great men' of Dutch planning in the 1930s, he was also obliged to become one of its first team players. Such evidence of the growing depth and diversity of planning expertise in the Netherlands was symptomatic of the wider change. By 1939, Dutch planning was becoming well-established as a distinctive national tradition and one that was beginning to have a very marked international resonance.

## THE NORDIC COUNTRIES

The 1930s saw the Nordic countries, and especially Sweden, assuming a more central position in international planning thought and practice. They were not yet comparable with the Netherlands, but interest in them was growing rapidly. Like the Netherlands, Sweden's influence was not a function of its size. The country had a population of 6.25 million in 1936, of which only a third were urban dwellers (Denby, 1938). This compared with four-fifths in Britain, three-quarters in the Netherlands, two-thirds in Germany and a half in France. The largest Swedish city, Stockholm, had barely reached a population of 500,000 by 1930. Why then were it and its neighbours beginning to become sites of pilgrimage for architects and planners, especially from the Anglophone world, by the later 1930s?

## SWEDISH PLANNING AFTER 1914

Some of the reasons were quite deep-seated. There had been a patchy international awareness of Swedish urban planning since before 1914. Sweden (along with Norway and Denmark) was neutral during the First World War which meant that overall development of all Scandinavian planning, though driven by many of the same underlying concerns as in the combatant nations, was rather less dramatic. Broadly, it evolved along lines that were already clear by 1914. The sense of urban planning as a distinct activity became stronger (T Hall, 1991a). Meanwhile Sweden's architects and planners, already familiar with lessons from Germanic and British experience, had begun to look across the Atlantic. Thus Stockholm's new commercial street, Kungsgatan, planned from 1916, could by 1924 boast Europe's first American-style skyscraper – soon to be joined by a twin (LO Larsson, 1984; Hultin (ed), 1998). It was, though, Stockholm's provincial rival, Göteburg, which led the re-establishment of the international planning movement when it hosted the first postwar gathering of the IGCTPF in 1923.

**Figure 5.2** *During the 1930s, Sweden began to embrace rational modern design. A common type of development was the narrow lamella block, orientated for maximum sunlight. The type is shown here at Hjorthagen in Stockholm, developed as workers housing.*

## The roots of international admiration

A decade later, international admiration was beginning to grow rapidly. Yet, apart from noting its relatively efficient operation, there was little interest in Sweden's statutory planning system. In fact, the legal framework of the 1907 legislation was strengthened in 1931 to make plan preparation compulsory for all but the smallest towns, an intent that was broadly fulfilled (T Hall, 1991a). At this stage, however, most attention focused on housing design and site planning. In part, this reflected a growing international interest in Scandinavian design. The 1930 Stockholm Exhibition of Industrial and Decorative Arts established Sweden's place in the new functionalism (Rudberg, 1999). The political hegemony of the Social Democrats from 1932 was also extremely important (P Hall, 1998). Socialist tendencies had long dominated Swedish politics, but this had been less remarkable in the 1920s. It was as the right wing held, or gained, dominant positions elsewhere in 1930s Europe that Scandinavian, especially Swedish, social democracy began to stand out. It was as if the Swedes had taken over the progressive flame that had ignited during the previous decade in Weimar Germany. Moreover, as we have hinted, specifically Anglophone interest was encouraged because in all the Scandinavian countries many leading municipal architects and planners were very proficient in English. The channels of communication that were being opened up could be two-way.

## Swedish functionalism and housing

The Swedes, in fact, had borrowed much from German developments in the 1920s (T Hall, 1991a). By the end of the decade the younger modernists were beginning to make their mark. In 1932, following the Stockholm exhibition, a group of Swedish designers including the urban planner, Sven Markelius, issued a manifesto which asserted functionalist principles. At the same time, the city of Stockholm was also encouraging public debate about social housing forms (K Åstrom, 1967). The resultant ideal building block, the lamella, had a precise form that fully reflected modernist principles. This narrow, low-rise apartment block gave a dual aspect and maximum natural light to each dwelling. Form definitely followed function, uncompromised by any residual historicism. Examples which impressed foreign visitors included Hjorthagen, built from 1935 (Graham, 1940).

By the later 1930s, such lamellas were being built in large numbers, for example in the Bromma district of Stockholm (T Hall, 1991a). Here, in the eyes of international modernists, was tangible proof of the Swedish commitment to address social problems by rational design and the mass-production spirit. The internal planning of these dwellings was much admired, although the buildings were soon criticised as being very monotonous from the outside. In fact, a reaction began to set in by the end of the 1930s. Because Sweden remained neutral, the Second World War marks less of a watershed in its planning history. Following late 1930s thinking, the early 1940s brought more varied forms, including some higher blocks of up to about ten storeys. These invariably attracted the interest of foreign visitors in the early postwar years.

*136* OTHER ASPECTS OF SWEDISH PLANNING

In a more general sense, American and British visitors also admired the strength of Swedish collectivist principles (Graham, 1940; Barlow, 1940). In particular, the strong tradition of municipal landownership and the requirement that private developers yield a substantial part of their land, usually 40 per cent, for public purposes, seemed enviable preconditions for good planning. In a predominantly rural country, Swedish engagement with the garden city tradition continued. Developments, for example at Enskedefaltet in Stockholm, were often self-built, on publicly provided land and with a very high degree of municipal supervision and coordination (Graham, 1940; Goldfield, 1979).

DENMARK

Although it was mainly Sweden that attracted foreign attention some international observers also examined its neighbours (eg Graham, 1940). Denmark and Norway had similar political climates to Sweden, and their housing and urban development

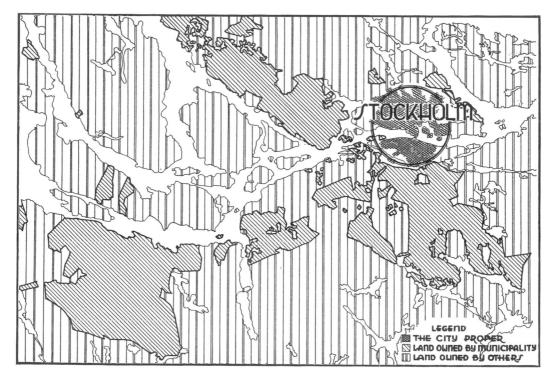

**Figure 5.3** *Stockholm, like most other Nordic cities, typically acquired large land holdings well in advance of development. This was hugely important in the long term planning of the city.*

policies followed parallel and related courses. The early postwar years saw moves in both countries to promote the development of urban planning thought and practice. A Danish laboratory for town planning, encouraging research and training, appeared in 1922 (Knudsen, 1988; B Larsson and Thomassen, 1991). The trend at this time was very much towards British ideas. Thus, from 1919 the ardent Anglophile Steen Eiler Rasmussen became a powerful voice in the shaping of Danish planning discourse. Over the following years, it too was touched by Weimar progressivism (and the 1930 Stockholm exhibition). Yet Danish planning remained noticeably more British-oriented than that in the other Scandinavian countries. Rasmussen's influences were revealed in his classic 1934 appreciation of the British capital, published in English as *London: The Unique City* (Rasmussen, 1948). On several occasions during these years he brought Raymond Unwin, the elder statesman of British planning, to Copenhagen with lasting impacts on Danish thinking about the planning of Scandinavia's largest city – it had a population of one million in the metropolitan area by the 1930s.

## NORWAY

Norway's interwar planning history followed a broadly similar course, with British ideas in the ascendant in the years immediately after 1914 (Lorange and Myhre, 1991; Jensen, 1997)). In Christiania (Oslo), for example, the new suburb of Ulleval Hageby was developed as social housing along garden city lines from 1916 to 1921. However, this interest in British planning did not go as far as it did in Denmark and there remained a more obvious willingness to draw on other approaches, such as those of Germany and Sweden. A National Association for Town Planning was formed in 1919 to promote interest and expertise in planning. Throughout the following years the planning of Oslo (as Christiania was renamed in 1925) was an important priority. Though still a rather small city, with a metropolitan population of only about 370,000 in 1930, its still relatively new role as Norway's capital gave special importance to its planning. In 1929, the city's chief planner, Harald Hals, published a major book on Oslo. The most important work on planning yet to appear in Norwegian, it was soon the basis for an advisory regional plan. The work revealed a planning approach shaped with wide reference to British, American, German, French and Swedish examples. In a sense, it marked the beginning of a more mature Norwegian planning discourse, derivative but no longer directly deferential.

## FINLAND

Finland followed a distinctly different path to its Scandinavian neighbours (Sundman, 1991). Despite its status within imperial Russia knowledge of western, especially German and British, planning had grown rapidly before 1914. And, in sharp contrast to the other Scandinavian countries, one Finnish planner, Eliel Saarinen, was already internationally known through his competition entries for Canberra, the new Australian capital, and Greater Reval (now Tallinn) in Estonia, from 1911 to 1913 (Reps, 1997). Saarinen's standing in Finland rose further in 1915 when he published a lavish plan commissioned by a development company for a vast garden suburb at

Munkkiniemi and Haaga in the northwestern suburbs of Helsinki (Aario, 1986; Sundman, 1991; ECFJS, 1997). Intended to house about 60,000 people of all social classes, along with communal facilities and factory districts, the plan displayed a detailed understanding of all the major British garden city plans. Only a small fragment of the suburb was ever built but it became a landmark in Finnish planning thought.

Saarinen and two other planners also produced another notable plan, for the whole of Greater Helsinki, in 1918 just as the civil war between the Soviet-supported Red Guard and the nationalist White Guard ended in victory for the latter (Hedman, 1997). Sponsored by a Finnish businessman as a gift to the new capital of the independent state, the plan's timing alone gave it symbolic significance. Though at the time it was little known outside Finland, it was a very early example of metropolitan growth using distinct satellite towns separated by planned corridor areas. Familiar problems of landownership and tight city boundaries prevented its implementation, but it confirms Saarinen's influential role in the international development of planning. His reputation was greatly enhanced after his move in 1924 to the larger

**Figure 5.4** *The garden city idea appeared in many architectural guises between the wars. Helsinki's 1920s' working class garden suburb of Käpyla used traditional Finnish wood construction. Since conservation secured its future, it has become a popular residential area.*

stage of the United States. Though he never cut his links with his homeland, Saarinen exerted an important influence on American planning through his work in the United States and, perhaps still more, through his teaching.

The dominance of conservative and nationalist sentiments in interwar Finland made fewer parallels with its Scandinavian neighbours possible in the 1930s, when the country's pro-German national outlook remained strong (Klinge and Kolbe, 1999). The upshot was that modernism had less impact in Finland at this time than it had in Sweden or its other western neighbours (Sundman, 1991; T Hall, 1991b). Classicist influences were dominant. Important exceptions were the new textile town at Sunila, designed by Alvar Aalto in 1936, and the village built for the cancelled 1940 Helsinki Olympic Games. The latter marked the first Finnish adoption of Swedish-style lamella blocks. It took a dramatic change of political and cultural climate to bring about the remarkable flowering of Finnish modern design after 1945.

## ITALY

At the other side of the continent, the only southern European country to win major international urban planning interest between the wars was Italy. Its central place in the history of western civilisation (and the education of western architects), almost guaranteed external attention for any important initiatives in urban planning. That these initiatives also came from the world's first Fascist regime, under the leadership of Il Duce, Benito Mussolini, intensified this interest. For many international observers, especially those on the right wing of politics, the regime seemed to offer a model of ordered modernisation. (The Germans, after all, had always appeared impressive in their urban planning, whatever the regime.) In most western countries the fear of communism ran too deep amongst dominant opinion to permit widespread admiration of Russia. Italy, though one of Europe's most populous countries, comparable in size to Britain and France, was traditionally backward and semi industrialised. Now the Fascists, who had run the country from 1922, seemed to be transforming it into a modern efficient state. Until the Abyssinian War in 1935 the regime's achievements were generally viewed positively throughout the west.

There were several reasons for this (Whittick (ed), 1980; Calabi, 1984; Ghirardo, 1989). Unlike Germany, Italy had not traditionally threatened European stability. Moreover, in the world of planning there were no internationally admired exiles to raise doubts. Nor was most of the urban design of the Fascist regime quite as overblown as its Nazi equivalent. In Italy, quite simply, the best architects and planners of the interwar years were Fascists. Several key figures of post-1945 Italian planning, most notably Luigi Piccinato, first achieved prominence in the Fascist period. Overall, their work was not limited to one official style. It varied between the rational simplicity of modernism, in which the Italian Futurists had played a significant formative role before 1914, and Italy's older, mainly classical, traditions (Mumford, 2000). Some projects (for example, those of Piccinato and his associates) won plaudits from international modernists. Yet Mussolini always remained anxious to stress the Italian dimension, on one occasion rebuffing Le Corbusier when he sought to work in Rome.

## THE AUTOSTRADA

As international awareness grew during the 1920s (for example at the IFHTP meeting in Rome in 1929) several aspects of Italian planning were admired. One was that well-developed dictatorial fondness for roads that Hitler later inherited. In Mussolini's case, it drew on both the road-building traditions of ancient Rome and the Futurists' fascination with speed. Despite presiding over what was still a largely undeveloped, semi-industrialised country reliant mainly on animal traffic, Il Duce saw the motor vehicle as a symbol of modernisation. In 1924/5 a private company, strongly supported by the new government, built the world's first high-speed, limited access road without frontage development or intersections at grade (RPA, 1936). Known as an *autostrada*, it covered 80 kilometres between Milan and the Italian lakes, and was operated as a toll route. By 1936, more of these roads had been built, extending to 450 kilometres. The most famous was the toll-free route between Rome and Ostia. In general, the *autostrade* were undivided, unlike the divided twin road beds of the *autobahnen* or many American freeways.

## THE NEW TOWNS

Italy's new towns, especially the five begun between 1932 and 1938 as part of Mussolini's scheme to drain the extensive malarial Pontine marshes near Rome (Calabi, 1984; Ghirardo, 1989; Nuti, 1988) were widely reported and admired abroad. The project caught right-wing imaginations almost everywhere but there was also a genuine professional admiration across the political spectrum. There had long been proposals for this reclamation but nothing had been achieved before the Fascists. Mussolini saw the project as a way of reinforcing agricultural life and combating the drift to the industrial cities. The five small towns were to be service and administrative centres for this new farming region which was centred on the first and largest of them, Littoria (now Latina), which had a population of 21,000 by 1937. The other Pontine towns – Sabaudia (1934) which was especially praised by modernists and certainly the most influential in its planning, Pontinia (1935), Aprilia (1936) and Pomezia (1938) – also fulfilled this role. In addition, seven other towns were created elsewhere. One of them, Mussolinia (1928) predated the Pontine towns. The others were less agricultural in orientation. For example, Guidonia (1935) functioned as an air-force training centre; Arsia (1937) and Carbonia (1938) were coal-mining towns, developed when international sanctions cut off imported coal; and Torviscosa (1938) was a textile town. In all, 12 centres were created, explicitly as new towns. In addition, Mussolini's home town of Predappio had been extensively rebuilt from 1925 and was, in some ways, a prototype for these.

## PLANNING ROME AND OTHER CITIES

As might be expected, the Fascists set great store by ambitious schemes to replan Rome (Fried, 1973; Calabi, 1984). In fact, their visions shared many of the same confusions as those of the Nazis, between monumentalism and functional needs and between anti-urbanism and a desire for impressive cities. Thus the new-towns programme partly reflected a desire to avoid major concentrations of industry in cities. The 1923 plan for Milan envisaged satellite town development to mitigate the effects of continuous urbanisation (Barlow, 1940). There was also a parallel confusion in plan implementation, between the relative power of the state and private interests. Many of these confusions were apparent in the 1931 Rome plan. The preceding years had seen two counterproposals being developed. One, thought to reflect Mussolini's own viewpoint, sought to monumentalise the classical city. The other, developed by a group of young modernists, was more functional in its approach and reflected the priorities of the contemporary city. Presiding over their efforts, in effect protecting them by his name, was Marcello Piacentini, the leading architect and planner of the period, who was already known for his plan for the new Bergamo (1914–29). He also played an important role in the building of the Via Roma, a grand new street in Turin, in the 1930s.

Recognising that different approaches were possible, Mussolini sought to embrace both contemporary and monumental historic intentions. The 1931 Rome plan, drafted by Piacentini at the behest of Il Duce's appointed committee, thus embodied all the contradictions that arose from this confusion. It was intended to allow the city to grow from about one million to two million inhabitants. Though it leant strongly towards the functional dimension it actually required major central changes, largely for monumental purposes. Initially work to implement the plan began at speed, evidence for western observers of Fascist decisiveness, but the money soon ran out. Meanwhile, the proposals to improve the suburban districts were frustrated by an unwillingness to curb private construction. Although the plan remained in force until 1959 it achieved little. Even the most important state decision about Rome's development in the 1930s – to create a site (now the EUR district) to host E42, a 1942 International Exhibition, was made without reference to it. Such opportunistic tendencies were hardly unique to Rome. Yet they belied the image of Fascist order that beguiled so many foreign observers.

## AUSTRIA

Austria, and specifically its capital Vienna, is the final example of a European country (or, more accurately, a large city) that became a significant international model between the wars. The new republic of German Austria that emerged in 1918 from the defeat of the Austro-Hungarian Empire bore little resemblance to its imperial predecessor (Blau, 1999a; 1999b). It was the German-speaking part of the old empire whose former non-German-speaking lands were now ceded to Czecho-Slovakia, Poland, Yugoslavia and Italy. Just under a third of its population lived in Vienna, which had 1.8 million inhabitants by 1918. Remarkably, the new country avoided the Bolshevik insurrections that affected Russia, Germany and its own former imperial partner, Hungary. 'Red Vienna', though, became a socialist stronghold and quickly embarked on a notable housing programme (Denby, 1938).

## WILD SETTLEMENTS AND COOPERATIVE HOUSING

In large measure the programme sprang initially from the spontaneous 'wild' settlement movement, a wartime self-help solution to chronic food and housing shortages (Korthals Altes and Faludi, 1995; Blau, 1999a). From 1919, cooperative housing modelled very much on British and, perhaps, Dutch approaches, began to formalise the wild settlements. The principal design inspiration was the garden city idea which was proving so popular almost everywhere, yet in Vienna this was combined with a stronger commitment to Howard's emphasis on communal ownership. In 1922, however, there came a major change, as the capital secured provincial status in the new republic but within very tight boundaries. Though the city gained a high degree of autonomy, 'Red Vienna' and all its problems were contained. So too, therefore, were its housing solutions. When the city itself began to build in 1923, taking over from cooperative endeavour, it had increasingly to turn towards higher density flatted solutions. In doing this, it created a new and distinctive approach. Initially, however, its efforts did not impress the arbiters of international planning and architectural thought.

## THE *GEMEINDEBAUTEN*

Progressive European thinking about the planning of housing was, by 1930, dominated by the open-housing pattern of the German *siedlung* (Blau, 1999a; 1999b). As we have seen, this was the modernist derivative of the garden city which won widespread international acclaim in the 1920s. The municipality of Vienna, however, famously followed a different course. The preferred form was a very large, high-density flatted housing complex, normally up to about six storeys. Thus the most famous scheme, the Karl Marx Hof, built from 1926 to 1930, housed about 5,000 people in some 1,400 apartments. Others were even larger. The important point, though, was that these *gemeindebauten*, as they were called, appeared to break all emergent understandings about planning sites to enhance sunshine and air. The blocks were arranged predominantly in a perimeter fashion along street frontages, with interior courtyards. Though this was mass housing on a scale unmatched almost anywhere else, there was no attempt at a mass-production approach or at standard architectural treatment. Exterior facade decoration, though restrained, was common; roofs were often pitched. Not surprisingly, therefore, these approaches were received with a certain coolness in mainstream international forums, such as the IGCTPF conference held in Vienna in 1926. Nor was CIAM any more sympathetic.

## THE VIENNESE MODEL

By the 1930s, however, these attitudes began to change. The heroic scale of Viennese social housing development was itself impressive (Ermers, 1942). Some 68,000 municipal dwellings were built between 1918 and 1934, almost all financed solely from the city's own resources. For comparison, the London County Council, with a population well over twice that of Vienna and with generous central government assistance, managed only 52,500 in the same period. Nor could anywhere else remotely match the scale of Viennese flat provision (63,000). Quite simply, no other city in the world had gained so much experience in the building of flatted communities. More even than this, however, it was the events of 1933 and 1934, which ended the housing programme, that engraved Vienna on the hearts of the left and a wide section of 1930s planning and architectural opinion (Blau, 1999a; Denby, 1938). As the Nazis took over in Germany and Chancellor Dollfuss drew Austria along the same road, the *gemeindebauten* became the centre of socialist Vienna's resistance. In February 1934 there was a short civil war and the militia shelled the Karl Marx Hof and other blocks. For a brief moment, the larger ideological meaning of social architecture and town planning, a theme that the modernists had self-importantly rehearsed for some years, slipped into painfully sharp focus.

## OTHER PARTS OF EUROPE

### SPAIN

Spain was notable more as a recipient of planning approaches developed elsewhere than as an innovator. Despite the country's great creative and technical capacity, Spanish planning thought in the interwar years was shaped largely by external influences (M Wynn, 1984a). In one sense, this reflected trends of deference that were already palpable as part of Spain's postimperial decline. But the most fundamental reason was acute political instability which precluded any very sustained development of an innovative urban planning movement of international significance. Thus the de Rivera dictatorship of 1923–30 was followed by a few, fragile years of republican democracy. In 1936, however, the republic, under socialist control, faced a fascist challenge in a long civil war. Eventually in 1939, after decisive assistance from Hitler and, to a lesser extent, Mussolini, a new and enduring dictatorship was established under the fascist leader General Franco.

These drastic swings in the political climate meant that new planning movements were soon curtailed and resulted in only limited practical achievements. Nevertheless, there were important developments in the late 1920s and early 1930s which connected Spain to the main strands of European planning thought. For example, following a competition in 1929 the Spanish architect Fernandino Zuazo collaborated with the German planner Hermann Jansen to prepare a major extension plan for Madrid. Earlier, the veteran Josef Stübben had been an entrant for the 1926 competition for an extension plan for Bilbao. Other international connections were apparent in the first moves towards regional planning in Madrid in 1932, following the publication of Unwin's reports for London.

By the early 1930s modernism, reflecting the creative optimism of the republican era, also began actively to shape thinking in Madrid and Barcelona, Spain's two biggest cities (Ravetllat, 1996; Mumford, 2000). Barcelona was at the centre of this brief flowering. Even before the republic was formed, modernist influences had been evident there at the 1929 International Exposition, with visions of a future, modern city. An important Barcelona-based organisation, GATCPAC (Grup d'Arquitectes i Tècnics Catalans per al Progrés de l'Arquitectura Contemporània) appeared in 1931, soon becoming GATEPAC (the E signifying Españoles), the Spanish chapter of CIAM. Its Catalan membership, which included the internationally known modernists Josep Luis Sert and Josep Torres, was particularly energetic. With the active collaboration of Le Corbusier, it produced the Plan Macià in 1934, effectively the Ville Radieuse superimposed on Barcelona. The civil war precluded any practical versions of these theoretical projects and wrought serious destruction, especially on Madrid (M Wynn, 1984a). As in Germany, the triumph of fascism and the repression that followed pushed some leading figures into exile, most notably Sert, first to France and then, more permanently, the United States.

## IRELAND

In contrast to the travails of the long-established Spanish state, we can briefly consider another, more obviously derivative approach: the small new nation-state of Ireland, created in 1921. Initially granted independence only as a dominion within the British Empire, and without the more industrialised and Protestant north, the resultant bitterness had fuelled civil war. This added to the earlier destruction associated with the 1916 rising, making Dublin's reconstruction as a capital fit into the major urban planning theme of the 1920s (Bannon, 1989). The 1921 settlement also left a predominantly rural and Catholic Ireland coexisting very uneasily with the United Kingdom.

Yet, despite this, it was the residual connection to Britain, rather than resentment that shaped Irish planning at this time. Despite a repudiation of pre-1914 attempts to plan Dublin, and repeated assertions of the need to avoid copying Britain, there remained a remarkable reliance on British planning. Alternative connections which might have been sought, for example with the United States, did not develop, presumably for reasons of distance. Like that in most other parts of the empire, the Irish planning legislation (passed in 1934) largely followed British precedent (Nowlan, 1989; Home, 1997). There was some Irish awareness of other examples, such as the regional initiatives in the Ruhr and New York, but this came largely through the British filter. Irish planners also continued to look to the British Town Planning Institute. Moreover, despite occasional expressions of disquiet, the tendency to call directly on British planning advice, principally that of Patrick Abercrombie, remained strong. Over subsequent years such obvious deference diminished, especially after constitutional changes in 1937 and 1949 gave full independence to Ireland. But British precedents in Irish planning matters have remained extremely important.

## CANADA

No other British dominion was as close to the imperial homeland or felt such nationalist resentment of Britain as did Ireland. Across the Atlantic, Canadians flocked to fight (and die) for king and empire in 1914, scarcely pausing to consider what their powerful neighbour to the south was doing. Pro-British sentiments in the nascent field of planning were also ostensibly strong as Thomas Adams, newly arrived from London, energetically beat the town planning drum throughout the country

(Simpson, 1985). Manitoba, Saskatchewan, Ontario and Prince Edward Island all adopted planning legislation based mainly on his advice. He was also the prime mover in forming a new professional body, the Town Planning Institute of Canada, in 1919, very much on the pattern of his British creation (Sherwood, 1994). When, in 1915, Edward Bennett, the English-born American former associate of Burnham, produced his grandiose city beautiful plan for the federal capital, Ottawa, and neighbouring Hull, Adams was a vocal critic of its American methods (Gordon, 1998).

## THE CITY EFFICIENT IN CANADIAN PLANNING

Yet Adams was more than just a carrier of British influence. As we have seen, he actively participated in the wartime development of American city planning and by 1918 was absorbing many of the new American emphases on the 'city efficient'. It is perhaps more accurate to see him as a figure who pointed to a postwar destiny for Canadian planning that lay between the British and the American models. A microcosm of these varied trends was the city of Kitchener in Ontario (Simpson,

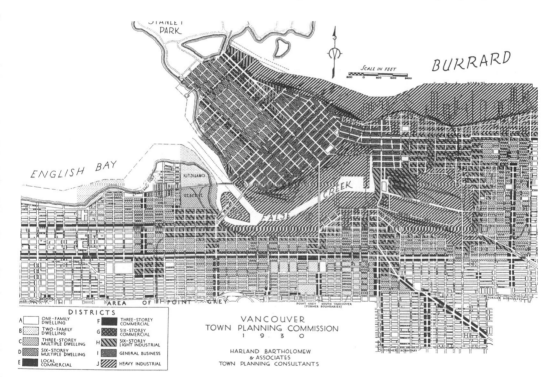

*Figure 5.5 Canadian planning moved strongly in an American direction during the 1920s, embracing the business ethos of the 'city efficient'. Vancouver hired the American planning consultant, Harland Bartholomew, to prepare a comprehensive plan that fully embodied these principles.*

1985; Hodge, 1991). Formerly called Berlin, this ethnically very German city was renamed (in memory of Britain's best known soldier) in 1916 to assert its fervent loyalty to the empire. Yet its planning showed a stronger awareness of American than British trends. In 1917, it established an American-style city planning commission and in 1922 hired Adams (now a private consultant after the recent demise of the Commission for Conservation) and one of Canada's first home-grown planners, Horace Seymour. Their task was to prepare what became the first comprehensive city plan and zoning scheme in Canada. As we will see, however, the trend towards American city planning became very much stronger later in the decade.

## AMERICAN INFLUENCES IN THE 1920s

The general trends towards Americanisation strengthened greatly during the 1920s. Canada shared fully in the growth and prosperity of its giant neighbour, as was clearly manifest in its biggest cities. By 1931, Montreal's metropolitan population stood at almost 820,000, Toronto's at over 630,000 and Vancouver's at almost 247,000 (McCann and Smith, 1991). Crucially, the decade also witnessed a long-term switch in the major source of external investment – from Britain to the United States. So it was with many other aspects of Canadian life, including urban planning. Although professional discourse in Canada retained its British flavour, actual practice became noticeably more American. The city of Kitchener, for example, followed up its earlier moves and adopted the first American-style zoning by-law in 1924 (Hodge, 1991). In 1925 and 1929, British Columbia and Alberta passed planning acts that were altogether more American than earlier legislation (Ward, 1999; Smith, 1986). The most expressive example came in 1926 when, despite protests, Vancouver retained the doyen of American planning consultants, Harland Bartholomew, to prepare an American-style comprehensive plan for the city (Perks, 1985; Ward, 1999). The Bartholomew plan, presented in 1929, was one of the pinnacles of Canadian urban planning before 1945 (Bartholomew, 1930). Yet its form, content and even its very language asserted the Americanness of Canadian planning.

## PLANNING IN THE DEPRESSION YEARS

From 1929, however, the paths of the two countries again diverged. Canada was acutely affected by the Depression, in many ways more than the United States. Despite Ottawa's best efforts from the mid-1930s, there was no New Deal (Carver, 1975; Ward, 1999). The country, especially the Prairie Provinces and some of the Atlantic Provinces, languished until the Second World War brought a return of prosperity, restoring fiscal stability to provincial and local governments. (Newfoundland, which was not yet part of Canada, actually went bankrupt in 1934.) Recorded unemployment was lower than in the United States, but in a country still dependent on primary production this was not the best indicator. Recovery came only slowly, and housing and urban growth were almost at a standstill despite two federal acts designed to boost the housing market, in 1935 and 1938. However, there were no federal works programmes, reflecting the opposition of the richer provinces. As public investments in infrastructure relied on provincial funding they were more modest than in America and were confined to the more wealthy areas. The major highway schemes of the United States or Germany found only a timid echo in the Queen Elizabeth Way from Toronto to Niagara which was opened in 1939. Yet the 1920s concept of planning dependent on market-led growth now had little relevance. The Town Planning Institute of Canada went into suspended animation for two decades from 1932. Nevertheless, the 1930s were important in generating, if not implementing, a more radical alternative to allowing market forces alone to determine the fate of urban communities (Hodge, 1991; Wolfe, 1994).

## VISIONS OF SOCIAL RECONSTRUCTION

The key body in formulating this new planning concept was the League for Social Reconstruction (LSR), the Fabian-style intellectual arm of the newly formed Co-operative Commonwealth Federation, a political movement that was moderate socialist in ideology and the forerunner of the present New Democratic Party (Purdy, 1997; Carver, 1975; Ward, 1999). As part of a wider programme of social welfare reforms, the LSR developed a new, more socially oriented concept of community planning. Its leaders in urban planning matters were a young garden city enthusiast, Humphrey Carver, who had moved from Britain in 1929, and Leonard Marsh, a British immigrant academic with a strong commitment to social welfare on the British pattern. They also had a keen interest in the ideas of the American RPAA and the New Deal initiatives; and figures such as Perry, Stein and Mumford were increasingly admired for translating the more social concepts of British planning into an American context. At the time, the timidity of the Ottawa government precluded any outlet for their labours but this was to change after 1939.

## AUSTRALIA

For most Australians in 1914, colonial status remained a much fresher memory than it did for Canadians. The war allowed them to prove their loyalty to Britain and the empire, yet also establish themselves as a distinct nation (Clark, 1995). The same mixture of deference and autonomy was apparent throughout Australian life, not least in urban planning. Australian urban reformers thus strengthened their hesitant prewar engagement with British models and used them to build an Australian planning movement (Freestone, 1989). More state town planning associations appeared during the war years and by 1916 all states had some form of organisation. In 1917,1918 and 1919 three major planning conferences were held, in Adelaide, Brisbane and Ballarat respectively.

A key figure in all this, an Australian equivalent of Thomas Adams, was the New Zealander Charles Reade (Tregenza, 1986; Home, 1997; Garnaut, 2000). He was the only person in wartime Australia with direct links to the London-based garden city and planning movement. Reade had a particular impact in South Australia, where he became official town planning adviser to the state government in 1915. His major achievement was the planning of a large garden suburb at Mitcham in Adelaide (now known as Colonel Light Gardens) in 1917, which was developed extensively during the 1920s (Garnaut, 1999; Hutchings, 1986). He also planned other suburbs, encouraged thought about overall metropolitan planning in Adelaide and helped to secure state planning legislation in 1920. By the end of 1921, however, he had moved to another imperial role, as town planning adviser to the Federated Malay States.

## WARTIME AND EARLY POSTWAR PLANNING

There were other ventures that reflected town planning in these years. As in the United States, several one-industry company towns were planned on garden city lines, the most impressive of which, for state electricity commission workers, was at Yallourn in Victoria in 1921 (Freestone, 1989). There were also a number of small model garden suburbs, designed for returning servicemen, and private developments inspired to some extent by the garden city. The most remarkable of these was Castlecrag in Greater Sydney which was promoted and planned by the American Walter Burley Griffin, from 1919 (Walker, Kabos and Weirick, 1994). Griffin's

**Figure 5.6** *Mitcham Garden Suburb (now Colonel Light Gardens) in Adelaide, planned by Charles Reade, was the most confident interwar Australian exercise in garden city planning. Again the interpretation is distinctive, with lower densities and housing in single storey bungalows.*

involvement in the ill-starred Canberra plan, meanwhile, was coming to an end. Frustrated by the federal government's indifference, he severed his connection with it in 1921. Much of the reason for this indifference lay in a wider reluctance to develop a strong federal government, which would obviously have needed the substantial national capital that he had planned. It is, though, interesting to speculate whether Griffin would have fared better had he been British. As shown in Chapter 3, the peculiar circumstances of the original competition meant there were no serious British contenders. The war years had brought a strengthening of imperial sentiment in Australia and certainly some criticisms of Griffin's proposals seem to mirror this.

## AMERICAN INFLUENCES

Assisted by protective tariffs, Australia's biggest cities began to industrialise on a significant scale in the 1920s, adding further momentum to their growth. By 1933, metropolitan Sydney had reached a population of 1.235 million and Melbourne 992,000. Adelaide and Brisbane were both over 300,000 and Perth 207,000 (though the new federal capital at Canberra had only managed to grow to 7,000). Like Canada, Australia became more open to American influences in the 1920s. Melbourne (1922) and Perth (1928) created American-style town planning commissions (Hutchings, 2000; Freestone, 2000b; Webb, 1979) and there were discussions along similar lines in Sydney. Moreover, the dominant city efficient model of American planning in the 1920s seemed increasingly appropriate. As in the United States, Australian cities grew largely by private low-density suburban development (increasingly favouring the 'Californian' bungalow style). British-style municipal housing was extremely rare. Yet apart from Griffin, who made Australia his home until 1935, there was no direct involvement of American planners.

## THE BRITISH CONNECTION

Nor, for that matter, was there any direct use of British planners. However, in urban planning, as in other aspects of Australian life such as trade and investment, the connections to Britain remained stronger than in Canada (Freestone, 1997; Ward, 1997). Australian planners and architects (for example, the young modernist Walter Bunning) visited the United States but they also went, in larger numbers, to Britain – and, by the later 1930s, a few also to continental Europe (Freestone, 1996b). Thus when Bunning returned, in 1939, he founded an Australian MARS group, on the CIAM-inspired British model. Such developments were important more for the future than for the present, however. Over the interwar period as a whole, it was the garden city model and its derivatives that retained the greatest potency. A notable example was the Perth Endowment Lands scheme, planned from 1925 as twin satellite suburbs separated by a wide green belt, though long delayed in its completion (Poole, 1979; Freestone, 1989). Many lesser schemes also claimed garden city lineage. More notable, though, were the rehearsals of green-belt and satellite-town solutions to the problems of metropolitan growth. Such ideas were being publicly aired by the later

1930s. Indeed, Alfred Brown, a New Zealander and former assistant to Louis de Soissons at Welwyn, had advocated such a strategy for Sydney from 1931. There were also tentative moves to give legal standing to Brisbane's agricultural belt.

## PLANNING AND THE DEPRESSION YEARS

As this implies, planning in Australia was not as completely disrupted by the Depression as it was in Canada (Hutchings, 2000). Although the country's economy depended on primary production, and was thus badly affected, the experience in this more urbanised society was less severe than in Canada. Nor was there the widespread incipient fiscal collapse of subnational governments that did so much to undermine Canadian planning. Nor, unlike Canada, was there yet a truly national professional body to be disrupted. Paradoxically, the Depression years actually brought the first important moves towards Australian professionalisation on the British model, when Brown founded the Town and Country Planning Institute of New South Wales in 1934 (Freestone, 1989). It took the effects of the Second World War and a strengthened political commitment to place Australian planning on entirely secure foundations, but much of the groundwork was done in the 1930s.

## JAPAN

From 1919 Japan, the only Asian nation sufficiently developed to be able to claim a place alongside the industrialised western countries, began to make more active use of the lessons it had drawn from their planning. In that year earlier debates about planning finally came to fruition and a city planning law was passed (Watanabe, 1984; 1992). It embodied many elements which had impressed Japanese observers of western planning before 1914. Perhaps because they were far removed from the main theatres of war, the Japanese did not turn against German ideas, as happened in Europe. Thus it was German and, to a lesser extent, American and British planning ideas that largely informed the new legislation (Hein and Ishida, 1998). A notable feature was the reliance on the original 1893 draft of the German *Lex Adickes* on land-readjustment powers, rather than the weakened version actually adopted by the Prussian parliament in 1902 (Ishida, 1988a; 1988c). Apparently done by mistake, this was an early sign of what was to be a continuing Japanese focus on land readjustment.

Though the new legislation did not really incorporate any of the features of the garden city (*den-en toshi*), the concept continued to be very potent within Japanese planning thought. Following pre-1914 initiatives, 1918 saw the creation of a garden city company which initiated commuter garden suburbs around Tokyo, including one of rather distinctive design at Tamagawadai, now Den-en Chofu (Watanabe, 1980; 1992). There were also moves to stimulate larger scale development of *den-en toshi*, financed by a mixture of private and public finance. Meanwhile, it was decided that, statutory planning for the capital should encompass both the city proper and its suburbs. By 1923 a regulatory scheme covering the suburbs was taking shape.

## The Great Kanto earthquake and the reconstruction of Tokyo

All this was, however, blown off-course by the Great Kanto earthquake of September 1923 (Cybriwsky, 1999; Ishizuka and Ishida, 1988; TMG, 1994). The earthquake and associated fire affected Tokyo and neighbouring Yokohama and wrought destruction greater than any caused to a single European city by the war. In Tokyo city alone 70,000 people (3 per cent of the population) were killed and 1.4 million (61 per cent) were made homeless. Most of the central and eastern districts were completely flattened and special legislation was enacted to facilitate rebuilding. The effect was to shift the emphasis in the capital's planning away from suburban concerns to reconstruction and land readjustment, pooling and re-sorting the property boundaries to create new street alignments, new building plots and many new parks (Ito, 1988a; Itoh, 1988).

The reconstruction was largely run by engineers, some with experience in Japan's colonies in Taiwan and Manchuria, others from the railways ministry (Shoji, 1988). Amongst them was Enzo Ohta, who initially headed the town planning operation. Surprisingly, when compared with the avid interest shown in the reconstruction of what were quite small war-damaged cities in Belgium and France, the immense task of rebuilding Tokyo was largely ignored by western planners. An American public administration expert, Charles Beard, from New York, was invited to make recommendations, but these had little immediate impact. During these years, Japanese planners, such as Shigeyoshi Fukuda (of Tokyo) and Hideaki Ishikawa (of Nagoya),

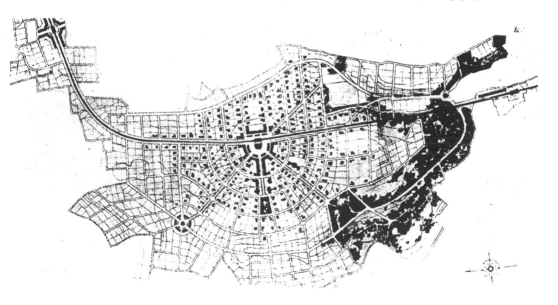

*Figure 5.7* Den-en-Chofu was the best known Japanese garden suburb of these years. Developed on the familiar Japanese pattern, by a commuter rail company, it offered space and easy access to central Tokyo.

continued, while on European trips, to seek advice from western figures like Schumacher or Unwin (Hein, 1998b). This hinted at a degree of uncertainty about using recently acquired western concepts. But, in the main, this vast rebuilding operation was an important formative experience for Japanese planning capacity.

## METROPOLITAN GROWTH AND WESTERN LINKS

Despite the devastating effects of the 1923 earthquake, Tokyo's astonishing growth continued with scarcely a pause. By 1940, it had a metropolitan population of 7.1 million, making it the world's third largest city after New York and London (KT Jackson, 1984). Osaka, with 3.4 million, was ninth largest. These spectacular increases reflected Japan's emergence as a major world power. By the 1930s, the country's expansionist tendencies, fuelled by a desire to find markets for its industrial economy, were increasingly seen by the west as a threat to peace.

Yet, despite the country's mounting international importance, western understanding of Japan and its urban planning remained extraordinarily limited. Western planners encountered their Japanese counterparts at international conferences, but very few of them spent any time in Japan (Hein, 1998b). For their part, the Japanese continued to make little use of foreign expertise, which probably discouraged western planners on speculative visits to the country. They did, however, keep reasonably abreast of mainstream, if not avant-garde, western planning and design ideas. Yet the dominant western impression of Japan was still that it was a traditional rather than an industrial society. Thus the only aspect of Japanese architecture and design which attracted spontaneous interest in the west was its traditional architecture. By the 1930s Japanese publications in English began to ensure some western knowledge of Tokyo's reconstruction after 1923. However, there were very few western accounts of Japanese planning that were based on a proper understanding of what lay behind it. Those that did appear, for example by the German modernist (and admirer of Japan's traditional architecture) Bruno Taut, scarcely represented the current climate of thinking in the west.

## METROPOLITAN PLANNING

The upshot was that Japanese planners continued to borrow far more from western planning than vice versa. One of the most potent concepts to enter Japan in the 1920s involved the use of green belts and satellite towns to articulate metropolitan growth. In the short term, at least, this made little impression on actual policies, let alone outcomes. Tokyo had finally adopted a zoning scheme in 1925, though it covered an area not much larger than the city (Ishizuka and Ishida, 1988; TMG, 1994). Already, however, in the aftermath of the earthquake rapid industrial and associated residential development was occurring beyond the limits of this scheme. This immediately underlined the relevance of the green belt-satellite idea. Firm proposals only came in the 1930s as the growing threat of war highlighted the need to control urban growth, especially of highly flammable buildings. In 1939, for example, a green-space plan proposed a green belt with wedges, ostensibly for recreational purposes though actually to provide spaces for air-raid protection and defence (Ishida, 1998).

## PLANNING AND HOUSING

There was also much interest in western concepts of planned residential extension. Building partly on earlier encounters with British garden city ideas, more examples of commuter suburban areas appeared in Tokyo and Osaka, promoted by railroad and land companies (Watanabe, 1992; Katoh, 1988). A more distinctive emphasis was put on land readjustment in suburban development (Ishida, 1988c). This drew explicitly on German precedents, though it also echoed certain aspects of traditional Japanese agrarian land practices. Land readjustment was widely used in Osaka, Nagoya and, though apparently less comprehensively, in Tokyo. Essentially, fragmented land-holdings were pooled to assemble larger parcels suitable for orderly development and provide the land necessary for planned infrastructures. The exact role of the planners in promoting readjustment varied (Ishizuka and Ishida, 1988). In some cases planners were directly responsible; in others they exerted varying degrees of encouragement or pressure on private owners to create voluntary associations. In fact, the rising land values associated with readjustment and infrastructure provision meant many landowners needed little coercion.

As this implies, most development was privately undertaken. An organisation called Dojunkai was, however, formed in Tokyo in 1924 to provide public housing in non-suburban locations in the aftermath of the earthquake (Satoh, 1988a; TMG, 1994). Although it operated on a much smaller scale than its European equivalents, it represented the first important Japanese experiment in social housing. After its first efforts to build wooden emergency barracks, the organisation began to construct concrete low- and medium-rise apartment blocks for white- and blue-collar workers. Many of these showed clear references to contemporary European modernist projects. Dojunkai itself published a two-volume study of western housing (1936–8), though this was apparently based on information derived from books rather than actual visits (Hein, 1998b; Ishida, 2000). Certain other parallels with western approaches were also evident. Thus, from 1927 Dojunkai became involved in slum clearance and redevelopment. However, again this was on a less ambitious scale than was typical in Europe.

## JAPANESE IMPERIAL PLANNING

In so far as Japanese planning ideas and practices spread internationally, it was to its own widening empire. Because the link with their development in Japan itself was particularly close, we will make an exception and briefly consider planning in Japan's neighbouring colonies of Korea, Taiwan and Manchuria (Hein, 1998a; 1998b). These were prizes from its late 19th- and early 20th-century wars with Russia and China. As many other parts of Asia found from the later 1930s, the Japanese proved to be heavy-handed imperialists. In familiar fashion, the powers relating to land rights in the colonies were much more draconian than those that prevailed in Japan. Drastic remodelling of existing cities, most notably Seoul, was usual.

It was, however, in Manchuria, the springboard for Japanese expansionism in the 1930s, that the most conceptually significant planning proposals appeared. A group led by a Tokyo academic, Yoshikazi Uchida, and including several others who played leading roles in the Japanese planning after 1945, generated several plans for agricultural colonisation and urban growth. These included a monumental one for the colonial capital, Shinykô (the present Changchun), and plans for standard settler villages. The most remarkable effort, however, was the plan for Datong, prepared in 1938 and 1939. It incorporated many western ideas, including the notion of satellite towns, green belts and planned neighbourhood units. Much was very directly borrowed, particularly the standard neighbourhood plan which was virtually identical to one applied in Detroit in the early 1930s. Overall, these Manchurian projects had a visionary quality that was virtually unknown in Japan itself, made possible by the inherent authoritarianism of the context. Yet, even in such an unconstrained setting, they confirm just how dependent Japanese planners still were on uncritically borrowed western planning models.

## Conclusions

### Diffusions in a turbulent time

For practically all historians, the outbreak of the First World War in 1914 forms the first main historical staging post of the 20th century. As we have seen, it brought to an end a period in the history of urban planning that was characterised largely by innovation and relatively unconstrained diffusion amongst most of the primary movers in this. Certainly the years immediately after 1914 were nothing like as innovative. They also brought a crucial fracturing in previously important diffusional flows, especially between the English- and German-speaking worlds. Yet, as we have shown, this interruption was more than offset by an intensification of other diffusions. Amongst the western allies, for example, some flows of ideas and expertise were hugely increased. The links between American and European, especially French, planning were greatly strengthened. Belgian encounters with the planning approaches of their neighbours (especially Britain) became far more intense than could ever have occurred in peacetime. Japan continued to borrow extensively from all western countries (including Germany). Yet the early 1920s saw a more self-confident Japanese approach to developing, in the wake of reconstruction after a catastrophe that would have taxed even the most advanced European states.

### Enriching the body of planning thought

Overall, the interwar decades stand out as hugely important in the further refinement and diffusion of 20th-century planning ideas. In most, though not all, places the gap between ideas and policies and, even more, actual outcomes was great. In this sense, in most countries these years have been judged as a period of largely unfulfilled promise, with only a few oases of enlightenment in a desert of disappointment. Yet, from the conceptual point of view, this largely misses the point. There was sufficient activity to broaden, deepen and, perhaps more importantly, add a richness of texture and finer detailing to the international body of planning thought and practice. Many ideas were applied, often in several different settings, and were being revised and refined in the light of experience. The very fact that there were now more centres that were perceived as international models, not just the 'big four' of pre-1914, was itself important. Diffusion by selective borrowing, usually from multiple sources, spawned new variants, giving the international planning movement greater diversity. Even where the borrowing was uncritical, the new applications still offered scope for refinement and unconscious, or unintended, adaptations. In many cases, important future parameters of planning action were being laid down that were to grow in significance after 1945.

## PROFESSIONALISATION, INNOVATION AND DIFFUSION

As these changes occurred, there were subtle shifts in the agents of innovation and diffusion. Everywhere professional expertise was gaining ground over the reformist 'amateur'. Though far from complete, the shift nonetheless had already begun noticeably to reduce the scope for the charismatic 'visionary' and 'missionary' figures. Henceforth, international planning arenas would be more professionally dominated, concerned increasingly with technical details and refinements rather than fundamental visions of the city. The international literature of urban planning was also becoming noticeably more professional and technical in character, with less of a campaigning, reformist edge. This meant, of course, that the technical content of planning could be cumulatively detached from the liberal reformist values and ideologies that had originally inspired it. This also meant that it could be reattached to other values and ideologies, a process most chillingly illustrated in Germany after 1933.

## THE NETWORKS OF INTERNATIONAL EXCHANGE

In general, though, ideas and knowledge spread in much the same way as before 1914. There were, it is true, more formal barriers to personal global movement in the form of visas and passports. The import and export of goods, services, capital and information were also more likely to be subject to controls of various kinds, certainly by the 1930s. On the other hand, the frequency, affordability and efficiency of international modes of travel and communication increased. So, too, did the volume of literature on planning matters and the number of organisations promoting planning ideas and practice. Both contributed in a variety of ways to international discourse, for example by reporting foreign examples or sending delegates to international gatherings. The numbers of explicitly international organisations dealing with planning matters remained quite small (mainly the IFHTP, IULA and CIAM). Yet they offered regular opportunities for international tours, conferences and networking. Important too were competitions, lecture tours and more limited invitations to tender.

## The international planning expert

Taking advantage of these opportunities were a growing number of international planning experts. Some of these, as we have seen, had internationality thrust upon them because larger events, particularly the rise of totalitarianism, forced them into exile. Others emigrated for different, less pressing, reasons to seek better opportunities. All, however, became exotic figures in their new land, their experience (and, often, their wider linguistic skills) giving them special insights and experience that could enrich and diversify home-grown expertise and connect it in new ways to international planning discourse. Others again trained or worked abroad, on a temporary basis, usually returning in due course to enrich practice in their homeland. Some planning consultants undertook work in other, perhaps neighbouring, countries to their own as a natural extension of their domestic work, or in the protected markets of their nation's empire, or simply because there was insufficient work at home. Most ambitious of all were the handful such as Jansen, Prost or Adams who developed consultancies with the specific intention of working in different countries.

## The rise of global planning?

These last individuals beg questions that permeate all aspects of international diffusion: was it any longer meaningful to refer to different national traditions of planning thought? Planning systems and specific policies might retain certain national idiosyncrasies, but surely the body of underlying ideas was now global? Such questions are difficult to answer definitively. Yet planners in different countries still mixed the international cocktail of ideas in subtly different ways. Even the most cosmopolitan figures almost always betrayed certain distinctive national charac-teristics in their projects. To some extent, indeed, they traded on the reputation of their own country's urban planning tradition. But the best, at least, had a virtuosity that could transcend such traditions, if that was what was required. Such skills were, however, little in demand in the years that immediately followed.

# CHAPTER 6

# RECONSTRUCTION AND MODERNISATION I: THE MAJOR TRADITIONS

Even before the outbreak of the Second World War in 1939, the wider internationalist hopes of the 1920s had diminished. More rapidly than in 1914, war confirmed this almost complete (though never quite total) breakdown of information flows between opposing camps. Yet, if war damaged the international planning movement, it also threw up demands that strengthened the prospects for decisive planning action. A key reason for this was that, for the first time, aerial bombing was used on a large scale against urban centres. Its result was much greater physical destruction than occurred in the 1914–18 war. Throughout Europe, large tracts of cities were totally destroyed or severely damaged.

War fostered planning in other ways. It strengthened the power of governments in relation to private interests. It also demanded efficiency and innovation in the organisation of all aspects of life. Not least, it required mass loyalty, obliging governments to make promises about the quality of postwar life as a reward for wartime sacrifice. In countries which had experienced defeat such sentiments went further, as planning became a vehicle of moral and ideological renewal, albeit conceived in a variety of ways. Taken together, these impacts made the war and postwar years into a watershed in planning history. Reconstruction and, through it, urban planning assumed huge importance for some time after peace was restored.

Rarely, however, was it literally *reconstruction* on the identical or near-identical pattern that had been usual after 1918. Almost everywhere, planners and their political masters chose to modernise, though to varying degrees, as they rebuilt. Urban planning was thus charged with immediate tasks that were more challenging and ambitious than ever before. The early postwar years were dominated by real policies, implemented on a mass scale. There was less scope now for abstract rehearsal or experimental refinement of ideas. Yet the large-scale implementation of long-cherished planning ideals itself taught new practical lessons and created tangible examples that themselves could be studied, admired, copied or adapted. In other words, an international planning discourse soon re-emerged around urban reconstruction and modernisation.

Not surprisingly, this discourse was dominated by those nations that had ended up on the winning side. Though German reconstruction generated some interest, there was no rapid restoration of its external reputation as had happened in the 1920s. Instead, the United States and the Soviet Union shaped the larger parameters of reconstruction, each in their own geopolitical realms. In the west itself, the United States, even more than before 1939, seemed to define future trends of urban change. In the specific field of urban planning, however, this Americanisation was, for various reasons, very incomplete. Thus it was that Britain, to a lesser extent France, and (as we will see in the next chapter) the Netherlands, Sweden and other countries became the key international models at this time.

# GERMANY

In fact, Germany remained central to understanding the international development of planning. This was no longer because the world followed its lead. Rather, it was because there was now an unprecedented and direct international presence in the country, with important implications for urban planning. Many larger trends were thus writ large in its planning history. The Soviet Union, the United States, Britain and France each occupied different zones of German territory and sectors of Berlin (Pulzer, 1995). These divisions achieved a degree of permanence when Germany was split in 1949 into two states: the Democratic Republic (East Germany) covering the Soviet zone, under Communist leadership; and the larger Federal Republic (West Germany) covering the American, British and French zones. Berlin was a microcosm of these divisions. It soon became an arena of extraordinary tension in the new cold war between the Soviet Union and the western powers, giving great international significance to its postwar planning.

Although planners had to work within these larger geopolitical forces, it was the extent of physical destruction that more directly set the agenda for their work (JM Diefendorf, 1993b). On average, larger cities, with populations of over 100,000 in 1939, had about 50 per cent of their built-up areas destroyed. In many, such as Hamburg, Bremen, Dresden, Cologne, Essen and Dortmund, the proportion was even higher. In a few, such as Munich or Leipzig, it was lower. Destruction in virtually all the large German cities was, however, on a greater scale than even the worst affected of British cities.

## WARTIME PLANNING

Most of this destruction occurred in the last two years of the war. This limited the extent of wartime work on reconstruction planning in Germany compared to that in Britain, Vichy France or even the occupied Netherlands. Instead the early war years saw continued planning activity on Hitler's extended 'representative cities' programme. There were also important planning initiatives in those conquered territories that were being incorporated directly into the Reich, such as the Westmark (covering Alsace and Lorraine) and parts of Poland.

The latter, which affected the regions around Danzig (Gdansk) and Posen (Posnan), illustrates Nazi planning at its most chilling, showing how military conquest can produce the most authoritarian forms of planning (Fehl, 1992). The replanning work, intended to make these areas into an agrarian and racially pure Nazi utopia, was directly undertaken by the SS, following guidelines defined by its head, Heinrich Himmler. His planning team included the geographer Walter Christaller, who had promulgated his well-known central place theory during the 1930s. Christaller's ideas (which themselves borrowed aspects of Ebenezer Howard's spatial vision of the social city) were used to remodel the settlement pattern. A network of similar-sized villages was created, functionally linked to larger market and service centres. These changes could be contemplated because replanning was preceded by a forced programme of repopulation. Jews and Poles were removed, their property was seized and settlers with German origins were brought in. The idea was that different German 'tribes' would be resettled together, adding further refinement to the Nazi vision.

## RECONSTRUCTION PLANNING BEFORE 1945

Fortunately, this project did not proceed very far. As the balance of the war turned in 1942 and 1943, the heavy bombing of German cities began. Hamburg was the first to experience large-scale firebombing (Gutschow, 1990). Partly for this reason, and partly because of the planner who headed the representative city initiative there – Konstanty Gutschow – it was also the city where reconstruction planning was most advanced when war ended. Gutschow had always been interested in the wider functioning of the city as well as in the grandiose projects of Hitler's programme (JM Diefendorf, 1993b). It was relatively straightforward to extend this thinking into replanning. And since Gutschow headed a national working group on reconstruction, Hamburg became a model for other cities.

*Figure 6.1  Kassel had one of the most radical of West German reconstruction plans. From the outset it proposed ambitious remodelling of street and movement patterns, with extensive pedestrianisation.*

A central concept in reconstruction was to be the *ortsgruppe als siedlungszelle* (literally, local Nazi Party chapter as residential cell), each with a population of about 7,000 to 9,000, with local shops, schools and other social facilities (Pahl-Weber and Schubert, 1991; Schubert, 1995; 2000). Developed by Gutschow and others, particularly Hans Bernhard Reichow, this concept consciously echoed Nazi ideology by postulating an 'organic' relationship between the natural landscape and the residential clusters. Yet it was also strikingly similar to the American, and increasingly British, concept of the neighbourhood unit. Thanks to the state intelligence services, who surreptitiously procured key British plans (particularly the 1943 County of London Plan) through neutral countries, Gutschow knew exactly the central role this concept was playing in British wartime reconstruction planning (Fischer, 1990). When the British occupation administration arrived in Hamburg they were surprised at the parallels.

## THE POSTWAR PLANNERS

A key question facing the occupying forces was who would actually undertake reconstruction planning. Few experienced planners in Germany were untainted by association with the previous regime (JM Diefendorf, 1993b). Albert Speer, much the most powerful urban planner of the Nazi era, was convicted as a war criminal, though not specifically for his planning work. A few others, for example Konrad Meyer, the leader of the SS team which had replanned the incorporated territories of Poland, were tried – and, in his case, acquitted (Fehl, 1992). More typically though, denazification required that planners, such as Gutschow, who were most prominently associated with the previous regime be removed from their posts. They were not, however, debarred from practising in the west. Many soon resumed active consultancy careers or gained other posts. A few figures, amongst them Fritz Schumacher, were beyond reproach but too old to play an active role.

There were energetic efforts to bring back the modernist émigrés such as Walter Gropius, Martin Wagner and Mies van der Rohe to fill the vacuum. However, none of these, by now Americanised, individuals returned except on occasional commissions. Ernst May eventually came home from Africa in the early 1950s, though he worked for a major housing association rather than in a mainstream urban planning role. Perhaps the most significant returnees were, however, those in the Soviet zone (Düwel, 1997b). Thus Kurt Liebknecht, exiled with others in Moscow, and Richard Paulick, in Shanghai, played key roles in East German planning. A few uncompromising modernists had remained in Germany under the Nazis (and were therefore denied any public role). The most prominent was Hans Scharoun, who played an important, if short-lived, part in leading Berlin's planning before the city was divided.

## CONTINUITIES WITH THE NAZI ERA

The upshot was that most of Germany's reconstruction planning, at least in the west, fell into the hands of figures who had been in senior, if not usually the most powerful, positions during the Nazi era (JM Diefendorf, 1993b). They had not necessarily been party members although they had clearly been obliged to accept many of the regime's values. A few chief planners were allowed to continue in their roles, sometimes after a brief interval. Others moved up a step to top positions, perhaps in other cities. Gutschow's deputy, Rudolf Hillebrecht, for example, headed Hanover's reconstruction planning and gave extensive consultancy work to his old employer. Rudolf Schwarz and Walter Hoss, who had worked on planning the Westmark, now led reconstruction planning in Cologne and Stuttgart. Another prominent postwar figure was Hans Bernhard Reichow, who managed to survive close Nazi associations to become one of West Germany's leading planners of the period after the war.

In Chapter 5 we noted how planning's increasing professionalisation allowed it to be understood as a purely neutral, technical activity. This tendency was especially strong in a totalitarian state, where the essentially political nature of planning was concealed by the very fact of an authoritarian regime. Certainly this was how the postwar German reconstruction planners perceived their work. They had little difficulty with either reorienting their technical skills to a new regime or coming to terms with their previous work. All of which ensured there were many continuities with the pre-1945 period.

## REINTERNATIONALISING GERMAN PLANNING: FRENCH AND BRITISH CONNECTIONS

Yet this continuity could occur only with the compliance of the occupying powers. Theoretically, of course, Germany's unconditional surrender could have allowed the institution of an authoritarian colonial-style regime. Such a punitive solution, involving complete de-industrialisation, was considered but never seriously pursued. Another possibility was that the occupying powers could have directly imposed their own planners and planning solutions. The French showed an initial inclination to do this. Thus the French modernists Marcel Lods and Georg-Henri Pingusson worked in Mainz and Saarbrucken respectively. Like Scharoun's Berlin proposals, their radical plans were unpopular, offending important interests and having little impact.

But this was not a common approach. With some important differences of emphasis, the three western occupying powers recognised and sought to encourage the traditional strengths of German planning. Once they had dislodged the most blatant Nazi supporters, they backed German planners, tried to accustom them to working within a democratic political framework and reintegrated them into international planning discourse (Fischer, 1990). These connections took a few years to develop, partly because the Germans found it almost impossible to travel abroad before 1950. Moreover, as after 1918, they were not initially welcome at international planning gatherings. The IFHTP, for example, did not readmit delegates from Germany until 1950, nor resume recognition of the German language until 1954 (Cherry, 1990). Despite this, German planners met a few of their British and French counterparts through the latter's lecture tours or visits or in other arenas during the late 1940s (JM Diefendorf, 1993b). The British won the approval of the planners in their zone by maintaining a system of tight building control which supported their efforts. Such moves allowed German planners to feel that they were now 'on the same side' as planners everywhere.

## AMERICAN INFLUENCES

Initially the Americans, whose zone included Frankfurt, Munich and Stuttgart, did much less to promote reconstruction planning (JM Diefendorf, 1993a). The punitive sentiment that the Germans should be left to flounder in their destroyed country was especially strong in the immediate aftermath of war. Gradually, however, this *laissez-faire* attitude changed, especially as relations with the Soviet Union worsened in the late 1940s. In 1949 Hans Blumenfeld, the German-Jewish (and former Communist) émigré planner who was working in Philadelphia, and another expert from the same city, Samuel Zisman, were asked to advise on what the United States ought to do on the urban planning front (Blumenfeld, 1987). Their recommendations reflected the shifting emphasis. Well aware of the traditional strengths of German planning, they rejected the imposition of the somewhat weaker American planning approach (JM Diefendorf, 1993a, b). They did, however, stress the critical importance of accelerating housing supply. Like the British, they also recognised that, unless the position of Germany's planners was supported, the reaction against the totalitarian bureaucracy of the Nazi regime might easily cause control of reconstruction to fall entirely into private hands.

At least some cities in the American zone, particularly Frankfurt, developed relatively *laissez-faire* planning regimes in the longer term. Yet the prevalent attitude changed after the Blumenfeld/Zisman report. The Americans began to promote contacts between German planners and the United States, especially with the émigrés, and encouraged more Germans in the occupation zone to gain American experience. Most importantly, and rather paradoxically, they helped to re-establish the very modernist, mass-production approaches to housing provision that their own housers and planners had learnt from Germany in the 1930s. As the major external paymaster for reconstruction, the United States could exert a powerful leverage, even though detailed planning influence was limited.

## THE SOVIET ROLE

The main countervailing external force was the Soviet Union (Düwel, 1997b; 1997c; Strobel, 1998). In its zone an altogether more punitive approach to the Germans was adopted, reflecting appalling Russian losses at the hands of the Nazis. The purge of planners from the previous era was far more thorough than in the western zones. Some of them, fearing the worst, were amongst the flood of refugees who fled westward from the Red Army as war ended. Fairly quickly, the Soviet administration established a much stronger ideological grip on urban planning than the other occupying powers (von Beyme, 1990). It soon became unwise for ambitious planners in the Soviet zone to espouse Bauhaus modernist sentiments. Thus, although the Soviet Union, as the first occupying power in Berlin, had appointed Scharoun, it was also the Soviet Union who insisted on his dismissal.

Links with planners in the western zones soon became difficult, largely because of the wider strategic tensions over Berlin in 1948 and 1949. Yet there was also a growing gulf between the ideological content of planning in the east and west which brought a deeper intellectual estrangement. Leading figures in early East German planning, such as Liebknecht, Paulick or Hermann Henselmann, soon lost the west's respect for their apparent willingness to compromise their former modernist views. Increasingly, the only close external professional linkages encouraged were those with the Soviet Union. Thus leading planning figures in the new state were despatched to Moscow for instruction on 'correct', socialist realist, perspectives in 1950.

## PRESERVATION OR MODERNISATION?: WEST GERMANY . . .

Despite this growing divide, common reconstruction problems faced the two Germanies. A critical question was whether planners should strive to keep as much as possible of what survived, and even rebuild what had been lost, or seek dramatic changes to modernise cities (JM Diefendorf, 1993b). The planners' raw material varied, of course, according to the extent of the destruction, where it was concentrated in the city and how far buildings could be retained. On balance, the modernising forces were dominant, though their influence varied a great deal. West Berlin, Hamburg and Frankfurt, Stuttgart, Hanover and Kassel adopted strongly modernising approaches.

The visual impacts of this dominance varied. In Hamburg, for example, the central area, largely built in stone and brick after a fire in 1842, had mainly survived the bombing, so modernisation affected adjoining districts (Gutschow, 1990; BFHH, 1958). In Frankfurt, by contrast, many largely wooden, medieval buildings in the centre were wholly destroyed, leaving fewer preservationist options. In some cases, for example Hanover, remaining older buildings were physically moved to create historic districts within a modernist approach. Kassel was the most radical, however, in that modernisation extended beyond individual buildings to the whole layout of the city centre (Hass-Klau, 1990). Its 1950 plan brought dramatic changes to the old medieval street pattern and provided for the total exclusion of private motor traffic. This option had been discussed elsewhere but no other city took such decisive steps at this stage. The shift occurred on a more incremental basis: during the 1950s a growing number of cities, led by Essen in 1952, began to pedestrianise some of their existing historic streets.

A few centres were altogether more wholehearted in their commitment to maintaining the historic city (JM Diefendorf, 1993b). Thus Nuremberg retained its old buildings where at all possible and rebuilt in the gaps with new buildings that respected the historic morphology of the destroyed city. In other cases, particularly Cologne and Munich, modernising plans were compromised to retain a strong sense of history, using virtually identical reconstruction. The effect was very marked in Munich, usually seen as the most traditional of the big German cities.

## . . . AND EAST GERMANY

The question whether to preserve or modernise took a slightly different form in East Germany. With the exception of Dresden, which was 85 per cent destroyed, cities in the east had experienced less war damage than those in the west (von Beyme, 1990; Paul, 1990; Soane, 1999). Stronger powers to acquire land allowed more freedom to

replan cities. And the greater economic weaknesses of East Germany limited the possibilities of either rapid restoration or new development. Together, these various factors encouraged a rather cavalier attitude to the historic environment in bombed cities. In Dresden, for example, large tracts of quite restorable Baroque and other historic buildings were demolished in 1950 (often at night because of popular disapproval). Frequently though, the resources for further development were lacking, so sites remained vacant.

A critical issue was also the form that new development should take. As we have seen, the Bauhaus tradition had, in Communist eyes, become ideologically tainted by its growing American associations. The correct approach was socialist realism, which combined national German traditions with admiration for the Soviet example. Ironically, therefore, the modernised city in Communist Germany initially took a historicist form (Strobel, 1998; Düwel, 1997c). In 1950, 16 principles expressing this approach were enunciated as a conscious counterblast to the Athens Charter. It was best exemplified in the famous 1952 plan for the Stalinallee (later the Karl-Marx-Allee) in East Berlin. This monumental axis quickly became the new regime's major planning showpiece, emulated in other cities.

## HOUSING IN THE TWO GERMANIES

The residential buildings in the first sections of the Stalinallee plan, notably those at the Weberwiese, were of very high quality and were used specifically to promote the new East German state. Yet the social realist approach was scarcely suited to its needs for rapid housing provision. This was a key issue in the popular uprising against the Communist government in 1953. Moreover, it was a field in which West Germany, with much external encouragement, was performing increasingly well (Hajdu, 1983; D Kennedy, 1984) by the early 1950s. An important initiative dealing with the planning, design and construction of housing was the Constructa exhibition, held in Hanover in 1951 (JM Diefendorf, 1993b). Inspired by Hillebrecht's recent visits to early postwar British housing schemes, its broad intention was to encourage more standardised housing types suitable for accelerated housing production. The exhibition featured three- to five-storey blocks of flats of types – entirely unremarkable in architectural terms – that soon came to dominate West German housing output.

## THE 1957 INTERBAU

The planning and design of housing became a key issue in West Berlin. It was here that most American aid for housing was deliberately concentrated, becoming a key part of the urban 'cold war' (Düwel, 1997a). Thus West Berlin hosted a deliberate

*Figure 6.2  Nuremberg's reconstruction involved retention of many more historic features. Modern buildings also echoed many features of the traditional city, though direct copying of older townscapes, typical of cities such as Munich, did not occur.*

counterblast to the Stalinallee in the 1957 Internationale Bauausstellung (International building exhibition), often called Interbau or simply IBA (JM Diefendorf, 1993b). This was conceived on the pattern of the Weissenhof exhibition of 1927. An array of modernist luminaries, including Gropius and Le Corbusier, were recruited to design examples of modern social housing. The final results looked forward to more exciting urban forms than the predominant blandness of West German housing. There were bigger and taller blocks, more innovative techniques and more *architecture* as opposed to *building*. The internationalism was calculated and deliberate, to highlight the openness and outward-looking nature of West Germany in contrast to the narrower and closed nature of East Germany.

## SOCIALIST MODERNISM

In housing terms, though, East Germany began gradually to change from the mid-1950s, following the increasing Soviet repudiation of Stalin and the wasteful excesses of socialist realism (von Beyme, 1990; Düwel, 1997a; 1997c; Strobel, 1998). Apart from the Stalinallee, it had actually managed to avoid the more grandiose urban planning projects of Stalinism. Thus, though they occasioned much propagandising, the new towns at Stalinstadt, now Eisenhüttenstadt (1951), Hoyerswerda-Neustadt and Schwedt (both 1957) were modest in conception (Whittick (ed), 1980). By the later 1950s East German housing policy was taking a more practical turn, towards mass production. By 1960 modernism's radical roots and 1930s connections with the Soviet Union were also being rediscovered, giving some legitimation to this volte-face. The leaders of East German planning could now begin to become modernists again. Following Soviet leads, references to acceptable western planning models also became more common. Yet, despite the reality of a growing convergence of approach with West Germany, these ideological somersaults scarcely strengthened western regard for the work of East Germany's planners. The building of the Berlin Wall in 1961, to stop the growing exodus of East Germans seeking a better life, was a more telling symbol of a deeper separation.

## BRITAIN

Germany had been, successively, the world's most important urban planning innovator and, after 1933, a nation unwilling to be seen taking lessons from anyone. Defeat in war obliged it to receive whatever the nations now occupying its territory chose to press upon it. By contrast, Britain's place amongst the victorious powers served to increase further the already high international standing of its urban planning. This was not simply because those who win wars usually define what follows. In a material sense, the war against Hitler and his allies was won by the actions of the Soviet Union and the United States. Britain certainly could not have 'done it alone'. Yet the fact that it fought longer than any other combatant, at one point entirely without allies, had given it a critical role, more moral than material, in demonstrating, and thereby sustaining, the long-term viability of democracy in Europe. Planning, both in its widest sense and more specifically understood as *urban* planning, reinforced this moral role. Britain was seen as representing the positive features of modern social democracy against both the long-standing evils of the city and the more immediate evils of Nazism.

These larger understandings effectively predisposed many parts of the world to look to Britain as a postwar model. This was reinforced by much impressive planning activity in the 1940s which gave a real basis for this abstract admiration (Ward, 1994). From an early stage in the war, British planners were set to work moulding earlier broad ideas into practical proposals capable of large-scale adoption. Although political considerations shaped their work, sometimes profoundly, they were less distracted by larger ideological questions than their German or French counterparts (Cherry, 1990). At the end of the war, for example, they did not have to play down associations and continuities with previous discredited political regimes. The new legal powers, techniques, design approaches and functional and social analyses could be carried forward without need for the ideological rebadging that was necessary in Germany. In a technical and professional sense, therefore, this sustained work meant that British reconstruction planning had great international resonance during the early postwar years. Thus it hosted the first postwar meetings of both the IFHTP, in 1946, and CIAM, in 1947 (Gold, 1997; Mumford, 2000). CIAM returned during the 1951 Festival of Britain, providing further testimony to the strength of international interest in British developments.

## BOMBING AND PLANNING

The actual scale of destruction in Britain was very much less than in Germany, some other parts of continental Europe (for example, Rotterdam or Warsaw) or Japan. Thus the worst affected British cities, such as Coventry, Plymouth and Southampton, lost less than a third of their housing stocks compared to a 45 per cent *average* loss amongst Germany's large cities (Hasegawa, 1992; Mason and Tiratsoo, 1990). Parts of east London were more badly affected but the capital as a whole survived remarkably well compared to Berlin or Tokyo, let alone Dresden or Hiroshima. Several large British cities were barely touched. Yet the timing of the destruction, very early in the war, was extremely important (Ambrose, 1986; Ward, 1994). British cities began to be seriously bombed in autumn 1940. Although there were later attacks, including the so-called Baedeker raids (named after the famous guidebook) on historic centres such as Exeter and Canterbury, the heaviest bombing campaigns against the big cities had largely ended by mid-1941.

These months coincided with the period of greatest fear that the war would be lost. This prompted the government to make commitments about planning that were certainly more radical than any it would have made later. These were partly intended to bolster civilian morale, about which there were much greater fears then than in later years. There was also a deliberate desire, while Britain 'stood alone', to send out positive propaganda messages to the world – especially to public opinion in the United States, which did not enter the war until December 1941 (Rodgers, 1998). A further, crucially important, factor was the collapse of confidence in urban land markets which converted what had been the main prewar opposition to stronger planning powers into a force pressing for their adoption. Together with what had been a growing prewar interest in the subject, evident in the Barlow Commission of 1937 to 1940, this conjunction of circumstances proved particularly conducive to the robust development of planning – which was not confined to the bombed cities themselves (Barlow, 1940). Several of these circumstances changed later in the war, fostering more cautious attitudes, but by then planning had acquired a powerful political momentum that was not easily stopped.

**Figure 6.3** *Coventry was much the most radical of the British plans for reconstruction. Its pioneering central shopping precinct was soon internationally known.*

## THE INNOVATORS

The key arenas of technical innovation in the 1940s were primarily in the teams which prepared the plans for London, in one or two provincial cities and in the hastily assembled planning contingent within central government. Behind those who stood at the head of the process of innovation, such as Patrick Abercrombie, or mediated between the planners and the wider administrative process, such as George Pepler, lay a wider group (Dix, 1981; Cherry, 1981). Mostly male, they included many who became leaders of the profession in Britain and other parts of the British world during the 1950s and 1960s. Most were British-born, but they showed a wide international awareness. One such in the County of London (and later Coventry) was Arthur Ling, a stalwart of MARS and enthusiast for Soviet planning (Gold, 1997). Another, who worked on the Greater London plan and in the Ministry of Town and Country Planning, was Gordon Stephenson who had trained at Liverpool, and in Paris with both Gréber and Le Corbusier (G Stephenson, 1992). He, too, had an interest in Soviet planning which was strongly encouraged by the ministry in the 1940s but destined to cause him problems when he tried to move to the United States in the colder global climate of the 1950s.

By 1947 other, more junior, talents within the planning ministry included the future doyen of British transport planning, Colin Buchanan, and Nathaniel Lichfield, an expert on the economics of planning. A significant émigré was the Hungarian modernist Ernö Goldfinger. There was also a leavening of planning talent from the empire, including a suave and urbane South African, William Holford (Cherry and Penny, 1986). Another, older, colleague in the planning ministry, Jock Stewart, brought experience from the Calcutta Improvement Trust.

## RECONSTRUCTION PLANS

The wartime government initially encouraged bombed cities to approach reconstruction planning boldly, unconstrained by existing landownership and planning powers (Ward, 1994). The extent to which provincial cities followed this advice varied. Still more varied was the extent to which they then stuck to their plans in the face of opposition from local traders, property owners and an increasingly cautious central government. Only in Coventry did modernism permeate all aspects of the plan, prepared from 1941 by the young city architect, Donald Gibson, and survive most attempts to dilute its novelty (Mason and Tiratsoo, 1990). Its principal feature was a fully pedestrianised shopping precinct, the first to be proposed in Britain.

The Plymouth plans, prepared by Patrick Abercrombie and the city's engineer, though less uncompromisingly radical than Coventry's, were also largely followed in reconstruction (Hasegawa, 1992). Other cities, for example Hull (also mainly Abercrombie's work) and Southampton, saw initial radical proposals subsequently compromised. Some, such as Portsmouth, never went through a radical phase, always favouring reconstruction broadly on existing spatial patterns. Finally, there were some conceptually important wartime 'reconstruction' plans prepared for cities that suffered very little bombing. Foremost amongst these was Max Lock's plan for

Middlesbrough which broke new ground in its social and functional analyses and the extent of public consultation (Lock, 1946; Hebbert, 1983).

## REPLANNING LONDON

Of the provincial plans, only that for Coventry received much international attention (eg BFHH, 1958). It was, rather, the wartime plans for London, especially those for the county of London (1943) and, above all, the Greater London plan (1944) that came to represent British big city planning to the rest of the world (Forshaw and Abercrombie, 1943; Abercrombie, 1945). Both were prepared by teams led by Abercrombie (jointly with JH Forshaw, the chief architect of the London County Council, in the case of the 1943 plan). Considering the prevailing wartime austerity regulations, both were surprisingly lavish documents, a sign of their importance.

They also contained many important practical innovations, giving specific and comprehensive expression to ideas rehearsed between the wars. Many were of American or continental European origin. The former included the neighbourhood unit, which provided the social underpinning for both plans. Traffic planning also drew on American and some European precedents, with proposals for major through-routes. These echoed the parkways of Robert Moses and Thomas Adams in New York, together with some examples of grade-separated crossings in Paris and street widening in Moscow. (In different circumstances, German examples might also have been explicitly cited.) Much of the traffic planning reflected the ideas of the Assistant Commissioner of the Metropolitan Police, H Alker Tripp (Hass-Klau, 1990). The broad concept was a roads hierarchy with local areas, called precincts, where through traffic would be minimised. Obviously these principles would mesh closely with neighbourhood unit ideas, though the Radburn layout with total separation of traffic and pedestrian circulation was not yet being advocated. Other important continental European ideas that appeared for the first time in Britain were residential layouts of *zeilenbau* type, often using mixed developments of high-and low-rise buildings (Bullock, 1987; 1993).

## THE STRATEGIC VISION

More distinctively British was the strategic planning vision for the whole metropolitan area of London (Ward, 1994; Hebbert, 1998). Drawing on Unwin and others (including his own interwar regional planning work), Abercrombie's proposals for Greater London envisaged a wide green belt encircling the built-up area, tightly enforced to prevent further suburban sprawl (Abercrombie, 1945). It was assumed that national policies for regional development would reduce future overall growth pressures. Yet the planned redevelopment of the bombed and slum areas of inner London at lower densities would still require additional land to rehouse those who were displaced. The solution lay in eight entirely new planned satellite towns, each with an average population of 50,000, to be built beyond the green belt. These were to be self-contained settlements with their own employment and communal facilities –

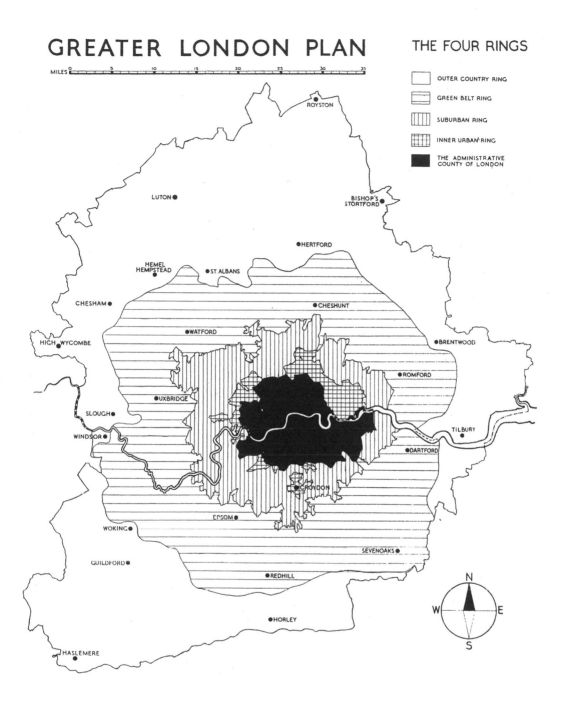

# GREATER LONDON PLAN

## THE FOUR RINGS

- ☐ OUTER COUNTRY RING
- ☰ GREEN BELT RING
- ▥ SUBURBAN RING
- ▦ INNER URBAN RING
- ■ THE ADMINISTRATIVE COUNTY OF LONDON

MILES 0 5 10 15 20 25 30 35

ROYSTON

LUTON

BISHOP'S STORTFORD

HERTFORD

HEMEL HEMPSTEAD    ST. ALBANS

CHESHAM

CHESHUNT

WATFORD

HIGH WYCOMBE

BRENTWOOD

ROMFORD

UXBRIDGE

SLOUGH

WINDSOR

TILBURY

DARTFORD

CROYDON

EPSOM

WOKING

SEVENOAKS

GUILDFORD

REDHILL

HORLEY

HASLEMERE

N
W E
S

**Figure 6.4**   *The Greater London Plan of 1944 was the most internationally important British plan of all time. Its wide containing green belt stopping further suburban expansion, and planned decentralisation to new settlements in the outer country ring defined the post-war British approach to metropolitan planning.*

modernised versions, in other words, of the garden city (Ward, 1992). In addition smaller country towns were to be expanded, reflecting similar planning principles.


## GREEN BELTS

Remarkably, all these proposals were quickly adopted and provided a model for the planning of many other British cities – and, often much less appropriately, for those in several other parts of the world. The 1947 Town and Country Planning Act took development rights into public ownership, allowing wide green belts to be enforced on privately owned land (Elson, 1986). By the mid-1950s, and with strong government encouragement, London's lead in designating a green belt was being followed by most other large British cities and several smaller, historic centres. By 1960, their central position in late 20th-century British planning was already assured.


## NEW TOWNS

Meanwhile the 1946 New Towns Act created very strong powers to build new towns on the Abercrombie model (JB Cullingworth, 1979; M Aldridge, 1979; Hardy, 1991a; 1991b). Fourteen were designated between 1946 and 1950 (though 20 was the original target). Again, although London's needs set the pace, these were not the only concern. As Abercrombie wanted, there were eight new towns around London, at Stevenage, Crawley, Hemel Hempstead, Harlow, Hatfield, Welwyn Garden City, Basildon and Bracknell, though only two (Stevenage and Harlow) were at the locations he proposed. Others were designated at Aycliffe and Peterlee in County Durham, East Kilbride and Glenrothes in Scotland, Cwmbran in South Wales and Corby in Northamptonshire. The 1950s brought a lull in designations, though Cumbernauld, a further new town for Glasgow, was added in 1955.

The new towns, especially those planned and built in the difficult early postwar years, became Britain's most admired (and most visited) planning achievement (Osborn and Whittick, 1977). The earliest developments disappointed many modernist architects. Although there were variations, the general approach was a rather dilute version of Scandinavian functionalism, with simple brick-built houses usually in terraced formation and with pitched roofs. Yet, in planning terms, the new towns were very innovative, both by their very nature and in many detailed aspects. Stevenage, for example, vied with Coventry as having Britain's (and thus one of the world's) first fully pedestrianised central shopping precincts (G Stephenson, 1992). The approach had been foreshadowed in the proposals for the unbuilt satellite town of Ongar, outlined in the 1944 Greater London plan. Its realisation at Stevenage involved a team led by Gordon Stephenson assisted (albeit briefly) by his close friend,

**Figure 6.5** *Stevenage was the first of Britain's very widely admired new towns, begun in 1946. Its central area was another pioneer of large scale pedestrianisation. The foreground statue celebrates the orientation of the new towns towards children and family life.*

Clarence Stein, the American doyen of vehicle-pedestrian segregation. Stein had lately begun to work on design principles for pedestrianised shopping malls.

In fact, the application of Stein's Radburn principles to residential development came only slowly. The continuing effects of petrol rationing ensured that motor vehicle use in early postwar Britain remained far below the American levels of even the late 1920s. The idea of planning for extensive vehicle separation throughout the new towns did not therefore seem appropriate until after the mid-1950s. The American concept of the neighbourhood unit was, however, applied rigorously, though usually to serve populations of about 9,000 or 10,000, larger than had been considered ideal in prewar thinking. The extensive use of terraced housing also brought some *zeilenbau* layouts, which allowed some separation of spaces for pedestrians and traffic. It was, though, the new towns that brought Radburn-type residential site plans to prominence in Britain during the 1950s. A few small examples had appeared slightly earlier, the first designed by Gordon Stephenson at Wrexham in north Wales, with other early examples in Northampton and Sheffield (KC Parsons, 1992b). As motor vehicles increased sharply in number in the later 1950s, however, Cumbernauld became, in 1958, the first sizeable town anywhere to be planned entirely on the Radburn principle (Osborn and Whittick, 1977).

## PLANNED REDEVELOPMENT

Meanwhile, and just as Abercrombie had envisaged, the rebuilding of the bombed areas gradually gave way in the mid-1950s to a resumption of the slum clearance programme begun in the 1930s (Burns, 1963; Johnson-Marshall, 1966). Planned redevelopment thus became another major arena of urban planning action. For many planners it was potentially more exciting than the new towns because the higher densities allowed greater opportunities for architectural virtuosity. The late 1940s and, even more, the 1950s saw several higher density flatted schemes that became models (though not all were actually on redeveloped sites). Those which attracted international attention were mainly in London. Most prominent amongst many notable examples were Churchill Gardens, from 1946, Lansbury, 1951, and Alton East and West, 1952–8 (Glendinning and Muthesius, 1994; Gold, 1997). The most important in planning terms was the Lansbury neighbourhood, a mixed development of terraced housing, low- and medium-rise flats and community facilities in a bombed area of the East End (Cherry, 1974). The scheme featured as a 'live architecture' exhibit at the Festival of Britain. Suburban Alton was, however, more avowedly modernist and a foretaste of much that was soon to follow in less verdant inner city surroundings (Benton, 1993). It showed clearly the influence on British social housing design at this time of both the Swedish *punkthus*, (Alton East) and Le Corbusier (Alton West). The *punkthus* is discussed in Chapter 7.

## THE INTERNATIONAL CONTEXT OF BRITISH PLANNING

The triumph of modernist design approaches in Britain owed much to imported ideas, mainly based on foundations which were already laid by 1945. During the war itself the emergency housing programme marked the first major use of prefabricated housing, borrowing very directly from American experience (Vale, 1995). There was some moderately active lesson-drawing from other early postwar examples, especially Rotterdam and Stockholm, that seemed especially close to British thinking (Cherry, 1990). Rather like the interest shown in Belgium during the First World War, there was also a special regard for the (rather different) approach being adopted to reconstruction in Poland, especially Warsaw. As in the case of Belgium, though, the exchange of planning approaches with Poland was not intense or even two-way in any very meaningful sense. A small, but significant, number of Polish planners received British professional training in the early postwar years before the formation of the Communist government in Warsaw severed connections.

By the 1950s, British planning was very much a net exporter of ideas and expertise. Early postwar international regard increased as foreign visitors came in larger numbers to see British planning achievements, especially the new towns. Meanwhile Britain's planning consultants, the authors of so many wartime plans, began to work extensively overseas. This was partly because the 1947 Act dramatically increased the role of salaried municipal officers, reducing the demand for consultants (Cherry, 1974). The reputation of British planning was, however, such that international outlets largely replaced the shrinking domestic market. The new planning opportunities lay mainly in the British Commonwealth (the new name for the empire), where urban planning featured strongly in colonialism's final chapter (Home, 1997). Several figures who had been central to the changes of the 1940s, amongst them Abercrombie, Pepler, Stephenson and Lock, undertook important commissions elsewhere (Dix, 1981; Cherry, 1981; G Stephenson, 1992; MLCERG, 1996). There was also a significant permanent outflow of British planning expertise, again largely to other parts of the English-speaking world. Thus several members of the team that had formulated the postwar planning process within central government emigrated to fill key government, consultancy or education roles in the white Commonwealth.

What these emigrants and consultants exported was more than just specific British planning formulations. It was also the wider ideology of a technical and professional approach to planning, underpinned by a legal code. It was reinforced by the British concept of planning as a professional activity (TPI, 1956). Spatially, the dominant international linkages reflected Britain's wider world view in the 1950s. They focused largely on the British world and, increasingly, the United States. Among planners there was less real understanding of Britain's closer neighbours. The European examples they admired tended to be those which appeared to reinforce their own approaches.

## FRANCE

Despite discontinuities of government and administration France, like Britain, showed great continuity in its reconstruction planning. In some respects this was even more pronounced than in Britain, and much of the basis of postwar planning, at least until the 1960s, was in place before the war ended. Yet this phase of French urban planning was less significant internationally than the corresponding activity in Britain,

Germany or, indeed, several other European countries. This was largely because the country's capital and much its largest city, Paris, was spared serious wartime destruction (Noin and White, 1997). France had fallen before the need to attack the city had arisen and Anglo-American air raids were few and affected only peripheral industrial districts. Most important of all, the German commander disobeyed Hitler's order to destroy Paris when retreat became inevitable. This fortunate outcome meant that the reconstruction of a city which still commanded world attention was unnecessary.

In fact, although Paris fared better than London, Berlin, Rotterdam or Warsaw, the destruction in parts of provincial France was as bad as that anywhere else in Europe (Couedelo, 1991; Voldman, 1991b). Successive waves of fighting touched a much wider area than in the First World War. The northern and eastern frontier zones again experienced serious destruction. The town of Douai, for example, rebuilt after 1918, was 50 per cent destroyed by 1944. This time, however, many coastal towns, mainly on the Channel coast and including Dunkirk and St Malo, were also seriously affected. Further south, the towns of the Loire valley such as Orléans and Gien, and the Atlantic coastal towns of St Nazaire and Royan were extensively destroyed. In Marseilles, the German occupation forces demolished sections of the old port district, ostensibly for strategic reasons. The worst affected large city, however, was the Channel port of Le Havre, with a prewar metropolitan population of about 150,000 (Clout, 1999). Its central districts and the port area were almost totally destroyed, along with over 50 per cent of the city's dwellings. The other large city that experienced serious destruction was Rouen (with 258,000 metropolitan population in 1939).

*Figure 6.6* Le Havre produced by far the most radical French reconstruction plan, though it was remarkable more for its architecture, which reflected the leadership of the veteran pioneer of concrete architecture, Auguste Perret.

## Planning under Vichy

The German invasion led to occupation and the formation in 1940 of a partly autonomous, but essentially collaborationist, French state based at Vichy. Although the Vichy regime directly administered only part of France, it was also charged with reconstruction planning throughout the whole country with the exception of the annexed territories of Alsace and Lorraine (Couedelo, 1991; Vaysierre, 2000; Voldman, 2000, 1991a). For strategic reasons the Germans wanted reconstruction of roads and infrastructure, which made a wider planning approach possible. The Vichy government, for its part, felt that efficiency in this sphere would increase the chances of winning greater independence back from France's conquerors. This prompted the creation of a strong central apparatus to promote reconstruction planning, and the encouragement of local replanning activity. In turn, this provided opportunities for many of the leading *urbanistes* (Voldman, 1989; 1990).

## Continuities after the liberation of France

Although the liberation of France outwardly saw a vociferous repudiation of the previous regime, the postliberation governments reaped much of the benefit of its planning efforts (Couedelo, 1991). The first minister of reconstruction and planning after the liberation, in General de Gaulle's short-lived government, was Raoul Dautry, an engineer planner from a railway background. He was an essentially practical man, unwilling to discard the sound technical work that had already been undertaken. Thus the ministerial experts and technicians, led by André Prothin, who had worked for the Vichy government were retained after the liberation. It was also a Vichy law of 1943 that created the postwar French planning system (Piron, 1994). This was remarkable when we remember that even Britain did not have a planning Act until 1947. It has even been claimed that there was contact between Vichy and the Free French administration in London to ensure the acceptability of the legislation. Whether or not this is actually true, the very citation of such an explanation certainly highlights the surprising nature of the legal and professional continuity in France.

## Traditionalism and modernism

One apparent discontinuity lay in the favoured design approaches before and after the liberation. Vichy was very much associated with traditional, regionalist approaches to rebuilding, as had been pursued after 1918. By contrast, modernism came much more to the fore after 1944. Yet this distinction has been much exaggerated as the climate of opinion was itself shifting between 1940 and 1944 (Baudouï, 1990, 1993; Voldman, 1991b). Le Corbusier remained in France during the Vichy period (he was a citizen of neutral Switzerland) and certainly sought opportunities to work for the regime. During these years he also published a spate of modernist tracts, including his long-delayed version of the Athens Charter. Contrary to the impression sometimes given, that these were manifestoes of resistance to the spirit of Vichy, they were readily available and actually received elaborate praise in the officially approved press.

The Vichy regime certainly appointed traditionalists to most reconstruction roles, for example in the Loire valley. At Rouen, the beaux-arts *urbaniste*, Jacques Gréber, was given charge of reconstruction in 1940 (Clout, 1999). Yet most of these appointments were not changed after 1944 and traditional reconstruction plans largely continued, most impressively at Gien (Baudouï, 1993). Modernist approaches were definitely favoured in reconstruction plans initiated after the liberation, particularly at Le Havre. Even then, however, a few towns continued to seek near-identical reconstructions, for example in the walled city of St Malo. Moreover, modernist tendencies had not been unknown under Vichy. In Marseilles, for example (where Gréber had prepared an important plan in the late 1930s), the modernist Eugène Beaudouin was placed in charge in 1940 (Voldman, 1991b). (Reversing the usual order of things, his 'reconstruction' proposals actually *preceded* destruction, giving the embarrassed French authorities some vestige of legitimacy when the German forces dynamited areas adjoining the old port in 1943.)

## RECONSTRUCTION PLANNING IN LE HAVRE

Symbolically, of course, the Loire valley reconstruction plans seem more representative of the spirit of Vichy, while the planning of Le Havre seems better to capture the post-liberation sense of progress (Baudouï, 1990a). Le Havre was certainly the most internationally significant French reconstruction plan of these years (Etienne-Steiner, 1999; Clout, 1999; van Roosmalen, 1997; Toulier, 1999). It was associated particularly with the veteran modernist, Auguste Perret, who was 71 when he was appointed by Dautry in 1944. Perret was a pioneer in the architectural use of concrete, a crucially important consideration given the acute shortage of traditional building materials. He had been an important early influence on the young Le Corbusier and, indeed, many other French architects. His Le Havre team was largely composed of his admirers and it is difficult always to distinguish his direct hand from their derivative work.

A complicating factor was, however, the work of another planner, Felix Brunau, who had been appointed to plan Le Havre's reconstruction in 1941. Though Perret was favoured by the central government his initial plan, based on a 100-metre grid, proved far too radical. Especially unpopular was his proposal to raise the street level of the entire inner city by 3.5 metres, solving problems of rubble disposal and drainage while creating space for infrastructure, public transport and storage. The city council favoured instead a compromise with the Brunau plan. The result was architecturally innovative, with medium-rise concrete blocks lining the streets and punctuated by occasional high rises. Overall, though, it was more conservative in planning terms than the contemporary plans for Rotterdam, Coventry or Kassel. There was, for example, no pedestrian precinct development. The street plan reproduced much of the previous layout, except for the irregular pattern that formerly existed within the area of the original fortifications.

## OTHER MODERNIST PLANS

Elsewhere other modernists, amongst them André Lurçat at Mauberge and Marcel Lods at Mayence, took charge of reconstruction work (Baudouï, 1993). Le Corbusier was involved in several places. Yet, despite openings at La Rochelle and St Dié in 1945, his ideas proved too controversial and he did not find a major planning role in the French reconstruction. From La Rochelle, he salvaged plans for his vast Unité d'Habitation slab block, the first of which was built in Marseilles from 1949. His wider planning ambitions eventually came closest to realisation in France in the mid-1950s, when he designed a new district for the industrial town of Firminy (Pouvreau, 2000).

## FRENCH RECONSTRUCTION IN ITS INTERNATIONAL CONTEXT

Whatever its form, French reconstruction planning was almost totally in French hands. Le Corbusier, as a Swiss citizen, should technically be seen as an exception but only in the very strictest sense. Even more than previously, of course, his ideas commanded international attention, partly through his continued involvement in CIAM. His Athens Charter became widely known in the early postwar years. It was, for example, translated into German in 1948 by Hans Kampffmeyer, a former member of the German occupation force (and son of one of Germany's garden city pioneers), who had encountered it in wartime Paris (Fischer, 1990). Alton West in London was inspired by Le Corbusier's Marseilles Unité block and he provided a clone for the 1957 Interbau in Berlin (Benton, 1993; Düwel, 1997a). As we have implied, however, Le Havre was the only large-scale French reconstruction plan that earned much international attention at this time.

For its part, French *urbanisme* probably received more from elsewhere than it exported. The re-establishment of the international planning movement was important, allowing French planners again to draw on external ideas. There were no direct foreign involvements in reconstruction planning in France in the manner of George Ford's work in Reims from 1917. Yet the immediate shortages of housing encouraged the French government to promote knowledge of foreign innovations, especially in prefabricated construction (Barjot, 1991). In 1946, for example, there was a large exhibition specifically on American techniques in housing and planning. In addition Canada, Switzerland, Sweden and Britain gave assistance with temporary housing. Another major international exhibition organised in 1947 shared the experience of nine European countries and South Africa.

## THE AMERICAN CONNECTION

Links with the United States were especially strong. Several notable French architects and *urbanistes* had spent the war years in America. Amongst them was Maurice Rotival, a former associate of Henri Prost, who had worked in Venezuela. His American teaching role and later involvement in urban renewal in New Haven, Connecticut, meant he remained an important link between the American and French traditions (Garvin, 1996). The early post-liberation period saw the most systematic connections, however. From 1944, when the new French government opened its offices in Washington, its planning ministry was strongly represented, gathering knowledge (Cohen, 1995). Dautry, ever alert to American innovations since his own visit to the country in 1912 as a young railway engineer, quickly sent groups of professionals to investigate relevant practice and the pattern continued. Several of the best known *urbanistes* in France (and its colonies) visited the United States during these years, amongst them figures such as Lods and Le Corbusier.

They came back deeply impressed by how effectively the country had mobilised its economy for war, and in particular by its rapid creation of new industrial plants and worker housing itself built on factory-production lines. They also saw, in New Deal ventures such as the Tennessee Valley Authority, a model for European reconstruction and colonial development. It seemed to the French visitors that everything that was supposed to come from Soviet communism was being delivered by the world's greatest capitalist state, mobilised in a great cause.

These more specific contacts need to be seen, of course, against the wider background of the key American role in the liberation of France and, from 1947, the material assistance it granted as Marshall Aid. As in Germany, relatively little of the aid found its way directly into housing or urban planning, though it played a more important part in re-establishing infrastructure (Bossuat, 1991a). It was also important in reinforcing France's cultural links with the United States and building up the idea of a Europe that was pro-American and anti-Soviet. These wider meanings found echoes in planning. Part of the conscious symbolism of the Porte Océane, in the Le Havre plan, for example, was that it would be France's Atlantic gateway, opening the city to bid a visual 'welcome' to the ships bearing Marshall Aid (Baudouï, 1993).

## L'AMÉNAGEMENT DU TERRITOIRE

Financial assistance from the United States became an endowment for French national economic planning. Though few other countries took much interest in France's efforts until the 1960s, the use of indicative state planning within an essentially capitalist western economy was soon to become one of the major French contributions to international planning thought. Particularly important here was the spatial dimension of these planning efforts. This involved the elaboration of the relationship of national economic priorities with the potentialities of specific regions and urban areas (Hansen, 1968). It brought a rapid growth in a comparatively new branch of urban and regional planning, beyond *urbanisme*. Extending the earlier use of the word *aménagement* in an urban context to signify the less architectonic aspects of planning, it was called *l'aménagement du territoire*. The term itself (meaning literally the management of territory) first appeared only in the late 1940s (Couedelo, 1991). It received authoritative official definition in 1950, when the then minister of reconstruction, Eugène Claudius-Petit, defined it as the pursuit of a better distribution of population in relation to natural resources and economic activities. Yet the goals were not to be purely economic and should also reflect broadly defined social welfare needs.

## GROWTH POLE THEORY

The new theory and practice of *aménagement du territoire* gradually took shape during the 1950s. In one sense, it was comparable to the shift towards a wider concept of spatial planning that had been noticeable in the United States, Britain and the Netherlands since the 1930s. Yet the French approach was much more theoretically grounded, especially in regional economics (Boudeville, 1966). It also became more firmly embedded in all levels of governance than in other countries. In part, this greater French interest reflected the prevalent unevenness in France's economic and social development, and a generally lower level of economic development than any other major western nation. A particularly notable contribution was the growth pole theory, developed by François Perroux (DW Parsons, 1986). Elaborated largely during the 1950s, it asserted that propulsive clusters of dominant industries could become poles for economic development. Initially, the theory rested on the rather abstract concept of economic space. Another leading French regional economist, Jacques Boudeville, translated the theory more directly into geographical space and, therefore, locationally based planning.

## PARIS IN THE EARLY POSTWAR YEARS

Until the 1950s France's most spontaneous growth pole had, of course, been Paris. As we have seen, however, the capital, France's greatest urban canvas, was untouched by the artistry of reconstruction *urbanisme*. This neglect largely reflected the geography of destruction. Yet it also echoed the active mood of antimetropolitanism that came to dominate early postwar France (Evenson, 1979; Noin and White, 1997). This was another important strand of continuity with the rural and small-town values of Vichy. It received powerful endorsement in an influential book, *Paris et le désert français* (Paris and the French desert) published in 1947. Its author, Jean-François Gravier, a professor at the academy of arts and crafts, argued that the capital's dominance was damaging to France as a whole. His broad arguments were also subsumed within the new discourse of *aménagement du territoire*, expressed more neutrally as a search for balanced development of the national territory.

This objective grew in relevance as the French economy boomed in the 1950s (Hansen, 1968). As always, metropolitan Paris grew very rapidly, adding 100,000 population a year for most of the decade. Until 1954, this growth followed the historical pattern of being at the expense of the rest of France. But important shifts in policy came in the mid-1950s, with positive measures to encourage regional development outside Paris. In 1955 and 1958 there were also the first negative controls limiting industrial and office growth in the capital. In 1960 the decentralist PADOG (Plan d'Aménagement et d'Organisation Générale de la Région Parisienne) was approved. It finally superseded the prewar Prost plan and proposed the halving of population increase in the Paris region and deflecting growth pressures to smaller centres. Meanwhile, there was a quickening of planning activity within the area.

## MAJOR PLANNING INITIATIVES IN 1950s PARIS

A critical decision was to create an alternative centre for major office development, limiting the pressures for commercial redevelopment in the historic core of Paris (Evenson, 1979). The location chosen, in 1956, was at La Défense, to the west of the city itself, a continuation of the grand axis from the Louvre through the Arc de Triomphe. Here, serviced by an impressive array of investments in public infra-structure, was to be the principal site for Paris' new office towers. Construction of a major exhibition hall began in 1958. The original plan, not finally approved until 1964, involved several leading architect-planners. The design work was undertaken by Bernard Zehrfuss, Robert Camelot and Jean de Mailly, with advice from leading planners in the central planning ministry and the Paris region. The first ideas for La Défense envisaged a mixed development with housing, other community facilities and office blocks no taller than 25 storeys. (There would, though, be many subsequent revisions, to which we will return in Chapter 8.) Another extremely important decision, in 1956, was to create the Boulevard Péripherique. This sought to avoid the need for major road construction and associated demolition in central Paris by creating a major ring route around the historic city. The first stage was begun in 1957.

## THE ORIGINS OF THE *GRANDS ENSEMBLES*

Already though, rapid growth was exposing a traditional weak point in French *urbanisme*: the provision of cheap housing. By the mid-1950s France faced a massive housing crisis with serious shortages. This applied especially to Paris (whose population grew by 100,000 a year between 1954 and 1962), and which had appalling slums in parts of its centre and ramshackle shanty towns in its suburbs (Evenson, 1979; Noin and White, 1997). The major response, which began to appear from 1953 (and on a very large scale from the later 1950s), was based on using nontraditional building methods to build large areas of low- and moderate-cost apartment blocks – the so-called *grands ensembles* (literally, big groups). This extremely important initiative, which was soon to change the face of French cities and had significant international impacts, is still surprisingly under-researched. There were certainly some continuities with the last of the interwar projects such as Drancy-la Muette, but the 1948 housing legislation triggered more dramatic changes. British examples of neighbourhood unit planning were influential in framing the first large housing schemes (eg Vollerin, 1999). More distinctively French, however, was the conscious central encouragement of new building technologies to accelerate large-scale housing production (RB White, 1971; *Urbanisme*, 1999).

## INDUSTRIALISED BUILDING

An important advocate of industrialised housing was, again, the reconstruction minister, Eugène Claudius-Petit. A leader in the promotion of the *aménagement du territoire* during the early 1950s, he was also a notable modernist architect – and close friend of Le Corbusier (Cohen, 1995; Pouvreau, 2000). An official French visitor to the United States in the early postwar years, he had returned with a growing conviction that mass production was needed. Following the wartime American examples, earnest efforts were made during the 1950s to involve major manu-facturers, especially in the motor industry, in housing production (Vollerin, 1999). Little actually came of this and it was, in fact, the building industry that changed. But the 1950s were important years of experiment. In Lyons, for example, there were important innovations in building technique in the neighbourhood of Parilly, and the earliest part of what became one of the city's largest *grands ensembles* at Duchère. The programme received a major boost nationally in 1958 when a new planning instrument, the ZUP (priority development zone), was introduced to expedite the planning of these very large areas of housing (Merlin, 1971).

## EXAMPLES OF *GRANDS ENSEMBLES*

One of the first, and eventually one of the biggest, *grands ensembles*, was begun at Massy-Antony in the southern suburbs of Paris, near the proposed Orly airport (Evenson, 1979; Noin and White, 1997). Planned for 40,000 people, its development began in 1954 with five-storey apartment blocks. Higher slab blocks and towers, produced by progressively more industrialised methods, became increasingly common in the later sections reflecting national trends. Like many such areas, community facilities, local employment and adequate transport links were slow to appear, and often remained inadequate. The most notorious *grand ensemble* in the whole of France was

*Figure 6.7* *Meeting the housing shortage became the overwhelming priority of French urban policy from the late 1940s, accompanied by a search for practical methods for industrialised mass production. Parilly, in metropolitan Lyons, was an early experimental prototype.*

designed by Henri Labourdette at Sarcelles in the northern suburbs of Paris (*Urbanisme*, 1999). Begun in 1955, and developed over a 20-year period it, too, had a 40,000 population target. Every medium-sized or large French city had its own equivalents of the *grand ensemble* under way by the early 1960s. In Lyons, Duchère was joined by Montessuy and the vast area in the southern suburbs at Vénissieux-Les Minguettes. Yet, despite their role in improving material housing standards and the great international interest in French building innovation they quickly generated (eg RB White, 1971), *grands ensembles* soon came to be seen as a problem. Their huge physical scale and growing social difficulties encouraged a growing negative perception by the early 1960s. They had become highly visible and easily labelled pockets of suburban disenchantment. It was, in part, the search for alternatives to this approach in the early 1960s which finally restored France as a universally admired planning model.

## THE UNITED STATES

We have seen that all three major European planning traditions showed clear American influences on their reconstruction planning. In one sense, this new ascendancy was paradoxical, because American cities themselves experienced no war damage. Yet the United States, though suffering much less than most European countries in relative terms, was profoundly affected by war (Patterson, 1998). The manner of American entry into the war in December 1941, following a pre-emptive Japanese attack on the Pearl Harbor naval base in its dependency, Hawaii, etched the air threat deeply on the national consciousness. It was, however, the vast mobilisation of the American economy and its people to fight, but above all to produce and provide for its beleaguered allies, that had the greatest impact (Scott, 1969). The resultant intensification of production finally hauled the United States out of the economic doldrums of the 1930s.

All aspects of life were affected, and urban planning substantially so. In part, this was because the enforced dynamism of the American war economy extended the principles of Fordist mass production into urban development. There were also important changes in American attitudes both to the role of government and to society in general. We saw in Chapter 5 how the New Deal brought a federal dimension to American city planning, orchestrated and funded from Washington. This had allowed the more confident development of a social agenda that made American city planning more directly comparable to European forms of urban planning. War now accelerated these trends so that Americans became more receptive to the notion of 'big government' (Funigiello, 1983). On a much greater scale than in 1917, they also accepted that under federal orders what were, quite literally, new industrial and military cities would be created almost overnight (Albrecht (ed), 1995). They also experienced a sense of common purpose and social cohesion that made more people question the deep divisions and inequalities that existed within American society.

### HOMES BY THE MILLION

The wartime development which drew these various elements together (and which excited greatest international interest) was the programme to develop housing and communities to serve the new war factories and shipyards (Crawford, 1995; Hise, 1995; 1996). Under a variety of programmes, governmental and private, some eight million Americans were housed in rapidly built dwellings. Many of these were prefabricated, or at least built using far more machinery and unskilled labour than was usual. Simple functional designs were preferred, totally free of stylistic affectation. Many site plans and layouts showed allegiance to the most advanced American thinking on community design from the previous decade. Modernist planners in particular were captivated by what they saw (Casson, 1946; Cohen, 1995). Thus the schemes designed by exiled modernists, for example Walter Gropius and Marcel Breuer at New Kensington in Pennsylvania, drew particular interest.

Yet the most accomplished exercises in new community planning were also the least known. These were the top secret 'atomic cities' at Oak Ridge in Tennessee, Los Alamos in New Mexico and Richland in Washington (Scott, 1969). In these, the hand of federal power had been supreme. More typical were the rather more ad hoc communities developed to serve major new private war factories. Particularly notable amongst these were the efforts of Kaiser Industries, for example, at Fontana in California (Hise, 1996). From 1946, the company used its wartime mass-production housing experience to adapt to peacetime needs. Underpinned by federal loans to war veterans, it built a new community for over 2,000 families at Panorama City in Los Angeles (Hise, 1995). Rather less successful was the settlement planned to serve the vast Ford bomber factory at Willow Run, in Ypsilanti, Michigan (Scott, 1969; Crawford, 1995). Although an ambitious plan proposed the adoption of neighbourhood unit principles and full provision for social needs, it was only partly implemented.

## AMERICAN INTEREST IN EUROPEAN WARTIME DEVELOPMENTS IN PLANNING

The wartime mobilisation of American production revealed a hitherto untapped capacity for national planning. Equally, however, it often encouraged expediency rather than considered, permanent solutions. As elsewhere, wartime experiences also triggered political, professional and public debate about profoundly important planning issues, in particular urban redevelopment and metropolitan planning (eg Justement, 1946; Bauman, 1983). The unfolding of the planning debate in Britain was watched especially closely (Rodgers, 1998). More than ever before, the two countries drew closer together during the war years. Even before the United States became a combatant, British government information services ensured that influential Americans were kept well informed of Britain's reconstruction plans. At a time when Hitler was declaring a new order for Europe, British propagandists realised that these plans were important in helping to convince Americans of the viability of democracy in Europe. For their part, growing numbers of Americans were drawn naturally into an interest in the war as they heard their own countrymen broadcasting from London during the Blitz. Nor did their interest diminish after Pearl Harbor. The wartime climate of thinking, coming hard on the heels of the New Deal and favouring more active government, was very receptive to British reconstruction proposals, especially Abercrombie's plans for London.

## SLUMS AND PUBLIC HOUSING

Admiration did not, however, turn into emulation. After a great deal of political hesitation the 1949 Housing Act was eventually passed, giving federal assistance to encourage slum clearance, redevelopment and public housing (Scott, 1969). Many American planners and urban reformers hoped this would facilitate large-scale housing-led urban redevelopment of the kind begun in Europe in the 1930s, and which was being resumed after 1945 on an even greater scale. They hoped, too, to see a major expansion in the United States of good quality European-style social housing in well-planned neighbourhoods of the kind they saw appearing in Britain, the Netherlands and Sweden. It was the oldest established cities of the Atlantic seaboard, traditionally those most open to European thinking, that sought to make fullest use of the new measure.

## PUBLIC HOUSING IN NEW YORK AND PHILADELPHIA

Some, indeed, had already taken the first steps. In New York housing became part of Robert Moses' empire in 1948 (Plunz, 1990). The city's first major postwar project, Stuyvesant Town, completed in 1949, was privately developed but with much public assistance and involvement. Its 35 13-storey residential towers were exclusively for white middle-income households. There were many criticisms of the scheme, on both design and racial grounds. Yet high-rise projects with low-site cover, which differed radically from the older developments they replaced, quickly became the preferred form of public housing in the city. By the early 1950s, slab blocks influenced by Le Corbusier's Unité d'Habitation were appearing in projects such as Sedgwick in the Bronx and North Harlem in Manhattan (Metzger, 1994). The Albany and Farragut projects in Brooklyn used five-winged asterisk towers. The later Baruch project in Manhattan's Lower East Side favoured a stepped slab form.

This reliance on very large-scale projects was not, however, universal. Philadelphia soon came to represent a far more enlightened approach, influential both within the United States and, increasingly, in Europe (Bauman, 1988). From 1947 the city's planning was under the spirited leadership of Edmund Bacon, already a leading figure in the city's housing (Bauman, 1983). An impressive array of talents contributed in various capacities in the early postwar years, amongst them the European émigrés, Oskar Stonorov and Hans Blumenfeld (Blumenfeld, 1987). The Philadelphia approach as applied in the areas of older row housing around the city centre involved redevelopment, but on a much smaller scale than in New York. Strongly influenced by the ideals of his mentor, Eliel Saarinen, Bacon's initial approach, exemplified most fully in the East Poplar just to the north of the commercial centre, was to retain and rehabilitate much of the existing physical fabric. Only the worst housing was demolished. Wherever possible churches, schools, shops and other community institutions were retained. Later schemes involved more clearance and larger public housing projects. The Temple area of north Philadelphia, for example, saw new public housing provided in high blocks and rows. By the early 1950s, however, solutions based on rehabilitation rather than replacement were beginning to be promoted nationally. East Poplar, along with notable schemes of neighbourhood revitalisation in other cities, such as Waverly in Baltimore and Woodlawn in Chicago, became the new national models (Scott, 1969).

## THE RETREAT FROM PUBLIC HOUSING

The larger truth was that the brief American flirtation with a broad-based, European-style subsidised social housing policy was ending. As private house building boomed in the suburbs in the early 1950s, white populations began to leave the older inner districts in ever larger numbers (McKelvey, 1968; Fox, 1985). In the industrial cities of the northeast and Midwest their places were taken by black migrants from the south. In turn, the endemic racism of American society further accelerated the outflow of whites. The political consequence was that white suburbanites, who had solved their own housing problems by leaving the cities, no longer cared much about public housing. The whole course of policy changed direction under President Eisenhower. The Korean War and increased tensions with the Communist bloc underpinned a growing reaction against anything that could be labelled as socialistic – such as public housing (or, indeed, city planning). After two decades which had seen a strengthening of the social dimension of American city planning, the 1950s saw a shift towards more individualistic, market-based ideologies.

## THE SWITCH TO URBAN RENEWAL

Moreover, the 1949 legislation had not worked as well as its original promoters had hoped (Bauman, 1988; Scott, 1969; Fox, 1985). There had been much hesitation, often for racial reasons, on the part of local political leaders. The actual impact of replacement public housing on wider housing conditions was also rather limited. Housing policies based on rehabilitation offered a cheaper and less socially disruptive method of improving housing conditions for a larger number of households. A larger policy shift was also taking place as, from 1954, redevelopment itself assumed priority over housing. This meant that run-down districts close to the downtown commercial areas of cities could now be more easily replaced by new development of much higher value – for example of offices, shops and expensive apartments. There remained an obligation to provide a minimum of public housing to rehouse those who were displaced but any wider commitment had gone. This diminution of its social content restored American city planning to its historic trajectory. In turn, it also encouraged the emergence of a distinctively American approach to the planning of urban renewal that was destined, in the longer term, to have important international influence.

## THE NEW MODELS OF URBAN RENEWAL

Beginning in Pittsburgh in 1943 and followed by Philadelphia in 1948, New Haven in 1954, Baltimore in 1955 and others, the older cities spawned ad hoc organisations of downtown business interests (Fosler and Berger (eds), 1992; Frieden and Sagalyn, 1989). Using the policy shifts of the 1950s, these soon became powerful voices in the redevelopment of downtown areas, working in increasingly close partnership with city halls. By the mid-1950s, the first urban renewal prototypes of this new public-private partnership approach in urban planning were appearing.

Again Philadelphia stands out as the major innovator with its widely studied Penn Center, planned from 1947 to 1953 (Bacon, 1974; Garvin, 1996). Built on the site of an old railway station and elevated approach tracks, its modernist office towers stood above a lower-level pedestrian concourse. Retailing and a replacement suburban railway station were moved underground. In fact, the completed scheme seriously compromised the original design, by Edmund Bacon, for a carefully planned multi-use development with much emphasis on pedestrianised public space. It became, essentially, a large-scale office development with only a small amount of shopping and rather unappealing public space. Yet its commercial success showed definitively that developers and planners could work together to achieve urban renewal in an innovative modernist design. Though none was quite as influential as the Penn Center, several important commercial redevelopments in other cities were under way by the mid-1950s. They included the Triangle district of Pittsburgh, the Prudential Center in Boston's Back Bay and the Charles Center in Baltimore.

## THE GROWTH OF THE SUBURBS

Such developments did not reduce, or even challenge to any great extent, the outward shift of cities. Without them, there would perhaps have been more extensive suburbanisation of offices. Yet the scale of suburban growth was still immense (KT Jackson, 1985; Fox, 1985). In 1960 almost 55 million Americans lived in suburbs compared to 35 million just 10 years earlier (and 20 million in 1940). In relative terms, the suburban proportion of the national population had doubled from 15.3 per cent in 1940 to 30.6 per cent in 1960. Moreover, although this growth largely occurred at the expense of the nonmetropolitan (mainly rural) population, the relative importance of the older core cities began, for the first time, to show a slight decline during the 1950s.

## THE AUTOMOBILE AND SUBURBIA

How much, though, was the suburbanisation of the United States a product of planning? The underlying strength of the garden city concept in American planning thought undoubtedly reinforced the sense that this was the way to solve urban problems. Yet the direct influence of such thinking on the acceleration of suburbanisation was very small. A critical factor was the ever greater motorisation of American society. Wartime scarcities had brought some restrictions on automobile use, but these were far less stringent than those in Europe. Moreover, the rapid growth in using vehicles soon resumed after 1945. An important area of public policy which encouraged this growth was the growing extent of freeway-type roads (Ellis, 1996). We have seen how, through state and city initiatives, these had begun to be more common in the years immediately before American entry into the war. A further boost came with the 1956 Federal Aid Highways Act (Fox, 1985). This gave federal support to build a national system of interstate freeway roads, though without considering the urban impacts of such developments. In fact, urban areas accounted for some $15 billion of the total of $27 billion spent on interstate highways in the 10 years from 1956. By the mid-1960s most large metropolitan areas had extensive orbital 'beltways' with radial 'spokes'.

## HIGHWAY PLANNING AND URBAN PLANNING THOUGHT

Some prominent city planners (including Harland Bartholomew and Rexford Tugwell) had contributed to a key federal policy report on the planning of interregional highways in 1944 (Ellis, 1996). But much of the detailed planning of specific routes (including their urban sections) lay in the hands of federal highways engineers. The most city planners could do was to try to mitigate the local effects (Altshuler, 1983). In fact, the engineers who did most of the planning work for the interstates made a major contribution to urban planning thought and technique (Bruton, 1975; P Hall, 1988). To generate and justify their proposals, they had to develop ways of measuring and predicting the traffic demands that arose from particular arrangements of urban activities. Such approaches also had to be dynamic, taking account of growth and spatial change in metropolitan areas. It was highly quantitative and relied on electronic computers to undertake a volume of data-processing that would otherwise have been quite impossible. The first application of this new scientific methodology was the Detroit Metropolitan Area transportation study of 1955, developed further in the Chicago study of the following year. Very soon it became routine. The approach also began to suggest a new scientific and rational basis for urban planning as a whole. If transportation, why not housing, employment, retailing or public services?

Such lines of thought were encouraged further by contemporary changes in American geography which was busily reinventing itself as a spatial science. The earlier work of German locational economists (amongst them Walter Christaller, the former SS planner of Nazi-occupied Poland) was revisited and updated for the computer era. The upshot was that urban planners were no longer supposed to see cities as mere physical entities within which people lived and worked. They were interrelated and dynamic systems of activity, capable of precise understanding. This seemed to be a way of replacing the intuitive element of urban planning with something that was entirely rational and objective. Within a few years, city planners were beginning to embrace the new techniques and use them as a new way of thinking about their discipline.

## THE FAILURE OF METROPOLITAN PLANNING

A more tangible consequence of the highways programme for cities was the impetus it gave to the spatial expansion of metropolitan areas. It was now rare for suburban growth to occur within the limits of any of the older cities. This created serious problems, prompting much postwar discussion on the need for metropolitan government and planning (Scott, 1969). London's wartime plans were particularly influential. The growing fear of nuclear war after the Soviet Union exploded its first atomic bomb in 1949 strengthened the case for a decentralised metropolis. Like much else in American society at this time, however, the reaction was to be individualised rather than collective. For those who could, it provided one more reason to get away from the cities. The growth of the suburbs was, of course, subject to the idiosyncrasies of local zoning controls in the new mosaic of suburban cities around the older city cores, but owed little to wider planning visions. As we will see in the next chapter, the only place in North America where effective mechanisms to undertake metropolitan planning were adopted was Canada.

## LEVITTOWN AS A PLANNED COMMUNITY

In a piecemeal sense, some suburban developers operated on a scale that conferred some wider planning interest on their operations. We have already mentioned the Kaiser community homes and there were a number of other early postwar schemes aimed at war veterans. By far the most important was William J Levitt and Sons' vast development, from 1947, of 17,400 inexpensive houses for about 82,000 residents at Hempstead, Long Island, in New York State (KT Jackson, 1985; Hise, 1995). Levittown, as it was called, depended heavily on federal financial support from the Federal Housing Administration and the Veterans Administration. In all promotional material it was styled as 'a garden community', and certainly owed some allegiance to the garden city concept. Densities were low with large gardens and many community facilities. Factories nearby provided local employment, the need for which was well understood. (Landia, an unfulfilled Levitt community proposed in 1951, also on Long Island, would have gone further by integrating industrial development into the overall project.) The two other Levittowns that were soon developed in Pennsylvania and New Jersey, close to Philadelphia, showed a similar awareness of local employment opportunities.

## THE SHOPPING MALL

The creation of planned environments through market mechanisms, rather than purposive action by public agencies, can be seen as the hallmark of American planning in the 1950s. Perhaps the most outstanding example of this was the shopping mall (Scott, 1969; Gruen and Smith, 1960; Garvin, 1996). As the world's first mass-consumer society, the United States had already taken the lead in retailing innovation during the 20th century. Yet, until 1946, there were only eight purpose-built shopping centres in the entire United States that followed the model of the Country Club Plaza in Kansas City (KT Jackson, 1985). The absence of war damage and, even more, of rationing, allowed consumerism in America to race far ahead of that in Europe in the early postwar years. Combined with the wider trends of motorisation and suburban-isation this triggered a rapid growth of large suburban shopping malls, planned in the early postwar years.

Several examples opened almost simultaneously (Gruen and Smith, 1960). The earliest, both from 1949, were probably those at Raleigh, North Carolina, and Memphis, Tennessee. In terms of planning innovation, however, Shoppers' World at

**Figure 6.8** *Levittown was a large-scale suburban community planned and built by the Levitt building company for war veterans, newly able to buy their homes with federal assistance. Though few would readily concede the point, it was, in many ways, the world's first private garden city.*

Framingham near Boston hold greater interest. Slightly earlier than the first completed European examples, this had an internal pedestrian area fully segregated from surrounding car parks and delivery areas. On the other side of the continent another early example, Northgate Mall, was opened in 1950 on a greenfield site in suburban Seattle.

## VICTOR GRUEN AND RETAIL PLANNING

Apart from some limited canopy shelter, the general circulation space of these early malls remained open to the elements. The next key development came in 1956 with the opening of the world's first fully enclosed, air-conditioned mall: Southdale in Edina, a suburb of Minneapolis (Gruen and Smith, 1960; Garvin, 1996). This had special advantages in a climate such as Minnesota's, which combined hard winters and uncomfortably hot summers. Although in the short term the circulation areas of most malls remained unenclosed, Southdale was a model that was borrowed throughout the

*Figure 6.9* *Developers also generated another influential American planning innovation, the shopping mall. During the early 1950s, rapidly growing numbers of these suburban malls, surrounded by great prairies of car parking, appeared throughout the nation. This example is in San Francisco.*

world, especially the Anglophone world, in the 1960s. Its designer, Victor Gruen, was an Austrian Jew who had fled Nazism in the 1930s. Like many other émigrés he became an American, though without ever losing his awareness of European developments. He kept a close eye on retail planning innovations in Rotterdam, Coventry and the new towns of London and Stockholm. It was, in part, this awareness that, within a few years, led him to advocate the building of malls in American downtown areas as a means of combating decline. In the later 1950s, however, his reputation was built on the perfection of the suburban mall which did so much to drain vitality from the downtowns. By 1960 he was firmly established as the leading planner of shopping malls in the United States and was beginning to have a great international influence.

## AMERICAN PLANNING IN ITS INTERNATIONAL CONTEXT

More generally, the years after 1945 saw American planning become less an importer, and more an exporter, of ideas about how cities should develop (cf Rodgers, 1998). Interest abroad did not grow from any belief in the superiority of American planning. It derived more from a perception of the United States as the world's most advanced country, able – whether through wartime collective action or the dynamics of the market – to generate new approaches to urban life. Although never a planning model to follow slavishly, it seemed now to be setting trends that would eventually affect the whole of the western world. In large measure, the growing introspection of American planning drew on these perceptions. Across the social spectrum, the majority of Americans were well aware that they enjoyed material comforts greater than those of their social equivalents anywhere else in the world. In almost every field of activity, American life seemed to most Americans to be superior to the alternatives. In the 1950s, moreover, these benefits appeared to flow from the free enterprise system rather than from public policy. This perception was reinforced because the only real threat to the American way of life came from the Soviet Union, the epitome of state power and antithesis of all things American.

Though American planners remained more outward-looking and more sceptical about the impact of unregulated free enterprise than the majority of their fellow citizens, they were not immune to these dominant attitudes. The xenophobic anti-Communist campaign led by Senator Joseph McCarthy in the early 1950s marginalised the champions of New Deal and wartime collectivism. The prevalent mood became much less conducive to receiving external ideas than it had been in the 1930s. Thus when a leading British planner, Gordon Stephenson, tried to take up a professorial post at the Massachusetts Institute of Technology in 1955, he was blocked by United States Immigration on the grounds of supposed former Communist sympathies (G Stephenson, 1992). Meanwhile a prewar émigré, Hans Blumenfeld, whose Communist sympathies had been genuine, now found his career blocked for political reasons despite much support from his fellow planners (Blumenfeld, 1987). Both Stephenson and Blumenfeld moved to the more welcoming atmosphere of Canada in 1955. Should there have been any doubt, these incidents gave further confirmation that the era of American deference to European progressive thought was definitely over.

## Interim Conclusions

Overall, therefore, the war and early postwar years brought dramatic changes to the relative standing of the main western urban planning traditions. Following its defeat, Germany saw its significance as an international planning model, already damaged by the impact of Nazism but at least treated with some respect, decline dramatically. Conversely the United States, which emerged much stronger from the war, saw the salience of its prewar ideas about cities enhanced. Yet, as we have seen, it soon tired of the collectivism of the Roosevelt era and left urban development to market processes. Nor did the United States have to face the huge task of urban reconstruction that affected Europe. In European eyes, therefore, the new and unchallenged leader of the west never quite fulfilled its promise as an innovative leader in urban planning.

French reconstruction planning meanwhile attracted some interest but, because Paris was spared (and perhaps because Le Corbusier was denied a major role), international interest was limited. However, as the concerns of modernisation started to dominate in the 1950s, the international salience of French planning efforts began gradually to increase, though their full impact only became evident during the following decade. It therefore fell to Britain, undefeated though economically exhausted by war, to stand pre-eminent amongst the major traditions as an international source of urban planning lessons in the 1940s and 1950s. To concentrate solely on these four countries is, however, more misleading than it was to do so earlier in the century. There were now other important lessons being drawn from several other European countries. It is to these that we now turn.

# CHAPTER 7

# RECONSTRUCTION AND MODERNISATION II: THE OTHER TRADITIONS

In Chapter 5, we saw how several countries other than those which spawned the major traditions of western planning were gaining significant international reputations in the 1930s. The Second World War gave even greater prominence to their planning experiences. In part, this was because some of them suffered very serious destruction that allowed planners a larger role than had ever previously been possible. As never before, it focused world attention upon their rebuilding efforts. This was certainly true of the Netherlands. Yet direct involvement in the war itself was not essential. Thus Sweden, the other great urban planning model of this period, attracted interest in large part because it was able to implement the planned vision of urban modernity more rapidly than its war-torn neighbours.

Apart from elsewhere in Scandinavia, where Denmark and Finland began to make important contributions, other European countries remained (or, in the case of Italy, reverted to being) more derivative in their planning traditions, borrowing more or less selectively from more innovatory countries. Once again, some of these hold particular interest as exemplars of lesson-drawing patterns at this time, in some cases (such as Belgium) confirming the salience of emergent as well as traditional models. Even more unusual was fascist Spain, where reconstruction after its own civil war took a path that was, at first, in the 1940s, unique in western Europe but had shifted towards the mainstream by 1960.

Outside Europe, Japan was very seriously damaged by the war. Like Germany, it suffered the ignominy of being occupied by its conquerors, in its case the United States. This had a major impact on the general character of postwar reconstruction. As in Europe, the American administration gave far less priority to urban planning than to economic and political reconstruction. Meanwhile, Australia and Canada embraced urban planning ideas more firmly than ever before. To varying degrees, their historic associations with Britain remained important. Now, though, these were leavened by increasingly confident and diverse lesson-drawing from other planning traditions. Amongst these was the emergent Dutch planning tradition, whose reconstruction efforts soon brought international admiration.

## THE NETHERLANDS

Like France, the Netherlands experienced destruction in several phases of the war (ISMRH, 1947). Apart from serious flooding and widespread transport dislocation produced by acts of war, many towns and cities experienced destruction, the result of bombing by both sides, land fighting and deliberate demolition by the retreating Germans. Worst affected of the bigger centres were Rotterdam, the Hague, Arnhem,

Nijmegen and Groningen. Like Paris, the city of Amsterdam (though not its port) escaped serious damage. In May 1940, however, Rotterdam became the first large western city to be heavily bombed. A 260-hectare tract encompassing the entire city centre and much adjoining housing was almost completely destroyed. This, combined with the effects of later Allied raids and German sabotage of the port, meant that in 1945 it was one of Europe's most seriously damaged cities. Yet, within a few years, it also became one of the most internationally celebrated western examples of recon-struction planning, much visited and extensively reported (eg Lock, 1947). The key reason for this was that no other city anywhere was quite so thorough or rapid in its acceptance of modernist principles in both planning and architecture. This approach reflected an important continuity with immediate prewar trends when Rotterdam had become the Dutch leader in architectural matters (Molema, 1996).

## DUTCH RECONSTRUCTION PLANNING TO 1945

Dutch planning had, of course, advanced rapidly in international estimation between the wars. By 1939 it showed a technical and conceptual sophistication that was comparable with the latest practice and thought elsewhere. The circumstances of the Second World War ensured that this momentum continued. Reconstruction planning began almost immediately, in 1940, so proposals were very advanced by 1945. As in France, these efforts were partly encouraged by the German occupation administra-tion. Shortly before the Netherlands fell the Dutch government had formed a recon-struction agency, led by JA Ringers (A Faludi and van der Valk, 1994; Wagenaar, 1993). This was retained by the Germans and in 1941 Ringers created a national planning authority. Through this, the Nazis hoped to reconcile the Dutch to German dominance. For their part, Dutch planners tried to use the resultant scope for a measure of autonomy to develop their own agendas. As in Vichy France, this gave an ambivalent quality to reconstruction efforts during the occupation (JE Bosma, 1990). Thus the virtually identical rebuilding of the historic town of Middelburg satisfied both German desires to shift the Dutch away from an outward-looking attitude, sympathetic to Anglo-American planning ideas, and Dutch wishes to assert their own threatened national traditions.

## RECONSTRUCTION PLANNING IN ROTTERDAM

Such compromises did not, however, occur in Rotterdam where national and local planners shaped a far-reaching reconstruction agenda (Wagenaar, 1993; van der Wal, 1997). Much urban planning activity took place behind closed doors, to minimise the opportunities for German interference (Lock, 1947). Working at high speed, the city's planning director, Willem Witteveen, in 1941 produced very ambitious proposals to remodel the bombed area. Remarkably, however, these were quickly judged to be too cautious by fellow planners, architects and business interests in the city. Alternative proposals proposed the adoption of a variant of the neighbourhood unit concept, or favoured different design treatments of key parts of the city. The resulting dialectics occurred against a background of growing German suspicions about Dutch loyalties.

Ringers, the key central-government figure, was imprisoned without charge in 1943. The last war years saw the gestation of more far-reaching local proposals which extended modernist principles to the whole city. Witteveen himself, worn out by overwork, was replaced in early 1944 by his former deputy, C van Traa. It was the latter who, amidst continuing counterproposals, brought to fruition the 1946 basic plan which set out the main principles on which Rotterdam's actual reconstruction was based.

## SPECIFIC INNOVATIONS IN ROTTERDAM

Apart from the sheer scale of the reconstruction and the uncompromising modernism of the architecture, several individual aspects of the new Rotterdam drew international interest. The social planning approach, for example, favoured neighbourhoods of up to 20,000 population, appreciably larger than contemporary Anglo-American norms (Lock, 1947). The Rotterdam wartime calculations reflected certain distinctive features of Dutch society, yet the result proved more universally realistic as a physical framework for intra-urban social planning than the 10,000-population neighbourhood units being adopted in early postwar Britain. Much the most significant individual innovation was the Lijnbaan pedestrianised shopping area, planned from 1947 and built from 1951 (Taverne, 1990). Though quite modest in scale, it was the first purpose-built central-area shopping precinct in the world, slightly predating the larger schemes at Coventry and Stevenage. Already, in Amsterdam, an incremental pedestrianisation of the historic Kalverstraat was under way, noted with approval by some international observers including Gordon Stephenson and Clarence Stein (G Stephenson, 1992; KC Parsons (ed), 1998). As this suggests, Dutch urban planning efforts other than those in Rotterdam attracted foreign visitors during the reconstruction period. None, though, rivalled Rotterdam as an exemplar and it was also widely reported at international conferences.

## NATIONAL PHYSICAL PLANNING

The other internationally significant development emanating from the early postwar Netherlands concerned national physical planning (van der Heiden, 1988; A Faludi and van der Valk, 1994). The Dutch were certainly not the first to promote the idea of national planning. They were, of course, able to draw on a strong indigenous tradition of national territorial management associated with water control and the reclamation of the polders. Yet the uniqueness of this tradition meant it did not readily provide more transferable lessons. As Dutch planners noted the examples of the United States during the New Deal, and Nazi Germany in the later 1930s, they began to recognise a wider basis for national physical planning. In the event, the Dutch national planning agency, created during the occupation in 1941, was directly shaped by Nazi German models. Its ideologically tainted parentage was not readily forgiven by many urban planners and politicians after 1945. By the 1950s, however, the Netherlands was being admired internationally for its success in translating a totalitarian command model of national planning into something more suitable for a democratic state.

**Figure 7.1** *The Kalverstraat in Amsterdam was one of the world's first major shopping streets to be largely given over to pedestrians, on the pattern soon to be widely adopted in Germany.*

## PLANNING RANDSTAD

The main meeting point of national and urban planning in the 1950s arose in connection with the spatial concept of Randstad (ring city). The term refers to the functionally related horseshoe of urban settlements, including Utrecht, Amsterdam, Haarlem, Leiden, the Hague, Delft, Rotterdam and Dordrecht, in the three provinces of Noord-Holland, Zuid-Holland and Utrecht. The concept, and term, first appeared in about 1930, apparently coined by a future head of the KLM airline (MHPPN, 1970). At the time, however, few recognised how closely interrelated this whole urban region was beginning to become. As the Netherlands emerged from the privations of war, the potential relevance of this concept became plainer. Unexpectedly rapid population growth intensified a massive housing shortage that would require a doubling of the built-up area of the Netherlands (van der Cammen, 1988). It was clear that much of the impact would fall on the west of the country, around the main urban areas. In 1951 the Westen des Lands committee was formed, bringing national and provincial planners together with city representatives (Berkelbach, 1997). A technical group

*Figure 7.2  Much better known throughout the world was the Lijnbaan in Rotterdam, usually regarded as the world's first purpose built pedestrianised shopping precinct. Despite its position, however, it never became the dominant focus of central shopping activity.*

undertook extensive analytical work. It was led by Jacobus Thijisse and included several well-known Dutch planners, among whom was Theo van Lohuizen, a veteran of the 1934 Amsterdam plan.

The group drew on the strong analytical traditions Dutch planning had developed between the wars. The prewar and wartime German influences were also there (but not, of course, mentioned). A more acceptable and very potent postwar exemplar was the approach to metropolitan-regional planning evident in the Greater London plan of 1944 (van der Heiden, 1988). In the Netherlands, this approach was applied to a much wider area which lacked an obvious primate city and had a lower population, of not quite four million in 1955. The final spatial outcome, unveiled in 1958, was quite different from the London model, of course, with a protected green heart of country-side within the urban ring, rather than a surrounding green belt (Berkelbach, 1997). However, several new-town locations were proposed including Zoetermeer, Almere and Lelystad (though these names had not yet appeared). The important link with the Abercrombie London plan was the notion of conceptualising a large functional urban planning region that transcended local boundaries. The novelty lay in using this to challenge conventional ideas of what was a metropolitan area.

## DUTCH PLANNING IN ITS INTERNATIONAL CONTEXT

Postwar Dutch planning had therefore continued the late 1930s trend of finding its most fruitful international connections within the Anglo-American world. Key American planning figures such as Lewis Mumford and Clarence Stein heaped praise on Dutch efforts in the early postwar years (Mumford, 1961; Parsons (ed), 1998). For their part, the Dutch were also inspired by aspects of planning in the United States. The principal planner of the Lijnbaan, for example, inspected the latest aspects of American shop design and layout in 1948 (Taverne, 1990). He sought to incorporate them into a plan that, outwardly at least, differed markedly from American trends in retail planning. The links with British planning were also close and even more of a two-way traffic, as we have seen (Lock, 1947; van der Heiden, 1988). There were also links with other European countries that were acquiring a more Anglo-American outlook. Sweden, for example, gave important assistance with emergency housing (ISMRH, 1947).

However, other, more traditional, linkages were now much weaker. Germany was completely unacceptable as a reference point – though the feeling was not mutual, and planners in cities such as Hamburg were quite open in their admiration of Rotterdam by the mid-1950s (BFHH, 1958). The prewar modernist network continued to be significant, with van Eesteren remaining a central figure in CIAM in the early postwar years (Mumford, 2000). This gave Dutch planners contacts with French developments, though it became less effective in promoting other connections. Finally, we should note that Dutch planning experienced varying fortunes outside the European and North American worlds. Thus the very acrimonious end of Dutch colonialism in the East Indies meant that, for two decades, it had no significant planning influence in newly independent Indonesia (van der Heiden, 1988). However, certain other new states, most prominently Israel, began to draw lessons from the Dutch approach to national physical planning.

# SWEDEN AND THE NORDIC COUNTRIES

For most western planners, Swedish social democracy became a potent model for urban reconstruction in the early postwar period (P Hall, 1998). This was rather odd because Sweden had remained neutral and therefore sustained no war damage. Yet, in a curious way, its neutrality actually heightened its importance. The fact that it suffered less wartime disruption than other nations gave greater continuity to the planning initiatives that had already begun to attract international admiration in the late 1930s. In relative terms, there was far more wartime house-building in Sweden than amongst its war-affected neighbours. When the war ended important housing and community developments were actually under construction or work could start on them immediately. Even more importantly, the critical investment decisions to make the Stockholm *tunnelbana* subway into a city-wide system were made in 1941 and work began in 1944. As a result Sweden, and especially its capital, had a lead of at least two or three years on most other European countries.

## ANGLO-AMERICAN ADMIRATION OF SWEDISH PLANNING

Sweden became an obvious destination for delegations of foreign planners and architects in the early postwar years (Y Larsson, 1964; K Åström, 1967). It especially influenced Anglo-American planners, who found there tangible expressions of many of their own aspirations. There was a definite narcissistic element in some of the interest in Sweden. In particular, the neighbourhood planning work of American innovators of the interwar years, such as Clarence Perry, Clarence Stein and Henry Wright, became well known in Sweden in the 1940s (Parsons, 1992a). Particularly important in establishing these connections was Lewis Mumford's book, *The Culture of Cities*, which appeared in Swedish in 1942 (T Hall, 1991a). Published by the Swedish co-operative society, it enjoyed a very wide circulation. Shortly afterwards, Abercrombie and Forshaw's *County of London Plan* (1943) became available in Sweden. Their adoption of the neighbourhood unit concept was also particularly influential. (It was, almost certainly, through neutral Stockholm that German intelligence services obtained this and other British wartime plans.) In 1945 the Stockholm town planning committee published an influential review of English community planning

## SWEDISH ADOPTION OF THE NEIGHBOURHOOD UNIT

This inrush of ideas found almost immediate expression in the new centres for the residential areas then being developed in south Stockholm (Andersson, 1998). Instead of providing local shopping on the ground floors of residential blocks, as had been the practice previously, shops were now to be grouped together, with other community facilities, preferably arranged in a traffic-free precinct. Much the most influential example of this formula was at Årsta, planned by the modernist Uno Åhrén from 1943 (T Hall, 1991a). Developed by the cooperative housing company which Åhrén directed, it combined strikingly modern architecture with an exceptional level of community facilities which included a library, theatre, study rooms and cinema as well as shopping. It became the prototype Swedish neighbourhood unit, a model for much that followed. Yet it was also, to some extent, a cautionary lesson because the scale of community provision was too great, given that the much better facilities in the city centre were also readily accessible to Årsta's residents.

## EARLY HOUSING DEVELOPMENTS

It was not just timing that made these Swedish examples so impressive. They also, for the first time, integrated Anglo-American community planning aspirations, represented by the neighbourhood unit, with functional design principles (K Åström, 1967). At about the same time as Årsta was being built, other projects were elaborating on the ideals of interwar modernism, especially in housing design (Holm, 1957; T Hall, 1991a). A particularly distinctive Swedish residential form that appeared at this time was the *punkthus* (literally 'point house' or more usually, in a term which soon became widely used by British housing architects and planners, 'point block'). The *punkthus* differed from 1930s French and Dutch high-rise flats by being entirely freestanding. In the Swedish context, it had the great advantage of having a small 'footprint' so that it could be used on rugged terrain more readily than larger horizontal housing forms. Two very influential examples of this type were at Danviksklippan in Stockholm and Guldhelden in Göteburg, both completed in about 1945 (K Åström, 1967; Göteborg, 1960).

At almost exactly the same time another new form, the star block, made its appearance at Gröndal in Stockholm (Holm, 1957; Andersson, 1998). These blocks (initially of three and four storeys) had three wings, each with one apartment per level, radiating from a central stairwell. The main attraction of this arrangement lay in the daylighting advantages, always a major consideration in these northern latitudes. Each apartment could have windows on three sides. Where the terrain permitted, the star formations could be linked together in a flexible fashion to create continuous but varied structures which resembled a partial honeycomb. These offered many possibilities for site planning to create partially enclosed external spaces adjoining the buildings. Gröndal was also the test site for this more ambitious use of the star block, though the most famous early use was at Rosta in Örebro, completed in 1952.

## SWEDISH URBAN GROWTH

These innovations in the field of housing and community development were part of a larger shift. To some extent it reflected the growing political and cultural hegemony of Swedish social democracy. A further aspect of the Swedish planning model at this time concerned the approach to planning the city as a whole (Tonell, 1997). This needs to be understood in the context of the onset of rapid urbanisation in Sweden from the 1940s (Holm, 1957; T Hall, 1991a). By 1956, approximately two-thirds of the population lived in urban areas, though fewer than 30 per cent lived in places with more than 30,000 people. Yet it was the growth of these larger centres that was especially marked. Metropolitan Stockholm, with just over a million population in 1950, was growing at a very rapid rate. It had added 130,000 between 1942 and 1947 alone. Such were the fears of homelessness that in 1946 the city had launched a nationwide advertising campaign to discourage migration (Vlassenrood, 1997). It was recognised, however, that this could only be a short-term measure. The 1950s, in fact, brought a further 16 per cent growth, taking metropolitan Stockholm to 1.162 million in 1960. The priority therefore was to plan for growth.

## THE 1952 STOCKHOLM PLAN

In 1944, a small team led by Sven Markelius and Göran Sidenbladh (Vlassenrood, 1997; P Hall, 1998) began work on a metropolitan plan for Stockholm. Preliminary principles appeared the following year, outlining proposals for satellite neighbourhood communities, each with a population of about 10,000 to 15,000. Around a *tunnelbana* station, there was to be a *centrum* with shopping and other community facilities. Surrounding this there would be a ring of high-rise residential development, itself then surrounded by a further ring of terraced and detached housing. These residential areas would contain some local community facilities. At a higher level, these neighbourhoods would be combined into larger groupings. One neighbourhood centre in the group would therefore provide better shopping and services. There would also be industrial areas and other sources of employment, largely associated with the bigger centre. Throughout there was to be extensive separation of vehicle and pedestrian movements, on Radburn lines. Radburn's planner, Clarence Stein, was nothing short of ecstatic about what he found when he first visited Stockholm in 1949. He returned several times in the 1950s and became a close friend of Markelius (Parsons, 1992a).

By then, work on the plan was substantially complete. The overall form had been strongly influenced by the 1947 'finger' plan for Copenhagen (to be discussed shortly) and Markelius and his team soon borrowed this same terminology. The *tunnelbana* routes were to provide the principal rationale for the 'fingers', with urban development clustered around stations. In fact, the plan proved extremely controversial and, despite lengthy debates, was not actually accepted by the socialist-led city council. Yet they did not entirely reject it either. As a result, it appeared in print in 1952, to become a hugely important influence on the subsequent development of both the city and – even more than the Copenhagen plan that had partly inspired it – international planning thought.

## VÄLLINGBY AND SWEDISH URBAN DECENTRALISATION

A key reason why the plan was so influential was the high quality of the planned environments that actually appeared. The most impressive early realisation was the group of neighbourhoods that comprised the first satellite town, centred on Vällingby in northwest Stockholm, planned from 1949 and developed during the 1950s (Pass, 1973; Lundén, 1994; P Hall, 1998). As well as Vällingby itself, the satellite included the neighbourhood communities of Råcksta, Grimsta, Hässelby Gård, Hässelby Strand and Blackeberg. Together they had a population of about 60,000 by the mid-1960s. Development closely followed the principles outlined in the 1945 report. All the

**Figure 7.3** *Vällingby was the first and remains the finest of Stockholm's satellite towns, a lasting monument to a golden age of Swedish social democracy.*

communities with the exception of Grimsta were centred on *tunnelbana* stations. Each had its own shopping centre adjoining the station. This was surrounded by residential areas with densities declining further from the centre.

Vällingby itself was the principal centre, intended as the main focus of employment for the whole cluster. In the terminology of the 1952 plan, it was the ABC community, signifying *arbete* (work), *böstader* (dwelling) and *centrum* (centre). The intention was also that, like the British new towns, there would be a very high degree of local employment in the satellites. In this respect, however, they failed, perhaps because they were so close to, and well connected with, the city centre in comparison with London new towns such as Stevenage, Crawley or Harlow. Despite energetic efforts, by 1960 Vällingby had 25,000 workers but only 9,000 jobs, of which only half were filled by local residents. Yet this too became an important international lesson drawn from Vällingby. For planners in many countries, it began to suggest that the British solution of self-contained new towns was, if not unique, certainly extraordinarily difficult to replicate elsewhere.

Vällingby itself set a model for subsequent development in the Swedish capital and, increasingly, elsewhere. Its counterpart in south Stockholm was Farsta. Capacity problems on the *tunnelbana* delayed development, which did not finally begin until 1953 when Vällingby was well advanced. Accordingly, much learning from the earlier satellite was apparent. The *centrum* was planned differently, with more attention to car parking and delivery arrangements. The housing mix was also different, with more houses for single families, although more flats were provided in high blocks. Other Swedish cities, for the moment at least, did not plan satellites that were much more than residential dormitories. Sweden's provincial cities remained relatively small, so it was easier to retain a stronger connection with the main city centre, but many maintained very high design standards. Kortedala and Biskopsgården in Göteborg, for example, were striking examples of this approach (Göteborg, 1960; T Hall, 1991a).

## SWEDISH LAND USE PLANNING

Other aspects of Swedish planning during the 1940s and 1950s held international significance, albeit for different reasons. The more general evolution of statutory physical and land use planning in Sweden under its 1947 legislation, was, in some respects, a story of failure (T Hall, 1991a; T Hall, Ponzio and Tonell, 1994). As in Stockholm, there was very widespread political reluctance to approve the general plans that were supposed to provide a formal framework for urban development. The reluctance grew from the fear of inflexibility yet, as in Stockholm, this did not stop the plans having an important informal role. Their preparation also brought a growth in master-planning skills. The key figure in this process was the Hungarian-Jewish émigré Fred Forbat. He reminds us that Swedish planning, despite its active postwar engagement with the Anglo-American world, retained still important connections with central European planning traditions. Forbat was a former associate of Walter Gropius in Weimar Germany and of Ernst May in the Soviet Union (Blau and Platzer (eds), 1999). He fled the anti-Semitism of his homeland to settle permanently in Sweden in 1938. His 1949 general plan for Skövde, through its analytical and evaluative approach, became a model for urban master planning throughout Sweden.

## CENTRAL AREA RENEWAL

Planners of bombed cities in other parts of Europe also looked to Sweden, and specifically Stockholm, for another reason, namely the bold approach that was being adopted to redeveloping the central part of the city. To an extent as yet unknown in other cities that had not been bombed, in 1945 Stockholm city council decided to embark on the complete remodelling of a key part of the central area, to create a new commercial district (T Hall, 1979). The building of the *tunnelbana* delayed work but from 1952 a dramatically modernist environment, showing some clear transatlantic references (Tonell, 1997), began to be created at Hötorgscity (Andersson, 1998). A line of five 18-storey office towers rose from a two-storey, largely pedestrianised deck, with shops and restaurants underneath accessible from a large street-level pedestrian precinct. Deliveries were entirely underground.

There were some rumbles of popular opposition to this breathtakingly radical transformation, which depended on the almost complete demolition of existing buildings. Yet such was the extent of political consensus that it was not even necessary to put the plan for the Hötorgscity to a vote of the city council. In view of the extensive battles still being fought in many cities about radical replanning, even where large areas had already been laid waste by bombs, this consensus for comprehensive planned modernisation was remarkable indeed. It is easy to see why in the 1950s urban planners everywhere looked on with envy at what their Swedish counterparts were able, democratically but without apparent struggle, to achieve.

## DENMARK

No other part of Scandinavia was able to remain neutral. Denmark was invaded by Germany in 1940, but avoided direct German administration until 1943. It also experienced very little serious war damage, except on the Baltic island of Bornholm (Hiort, 1952). Danish planners, already well informed about and enthused by British planning thought and practice before 1939, shared their Swedish neighbours' growing engagement with Anglo-American developments (B Larsson and Thomassen, 1991). The 1942 Swedish translation of Mumford's *The Culture of Cities* was read by many Danish planners during the war. It seems likely that they were also aware, via Sweden, of the key wartime developments in British planning. Much of this interest remained at an abstract level, however. In typical Scandinavian fashion there had been extensive municipal land acquisition around Copenhagen, giving the city a mechanism to shape some aspects of urban development (Graham, 1940). But Denmark had no formal planning powers until 1938. Naturally very little had been achieved by the time war broke out, particularly outside the capital.

*Figure 7.4 Hötorgscity in central Stockholm took shape during the 1950s. It was for many years an international model of planned urban reconstruction, all the more remarkable because there had been no bombing to give a pretext for such a radical transformation.*

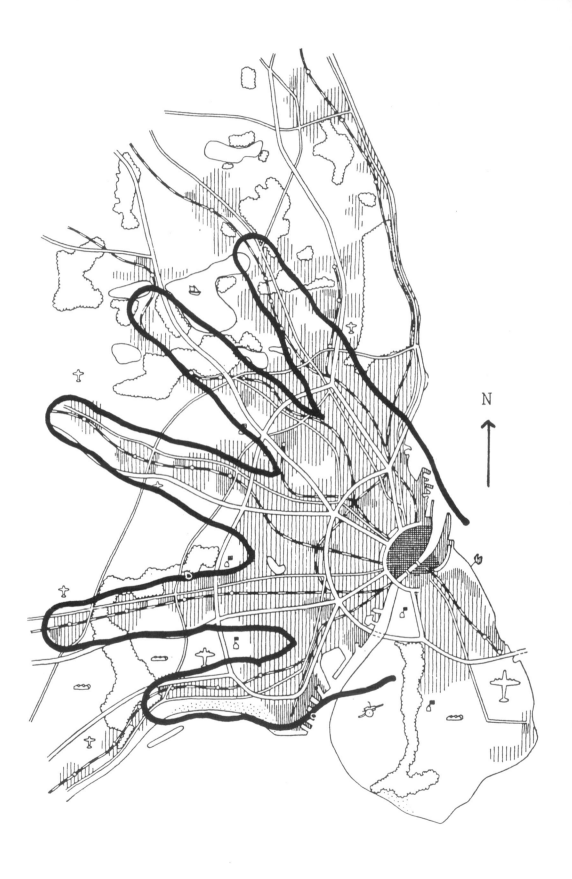

N

## THE COPENHAGEN 'FINGER' PLAN

The main aspect of postwar Danish planning that attracted international attention was the 1947 'finger plan' for Greater Copenhagen, already mentioned as an influence on Stockholm (Knudsen, 1988; B Larsson and Thomassen, 1991; Lemberg, 1997). It was led by the architect planners Steen Eiler Rasmussen, who attended to political matters, and Peter Bredsdorff, who actually led the planning team. Both were great enthusiasts of the ideas of Mumford, Unwin and Abercrombie. Their plan called for fingers of urban development along rail routes, separated by clearly articulated green wedges. The use of the finger analogy idea proved very easy to understand and helped ensure a sympathetic reception. The real problem was that the implementation of the plan depended on persuading authorities outside the city itself to act on its proposals.

There was a sharp contrast here with Stockholm, where the fingers lay within the city giving a very direct control of implementation. The clarity of the green wedges therefore became seriously compromised, especially in the north. Moreover, Copenhagen could boast nothing so impressive as Vällingby or Farsta. Some good-quality housing was built in the early postwar years, for example at Voldparken and Fortunbyen (Hiort, 1952). Much of it was low rise and rather more traditional in design and construction than in Sweden. However, high-rise industrialised building appeared from 1950, at Bellahøj, though it never became very common.

## NORWAY

Norway experienced the worst war damage of any Scandinavian country (Lorange and Myrhe, 1991; Jensen, 1997). Several smaller towns in the north suffered substantial destruction and there was significant damage in Bergen. Yet, perhaps because Oslo was unaffected, none of this prompted anything remotely as influential as contemporary Swedish or Danish innovations. Like its neighbours, Norway showed a growing engagement with Anglo-American planning thought. A distinctive feature was, however, the Norwegian interest in the Tennessee Valley Authority as a model for reconstruction in some of its remoter areas, particularly Finnmark and Troms. Metropolitan planning in London and in the other Scandinavian countries also served as influences on the planning of Norway's capital. Several planned satellite communities, mainly in flatted form and with their own shopping facilities and services, appeared. The first, planned for 10,000 inhabitants in 1950, was to the southeast of Oslo, at Lambertseter.

## FINLAND

Finland's wartime experience was, in several respects, very different to that of its neighbours (Klinge and Kolbe, 1999). Its war was against Soviet invasion, in which it

**Figure 7.5** *The famous 1947 finger plan for Copenhagen provided an important alternative model for spatial development to the containment/decentralist model of Greater London. With Stockholm's later plan, it was widely studied.*

was supported only by Germany. This meant it ended up on the losing side and experienced a sudden influx of refugees from former national territory now ceded to the Soviet Union. Yet Finland retained much sympathy in the west, especially as tension with the Soviet bloc increased. As regards the postwar state of the country, the ineffectiveness of Soviet bombing had left historic Helsinki little damaged. As in Norway, it was the remoter rural areas that were worst affected (Sundman, 1991). The most profound effect of the war was, however, on Finland's national outlook: it eclipsed the country's cultural conservatism and deference to Germany. There was the familiar postwar borrowing from Anglo-American planning thought, yet this was combined with a belated (but truly splendid) flowering of modernist design (Becker and Schlote, 1964). The works of Mumford, and Abercrombie's London plans, became well known in the first years of peace. Finland's premier modernist architect and planner, Alvar Aalto, also developed strong links with the United States, whence he borrowed ideas about regional and rural reconstruction.

## TAPIOLA GARDEN CITY

The example of early postwar Finnish planning that most successfully brought together these influences to win great international admiration was Tapiola garden city, immediately to the west of Helsinki (von Hertzen and Speiregen, 1973; Aario, 1986; ECFJS, 1997)). The main driving force in its development was Heikki von Hertzen, a lawyer and garden city enthusiast, whose fluency in English did much to establish its international reputation. Tapiola was planned in the late 1940s for about 12,000 inhabitants, and was intended to be a self-contained community with shopping, services and employment. Despite a large measure of success in this respect, the reality was that, like Stockholm's satellites, it functioned more as an integrated part of a wider metropolitan whole. There were changes, too, in the favoured residential forms. The first plan (1946), prepared by Otto Meurman (who had worked with Saarinen on the influential 1915 plan for Munkkiniemi), envisaged individual houses with gardens. In the event, construction economies required a reliance on apartment blocks carefully placed to reflect topography. Overall densities remained low, reflecting the extensive forest and parkland settings, the whole becoming a distinctive new interpretation of the garden city.

## OTHER PARTS OF EUROPE

### BELGIUM

Finland can be seen as a country that claimed international attention in the postwar west partly against the odds. Belgium, by contrast, was a country at the very heart of western Europe, which was all but invisible as an international source of planning lessons. Despite its brief moment of prominence during the First World War, post-1945 Belgian reconstruction failed to develop features of international significance. In part, this might have been because it was the only combatant nation where urban destruction was *less* extensive than in 1914–18. Yet reconstruction efforts began in earnest in 1940, under the decree promulgated immediately after the German occupation (Uyttenhove, 1990a).

## RECONSTRUCTION PLANNING IN WARTIME BELGIUM

This alacrity was, in part, a reaction to memories of the inertia that had pervaded the early reconstruction. It also reflected the mature state of the national discussion about planning which, as in Britain, had been very extensively rehearsed during the later 1930s. A further factor was that the Belgian administrators felt more at ease with their occupiers than they had done in 1914–18. Quite apart from the less extensive damage to the urban fabric, the Belgian king and government remained in the country. Moreover, until 1943, Belgian administrators were granted considerable autonomy in their work, less impeded by the German occupiers than they were by the interference of politicians in peacetime. The content of their work is interesting on several counts, especially for the evidence it provides of the new ascendancy of planning ideas from the Netherlands. Thus the Dutch concept of *planologie*, signifying a rigorously analytical, social-science-based approach to planning, began to be applied with some commitment during the war years.

## BELGIAN RECONSTRUCTION AFTER 1945

The integrated approach to national and local physical planning that the wartime technocrats espoused became ideologically tainted after the liberation. In sharp contrast to French and Dutch experiences, a totally new reconstruction agency was created in 1945, staffed by quite different people. (Several of those who were removed subsequently occupied important colonial roles in urban planning during the inglorious twilight of Belgian rule in the Congo.) Combined with the impact of Marshall Aid projects and the re-establishment of market processes, these changes meant that Belgium, though it kept some affinities with Dutch planning, came to represent a rather weak planning approach (K Bosma and Hellinga, 1997a). Nevertheless, there were some important continuities and the 1940 decree provided the essential basis of the Belgian planning system until 1962.

## ITALY

Despite many unique features, Italy showed certain similarities with both Belgium and Finland. Although it had supported Germany for much of the war, by 1945 it had partly redeemed itself in western eyes by overthrowing Mussolini and allying itself to the anti-Nazi struggle. This spared it the relentless Allied air raids that preceded final defeat in Germany and Japan. Nevertheless, bombing and land fighting together brought serious destruction (Whittick (ed) 1980; Calabi, 1984). Although Rome, like Paris, emerged largely unscathed, many other Italian cities over the length of the country experienced serious damage. These included Milan, Naples, Genoa, Bologna, Leghorn, La Spezia, Reggio di Calabria and Catania. This destruction, combined with the prewar interest in modernisation, ensured that there was much urban planning activity through the war and early postwar years. As in Belgium and France, enduring planning legislation was passed during the war itself, in 1942. In the event, however, postwar Italian urban development in the 1950s and 1960s owed very little to the hand of planning.

## ITALIAN PLANNING IN THE 1940s

In fact, the planning efforts of the 1940s held some potential interest for planners elsewhere, more so perhaps than did the later opportunism. A particularly important feature was the strength of modernist thinking, even under the Fascists. A 1942 plan for four satellite towns around Milan, for example, clearly showed the influence of CIAM thinking, as did the 'AR' plan for the whole city region produced in 1945 (Bianchetti, 1993). The same trends were apparent in many early reconstruction efforts, such as the QT8 district of Milan, planned from 1946 (Loach, 2000). These efforts, combined with the prewar admiration for aspects of Italian planning, allowed leading planners to find international outlets for their expertise during the early postwar decades. Thus Luigi Piccinato, one of the acclaimed young modernists of the Mussolini era who was now widely seen as the leading Italian planner, worked in Buenos Aires (1947) and Istanbul (from 1958). He also prepared plans for Padua (1954), Siena (1955) and Rome (1957) (Fried, 1973; Whittick (ed) 1980).

## THE DRIFT TO *LAISSEZ FAIRE*

There was, by contrast, very little international interest in the detail of Italian reconstruction planning, perhaps because it was so soon swamped by a noninterventionist political culture. In the immediate aftermath of war, the western allies (principally the United States) were anxious to prevent Italy from falling wholly or partly into Communist hands. This fate was soon averted, in part because of Marshall Aid (Ellwood, 1993). As in most other countries, the aid was more concerned with big infrastructure projects and the re-establishment of capitalism than with laying down a framework for planning. Because Italy was successfully reclaimed for western capitalism, there were none of the internal and external imperatives to encourage urban planning for the kinds of ideological reasons that were typified in Germany during the cold war era. Significantly, the most notable planning-related initiative of the postwar period, the INA-Casa housing programme introduced in 1948/9, was driven mainly by employment considerations (Pace, 1993). The architecture and planning bore some resemblance to contemporary developments in Scandinavia, though there was no explicit official endorsement of these as models.

## SPAIN

The final European example is interesting because of its initial disconnection from either of the ideological mainstreams of European reconstruction planning. The

Spanish civil war had ended in the spring of 1939 with the victory of the fascists under General Franco. It left significant destruction of many towns and cities, including the capital. The Madrid reconstruction plan which followed in 1941 (approved in 1946) was in some respects a typical fascist plan, with triumphal ways and grand central assembly spaces and buildings (M Wynn, 1984a). Yet it showed some continuity with pre-1936 plans. In its wider structure it was also reminiscent of Saarinen and Abercrombie's ideas for urban decentralisation. It was originally conceived in a context which anticipated a fascist-dominated Europe. In fact, Franco skilfully resisted being drawn into the wider conflict. From 1943, when the defeat of fascism began to appear inevitable, he also tried to reposition Spain to give a more favourable impression to the western allies. Despite this, the country was shunned by the west, excluded from the wider plans for European recovery and for some years denied material aid by the United States. This began to change in the 1950s, when the Spanish role in combating Communism began to be valued.

These shifts were faithfully reflected in the course of Spanish planning history. The 1953 Barcelona Pla Comarcal (county plan), for example, clearly showed growing awareness of other European thinking about land use planning (Ferrer, 1996a). The 1956 national legislation on land and urban planning was reportedly modelled on French, Italian and Belgian precedents (M Wynn, 1984a). Meanwhile, Spanish planners and architects were becoming more familiar with the latest fashions in contemporary international modernism, such as the 1957 Berlin Interbau (Salvadó and Miró, 1996; Ferrer, 1996b; Subias, 1996). In Barcelona, for example, the first tower blocks, still of rather singular appearance, appeared in 1952 at the Passeig Cavell. Later, and increasingly larger, schemes such as the Eucharistic Congress District (1952–62) and Besòs and Montbau (both 1960) became progressively less distinguishable from those of the international mainstream.

# JAPAN

The most severe destruction outside Europe occurred in Japan where 112 towns and cities were classified as war damaged. Even the last raids on Germany could not compare with the destructive power of the onslaught on Japan in the final months of war. In absolute terms Tokyo, in 1940 the world's second largest metropolis, was most heavily bombed (TMG, 1994). 28 per cent of the city proper was completely destroyed, including about half the housing stock, leaving about 750,000 households without shelter. In total, approximately 100,000 people were killed, three-quarters of them in a single air raid in March 1945. It was, however, the bombing of the smaller cities of Hiroshima and Nagasaki in August 1945 that moved war destruction to a new scale of horror (Allinson, 1997). These were the first, and only, cities ever to be the targets of atomic bombs. The Hiroshima bomb destroyed over two-thirds of the city's buildings, the Nagasaki bomb about one-third. These were also the only cities anywhere in the world whose destruction provided confirmation of the prevalent theory that bombing civilian populations would undermine the will to fight.

Like Germany, Japan entered the postwar world defeated and humbled. Only the awful way in which the war had ended generated any degree of international sympathy. Unlike Germany, its occupation and early postwar development (until 1952) was exclusively under American control. This was an important difference because, as we have seen, the American concept of reconstruction did not usually accord high priority to the finer points of urban planning. Aside from punitive concerns, the United States' major intentions were economic and ideological – to make Japan, the most highly developed Asian nation, into a firm base on which the values of capitalist democracy could develop throughout the wider region. As Communism spread rapidly in east Asia in the immediate postwar years, these priorities became more important. They had major implications for the role that urban planning came to play in the postwar reconstruction of Japanese cities.

## RECONSTRUCTION PLANNING IN TOKYO

Unlike Germany, relatively little reconstruction planning took place in Japan until the very last weeks of the war. However, by the time of the country's surrender and the ensuing American occupation the process was moving quickly (Ishida, 1998; Ishimaru, 1996). In 1946 the war damage rehabilitation plan for Tokyo was issued. Overseen by Eiyo Ishikawa, a longtime proponent of planned decentralisation, it showed strong underlying garden city influences (Ishizuka and Ishida, 1988; Ito, 1988b; TMG, 1994). Many of its leading figures had been involved in the planning of Manchuria during the 1930s when the colony had been a testing ground for a bolder planning approach. The Tokyo plan was indeed bold, envisaging a permanent reduction of population in the city proper (known as the ward area) from a prewar 6.5 million to 3.5 million. A green belt, comprising a third of the ward area, would separate it from surrounding suburban areas. New satellite communities of about 100,000 inhabitants were to be developed 40 to 50 kilometres from the city. In total, some four million people would be housed in the suburban and satellite areas. It proved to be an unattainable ideal (*CPIJ Newsletter*, 1996a). Within two years, the ward area was regaining its prewar dynamism and the population raced through the planned 3.5 million ceiling. Also, the American occupation administration disapproved of such idealism in a defeated and shamed country. The huge cost of the land adjustment needed in the replanning of the ward area became a target in the 1949 austerity budget. In 1950 the area slated for readjustment was cut back to less than a quarter of that originally envisaged (Hatano, 1988).

## RECONSTRUCTION PLANNING IN OTHER CITIES

Planning thus played a far smaller role in the rebuilding of Tokyo than was envisaged. This trend was less pronounced in most other Japanese cities, some of which had been quicker off the mark before the 1949 economies. Of the biggest cities, Nagoya underwent the most extensive reordering, comparable with that of many European cities (Niitani, 1992; *CPIJ Newsletter*, 1996a). Yet it was only in Hiroshima that urban planning became a decisive force in shaping reconstruction (Ishimaru, 1998; Hein, 1998b). The terrible circumstances of the city's destruction gave great symbolic significance, understood throughout the world, to its replanning. Uniquely in Japan a competition was held, to create a space dedicated to peace at the heart of the city.

The winning design, by Kenzo Tange, the first Japanese architect to gain a global reputation, proposed a peace park, museum and wide boulevard. Tange made his proposals the subject of the first-ever Japanese presentation to CIAM, in 1951 (Mumford, 2000). Inevitably, even this plan was compromised in its implementation. Yet, although other war-damaged cities (such as Coventry and West Berlin) kept individual ruined buildings as testament to the destructive force of war, Hiroshima remained unique in the world by giving priority to such concerns.

## URBAN GROWTH AND PLANNERS IN THE 1950S

The Korean War of 1950–3 underlined for the United States the role that a thoroughly westernised Japan could, through its economic prowess, play in limiting the international spread of Communism (Allinson, 1997). The war gave a huge boost to Japanese industry and urban growth pressures were intensified as a result. Thus the population of the ward area of Tokyo grew from 5.4 million in 1950 to 8.3 million in 1960, and that of the wider metropolitan region from 12.7 million to 17.8 million (TMG, 1994). Japan's other main metropolitan areas also grew rapidly. National economic planning played an important role in shaping this growth and its broad spatial concentration. But, despite the strong hand of economic policy, the more detailed role of urban planning remained rather small, even though planners themselves were consciously trying to assert and strengthen their professional status. In 1951 Uchida Yoshikazu, who had led the innovative Manchurian planning team in the 1930s, formed the City Planning Institute of Japan with several other leading figures as a focus for professional expertise (Masser and Yorisaki, 1994). It was, though, very small with only 152 members in 1952.

## THE NATIONAL CAPITAL REGION PLAN 1958

Despite such efforts, the reality was that the 1950s repeated the 1940s tendency to formulate bold but impractical schemes for planned metropolitan development. The scale of Tokyo's growth led to the national capital region development law in 1956. Yet the national capital region plan, which followed in 1958, was ill-matched to the growth pressures (Satoh, 1988b; TMG, 1994). Although several options were considered, the selected alternative followed the 1944 Abercrombie plan for Greater London, with a green belt, suburban zone, and satellite towns. From the very outset the intended restrictions proved unpopular. In 1956, 16 municipalities in the intended green belt formed a league to oppose its formation, taking pre-emptive action with the new and powerful Japan Housing Corporation to encourage housing development (Ishizuka and Ishida, 1988; Cybriwsky, 1999). The result was that the necessary restrictions could never be implemented (and were dropped in 1965). There was more success in designating satellite towns at Machida-Sagamihara, in 1958, and Hino and Hachioji, in 1959 (Kurokawa, 1978). Even here, though, the intended co-ordination of housing and employment failed to materialise, especially so in Machida.

## AUSTRALIA

### CHANGES AND CONTINUITIES

It was not only the Japanese who discovered the limitations of uncritical reliance on imported planning models. Early postwar Australian planners continued to draw planning ideas and approaches overwhelmingly from Britain, despite a way of life that now began to diverge increasingly from the old imperial homeland (Bolton, 1996; Howe, 2000; Freestone, 1997). For one thing, Australia experienced only very limited war damage (confined to the remote northern city of Darwin). Rather like the United States, its economy was stimulated by war, ending the doldrums of the 1930s and allowing an affluent consumer society to emerge more rapidly than in Europe. In a real sense, too, Australia's strategic and economic ties with the United States were strengthened by the war. At the same time, though, postwar prosperity brought both a postwar baby boom and a resumption of immigration from Europe. The main cities grew more rapidly than ever before in the years from 1947 to 1954 with Melbourne, Adelaide and Sydney especially receiving large numbers of immigrants (Forster, 1995). Britain (and Ireland) remained an important source of new settlers but these were increasingly joined by growing numbers from other parts of Europe, especially its southern and eastern fringes.

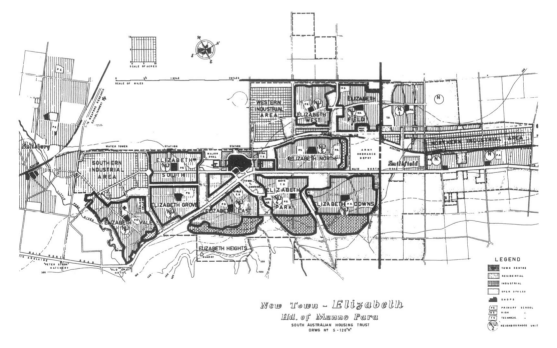

**Figure 7.6**  *The South Australian new town of Elizabeth was effectively a British new town built for new British migrants. The characteristically strong emphasis on the neighbourhood unit is very clear in this plan of the mid-1950s.*

Britain also remained the main source of planning expertise. Many Australian planners still trained in Britain and British-born planners were among the new waves of immigrants (Colman, 1993). A regular flow of eminent visitors from Britain also continued to carry the word. Once again, the idea of professionalising planning expertise was amongst the main exports. In 1951 the Australian Planning Institute was founded as a national organisation, replacing the state-based bodies formed in the 1930s and 1940s (Cherry, 1974; Wilks, 1993). Representatives of the British Town Planning Institute, George Pepler and William Holford, were present at the birth, giving guidance and encouragement. In 1955 the new body became an affiliate of the TPI, which also validated the planning schools at Sydney (1952) and Melbourne (1958). Both, significantly, were headed by recent British immigrants: Denis Winston and Fred Ledgar.

## SYDNEY METROPOLITAN PLANNING

The British influence was fully reflected in early postwar Australian planning (Alexander, 2000). The clearest example was the Cumberland County Planning Scheme, prepared for the Sydney metropolitan area (Winston, 1957; Freestone, 1989). Published in 1948 and approved in 1951, this important plan directly echoed the style and language of the Abercrombie plan for Greater London. Despite fundamental differences in both the prevailing urban conditions and the planning powers available, its proposals also leant heavily on the Abercrombie model. Crucial to the whole plan was a containing green belt, intended to stem suburban sprawl, though there was no equivalent of London's planned new towns. As in Tokyo, however, the concept of a permanent and inviolate green belt proved fatally flawed in a rapidly growing metropolitan city, where the interests favouring suburban expansion were deeply entrenched. By 1959, large-scale development in the green belt was sanctioned, marking the effective end of Sydney's containment strategy.

## MELBOURNE AND PERTH

Other notable metropolitan plans were those for Melbourne, published in 1954, and Perth (1955). Neither went quite so far as the Sydney plan in regard to urban containment. Thus they did not call for green belts, though both specified a more compact form of suburban development than, in the event, occurred. Nor were they completed as quickly as the Sydney plan, indicating greater caution about taking too rigid a planning approach at a time of very rapid growth. Despite this, both plans provided ample evidence of the British connection. The pedigree could scarcely have been mistaken in Perth where two British planners, Gordon Stephenson and Alastair Hepburn (who later played an important role in Melbourne), led the planning team (G Stephenson and Hepburn, 1955; G Stephenson, 1992). Much of the style, language and technique of their plan directly echoed the Greater London plan, in the preparation of which Stephenson had played a prominent part.

Yet both plans also revealed something of the growing Americanisation of Australian planning. Melbourne's efforts were suffused with an admiration of Los

Angeles, reinforced by a sponsored visit from that city's planner in 1953 (Freestone, 1997; McLoughlin, 1992). For its part, the Perth plan contained several American images: it admiringly presented out-of town malls, industrial parks, freeways and a Radburn-type residential environment at Greenbelt. Surprisingly, perhaps, there were no British images. (On a relevant personal note, Stephenson prepared the Perth plan during a period when he hoped to move permanently to the United States, an aspiration which, as we saw in the last chapter, was thwarted by McCarthyism. The result was that he spent longer on the Perth planning team than originally envisaged, then spent five years in Toronto before settling permanently in Perth from 1960.)

## NEW TOWNS OF THE 1950S

One factor that had prompted the Perth metropolitan plan was the development of a new town for 25,000 people at Kwinana, to the south of the continuous built-up area (Freestone, 1989; Melotte, 1993). Begun in 1952, it was to be the company town for nearby heavy industrial developments, especially a new British Petroleum oil refinery. It was, perhaps, predictable that the town would follow the latest British thinking, particularly since an Australian who had trained in Britain was given the responsibility for its planning. Not everything ran so true to type, however. The planner concerned, Margaret Feilman, was, at the remarkably young age of 31, the first woman in Australia (and probably the world) to be given professional leadership in new settlement planning.

The new town of Elizabeth, developed to service the expansion of manufacturing in metropolitan Adelaide and provide a home for large numbers of new (and overwhelmingly British) immigrants (Peel, 1995; Forster and McCaskill, 1986), was better known than Kwinana. Planned and developed by the South Australian Housing Trust (SAHT), a state public housing agency founded in 1936, Elizabeth itself was conceived in 1950 for some 25,000 inhabitants (Hutchings, 2000). This target was soon increased, however, so that it became more comparable in scale to the early new towns in Britain. In fact, its planners relied very heavily on the British example. (The town's name was, of course, that of the British and Australian royal head of state.) SAHT staff regularly visited the British new towns during the 1950s, ever eager to glean the latest thinking on neighbourhood units, shopping centres, industrial estates and much else.

There were, however, some detailed differences. The most obvious was the absence of measures to prevent the new town being surrounded by the later suburban sprawl of Adelaide. There was also the ubiquitous Australian reliance on the bungalow as the main housing form, the adoption of a smaller population size for the neighbourhood units and more private housing than in the early British new towns. But the overall result, especially when the town was peopled by many thousands of new immigrants from Britain, looked very derivative. Behind this lay an interesting paradox, in that Elizabeth's principal employer was American-owned. Still more significantly, it was also a car plant whose products in the 1950s were beginning to reach all sections of an Australian society that had never been more prosperous. In doing this, it was laying the foundations for a more motorised, and more American, suburban lifestyle, the consequences of which planners had to begin to address by the end of the decade.

# CANADA

## AMERICANISATION AND EUROPEAN IMMIGRATION

As previously, Canadian planning followed a similar, though not identical, course to that in Australia (Ward, 1997). There was no war damage and the Depression which had affected the country so badly quickly gave way to a wartime boom which was maintained after 1945 (Wolfe, 1994). However, to a far greater extent than in Australia, Canada's economic destiny became even more closely tied to that of America. By the early 1950s, for example, the United States accounted for more than three-quarters of the foreign investment in Canada (Ward, 1999). American companies controlled over half the country's mineral assets and just under half of its manufacturing. The British economic connection, supreme in Australia until the mid-1960s, declined commensurately. As in Australia, however, the large postwar influx of new immigrants (over two million from 1941 to 1961) served to bolster Canada's cultural links with Britain and other parts of Europe, particularly Germany, Italy and the Netherlands (GM Anderson and Marr, 1987).

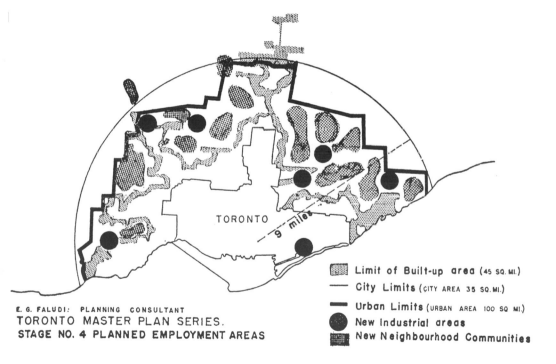

E. G. FALUDI: PLANNING CONSULTANT
**TORONTO MASTER PLAN SERIES.**
**STAGE NO. 4 PLANNED EMPLOYMENT AREAS**

Limit of Built-up area (45 SQ. MI.)
City Limits (CITY AREA 35 SQ. MI.)
Urban Limits (URBAN AREA 100 SQ MI.)
New Industrial areas
New Neighbourhood Communities

*Figure 7.7* War awoke Canada from the economic doldrums of the 1930s. This triggered a flurry of planning activity in the 1940s, including this metropolitan plan for Toronto, prepared by Eugenio Faludi.

## The Canadian planning profession

The scale of this immigration, combined with an extremely high birth rate during the early postwar years, generated great housing and urban planning needs (Wolfe, 1994; Spence-Sales, 1956; Carver, 1948). As noted in Chapter 5, these had been badly neglected in the 1930s, especially in the impoverished prairie and maritime provinces (which, from 1949, included Newfoundland). One consequence was an acute shortage of professional expertise (Ward, 1999). In 1949, for example, there were only about 45 qualified planners in the entire country. The prewar use of foreign, usually American, consultants continued but this was no longer a substitute for indigenous expertise. In fact, it was migrating planners, mainly from Britain, who bridged the expertise gap. As in Australia, they also played a central role in founding planning educational programmes, in Montreal in 1947, Winnipeg in 1951, Vancouver in 1952 and Toronto in 1956 (Hodge, 1991; G Stephenson, 1992; Wolfe, 1994).

The impact of this imported expertise on Canadian planning was, however, rather different to what it might have been earlier in the century. It was also slightly different to what was happening in 1950s Australia. Thus neither Canada's new planning schools nor the Town Planning Institute of Canada, reanimated in 1952 after two decades of suspension, was as directly dependent on the British TPI as their Australian equivalents (Sherwood, 1994). We can, perhaps, characterise these years less as a period when Britishness was reasserted and more as one when it added a distinctive 'edge' to an urban process that would otherwise have been wholly American.

## The 'outsiders' and their influence

Few in number though they were, the non-British and non-American planners who contributed to Canadian planning as consultants or immigrants reinforced its growing distinctiveness. Thus Jacques Gréber, the French consultant *urbaniste* responsible for Ottawa's postwar planning, reminded Canadians of their French roots (DeGrace, 1985; Taylor, 1996). Another was Eugenio Faludi, a Hungarian Jew who had trained and worked successfully in Fascist Italy (Sewell, 1993; EG Faludi, 1947–8; 1950). He left Italy in the wake of Mussolini's growing anti-Semitism, and settled permanently in Canada in 1940 where he became an influential consultant in postwar Toronto. Not least, there was also one of urban planning's greatest drifters, Hans Blumenfeld (Blumenfeld, 1987). In 1955, disenchanted with much about the United States, he took Canadian citizenship to become another key voice in the planning of Toronto. Such figures gave a cosmopolitan quality to planning in Canada. With the British input, they allowed urban planning to escape, at least partially, from its American destiny.

## Canadian reconstruction planning

This more distinctive form of Canadian planning began to take shape in the later war years (Wolfe, 1994). An official advisory committee on postwar reconstruction issued an influential report on housing and community planning in 1944 (Hodge, 1991;

Purdy, 1997). Reflecting these emergent concerns, the Central (later Canada) Mortgage and Housing Corporation (CMHC) appeared in 1946, and soon became a hugely important federal agency (JB Cullingworth, 1987). It also largely began the trend of attracting planners from across the Atlantic. Early and important recruits included Harold Spence-Sales and Peter Oberlander, both former members of the innovative planning technique section of the British Ministry of Town and Country Planning (G Stephenson, 1992). Humphrey Carver, an earlier British immigrant, now became an important figure in CMHC's planning work (Carver, 1975).

The new recruits found themselves working in an organisation that was prepared to use its control of housing funds to enforce good planning practice throughout the country for the first time. Another important initiative was the formation in 1946 of the Community Planning Association of Canada as a public voice on planning matters, similar to the Town and Country Planning Association (the former Garden City Association) in Britain. At provincial level there were comparable shifts. Ontario, for example, established its own housing and development department in 1944 and revised its planning legislation in 1946 (Hodge, 1991).

## CANADIAN METROPOLITAN PLANNING

Canadian cities also began to set examples in metropolitan planning matters that were of international importance. In 1943 the provincial government of Manitoba established an advisory planning body (the first in North America) for the Winnipeg metropolitan region. Similar agencies followed for British Columbia's Lower Mainland (Vancouver) region in 1949, and for the Alberta cities of Edmonton and Calgary in 1950. Of greatest international significance, however, was the creation in 1953 of Metro Toronto, the first statutory metropolitan government anywhere in the west. Through the Metro Toronto Planning Board, the new authority soon became a key player in shaping the development of the whole metropolitan area. This was because it was now backed by a metropolitan government with real powers (especially in relation to infrastructure investments). The authority also covered a much wider area than Metro Toronto itself.

As in Australia, there was a strong predilection for the British model of planned metropolitan development (Ward, 1999). Thus Faludi's important 1943 advisory metropolitan plan for Toronto, a powerful contribution to the whole metropolitan debate which set a postwar agenda for the city, envisaged new satellite communities beyond the existing built-up area, associated with new industrial growth (Sewell, 1994). An inner and outer green belt system was proposed to articulate the new settlements and separate them from the existing built-up area. More significant still was Gréber's plan for Ottawa, presented in 1950 (DeGrace, 1985; Taylor, 1996). Amongst many other things this proposed a green belt, which began to be created later in the decade. However, this was a restricted belt of publicly owned land, quite different from the very wide privately owned green belt championed by Abercrombie. Public ownership was not an option that could be widely followed, so Ottawa's green belt remained unique. Other efforts had more limited impacts, scarcely modifying the 'natural' process of suburban expansion.

## NEW COMMUNITY PLANNING

Nor were there any near equivalents to Britain's metropolitan new towns. A notable new nonmetropolitan settlement was the town of Kitimat. Ultimately for some 50,000 inhabitants, it was developed from 1952 to service a vast new aluminium-smelting plant in northern British Columbia (Parsons (ed), 1998). Designed by the American planner Clarence Stein, its use of neighbourhood unit principles and Radburn layouts gave it major international interest. The more usual Canadian approach was to render peripheral expansion more orderly by planning new suburban communities (Sewell, 1994). An early example was the settlement developed for munitions workers at Ajax, to the east of Toronto, from 1941.

Far more influential was Don Mills, a large planned community in northeast Toronto, which was privately developed from 1952 to house about 30,000 people in four planned neighbourhoods (J Hancock, 1994). Its chief planner, a young landscape architect called Macklin Hancock, was heavily influenced by the latest thinking in Britain, the United States and Sweden. He planned a socially mixed community with a full range of dwelling types, set in a green landscaped setting, with local employment and full local services. Unfortunately, its very success restricted its social diversity and it became a predominantly middle-income development. Within a few years many other Canadian developments were following this lead. Another early and influential example was Sherwood Park, Edmonton. In Toronto, Hancock followed Don Mills with another large new community development in a neighbouring area at Flemingdon Park, begun in 1958. Although it had many similarities to Don Mills in its planning, it was developed at a higher density and pioneered the extensive use of high-rise apartment blocks in suburban locations.

## OTHER ASPECTS OF URBAN PLANNING

Despite these obvious differences to American experiences, there were many of the same pressures for change in Canadian cities as there were south of the border. Thus new urban expressways, such as Toronto's Don Valley Parkway and the Gardiner Expressway, started to appear in the 1950s (Sewell, 1994; Lemon, 1996). (These were another proposal in the 1943 Faludi plan.) Automobile-oriented out-of-town shopping malls also began to be introduced only a few years after the initial American examples, the first at Park Royal in West Vancouver in 1950 (North and Hardwick, 1992). Yet there was never the strong federal push for building freeways that became so important in the United States by the late 1950s (Jacobs, in Sewell, 1993; JB Cullingworth, 1987). This meant that Canadian cities lagged well behind their American equivalents in bringing forward such proposals. As a corollary to this, they also cherished their public transit systems in a way that was unknown at the time in the United States. Toronto, for example, embarked on a new subway system immediately after the war.

There was also rather less commitment to urban renewal than there was in America (JB Cullingworth, 1993). Toronto saw a notable and large-scale example at Regent Park, where an older area was cleared and redeveloped in two phases in the late 1940s and mid-1950s (Sewell, 1994). The first phase, Regent Park North, aired initially in Faludi's 1943 plan, was important in bringing modernist public housing forms and layouts into Canadian cities, replacing grid streets lined with row houses. However, relatively little redevelopment of the older inner-city housing areas followed this intended model, in part because it was never as generously funded as in the United States (or Britain). Yet the relative absence in Canadian cities of racism, crime and discriminatory practices by mortgage providers, combined with this relative neglect of planned renewal and freeway building, meant that most inner city areas did not decay.

## INTERNATIONAL INTEREST IN CANADIAN PLANNING

The full implications of these divergences from American cities did not become apparent until the 1960s and 1970s, when Canadian cities escaped the rioting, racial tensions, increased crime and social problems of those in the United States (Goldberg and Mercer, 1986). But Canadian cities, especially Toronto, had already begun to be seen as sources of international lessons (Lemon, 1996). Metro Toronto, especially, prompted interest, particularly amongst American planners who had also started to admire the more ordered Canadian approach to suburban development. As the social and economic problems of American cities grew in the following decades, this admiration became stronger.

## CONCLUSIONS

We are now in a position to make more general statements about the evolution and spread of urban planning in the more advanced countries during the decades spanning the mid-point of the 20th century. Much that was already apparent by 1939 continued to be relevant, of course. Many ideas that had been rehearsed between the wars were now adopted on a large scale. Yet, in larger sense, this was a decisive period which brought a new pattern of geopolitics that was to structure international relations for most of the rest of the century. These changes alone would have had a major impact on the international diffusion of planning ideas and practices. In particular, the heightened significance of the ideological division between the capitalist and Communist worlds severed, or seriously disrupted, some established information flows. Everywhere, however, these same years simultaneously saw a heightening of the significance of urban planning. This unprecedented ascendancy grew on the destruction and strategic imperatives of war, the subsequent functional and symbolic need for reconstruction, variously understood, and the increasingly potent idea of modernisation. Indeed, by the 1960s, when the traumas of war had been healed, modernisation had itself become the dominating theme.

## THE PERSISTENCE OF NATIONAL DIVERSITY

As we noted in the previous chapter, though urban planning in the west and Japan shared important common features between countries, it still showed diverse national characteristics. Homogenising tendencies were stronger than ever before, but they were not absolute. Innovations arose in many different (and sometimes improbable) settings. As well as the countries with major traditions, many smaller ones also contributed disproportionately to the international body of planning ideas and practice.

The national experience that might have been expected to dominate, that of the United States, the new hegemonic western power, did not. At least, it did not in the way that the great European powers had largely shaped western urban planning in the early 20th century. Although American cities seemed always to be in the vanguard of change, this did not translate into an equivalent leadership in the conscious planning of urban change. In part, as we have noted, this was because the United States was spared the destruction that directly stimulated so much planning activity in European cities. It may well have been significant, too, that America had never presided over a formal empire of any size, an experience which had done so much to sharpen the planning expertise of countries such as Britain or France. Yet, beyond such specific considerations, there was also something in America's global 'style' which prioritised capitalism, market processes and democracy, rather than wishing to specify the finer grain of state policy. Whatever the source, however, the United States reproduced this style in its massive assistance to the reconstruction of western Europe and Japan, and the aid it was beginning to give to developing countries.

## International diffusion

The absence of a hegemonic American planning model allowed the multiple western traditions to persist and develop further. In turn, this diversity depended on effective means to spread knowledge of the many different innovators. As we have seen, the prewar international networks resumed, albeit with some changes that reflected war guilt and the new ideological divisions between the west and Communist worlds. These networks were also strengthened by more deliberate measures to publicise reconstruction widely, in exhibitions, the print media and film. Much effort was domestically focused, of course, but, to a greater extent than before 1939, there was also international publicity. More of this was now being published in English. The United States, in its role as the paymaster of much European reconstruction, stimulated this development. In doing so, however, it automatically made much information on planning and reconstruction in Europe available to a wider English-speaking world.

Other factors also affected the diffusion of planning. The somewhat random disruptions of war caused some planners to form new international contacts and connections, with implications for the spread of knowledge. The postwar resumption of migration also created some significant movements of planners, especially to countries such as Canada and Australia. Finally, we should note the postwar appearance of new international agencies such as the World Bank (1944) and the United Nations (1945). The creation of these bodies was largely orchestrated by the United States to provide an effective framework for stable and peaceful postwar international relations beyond the west. Within a few years of the ending of the Second World War, however, these wider aims had begun to have urban planning implications.

The detailed story of all this lies beyond the already wide remit of this book. We should, though, be aware of the extent to which the international development aid industry became an increasingly important vehicle for the wider global diffusion of the various versions of western planning during the later 20th century. In the pages that follow we will occasionally glimpse this important parallel and related story. It is, though, to the vaulting ambitions and disappointing outcomes of urban planning within the advanced capitalist countries during the years after 1960 that we must now turn.

# CHAPTER 8

# THE ZENITH OF MODERNISATION AND BEYOND I: THE MAJOR TRADITIONS

Everywhere, the 1960s saw the commitment to self-consciously modern urban planning reach its zenith. The visions which inspired this modernisation belonged to the earlier part of the century. Postwar reconstruction had brought more widespread adoption of the concept. As we have seen, however, the reality for most rebuilt cities was a compromised modernisation. But as the phase of reconstruction ended, western societies did not return to the economic uncertainties of the 1930s. They began to realise instead that they (and the world) were experiencing the longest economic boom of the century. They were also enjoying a high degree of geopolitical stability. The world, certainly, was ideologically divided. Yet the feared nuclear confrontation did not materialise. All advanced capitalist countries were able to concentrate on becoming mass-consumer societies based on advanced technology, with the rest of the world following them, or trying to do so. As never before, the richer nations could look to the future with a large measure of material confidence.

These circumstances allowed urban modernisation finally to become mainstream, implemented on a massive scale. The expectation was that technological change and economic progress would bring a future radically different to what had gone before. Meanwhile cities should reflect the bold, scientific materialism of the coming age. Yet, no sooner had the zenith of modernisation been reached than the vision began to atrophy and wither during the 1970s. The long postwar boom, of which planned modernisation was such an integral part, came to an end. Economic problems mounted and birth rates fell sharply. It was no longer possible to maintain the pace of urban change of the 1960s. Nor was it any longer desired. To many consumers of the planned modern city, the reality seemed flawed and inferior to what it had replaced. To more radical voices, planned modernisation was one symptom of a self-satisfied capitalist society that had no purpose other than to consume, and squander, the world's resources.

In this and the next chapter we examine the zenith of modernisation and what immediately followed it. As previously, a distinction is made between the major traditions, the other innovators and more derivative traditions. The latter two appear in the chapter that follows. Our immediate concern, however, is the shifting significance of the four founding traditions. Thus West Germany saw some return of international esteem, though not yet as great as it had been in former years. Britain, by contrast, remained an important reference point for planners elsewhere, although the lessons it offered were, increasingly, those of the recent past. There was, though, growing interest in the United States. In part, this was because it was the world's most powerful and affluent nation, a portent of the global future. It was, however, France which saw the most dramatic rise in international planning interest.

# FRANCE

By the early 1960s, France was changing more profoundly than ever before (Cole, 1998; McMillan, 1992). Previous waves of modernisation had been partial and spatially uneven in their impacts. After 1945, however, this changed rapidly, partly because of national economic planning adopted initially with Marshall Aid funding in 1947 (Bossuat, 1991a). There was huge public investment in economic and social infrastructure, direct investment in industries and utilities owned by the state and there were powerful financial incentives for industrial development. Spectacular growth rates were recorded from the late 1940s. Even between 1960 and 1975, the gross national product increased at an average of 5.8 per cent annually, a rate exceeded in major industrialised nations only by that of Japan. By the 1970s France was a major force in the European Economic Community (EEC), of which it was a founder member (Bossuat, 1991b).

Alongside these economic changes the French population, hitherto static and starting to decline, grew at a rate that was also spectacular. From being one of Europe's slowest growing large countries, it became one of the fastest. Between 1946 and 1962 the population grew by six million, to 46.5 million. By 1975 it reached 53 million. Natural increase, including the higher birth rate for which patriotic Catholics and conservatives had long prayed (never more fervently than in the Vichy years), accounted for most of the growth. The resultant pride in the fecundity of the French race was not unqualified, however. As France's empire crumbled, roughly a fifth of this surge in its population came from former colonies, including growing numbers of Arab and black immigrants (R King, 1998).

The combination of economic and population growth also brought a belated growth in the relative importance of urban areas (Lecoin, 1988). Their populations increased from just over half the national total in 1945 to about two-thirds by the mid-1960s. That of the continuously built-up Paris metropolitan area also grew rapidly, from about six million in the 1930s to 6.6 million in 1954, 7.4 million in 1962 and 8.5 million in 1975. But this expansion was no longer at the expense of the rest of France, as it had been in former days. The metropolitan area actually reached its all-time peak of relative importance in 1968, at just under 17 per cent of the national population, but this was very close to the position maintained throughout the entire second half of the 20th century.

## DELOUVRIER, DE GAULLE AND PARIS

The growth of the capital was the subject of the Schéma Directeur d'Aménagement et d'Urbanisme de la Région de Paris (SDAURP) of 1965 (Merlin, 1971). Hugely influential in French planning, particularly for the 1967 reforms of the planning system (Booth, 1996), it was also the most important metropolitan plan produced anywhere in the western world in the 1960s. It encapsulated a national approach to the urban future and was comparable in significance to the 1944 Greater London plan or the 1952 Stockholm plan. Covering an area slightly wider than metropolitan Paris, it reflected the optimism of France's postwar boom (Evenson, 1979; P Hall, 1988). It also expressed the political dominance of President Charles de Gaulle, at the very pinnacle of power in the early 1960s. The loss of empire had removed the traditional arena for French power and influence. Now de Gaulle was eager to take any opportunity to assert an economically powerful France's place in the world, and especially in the emergent European project represented by the EEC. Appropriately, SDAURP surpassed in its ambition all previous (and subsequent) efforts for the city.

The driving personality who shaped the plan was Paul Delouvrier, a long-standing associate of President de Gaulle and a brilliant administrator (van Hoogstraaten, 1997). In a real sense, he symbolised the transition from the old imperial France to the modern dynamic state. He had played a significant role in facilitating the French withdrawal from Algeria in the early 1960s. Shortly after Delouvrier's return, in 1961,

**Figure 8.1** *The 1965 Paris regional plan was a hugely ambitious attempt to organise metropolitan growth along two major axes to the north and south of the historic city itself. There was to be massive investment in transport and major new town development.*

de Gaulle asked this trusted functionary to take charge of the planning of the Paris region, to 'establish some order in this pigsty'.

## THE BACKGROUND TO SDAURP

Fully reflecting the technocratic style which typified French governance at this time, Delouvrier became head of an entirely new planning authority for the capital (Rubenstein, 1978; Lecoin, 1988). This centralised body had its own taxation, borrowing and other financial powers. Such a powerful mandate for urban planning was, of course, very rare indeed, and proved crucially important for the subsequent impact of the plan. Delouvrier himself was also an inspired choice, capable of leading and harnessing the technical efforts of many planning specialists while steering the plan around the many pitfalls and jealousies of the French administrative system. When appointed, he had intended merely to adapt and implement the decentralist PADOG, produced in 1960. Yet he quickly decided that this plan would inhibit meaningful improvements to living and working conditions in the Paris region. Instead of denying any longer the reality of an expanding Paris, he now proposed a strategy that would bring order to its sprawl. He outlined his ideas in an official document in 1963. These were then elaborated by the planners and researchers of the Institut d'Aménagement et d'Urbanisme de la Région Parisienne (IAURP), itself formed in 1960 (and also headed by Delouvrier).

## MAIN PROPOSALS OF SDAURP

Far from denying Parisian growth, the plan unveiled as SDAURP in 1965 envisaged a Paris region that, by 2000, could accommodate 14 million people out of a projected national population of 75 million (Merlin, 1971; Evenson, 1979; van Hoogstraaten, 1997). (For comparison, the reality in 2000 was about 59 million, with the Paris region proportionately smaller.) In its conceptual approach, this was an indicative spatial plan for social and economic development, an exercise in broad brush *aménagement du territoire*. Despite its title, Prostian or Corbusian ideas of *urbanisme* were completely absent, as was any type of detailed land use zoning. (The distinction between a broad SDAU and a detailed land use plan, called a *plan d'occupation des sols*, was reproduced in the 1967 planning reforms.)

The principal substantive proposal of SDAURP was that the outward sprawl of the city would be reconfigured into two major axes along the plateaux overlooking the Seine and Marne valleys (and leading ultimately to Rouen, Le Havre and Caen). Along the axes, new towns would focus growth and activity. In contrast to the Howardian tradition, however, these were to be fully integrated with the whole metropolitan area. Major investment in public transport would tie them into the concentrated core of Paris. Meanwhile, new roads would reinforce the development axes and provide a major means of movement within the suburban areas themselves. The existing suburbs, a muddled mix of industry, other business activity, *grands ensembles* and other more piecemeal residential development, were also to be refocused on several new service centres.

## THE IMPACT OF SDAURP

Though SDAURP was not costed, it was clear that implementation would cost tens of billions of francs (Rubenstein, 1978; Noin and White, 1997). The plan was not formally adopted until 1971, yet the funds to build the RER (Reseau Express Régionale – the regional express metro system) and many new highways, including much of the Péripherique, had already been allocated in successive national plans. Suburban centres were also successfully created in several of the projected locations, most notably Bobigny, Créteil and La Défense. (The last had, of course, been started several years earlier.) There was some dilution of the original plan, as its forecasts of national growth were toned down in the late 1960s. Thus only five new towns were finally designated (instead of the projected eight).

## NON-FRENCH INFLUENCES

In shaping (and subsequently elaborating) these proposals, Delouvrier and his planners took great pains to learn from other countries (Merlin, 1971; Rubenstein, 1978). This was very unusual by French standards. As we have seen in earlier chapters, France did not readily seek lessons from other countries. This was especially so in connection with the capital. Paris was traditionally thought to be the model for other cities, not an emulator of them. Yet the decline of empire and the emergence of the idea of Europe had helped to change thinking by the early 1960s. Paris had missed any major opportunity to rethink its strategic development in the 1940s and 1950s. By the early 1960s, there was a growing perception of a need to catch up with what other major cities had been doing since 1945. Nor was this borrowing from other countries confined solely to governmental planning. In 1962, in a very significant development of single-family housing at Versailles, William Levitt, the leading American builder of houses, introduced Parisians to the highly packaged residential development methods he had pioneered in the United States in the late 1940s. French developers quickly learnt that the market for American-style suburban living in France was stronger than many planners would have them believe.

For their part, French planners had already become more internationally minded during the 1950s, with steadily growing participation in the International Federation of Housing and Planning (IFHP) as the IFHTP was now renamed (Whittick (ed), 1980). Bordeaux and Paris hosted the federation's conferences in 1955 and 1962 and a French planner, Jean Canaux, served as its president from 1958 to 1962. Even so, Delouvrier's desire in the early and middle 1960s for expert studies of foreign practice was remarkable. Knowledge about new towns in metropolitan settings was eagerly sought (Merlin, 1971; Rubenstein, 1978). A team led by Pierre Merlin of the IAURP carefully examined the experiences of Britain, Sweden, Denmark, Finland, the Netherlands, Poland, Hungary and the United States. Of these, Britain, the Nordic countries and eastern Europe were judged most successful on a variety of criteria. Carefully synthesised, these lessons had the greatest impact on French new town planning. It is difficult to establish SDAURP's general pedigree quite as clearly. Yet it was, in several respects, a scaled-up version of the early postwar plans for

Copenhagen in 1947 and Stockholm in 1952 (P Hall, 1988). The heavy investment in the RER made the resemblance to the Stockholm approach especially striking.

## THE *GRANDS ENSEMBLES*

French interest in planning large new settlements had been growing before SDAURP. The *grands ensembles* had actually provided large numbers of modern dwellings. By 1969, they accommodated about two million people nationally, and about one person in six in the Paris region (Merlin, 1971; Evenson, 1979; Noin and White, 1997). They were of comparable importance in the big provincial cities. Lyons, for example, built large areas of this type at La Duchère, Les Minguettes and Vaulx-en-Velin during the 1960s and 1970s (Vollerin, 1999). Yet the dormitory character, monotonous architecture and generally poor social and cultural facilities of all *grands ensembles* posed mounting questions. French social expectations had risen dramatically since the early 1950s, and material improvements in housing conditions alone were no longer enough. In fact, some large *grands ensembles*, such as Sarcelles, the biggest in the Paris region, were significantly improved in the 1960s with more employment and services. Nevertheless, they rapidly fell from favour after 1973 because of mounting criticisms and shrinking growth forecasts (*Urbanisme*, 1999).

## TOWARDS THE NEW TOWNS

As ever-larger developments were begun in the later 1950s, ambitions grew to plan 'real' communities (Merlin, 1971). This was especially so in several major developments on the edge of smaller provincial towns and cities. Notable examples were Hérouville-Saint-Clair near Caen for 30,000 people, and Toulouse-Le Mirail, for a population of 100,000, both planned in the early 1960s. The latter sparked a good deal of international interest. It was designed by a Greek architect-planner, Georges Candilis (who had moved to France following the Greek civil war of 1944–5), and his associates, who included a French-based American, Shadrach Woods (Woods, 1975; Marconis, 1996). Conceived with large areas of local employment, their design aimed for a richer community life than was possible in purely dormitory developments. Le Mirail followed the 'stem' principle. This focused residential development along pedestrian routes which were largely segregated from traffic and intended to provide a setting for social interaction. The housing forms were also more varied than was usual in the *grands ensembles*.

## VILLES NOUVELLES

Despite its size, Le Mirail was essentially a local government project. The new towns proper (*villes nouvelles*), usually understood in France (as in Britain) to mean settlements created directly by central government action, came only in the wake of SDAURP (Merlin, 1971; Rubenstein, 1978). By the late 1960s, nine such towns had been designated. Five were around Paris in locations identified by SDAURP, at Marne la Vallée, Melun-Sénart, Cergy-Pontoise, Evry and Saint-Quentin-en-Yvelines. Of the remainder, three were associated with provincial cities identified as *metropoles d'équilibres* (metropolitan growth poles intended to balance Parisian dominance) in the 1965 national growth plan (Hansen, 1968). Thus Lille-Est (now named Villeneuve d'Ascq) was associated with a major new university development on the eastern fringes of Lille (Cuñat *et al.*, 1996). L'Isle d'Abeau was adjacent to the new airport at Lyons and Rives de l'Etang de Berre was a multicentred development associated with a major port expansion at Marseilles. Finally Le Vaudreuil (Val de Reuil), near Rouen, was to be a focus for growth in the Paris–Le Havre development axis.

The provincial new towns were the result of metropolitan regional studies initiated by DATAR, Délégation à l'Aménagement du Territoire et à l'Action Régional (Rubenstein, 1978; Hansen, 1968), the national agency for regional policies created in 1963. It assumed responsibility for the controls on business development in the Paris region introduced in the 1950s. It was also the main supporter of the concept of *metropoles d'équilibres*. This ensured, in turn, that it was a strong opponent of major investments in the Paris region which, in its view, would trigger new growth pressures. SDAURP was therefore a major challenge to DATAR. It is a measure of Delouvrier's political skills that he was able to win the latter's agreement. One of the main ways he did this was by strongly encouraging DATAR to propose its own provincial new towns and incorporate them in its *metropoles d'équilibres* strategy. However, only in Lille, where the new town was a contiguous extension of the core city, were these aspirations shared by key local politicians. By contrast, the mayors of Lyons, Marseilles and Rouen viewed their own, more distant, new towns with indifference or active hostility.

## NEW TOWN PLANNING

Overall, at their inception the French new towns were planned to accommodate roughly 2.4 million people, those in the Paris region accounting for 1.4 million (Rubenstein, 1978). With a planned average target population of over 260,000, their size was to be one of their most impressive features. Even the smallest, Le Vaudreuil, planned for 140,000 inhabitants, was to be bigger than any earlier British examples (*Urbanisme*, 1999). The most ambitious, Rives de l'Etang de Berre, which comprised three distinct settlements, had a target of 375,000. Most of the Paris new towns were to be 300,000 or more. All would also be major employment centres, although the British (and the original, if unfulfilled, Swedish) goal of self-contained new towns was not pursued. By the 1960s it was, of course, clear that all western societies would be far more mobile than had seemed likely anywhere in Europe in the 1940s, widening journey to work areas. Yet there was also an important cultural difference (Ward, 1992). French planners found it difficult to understand why the British had ever wanted new-town labour markets to be separate from those of the wider metropolitan areas of which they were part.

In fact, the original population and employment targets were much too optimistic and were reduced sharply as growth projections were reined back in the mid-1970s. Despite this, however, the new towns, particularly those around Paris, were sufficiently large to support the formation of major new centres at public transport hubs (Evenson, 1979). These had extensive shopping, office-based development and, close by, high-density apartment developments. Industrial areas and, increasingly, lower density housing were developed at a greater distance from these centres.

## NEW TOWNS AND PLANNING INNOVATION

The new towns attracted great interest for their innovation in the organisation of urban life (Chaline, 1985). Most immediately striking was the exuberant modernism of their architecture, a sharp contrast with both the dreary monotony usual in the *grands ensembles* and the well-mannered plainness typical of British and Swedish new communities (Evenson, 1979). Early schemes such as the pyramidal Evry I housing project, built in the mid-1970s, attracted widespread international comment. Other, even more astonishing, apartment schemes followed, especially in Marne la Vallée and Cergy-Pontoise. From 1977, however, housing provision began to become more conventional, in order to lure private suburban developers into the new towns (Rubenstein, 1978).

Another important area of innovation lay in transport. The new towns were quick to adopt ideas that were becoming current in the 1970s, such as bus lanes, dial-a-bus and electric buses. Evry was notable for its busway system, an innovation borrowed from Runcorn new town in Britain. The RER link was, however, the principal contribution to the Paris new towns, beginning with Marne la Vallée though long delayed for some of the others. On a smaller scale, the new automated VAL metro system linking Villeneuve-l'Ascq with Lille was equally significant (Cuñat *et al.*, 1996). Yet what would have been the most remarkable innovation, the high-speed aerotrain proposed for Cergy-Pontoise, was never built.

## URBAN RENEWAL

If the new towns became the most complete symbol of French modernisation, the older cities certainly did not escape redevelopment. The new suburban centres for Paris envisaged in the SDAURP had a dramatic impact, none more so than La Défense (Evenson, 1979; Noin and White, 1997). Although started in the late 1950s, its new strategic role and progressively better transport links encouraged more rapid development. In 1966 came the first skyscraper – over 25 storeys – though this was itself dwarfed by later blocks in the 1970s, reflecting a liberalisation of the planning guidelines. Thanks to La Défense, however (and reinforced by tighter planning guidelines in 1977), the historic city of Paris was largely spared skyscraper developments.

There were, though, notable pieces of redevelopment. Especially significant was the demolition in 1971 (though this had been decided upon in 1960) of the former wholesale food-market buildings at Les Halles. In the following years a massive underground RER/Metro transport interchange and large shopping centre was created, with a new green space at ground level. Yet, if this modernisation was largely subterranean, the same could not be said for the massive new national arts and cultural centre built on the nearby Plateau Beaubourg. Commissioned by President Pompidou in 1968 and opened in 1977, the Pompidou Centre was a remarkable and audacious symbol of the new France.

## CONSERVATION

Modern France also led internationally in moves to conserve the historic quarters of its cities, reconciling modernity with the past (Kain, 1981; Noin and White, 1997). As we have seen in earlier chapters, a sense of the past had permeated much of the rebuilding of towns and cities after both world wars. Individual building groups and monuments in public ownership had also long been the subject of attention. The major change of the 1960s was to develop a positive approach to area-based conservation, under the Malraux Law of 1962. This measure was largely the work of de Gaulle's Minister for Cultural Affairs, André Malraux, a famous novelist and heroic figure of the wartime resistance who was widely admired in France and abroad.

The basic aim was to maintain historic townscapes while modernising living conditions, improving traffic arrangements and establishing a viable social and economic base. The major planning instrument introduced was the *secteur sauvegardé* (safeguarded sector or, more freely, conservation area). By the end of 1976, 60 of these had been approved, mainly covering the historic cores of French provincial towns. The best known, however, was the entire Marais district of Paris, where the

*Figure 8.2*  *Within Paris, the historic environment would largely be protected, though the extensive central abattoir and meat market at Les Halles was demolished and replaced with a vast underground shopping complex, providing a new park on the surface.*

conservation process created a historic tourist quarter in a declining Jewish working-class area. In general outcome, therefore, as well as intention, the French anticipated approaches that soon spread widely in western planning.

## THE WIDER INFLUENCE OF FRENCH PLANNING

In fact, the remarkable achievements of French planning as a whole brought wide international attention during the 1960s and 1970s (Lortie, 1995b). To some extent, this was the attention that fast-growing places have always generated. Now, though, the links between that growth and planned action seemed closer than they had ever before been in a western capitalist democracy. Thus the work of Perroux and Boudeville on growth points, and the practical applications of these in DATAR policies, won interest in Britain, the United States and elsewhere (Boudeville, 1966; Hansen, 1968). International borrowing from the industrialised building methods used for the *grands ensembles* also grew, spreading to the Communist bloc even when western interest had faded by the late 1960s (eg RB White, 1971).

SDAURP took centre stage, however, particularly as its proposals began to form the basis for real achievements. As the RER and new towns took shape in the 1970s, international interest was palpable. For urban planners everywhere the sense that metropolitan new towns could be contemplated on this scale was especially impressive. Almost immediately the planners of IAURP (or IAURIF as it became in 1976, when the Paris planning region became the Ile de France region) found their expertise in demand (Lortie, 1995b). At first this was on a fairly random basis. In 1967, for example, Buenos Aires requested their assistance, reviving an older Latin American admiration of Parisian *urbanisme*. By the time of their most notable commission, the SDAU for Greater Cairo, 1981–2, a more systematic pattern was emerging which mainly involved links with cities of the Francophone world, such as Tunis, Abidjan (the Côte d'Ivoire) and Beirut. From 1972 to 1977 the Paris city planners (whose international operations had remained more occasional than those of IAURP) also prepared an urban plan for the Lebanese capital.

Ever since the 1860s Paris has never needed to do much to win international attention. Yet the 1960s and 1970s were vintage years. As well as the examples already given, specific projects such as La Défense, Les Halles, the Pompidou Centre and the Marais quickly became part of the vocabulary of western planning. Each was unique, but all also became grand archetypes of the possibilities of planning.

## JE PARTICIPE . . .

Urban planners in other western countries admired the opportunities France provided for bold and decisive planning action backed up, it seemed, by the full power and resources of the state. In fact, the notion of a centralised technocratic planning approach that transcended the narrowness of ordinary politics did not go unchallenged in France itself. The widespread industrial and student unrest of 1968 and the deposing of the aged de Gaulle in the 1969 referendum were not centrally about urban planning (Cole, 1998; McMillan, 1992). They did, though, point to the growing popular reaction, not just against de Gaulle himself, but against the modern state apparatus he had forged, of which urban planning was part. One (of the many) slogans rejected the 'sham towns' that postwar planning had created. More pervasively, there was also a desire for opportunities to challenge, or at least debate, the process of governance and its outcomes. France accordingly claimed a place at the very centre of the new discourse of popular participation and citizen activism that emerged throughout the west from the late 1960s. It also became, in 1971, one of the first countries in Europe to have a Friends of the Earth organisation, following the lead of the movement's American founder.

## . . . ILS PROFITENT

For the most radical critics, however, participation served only to legitimate the unacceptable by making the masses appear to be complicit in the state's work. Paris soon became the centre of the new Marxist urban theory developed in the 1970s by Henri Lefebvre, Manuel Castells and others (Lefebvre, 1968; Castells, 1977). These new approaches squarely challenged post-1945 western social democratic understandings of the state under capitalism. They saw the state not as a barometer of collectivist sentiment or a benevolent corrector of the inequities of the market, but rather as a major facilitator of capitalist accumulation and the reproduction of labour. Capitalism, in other words, needed an interventionist state, and the capitalist city needed urban planning. This, in turn, inexorably drew urban planning into the arena of class conflict as its actions to promote capitalist interests were challenged. These new critical understandings, quite literally the anti-thesis of the west's most confident national project of planned modernisation, in turn fed a wider, more intuitive western unease about urban planning during the 1970s.

## BRITAIN

By the early 1960s, it had begun to dawn on the leaders of France's offshore neighbour that the complacent superiority with which they had been regarding the rest of western Europe since 1945 was no longer justified. Although Britain shared in the postwar boom, its national economic growth performance languished well below those of other western European countries, especially France and West Germany (Shanks, 1977). In part this reflected Britain's early industrialisation and the lesser impact the Second World War had on the country. Compared to France, Britain had no backward, undeveloped regions to modernise; compared to West Germany, it had not had to undertake total reconstruction of its economy. Yet, even as continental European countries began to leave these problems behind, their growth continued to outpace Britain's. The truth was that there were serious structural weaknesses in the British economy, reflecting its older industries, relative lack of investment, low productivity and failure to embrace new production technologies.

The answer to these problems, of course, was found in an accelerated modernisation, of the economy and all other aspects of life, including cities (Ward, 1994). The dominant mood of Britain's leaders in the 1960s was reflected in a much-quoted phrase of Harold Wilson, its prime minister from 1964 to 1970. Shortly before gaining office, he spoke of creating a new Britain forged in the 'white heat of the technological revolution'. This set the tone for much that followed. It seemed relevant in the 1960s because very high rates of population growth were confidently being expected. The early years of the decade saw both a high birth rate and historically high immigration. Almost three million people were foreign-born by 1971, including a rapidly growing proportion from nonwhite Commonwealth countries. In the mid-1960s, official forecasts predicted there would be 75 million people in 2000 (the reality was 59.5 million). The housing and provision of jobs for these extra millions accordingly formed a major planning theme in the 1960s.

In the event, this growth soon dwindled. Overall, the United Kingdom population actually increased by less than a tenth in the 1960s and 1970s, amongst the lowest western growth rates. Meanwhile, the underlying weaknesses of the economy began to have real effects in the 1970s that were more serious than elsewhere in Europe. Older, less efficient industries began to falter as global competition intensified and unemployment rose.

## Regional economic planning

The 1960s brought growing British awareness of the regional economic planning adopted with such success by its European neighbours, especially France (DW Parsons, 1986). Perroux and Boudeville's work on growth poles began to be more widely known, if not entirely understood. Their accompanying notion of propulsive industries was not pursued with anything approaching the French commitment. The link between the location of employment and physical planning remained rather more opportunistic than in France. There were, however, some partial applications of the growth pole concept, particularly in Scotland. The thinking behind the new town of Irvine, designated in 1966, came closest to the French ideal (Osborn and Whittick, 1977). Even here, though, reality soon frustrated the original intentions as planned major industrial developments failed to materialise on the scale anticipated.

## Planning reforms

Also notable was the failed attempt by the Labour government in 1964 and 1965 to forge a French-style link between broader economic and physical planning (Shanks, 1977; Ward, 1994). Against the background of Britain's first and only national plan, intended to boost Britain's growth, new regional economic planning councils were created by Deputy Prime Minister George Brown. However, the jealousies of existing ministries ensured that they were left powerless. More significant were the changes to the local physical planning system, rehearsed in 1965 and introduced in 1968 (PAG, 1965; Ward, 1994). The reliance on a single detailed land use development plan, introduced in 1947, ended. A new distinction was now made between a broadly indicative structure plan, covering a wide area, and a detailed local plan, for an area undergoing change. The structure plan was seen as flexible and more suitable for a period of rapid growth. It was also seen as a link point with national and regional economic planning. By 1968, this two-level approach was already evident in neighbouring parts of Europe, particularly the Netherlands and, as we have seen, France (Whittick (ed), 1980). Its introduction in Britain was not, however, done with explicit international references so it is not clear what role, if any, these examples had played.

## TRAFFIC IN TOWNS

Much more explicit in its lesson-drawing (and itself subsequently of great international significance) was *Traffic in Towns* (1963), the report of a Ministry of Transport working group led by Colin Buchanan (MT, 1963). Buchanan had prewar imperial experience in the Sudan and the Ministry of Transport (Bruton, 1981). He joined the Ministry of Town and Country Planning in the 1940s, and remained with its successor, the Ministry of Housing and Local Government, to become its top planning inspector. He also published an acclaimed book, *Mixed Blessing*, in 1958 (Buchanan, 1958).

The Buchanan report foresaw huge increases in the number and use of motor vehicles, especially private cars. To meet this inevitable (though, in the event, overestimated) increase, it recommended primary urban road networks where traffic could move as freely as possible. However, there should also be 'environmental areas' in which pedestrians and environmental conditions enjoyed a clear priority. The expectation was that far more redevelopment than previously anticipated would be essential to achieve both these major proposals. In addition, great improvements in planning for transport and close integration with land use planning would be needed. Though the reception of the report was favourable, these conclusions were not all pursued with equal commitment (Hass-Klau, 1990). The primary road networks were more easily understood and acted upon. Yet environmental areas appeared only slowly, especially where redevelopment did not occur. An early example was Pimlico in London. More followed in the 1970s, when the retreat from comprehensive development shifted the emphasis to gradual improvement of older housing areas. Even so, however, British moves came more slowly than those in the Netherlands and West Germany.

## AMERICAN AND OTHER INFLUENCES ON BUCHANAN

The Buchanan report naturally drew on relevant British experience, primarily from the new towns and blitzed cities, especially Coventry (MT, 1963). It also referred to some extent to the experience of West Germany, mainly highlighting the growing trend there to pedestrianise central streets (in contrast to the British creation of entirely new pedestrian shopping precincts). There was also recognition of the continued importance of trams in urban transport and the quality of design associated with major roads. There was also a briefer consideration of Stockholm and Venice (the latter a totally car-free environment).

Far more important, however, was the experience of the United States. This permeated the whole report which reflected the sheer extent of American motorisation and the confident expectation that Britain would follow the same trend. The report certainly did not advocate following the American urban experience. Buchanan criticised the way dependence on the automobile and weak control of peripheral urban growth had produced the characteristic sprawl of American cities. He also disliked the intrusive impacts of many freeways on older city areas. Yet he also found much to admire. Urban renewal projects, particularly the Penn Center in Philadelphia, apparently showed how planners and private developers might together rebuild cities. As well as creating modern commercial premises, such developments seemed to promise that careful design, using what Buchanan called traffic architecture, could reconcile car access with other needs. The treatment of urban freeways in some cities, especially the cuttings used in Philadelphia, also met with approval. So, too, did the Radburn residential layout developed in the late 1920s (but little used in the United States) which had already become more common in Britain since the early 1950s. Despite sprawl, Buchanan was also impressed by the sheer convenience of car-based out-of-town shopping. Above all, though, he admired American technical expertise in traffic and transportation planning. He was eager that it be quickly integrated with Britain's strong land use planning tradition.

*Figure 8.3* *The Buchanan Report was a major contribution to international planning thought and practice. In Britain, however, it was largely understood by decision-makers as favouring massive urban redevelopment, of the type suggested in this illustration from the report.*

## THE INTERNATIONAL IMPACT OF *TRAFFIC IN TOWNS*

The Buchanan report was much the most important British contribution to international planning thought in the 1960s. It was translated into German in 1964 and widely studied by German planners (Hass-Klau, 1990). Its importance was also soon recognised in France and key parts of Buchanan's ideas appeared in French in 1965 (*Urbanisme*, 1999). His name rapidly became known throughout the world. For an international readership, however, the primary British purpose of the Buchanan report, as policy advice, was far less significant. As we will see, it turned out that its full conceptual implications would be more thoroughly grasped outside Britain. Meanwhile Buchanan himself formed a planning consultancy in 1964, largely comprising the *Traffic in Towns* team (Bruton, 1981). It undertook several major British commissions, mainly elaborating the report's principles for specific towns. International work quickly followed in many parts of the non-European world, such as Kenya, Salvador and Kuwait.

### REDEVELOPING THE SLUMS

The 1960s saw a huge acceleration in slum clearance and redevelopment for public housing, increasingly in high blocks of flats (Burns, 1963; Cooney, 1974; Ward, 1994). The increased scale of this redevelopment also reflected the growing recognition, after Buchanan, of the need to restructure urban roads. The slum areas that surrounded the commercial cores of big cities offered great potential for forming new road systems. By the mid-1970s a new urban landscape had arisen in these districts (Higgott, 2000). Motorway-type roads, separate from existing streets, were flanked by futuristic tower or slab blocks. There was also much lower or medium-rise housing development, again of modern design.

As elsewhere in the west, the modern movement finally became the new orthodoxy of the 1960s. Architects and planners weaned on Corbusian and other modernistic visionaries were now sufficiently senior to wield important influence. Such people provided a large part of the explicit rationale for remaking cities in this image. Meanwhile, the small number of major construction companies capable of producing large numbers of dwellings by nontraditional methods (or handling major road-building projects) allowed the vision to be realised. They were enthusiastically backed, at least in the 1960s, by governments from both main political parties. In fact, many of the most celebrated schemes (some begun in the 1950s though not completed until later) did not use mass-production system building in the strict sense (Glendinning and Muthesius, 1994). They included Park Hill in Sheffield, the Barbican in the City of London, Trellick Tower and its clones elsewhere in inner west and east London, and the last major example nationally of this type of redevelopment: the Byker Wall in Newcastle.

### INDUSTRIALISED BUILDING

True industrialised building came later and was less important in total housing production than it was in, for example, France, Sweden or the Communist bloc (RB

White, 1971; Russell, 1981). In the mid to late 1960s, however, industrialised system building, involving package deals between building companies and local authorities (and with much potential for corruption), became common (Dunleavy, 1981). The companies effectively took charge of many aspects of planning and design. Many of the systems used by British builders were of foreign origin (Glendinning and Muthesius, 1994). In a pattern presaged by the Quarry Hill scheme in Leeds during the 1930s, British construction companies adopted several French industrialised systems in the 1960s. The best-known were Sectra, pioneered in Lyons, and Camus. Scandinavia was another source of systems, including that misapplied so catastrophically in the 22-storey Ronan Point block in east London, which partially collapsed following a small gas explosion in May 1968. Fewer tower blocks were built after this time (partly because the extra subsidies were dropped in 1967). Lower rise system-built forms, including 'streets in the sky', deck-access flats, became more common. The wheels of industrialised production, once in motion, were not easily stopped, however. It was not until large-scale slum clearance and redevelopment was

*Figure 8.4* One of the last large scale British schemes of slum clearance and housing was at Byker in Newcastle. The wall of multi-storey flats (on the right) contain the otherwise low rise scheme, protecting it from the noise of a proposed (but never built) motorway. The remnants of old Byker can be seen on the left.

itself wound down in the early 1970s, in response to growing social criticisms and mounting costs, that this way of providing housing also declined.

## REDEVELOPING THE CITY CENTRES

The 1960s and early 1970s brought a great deal of modernisation of city centres as well as of slums (Burns, 1963; Ward, 1994). Unlike Paris or some other European cities, British planners made no serious attempts to deflect office developers to off-centre locations. Nor was Buchanan's admiration for American out-of-town car-based shopping widely shared as an alternative to central areas. Early proposals for this kind of development were blocked during the first half of the 1960s. It was not until 1976 that anything close to the American out-of-town mall appeared in Britain (at Brent Cross, in northwest London). The result was wholesale commercial redevelopment of existing city centres, often extending them to the new ring roads being built in the adjoining former housing areas. Office development was usually undertaken on a more individual, speculative basis by private developers. By contrast, shopping centres were usually built by private developers in partnership with local authorities, strengthening the role of planners (at least in theory).

## PLANNING SHOPPING CENTRES

The open pedestrianised precincts that had appeared in the 1950s in Coventry, Stevenage and elsewhere now gave way to enclosed central-area malls. In the United States, Victor Gruen was also advocating downtown malls by the early 1960s (Gruen, 1964). Yet it was in Britain that this approach dominated retail planning. The first enclosed mall in Britain was the Bull Ring Centre in central Birmingham, planned after careful study of examples in the United States and Canada and opened in 1964 (Higgott, 2000). It incorporated all the elements of traffic architecture, pedestrian segregation, integration of car parking and public transport access that Buchanan advocated. During the late 1960s and 1970s centres of this type, including the vast Arndale Centre in Manchester and the Eldon Centre in Newcastle, appeared in almost every city in Britain. British developers also re-exported the American mall concept, to cities as varied as Lyons and Adelaide.

Yet although the mall, turning its back on the street, dominated the planning of central shopping it was not the only approach. A notable move was the pedestrianisation of existing streets in the historic city of Norwich in 1968 (Hass-Klau, 1990). The city had featured in the Buchanan report, which had suggested this response (MT, 1963). Implementation followed study of West German cities, and particularly of the oldest of the larger pedestrianisation schemes, in Essen. The German approach was not quickly or widely followed, however. There was more interest in this in the 1970s, when political and popular opinion became more critical of relentless redevelopment and began to favour conservation. Even then, big cities in Britain were much slower to adopt this approach than those in West Germany. Leeds was the first, beginning in the late 1960s (Smales and Whitney, 1996). It was some years, however, before a sizable traffic-free area was created.

# NEW TOWNS

The new towns remained the specific British planning achievement most widely admired throughout the world. After a lull during the 1950s when Cumbernauld alone was added to the early postwar designations, the 1960s became a period of great activity (JB Cullingworth, 1979). A further 13 new towns were started between 1961 and 1970, most to receive people moving from provincial cities. Thus there were Skelmersdale and Runcorn (Liverpool), Livingston and the already mentioned Irvine (Glasgow), Redditch and Telford (Birmingham), Warrington and Central Lancashire (Manchester) and Washington (Newcastle). London had three further new towns at Peterborough, Northampton and, best known, Milton Keynes. In addition, the appropriately named Newtown in mid-Wales became a small new town that provided a focus for rural development.

The main reasons for this renewed activity lay in the combination of high growth projections and accelerated urban redevelopment during the 1960s (Ward, 1994). Both required more land to house the extra, or displaced, population. The average target size of the new towns designated in the 1960s, especially after 1966, was rather higher than those started in the late 1940s (though many of these had their targets increased). Thus Telford, Northampton and Milton Keynes were each intended to house over 200,000 inhabitants. Central Lancashire, initially targeted for 325,000, was projected eventually to reach perhaps half a million. Like the Parisian new towns, each of these 'new cities' also incorporated extensive areas of existing urbanisation.

## NEW TOWN PLANNING

As with the early new towns, the later examples attracted leading planning and design talents and had many novel features (Osborn and Whittick, 1977). Reflecting the higher growth projections of the period, the planned densities in these towns were appreciably higher than in the early ones. There was much use of high-density low-rise housing, often in terraces or more complex clusters and of more obviously modern design than their predecessors. Elements of the neighbourhood unit survived, but in rather different guises that reflected changed shopping patterns and greater mobility. Generally there was much greater provision for car use. Virtually complete segregation between traffic and pedestrians was now usual. There were significant differences, however in transport arrangements. Runcorn, for example, planned by Arthur Ling, a former member of Abercrombie's London team and Coventry city planner, stood at the public transport end of the spectrum. Ling's plan adopted a closed linear structure arranged around a figure-of-eight busway. Washington, by contrast, planned by the consultants Llewelyn-Davies and Partners, was conceived around a road grid system (albeit altered in the plan's detailed elaboration), indicating an expectation of high car use.

## MILTON KEYNES

The same consultants, led by Richard Llewelyn-Davies and Walter Bor, a former chief planner of Liverpool, were also responsible for the plan for Milton Keynes which, internationally, became the best known of all British new towns (Bendixson and Platt, 1992; Clapson, Dobbin and Waterman, 1998). In large part, this reflected a highly innovative planning approach that leant heavily on American thinking, particularly Melvin Webber's influential work on urban society. Webber, in Britain at the critical time, became an adviser to the consultancy team. In a notable 1964 essay, he had written of the 'non-place urban realm'. Its essence was that community in future urban society would not depend on spatial proximity but would reflect common interests, facilitated by enhanced mobility and communications. This stood in sharp contrast to the nostalgic tone of much contemporary British social criticism of urban planning – that it was destroying working-class communities. In effect, Webber argued that such communities were in any case doomed and that planners should not be trying to re-create them within rigid planned neighbourhood units of the type found in almost all previous new towns.

The master plan for Milton Keynes, published in 1970, reflected these principles in a truly original way (Clapson, 1999, van Es, 1997). Despite the earliest suggestions for a high-density linear city based around a monorail, the consultants produced a truly iconic plan for a Los-Angeles-style road grid. Instead of local neighbourhood centres, there were to be activity centres readily accessible by road from anywhere in the city. The main city centre was to be merely the first amongst equals, rather than providing a completely different order of shopping provision as in conventional cities (or other new towns). There were to be extensive parks and, of course, pedestrian and cycle movement entirely separate from motor roads. Above all, the plan was to be flexible, to reflect the uncertainty of change, and the planners did not try to specify the exact balance of ultimate land uses.

As so often, many aspects of the plan were diluted as it was implemented, though Milton Keynes proved very successful in attracting residents and investment. It also attracted immense international interest. It seemed to be a credible answer to the fundamental problem that Buchanan had addressed. The new city embraced the affluent suburban lifestyle of the United States. Yet it also promised to tame its less attractive features by providing, through public planning, a richer and more ordered civic realm. Since many planners throughout the west faced variants of the same problem, this memorable plan was bound to win attention. Its influence spread even more widely, most notably in the direct involvement of planners from Milton Keynes in the planning of the central parts of the new Nigerian capital, Abuja, during the late 1970s (Lafrenz, 1999).

## THE LIMITS TO MODERNISATION

By the late 1960s and early 1970s Britain's planners began to come up against increasingly serious limits to the physical modernisation of urban life. As in France, public reactions to unpopular planning measures became more vocal. The main target was urban redevelopment, which destroyed established communities and replaced older buildings and streets with increasingly unpopular public housing schemes, office blocks or, especially disliked, urban motorways. Much of the familiar texture of cities was being lost, or degraded. Gordon Cullen's influential 1961 book, *Townscape*, stressed the aesthetic and other qualities of streets and urban spaces (Cullen, 1961).

Some of these concerns found formal expression in planning measures, particularly the 1967 Civic Amenities Act which introduced conservation areas. Ministerial sympathy for this new approach had been boosted by a visit to France to see the Malraux Law in operation (Delafons, 1997). The emphasis also shifted steadily away from slum clearance as the 1969 and 1974 Housing Acts encouraged area-based rehabilitation of existing older housing (Ward, 1994). Meanwhile public participation in planning, officially encouraged by the Skeffington report of 1969, allowed criticisms of purely expert judgements of what was in the public interest.

The 1970s brought more active opposition, especially to road building. It also saw the growth (albeit this was less spectacular than in West Germany and North America) of an organised environmental movement (Porritt and Winner, 1988). This effectively began in 1971, when a British Friends of the Earth pressure group was formed, following a European initiative by the founder of the American body. The world's first environmental political party – PEOPLE, later to become the Green Party – was also formed in Britain in 1973. The idea was soon borrowed by other countries in Europe, where it found far greater success.

## RATIONAL SCIENTIFIC PLANNING

Despite increasingly articulate and informed public challenges planners remained confident, at least for a few more years, of their expertise. British planning thought and practice underwent an important shift from about the mid-1960s, as ever more statistically based approaches were adopted from the United States (P Hall, 1988). These moves followed Buchanan's admiration of American transportation planning expertise. Many American consultants in this field (such as Wilbur Smith and Alan Voorhees) actually worked in Britain during these years. Transport planning, with its connections to engineering, economics and quantitative science, continued to set the pace but the approach spread to other spheres of planning.

The growing numbers of geographers who entered planning in the 1960s and 1970s also played a part, since those in Britain soon followed their American counterparts down the scientific road. These new geographers were soon eager to lay down markers for a more rational approach to planning. An innovative series of late 1960s/early 1970s subregional studies (for Leicester and Leicestershire, Coventry and Solihull, and Nottinghamshire and Derbyshire) became demonstration projects for the new structure-planning process (Ward, 1994). Modelling of various critical urban relationships, between basic employment, service provision, residential patterns and commuting patterns soon became common. The American Garin-Lowry model, which predicted future spatial patterns from employment and transport data, was the one that was most often used. Already in the 1960s planners had become increasingly familiar with many varieties of statistical forecasting and cost-benefit analysis.

## SYSTEMS AND CORPORATE PLANNING

By the early 1970s, all these self-consciously 'rational' and 'scientific' techniques were being pulled together under the grand umbrella of the systems approach (not to be confused with systems building). This was extensively used in the American space and weapons programmes, and already enjoyed wide currency in planning in the United States. It fell, however, to the British planning academics Brian McLoughlin and George Chadwick to give the most complete expositions of the systems approach in urban planning in their books on the subject (McLoughlin, 1969; Chadwick, 1971). Both these works had significant international impact, particularly McLoughlin's which, in West Germany for example, helped to encourage the growing sense that planning was more than just an adjunct of architecture or engineering.

Meanwhile, yet more new planning ideas about organisational methods came from the United States (Friend and Jessop, 1969). Known overall as corporate planning, the approach came from business management and focused on managing the delivery of public services, something which some planners now saw as an obvious area to colonise. Corporate planning enjoyed a short vogue when the new local government system became established from 1972. Not surprisingly, however, in the 1970s many British planners were increasingly uncertain as to what exactly their expertise was about.

## THE INNER CITY

The biggest challenge to British planning in the 1970s was actually driven by far larger forces than uncertainty. As oil prices rose rapidly in 1973 and 1974, the long postwar boom in the international economy finally came to an end. It was now that the relative weakness of the British economy, long a source of growing anxiety, became a serious problem (Robson, 1988; Ward, 1994). Although growth expectations shrank throughout the world, many parts of Britain, especially those tied to older industries, began to face the prospect of very serious decline. The bigger cities, especially their inner areas, were the worst affected. Planners had sought the physical modernisation of living environments in these areas. Yet both they and their political masters had failed to modernise economic activity. Inner-city economies were, accordingly, extremely vulnerable to even a slight intensification of competition and began to suffer serious distress. Populations in these areas, already declining before 1970, now began to fall alarmingly as those who could find jobs elsewhere (or wanted to buy their own houses in the suburbs) left them. Between 1971 and 1981 some Inner London boroughs lost more than a quarter of their populations, while Glasgow lost 22 per cent, and Manchester and Liverpool each over 16 per cent. The people who remained in the inner cities were increasingly the less skilled, the old and those least able to thrive through their own efforts. These features reproduced themselves in all the other dimensions of social deprivation.

## RECASTING PLANNING POLICIES

Planning since 1945 had, of course, sought to reduce the populations of these inner city areas through redevelopment and decentralisation policies. Now wider changes were producing a much faster decline and more industrial dereliction. It did not help, either, that a good deal of the social housing built to replace the slums in such areas was itself increasingly unpopular. The orthodoxies of postwar planning, while not the primary cause of the inner city problem, did not seem to be contributing towards any effective solution. Already, by the mid-1970s, in the worst affected cities, most notably Glasgow, decline was so serious as to threaten an American-style emptying out of the inner areas. The result was a marked change of policy direction. Slum clearance was finally ended and the rehabilitation of older housing intensified after 1974. The new towns were also downgraded. Two were actually abandoned, at Llantrisant in South Wales and Stonehouse near Glasgow (Ward, 1992). Meanwhile, vaguer proposals for ambitious planned growth areas (for example in south Hampshire) were diluted and existing new towns had their targets reined back.

More positive policies to regenerate the inner cities began to emerge. Glasgow set up the GEAR (Glasgow Eastern Area Renewal) project in 1976 and a full national review of inner city policy came in 1977. In 1978 legislation following earlier local efforts in Newcastle and its neighbours saw the tentative beginnings of local economic development policies. Unfortunately the main political response to mounting national economic problems was to cut public expenditure, severely limiting the effects of these new policies.

## THE INTERNATIONAL CONTEXT OF BRITISH PLANNING

The faint signs of insecurity apparent within the political elite in the early 1960s had thus grown into something much larger by the late 1970s. As so often, insecurity fostered a belief that others could do things better. Those who shaped the British planning debate began to find more to admire elsewhere than their foreign equivalents had to admire in Britain. The distinguished legacy of British planning remained internationally important, of course. Yet, apart from the Buchanan report and Milton Keynes, genuinely innovative planning achievements that had real international salience were becoming fewer. Meanwhile, British planners were being increasingly influenced by their French, West German and, above all, their American counterparts (eg Burns, Lane and Thomas, 1962).

At one level, this growing American connection was a paradox. By the mid-1970s, Britain had largely dismantled its empire and ostensibly reduced its dependence on what had once been its primary international network. It had also finally joined the European Community (in 1973). Yet the British had joined with a sense of their own special distinctness from Europe. In many ways, they remained more at ease with their multidimensional links to the Anglophone world. Above all, there was the 'special relationship' with the United States, whose experiences – as a result of motorisation or, increasingly, urban decline – seemed the most accurate pointers to Britain's own future. Such attitudes help to explain why British planners in the 1970s, like their fellow countrymen and women, tended to look across the Atlantic rather than the Channel or the North Sea.

## WEST GERMANY

The broad course of planning history in West Germany in the 1960s and 1970s showed many similarities to France and Britain. The long slog of reconstruction, a far bigger task than in any other western country, was virtually completed by 1960. The main pressures on planners in the 1960s and 1970s were no longer those attributable to Hitler's war. At last, their problems were essentially the same as those of their neighbours – those of growth and rising expectations (Pulzer, 1995). Yet the sheer success of the spectacular 'economic miracle' of the 1950s, based largely on manufacturing, ensured that West Germany's planners also had to tackle urban modernisation with greater energy than their counterparts in most other countries. In fact, the 1960s saw a slightly lower growth rate, with a much lower rate in the 1970s. This was still sufficient, however, to make the German Federal Republic into western Europe's biggest economy (and the world's fourth biggest, after the United States, the Soviet Union and Japan) in 1980.

As in France, economic success produced important social changes. One that was common to all western European countries, but an especial challenge to West Germany in view of the painful memories of the acute racism of the Nazi era, was the growing ethnic diversity of cities (Friedmann and Lehrer, 1998; Elkins, 1988). As the immigration of Germans from eastern Europe dried up, the buoyant West German economy began to depend on a growing low-paid labour force from southern Europe (R King, 1998). By 1976 there were 2.17 million 'guest workers', mainly from Turkey and Yugoslavia. As in Britain, these ethnic minorities were concentrated in the older, inner parts of the big cities, which affluent West Germans were leaving for commuter suburbs and smaller towns.

Also moving into these older city areas were many younger West Germans, who were less committed than their parents to the dominant values of postwar society. In some ways, their opposition to the material smugness that followed prosperity went further than in France (and certainly than in Britain, where the prosperity itself always proved more elusive). Not surprisingly, the inner parts of German cities witnessed important, often violent, confrontations over urban planning in the 1970s (Hajdu, 1983). These had an immediate impact on the nature of planning actions. Yet they were also extremely important in the longer term, and not just in West Germany, because they stimulated the growth of what, by the early 1980s, was Europe's most advanced and politicised environmental movement. For the moment though, the wider international resonance of German environmentalism was rather limited, seemingly only more serious versions of protests that were being experienced everywhere in the west.

## PLANNING URBAN GROWTH

Housing continued to be one of the principal pressures on planners (D Kennedy, 1984). Instead of the need to rebuild bombed areas, the pressures were those of natural increase and heavy migration. The major movement from East Germany was greatly diminished after the building of the Berlin Wall in 1961, but now the inflow was of guest workers mainly from south and east Europe, especially Turkey. The main shortfall was met by the planning, from the late 1950s, of large areas of peripheral housing, known under various names, principally as either *trabantenstädte* (satellite towns) or *grosswohnsiedlungen* (big housing projects), around the main cities (Hajdu, 1983; Whittick (ed), 1980). Neither label has a precise meaning, though the former implies a more ambitious planned intent regarding the development of the community (Mullin, 1978). Yet both differed from British-style freestanding new towns which were created by development corporations and with their own employment. There were a few examples closer to this type of development in the Land of Nordrhein-Westfalen, notably one at Sennestadt (near Bielefeld) which was planned by Hans Bernhard Reichow, now one of West Germany's leading planners despite his Nazi past. Others were at Wulfen and Marl on the northern rim of the Ruhr coal district. But this model was not generally followed. Instead large settlements on the edge of the big cities were preferred, usually developed by public-private consortia underwritten by public housing subsidies.

## TRABANTENSTÄDTE AND GROSSWOHNSIEDLINGEN

Examples of these peripheral settlements included Langwasser on the edge of Nuremberg and Perlach in Munich (both planned for about 60,000 inhabitants). Bremen had Neue Vahr (30,000), Düsseldorf had Garath (30,000) and Frankfurt had Nordweststadt, planned for a population of 45,000 (Whittick (ed), 1980; Hajdu, 1983; Elkins, 1988; Bullock, 1999). West Berlin spawned the satellites at Falkenhagener Feld (for about 35,000), Buckow-Rudow (for about 40,000), also called Gropiusstadt, to mark involvement in its planning by the Americanised Bauhaus exile Walter Gropius, and the Märkische Viertel (about 50,000). With some variations, the essential concept was similar to the *grand ensemble* – an essentially dormitory settlement, with most dwellings provided in flats and with many taller blocks. In general, though, there was more rapid provision of good shopping facilities, public transport links and other services than there was in the French examples. Nor were the German designs and environments, blandly modern and mass-produced though they were, usually quite as monolithically dreary as those around French cities

## MÄRKISCHE VIERTEL AND NORDWESTSTADT

There were exceptions, however. One of the most notorious was the Märkische Viertel in West Berlin, the nearest equivalent in popular demonology to Sarcelles in Paris, with vast walls of high-rise flats (Elkins, 1988; Bullock, 1999). Partly because it was originally planned for a smaller population, shopping facilities were inadequate. There was also very poor public transport for many years. Such problems were a direct result of Berlin's specific difficulties as a divided city, which both restricted land supply and created a fragmented transport system. Yet they immediately helped to make the area less desirable. This was compounded by lettings policies which allowed it soon to become a focus for many social problems.

In the less pressured setting of Frankfurt, however, many of these difficulties could be avoided. Nordweststadt had interesting connections with some of the main currents of 20th-century German planning (Schwagenscheidt, 1964; Kampffmeyer, 1968). Its initiator and driving force was Hans Kampffmeyer, the son of one of the German garden city pioneers. He had also translated Le Corbusier's Athens Charter into German (Fischer, 1990). As a Frankfurt councillor in the late 1950s, he put his experience to use organising a design competition for the new satellite. The winning team was led by Walter Schwagenscheidt, who had worked with Ernst May in the Soviet Union in the 1930s. Yet this did not stop the new satellite all but overwhelming May's neighbouring *siedlung* from the Wiemar era at Römerstadt.

Despite this, Nordweststadt, was actually one of the more interesting examples of a 1960s *trabantenstadt*, and was widely reported (mainly by Schwagenscheidt and Kampffmeyer). Ninety per cent of housing was provided as flats, including many blocks of eight or more storeys. There was, however, a more diverse social mix than at the Märkische Viertel. Moreover, Nordweststadt retained something of the garden city legacy of the May era, with extensive wooded landscaping. It also used classic Radburn cul-de-sac layouts which gave very extensive segregation of motor traffic from pedestrians and cyclists. However, this is not to say that Nordweststadt entirely

**Figure 8.5**  *Nordweststadt in Frankfurt was characteristic of large planned developments which began to appear on the edge of many West German cities during the 1960s. The detailed planning showed a mixture of high and low rise development, with segregation of pedestrians from road traffic.*

escaped the familiar social problems. A particular focus of disenchantment was the main shopping centre, which proved unpopular in its original open precinct form.

## URBAN REDEVELOPMENT

The extent of wartime destruction meant that by the 1960s there was less enthusiasm (or indeed scope) for slum clearance and comprehensive redevelopment. Hamburg had been a traditional enthusiast for this British-style solution and produced one of the most celebrated postwar West German efforts of this type (BFHH, 1958; Harms and Schubert, 1989). This was the Neu Altona scheme, unveiled in the late 1950s, for a large area on the eastern side of central Hamburg. It was planned by a sizable team, including Ernst May, on behalf of the Neue Heimat housing association which was the main developer, and the Hamburg city planner Werner Hebebrand. The intention was that 36,000 people would ultimately live in the area, though commitment to the scheme was only partial and it was aborted well before completion. Many of the remaining older buildings were retained and the resident population is currently only about a quarter of the planned target.

In 1964, the West Berlin government also decided to embark on extensive clearance in what had long been Germany's most overcrowded city. The first area, Kreuzberg, was originally scheduled for wholesale clearance and comprehensive redevelopment with a new motorway (Elkins, 1988; Bullock, 1999). This was soon diluted but even the partial clearance option provoked opposition. Socially, the area was a microcosm of inner areas in many big West German cities at that time, with a growing population of immigrants and radical young Germans. Together these groups began to challenge the official planning process (Kündiger, 1997a). During the early and mid-1970s activism against the Kreuzberg proposals and the whole style of planning it represented was at its height. A local priest acted as a catalyst in the development of self-help solutions and launched alternative strategies for the district. There were also street battles with police to combat evictions. A significant victory for the activists, peaceful and otherwise, came in 1976 when the motorway plan was dropped.

## A CRITICAL PLANNING APPROACH

More considered critiques reinforced direct action in producing a wider questioning of the way urban planning was changing cities. Many West German planners were aware of important English-language, especially American, literature on the theme. Jane Jacobs' trenchant critique of the failures of planning in *The Death and Life of Great American Cities* (1961) soon became known. There was also equivalent work that referred directly to the West German scene. Most important was *Die Unwirtlichkeit unserer Städte* (literally, the inhospitability of our cities) by Alexander Mitscherlich, published in 1965 (Hajdu, 1983; D Kennedy, 1984). In contrast to the international impact of Jacobs' book, it made no impression outside West Germany. Though Mitscherlich criticised the social and psychological weaknesses of modern cities, his work was less a generic assault on planners and more a critique of a collective political failure. (He also favoured far greater public control of the land market, a rather different emphasis to Jacobs' preference for small ownership.)

By the early 1970s, the criticisms were becoming more focused and more positive suggestions were emerging. For example, a 1971 exhibition in Munich, 'Profitopolis or Mankind Needs Another Kind of City', called for more attention to be paid to older residential districts. These offered a street life, variety and colour lacking in newer areas but suffered from traffic, noise and pollution. Arguments like this triggered a major new initiative in the planning of older districts, in 1977, with the announcement of another Berlin IBA (international building exhibition) that would focus on just this theme (Kündiger, 1997a). In the 1980s, as the IBA came to fruition, its importance as a contribution to international debate about the planning of older parts of cities became clear.

## Planning city centres

West German efforts to plan their city centres were already being widely admired. Occasionally there were attempts to deflect office development pressures to off-centre locations, La Défense style, for example at City-Nord in Hamburg. However, this kind of specific decentralisation policy was not pursued so rigorously in the emergent financial capital of Frankfurt where such pressures were greatest. In keeping with its early postwar American connections (and reflecting a planning regime that was unusually liberal by German standards), the city skyline began to change dramatically in the 1970s (Hajdu, 1983). Much of this development took place in Westend, the older residential neighbourhood adjoining the historic centre. Despite violent confrontations in 1973 between police and activists who were trying to stop the property developers, tall office blocks soon began to tower over formerly low-rise streets. Such Americanisation had its limits, however. In all cities, major retailing remained firmly anchored in central locations. There was also a sharp contrast with the widespread British fondness for new American-style enclosed shopping malls in central areas. The dominant German approach was to keep the traditional city centre street, with shop and other building frontages, but exclude traffic, especially cars.

## Central pedestrianisation

As we noted in Chapter 6, moves towards excluding traffic had started in the 1950s. In 1955, 21 cities, mainly in Nordrhein-Westfalen where car ownership was high, had traffic-free central streets (Hass-Klau, 1990; Hajdu, 1983). By 1966, the number of pedestrianised areas had grown to 63. Most were still on a small scale but an increasing boldness in central traffic restraint was evident (Hajdu, 1988). In Bremen, for example, cross-centre movements of motor traffic were entirely stopped in 1960, making wider traffic-free areas feasible. Yet until the early 1970s the first central pedestrianised scheme, in Essen, remained the largest. It was the very extensive and stylish one in Munich, opened in 1972 to coincide with the city's hosting of the Olympic Games, that finally ensured that extensive pedestrianisation became the usual treatment even for the biggest cities.

The Olympic Games (although marred by terrorism) focused world attention on the city and this helped to spread the pedestrianisation concept internationally (Chalkley and Essex, 1999). However, foreign observers did not always appreciate the specific circumstances that underpinned this innovation in West German cities. Bombing had often allowed significant changes to be made to road systems, easing the possibility of closing narrower streets that were less significant for traffic movement. Even more importantly, the West Germans, despite their deep affection for the motor car as both contributor to, and reward for, their postwar economic success, had maintained excellent public transport. Unlike the British, French or Americans they had continued to invest in street tramways. These were effective movers of large numbers of people, but also proved far more acceptable than buses within pedestrian areas. In the 1970s, growing investment in public transport also allowed more cities either to take the tramways underground in the central areas or to create entirely new subway systems.

*Figure 8.6* *By the 1960s, West Germany's early adoption of pedestrianisation of extensive networks of existing central shopping streets, evident here in the pioneering city of Essen, was winning strong international interest.*

## TOWARDS TRAFFIC RESTRAINT

Apart from central pedestrianisation the West German authorities had not sought any significant restraint on motor-vehicle use (Hass-Klau, 1990). (Even urban speed limits were slow to be imposed.) Also, the very same postwar building of central roads that facilitated partial pedestrianisation could often preclude completely traffic-free schemes. Frankfurt and Hamburg, for example, had bisected their centres with major new roads. As traffic volumes began to increase in the 1960s, however, attitudes began to change. We have already noted the importance of the proposed motorway in Kreuzberg as a focus for political opposition. Encouraged by this, the victories of central pedestrianisation and the more general rise in political activism in the late 1960s and 1970s there was mounting criticism over urban traffic and roads building (Hajdu, 1983). (New legislation in 1971 also gave improved rights for public participation in planning.) There was a growing awareness, too, that without wider restraint pedestrian areas often worsened traffic on adjoining nonpedestrianised streets.

At a different level, German planners also read *Traffic in Towns* (which was, as already noted, soon translated into German) and an official West German report on the same subject was published in 1965 (Hass-Klau, 1990). Though the two reports had certain similarities it seems unlikely that the German report, which essentially backed a dual strategy of road building and public transport spending, was influenced by the Buchanan report. In particular, it lacked any reference to the environmental areas that formed Buchanan's second major proposal. This was, however, an idea that greatly interested a growing number of German planners. They could, perhaps, appreciate its significance and possibilities more clearly than the British because of their own experience with pedestrianisation.

## EARLY TRAFFIC CALMING

In the mid-1970s the combination of wider pressure and conceptual understanding triggered the first German experiments with traffic calming (Hass-Klau, 1990; Ewing, 1999). By this time, however, Buchanan was only a starting point. It was the Dutch experiments with the *woonerf* (home zone) concept since 1965, particularly in Delft, that had largely focused German thinking. (There is more detail about these Dutch innovations in Chapter 9.) The first West German experiments with the Dutch ideas came in 1976 when Nordrhein-Westfalen, the Land closest to the Netherlands, again scored a first by adopting *woonerf*-type schemes. A notable plan was also initiated in Munich in the same year. Meanwhile, however, Dutch practice was itself shifting towards traffic calming with road humps and other physical restraint measures, as a simplified and cheaper form of *woonerf* (which involved a complete change of the road space). It was this variant which the West Germans also began to pursue and which they developed further in the late 1970s. By 1979 there were 96 traffic-calmed areas in West Germany, mainly in older housing areas. In 1980 the federal government sponsored a major research project on the subject, monitoring the effects of traffic calming in order to define good practice.

## THE INTERNATIONAL CONTEXT OF WEST GERMAN PLANNING

This last example makes it clear that West German innovations in planning certainly did not arise in isolation. There had always been a strong German interest in drawing lessons from planning in other countries. The post-1945 occupation period had, as we have seen, enforced some of these international connections. By the 1960s and 1970s, however, West Germans were making full use of their affluence and the easing of foreign travel to draw international lessons in a much freer fashion. A rapidly growing number of educated West Germans were also fluent in English (and, to a lesser extent, other languages). As previously, Britain remained an important referent. Thus its new interest in the systems approach, for example, had a significant impact on German planning thought. This British work was, of course, building on American developments in planning methodology. Increasingly, West German planners were also taking a more direct interest in the United States. Meanwhile, the growing salience of the European Community created a climate in which a much closer awareness than ever before of what was happening in France could develop. The keen interest, by the 1970s, in the experiences of Germany's smaller neighbours, particularly the Netherlands and Denmark, was another important development.

The 'export' side of the trade balance in planning knowledge also rose markedly during the 1960s and 1970s. The sheer quantitative scale of reconstruction, especially housing production, had, of course, already impressed many foreign observers by the early 1960s. At that time, however, there had been little that was genuinely innovative in a qualitative sense. This soon began to change. In particular, West German leadership in pedestrianisation and the emergent area of traffic restraint won increased international attention as environmental concerns began to strengthen throughout the west in the 1970s. Nor was it simply a transfer of professional knowledge. Battles such as those for Frankfurt's Westend or Kreuzberg in Berlin had more than local significance. With the others that followed in most major cities, they helped to make West Germany a hothouse for the new, socially radical green politics that began to blossom in the 1980s (Pulzer, 1995). In turn, this new movement helped to redefine the nature and content of urban planning discourse throughout the west in the decades which followed.

## THE UNITED STATES

As we have seen, the American way of life (and of organising cities) continued to generate interest in major European countries. The lessons drawn were a complex mixture of positive exemplars and increasingly awful warnings. The key defining trait of the United States was that it was the most materially successful society the world had ever known (Patterson, 1998). Despite its already advanced state, the American economy grew at a rate not far behind that of most of western Europe in the 1960s. It also slightly outperformed West Germany in the 1970s. Like every other nation, its population was expected to grow rapidly. Official predictions in the early 1960s were that there would be roughly 300 million Americans by 2000 (Scott, 1969). This did not happen, but high natural increase and substantial immigration ensured that growth was still very rapid by western standards. Between 1960 and 1980 the population grew by just over a quarter, to 227.7 million in 1980. (By 2000, it had reached 273 million).

The benefits of American prosperity were, however, far less evenly spread than was usual in the social democracies of western Europe. In 1964, almost a fifth of the population, and a very much higher proportion of black Americans, were defined as living in poverty (McKelvey, 1968; Fox, 1985). If this was not absolute poverty in the Third World sense, there remained urban and rural deprivation on a scale that resembled that in far poorer countries. Nor did the negative side of the American experience appear only in broad social indicators (Morgan, 1991). The specific moments which have come to define the 1960s and 1970s, the assassinations of President John Kennedy, Martin Luther King and Robert Kennedy, and the demise of Richard Nixon's presidency in a criminal conspiracy, also reveal the nation's pessimism and shame.

These contradictions were deeply rooted in the wider American experience. In retrospect, we can see that the United States actually strengthened its global position by 1980. During the 1960s and 1970s, however, this outcome was by no means clear and many Americans remained deeply insecure about themselves and their place in the world. 1962, for example, saw the United States and the Soviet Union come terrifyingly close to nuclear war over Cuba. Until the later 1960s national techno-logical prestige was also dented by fears that the United States was being left behind in space exploration. Most troubling in the long term for American self-esteem was the Vietnam war, with the country's increasingly controversial military involvement, especially from 1964 until the humiliating withdrawal in 1973.

The war provided a major focus for the heightened domestic political activism throughout the west in the late 1960s and early 1970s, especially in the United States itself. Here was the radical cause that gave a hard edge to the counterculture that had been coalescing since the mid-1960s. Yet it was neither the first nor most profound source of social and political unrest in that decade. From the late 1950s, the civil rights movement to end racial discrimination had begun to shake up mainstream affluent (and increasingly suburban) white American society. Though the leaders of the movement were not involved, their message was underlined by disorganised and violent urban disorder. Between 1964 and 1970 every major metropolitan city experienced at least one outbreak of serious rioting, largely by black people.

## METROPOLITAN SOCIAL CHANGE

These events need to be set within the profound demographic shifts that had been under way in metropolitan areas since the 1940s (Fox, 1985). By 1970 the movement to the suburbs, which was to date overwhelmingly white, had become so great that, for the first time, suburban populations outnumbered those of the core cities. The gap opened up dramatically in the 1970s. By 1980, some 101.5 million Americans lived in suburbs, 26 million more than had lived in them 10 years earlier. This was almost 45 per cent of the total population, compared to just 30 per cent in the core city areas. The social and political changes in the status of black Americans are crucial to understanding this. The historic flow of black people from the rural South, where racism had been most severe, to the core cities of metropolitan areas was ending.

And, for the first time, growing numbers of more affluent black Americans were beginning to follow the white flight to the suburbs. As a result core city populations, which were predominantly black in a growing number of cases, were either static or declining. They also contained ever-larger proportions of the poor and disadvantaged, the groups least able to aspire to suburban living.

## URBAN RENEWAL

The most obvious impact of urban planning on the older parts of metropolitan areas in the 1960s was through urban renewal (Fox, 1985; Garvin, 1996). As we saw in Chapter 6, by the later 1950s what had originated as a public-housing-led programme had become a vehicle for high-value residential and even commercial development. The tendency became even stronger in the 1960s as legislative constraints were further relaxed. All this, of course, made this approach to urban renewal – which reached its peak during the middle 1960s – increasingly attractive to private developers and most city governments. They welcomed the opportunities to enhance property values and to reverse the middle-class exodus to suburbia.

Some cities used urban renewal to create memorable environments (though not for those who were displaced). The Washington Square East project in Philadelphia, better known as Society Hill, developed from 1960 to 1964, was the one that was most widely admired. To North American planners, this was urban renewal at its best. To Europeans, it reinforced the general perception of Philadelphia as an American city where planning really counted. It was conceived in outline by Philadelphia's formidable city planner, Edmund Bacon, but also owed a great deal to the developer and his architect (Bacon, 1974). The project combined outstanding modern architecture in new apartment towers, extensive renovation of older row houses, infilling with smaller groups of new town houses and exceptionally fine public open spaces. Another notable example (which originally involved the same developer and architect as Society Hill) was the South West Washington project, begun in the mid-1950s but not completed for more than 20 years.

## OPPOSITION TO URBAN RENEWAL AND FREEWAYS

There were, however, growing criticisms that, far from gaining from projects like these, the poor (and, increasingly, black) residents of areas being cleared were actually the main losers. They suffered social disruption and often found themselves in new, often high-rise housing that soon became a source of new problems. By the early 1960s major criticisms of this approach were being published, most notably by Jane Jacobs in 1961 and Herbert Gans in 1962 (Jacobs, 1964; Gans, 1962). Both were also critical (along with a growing number of other commentators) of the effects of freeways in cities. As we saw in Chapter 6, the impact of these was growing during the 1950s (Altshuler, 1983). At the outset, they were usually driven through more run-down neighbourhoods, many of which had black (or, on the west coast, Chinese or Hispanic) populations. However, as more middle-class and settled communities were threatened highly organised and more influential protest movements began to emerge.

The earliest were in San Francisco during the late 1950s, but they became much stronger in the early 1960s as proposals for major extensions were unveiled (Woodbridge, 1990). By 1966, all planning of freeways in the city had ceased. Other challenges soon appeared elsewhere, for example in Boston, Philadelphia, Richmond, Seattle, New Orleans and Washington. The later campaigns, such as that in Boston against the proposed South West Expressway in 1968/9, show the beginnings of a widening environmental critique (LW Kennedy, 1992). Options which relied more on public transportation were already being unveiled, the first being San Francisco's Bay Area Rapid Transit, approved in 1962 and constructed from 1964.

## MODEL CITIES

Traditional urban renewal was also superseded in the later 1960s by approaches that addressed the social and economic roots of urban decay, rather than just their physical symptoms. An important precondition for these policies was the creation of the cabinet-level Department of Housing and Urban Development (HUD) by President Johnson in 1965 (Scott, 1969; Fox, 1985). It was important both as a sign of the priority given to urban affairs and as a vehicle for advancing and implementing urban policies. It was also headed by the first black American ever to reach this level of government: Robert Weaver. The 'model cities' programme, unveiled in 1966, was the most ambitious actual policy that HUD promoted. It was a response to both the epidemic of urban unrest amongst black populations in the big cities and the more considered representations of the civil rights movement. Well-funded at the outset, it was typified by the identification of very wide areas within which planners envisaged a mix of partial redevelopment, rehabilitation and area improvement, and various community development measures.

## CHANGES IN THE 1970s

In the event, the ambition of the model cities programme greatly exceeded the duration of the funding (JB Cullingworth, 1993). Big federal projects of any kind, especially those with a largely social purpose, always tended to have many political enemies. And by the early 1970s a combination of several different factors strengthened the opposition to such projects. The growing popular dislike of, and opposition to, the results of modernist urban planning was difficult to ignore. The widely publicised 1972 demolition, with explosives, of the Pruitt-Igoe public housing in St Louis was seen as symptomatic of widespread attitudes (P Hall, 1988). Although the balance of policy had already shifted away from this kind of project, for many Americans the incident confirmed that they did not want to see federal money being used for ambitious urban policies. The Republican President Nixon was also instinctively less committed to a social urban policy than the Democrat presidents Johnson or Kennedy.

These attitudes were strengthened as the American economy, the world's most profligate consumer of oil, much of it imported, slowed down when world oil prices rose dramatically in 1973 and 1974 (Fox, 1985). Nixon imposed a complete halt on spending on urban policies in 1973. A different programme followed in 1974, and finally saw the eclipse of slum clearance. As in Britain, the new approach favoured rehabilitation and other measures of neighbourhood improvement and economic development (Garvin, 1996). In 1976 another, more targeted, programme appeared under President Carter but with lower funding and, again, only a short life. A few cities achieved notable successes, however, even in the less favourable funding climate of the 1970s. Thus New York managed to bring significant improvements to the better parts of Washington Heights in Harlem with housing rehabilitation policies. These relied on the cooperation of private investors. Yet the most run-down parts of Harlem proved more difficult to ameliorate by this means. This was because private investors, not surprisingly, were unwilling to put funds into housing from which they did not anticipate an adequate return.

## METROPOLITAN PLANNING

Growth projections and the obvious pace of outward suburban growth rekindled interest in strategic metropolitan planning in the 1960s (Scott, 1969). This scale of planning continued to be handicapped by a complete lack of effective metropolitan government. Outside cities with areas that had usually not been extended (in the older industrial regions, at least) since the 1920s, lay a mosaic of suburban cities, all eager to escape the tax burdens of metropolitan services (KT Jackson, 1985). They were only willing to pool their autonomy for the most pressing matters, and planning future growth was not generally seen as one of these. Moreover, neither state nor federal governments were willing either to knock heads together or to give the financial assistance that would have encouraged cooperation, at least on this matter. Metropolitan regional planning bodies existed as legal entities in several cities, for example Baltimore and Chicago. In some cases they came up with interesting proposals, such as the creation of 'metrotowns' to give focal points for the outward expansion of Baltimore (Whittick (ed), 1980). But legal enforcement remained at the local level and, as always in the United States, this tended to mean that developers shaped events. Thus the most ambitious efforts of the 1960s and early 1970s came to almost nothing.

## THE WASHINGTON REGIONAL PLAN 1961

Much the most notable example of this was the National Capital Planning Commission's proposals for the Washington region, unveiled in 1961 (Scott, 1969). Envisaging that the population would grow from about two to five million by 2000, the plan advocated a memorable spatial form. It was based on linear corridors of development extending out from the District of Columbia like the spokes of a wheel, interspersed with open green wedges. The spokes would include a series of new towns as nodes on the main communication routes that were to be the functional basis of the spokes. This was the American equivalent to the Greater London plan of 1944, the 1947 Copenhagen 'finger' plan, the Stockholm satellite plan of 1952 and the slightly later Paris plan of 1965. The earlier European plans were very well known to the

Washington planners, who were led by William Finley. There was obvious admiration for the Scandinavian approaches which, because of their possibilities for extension, were seen as more suitable for high growth predictions than the London approach. The strong public agencies created to build British new towns were, however, admired as a possible model for building the new communities.

The problem was that, even in the heady optimism of the Kennedy years, Washington remained in the United States. It had not shifted to western Europe (nor to Canada). There was, accordingly, no enthusiasm for the regional rapid transit system that would, in the manner of the Parisian RER, have created the essential functional network for implementing the plan. Washington acquired a superb metro system, but one that barely extended beyond the District of Columbia. Nor was there enthusiasm for the higher density development around the transit nodes that made up the spokes, nor any likelihood of strong public agencies to build these new communities. Meanwhile, in the absence of any strong controls on building in the urban fringe, suburban developers were busy acquiring and building on the would-be green wedges.

The fact that little came from this, the most influentially supported exercise in American metropolitan planning during these years, speaks volumes for the fate of the others. It also makes it easy to appreciate why American planners looked with such wonderment at the massive political commitment that allowed the implementation of the 1965 Paris plan on such a grand scale. Despite this, however, the Washington plan attracted international attention in the 1960s, before the size of its implementation gap became apparent. Buchanan, for example, cited the plan in 1963 as evidence that the United States was capable of developing planned models as an alternative to sprawl (MT, 1963). More generally, it helped to establish an interest in corridor plans in the Anglophone world, especially in Australia (Morison, 2000).

## NEW TOWNS: RESTON, COLUMBIA AND IRVINE

Nor was the idea of planning new communities entirely fanciful. The 1960s saw two widely admired private sector attempts to build new towns close to Washington at Reston, Virginia, begun in 1962, for an original target population of 72,000, and Columbia, Maryland, in 1963, for 110,000 (Garvin, 1996). Both were the products of remarkable developers: Robert E (Bob) Simon at Reston (his initials are incorporated in the name) and James Rouse at Columbia. Of the two, Reston's links to the mainstream of American garden city thought were the more obvious. Its planner was Julian Whittlesey, a long-standing associate of Clarence Stein.

Whittlesey's awareness of both the Radburn tradition and more recent European efforts was palpable, not least in his pervasive desire to achieve community through physical design and local service provision (KC Parsons, 1992b; Birch, 1983). Reston's planning also had many Radburn touches and showed the characteristic desire to create community through design and providing local services. Columbia's planning was generally seen as more innovative. Rouse relied mainly on his company's in-house expertise (with Morton Hoppenfeld as head of planning and design). However, the important point was that he also created an advisory panel of many nationally known experts. In its essentials, the resultant plan was rather similar to that for

# Homes as complete as Columbia itself!

At Running Brook every Levitt home is centrally air conditioned. Every home is equipped with major kitchen and laundry appliances—all by General Electric. Those items alone add up to about $2,000. All are included in the price of the house!

And there are other features you'd normally expect to pay extra for—things that add to the beauty, privacy, comfort, and convenience of these fine homes...without adding to your cost! Hardwood kitchen cabinets, for example; and a stainless steel sink and range hood, built-in vanities, sliding glass doors, decorator-selected lighting fixtures. At Running Brook these are all part of the stated purchase price! Complete landscaping, too.

**Outstanding value!** With all these extra features, prices at Running Brook are surprisingly low. A three-bedroom ranch home with two baths and attached garage costs as little as $27,990. And there are five different home designs to choose from! All are on gently rolling property, many on lots along the fairways of the beautiful Allview Golf Course.

**In America's newest city!** Residents of Running Brook, as part of Columbia, will enjoy concerts, sports, shopping, shows, dance groups, and many other cultural and social advantages of this complete new city. Levitt and Sons invites you to see downtown Columbia and the main exhibit center—then inspect the amazingly complete homes at Running Brook. Decorator-furnished models are open weekdays 'til seven, weekends until six at night.

**Only 10% down...no closing costs!**

*From Baltimore:* Baltimore Beltway to Exit 16. Take Route 70N to Route 29, then south on 29 to Route 108 (Clarksville Pike). Turn right, drive to Ten Mills Road. Turn left to Exhibit Area (Columbia Tour Bus Stop No. 17).

**The Regency**
*4 bedrooms, 2½ baths,*
*2-car garage—$34,250*
*including central air conditioning.*
*Also available with*
*1-car garage.*

## Running Brook at Columbia *by Levitt and Sons* INCORPORATED
5083 Whetstone Rd., Columbia, Maryland · Tel. 737-8850
OUR 40TH YEAR

Reston, with a hierarchy of retail and service provision. The smallest unit was the residential cluster, with nine villages (each of four or five clusters) and a town centre serving the villages.

Both new towns were widely admired by garden city enthusiasts in the United States, Britain and elsewhere. They appeared to have combined a privately orchestrated development process with many of the planning aspirations of publicly initiated new towns. Amongst other things, both Reston and Columbia subscribed to the principle of social mix, with some provision of lower-income housing. This mixing was modest by European standards but daring in American suburbia. Reston actually had a small amount of public housing, usually unknown outside core city areas. Garden city purists also approved of the extensive provision of employment, although the numbers of residents actually working in the towns in this highly motorised society fell far below British standards. Some of these features were found in another private new town begun in the early 1960s, though it had fewer pretensions to the garden city legacy. This was Irvine near Los Angeles. The biggest of the three (planned originally for a population of 430,000, and with 110,000 in 1990), it also proved the most successful, both financially and in providing jobs.

## A NEW COMMUNITIES PROGRAMME

These three examples suggested that new towns could be built without the heavy governmental involvement typical in Europe (Garvin, 1996). This was very important because the British-style development corporations admired by many American planners were politically impossible in the United States, except during national emergencies. The federal new communities programme of the late 1960s and early 1970s accordingly relied mainly on loans guaranteed by HUD for the private capital used to build substantial new settlements (Biles, 1998). There was also some grant aid available through other federal programmes. In all, 15 new communities approved by HUD were started. Two were 'in town', large developments within existing metropolitan cities, at Cedar-Riverside in Minneapolis and Roosevelt Island in New York City. The remainder were in urban-rural fringe locations and were more directly comparable to Reston, Columbia, Irvine and European examples. The most interesting in the context of the late 1960s was Soul City, North Carolina. This was to be developed by a black-owned company with direct links to the civil rights movement.

## THE FAILURE OF THE NEW COMMUNITIES

In the event, federal commitment proved short-lived, and the programme foundered during the 1970s. Almost all approved new communities defaulted on loans

**Figure 8.7** *Columbia was a private new town, the widely studied brainchild of the Baltimore developer, James Rouse. America's major house builders, including William Levitt, played their part in its construction.*

guaranteed by HUD. Seven were completely aborted and a further four changed beyond recognition. The two in-town new communities have gone ahead, though hesitantly (at Cedar-Riverside) and with many changes (at Roosevelt Island). Only two freestanding new communities, at St Charles in Maryland and Woodlands in Texas, have proceeded on broadly the intended lines and become profitable. Woodlands, which is close to the buoyant metropolis of Houston, is the more successful. It was developed by a large energy company with deep pockets (though, as elsewhere, development slowed following the oil crisis). Woodlands' plan was by William Pereira (also planner of Irvine) and followed the residential community grouping principles used at Reston and Columbia. By 1990, its population was 30,000, compared to its planned target of 150,000.

## AN ENVIRONMENTAL AGENDA

As in Europe, therefore, the 1970s brought a retreat from many of the bold 1960s planning aspirations. The American formation of the Friends of the Earth pressure group in 1969, soon the base for an international movement, was symptomatic of the emergent thinking. Reflecting this highly organised environmental lobby, smaller and more environmentally sensitive planning initiatives became more common. We have already noted the retreat from urban freeway construction and the shift in housing policies towards encouraging rehabilitation. Historic preservation of larger districts gradually became more common in the wake of historic-preservation legislation in 1966 and wider environmental-protection legislation in 1969 and 1976 (Garvin, 1996; B Cullingworth, 1997). A notable early example of a large historic district, declared in 1970, was at Pioneer Square in Seattle. It was already deemed a major success by 1976 (Park Lee, 2001).

A few modest experiments in managing growth to moderate suburban sprawl also began in the late 1960s and early 1970s. Leaders in this were Ramapo and Petaluma, two obscure towns in the states of New York and California. Both places were the subject of major litigation (in 1972 and 1976) which helped to define what was permissible by the use of zoning powers. The city of Boulder, Colorado, was also a leader. It found ways of protecting land from development by means other than zoning, including the withholding of city water supply (deemed illegal in 1976) and the purchase of development rights. Meanwhile some states were beginning to take action, most notably Oregon which laid the basis for a statewide growth management policy in 1973. A few other states, including Florida and New Jersey, also showed interest during the 1970s, though with few tangible impacts until later.

## CURBING THE AUTOMOBILE

There were a few rare instances where environmental consciousness even began to encourage restrictions on the automobile (Ewing, 1999). For example, there were cautious experiments with traffic calming in a handful of residential areas, particularly on the west coast in Seattle, Berkeley, Eugene and San José. For the moment these experiments were undertaken in a rather crude fashion, with limited awareness of how European practice was evolving. A few cities also experimented, generally much less successfully, with German-style central pedestrianisation of former traffic streets, partly to combat the effects of out-of-town shopping malls (Garvin, 1996; Robertson, 1997). The first small example had been opened in Kalamazoo, Michigan, in 1959 and was extended in 1970, by which time more were under way. Quite a number of these, such as the ambitious scheme opened in 1973 in Louisville, Kentucky, proved failures.

In part, the divergence between American and European experience reflected the extensive development in the United States of out-of-town malls easily accessible by car. Nor were traffic flows on the street grids of most American downtowns usually very high compared to the more convergent historic street patterns of European cities. The more successful American examples of pedestrianisation were usually partial, reducing but not entirely eliminating traffic, especially public transit. Along with high quality design, this was the key to the highly influential Transit Mall in Portland, Oregon. Opened in 1977, it was served by buses and crossed, from 1986, by the new MAX light-rail system. In the late 1970s Denver was also in the process of adopting a similar scheme, though without the light-rail system, which was completed in 1982.

## AMERICAN PLANNING METHODOLOGY AND PRACTICE

Important though these initiatives were in a North American context, few held much real interest from the European point of view. More relevant and successful examples were invariably available closer to home. The wider truth was that American planning in the 1960s and early 1970s was largely a story of high ambitions unfulfilled. Despite (or perhaps in part because of) this, American contributions to planning thought and technique were admired by many European, and especially British, planners. We have seen how urban transportation planning, systems planning and corporate planning techniques crossed the Atlantic in the 1960s and 1970s.

There was also European interest in some of the more radical American alternatives to these technocratic approaches, which sought more direct professional relationships with poorer communities than those familiar to European planners. The rise of these alternatives reflected the ethical dilemmas of working in core metropolitan cities during a period of social and racial tension. One important idea, developed in the mid-1960s, was advocacy planning (Davidoff, 1965). This involved planners directly representing the interests of specific deprived communities rather than some generalised (and therefore, it was argued, mythical) 'public interest'. Another concept was equity planning, associated in the 1970s with Norman Krumholz's work in Cleveland, Ohio (Krumholz, 1983). Krumholz asserted that the planner should always act as guardian of the interests of the weak and disadvantaged. In many respects, such alternative self-images of the planner were naive and romantic (Sandercock, 1998). Thus the advocate planners practising in Harlem and Boston soon realised that what the disadvantaged really lacked was power, rather than planning expertise. Yet to many young Europeans, entering planning employment in the 1970s when traditional certainties were starting to erode, the radical intent of the concept could still be inspirational.

## AMERICAN PLANNING LITERATURE IN THE 1960s

Extremely significant as a general underpinning for such experiments was the growing volume of American literature about planning and the issues surrounding it. In contrast to much of the most important European material this did not, in the main, originate from official sources. It included critical commentaries, research on planning's impacts and work of a more speculative or theoretical nature. By the 1970s, no other western country had a comparable corpus of recently published material written from viewpoints independent of governmental agencies. Several of these works became key texts in international planning thought.

Thus Jane Jacobs's 1961 classic polemic, *The Death and Life of Great American Cities*, was quickly absorbed by the opinion formers of planning throughout the west (Jacobs, 1964). Herbert Gans's various works similarly sowed seeds of doubt before comparable studies of planning's social impacts existed elsewhere (Gans, 1962; 1967). They also inspired many social researchers to replicate his work in their own countries. Another important American text from this time was Kevin Lynch's *The Image of the City* (1960), which showed that urban design had social meanings that were far more important than how it was judged by professionals. As well as showing how urban design could be investigated systematically, Lynch's work contributed to the growing antifreeway and preservation movements (Banerjee and Southworth, 1994). Meanwhile, though Rachel Carson's *Silent Spring* (1962) was not a specifically urban text it became one of the earliest contributions to the environmental movement. Less innovative (because his ideas were already widely known) but profound nonetheless was Lewis Mumford's *The City in History* (1961).

## AMERICAN PLANNING LITERATURE IN THE 1970s

The critical dimension grew stronger in the following decade. A work which enjoyed a short but intense vogue elsewhere was Oscar Newman's *Defensible Space* (1972). The author (actually a Canadian) tried to show exactly why modernist housing environments had so often failed. They created too much space that apparently belonged to no one, creating an ideal environment for vandalism and crime. The message was a positive one, however, suggesting that physical design and planning principles (which were actually borrowed from Montreal's older neighbourhoods) could also largely provide the answer (Germain and Rose, 2000). More far-reaching and insidious was Robert Venturi, Denise Scott-Brown and Steven Izenour's *Learning from Las Vegas* (1972). This explored the exuberant, colourful artlessness of American commercial architecture at its most kitsch. In doing so, it highlighted the sheer emptiness of modernist rational design, and pointed the way to a Post-Modernist approach.

More surprisingly, the United States also began to claim a central place in the emergent Marxian critique of planning that grew from the late 1960s, and which had initially been more readily grasped by European critics of planning than by American ones because it connected to work already in progress, especially in France. To a large extent the reason for this development was that American universities recruited some of the European leaders of this emergent discourse in the 1970s. The British geographer David Harvey moved to Baltimore and published a seminal text there in

1973. Called *Social Justice and the City*, it offered Anglophone geographers and planners a radical alternative to their positivist belief in systems theory. Manuel Castells, the Spanish sociologist, similarly moved to Berkeley in 1979. His key work on planning, *La Question Urbaine* (1972) had appeared while he was in Paris. Translated into English in 1977, it quickly established him as the leading critical theorist of urban planning (Castells, 1977). As so often before, the United States made sure that it was close to the centre of new thinking even when, like Castells' work, it essentially opposed the capitalist system of which planning was a part.

## TOWARDS THE POSTINDUSTRIAL CITY

For planners, one of the key problems was that this critical planning discourse could not be translated into practice. In fact, the most internationally significant American planning innovation of the 1970s developed in a far more pragmatic fashion. This was the emergent interest in building new postindustrial identities for the declining industrial and port cities. We have seen that economic development began to creep on to the urban policy agenda in the 1970s. Already, however, several cities were using local or state subsidies and tax exemptions to stimulate business investment in their downtown areas (Frieden and Sagalyn, 1989). In Boston for example, local tax reliefs were used from 1960 to promote office development such as the Prudential Center in the Back Bay (O'Connor, 1993). These measures were the latest instalment of a longer term partnership between city government and local business leaders. Other cities such as Pittsburgh and Baltimore were moving in similar directions, and for similar reasons (Fosler and Berger (eds), 1992).

The 1970s saw many cities follow this path, and with far more tenacity than ever before. The background was that the long-term outward movement of people and business combined with the international economic slowdown from 1973 to intensify already serious local economic problems. This, in turn, triggered a disastrous fall in local-tax income and a simultaneous rise in spending demands that was particularly serious because federal generosity was declining. Several cities including New York (in 1975) and Cleveland (in 1978) came, literally, to the brink of bankruptcy. From such experiences grew a wider determination to attract new investment and new sources of economic activity (Ward, 1998).

## FINANCING REGENERATION

A notable, though not conspicuously successful, early initiative in a particularly troubled city was the vast Renaissance Center in Detroit, opened in 1977 (Garvin, 1996; Neill *et al.*, 1995). The centre, located near but not quite in the downtown area, included offices, hotel facilities, convention facilities and retailing. Unusually, it was funded almost entirely from private sources. Even more unusually, this was not mainstream development finance but came largely from the business leaders of this motor city, led by Henry Ford II. Ford saw this as a corporate gesture of good will in the city's far from certain future (not unrelated to major withdrawals of manu-facturing investment by these same corporate leaders). Quick profits were not anticipated, which was just as well because they did not materialise, limiting the centre's role as a model for other cities. A more viable strategy for most cities was to seek a mixture of public and private funding in regeneration and this became the dominant approach at about this time (Frieden and Sagalyn, 1989; Fosler and Berger (eds), 1992). City spending whether direct, or indirect through tax exemptions, began to be redirected increasingly to win (or 'leverage') as much private investment as possible. It was an approach that President Carter's administration further encouraged by the federal Urban Development Action Grant (UDAG), introduced in 1977 (Barnekov *et al.*, 1989).

## PLANNING AND THE POSTINDUSTRIAL CITY

As well as UDAG, which was soon being admired in Britain, the actions of individual cities began to spell out a new approach. Several big ones began to promote major downtown shopping malls that would, they hoped, stop major chain stores abandoning the centres of cities for the suburbs (Frieden and Sagalyn, 1989). This practice was already known in Britain but, despite Victor Gruen's urgings in the 1960s (Gruen, 1964), came a little later to the United States. Two early and influential examples, which adopted dramatic and high quality multistorey designs, were at Water Tower Place in Chicago (opened 1976) and the Gallery in Philadelphia (1977). Meanwhile, however, even more significant innovations were in hand in Boston and Baltimore, where pioneering forms of development reused the spaces of the industrial era to create the basis of a postindustrial economy (O'Connor, 1993). Boston had already implemented key parts of what became the postindustrial formula, particularly in a convention centre (1965) and an aquarium (1969). In the 1970s, working with the developer James Rouse, it pioneered an entirely new form of tourist-oriented space, called the festival market place. Opened in 1976, the first example reused the derelict Quincy Market buildings to create speciality retailing and food outlets in a pedestrianised precinct. It was an instant success and was soon implemented elsewhere.

The second example, in Rouse's home city, was even more influential (Breen and Rigby, 1994; 1996). This was the Baltimore Harborplace, begun in 1978. It became the centrepiece of the ongoing redevelopment of the city's inner harbour, allowing Baltimore to become the archetypal postindustrial city and a major tourist destination (Harvey, 1989). Here, so it seemed to many city leaders in the United States and, increasingly, elsewhere, lay the answer to the problems of postindustrial decline. There was, of course, a gap between this perception and reality. But, as we have seen with previous planning innovations, once something is seen as successful there has always been a tendency to overlook limitations. In this case though, the simultaneous rediscovery in the later 1970s of a much older American urban tradition – boosterism – ensured that image triumphed easily over more sober reality (Ward, 1998). The model was New York, which in 1977 launched the famous I ♥ NY image campaign. Although actually a state campaign, it was widely credited as being an essential element in the city's return to fiscal probity. More importantly, this archetypal advertising campaign launched what soon became a global practice, whereby cities trumpeted their postindustrial reinvention.

## INTERIM CONCLUSIONS

By 1980, therefore, there had been important shifts in each of the four main planning traditions. The universal desirability of technocratic and comprehensive urban modernisation that had everywhere been the watchword of planning in the 1960s was now in question. The early 1970s brought different manifestations of crisis, whether in the violent confrontations of street battles, spectacular demolition of former modernist showpieces or quieter policy reversals. The achievements of 1960s planning were most spectacular, and its legacy most enduring, in France largely because the modernisation of which it was part genuinely permeated all aspects of French life. The technocratic approach to planning was questioned and aspects of the product were changed in the 1970s. But the reaction was less profound than elsewhere. In comparison, British planning, though it still attracted international attention, held less interest than in former years. The roots of modernisation were less deep in Britain than in France and its physical results were, in general, less convincing. Largely for economic reasons, in the 1970s planning began to change more profoundly in Britain than anywhere else.

*Figure 8.8* Rouse was also centrally involved in a key American contribution to urban regeneration. Boston's Quincy Market, opened in 1976, was the first of his festival market places, soon being widely reproduced elsewhere.

By comparison, the challenges that urban planning faced in West Germany were more overtly political. The more extreme of these would certainly have required nothing short of radical social transformation. Yet the specific form that West German urban modernisation had taken in the 1960s allowed its planners to respond more convincingly to the emergent environmental critique than their counterparts in other major planning traditions. This, in turn, gave a growing international significance to West German experience by the late 1970s. Finally, the United States exerted an international influence that was profound but even more contradictory than ever. Its innovative planning methodologies, evaluative research tradition, critical discourse and attempts at critical, socially aware practice were very influential. This was despite the limited impact they appeared to have on the reality of American cities. A few specific physical outcomes were admired and emulated to varying degrees, particularly those which harnessed the financial muscle of private developers to city planning. Yet, against these models there were also the negative lessons of urban decline and ethnic tension, which became all the more potent as planners in other countries began to see certain parallels in the way their own cities were changing. In fact, there was nowhere in the west that could remain uninterested in developments, whether positive or negative, within its most powerful member. We will find further support for this in the next chapter.

## CHAPTER 9

# THE ZENITH OF MODERNISATION AND BEYOND II: THE OTHER TRADITIONS

As in the major planning nations, planned urban modernisation throughout the rest of the advanced capitalist world failed, to varying extents, to fulfil its vaulting ambitions. Each country went along this road in ways that were broadly similar, though never exactly identical. In relative terms some of them, such as Sweden, the Netherlands and Japan, showed even more zeal for modernising their cities than countries with major national planning traditions. In the first two, at least, the domestic and international acclaim which had greeted their earlier model schemes was now to be severely tested by some later examples of their planned modernisations. Japan, its economic performance still outstripping that of the west, continued to find new ways to modernise, its faith in this paradigm comparatively undimmed even by the late 1970s. Other countries, for various reasons, were more cautious or simply slower in their pursuit of this goal.

Everywhere, though, a reaction of some kind had begun to set in during the late 1960s and early 1970s. Each country could point to some defining event that marked its own particular watershed. In many cases, the issues were similar to those we have noted in the major planning traditions: against roads, urban renewal, monolithic housing developments, other major construction projects or the loss of valued environments. But the intensity, singularity and wider significance of the reactions varied. Some assertive social movements that were formed out of an opposition to modernist planning, such as those in the Netherlands, Denmark, Australia and Canada, transcended the local and the national. They managed, or helped, to change the planning agenda in ways that were often to prove very creative. In effect, they encouraged new planning themes and responses that gave a wider or more coherent significance to developments already stirring on the margins of the professional mainstream.

The overall result was that, by the end of the 1970s, a new set of national planning exemplars from which positive lessons could be drawn was beginning to be identifiable. For some countries, such as Denmark or Canada, it marked a promotion to the international 'big league' of planning discourse. Japan, too, where faith in modernisation remained strongest, also became a more potent urban planning exemplar. Sweden, meanwhile, moved in the opposite direction to become less influential. By contrast, the Netherlands, its fellow champion amongst the minor national traditions of planned urban modernisation, proved much more successful in embracing and leading the emergent ideas and practices.

# THE NETHERLANDS

We have seen how international regard for Dutch urban planning rose rapidly during the middle years of the 20th century. This trend continued in the 1960s and 1970s, although the lessons to be drawn were not all as positive as previously. As everywhere in the west, the issues faced by planners in this small country were growth-related. The economy of the Netherlands grew more rapidly than that of all its neighbours except France. Dutch population growth, meanwhile, was the highest in northwestern Europe, rising by almost a quarter between 1960 and 1980 to reach over 14.1 million. As elsewhere, this was a product of high natural increase and immigration, mainly from the Caribbean, Turkey and Morocco (R King, 1998). As elsewhere, too, the high growth was expected to continue. In the mid-1960s, the forecasts for the national population in 2000 were about 20 million. The actual figure turned out to be just under 16 million, a proportionately similar shortfall to that in Britain and France.

## NATIONAL PHYSICAL PLANNING

Accommodating this growth was, accordingly, one of the major priorities. National planning reports in 1960 and, more especially, 1966 identified growth areas (Faludi and van der Valk, 1994; K Bosma and Hellinga, 1997b). Both drew on the original 1958 report on the Randstad and adopted many of its proposals (Berkelbach, 1997). It was through them that the concept of Randstad became widely known, reported extensively in international planning literature. The preferred strategy was *gebundelde deconcentratie* (literally bundled, or clustered, deconcentration). This was intended to give order to the outward movement of population from the bigger Randstad cities (van der Cammen, 1988). Definite growth centres were identified, often in locations which had been discussed in earlier reports.

One of the most significant of these, Zoetermeer near The Hague, was now endorsed as a major overspill location. This was despite the fact that it actually compromised a Randstad planning intention to limit development around The Hague and Rotterdam. More importantly, two large and entirely new towns were to be developed on the Flevoland polder at Lelystad and Almere (van der Wal, 1997). Work on Zoetermeer and Lelystad was already under way by 1966. (The site of Almere was still being reclaimed from the IJsselmeer.) In addition, many villages and smaller towns were to be expanded, especially to the north of Amsterdam (for example Alkmaar) and in the less populated northern part of the Netherlands. One especially notable example here was the proposed new town of Emmen, where major new industrial development in 1950 had already triggered expansion of this previously rural area (Huygen, 1997).

## PLANNING THE NEW TOWNS

The apparent clarity expressed in these national physical plans was not always reproduced in detailed schemes. Although there was national funding for social housing and infrastructure, much planning of this growth remained in the hands of municipalities or the polder reclamation authority. There were no special agencies to develop new towns on the British (or, later, the French) pattern. Nor was there an executive Randstad planning body comparable to the IAURP in the Paris region. A great deal needed to be resolved by negotiation between different levels of government and between different local authorities (Faludi and van der Valk, 1994). Allied with continuing national uncertainties about how big the new settlements should actually be, this gave a rather idiosyncratic character to the development of the new towns. Despite some important innovative features, all this certainly limited their international impact. They did not seem to constitute a model that could readily be borrowed. Thus the Paris team sent by Delouvrier to review new-town planning in the Netherlands, while finding much to admire, saw that the approach to the planning of Lelystad was confused (Merlin, 1971).

## LELYSTAD

The first Randstad overspill new town in Flevoland was named after Cornelis Lely, the engineer who had conceived the vast Zuider Zee reclamation scheme in the late 19th century (K Bosma, 1997a). As befitted the culmination of a heroic national battle with nature, the leading Dutch modernist planner, Cornelis van Eesteren, was commissioned to prepare a plan in 1959, which he presented in 1964 (Brouwer, 1997a; van der Wal, 1997). Throughout the planning process, however, he had no clear advice about the intended size of the town. There was dispute as to whether he been told to plan for 50,000 or 100,000 inhabitants. After several years of dithering (during which national population forecasts were falling) his plan was rejected as too ambitious. (Of course, this controversy was not only because of the deliberative, nonauthoritarian style of Dutch democracy. Other interpretations would note the personal tensions or, at the other extreme, see it as an early sign of the coming crisis of modernism.)

## ALMERE

At any rate, by the time Almere was planned in the 1970s more was being learnt about how uncertainty and flexibility could be built into the planning process (van der Wal, 1997; Brouwer, 1997b). Its plan, prepared by a team led by Teun Koolhaas and published in 1977, had to allow for a possible target population of about 250,000. Yet, by adopting a multinuclear structure that could be developed (or not) as necessary, it avoided the problems of its predecessor. Almere is generally considered to be the most successful of the Dutch new towns, growing to over 100,000 in the 1990s. Its location, much nearer Amsterdam than Lelystad and more centrally placed on national communication routes, helped a great deal. It was developed entirely as a low-rise and, by Dutch planning standards, low-density settlement (at about 35 to 40 dwellings per hectare). Two of the nuclei centres, at Almere-Haven and Almere-Stad, mimicked historic Dutch towns, with higher densities and mixed use. Overall, however, public transport use was, by Dutch urban standards, quite low. Yet, in striking contrast to Milton Keynes (a new town with which it has often been compared), car use has remained moderate, especially for nonwork travel (J Roberts,

1992). Almere might be the nearest Dutch planning has gone towards a suburban car-based lifestyle, but its design also gives great encouragement to bicycling and walking.

## PLANNING AMSTERDAM

The big cities remained powerful actors in Dutch planning. Much of what actually happened on the ground reflected their actions. After being internationally overshadowed by Rotterdam in the early postwar years, Amsterdam now became much more significant (DRO, 1994). Much activity was focused on the plan for Amsterdam and neighbouring areas, prepared by the city planners under Ko Mulder from 1958 to 1962. Its major proposals were large new residential extensions of the city, mainly to the north and in the southeast, each for 100,000 to 120,000 people, with further development in the south and more industrial expansion to the west. The northern development began first, in 1966. Increasingly, compared to earlier extensions, the trend was towards developments of the type found in France and Germany – high-density, high-rise blocks, here with semi-elevated roads and full

*Figure 9.1* *The Polder new town of Almere has offered a car-based suburban lifestyle to many of its residents. Its many admirers in other (especially Anglophone) countries are, however, struck by its relative compact residential areas, busways (borrowed from the British new town of Runcorn) and high rates of walking and cycling.*

pedestrian and cycle segregation. These earlier schemes were a rehearsal for the most ambitious development of this type southeast of Amsterdam, at Bijlmermeer.

## BIJLMERMEER

Two alternative plans were prepared for Bijlmermeer. One was low- to medium-rise, closer to the traditional postwar Dutch pattern. The accepted plan, however, relied on industrialised high-rise construction in a particularly overpowering design (DRO, 1994; Docter, 2000). Vast slab blocks, containing nine storeys of dwellings above a two-storey service level, were arranged honeycomb fashion to enclose large hexagonal open areas. A three-level movement system was adopted, with through traffic on top, local traffic underneath and pedestrians and cyclists at the bottom. Widely known internationally, it came to represent the nadir of postwar modernist planning in the Netherlands. In popular perception, it quickly became the Dutch equivalent of Sarcelles or the Märkische Viertel. Few Amsterdammers who had the choice wished to move there and it was soon occupied by large numbers of immigrants. The move to small-scale neovernacular development (*kleinschaligheid*), apparent at Almere and Lelystad, was, in part, a reaction to Bijlmermeer (van der Wal, 1997).

## TOWARDS THE COMPACT CITY

This was not, though, the only reaction to modernism. In fact, the Netherlands became an international leader in adapting to the popular and environmental pressures of the 1970s. There were several reasons for this. One lay in the early emergence there of environmental radicalism. This was especially so in Amsterdam, where the anarchist Provo movement challenged many aspects of planning policy from 1966 (DRO, 1994). A particular object of their anger was the urban renewal of the city's older quarters. This began from 1968 as more people moved out to the periphery or overspill towns. The usual modernist formula of large-scale development – changing the traditional street network – was strongly resisted.

Many of the most fiercely contested demolitions were those associated with road construction and the creation of a new underground metro system in the 1970s. In part, these investments in transport infrastructure were seen as necessary because the outward movement of population had triggered a substantial rise in commuting. (Unlike British and American cities, there was no substantial loss of jobs in the older cities.) The Provos wanted to see a more localised city and championed bicycle use. Although their radical actions alienated some, they played a key role in raising consciousness and encouraging a wider questioning of authority. During the 10 years from 1968 many proposed renewal projects were halted, or realised only in part.

By the late 1970s, planning policy had been shifted into something that was smaller scale and more respectful of the existing morphology and social fabric. In 1978 the city leaders rejected clustered deconcentration, and affirmed a wish that Amsterdam should become a compact city again. This involved retaining population and keeping as many activities as possible within the city, using traditional transport forms such as the tram, walking and the bicycle.

## THE ORIGINS OF THE *WOONERF*

In fact, as shown in the previous chapter, the key lesson drawn from the Netherlands in the 1970s and 1980s was in relation to traffic restraint. The ideas were rehearsed first in the small northern growth point of Emmen, near the German border (Huygen, 1997). Here two young planners, Niek de Boer and AJM de Jong, began planning expansion from the mid-1950s. De Boer supported the concept of an 'open green city' and he and de Jong worked on how this might be elaborated in detail. One aspect involved reclaiming residential streets from vehicles and allowing them to be part of the usable public space of the city. The idea was that drivers would feel they were in their own gardens and drive accordingly. The new term *woonerf* ('living street' or today, more usually in English, 'home zone') was coined in Emmen in about 1963 to describe this innovation. The concept was gradually implemented in Emmen's residential district plans, especially the second, for Emmerhout.

De Boer and de Jong's ideas became far more widely known when they were implemented in an older housing area in Delft in the late 1960s (Hass-Klau, 1990). By this time, there was greater theoretical underpinning for such an approach, most notably from the British Buchanan report's concept of environmental areas (MT, 1963). There were also some very specific local factors. The district chosen had a large student population which was more willing than others to take part in an experiment. It also helped that unstable soil conditions in the western Netherlands frequently required the complete renewal of street surfaces, facilitating the experimental redesign of street space. The experiment proved very popular with residents, including those who owned cars as it was possible to park close to where they lived.

## THE DIFFUSION OF THE *WOONERF*

The lessons learnt in Delft spread rapidly to other Dutch towns and cities. It helped that there was, simultaneously, publicity about vandalism to cars at Bijlmermeer which had been designed on Radburn lines with large unsupervised car parks (Hass-Klau, 1990). In 1976 the concept of the *woonerf* gained legal status and a special traffic sign was introduced. By 1978, 175 out of 800 Dutch local authorities had implemented *woonerf* schemes. This rose to 260 in 1980. Gradually though, there was a retreat from a full redesign to a cheaper traffic-calming approach. By this time, the innovation had also diffused beyond the Netherlands. Delft, a major historic city close to The Hague and Rotterdam and with a university prominent in architecture and planning, was well known internationally. Academics played an important role as intermediaries in spreading the idea and the practice, both as visitors to, and ambassadors from, Delft. Danish and, as we have seen, West German planners were quick to adopt (and adapt) the Dutch experiments (Ewing, 1999).

## DUTCH PLANNING IN ITS INTERNATIONAL CONTEXT

As all the above suggests, the Netherlands in the 1960s and 1970s possessed many of the preconditions for innovation. It had a planning movement that was highly developed in terms of technical expertise, and an articulate and questioning civil society. These characteristics were combined with a strong sense of the country's international position, and very high linguistic skills, especially in English, that allowed good contacts with all nearby countries and further afield. Several leading Dutch planners, for example, had received some educational training in the United States. The Netherlands'own planning schools also recruited staff from other countries. Most Dutch planners were therefore very well informed about planning developments elsewhere. In turn, many of these same factors helped to increase international knowledge of Dutch planning. Its innovations (positive and negative) were quickly noticed in other countries. During this period foreign observers of planning in the Netherlands saw developments about which they had doubts – so it was with planning everywhere, of course. Yet this, too, was evidence of the quality of the information flows. It also implied that admiration for the new directions Dutch planning was taking in the 1970s was part of a balanced and critical perspective.

## SWEDEN

Since the 1930s Sweden had been the other smaller European country whose urban planning had won very wide international attention. Yet the basis of its external appeal turned out to be narrower than that of Dutch planning. It rested on the single-minded Swedish commitment to creating, as part of a wider welfare state, the social democratic city through modernist planning. In the 1940s and 1950s Stockholm seemed to point the way to the kind of society many planners in other western countries thought that they wanted and their own societies needed. At that time there was still an innovative quality to what was being done in Stockholm and other cities. Viewed in the northern sunshine, there was a sparkling purity and freshness to planning and urban design in Sweden that entranced visiting groups. During the 1960s, however, the Swedish quest became more relentless, standardised and dreary (P Hall, 1998).

## PLANNING STOCKHOLM

In the 1960s there was actually a high degree of planning continuity with the earlier period. In Stockholm the spatial model of satellites linked to the centre by a high-capacity *tunnelbana* metro system remained the essential basis of metropolitan planning. Now, however, it was extended beyond the city boundaries. These proposals were formalised in a new Stockholm regional plan, published in 1966 and approved in 1973. Yet, despite the creation of new bodies with responsibilities for this wider area, the administrative basis was less clear cut than within the city. There was much scope for disagreement between Stockholm and the suburban local authorities. These problems were hardly unique to the Swedish capital, but few other cities were as ambitious in what they tried to achieve within this kind of framework. It certainly did not help as wider problems began to arise in the 1970s.

## THE MILLION HOMES PROGRAMME

The political ambition that took Swedish modernism over the edge was the 10-year million homes programme, adopted in 1965 (T Hall, 1991a; Nyström, 1996; P Hall, 1998). This was the great push that would solve the Swedish urban housing problem. It would meet the shortfall, allow slums to be eliminated and provide more spacious and better-equipped homes. Its scale can be gauged by the fact that in 1965 Sweden had a total housing stock of only three million. (Moreover, Sweden added only 0.8 million to its population in the 1960s and 1970s, to reach 8.3 million in 1980.) The programme's heroic aspiration could only be realised through greater industrialisation of housing production. Sweden began to adopt system construction methods on a very extensive scale, using large prefabricated panels. As we have seen, these methods were mainly pioneered in France. During the 1960s, however, different variants were being developed and diffused throughout western Europe, and adopted to varying extents in national housing programmes.

**Figure 9.2** *By the 1960s, Stockholm's development was sufficiently advanced to form an international benchmark for the kind of complex multi-level central cities now being aspired to elsewhere.*

## LATER SATELLITE TOWNS

Sweden became one of the most committed users of industrialised construction, with dramatic effects on the planning and design of the resulting residential areas (Andersson, 1998; Lundén, 1994). In contrast to the mixed-height development and careful attention to topography that was characteristic of early satellites such as Vällingby and Farsta, this later generation had designs and site planning directly shaped by the requirements of industrialised production. While the old lessons of maximising sunlight were not forgotten, sites were now levelled and completely uniform building layouts were adopted, to facilitate the movements of tower cranes and allow continuous delivery of building components. As elsewhere, these methods tended to work best with large high-rise structures.

## GROWING CRITICISMS

Serious criticisms of these new approaches began about 1970. The first target was the new Skärholmen satellite, in the southwest fringes of Stockholm (P Hall, 1998). This

*Figure 9.3* *Increasingly, Swedish planners were not being as successful in meeting the aspirations of their own people. Skärholmen was the first satellite town to experience serious problems, attributable partly to bleakness and increasing standardisation of the production process.*

was by no means the worst example, however. The slightly later Tensta-Rinkeby satellite was exceptionally bleak and its transport links and community facilities were for a long period inadequate (Andersson, 1998). Other later satellites such as Fittja and Alby, more distant from the centre and outside the city, faced similar problems. The other big Swedish cities had comparable areas, such as Hammarkullen in Göteborg and Rosengård in Malmö (T Hall, 1991a).

Meanwhile, the housing shortage had begun to ease markedly, with the result that many of these unpopular areas found it difficult to attract residents. A growing number of Swedes were rebelling against their leaders' presumption that they should live in rented multistorey blocks of flats. Instead they were showing an ever stronger desire to live in single family houses that they could own. Areas of such housing were appearing in other kinds of suburbs immediately beyond the boundaries of Sweden's cities. As happened throughout western Europe, the long-term residents of high-rise rental housing became those with fewest options. They were the people who were experiencing other social problems, together with a growing number of recent immigrants, in the 1970s mainly Yugoslavs and Greeks (Nyström, 1996).

## A CHANGING AGENDA

The 1970s recession hit Sweden particularly hard, which put further pressure on the hugely expensive housing programme. Construction, especially of flats, fell rapidly in the later years of the decade. Far more emphasis was placed on lower rise developments, private building of single family homes for ownership and the renewal of older dwellings. As elsewhere, the new western interest in the environment also began to exert an influence (Tonell, 1997; P Hall, 1998). In 1971, on an American initiative, but feeding on genuine local sentiments and a new willingness to challenge authority, an arm of Friends of the Earth was established. Yet Swedish planners were not to be in the first wave of international trendsetters, interpreting what the new environmentalism would mean for urban planning.

## THE INTERNATIONAL CONTEXT OF SWEDISH PLANNING

These changes also marked a significant shift in Sweden's international balance of trade in planning ideas. Swedish, especially Stockholm's, planners had played a central role in articulating modernist western urban planning after 1945. After prewar borrowings from Germanic modernism, they had shifted to a more Anglo-American frame of reference over the postwar years (T Hall, 1991a; 1991b). In turn, their models had very directly influenced their Nordic neighbours. Finnish planning, for example, was said to follow Sweden 'as the carriages follow the engine' (Sundman, 1991: 93). Such links were also institutionalised in the training of planners. Thus in 1968 a Nordic planning institute was formed in Stockholm to give advanced training to practising planners from all Nordic countries (including Iceland).

Gradually, however, this pre-eminence began to diminish, most noticeably in the new practice of traffic restraint. Swedish planners, while acknowledging Buchanan's seminal theoretical role (and his compliments to their own practice), increasingly drew their practical lessons from the Netherlands, West Germany and Denmark. This is not to imply, however, that Swedish planners were particularly slow to adopt such ideas, particularly in the cities closest to the most innovative countries. Thus during the 1960s Göteborg became the first city to follow Bremen in preventing through movement of traffic in its central area (Hass-Klau, 1990). With Malmö, it also became a Swedish leader in traffic calming in the 1980s. Internationally, however, the style of planning that had been particularly associated with Sweden, and especially Stockholm, was now being eclipsed.

# DENMARK

Though its influence was never as pervasive as Sweden's had been, the new Nordic innovator of the 1970s was Denmark. Although the country's population growth was, like Sweden's, relatively low by international standards, the Danish economy was Scandinavia's fastest growing in the 1960s. And though, as everywhere, its economic growth rate fell in the 1970s, it remained higher than Sweden's. Denmark was also geographically closer to the Netherlands and West Germany, where the new thinking was moving most rapidly. There were other factors reinforcing such connections. Thus West Germany became its major trading partner during the 1960s, replacing Britain. Like the Netherlands, Denmark was a fairly flat, temperate country with a strong bicycling tradition. Moreover, its fragmented island structure had not encouraged the early growth of a strongly car-oriented society. Rather like the Dutch (and far more readily than the Swedes), the Danes also embraced the new anti-authority political and environmental activist movements of the late 1960s and 1970s (Lemberg, 1997).

## PLANNING URBAN EXPANSION

Although, as we saw in Chapter 7, Denmark had followed a more conventional approach than Sweden in the design of new housing areas since 1945, in the 1960s it too embraced large-scale industrialised construction. Very standardised layouts to allow cranes to be used became common, and traditional references in the architecture disappeared. To the west and southwest of Copenhagen new satellite areas appeared, often with high-rise flats, implementing and elaborating the famous postwar 'finger' plan. The most interesting part of this was the extension to the plan's 'thumb', southwest of Copenhagen, along Køge Bay (Harvest, 1978; Lemberg, 1997). In 1961, a committee of the 10 local authorities in the area began to coordinate its development as a primarily residential linear new town, influenced by, without directly copying, British models. In the 1966 plan there were 10 development nodes along a commuter rail link, with multistorey development at stations and lower density beyond. From a population of about 12,000 in 1960, the area was planned to reach about 150,000 by 1990. Of course, as growth projections fell, these targets were not fulfilled and the outer nodes were smaller than originally envisaged. In the late 1970s, the shoreline was developed (by Dutch planners) as a coastal park and resort.

Alongside these attempts to create more consciously planned communities, there was also a great deal of relatively unplanned development in the 1960s and early 1970s (B Larsson and Thomassen, 1991). Much of this was single family 'catalogue' homes (also produced by industrialised methods), especially northwest of Copenhagen and around other larger centres. Such developments were usually poorly coordinated with employment location and service provision, and contributed to a rise in commuting, especially by car. There were, however, some attempts to focus development into major planned expansions of provincial cities. Especially notable were the overambitious plans in the early 1970s for urban extension associated with large new

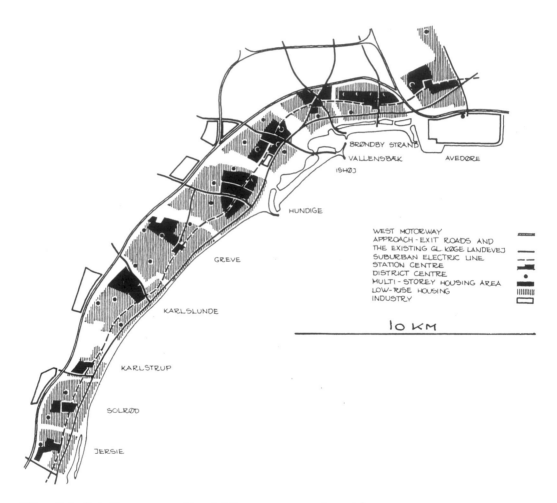

**Figure 9.4** *Køge Bay was a multi-nodal linear new town planned for Copenhagen along a commuter rail link in the 1960s. The avoidance of a single large-scale development was very typical of the generally modest scale of much Danish planning.*

universities at Odense and Ålborg. Both were strongly influenced by the important British new town plan for Milton Keynes and borrowed its characteristic grid layout.

## DANISH HOUSING

Many of the high-rise expansion areas around Copenhagen and other urban areas experienced social histories similar to their equivalents elsewhere (B Larsson and Thomassen, 1991; Lind and Lund, 1996). Yet the story is not quite the same. Overall, the Danes made rather less use of high-rise forms than planners elsewhere, especially in Sweden. From an early stage, low-rise, high-density housing became a more typical Danish solution. One of the best known was at Albertslund where, early in the 1970s, there were conscious attempts to plan for community interaction, using very standardised housing types but with more inventive site layouts and public space. During the 1970s more irregular low-rise plans evolved, often developed with public involvement (and approval). Some higher rise developments continued, though these also benefited from a less technocratic and more participative planning approach.

## PLANNING OLDER CITY AREAS

It was, however, in the planning of already built-up parts of the Danish capital that emergent trends and newer external influences were most apparent. In 1962, for example, the Strøget, Copenhagen's most famous shopping street, was pedestrianised (Gehl and Gemzøe, 1996; Lemberg, 1997). This was by no means the first such European effort – many West German cities and the Kalverstraat in Amsterdam were earlier. But the bold decision to pedestrianise the main shopping street of a capital city made this the most influential initiative of its kind anywhere in the world at this time. Despite fierce opposition from retailers at the outset, its tremendous success, commercially and otherwise, encouraged significant extensions in Copenhagen from 1968. A relevant factor in this success in making changes in the Danish capital was that the population had been declining since the early 1950s. Car use in the city also began to fall from about 1964.

The growing international impact of this Danish experience with pedestrianisation was helped by the publication, in 1971, of a very important book, *Livet mellum husena* – 'Life between buildings' (Gehl, 2001). Its author, Jan Gehl, drew on Copenhagen's experience to consider pedestrianisation as being a part of urban design and social and cultural life, rather than merely a matter of highways engineering and administration. For the moment, however, his readership was limited largely to the Nordic countries.

## THE RISE OF THE GRASS ROOTS

As well as underpinning pedestrianisation schemes, declining car use also encouraged public opposition to new roads schemes. These were built in suburban districts, not in the city of Copenhagen. Urban renewal to replace older housing also began in earnest in the 1970s. However, this too prompted growing public opposition. None of these shifts were unusual, of course, and reflected trends evident throughout the west. What was more distinctive about the Copenhagen planning scene was the rapid growth of highly organised grass-roots activism (Lemberg, 1997; Lind and Lund, 1996). This took various forms. At times there were violent confrontations, similar to those in West German cities, though this was not the most typical response. The later 1960s, for example, saw the creation of 12 entirely unofficial 'councils' throughout the city which harried the official city council and its new planning department (created in 1968) on many issues. Later the city accepted their existence in a more formal way and used them as advisory boards.

A more autonomous grass roots movement in Copenhagen was the 'free town' of Christiania, declared in 1971. This came into being when the military barracks in the old fortified area of Christianshavn in central Copenhagen were closed. Official plans were made for the area but, before these could be implemented, the area was taken over by 1,000 or more young people who declared it a 'free town' that operated according to its own rules. The 'christianits' were influenced by comparable counter-cultural movements in the United States and the Netherlands, which had broadly anarchist/environmentalist approaches. Yet there were many distinctive features, not least of which was the way Christiania was increasingly tolerated by the city and its wider population. The settlement now pays for water and electricity and contributes some taxes. Its scale and persistence for three decades, within a capital city, make it perhaps the most remarkable western example of 'alternative planning'.

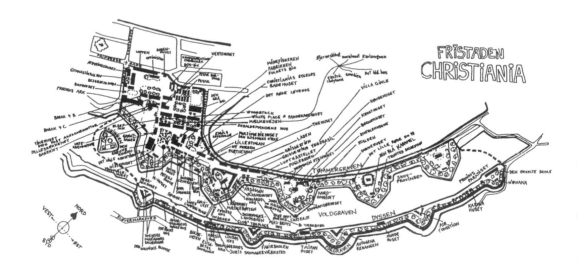

**Figure 9.5** *An alternative plan for the free town of Christiania in Copenhagen. Denmark moved relatively easily into the new thinking about the grass roots and 'bottom-up' planning in the 1970s.*

## DANISH PLANNING IN ITS INTERNATIONAL CONTEXT

It would be wrong to imply that official planning smoothly accepted this insurgent agenda. There were certainly tensions, which usually reflected periodic political shifts or moral panics. Yet there was also considerable tolerance and understanding. The result was that, as elsewhere, these radical initiatives helped to reorient the discourse of planning in Denmark, and especially in Copenhagen. Not surprisingly, the country became one of the leaders in the new thinking about urban traffic management in the 1970s. With the Dutch and the West Germans, Danish planners were the earliest international exponents of *woonerf* and traffic-calming concepts (Hass-Klau, 1990; Ewing, 1999). Thus it was that the *stillje veje* (quiet road) spread widely in Denmark during the later 1970s. As we have seen, it was also largely through Denmark (the first Scandinavian country to join the European Community, in 1973) that these ideas spread northwards. By the 1970s the Anglo-American frame of reference, so important in Danish planning for much of the 20th century, was being significantly modified by these growing links with its more immediate continental neighbours.

## OTHER PARTS OF EUROPE

### NORWAY

There were many parallels with Denmark and Sweden in the planning history of Norway over these years (Jensen, 1997; Lorange and Myhre, 1991). The country, traditionally seen as the most 'provincial' part of Scandinavia, underwent very rapid economic growth. Relative to the rest of Europe its economic performance was exceptionally high in the 1970s, when the huge growth of its offshore oil industry allowed it largely to avoid the economic slowdown apparent elsewhere. These growth pressures were reflected in particularly ambitious plans to modernise its cities, especially Oslo. Housing policies generally followed the pattern of those of neighbouring countries, with large-scale high-rise developments in suburban districts such as the Grorud valley to the east of central Oslo.

More notable, however, were the efforts to adapt the capital to motor traffic. This was because, in a major planning exercise for Oslo in 1963 and 1964, Norwegian planners were amongst the first in Europe to adopt American land use and transportation modelling techniques. The study itself attracted international attention. However, such methodological innovation did not overcome popular opposition to the new roads that were proposed. There was growing interest in the new ideas of traffic restraint and management during the 1970s, though the most important Norwegian contributions in this field were to come after 1980.

### FINLAND

Like Norway, Finland's economy was changing more rapidly than those of Sweden or Denmark. The burden of war reparations to the Soviet Union had become a catalyst for the growth of manufacturing industries. By the 1960s, rapid urbanisation was under way as Finnish people migrated into the growing industrial economy (Klinge and Kolbe, 1999). This was quite different to the pattern in many more developed parts of western Europe, where urban labour shortages were increasingly met by foreign immigrants. In the early 1960s Finland's preferred model for planned urban expansion reflected this experience in the distinctive 'forest town', with modern housing in a characteristically Finnish rural setting, pioneered at Tapiola (von Hertzen and Speiregen, 1973).

This approach was increasingly criticised by the mid-1960s, however. Finnish architects and planners followed their Scandinavian colleagues into industrialised construction (usually with Swedish building systems) and austerely rectilinear layouts, influenced by both Swedish high-rise and Danish-low rise examples (Sundman, 1991). Despite this, design quality remained high. Moreover, large developments, especially of high-rise housing, were rare. There was also much less reliance on public rental housing than elsewhere in Scandinavia. Private co-ownership was more typical. The almost complete absence of non-Finns also allowed an unusually high degree of social homogeneity. Housing areas of this period have generally experienced fewer problems than elsewhere, despite some outwardly common features.

Other aspects of Finnish planning were also distinctive. In Helsinki, for example, Alvar Aalto's early 1960s plan to create a new modernist cultural complex along the shore of Töölö Bay was especially striking (though only Finlandia Hall was realised). Another notable feature was the planning, in two stages in 1971 and 1979, of an off-centre commercial district at Pasila (ECFJS, 1997; HCPD, 2000). This was intended, La Défense-style, to relieve office-development pressure on the historic core of the city.

## ITALY

On the other side of Europe Italy's economy also grew very rapidly, almost at French levels, during the 1960s, though its performance was less dramatic in the 1970s. As in Finland, this brought a rapid growth in urban population, though there were few other similarities. In the 1950s and early 1960s workers from the country's rural south had gone to France, West Germany and Switzerland to become Europe's first international economic migrants. Now it was Italy's own industrial towns and cities, mainly in the north but increasingly also in the south, that attracted the migrants from the south (R King, 1998). As with France there was international interest in the rapidity of Italy's economic modernisation. Unlike France, however, there was almost nothing in Italian urban planning to stir the interest of planners in other countries.

Most of the reasons for this were political rather than because there was any lack of expertise on the part of the leading Italian planners, who were certainly aware of planning innovations in other countries (Whittick (ed), 1980; Calabi, 1984). The French concept of *aménagement du territoire* was, for example, borrowed in a national spatial plan drawn up in 1971. It was intended to facilitate a more balanced and ordered approach to economic and territorial development. Invariably, however, all grand strategies were compromised by a political opportunism that was more venal than almost anywhere else in western Europe. Plans for the big cities were delayed and overridden by powerful interests. Major reforms of planning were heavily compromised and building codes were ignored. At all levels of government corruption was common. This had important effects on the timing and execution of many public projects. Meanwhile, illegal (and often defective) private construction remained common, especially in the south and in tourist areas. Natural disasters, such as the 1967 Agrigento landslide, revealed (because they were worsened by) this culture of corruption and neglect. Even in Rome, in the mid-1970s, 0.65 million people were living in illegal dwellings built without permits, with a further 0.1 million in self-built shanty towns – together, roughly a quarter of the metropolitan population.

## SPAIN

Spain shared some of Italy's underlying features of economic growth, migration and urbanisation (M Wynn, 1984a). Rapid industrial growth and an even faster expansion of international tourism ensured that the country's economy grew as never before. There was a huge population shift to Madrid, Barcelona, Bilbao and other big centres. By the 1960s, however, it was the wider regions of these cities that were growing most rapidly. To a greater extent than in Italy, and more like most other parts of western Europe, the Franco dictatorship continued the very active housing policy it had begun in the 1950s, subsidising public and especially private builders (M Wynn, 1984b). Large peripheral housing projects, usually high rise, were built with industrialised methods (Salvadó and Miró, 1996; Ferrer, 1996b). Examples included San Ildefons in Cornellà, Montbau, Bellvitge, La Mina and Canyelles around Barcelona. The largest of these, such as Bellvitge (planned for up to 40,000 inhabitants), were comparable in size to their equivalents in France or West Germany.

This active housing policy eased (though it did not eliminate) the pressures for illegal construction. Yet it tended to take priority over local planning which largely failed to give effective direction or control to urban growth. Important national planning initiatives invariably overrode the local system, even where this sought similar outcomes. 1970 saw the most ambitious national planning policy – to house 0.8 million people in eight new towns built up to 30 kilometres from their parent cities and with local employment and services (M Wynn, 1984a). There were to be three of these for Barcelona (which had sought such a solution in local planning efforts) and one each for Madrid, Valencia, Seville, Zaragoza and Cadiz. There was, though, much opposition, including dissent from many planners at the proposed reliance on large private developers. In the event, the programme achieved almost nothing. Only one of these Tres Cantos – the Madrid new town – made any real progress (and then it was with some important organisational changes).

The programme had become caught up in a much bigger change: the end of Franco's dictatorship. By the 1970s there was widespread opposition to the regime, even though this was by then generally far less repressive than it had been in its early years. Franco's chosen successor, King Juan Carlos, put Spain on the road to democracy in the later 1970s. The vast majority of planners, in common with most Spanish citizens, welcomed these changes, in part because they felt they would allow them a fuller international acceptance. In fact, Spain had been tolerated by the west since the 1950s, and there had been much interaction with other western countries at a variety of levels. In the field of planning and development foreign consultants (for example, Doxiadis Associates) and developers had operated in Spain in the 1960s and 1970s, and Spanish planners had been able to travel fairly freely. Yet international acceptance was not complete. The new post-Francoist path which began in the late 1970s allowed Spain to assume a much more prominent role in the international development of planning in the following decades.

# CANADA

We now have a picture of the main currents of planning activity that evolved during the 1960s and 1970s in the most urbanised parts of western Europe. Some gaps remain but filling them would not add anything substantially new to the story. Countries such as Belgium and Ireland, for example, continued to follow already established paths towards the modernisation of their cities, with relatively little of international interest. Outside Europe, however, the transformations of cities in the advanced capitalist countries were more dramatic.

Canada's economic growth put it amongst the best performing of the western economies. Even more dramatically, its population increased by roughly a third from 1961 to 1981 to over 24 million, an exceptionally high growth rate for a western country (GM Anderson and Marr, 1987). This reflected a combination of high natural increase and immigration. The 1970s saw one of the largest ever net inflows. In part this reflected the relative strength of the Canadian economy. It also reflected a reorientation of immigration policies in 1967, which greatly eased the entry of non-whites. From this date, rapidly growing numbers of immigrants came from south and east Asian countries, and from the Caribbean. Although there had occasionally been earlier nonwhite immigration, these more sustained shifts changed the social character of all the larger cities, especially Toronto and Vancouver. Meanwhile, white Canada's French-speaking minority also sought greater recognition, with a strong independence movement emerging in Quebec. The upshot of these diverse pressures was to lay the basis for a multicultural Canada, opening or strengthening international connections other than with Britain and the United States.

## URBAN RENEWAL AND FREEWAYS

As we saw in Chapter 8, Canadian urban planning and management had some quite distinctive features by 1960. Nevertheless, the tendency to follow the United States remained strong. So it was with urban renewal which in 1964 expanded, American-style, to encourage the redevelopment of housing areas for nonresidential purposes. The most active city in slum clearance was Montreal, where many older dwellings were removed under the Plan Dozois (named after the Quebec minister responsible for it, and dubbed Bulldozois by some critics) in the early 1960s (Germain and Rose, 2000; Blumenfeld, 1987). Even here, though, the destruction never reached American levels, a pattern common throughout Canada.

As in the United States, freeway plans had often been an important trigger for renewal schemes. Many of Canada's British planning elite were amongst the strongest enthusiasts for these. In Vancouver, for example, the formidable Gerald Sutton-

Brown, chief planner from 1952 (and city commissioner from 1964), was a tireless advocate, hiring American consultants in 1963 and 1966 to elaborate the proposals (Ward, 1999). By the late 1960s, however, a mighty reaction was building. Sutton-Brown and his political masters were surprised at the strength of opposition to the proposed renewal of Strathcona (Chinatown) and the associated Burrard Peninsula Expressway (Hardwick, 1974). The success of the activists, both in Vancouver and Toronto, over the proposed Spadina Expressway in the early 1970s were national turning points (Sewell, 1993). In Montreal, popular opposition to freeways was less significant (Germain and Rose, 2000). (In the early 1960s the port authority had forced important modifications of freeway plans, reducing their destructive impacts.) Instead, popular activism in the city came in reaction to the proposed renewal of the inner residential neighbourhood of Milton Parc with 16 50-storey apartment towers. In 1973, however, federal support for urban renewal ended and freeway systems were largely abandoned half built. Vancouver remains the largest North American city never to have built freeways, but all Canadian cities built fewer than equivalent American cities (Sewell, 1993; JB Cullingworth, 1993).

## COMMERCIAL REDEVELOPMENT

Yet the resultant survival, relatively intact, of the inner residential neighbourhoods did not imply any absence of redevelopment of downtown or inner nonresidential areas. All the big Canadian cities, particularly Montreal and Toronto, underwent dramatic changes during the 1960s and 1970s (Germain and Rose, 2000; Sewell, 1993; Lemon, 1996). As in the United States, commercial developers played a key role, in partnership with planners, in creating public spaces. A distinctive feature of Montreal and Toronto was the creation of extensive subterranean pedestrian shopping precincts that linked the new office towers and integrated with public transit. (Montreal opened its new Parisian-style subway system, built with French advice, in 1966.) Central Toronto also acquired one of the world's most outstanding enclosed shopping malls, the Eaton Centre, in 1971. The first phase of the redevelopment of Toronto's railway lands (between downtown and Lake Ontario), begun during the 1970s, also gave the city a new iconic structure: the vast Canadian National Tower, completed in 1976.

## URBAN BOOSTERISM

Such projects reveal a growing desire during this period to promote Canada's cities on the world stage, anticipating a more universal trend during the 1980s and 1990s. In part, it was a consequence of the country's very rapid growth but there was also more specific rivalry between the two biggest cities, Montreal and Toronto. The pace was set by Montreal, which was led for 26 years from 1960 by a remarkable mayor, Jean Drapeau (Germain and Rose, 2000). In 1967 the city hosted Expo 67, a major international exhibition, notable for producing Canada's best-known contribution to the design of cities during these years: Habitat 67. Designed by Moshe Safdie, this was a mass housing complex of very striking design, which extended the gospel of

modernisation. The most grandiose project was for the Montreal Olympic Games of 1976, ambitious in its (French) designed stadium complex (Chalkley and Essex, 1999) but financially crippling. Although Toronto showed similar tendencies, the approach was less profligate with public funds. In fact, the city did not need to try quite so hard. Despite Montreal's efforts, the Ontarian capital became Canada's biggest city in the 1970s (McCann and Smith, 1991).

## NEW APPROACHES IN THE 1970s

Alongside this boosterism, however, a much softer planning agenda was growing (Wolfe, 1994). As elsewhere, the anti-roads and anti-renewal movements revived traditional ideas of cities based around traditional neighbourhoods, local shops and less commuting, where people walked, bicycled, or rode on buses, trams or subways (Sewell, 1993; Hardwick, 1974, 1994). This meant rehabilitation, conservation, greater environmental awareness and, above all, greater public involvement. The shift was important for the international reputation of Canadian cities, which had never abandoned these qualities as completely as their American counterparts. It was, for example, no accident that the first critic of modernist city planning, Jane Jacobs, moved from New York to Toronto in 1968. Thereafter she regularly lauded the virtues of a city which, as she saw it, had avoided American mistakes. It is also significant that Oscar Newman's American-published critique of modernist residential design, *Defensible Space* (1972), was a celebration of the traditional inner-area residential environment of his native Montreal (Germain and Rose, 2000). His ideas were not directly associated in readers' minds with the city, however, so he was less significant for Montreal's reputation than Jacobs was for Toronto's.

However, for Canadian planners and their political masters the general point was that the increasingly negative image of American urbanity encouraged them to appreciate the virtues of their own cities (cf Goldberg and Mercer, 1986). The increasing violence and obvious decay of core American cities from the mid-1960s heightened the contrast. This point grew hugely in significance as Canadian cities became more ethnically diverse in the 1970s.

## THE LIVEABLE CITY

Vancouver led the new thinking. It was the country's most rapidly changing city, where the emergent Pacific-oriented, multicultural Canada first appeared (Ley *et al*, 1992). It was also the birthplace, in 1971, of the international Greenpeace environmental movement. The city's closeness to American west coast radicalism was important. So too was timing. Many young Americans fled to Canada to avoid the draft during the Vietnam war. (Unlike Australia, Canada did not join the United States in

*Figure 9.6* *From the late 1960s, Canadian cities began to be widely recognised as far better planned than their American equivalents. Toronto's Eaton Centre gave all the advantages of enclosed mall shopping translated into multi-level form within the downtown area of a major city.*

Vietnam.) Vancouver, the Canadian city closest to the border, was an especially popular destination. A few draft dodgers played important organisational roles in founding both Greenpeace and neighbourhood-action groups in the city, including the group that fought the Chinatown freeway (Ward, 1999). Yet it would be wrong to think of the reorientation of planning in the 1970s solely in American terms. Local feeling was already running high. There were important political shifts towards the liberal left at city, regional and provincial levels. Broadly similar changes were also under way in Toronto. Their impacts for planning discourse can be summed up in a term widely used at this time: 'the liveable (or livable) city'.

## PLANNING LIVEABLE CITIES

Vancouver's new city planner, Ray Spaxman (another Briton, though long resident in Canada), implemented the new agenda in the 1970s (Hardwick, 1994). False Creek became a celebrated moderate-cost housing area on a former derelict waterfront. Granville Island was transformed into a leisure-oriented area, with arts, crafts and a public market (Breen and Rigby, 1994; 1996). Champlain Heights applied the new thinking in the suburbs. Meanwhile Gastown and Chinatown, reprieved from freeway construction, became historic districts in 1971. Similar shifts occurred in other cities. In Toronto, The Annexe and Cabbagetown were spared by the ending of renewal and freeways. The St Lawrence area was redeveloped with respect for the traditional social fabric. The city's strategy from 1976 was to put more housing in the downtown area, to move away from the concept of a specialised central district without a resident population.

## PLANNING URBAN REGIONS

This policy shift coincided with growing worries about Toronto's declining population because of suburbanisation beyond it and the administrative area of Metro Toronto. There were, in fact, some notable exercises in planning for wider urban regions in Canada during these years. Canadian cities had relatively strong frameworks for metropolitan government. The pioneering Metro Toronto was joined by comparable bodies for Montreal in 1959, Winnipeg in 1960 and Vancouver in 1967 (Hodge, 1991). With provincial encouragement, such bodies helped build support for planning urban regions.

The two most notable exercises were those for Toronto and Vancouver. The first covered an area much greater than Metro Toronto, and was referred to as the Toronto-Centred Region – TCR (JB Cullingworth, 1987; Sewell, 1993). Following an important regional transport study undertaken from 1963 to 1968, the Ontario government believed it needed to plan for a massive growth in the TCR, from 3.6 million in 1966 to eight million in 2000. Led by yet another British immigrant, Nigel

*Figure 9.7* Vancouver's Gastown was saved from the developers to become an attractive and popular historic district in the 1970s.

Richardson, the TCR exercise, published in 1970, envisaged a three-zone plan. This comprised a lakeshore urban complex, a green belt with transportation corridors but little development and a wider zone of selective urban growth. In the event, the growth projections were so inflated that the plan was soon sidelined.

The Greater Vancouver Regional District's Livable Region Proposals (LRP), prepared between 1972 and 1975, were less grandiose (GVRD, 1975; Lash, 1976; Ward, 1999). The chief planner was Harry Lash, formerly of Montreal (where, despite his efforts, regional planning made less headway). The LRP encouraged a local jobs balance, regional town centres based on public transit to relieve downtown Vancouver, growth management and rural protection. There were also truly heroic levels of public participation. Despite all this, however, most of the LRP fell by the wayside as Vancouver planning took a more developer-friendly and pragmatic turn in the 1980s.

## CANADIAN PLANNING IN ITS INTERNATIONAL CONTEXT

By the 1960s and especially by the 1970s, Canadian planning had become a fully distinctive national tradition. Planners remained very aware of what was being done in other countries. Harry Lash's team, for example, borrowed ideas from the United States, Britain, France, the Netherlands, Scandinavia and West Germany (Ward, 1999). Yet the engagement was critical, adaptive and synthetic. In particular, Canadian planners were too close to American cities to harbour illusions about them. Compared to their own relatively clean, safe and well-ordered cities, they found big American cities in the 1970s unpleasant and increasingly frightening places (eg Lash, 1976). For their part, planners in other countries began to look to Canada as a model. Americans, always apt to treat their northern neighbour with some disdain, were increasingly open in their admiration of Toronto (Lemon, 1996). In the 1960s, it was mainly urban administrators fascinated by its metropolitan government who came there to draw lessons. When Jane Jacobs gave the city her approval, however, the admiration became more widely (and internationally) based. In their different ways Montreal's boosterism and Vancouver's environmentalism also began to be noticed by the world. Meanwhile, Canada's growing wealth also allowed the beginnings, in the 1960s, of foreign aid to the developing world (Aubry and Bergeron, 1994). This began, albeit in a very small way, to export Canadian planning expertise in a more deliberate fashion.

## AUSTRALIA

Australia's population grew at a faster rate than that of any other western country, from 10.5 million in 1961 to 14.9 million in 1981. The economy was also booming until the wider problems began to affect the country during the 1970s (Forster, 1995). As in Canada, population growth reflected high natural increase (in the 1960s) and very high immigration. The new immigrants were increasingly from non-European sources (though large-scale immigration from Asia, so long resisted, did not begin until the later 1970s). The big coastal cities, as always, accommodated almost all the growth, with new immigrants predominantly settling in the inner suburbs. Much of the natural increase of population occurred both there and, even more, in the great outward sprawl of very low density suburbia. To a greater extent than in any other western country, the accommodation of metropolitan growth was therefore the most pressing problem facing planners during these years. From an international perspective, it is also one of the most interesting aspects.

## THE EMERGENCE OF CORRIDOR PLANS

Especially notable was the widespread adoption of the growth corridor approach (Morison, 2000). The first was for Adelaide, proposed in 1962 though not approved until 1967 (Forster and McCaskill, 1986). It was, however, the planning of the rapidly growing federal capital of Canberra that embedded the concept of corridor growth in the collective consciousness of the Australian planning profession. In part, this was because the approach drew on major international advice and precedents. The consultancy of the South African-British planner, Sir William Holford, played an important role in Canberra's planning from 1957 (Cherry and Penny, 1986; Birtles, 1997). A string of other British planners gave advice on specific aspects. Canberra's chief planner, Peter Harrison, also drew on Ebenezer Howard's decentralised social city, albeit updated for the car.

An important shift took place in the middle 1960s, however, as growth projections for Canberra moved upwards (to one million population, from just 36,000 in 1957). The most salient international reference now became the 1961 plan for the American capital region (Morison, 2000). There were direct contacts between the Washington and Canberra planners. These led to the appointment, in 1966, of Alan Voorhees, a leading American transportation consultant, who devised options for the projected growth of the Australian capital. Voorhees's work was central to the emergence of the general spatial concept, elaborated from 1968 to 1970. Known as the 'Y plan' it consisted of three corridors of distinct new towns developed along a public transit spine and flanked by freeways.

## LATER CORRIDOR PLANS

Growth corridors were also proposed for most of the other metropolitan cities, including Melbourne (1966–7), Sydney (1968) and Perth (1971). The most interesting, from the point of view of the extent of international and purely local influences, was the four-corridor plan for Sydney. The collapse of the original Abercrombie-style green belt-satellite town strategy in 1959 had left a void. Massive population growth, from 2.2 million in 1961 to perhaps five million by 2000 was being expected. By 1965 the influential voice of Australia's leading modernist architect, Walter Bunning, was advocating a 'five finger' growth solution that was literally a left-handed version of the 1947 Copenhagen plan (Freestone, 1996b). Meanwhile, Bunning's fellow modernist and friend, Nigel Ashton, had just become chairman of the responsible planning body. Ashton had an especial fondness for Stockholm, which he had visited in 1938, 1961 and (in an official capacity resulting in a detailed report)

1967 (NAW Ashton, 1969). He clearly saw potential in Stockholm's close integration of transport routes and satellite development. Such views (and perhaps also awareness of Washington) structured a general climate of thinking though they did not directly shape the plan. Its actual formulation, led by Peter Kacirek, a recent immigrant from Britain, and the Australian Tony Powell, evidently proceeded on its own, more technical logic (Cardew, 1998).

The most explicitly articulated corridor plan was that for Perth (1970), prepared from 1966 under the leadership of David Carr, a New Zealander with American training (Carr, 1979; Stokes and Hill, 1992). The plan proposed accommodating a population increase from 650,000 people in 1970 to 1.43 million in 1989 in four corridors. Carr and his team made overt reference to other corridor proposals, specifically Washington, Copenhagen, Melbourne and Sydney. There was considerable opposition, including an alternative growth model based on a directional grid borrowed from Colin Buchanan's 1966 *South Hampshire Study* in Britain. In the event, though the original plan was accepted it proved too optimistic for the actual level of growth.

## NEW TOWNS

The implementation of these corridor plans relied, to some extent, on the conscious creation of new settlements. The most ambitious planning efforts, as might be expected given the absence of private landownership, were in Canberra (Birtles, 1997; Brine, 1997). The first of the city's suburban new towns was Woden, begun in 1962 and later extended to include Weston Creek, followed by Belconnen (1967), Tuggeranong (1974) and Gungahlin, begun in the 1980s and still at an early stage. The planned populations varied from 55,000 at Woden, 90,000 with Weston Creek, to 120,000 at Belconnen. Tuggeranong was intended to have the same number of inhabitants as Belconnen but this was reduced for environmental reasons. The design concept of the new towns followed those in Britain, though at about half the density and with Australia's characteristic single-storey bungalows. There was, of course, some evolution, so Woden resembled the early postwar wave of British new towns, while Belconnen's planning (not fulfilled in execution) had a touch of Cumbernauld. All, however, were more car oriented than their British equivalents, a contrast especially noticeable in their town centres.

In 1976, a British-style development corporation was created to build the new town of Joondalup for upwards of 150,000 people in the northwestern coastal corridor of the Perth plan (Stannage, 1996). Even before designation, the federal government under Gough Whitlam's radical Labor administration had launched an ambitious new-cities programme, funding land purchases. This came to an abrupt end in 1975 and Joondalup was lucky to survive. Its first planners included the grand old man of Western Australian planning, Gordon Stephenson, and Simon Holthouse, who prepared the first land-use plan. Some British new towns were influential, including Stevenage on which Stephenson had actually worked. Even more, though, the design of the three private American examples, at Reston, Columbia and Irvine, impressed both decision-makers and planners. Macarthur meanwhile fulfilled a similar function to Joondalup in the southwestern Sydney corridor (M Huxley, 2000). Some new cities were also proposed from 1972 to 1975 as major new growth centres outside metropolitan growth corridors. Of these, only one – Albury-Wodonga on the New South Wales/Victoria border – has prospered. Monarto, near Adelaide, and Bathurst-Orange in New South Wales were soon aborted (Forster and McCaskill, 1986).

## GREEN BANS

As occurred elsewhere, new pressures began to shift the planning agenda during the 1970s. Some of these shifts followed international trends. The manner in which the antidevelopment environmentalist movement took shape in Australia was, however, unique (Davison, 1991). In 1971 the residents of Hunters Hill, an elite district of Sydney, were trying to stop the development of a remaining fragment of unspoilt bush land. They appealed to the communist leader of the builders' trades union, Jack Mundey, for help and, to everyone's surprise, got it. Work stopped in the first 'green ban'. Between 1971 and 1974, similar bans were instituted on key historic sites in Sydney and Melbourne that were threatened by development. Mundey's argument was that it was no good having higher wages and better working conditions if the environment had to be destroyed in the process. It was almost possible to hear the ghost of William Morris cheering from the other side of the world.

## THE CONSERVATION MOVEMENT

Another key change was the revival of historic inner suburbs. Many immigrants from the Mediterranean countries actively preferred their denser character. There was also a more familiar process of gentrification. Together, these factors helped to change the planned destiny of the areas. An early sign was the defeat of a proposal for a major road through Paddington in Sydney in 1968, which pioneered conservation zoning. The green bans helped to raise the temperature still further. A critical case was the Rocks district of Sydney, where Europeans first landed on the Australian continent, which had many historic buildings (Blackmore, 1988). In 1970 a plan for a vast redevelopment of skyscrapers was unveiled, championed by Australia's leading modernist, Walter Bunning (Freestone, 1996a). There was much public criticism and in 1971 Mundey, in consultation with the new, largely working-class, residents association, instituted a green ban. In 1972 it was partially lifted to allow restoration work to proceed. However, as the Australian economy followed the world into recession from 1973 the market for office space evaporated. A largely conservation-based solution became the only viable option. Broadly the same pattern was repeated in other areas and cities over the next few years.

## AUSTRALIAN PLANNING IN ITS INTERNATIONAL CONTEXT

The green bans gave a wider political base to Australian conservation than was usual elsewhere. In most respects, though, Australian planning followed that in Britain and, increasingly, the United States. Many planners from Britain still held senior positions, especially in planning education, and there was also a small, but sometimes significant, presence from other parts of the British world. Consultants based in Britain, most prominently Holford, continued to find work in Australia. There were, though, growing numbers of Americans, particularly in highways and transport planning. De Leuw, Cather and Company, for example, advised both Sydney and Perth on freeway systems in the 1960s (P Ashton, 1993; Newman, 1992). Edmund Bacon, from Philadelphia, also gave advice on the design of Canberra (Birtles, 1997).

Apart from the modernists' long-established fondness for Scandinavian design (spectacularly renewed by Jørn Utzon's Sydney Opera House), there were few direct contacts with planning in non-Anglophone countries. Certainly Australia was becoming more ethnically diverse and gradually shifting towards a more Mediterranean inner urban lifestyle, with new ways of managing public space. Yet, although these cultural changes influenced planners they were not reflected in their international lesson-drawing. For example, despite an obvious relevance to corridor new towns, the 1965 Paris plan evoked no interest. Moreover, when Australian cities began to adopt traffic calming during the 1970s, their initial interest derived principally from

*Figure 9.8  The Rocks in Sydney was threatened by redevelopment of the kind which can be seen in adjoining districts. The opposition to the redevelopment led to one of the most celebrated of the green bans declared by the building trades unions, leading to a famous victory for the Australian conservation movement.*

the Buchanan report rather than direct knowledge of Dutch or German innovations (Ewing, 1999). The shift towards conserving inner suburbs in Sydney, Melbourne and Adelaide encouraged adoption of Buchanan's environmental area approach.

Overall therefore, the flow of planning ideas was still largely inward. For the moment there was little by way of export, except to Papua New Guinea. Yet the growth of professional, and especially educational, capacity was important for the future. A growing number of students from Southeast Asia received planning training in Australia. The impact of this became more apparent as Australia began to build firmer links with its Asian neighbours in the 1980s.

## JAPAN

Throughout these years Australia, like the rest of the world, was feeling the impact of one Asian country which was becoming the major economic force in the whole Pacific region (Allinson, 1997). The annual economic growth rate in Japan during the 1960s was 11 per cent (nearly twice the rate of France, the best performer amongst the larger western countries). Even in the more troubled 1970s, it managed close to 5 per cent, substantially above that of the next best performer, again France. By 1980 it was the world's third largest manufacturing nation after the United States and the Soviet Union, comfortably ahead of any European nation. Population growth was also substantial, with an increase that approached a quarter between 1960 and 1980, when it was nearly 117 million. (Unlike western countries, however, foreign immigration was an insignificant part of this increase.) Tokyo became the world's largest city, with a (conservatively measured) agglomeration population of 16.9 million, compared to New York's 15.6 million) (Cybriwsky, 1999; TMG, 1994).

## URBAN CONDITIONS

Yet, if Japan was a phenomenal growth machine, in western countries perceptions of the quality of its cities were mixed. The 1964 Tokyo Olympic Games, which effectively marked the re-entry of Japan into the international fold, drew external attention to the tremendous contrasts evident in the city, and the whole country. There were modern buildings (not least the spectacular structures created for the Olympics themselves), expressways, a monorail from the airport and the first high-speed intercity *shinkansen* bullet trains to Osaka (Kudamatsu, 1988a). On the other hand, there were serious water shortages, appalling congestion of commuter rail services and extremely cramped and primitive housing conditions for many. Water and air pollution were also serious problems.

In part, these negative western perceptions of Japanese social conditions grew on an underlying suspicion or resentment of Japan's postwar economic prowess. Yet the problems were not conjured up out of western jealousies. They were acutely felt by Tokyo's citizens. In 1968, for example, over a third of the city's population considered themselves badly housed, principally because of lack of space; and 45 per cent lived in tenements where sharing of toilets and kitchens was normal, with only about 10 square metres of private space per family. The average peak congestion levels on

Tokyo commuter trains and subways in the mid-1960s were such that passengers found it impossible to make voluntary movements. Some trains were regularly so crowded that there was real physical danger of crushing. The principal challenge to Japanese urban planners was, therefore, to address these stark deficiencies in the social infrastructure and environment of their cities, especially of Tokyo.

## Planning a World City

During the early 1960s there was growing Japanese interest in the future of Tokyo, whose destiny as the world's largest city now seemed clear. The prominent Japanese architect-planner, Kenzo Tange, who designed the main Olympic buildings, launched 'Tokyo Plan 1960', a visionary scheme for the city to grow by extending a building complex across Tokyo Bay (TMG, 1994; Ishizuka and Ishida, 1988). Although the plan was not followed, the pace of land reclamation from the bay increased. More importantly, Tange's ideas helped encourage large-scale thinking about developing the city as befitted its new global significance. Meanwhile many, more specific, projects for the city's development were taking shape, particularly the implementation of major schemes to ease movement. The expressway plan was approved in 1959 and the first sections were opened by 1962 (Suzuki, 1988). A major programme to expand the subway system and link it directly with suburban rail lines was adopted in 1964.

Another important trend was the beginning of planned urban renewal. The best-known example was the creation of a massive new commercial subcentre at Shinjuku, on a major rail junction about 8 kilometres from downtown Tokyo (Kudamatsu, 1988b; TMG, 1994). The concept had been discussed before the war but was not finally pursued until 1960. Detailed plans that encouraged high-rise construction followed in 1965. By 1980 a major new district of office towers and hotels was taking shape. Railway companies and planners had similar schemes in mind in the vicinity of other railway stations. The removal of industries from the inner and central parts of the city also created many opportunities for commercial development.

## Improving Living Conditions

Real improvements in living conditions only came later in the decade. Some had been begun by the mid-1960s, but their importance was underlined by political changes in 1967 which saw the election of a left-wing governor of the city, Ryokichi Minobe, who held office from 1967 to 1979 (Cybriwsky, 1999). There was also growing direct political activism over issues such as the continued American presence in Tokyo, which occupied land that could be used for housing or other needs, pollution and rail congestion. Minobe launched or accelerated many expensive social and environmental improvement schemes. Water supply and sewerage began to improve and there were tighter pollution controls. In 1970 the first traffic-free days in the central Ginza district were introduced and other partial pedestrianisation measures followed (TMG, 1994).

## THE *DANCHI*

Most importantly, there was an acceleration of the housing supply (TMG, 1994; Cybriwsky, 1999). By the mid-1960s the Japanese Housing Corporation had created large multistorey housing complexes (known as *danchi*) in the outer parts of Tokyo city, for example at Ogikubo, Asagaya, Aoto and Harumi. These were broadly similar to the planned settlements found in most western European countries. The individual apartments were very small by western standards but were entirely private, without the shared facilities of the older tenements. The blocks were particularly drab and there was little except identifying numbers to distinguish one from another. Like their equivalents elsewhere, they played a vital role in improving physical housing conditions. The scale of the *danchi*, each with several thousand dwellings, often led to local shopping and other services being created. By the 1970s, the main setting for these kinds of housing schemes was on cleared sites where older housing had been removed.

## DORMITORY NEW TOWNS

From the mid-1960s, the emphasis shifted to dormitory satellite new towns, on a larger scale than previously (Kurokawa, 1978). Provincial Japanese cities had led in planning these. Thus Senri (begun in 1961, for 150,000 inhabitants) and Senboku (1964, for 188,000) served Osaka. The much smaller new town of Kozoji (begun in 1965, for 68,000 inhabitants) was planned to serve Nagoya. In the Tokyo region, the formal relaxation of the 1958 national capital region plan in 1965 was important. It acknowledged what had been reality for several years – that the green belt was impracticable as a containing device. Tama district, west of Tokyo city, saw two huge new towns being developed (Cybriwsky, 1999). The first, Tama Den-en Toshi (Tama Garden City), was begun in 1963. The developers were the massive Tokyu Group. This major railway and property development company (which also owned hotels and a major retail business) had created some of the early suburban garden cities (most notably Den-en Chofu, by now an elite suburb). Tama Den-en Toshi was, however, on a quite different scale, conceived ultimately for some 400,000 residents.

Public planning was much stronger in Tama new town which was designated in 1965 and planned from 1966. The most famous of Tokyo's new towns, it is seen as successful by both planners and residents. Its developers have been, and remain, the Tokyo Metropolitan Government and two public corporations (Kudamatsu, 1988c; TMG, 1994). The original target was 300,000 inhabitants. This was increased to 410,000 by 1970, but subsequently reduced to 375,000. Its form is linear, stretching for about 14 kilometres along two competing suburban rail routes. Most dwellings are in middle- to high-rise buildings, with some individual houses. The quality of local services is high and, although densities are above those usual in new towns in most other western countries, they are much lower than in central Tokyo, which allows green space close to residential areas. Other new towns followed at Kohoku (1968), planned for 220,000 inhabitants working in Tokyo and Yokohama, and Kitachiba (1966, for 330,000) and later Ryugasaki to the northeast of central Tokyo.

## OTHER NEW TOWNS

Not all new towns had a dormitory function. The new airport at Narita was associated with a small one planned for about 60,000 from 1969. The most interesting and innovative (though not entirely successful) Japanese new town of this period was, however, Tsukuba Science City, roughly 60 kilometres northeast of central Tokyo (Castells and Hall, 1994; www.info.tsukuba.org). The 1958 plan identified it as a possible satellite town, and development was authorised in 1963 following national decisions to decentralise government research facilities from Tokyo. In March 1966, as its planning was taking shape, there were international official visits to other conventional planned new towns, most notably Harlow in Britain and, more importantly, to other attempts to link academic research skills with innovation. Stanford University's participation in the emergence of Silicon Valley in California was particularly relevant. The Japanese also kept a close eye on parallel developments that were just beginning in other western countries. These included France and Belgium, where Sophia-Antipolis, Ile-de-France Sud and Louvain's new university city were just starting in the late 1960s. Yet Tsukuba was probably the first attempt to engineer this type of development by conscious planning. The intention was that 220,000 people would ultimately live there. The planning approach was, however, rather heavy-handed in the early years. There was much resistance to transferring government and academic jobs to what was seen as a rather remote and sterile environment. Private firms were also reluctant to develop their research facilities in Tsukuba, so for many years the town's development was rather lopsided.

## A DERIVATIVE PLANNING TRADITION?

The rather ambiguous nature of international lesson-drawing in the case of Tsukuba illustrates a more general tendency. Japanese planners remained very interested in western planning and were diligent in keeping up with the latest developments in other countries. As had always been the case, they learnt the skills rather than bringing in western planners. There was active Japanese participation in the IFHP and other international organisations. Much use was made of formal visits, study tours and bilateral links between cities, prefectures and educational institutions to improve the flow of information. Increasingly, this was two-way, but western countries certainly learnt much less from Japan than the other way around. In effect, they still perceived Japanese planning very much as a variant of their own approaches, with few distinctive features that they could apply to their own practice.

However, it would be incorrect to assume that Japanese lesson-drawing from the west had not moved on from earlier patterns. Even in the past, when ideas had been received rather uncritically, the tendency to draw from multiple western sources had required some selectivity in applying them. The huge growth in Japanese planning capacity during the 1960s and 1970s intensified this ability to be selective. For example, there were aspects of planning that were adopted in all western countries during these years but were virtually ignored in Japan. There was, as we have seen, a Japanese interest in the environment that grew in a similar fashion to that in the west (albeit there were more serious problems to address). Yet the historic conservation of buildings, a significant element in western planning from the later 1960s, was only a very small issue in modern Japanese cities. Cities which were primarily historic tourist centres, such as Kyoto, were well protected, but more workaday ones, such as Tokyo, were thought of quite differently. This was despite the immense wartime loss of buildings which, in western thinking, would have made those that remained more precious. Even as late as 1980 it was possible to demolish a major and highly distinctive historic building such as the old Tokyo Stock Exchange with little difficulty (TMG, 1994).

## THE EXPORT OF JAPANESE PLANNING

Since the very beginnings of modern urban planning it had been apparent that the perceived economic success of a particular country often triggered foreign interest. How far, then, did this occur as Japan became an economic powerhouse and Tokyo, its control room, the world's largest city? By 1980 there was certainly growing western interest in Japanese industrial practices, but this did not yet extend very far into the urban field. The story was different in Asia, however, where the interest was stronger (Whittick (ed), 1980). Contacts developed in several different ways. Japanese planners were major players in international regional organisations such as the East Asia Regional Organisation for Planning and Housing which held conferences, study tours and exchanged information. At the request of the United Nations the government also organised training programmes on regional development and related matters, using Japanese examples. The first such programme took place in 1969 in Nagoya, with participants from Sri Lanka, India, Indonesia, Iran, Malaysia, Singapore, Thailand, Vietnam (ie South Vietnam) and Brazil.

The international success of Japanese business also led to a growing economic presence in other countries, particularly Japan's Asian neighbours. In property development and construction this often meant some export of Japanese professional services, including, to some extent, planning. The 1960s and 1970s saw a marked growth of Japanese consultancies in planning-related activities. Some consultants worked in other countries, often in conjunction with Japanese-funded projects. There was also some Japanese property development in western countries bordering the Pacific Rim (itself a new spatial construct that appeared in the 1970s), including Australia and North America. In 1973, for example, the giant Tokyu company that developed Tama Den-en Toshi began, with another Japanese company, to develop a very small private new town at Mill Creek near Seattle (J Hancock and Sotoike, 1988). There was, however, nothing overtly Japanese about such developments which corresponded largely to local tastes. Nevertheless, by such means some elements of the Japanese style of planning began to become slightly better known in western countries.

## CONCLUSIONS

On a larger scale than ever before, the planners of the affluent first world in the 1960s and early 1970s promised rational and functional order in urban space, activities and buildings. As never before, too, their political masters shared and promoted this same project, often with fewer misgivings than the planners themselves. Cities would be a confident expression of modernity and technological progress. Even when important older structures and districts were conserved, an emergent theme of these years, they too were caught up in the wider functional and spatial modernisation. Increasingly, too, the very process of arriving at the planning solutions was made to seem rational. Truly, modern planning was seen as the very epitome of progress, the optimistic triumph of human artifice over nature, of science over superstition and the future over the past.

## INTERNATIONAL CONVERGENCE

At no other time in the 20th century was there such a high degree of international convergence about the theory and practice of urban planning in advanced capitalist countries. This chapter has essentially confirmed the broad findings of the previous one in this respect. This would not have been possible (or necessary) without global economic prosperity and growth. Yet this alone did not explain the convergence. Long before 1960, planners in most countries had received the conceptual raw material for the kind of planning that was now being implemented on a large scale. By the 1960s, the visions had been deeply assimilated everywhere, so that modernism now constituted the orthodoxy. But refinements, elaborations and variations continued, producing different outcomes in different places. These were then diffused more freely than ever before and it was this, ultimately, that created such similar interpretations of modernism across the world. In part, this rapid diffusion of every twist and turn of modernist planning took place because there were already so many shared understandings on which these refinements could build. But it also reflected a strengthening of the mechanisms of diffusion.

## EASIER TRAVEL AND DIFFUSION

In some cases, this diffusion was part of normal international economic relationships, as technology and know-how were exported, for example in construction, public transit or information technology. As always, however, the more typical diffusion relationships between advanced capitalist countries did not appear in international trade figures. The growing ease of communication was speeding up such flows compared to earlier years. During the 1960s, for example, major planning consultants flew regularly between countries and communicated internationally by telephone. Mass air travel also extended the horizons of the much wider group of planners and politicians who actually operated the planning systems. All the traditional methods of planning's diffusion – international professional conferences, study tours, visits to inspect specific developments or places in other countries – became more common. Not least important were the widening perceptions of the consumers of planning. For example, international events such as the Olympic Games or world fairs could now expect many more visitors from other countries than previously. These visitors' experiences of a host city (such as Munich or Tokyo) which had undergone a programme of planned improvements could be important in shifting thinking in their own country.

## MIGRATION AND PLANNING EDUCATION

International migration of planners also continued, especially to Australia and North America. However, the universally good employment prospects for planners and the relative absence of political persecution meant that these migrants were now less likely to include seminal figures. (The Vietnam war did, though, produce some outflow of radicals from the United States, with effects on community and environmental activism in Canada.) A small, but growing, number of students were also able to contemplate seeking planning-related education in other countries. Even if they did not, foreign study tours became familiar parts of planning education in most western countries. At least some of their teachers were also likely to have inspected planning efforts and established personal contacts with their peers in other countries. The continued rise of English as an international language facilitated many of these interactions, though French retained some importance especially in the formulation of critical planning theory.

## THE INTERNATIONALISATION OF POPULAR OPINION

Nor were these interactions confined to professionals, academics and decision-makers. Images of modernity spread rapidly in the mass media, especially television, allowing much wider awareness of the urban lifestyle that planning could deliver. It largely served to enhance the notion that what the United States had today, whether for good or ill, the rest of the affluent world would probably get tomorrow (or would have to vigorously pursue another course of action if it did not want it). The media could also help to diffuse doubt. Thus popular reactions to the system that modernist urban planning served spread equally rapidly, as images of civil unrest, protest movements and alternative approaches flashed across the globe, especially in 1968 and succeeding years.

## SHIFTING DIFFUSION PATTERNS IN THE 1970S

The popular reactions to modernism, and the professional misgivings that accompanied them, began to foster new patterns of innovation and diffusion. In this chapter, for example, we have seen how the Netherlands, despite occasional modernist horror stories at least as bad as anywhere else in the west, rose sharply as a source of positive lessons because of the new approaches being pioneered there. The demise of Swedish welfare modernism shifted the patterns of borrowing in the Nordic countries, with Denmark especially becoming more significant. Canada's planners began, in a small way, to shift the balance of trade in planning ideas with their giant neighbour. Meanwhile, for quite different reasons, Japan was also beginning to be noticed, largely for its extraordinary economic growth. Western planners (and in large measure

Japanese planners themselves) still saw its planning efforts as essentially catching up with the west. But signs of real planning innovation were beginning to appear (notably at Tsukuba) where the Japanese were moving, rather uncertainly, towards something slightly in advance of the west. Western planners had barely begun to realise this by 1980, though Japan's Asian neighbours were quicker to see things from which they could learn.

# CHAPTER 10

# GLOBALISATION, COMPETITIVENESS AND SUSTAINABILITY I: THE MAJOR TRADITIONS

Western urban planning in the 1980s and 1990s largely reflected two policy imperatives, one economic and the other environmental. As we saw in earlier chapters, popular opposition and falling growth rates in the 1970s made the planning strategy of relentless top-down modernisation increasingly untenable. Cities throughout the developed world, and especially in Britain and the United States, began to experience serious industrial decline. Specific local factors influenced the exact contours of urban change in individual countries, but broader spatial changes were also under way. Many new emergent economies, especially in Asia, were challenging the west in industries where it alone had formerly held sway.

Yet global shift was only a part of the story. The postwar system which had managed and stabilised international trade and currency flows finally broke down in the 1970s. Orchestrated by the United States, a more liberal economic regime took its place with fewer barriers to international trade, tourism and investment. Very large multinational free trade areas appeared in Europe, North America and elsewhere. (The EU went further still, to assume something of the appearance of an emergent supranational state.) The effects of these changes were intensified by a tremendous acceleration of the international diffusion of information. To a far greater extent than ever before, the world began to function as a single market economy. Investment and disinvestment decisions were increasingly made globally and international flows of capital, unrestricted by currency regulations, became common. The transnational company, though long familiar as a form of capitalist endeavour, now became an increasingly dominant element within global manufacturing and services. The volume and spatial reach of international tourism also increased at an astonishing rate. Together these various trends contributed to an internationalisation of culture, spreading western (mainly American) values, signs and symbols almost everywhere on earth.

Cities were, of course, the epicentres of all these changes, which are usually signified by the label 'globalisation'. In these circumstances, urban decision-makers and planners had to ensure that their cities could win, or at least retain, investment, business activity and cultural consumption. In many countries during the 1980s, and nowhere more than in Britain and the United States, this embrace of global capitalism seemed to marginalise traditional understandings of urban planning. It was, in fact, profoundly difficult for any nation, still less an individual city, to resist or moderate this economic and cultural globalisation. Almost everywhere, Communism, the 20th century's main alternative to international capitalism, collapsed during the late 1980s and early 1990s.

In the west, the strongest voices against global capitalism included some of the most radical champions of environmentalist thinking. The late 1960s and 1970s had seen the growth of a countercultural environmental radicalism that pointed to an alternative path to that of large-scale capitalism and government. From the first, it offered a global perspective that now, presciently, seemed to match the economic and cultural dimensions of globalisation. In the 1980s and 1990s these ideas, underpinned by a fast-growing corpus of scientific research, began to exert a growing influence on influential and more moderate opinion throughout the west. The result was that the language of environmentalism was increasingly adopted in the mainstream of public policy.

Critically important was the new hybrid concept of sustainable development, which became widely known from the late 1980s. In contrast to the usual antigrowth stance of the environmentalists the new concept seemed to offer a middle way, reconciling environmental priorities with the pressures for economic development at local, national and global levels. At varying rates, countries throughout the world subscribed to this new language of sustainability. During the 1990s it formed the basis for a new self-confidence amongst western urban planners. Of the four major planning traditions, it was (West) Germany that took the lead in this emergent area. In part this was because Germans were more cautious than the others in sacrificing their interventionist state on the altar of global competitiveness. France was less of a leader in the new discourse of sustainability, but it too maintained a relatively strong governmental planning tradition during the 1980s and used it to enhance its global economic position.

The main contrast was with Britain which, with the United States, wholeheartedly embraced market-led approaches to urban development during the 1980s. The resultant downgrading of the idea of governmental planning meant that the new, more interventionist agenda of sustainability took much longer to gain meaningful acceptance in either country. In a sense this more *laissez-faire* approach enhanced what had always been a strong theme in American planning. Far more remarkable, however, were the changes in Britain. These appeared to seek a wholesale rejection of 20th-century planning and reverted to a much older style of rampant, free-enterprise capitalism.

## BRITAIN

The background to developments in Britain was the long-familiar story of the country's relatively poor economic performance. By the late 1970s, large-scale decline of older industries had begun. Unemployment was rising and faith in interventionist government was falling. In 1979 the right-wing Conservative Margaret Thatcher became prime minister. She was intent on 'rolling back the frontiers of the state' to create a new enterprise culture (Thornley, 1991; Ward, 1994). It was an approach that seemed to set an international trend for the 1980s. This was largely because from 1980 it was hugely reinforced by similar policies in the United States under President Ronald Reagan. The result was that a distinct Anglo-American model of public policy was identifiable by the later 1980s (eg Barnekov et al., 1989; Parkinson et al. (eds), 1988). This advocated the privatisation, deregulation and marketisation of activities which had come to be seen as the prerogative of governments. In both countries this economic dimension was combined with an international assertiveness of national strength (and English-speaking civilisation). This was an especially potent line to follow in a Britain that had lost an empire but, in many ways, had also failed to come to terms with the reduced global role that followed.

In a curious way, therefore, Thatcherism combined a genuinely dynamic project of market-led economic modernisation with quasi-imperial retrostyling. It was purveyed with a stridency that quickly became tedious, especially to Britain's European neighbours. Despite enthusiasm for a single European market that removed all barriers to business and trade, Thatcherite revulsion at an ever closer governmental union was palpable. Eventually (in 1990) Thatcher became too much for all but the most masochistic of her supporters and was replaced. Yet the essence of her approach, albeit implemented by other, softer, hands and explained by less hectoring voices, remained profoundly important in the 1990s. In economic terms, the Thatcher decade probably did mark a turning point. By the mid-1980s, Britain was set on a largely postindustrial destiny that embraced with enthusiasm all aspects of global capitalism. Its overall economic growth performance in the 1980s and 1990s was slightly above the (fairly low) western European average, higher than in Germany and France (though below the United States). By any standards, this was a remarkable change.

Because urban planning was closely associated with state intervention and regulation, it soon became a target of Thatcherism. Yet the new reverence for market processes also stimulated significant planning innovations. The international salience of these varied. The broadly Anglo-American frame of reference which Thatcherism fostered tended to be reproduced, albeit with increasing reluctance, in the British planning community. It also delayed close British engagement with the important innovations occurring in continental Europe until the very last years of the century.

## LEVERAGE PLANNING

Thatcherite influences on urban planning were strongest in the inner areas of metropolitan cities (Robson, 1988; Ward, 1994). It was here that deindustrialisation, which became acute in the recession of the early 1980s, had the greatest impact. For the first time, the social peace of postwar Britain was seriously challenged. In 1981 there was rioting in some of the most deprived inner areas in London, Manchester, Liverpool and other cities. The proposed solution to social and economic decay, and physical dereliction, was a planning regime that would encourage large-scale private development. In the political rhetoric of the time, this would restore the spirit of free enterprise and lift the dead hand of socialism. This approach was quite contrary to the previous planning regimes which, in the 1950s and 1960s, had promoted large-scale public sector redevelopment of slums for housing, followed in the 1970s by subsidised rehabilitation of older housing areas. The new intention was to use public spending to draw in (or, in the favoured American term, to 'leverage' ) as much private capital as possible. As this implies, many of the ideas behind the new approach were borrowed from the United States, as were some of the specific instruments.

# THE URBAN DEVELOPMENT CORPORATION

The most important of the Thatcher government's innovations in this field were the urban development corporations (UDCs), introduced from 1980 (Imrie and Thomas (eds), 1993). These were centrally appointed public corporations with wide-ranging planning and urban development powers. They were created in 13 inner city areas, including London Docklands and large tracts of dereliction in Liverpool, Manchester, Newcastle, Birmingham and other metropolitan cities. Here they assumed leadership of urban redevelopment and effectively superseded the elected local authorities for varying periods during the 1980s and 1990s. Their most obvious inspiration was the new town development corporation, the uniquely powerful agency the post-1945 Labour government had invented to build the new towns. Now, though, this kind of powerful single-minded agency, able to sidestep local elective politics (invariably left-wing), proved uniquely attractive to the radical right-wing Thatcher government.

Unlike the new town development corporations, which themselves acted as developers to a very large extent, the UDCs became uncompromised flagships for the new, American-style, leverage planning. In contrast to previous experience, they showed that inner city areas, nowhere more so than the London Docklands, could attract very large amounts of private development capital (Brownill, 1990). American precedent was important in devising this approach, in particular the New York State Urban Development Corporation (P Hall, 1998), which had been created in 1968 as a response to the riots of the late 1960s. With some awareness of the British new town development corporations, New York State governor Nelson Rockefeller had created the corporation to act as a very powerful development agency (Garvin, 1996). Amongst other things it developed Roosevelt Island, New York's new town-in-town, referred to in Chapter 8. The key point was that the corporation could work autonomously, even in New York City, without needing detailed approval from city, county or state governments. This was also the intention (and broadly the reality) of the British UDCs.

## ENTERPRISE ZONES AND OTHER INITIATIVES

An even stronger transatlantic connection was apparent in the Urban Development Grant introduced in 1982 (Barnekov *et al*, 1989). This was a leverage-based public subsidy directly copied from the American Urban Development Action Grant introduced in 1977. However, the origins of the enterprise zone, which appeared in 1980, were more complex. Its invention is attributed to the influential British planning commentator Peter Hall (P Hall, 1988; Ward, 1994). In 1977, with others, he had sketched out the concept of 'non-plan', an essentially libertarian notion of a planning-free zone where development would be entirely unregulated (Hughes and Sadler (eds), 2000). Hall had in mind the remarkable flowering of economic activity that had occurred, less consciously, in similar zones of minimal regulation in Hong Kong and other emergent Asian cities. (He later admitted, however, that he had not appreciated the role that state-subsidised housing had played in facilitating such rapid economic growth.) Such an idea seemed to symbolise the very essence of the Thatcher revolution. It was taken up, albeit in rather cautious fashion, mainly in inner city areas. In practice, the planning regime was streamlined rather than free; the tax exemptions proved more important factors in its success.

## THE LONDON DOCKLANDS

These measures, allied with a huge property development boom in the late 1980s, brought spectacular changes to a few declining inner city areas. Nowhere was this more so than in the London Docklands, where several of the instruments of Thatcherite planning operated together (Brownill, 1990; Ward, 1994; P Hall, 1998). The vast tracts of derelict dock areas east of the city of London were rapidly transformed in a surge of profit-seeking development without equal at the time in any similar section of a major western city. American examples such as Baltimore and Boston, to be described below, provided a general inspiration, but the regeneration of London Docklands, covering 22 square kilometres, was on a far bigger scale.

Few planners could bring themselves to recognise this transformation as planning. Certainly it showed little by way of strategic master-planning, regulatory process, social awareness or community consultation. It was largely a combination of major public investment in land preparation and road construction, substantial private commercial development and a good deal of expensive housing. Investment in public transport was woefully inadequate for many years, a consequence of the unfulfilled assumption that because developers would pay governments need not. The new Docklands Light Railway (a light rapid tramway system) opened in 1987, giving some relief, but it was on too mean a scale for projected movement needs as employment grew. Links with the rest of the London underground railway system remained poor until 1999.

Though there was some mellowing in later years, the opportunistic tendencies of early Docklands 'planning' set the pattern. Much of the development which resulted, especially in the 1980s, was bland and mediocre but enough was sufficiently good to deserve praise. A good deal of the best involved the adaptive reuse of the rich legacy of historic buildings along the Thames, much of this for expensive apartments which were often combined with retailing, restaurants and other activities.

## CANARY WHARF

By far the most significant single piece of new development was the vast new commercial centre at Canary Wharf, which included Britain's (and briefly Europe's) tallest building. Initiated by an American, and with an American master plan, Canary Wharf was brought to fruition by Canadian developers Olympia and York. This was an off-centre office development on a major scale, which directly challenged the City of London several miles upstream. Though the concept had some similarities to La Défense in Paris, the critical difference was that the French example had been the product of strategic planning decisions about Parisian office development. Canary Wharf grew within a far more deregulated planning regime, with only outline controls. Despite serious financial problems in the early 1990s, it became the showpiece of

Docklands, just as Docklands had become the showpiece of Thatcherite planning. And, despite all the planning criticisms, it would be churlish not to recognise its major significance. Combined with the other deregulatory changes to London's functioning as a financial and stock market centre in the 1980s, the scale of Canary Wharf helped to reinvigorate London's reputation as a leading world business city.

## OTHER WATERFRONT RENEWAL SCHEMES

Similar tendencies were reproduced in scaled-down form elsewhere (Middleton, 1991; Imrie and Thomas (eds), 1993; Breen and Rigby, 1996). Across Britain there was a spate of waterfront renewal schemes, in Liverpool, Salford and Trafford (Manchester), Cardiff, Tyneside, Hull, Leith (Edinburgh) and several other cities. By the 1990s, the inland city of Birmingham was also extending the approach to its extensive canal network. Compared to London, there was rather less interest in these provincial centres from international developers. But all these cities looked to transatlantic examples, especially Baltimore and Boston, and often used American expertise. There were also some very direct borrowings. The festival marketplace concept, offering tourist-oriented shopping, was common. So, too, was the creation of cultural-leisure quarters in former dock areas, with museums, galleries, cinemas, sports facilities, etc. One of the most direct applications of the American formula was in Birmingham (Smyth, 1994). There an existing cultural quarter was extended by a massive

**Figure 10.1** *Canary Wharf in the London Docklands was the flagship of the rather cavalier Thatcherite approach to planning. Almost certainly the development would not have occurred if the planners had been in a more dominant position.*

convention centre, international hotel, festival marketplace, indoor sports arena, aquarium, offices and expensive housing.

## AMERICAN AND OTHER INFLUENCES

The general style of leveraged property-led urban regeneration combined with the generally flexible planning in these and other, nonwaterfront, regeneration areas accelerated the appearance in Britain of other American types of development (Goobey, 1992). One of the most significant was the long-resisted large out-of-town shopping mall, on a scale that competed directly with traditional major central areas. The first examples were the Gateshead MetroCentre on Tyneside (opened 1986), Merry Hill at Dudley in the West Midlands and Meadowhall in Sheffield (both 1990). These were, though, only the most extreme examples of a more widespread phenomenon. Other forms of noncentral car-based shopping and leisure development multiplied everywhere in Britain (as in many other western European countries) during these years. Large freestanding superstores (in which the French were European pioneers), retail warehouse parks, drive-in fast-food restaurants and multiplex cinemas became familiar parts of the urban scene.

Another approach borrowed from the United States by cities seeking to regenerate themselves, but increasingly used more widely, was place marketing (Ward, 1998). As well as the UDCs, which had sizeable marketing and promotion budgets, the main pioneer was Glasgow. In 1983 it launched its famous 'Glasgow's Miles Better' campaign, inspired directly by 'I ♥ New York', as part of a wider (and rather effective) strategy to promote the city as a centre for cultural tourism. However, although most of the new policy ideas came from the United States, there were also some European influences. Garden festivals, a rather opportunistic application of a German idea used successfully to promote the reuse of bombed areas (and popular also in the Netherlands), enjoyed a brief vogue in regeneration areas from 1984 to 1992. The Council of Europe's annual designation of a European city of culture, the idea of Greece's Minister of Culture, the former film star Melina Mercouri, was used to great effect as a marketing tool by Glasgow in 1990 (Booth and Boyle, 1993).

## OUTSIDE THE CITIES

Outside the older declining cities and industrial areas, the developers did not find such a liberal planning regime (Brindley et al, 1988). The general Thatcherite encouragement of cars, commitment to road building and reductions in public sector house building created a great deal of pressure for greenfield development in the urban periphery. Yet fears that traditional restraint policies would be relaxed proved groundless, largely because the government's political heartlands were in just such areas. Green belt and countryside protection policies were usually rigorously enforced (Elson, 1986; Ward, 1994). The strong pressures during the 1980s for private new town construction within a deregulated planning system came to nothing. By the later 1980s, a definite greening of Thatcherism was under way.

## 314  THE GREENING OF THATCHERISM

In part this growing environmental consciousness came from domestic political pressures in the urban fringe and rural areas. As the economic position improved, the arguments for ever more deregulation became increasingly difficult to maintain. Quality of life matters assumed greater prominence. This was reinforced by a growing environmental awareness (Porritt and Winner, 1988). Much pressure to act also came from the EU and international reports such as *Our Common Future*, the report of the World Commission on Environment and Development (the Brundtland report) of 1987 (Brundtland, 1987). The Thatcher government was slow to react to European pressures for greater environmental regulation until its own supporters began to send obvious signals (Ward, 1994). In 1989, for example, the Green Party gained its biggest percentage vote in the European elections in Britain, largely in Conservative areas. The following year, it became obvious that a shift, at least in presentation, was under way. The publication of *This Common Inheritance* (DOE *et al*, 1990), a major environmental policy document, underlined government commitment to the environment.

*Figure 10.2* The ethos of the market was widely adopted by urban policy makers during the 1980s. It was led, rather surprisingly, by the socialist stronghold of Glasgow, which imitated New York to produce this memorable marketing campaign.

## TOWARDS SUSTAINABLE URBAN DEVELOPMENT

The important shifts came after the Thatcher era was over, however. Although there was no sudden change of direction, the deregulationist impulse was never again quite as strong as in the 1980s. The Brundtland report had called for sustainable development. This was defined, with beguiling vagueness, as 'development which meets the need of the present without compromising the ability of future generations to meet their own needs' (Brundtland, 1987: 218). In effect, it pointed towards a middle way between economic development and environmental protection. In Britain, as everywhere else in the west, this compromise became the basis of the new planning discourse of the 1990s, reinforced especially by the 1992 Earth Summit held in Rio de Janeiro. From Agenda 21 of the summit came objectives that could be translated into actual urban policies. The EU also took a lead on these issues from 1990, fostering especially the idea of the compact city as the desired sustainable urban form (CEC, 1990a, 1990b; RH Williams, 1996). This would, in theory, be more economical in the demands it placed on the conversion of unbuilt land to urban use. The hope was that it would also increase the possibilities of good quality public services and, especially, permit lower reliance on the motor car (Jenks *et al* (eds), 1996; K Williams *et al*, (eds), 2000).

## FROM DOCKLANDS TO THAMES GATEWAY

There were other optimistic signs in the early 1990s. Strategic planning slowly began to re-emerge from the cold storage of the Thatcher years. The most positive evidence was the planning of the East Thames Corridor, begun in 1991 and rebadged as the Thames Gateway four years later (P Hall and C Ward, 1998). This was effectively an eastward extension from London Docklands along the Thames estuary, stretching for some 48 kilometres along both sides of the river. In many ways, it learnt from the docklands experience, and gave far more attention to transport, overall planning and public consultation. The London Docklands Development Corporation itself was wound up in 1998, but echoes of its opportunistic, project-driven, boosterist style continued. The clearest example was the Millennium Dome in north Greenwich, opened in 2000 as a child-oriented celebration of the new millennium. It was far less successful than originally projected.

Yet the strategy for the new development corridor, published in 1995, appears more hopeful. It adopts the new language of sustainability and, unusually for British planning, uses rail links as the main defining element. Peter Hall, who influenced the overall strategy, has likened it to the development axes in the 1965 Paris regional plan, occasionally referring to it as a 'Thames-la-Vallée' (Hardy, 1992). Such thinking was also encouraged because the corridor followed the new Channel tunnel rail link to London. Along this route there will be living and working areas, focused particularly around rail stations. The most prominent single node of new development is projected at Ebbsfleet, where what will effectively be a new town will appear around a Channel tunnel rail station.

## *316* THE WEAKNESSES OF BRITISH PLANNING

One of the most telling aspects of this whole story was, however, the extraordinary delays in building the new rail link. The Channel tunnel opened in 1994, four years before work on the link even began, and 13 years before its final completion. This delay was symptomatic of a wider weakness. Belief in a *laissez-faire*, market-led approach was faltering, but there was still precious little real commitment to any effective alternative. When measured against the new ideals of compact sustainable urban development, practically nothing that British planning did during the 1990s was innovative or impressive in international terms (eg Beatley, 2000). The best practice and the new ideas lay elsewhere. Largely for reasons beyond their control, British planners struggled to keep up.

The most serious problem of Thatcherism was the pattern it had established of chronic underinvestment in all public services, which persisted throughout the 1990s. This made it extremely difficult to deliver sustainable urban development. Public transport, critical to the compact-city approach, was especially poor compared to continental European equivalents. And, despite the sometimes impressive waterfront and other regeneration developments, the general quality of the urban environment declined as the public realm was neglected. No deals with the private sector could meet this shortfall through leverage or similar arrangements. Efforts to do so often distracted planners from their core concerns with creating a good quality urban environment. Many also suffered directly from a funding regime that emphasised quantitative rather than qualitative performance, discouraging both reflective practice and active knowledge of planning innovations in neighbouring countries. All too often, British planners were working with at least one, and sometimes both, hands tied behind their backs.

## BROWNFIELD DEVELOPMENT AND URBAN VILLAGES

The key planning debate of the later 1990s was about meeting future housing needs (P Hall and C Ward, 1998). From 1996, it was generally accepted that 60 per cent of new housing should be built on previously developed 'brownfield' land. Since most such land lay within existing urban areas, this was effectively an acceptance of the European compact-city model. The 1990s saw a number of important projects that tried to demonstrate how this might be done, posing alternatives to a suburban style of development (UVG, 1992; Barton (ed), 2000). Many have been referred to as 'urban villages', the rather imprecise label (used also in other parts of the English-speaking world) signifying attempts to create compact and socially cohesive residential areas with good local services, and sometimes with ecologically advanced designs.

Usually these are within existing urban areas (though one of the best known, Poundbury, developed by the Prince of Wales, is actually a greenfield development on the edge of the small town of Dorchester) (Thompson-Fawcett, 1998). The most notable effort on brownfield land has been the ambitious redevelopment of Hulme from 1992. This was a large area of derelict public sector flats, mainly of indus-trialised system construction, in Manchester. The new Hulme, comprising about

4,000 dwellings – a mixture of social rental and housing for sale – has been developed by a public-private partnership, with extensive community consultation. It has returned to a traditional street-based urban structure, partly reflecting principles advocated by the American 'new urbanist' movement (to be discussed below), though at higher densities. The results have been widely admired, attracting some attention from planners in other countries. A later example, which promises more environmental sensitivity, is the Millennium Village of about 1,400 dwellings, mainly for sale, in Greenwich close to the Millennium Dome.

## BROWNFIELD VERSUS GREENFIELD

Despite such demonstration projects, there continue to be grave doubts as to whether a 60 per cent brownfield target will be realistic in anything but the short term. As we have seen, 20th-century British planning had traditionally a strong decentralist impulse which seemingly reflected deeply held anti-urban cultural values. Important sections of British planning opinion, in fact, continued to argue that garden city or new-town-type development in greenfield locations would also be essential in delivering sustainable urban development (eg P Hall and Ward, 1998). However, this was not a fashionable argument in the late 1990s since it was feared that any early encouragement of this line would prejudice the success of a predominantly brownfield approach. Yet this was not the real problem. Housing values in Britain have traditionally been wedded to the suburban ideal. It is unlikely that this can quickly change, particularly when the environments and public services of inner urban areas remain so unattractive to most people. Clearly if the new approach was to succeed, something would need to be done to increase confidence in urban living.

## THE ROGERS REPORT

The urban regeneration projects of the 1980s had begun to suggest that the population decline in inner metropolitan areas could be reversed, especially in London. The problem was how to achieve this on a wider scale. In 1998, the Blair Labour government which had been elected, amidst high expectations, with a landslide majority the previous year, asked the prominent architect Lord (Richard) Rogers to recommend how this might be done. His task force's report, *Towards an Urban Renaissance*, published in 1999, may perhaps prove to be a turning point in British urban planning (Rogers, 1999). Certainly it marked a shift in international lesson-drawing. Rogers, designer of the Pompidou Centre in Paris and London's Millennium Dome, was one of a small group of British (in fact, he is half-Italian) architects who had become international figures. He had intermittently made notable contributions to the urban planning debate in Britain, arguing essentially for sustainable development with good architecture (Rogers, 1997).

This was also the tenor of the 1999 report. It made very full use of international examples (more so than any major British planning report since Buchanan in 1963). Yet, in contrast to the long-established American bias in British planning thought which peaked in the Thatcher years, Rogers favoured European examples. His task force visited the Netherlands, Germany, Spain and the United States. The last, though still the source of positive ideas about financing, was generally seen in a more negative light than previously. (This reflected America's long-familiar suburban sprawl and freeway-dominated cities, but there were now fewer positive lessons to counter-balance these.) By contrast, the lessons drawn from Europe were unvaryingly positive, sometimes suspiciously so. The report, significantly (and uniquely for an official British planning report), had a foreword by Pasqual Maragall, the charismatic, influential (and left-wing) former mayor of Barcelona. The Catalonian capital was one of the European cities most fulsomely admired. The greatest number of specific references were, however, to the Netherlands and to Germany. Typically, what were admired were compact housing design, pedestrian-friendly home zones (*woonerven*), social-class mix, community policing, public transport provision, pedestrian and cycling provision, and much else in similar vein.

## THE INTERNATIONAL CONTEXT OF BRITISH PLANNING

If the Rogers report is to have a long-term impact on Britain's cities, deeply embedded British attitudes about suburbs, cities and cars will need to be tackled. Nevertheless, the recommendations are a clear sign of a growing Europeanisation of British planning discourse. Having moved at least halfway across the Atlantic in the 1980s, the planning outlook of Britain had begun to shift closer to its true geographical position by 2000. Official rhetoric increasingly embraced the European ideal of the compact city, Dutch and German-style home zones and non-car-based urban transport solutions. The regeneration of run-down areas was another area to benefit from lesson-drawing across the EU in the late 1990s. There were some continuing American references, for example to movements such as the new urbanism, but these were a secondary theme. (And, as we will see, American planners were also beginning to look more to continental European examples by the end of the century.)

On balance, the extent of international learning from Britain during the 1980s and 1990s was more limited, particularly in the planning field proper. Most advanced capitalist countries drew lessons, negative as well as positive, from the regeneration of London Docklands (eg Breen and Rigby, 1996; Meyer, 1999). With the smaller projects in other cities, the Docklands served, to some extent, as a staging post in the transfer of the American model of waterfront development to continental Europe. Even Americans drew lessons from the vastly greater scale at which the model was applied in London Docklands. In a more general sense many European countries sampled the deregulated market-led approach to urban policy, sometimes directly encouraged by British developers. But they never accepted the model to the extent that Britain did. Moreover, as the paradigm shifted towards sustainability in the 1990s, there was, at least on the bigger matters, precious little good practice in Britain that could be emulated. It is significant that in those examples, such as Hulme, from which European lessons were drawn the principal novelty remained the harnessing of profit-seeking private sector funding to social regeneration. The Americanisation of British planning during the Thatcher era was still casting its long shadow.

# Germany

The international reputation of German planning, already climbing, finally returned to something like the level of the late 19th and early 20th centuries in the 1980s and 1990s. To a substantial extent, this mirrored larger events. German unification, in October 1990, saw the Communist East German state absorbed by West Germany (Harris, 1991; Lewis and McKenzie (eds), 1995; Pulzer, 1995; C Anderson *et al*, 1993). This created a large nation, with some 82.8 million people in 2000. The increase was less than 6 per cent on the combined populations of East and West Germany in 1980 (a similar growth rate to, for example, the United Kingdom and Sweden, though below France, the Netherlands and, especially, the United States). Yet Germany was again, by a large margin, the largest wholly European country. The wider collapse of Communism also allowed it to reclaim its central position in continental Europe and emphasised the significance of German speakers as the continent's largest linguistic group. Already, of course, the West German economy was Europe's largest. The absorption of the disintegrating East German economy (and the country's much poorer population) in 1991 was more headache than endowment. Like the rest of western Europe, German economic growth rates in the 1980s and 1990s were lower than in previous decades. Also its workers experienced higher unemployment as older industries declined, especially in the East. As a whole, though, the economy remained strong. In the longer term, the wider collapse of Communism also gave Germany a favoured position for taking advantage of the trading and investment opportunities that were emerging in all the former Communist eastern European countries.

Such background features are extremely important for understanding the growing international salience of German ideas and expertise. A more specific factor in western Europe was that Germany also became much the biggest member of the EU, which was enlarged to reflect unification. Under the dominating presence of Chancellor Helmut Kohl, who led Germany from 1983 to 1998, the country set the pace for an ever closer EU. The creation of a single European currency was the most important manifestation of this larger project, but the sentiments were reproduced across a wider range of activity, including environmental and urban policies. Unlike Britain, Germany was in all respects at the heart of the European project, so German attitudes and understandings contributed very directly to the wider European policy discourse.

## Globalisation and the new Germany

Germany's growing international resonance can be seen as a peaceful achievement of the continental hegemony that had so often eluded it in past military actions. The difference was, though, that the new dominance brought no very obvious Germanisation. West Germans had, of necessity, long learnt to live and prosper in a world shaped by the United States, where English was the dominant language of international contact. From the outside, East Germans also yearned to live in the same world though, when they finally entered it, it turned out to be far harsher than they had imagined. The unified Germany they found in the 1990s was, like the rest of Europe, feeling the effects of a particularly unforgiving phase of western capitalism. The centrally planned Communist economy was quickly replaced by one based on private enterprise and market principles. In other respects, however, Kohl did not roll back the frontiers of West Germany's social democratic state in the dramatic manner of Margaret Thatcher in Britain. But he accepted some of the same agenda, which reduced the government's ability to soften the impacts of global capitalism.

Globalisation was, of course, cast very largely in an American mould that reproduced itself across many different aspects of German – and continental European – life. Thus it was with a certain resignation that a leading German planning academic, Klaus Kunzmann, wrote in 1997 that 'Los Angeles seems to be creeping gradually into Europe: first mentally, then physically and economically' (Kunzmann, 1997: 16). Overall, though, Germany has suffered less, and gained more, from globalisation than all but a very few other countries in the world. Its size, economic prowess and new sense of itself gave it a greater ability – and confidence – to moderate globalisation's most damaging and intrusive aspects. More than any other part of Europe (certainly far more than Britain), Germany felt able to seek ways of modifying the dominant American shape of globalisation. In turn, its core position in Europe helped to bolster the collective European ability to do the same. These were themes that were played out in German (and European) planning history during these momentous years, nowhere more so than in the once and future capital: Berlin.

## THE REUNIFICATION OF BERLIN

Following the dramatic breaching in 1989 of the wall that divided the Communist East from West Berlin, the former capital once more became a single city (www.stadtentwicklung.berlin.de). In 1999, with the relocation of the federal government from Bonn, it was restored as the German capital. In world or European terms unified Berlin was not especially large, with roughly 3.5 million population (4.3 million with neighbouring, functionally related areas) in 2000. This was comparable to Athens or St Petersburg but smaller than London, Paris, Moscow or Istanbul (or the polycentric Ruhr metropolitan region). Nor, reflecting post-1945 history, was the city well connected with the main axes of European development. Suddenly though, it seemed that much of this historic disadvantage could be swept away as the political maps of city, nation and continent were simultaneously redrawn. Truly, all that was solid had melted into air. Berlin, it was confidently expected, could now reclaim its place as a major European and world city. If ever there was a moment to make plans, this was it.

## CONCEPTUAL REHEARSALS: THE BERLIN IBA 1984–7

As it happened, many of the arguments that were to be central to the planning of Berlin throughout the 1990s had been honed just a few years before (but with no expectation of) the city's reunification (Kündiger, 1997a; Bullock, 1999). The event which had triggered these arguments was the West Berlin IBA (Internationale Bauausstellung – International Building Exhibition) of 1984 to 1987. Like previous IBAs, this was an extended exercise in architecture, planning and related professional areas. Unlike the usual kind of exhibition, IBAs were intended to create permanent solutions to real planning problems, promoting international diffusion of best practice and encouraging further innovations. In comparable fashion to West Berlin's 1957 IBA, which played a critical role in the mainstreaming of modernism, the 1984–7 exhibition pointed to a way of reconciling modernity with the morphological memory of the city. The decision to proceed was taken in the late 1970s and work began in 1981. In some ways, though, the basic framing of the IBA was not promising. The sites were fragmented and there were important divergences regarding the underlying philosophy. There were, in fact, two IBAs. IBA Altbau (Old IBA), directed by Hardt-Walther Hämer, adopted an approach to urban renewal that combined conservation and rehabilitation of older blocks with selective demolition (for example to create interior courtyards and gardens within closely built blocks) and limited redevelopment. In political terms, it was a 'bottom-up' approach based on very close working with local communities. The focus was in two areas of Kreuzberg, the district which in the 1970s had seen such fierce resistance to the more traditional nostrums of postwar planning.

It was, however, the IBA Neubau (New IBA) which became most influential on subsequent thinking. Under the direction of Josef Paul Kleihues, it was focused on four areas. The main efforts were concentrated in the largely cleared areas of south Tiergarten and south Friedrichstadt, though there were other sites at Tegel and Prager Platz. Kleihues's central philosophy was summed up in the term *kritische rekonstruction* (critical reconstruction). This involved rebuilding in a way that remembered the essential physical, social and economic characteristics of the 19th-century block. There would be links with the past in terms of the plan, building lines and roof lines, and in far greater diversity of ownership and use within blocks than had been typical in Berlin's recent history. Yet the architectural expression was to be contemporary rather than nostalgic. There was a definite sense of updating an essentially European urban form, creating a real alternative to the rampant Americanisation which seemed to be shaping West German cities in the 1980s.

## PLANNING AFTER REUNIFICATION

The IBA was tremendously successful in attracting national and international attention (eg Omura, 1988b; Inghe, 1999). Although its achievements were limited, its different approaches fostered much debate. When the city was reunified it was therefore natural that planning discussions drew on this earlier work. There was no equivalent input from planners in the former East Berlin. More even than after the fall of Nazism in West Germany, the great majority of those from the previous regime, including all senior figures, were removed from office. The experience of the rest of former East Germany was similar, though less draconian, as planning was reconstructed on the western pattern. The general result was that West Germans took over professional leadership of planning in the east during the 1990s, especially so in Berlin. Meanwhile the tremendous development boom in that city was creating its own powerful imperatives, signalling the large-scale arrival of capitalist urbanisation (Stroschein, 1994). International competitions, organised to plan major districts, partially pre-empted IBA principles, most notably for the Potsdamer Platz (von Petz, 1996; Schlusche, 1997). Commercial developers and their architects probed for the loopholes in what was little more than a loose philosophy.

## CRITICAL RECONSTRUCTION AS THE NEW FORMULA

To combat these pressures, critical reconstruction was converted into a more robust and rigid formula (Kündiger, 1997a). In part this shift also reflected changes in the political control of the Berlin planning agency, the department of urban development. Under Christian Democrat leadership in the early 1990s, there was more scope for business and other interests to voice their opinions in the newly created *Stadtforum*, allowing greater pragmatism. By the mid-1990s, however, the Social Democrats had secured control of the department, which was led politically by Peter Strieder and professionally by Hans Stimmann. The more formulaic approach to critical recon-struction was pressed with increasing confidence, culminating in the *Planwerk Innenstadt* (inner city plan) of late 1996 (Süchting and Weiss, 2001). Yet critics now claim that the communicative, democratic approach of the IBA philosophy has been sacrificed. The former dialogue has, they say, become a monologue. There is also criticism from many former East Berlin architects and planners that the insistence on a return to 19th-century principles as the only legitimate basis for shaping the city rejects much of the reality of Berlin's 20th-century history (Hain, 2001). History, it is claimed, is being used very selectively.

## BERLIN AS A EUROPEAN CITY

Of course, these criticisms are not the only possible reaction. They also miss the main point for this international history – that Berlin simultaneously seeks to become again a global city, yet one with a distinctive *European* identity. Few cities in the 1990s have been more open in welcoming the world's architects and developers (www. stadtentwicklung.berlin.de). Yet its planners block 'global' planning and design approaches that derive from the American city. The legitimacy of this approach rests on Berlin's own past, though it alludes to traditional city-making principles through-out central Europe. This gives the Berlin approach a wider resonance, most obviously within the model of urban sustainability being promoted by the EU in the 1990s. The planners' vision of the new Berlin promotes compactness, mixed land and building uses and public transport. It tries to discourage large monofunctional zones, high-rise towers and residential decentralisation. In 1994 the Berlin government agreed to meet 90 per cent of their (substantial) requirements for housing on previously urbanised land (Beatley, 2000). The peculiar interest of Berlin, however, is that this European vision of urban compactness has been pitted more sharply than elsewhere against the 'global' American alternative.

## PLANNING URBAN REGIONS

Even in Berlin the planners' vision has had to face powerful and insidious American-ising tendencies, some from other fields of public policy. Rather unusually amongst major western cities at the very end of the 20th century, Berlin was busily engaged on urban motorway construction. This was ostensibly to direct traffic away from the newly re-created central area, an approach long ago applied elsewhere. Yet, as always, it encouraged a way of living that was the very opposite of the ideal of European urbanity. (Given the central role that the car continued to play in national life, however, it would be difficult to claim that it was any less German.)

Berlin's newly reborn love affair with automobilism interacted with other forces. German unification ended many of the peculiar features that had enforced Berlin's compactness. West Berliners, previously constrained by the Communist state that surrounded them, now found they could move to semirural areas beyond the city, commuting ever longer distances (Frick, 1999). East Berliners also had the possibility of greater freedom of residence than before unification. (In both parts of the city, the economic changes that followed the ending of subsidies also contributed to population change.) The result was that population fell, and especially so in the inner city where the property boom was pushing up land values, a novel experience in former Communist Berlin. Yet, despite these unique features, Berlin was belatedly following the pattern of many West German cities. Frankfurt-am-Main was a particularly striking example (Friedmann and Lehrer, 1998). That city itself had some 660,000 inhabitants in the early 1990s (of whom a growing proportion comprised ethnic minorities) and the immediate metropolitan region had 1.5 million. More significant though was the way the commuting hinterland was creating a Rhine–Main conurbation of some 3.5 million people.

Unlike most West German cities, however, Berlin in the 1990s had the space to allow a good deal of suburbanisation within its own boundaries (which were those of a Land, not merely of a city). But the rapid growth of the commuting area into the surrounding Land of Brandenburg posed major problems (Mäding, 1999). As Hamburg and Bremen, the other free cities (with the status of Länder), increasingly found, metropolitan planning conducted across Länder boundaries could often be very difficult. Despite this, a proposal to unite the Berlin and Brandenburg Länder was rejected by cautious electorates in 1996 (BSSUT/MUNRLB, 1998). Metropolitan planning proceeded on a cooperative basis but without powers to enforce any tight containment of Berlin. Surrounding towns, newly freed from the restrictions of Communist planning, were not minded to forgo opportunities for lucrative new developments. The strategy favoured by the two Länder, published in 1998, anticipated that the major outward movement of people from Berlin would continue. It sought, however, to give some order to the process by reinforcing the star-shaped expansion pattern that had long characterised the region's growth.

## AMERICANISING THE GERMAN CITY

Nowhere was the 'American' character of late 20th-century German urbanisation more visible than in Frankfurt. The outward spread of the travel to work area was just one dimension; more immediate evidence could be seen in the very heart of the city. Its postwar American occupiers had, in fact, helped set Frankfurt's destiny as a major international financial centre. They had also bequeathed a more market-led planning regime than was typical of other German cities, which intensified in the new age of global competition that opened in the 1980s.

Already in the late 1960s and 1970s, the transformation of central Frankfurt had been under way as office towers began to multiply (Kaulusche and Setzepfandt, 1997).

The process became even more intense during the 1980s and 1990s as Frankfurt embraced, with other European cities, the promotional point-scoring that had first led American cities to build skyscrapers. In 1991, for example, London's Canary Wharf tower, the symbol of Thatcherite planning, was quickly overtaken as Europe's tallest building by Frankfurt's Messeturm. (It was no accident that Frankfurt was also challenging London's position as Europe's premier global financial centre.) The 'Mainhattan' long anticipated by journalistic and boosterist fancy seemed to have arrived. By the 1990s, however, the high-rise buildings, many by major international architects, were increasingly Post-Modern and environmentally friendly variants of the classic skyscraper.

## CREATING THE CULTURAL CITY

Frankfurt's global ambitions had also caused it to adopt the city-marketing practices pioneered by American (and, increasingly, British) cities (Friedrichs and Dangschat, 1993). By the 1980s, it was widely criticised as a harsh and dreary place. It was felt that its future growth as an international financial centre would be prejudiced unless it could offer a richer and more diverse life outside working hours. To combat this negative image, the city embarked on massive cultural investment. The main setting for much of this was in the Römerberg quarter, the core of what had once been the medieval city. The early years of the 1980s brought moves to re-establish a sense of the area as a historic district, much as Munich (and, elsewhere, Warsaw) had done in the early postwar years. Using Polish craftsmen, a small but extremely significant group of historic buildings was painstakingly re-created together with associated, sympathetically designed but frankly modern buildings. The result did not receive universal professional approval. (It was, of course, soon overshadowed by the new, and more sophisticated, concept of critical reconstruction.) Still more dramatic was the rapid enlargement of the city's cultural infrastructure, also mainly in Römersberg. By the early 1990s, no less than 22 museums, 80 galleries, 17 theatres and four concert buildings had recently been opened or were under way.

## THE MALLING OF GERMANY?

Such policies for culture and heritage thus offered another way in which cities could respond to globalisation while apparently retaining, or even enhancing, local distinctiveness. It was less easy to achieve this with many of the other new urban forms that appeared throughout the world during these years. Even in this context, though, Germany sometimes managed to avoid uncritical borrowing of American models. Hamburg, for example, did not rush blindly into waterfront redevelopment as did many other western port cities. Its HafenCity project did not finally proceed until the later 1990s, allowing an approach that was rather more reflective and critical in its

*Figure 10.3  The creation of a 'Mainhattan' in Frankfurt's West end had begun amidst much tension during the 1970s but accelerated in the 1980s and 1990s as the towers of international banks soared above what had been a pleasant inner residential district.*

reference to other models (www.hafencity.com). Here, at least, the debt to Baltimore (or London Docklands, a more likely referent given Hamburg's historic links with the British capital) will be more indirect.

Distinctively German solutions were more difficult to maintain in retailing. Purpose-built enclosed shopping malls of the American or British type had been rare in German cities, which had preferred to pedestrianise existing streets. By the 1990s, however, there were clear signs of change. The Zeilgalerie 'Les Facettes' (its very name a signifier of internationalism) in Frankfurt, developed in 1992, was a stylish multilevel translation of the North American mall into the heart of a European city (Kaulusche and Setzepfandt, 1997). The later shopping mall at the Potsdamer Platz in Berlin was another high profile development and asserted a new centrality in a district formerly divided by the wall (www.stadtentwicklung.berlin.de). Like all enclosed malls, these recent examples are separate from the life of the street. Yet they come closer to being a real part of city life than the many older blind-walled examples that mar the centres of British, and some American, cities.

More telling were the changes on the urban fringe, where car-based retailing based on large superstores was proliferating (as it was almost everywhere in western Europe

**Figure 10.4** *As Frankfurt's leaders became sensitive in the 1980s to accusations of their city's dullness compared to London, they created a cultural quarter in the central Römer district. This included the recreation of a medieval streetscape, now hugely popular with tourists.*

during these years). The out-of-town regional shopping centre also made its appearance in 1994/6 at CentrO in Oberhausen in the Ruhr (www.centro.life.de). Following and extending the approach pioneered slightly earlier at Meadowhall in Sheffield, CentrO's British developers created continental Europe's largest shopping centre on the site of a former steelworks. Like Meadowhall, it was relatively well served by public transport but the surrounding associated development (including a leisure park) also took it closer to the American concept of a new 'edge city', to be discussed below. The developers claim it is the new town centre of Oberhausen (one of the Ruhr's smaller settlements). This is rather disingenuous, however, since CentrO clearly challenges the shopping centres of nearby cities.

## THE GREEN MOVEMENT

In sharp contrast to such initiatives, it was in the planning of sustainable cities that Germany made its most influential contributions to international planning discourse during these years. By 1980 West Germany, with the Netherlands and Denmark, was already an important formative force in the international green movement (Pulzer, 1995). These trends strengthened over the following decades, especially in the 1990s. In part, the salience of green issues was a function of national wealth, but it also reflected an unusually high popular awareness that was mirrored in the political strength of the Green Party (www.gruene.de). By 2000, there were Green ministers in Gerhard Schröder's federal coalition administration, and in Land administrations in Nordrhein-Westfalen, Hamburg and Schleswig-Holstein. There were also Green members in 11 of the 16 Land parliaments. (These were exclusively in the former West Germany, neatly highlighting the way economic wellbeing underpinned concern for green issues.) Finally, we should note the strong role of the Greens in many local governments. Overall, this level of political representation was without parallel in any other large country in the world.

Concern about the environment was nowhere, of course, the exclusive prerogative of green parties. But the strength of the Green Party in Germany ensured that the political agenda was skewed more towards green issues than was usual elsewhere. Nor were these issues defined in a narrow fashion. In Frankfurt, for example, the Greens were in 1989 the driving force behind the new city department of multicultural affairs, designed to combat racism (Friedmann and Lehrer, 1998). (The initiative was led by Daniel Cohn-Bendit, a central figure in the 1968 Paris student revolutionary movement. This hints at how the German Green Party became a home for radical sentiments that had at other times sought quite different solutions.) The main point, though, is that the German Greens saw environmental issues in broad terms, indivisible from social, economic and other matters. It was a philosophy that readily embraced the emergent integrative concept of sustainability.

## PLANNING FOR SUSTAINABILITY

Nowhere in the west did the commitment to sustainability come as an overnight conversion. This was especially so in Germany. Many policies which German cities had long been pursuing became central elements in the new thinking. We have already seen something of how the Berlin IBA contributed to the ideology of the compact city. Long-cherished West German commitments to pedestrianisation, cycling, public transport provision and traffic calming now also repaid earlier efforts (Hass-Klau, 1990). During the 1980s traffic-calming schemes appeared throughout West Germany, although mass implementation brought design standardisation and degradation, particularly as economies were sought. Yet the principles of traffic restraint became widely accepted and understood, allowing for ever more ambitious policies to improve the attractiveness of cities, especially their centres, for non-drivers.

By the 1990s, the main innovators tended to be smaller western cities such as Freiburg, Münster and Heidelberg (Beatley, 2000). The most complete attempts to create car-free or pro-cycling environments could be found in such settings. Here, too, some of the most interesting individual initiatives to promote energy efficiency and, indeed, other aspects of the environmental agenda could be found. The most significant example of entirely new development was at Kronsberg in Hanover (KUKA, nd, c1999). This was conceived in conjunction with the international Expo 2000 exhibition as a model of a sustainable new urban community and accords fully with the Agenda 21 principles of the 1992 Earth Summit. Developed on farmland, it was planned as a compact, high-density development. The scheme also showed ecological water and waste management, efficient energy generation and use, emphasis on public transport, cycling and walking, and exemplary provision of local social facilities for a diverse population. It is planned that Kronsberg will house some 15,000 people by 2006.

## IBA EMSCHER PARK

The qualitative interest of these smaller cities and one-off model ventures was undeniable. Yet the initiative that most convincingly harnessed environmental planning to the wider concerns of urban planning occurred where the challenge was greatest – in Germany's largest urban region, the Ruhrgebiet (IBA Emscher Park, 1999). As in similar regions throughout the western world, the coal and steel industries that had been the mainstay of the Ruhr's economy experienced serious contraction during the late 20th century (von Petz, 1997a). Mines, coking plants and steelworks were closed. What remained were the obsolete, massive buildings and structures of heavy industry, waste heaps, contaminated land and polluted watercourses, together with high unemployment and communities which felt they had lost their purpose. In 1989, the Land of Nordrhein-Westfalen launched a 10-year programme to allow the region to move on. The focus for this effort was essentially environmental and involved the creation of a massive landscape park, with over 90 individual linked projects. The park largely followed the Emscher river, which had traditionally served as the Ruhrgebiet's open sewer. Taking the form of an Internationale Bauaustellung (IBA), the Emscher Park covered 784 square kilometres and directly affected some two million inhabitants.

*Figure 10.5* The IBA Emscher Park remediated and reused the redundant spaces of the Ruhr's heavy industry. Huge industrial complexes were turned over to leisure and arts activity, as here at the former Zollverein Coking Plant in Essen.

By 1999, when the IBA's life ended, a huge amount had been achieved, funded largely by Land and EU moneys, with about a third of the investment from private sources. As with other IBAs, Emscher Park set high design standards and drew on international expertise. (Austria, Britain, Denmark, France, Switzerland and the United States were represented in addition to Germany.) The IBA's defining work was to clean up the Emscher itself and make specific landscape and access improvements. However, individual projects embraced economic, heritage, housing and social themes. There were science parks, technology centres, employment retraining centres and new cultural facilities. As well as many new buildings, major industrial structures were integrated into new uses. These were particularly important because they retained important landmarks, maintaining industrial memories in a postindustrial age. The huge Oberhausen gasholder became a setting for drama, concerts and exhibitions. A steelworks, complete with blast furnaces, became the Duisburg Nord landscape park. The surface buildings of the immense Zollverein coal mine in Essen became a centre for art, design and culture. There were also many small new housing projects that reflected and reinterpreted the Ruhr tradition of industrial garden villages.

## GERMAN PLANNING IN ITS INTERNATIONAL CONTEXT

In their different ways Emscher Park and Berlin encapsulated the distinctive contribution of Germany to international planning discourse in the late 20th century. As we might expect, the external impact of this approach was strongest in other parts of German-speaking Europe, and in those countries which historically had tended to look to Germany. In Finland and Scandinavia, for example, there were signs of a return to this traditional reference point (eg Ilmonen *et al* (eds), 1999). Parts of the former Communist world also became more open to German influence, even though it was the generic tendencies of global capitalism that more immediately shaped post-Communist urbanisation. It remains to be seen whether the finer aspirations of recent German planning will manage to express themselves in these settings. Further west, however, interest in German planning thought and practice was clearly growing by the late 1990s, especially in Britain and the United States.

On the other hand, the German planning agenda was clearly influenced by the Anglo-American market-led approach. But the reluctance of most planners in Germany to embrace this approach closely was palpable, especially so in the 1990s. They remained well connected to the main currents of international thinking about the design of cities, noting, for example, the rise of new models such as Barcelona. The frenzied rebuilding of postunification Berlin also provided many opportunities to engage with the global superstars of late 20th-century architecture. (At times in the 1990s, for example, it seemed that the German admiration for the British architect Norman Foster knew no bounds.)

However, at least one commentator, the Dutch architect Rem Koolhaas, well known for his writings on New York and Asian cities, has spoken of a self-centred conceit in German thinking about urban design, especially in Berlin (www.feedmag.-com/re/re114.2.html). It is not necessary completely to accept this argument in order to agree that German planners are, for the moment, finding relatively little elsewhere that they genuinely feel able to admire and from which they can draw lessons. Yet a century of planning history suggests that, compared to the other main national traditions, German self-confidence has a brittle edge that quickly turns to insecurity. If this is still so, then change may soon come.


# FRANCE

In their different ways, the Britain and Germany that entered the 21st century had changed radically since 1980. The other main European planning tradition was also touched by many of the same global pressures. Yet the elements of continuity in the French approach to urban planning have been rather stronger than in the other two countries. As we have seen, the third quarter of the 20th century brought a dramatic state-led modernisation of France (McMillan, 1992; Cole, 1998). The most remarkable aspect of national development in the last decades of the century was the extent to which this project of modernisation was maintained, even in the new era of global capitalism. This is not to say that the economy was untroubled. France experienced many of the problems of industrial decline and unemployment that afflicted its neighbours. The years of spectacular economic growth were over. In the 1980s growth performance mirrored the historically rather low western European average, and fell a little lower for much of the 1990s. (The population, meanwhile, grew by about a tenth, higher than that of most of its neighbours.) As we will see, this experience helped to trigger many of the urban anxieties that shaped planning and other policies else-where. Yet even this, rather sluggish, growth rate was still deemed sufficient to delay the kind of drastic pruning of state activity that occurred in Britain.

In this, though, politics was as important as economics. During the 1980s and 1990s the left was a much more important force in French national government than in other large western countries. The socialist François Mitterand was president from 1981 to 1995, with left-wing domination of the national assembly for 10 of these years. Although the Gaullists under Jacques Chirac managed to achieve short periods of government, their impact under Mitterand was limited. Even after Chirac became president in 1995 his dominance was quickly compromised by the election of a socialist-dominated national assembly in 1997. Paradoxically, however, it was the new socialist prime minister, Lionel Jospin, who showed the greatest interest in adopting the Anglo-American model of privatisation. Even so, by 2000 France retained a rela-tively large state sector. With this went an unusually strong faith in public planning.


## THE DECENTRALISATION OF GOVERNMENT

There were important changes. The most important was governmental decentralisa-tion, devolving power from the centre to local and regional levels (Newman and Thornley, 1996). The pressure came from the leaders of the bigger provincial cities, who resented the power of centrally appointed officials, the *préfets*, to shape local decisions. This was especially so when there were political differences in the com-position of local and national governments. Thus, after years of conservative domin-ance of national politics, it was the socialist mayor of Marseilles, Gaston Defferre, newly installed as a minister, who pushed through the administrative reforms

(*Urbanisme*, 1999). The principle of independent local government was established in 1982, and elected regional bodies followed in 1986. The *préfets* retained only residual, long-stop powers. Although these changes left the very fragmented structure of local government unreformed, they represented a major change in the locus of planning activity.

These, and related changes in voting systems, also gave more scope for political interests outside the coalitions of left and right which had dominated France since 1945. At local, regional and (though to a smaller extent) national levels, green interests began to become a significant voice, more than in Britain but much less than in Germany (Cole, 1998). Another trend that was rather stronger in France than its neighbours was the growth of the extreme right wing as a party political force. This highlighted a strong undertow of resentment against immigrants and ethnic minorities in French society, especially in the south but also in many cities. In their different ways, both these minority political interests contributed to French thinking about planning and urban policies in the 1980s and 1990s.

## LE MARKETING URBAIN

Despite the French socialists' ostensible resistance to the market philosophy that so animated British and American governments in the 1980s, their own project of decentralisation encouraged some quite similar outcomes. Cities and regions used their new autonomy to enhance and trumpet their international competitiveness, within France, the EU and the world (Newman and Thornley, 1996). Like their equivalents in the United States, Britain and elsewhere, French cities, especially provincial ones, and their planners began to practise urban marketing. Their advertising matter proliferated in the world's business press. Major urban development projects became flagships of the new approach, supplying the striking images that were supposed to attract international investors.

All this had important consequences for the international perception of France as a source of urban planning knowledge. Paris was no longer the only example deemed worthy of attention. The same shift to provincial cities had to some extent happened during the 1980s in Britain, the other highly centralised, nonfederal state amongst those with major planning traditions. In Britain, though, the very idea of planning had at the same time become so marginalised politically that international planning interest was always cautious. As we have noted, urban planning retained much of its potency in France. Moreover, the international blossoming of the regional cities was all the more surprising (and welcome) because it contrasted so sharply with what had until recently been the strongest tradition of centralist government anywhere in the west.

## PUBLIC-PRIVATE PARTNERSHIPS

Other aspects of French urban entrepreneurialism showed significant variations from the dominant thinking across the Channel and the Atlantic. Thus, although the public-private partnership, a fundamental principle of the Anglo-American model, was almost as important in French practice, there were significant differences. The Anglo-American approach ideally (if not always in practice) wanted private investment to be dominant. In France, the favoured partnership structure was the SEM (*société d'economie mixte* – mixed economy society). This organisational form had been introduced in 1958 but was used more freely from 1983 as decentralisation reduced the direct role of national government. Its main advantage was that it allowed private funding to be fed into projects where the public sector had a major stake, but with a management style that was more that of a private company. The exact mix of financial resources and control varied with each SEM. It was, however, usual for the public sector to be the dominant actor, with the local mayor often in charge. (Mayors of important cities also often had ministerial experience at national level, further strengthening their personal influence.) The result was more an entrepreneurial version of the public sector rather than the more completely developer-led approach that was typical of Anglo-American efforts.

## MONTPELLIER ANTIGONE

One of the earliest, and extremely influential, French uses of an urban development project to assert a city's advantage in a period of mounting place competition was at Montpellier (Volle and Lacave, 1996). As part of the planned modernisation of France, this relatively small southern city had undergone major investment and growth since the 1950s. A left-wing mayor, newly elected (to general surprise) in the late 1970s launched an extraordinary initiative (Negrier, 1993). Over the following years an entirely new international business district called Antigone took shape, adjoining Montpellier's central area (*Urbanisme*, 1999). In part the motivation (and the name) sprang directly from the new mayor's desire to upstage his predecessor, who had created a central commercial district called Polygone. Yet the project was also a response to more competitive conditions, when growth could no longer be taken for granted and other places might steal some of Montpellier's momentum.

Antigone's designer was the Catalan architect Ricardo Bofill, a particular favourite of President Valéry Giscard d'Estaing, Mitterand's predecessor. Bofill had already worked in Spain and Algeria and, notably, in several Parisian new towns, initially St Quentin-en-Yvelines. He specialised in using classical design principles to create a rather fantastic Post-Modern architecture and *urbanisme*. The distinctiveness, imageability and consequent marketing potential of this made it a deeply appropriate physical form during these years of economic insecurity. For Montpellier it complemented other key investments of the late 1970s and 1980s, in university, road and airport facilities.

## EURALILLE

Another seminal example of using a major planned urban development to promote a city was Euralille. This is an international rail hub with a major office, commercial, residential and leisure development which began to take shape from 1987 (Newman and Thornley, 1996; Cuñat *et al*, 1996; *Urbanisme*, 1999). For some years Lille had been seen as a city with great potential within France and Europe. The new town of Villeneuve d'Ascq and investments in the area's knowledge infrastructure had been under way since the late 1960s, and were continuing. It was, however, the creation of the TGV network (the high-speed rail system and itself the towering achievement of French state planning in the 1980s and 1990s) and the building of the Channel tunnel that finally allowed Lille's international aspirations to become reality. After the projected route had been repositioned closer to the centre of the city, it was decided to redevelop a 70-hectare area around the station as an international flagship development.

The process was orchestrated by a SEM dominated by the local governments of the Lille area, led by the city's socialist mayor, Pierre Mauroy. Other public sector investors including SNCF, the state railway company, were involved. Private sector investment was less significant but included modest participation by several foreign private investors from the Netherlands, Britain and Sweden. These were mainly of symbolic importance in giving the project an authentic international dimension. Important, too, was the retention of an international 'name' (Rem Koolhaas) as lead architect to create a suitably imageable environment. Meanwhile the old centre of Lille was rehabilitated and conserved, completing the marketing package.

## INTERNATIONAL PROJECTS IN DUNKIRK AND LYONS

It was inevitable that other cities would pursue comparable, internationally oriented, boosterist exercises. One example directly inspired by Lille was Dunkirk-Neptune, intended to transform the city's dock area (Bachofen and Picheral, nd). The London practice of Richard Rogers prepared the master plan in 1990, distilling lessons from the Docklands experience. Another notable example was Lyons, which developed its Cité Internationale from 1992 (Vollerin, 1999). Designed by the Italian architect Renzo Piano, it combined an art museum, conference centre, multiplex cinema, casino and international hotel and opened between 1995 and 2000. Far more ambitious in scale is the Lyons Confluence project to redevelop 150 hectares of the lower peninsula between the Rhône and Saône rivers (Lyon Confluence, 1998). A project of the new mayor, Raymond Barre (a former French prime minister) from 1995, it drew on much international experience of major development projects in Europe, the United States and elsewhere. There was a major international competition in 1996/7, with invited entries from Bofill, Kenzo Tange and other major names. The winner was a Franco-Catalan group led by Oriol Bohigas, an architect-planner closely associated with the transformation of Barcelona. The financing and development arrangements were not finalised at the time of writing in 2000.

## MARSEILLES EUROMÉDITERRANÉE

Still more ambitious is the 300-hectare Euroméditerranée project, adjoining central Marseilles, which began to take shape during the 1990s (www.marseilles.com/miseuro.html). France's major southern port city had suffered from increasingly intense competition with Barcelona and Genoa. It also suffered from a serious decline of its inner city and an outward shift to suburban areas, with many associated problems of high unemployment and racial tension. The Euroméditerranée project was a response to these problems. It asserted the city's international significance by the creation of a multiple-use internationally oriented district, and promised an extra 24,000 jobs by 2015. Its planning evolved in familiar fashion from a host of international star contributions, including those of Antoine Grumbach, Ignasi de Solà Morales and Aldo Rossi. An important difference to other comparable projects was, though, the more overt role of national government, which reflected Marseilles' huge importance for the French economy. In this respect, Euroméditerranée highlighted the key contrast with the more privatised Anglo-American model of property-led regeneration.

## PLANNING PARIS

Although the internationalisation of planning in the provincial cities was certainly the most striking feature of the 1980s and 1990s, Paris remained the major single showcase for French planning and development. The strategic plans for the whole region, made in the 1960s and subsequently scaled down to reflect lower growth forecasts, broadly came to fruition in the 1980s. A new round of planning for the region began in 1990 with the revised SDAU for the Paris region approved in 1994 (Ascher, 1997).

The essential background to this is that during the 1980s the capital and its region were touched by the same heightened international competition that affected all western cities. As elsewhere, though they also followed a Parisian tradition, grand urban projects played a key role, continually refreshing the city's reputation for architectural and urbanistic spectacle (Cohen and Fortier (eds), 1992; Noin and White, 1997). The creation in the late 1970s of an elective local government for Paris, headed by a strong mayor in the person (until he became French president) of the Gaullist Jacques Chirac, introduced a new tension between city and national state. Presidents Giscard d'Estaing and Mitterand certainly did not abandon their own ambitions to leave personal monuments in the capital. The emergence of another, local, power base in the Hôtel de Ville therefore added a new piquancy to this time-honoured practice. Chirac (who combined his mayoral role with the post of prime minister from 1986 to 1988) saw himself as a president in waiting. Accordingly, he tried both to thwart the ambitions of his rivals and produce his own projects.

## THE GRANDS PROJETS

While some projects were delayed in various ways, the 1980s and 1990s saw an unprecedented spate of dazzling embellishments of the city. Some were individual buildings or structures, such as the Bastille Opéra and the Grand Arch at La Défense (both completed 1989), and the Louvre pyramids (1993). Yet many also had important planning significance. The Grand Arch, for example, commissioned for the 200th anniversary of the French Revolution, also completed (at least for the moment) the grand historic axis which began in the Louvre and extended along the Champs Elysées to the Arc de Triomphe and La Défense. In other cases the grands projets involved

*336*

the redevelopment of sizeable areas. At the 50-hectare Parc de la Villette (completed 1993), the former city abattoirs were redeveloped as a museum and cultural quarter within a futuristic waterfront park setting (*Urbanisme*, 1999). La Villette's plan, following a 1982/3 competition, was by the Swiss architect Bernard Tschumi. The public agency that developed the park was also notable as providing the last major role for the veteran Paul Delouvrier, the Paris region's most famous 20th-century planning administrator.

## REGENERATING PARIS-EST

La Villette became part of a general planning strategy during the 1980s to upgrade the poorer eastern part of the city (Cohen and Fortier (eds), 1992; Newman and Thornley, 1996). In the southeast, on opposite banks of the Seine, two major redevelopments took place. The first was at Bercy, on a site formerly occupied by wine warehouses adjoining the Lyons rail station. Largely completed by the mid-1990s, the Bercy

*Figure 10.6 Planning efforts since the 1950s had firmly established La Défense as Paris's office and financial centre by the 1980s when the grand arch was created to commemorate the bicentennial of the French Revolution in 1989. To the right can be seen the first building on the site, the CNIT exhibition centre, completed in 1958.*

redevelopment included a vast government building along with a major sports centre, a park, housing and an American cultural centre. Across the river, adjoining the Austerlitz rail station, another SEM undertook a vast redevelopment covering over 130 hectares, in conjunction with Mitterand's last *grand projet*, the national library. The library itself was completed in 1997 and housing, university buildings and large areas of offices followed, the last constructed on decks built over the rail tracks.

## THE FEAR OF THE SUBURBS

One effect of the interventions in eastern Paris was to erode further the city's less affluent population, including its black and Muslim communities (Rey, 1996). The result was to heighten the polarisation between a bourgeois, largely white, city of Paris, within the Péripherique motorway and a poorer and more ethnically varied suburban ring (Noin and White, 1997). In the capital, as in other large French cities, the areas worst affected by economic change and social deprivation were generally in the suburbs. The greatest social problems were usually in the *grands ensembles*. These tended to have the largest concentrations of black and Muslim immigrant populations, many of whom felt alienated, or excluded by racism, from mainstream French society. In comparable fashion to British inner cities, there were serious riots in several of these areas beginning with Les Minguettes at Vénissieux in Lyons, in 1981 (Vollerin, 1999). Many others followed. Early remedies included the spurious catharsis of demolition, Pruitt-Igoe style, using dynamite (*Urbanisme*, 1999). The scenes of the early riots, in Vénissieux and at La Courneuve in Paris, were first in line for this treatment in 1986 and 1987.

## REGENERATING THE SUBURBS

From 1984 a more concerted policy, focusing attention on deprived suburban areas, was beginning to take shape at national level (Noin and White, 1997). This addressed both the social and economic dimensions of the problem. It involved many related measures, including transferring funds from richer to poorer communes. Another key initiative was the continued improvement of public transport in Paris, extending the radial Metro lines into the inner suburbs and the orbital scheme, and creating tramways to link these same areas. But such improved linkages to the wider urban labour market did not occur everywhere. Lyons' new metro, which had opened in the late 1970s and continued to expand, still had not reached any of its peripheral *grands ensembles* by 2000.

Economic change was also a key factor in the problems of the suburbs, as it was for the equivalent spaces of all western cities. In Paris the decline of the inner suburban industrial areas brought unemployment and physical decay. The areas included La Plaine St Denis and Gennevilliers to the north of the city itself, Boulogne-Billancourt to the west and the industrial belt at the Seine-Marne confluence in the southeast. Bringing these back into productive use became a major goal during the late 1980s and 1990s (Newman and Thornley, 1996). The most dramatic (if not the most typical) single result of these moves was the creation during the later 1990s of the national

*338*
___

sports stadium (the Stade de France) in the Plaine St Denis, which was the principal venue for the 1998 World Cup.

## THE URBAN FRINGE

If France's planning during this period was distinguished by unusually interventionist (and rather distinctively French) approaches, global or Americanising tendencies were certainly not unknown. By the mid-1990s, the fringes of French towns and cities were characterised by developments that could be found anywhere in the west. In fact, French retailers were European leaders in the creation of car-oriented out-of-town superstores and hypermarkets. These became anchor stores in the planned malls created in suburban and new town centres, or they occurred in more developer-led, freestanding forms on the edge of smaller towns (Noin and White, 1997). There were periodic restrictions, usually orchestrated by the small business interests which had traditionally dominated shopping provision. But the big French retailers responded by finding outlets in other countries. Meanwhile, all the familiar European

*Figure 10.7* *The 1980s saw worsening problems in the suburban grands ensembles. Many were still distant from employment, shopping and other services and transport often remained poor. Les Minguettes in metropolitan Lyon was amongst the worst and experienced serious rioting.*

and North American names in retailing and closely related activities (such as fast food) made their appearance on the French scene during the 1980s and 1990s, usually in urban fringe locations.

## EURODISNEY

France also conclusively proved that, in some respects, it could out-Americanise the rest of Europe (Noin and White, 1997; *Urbanisme*, 1999). The Eurodisney theme park and leisure resort was opened in 1992 in the outer reaches of the Paris new town of Marne la Vallée. This was very much a developer's project, its style more a greenfield version of the London Docklands than the kinds of urban redevelopment more usual in French cities. Criticisms that it was an assault on France's cultural identity were rebuffed with the argument that if Europe was going to have a Eurodisney, better in France than anywhere else. Certainly the Disney Corporation were made to feel welcome. Large amounts of cheap land that was no longer needed for new town expansion because of reduced growth forecasts were a powerful incentive. Others included a direct connection to the Paris RER, the national TGV and equivalent international links. Disney were also given a very free hand in planning and developing the area. Rather like London Docklands, however, Eurodisney became for a time a good advertisement for the limitations of market-led approaches. Following disappointing early visitor numbers, substantial management and financial changes were made, including the resort's rebadging as Disneyland Paris.

## *TECHNOPOLES*

In its revised form Disneyland helped to confirm Marne la Vallée as, in the term adopted in the 1994 plan for the Paris region, a centre of European significance (Ascher, 1997). It was the only new town to win this appellation, though the other centres, apart from the city of Paris itself, also lay in the suburbs. One, not surprisingly, was at La Défense, which by the 1990s had matured as a hugely important commercial centre. Areas close to Paris' two airports at Roissy and Orly accounted for the others. The one near Orly, known as Ile de France Sud and centred on the town of Massy, was particularly interesting since it represented the major concentration of high technology industries in the Paris region (Castells and Hall, 1994). To a substantial extent, this arose from policies and actions outside spatial planning proper, including government decisions on the location of research and advanced educational facilities. From the 1980s, however, urban planning began to play an increasing role with more deliberate actions (including the opening of a TGV station at Massy) to support and enhance this *cité scientifique*.

Elsewhere in France, the idea of creating deliberate concentrations of innovative high technology activity – *technopoles* – spread rapidly during the 1980s. In a sense, they were the greenfield equivalents of the urban development projects that had multiplied in the promotional scramble that followed decentralisation. By 1990, they were part of the marketing armoury of any region that was serious about winning global investments. The earliest, at Sophia-Antipolis near Nice, had begun during the 1970s as a private development initiative. It was, though, during the 1980s that it achieved real credibility, with much stronger regional government involvement. It also began to change from being merely a technology park: new housing and a full living environment were added, making it more directly comparable with Tsukuba in Japan.

## GREEN PLANNING

As we have seen, the use of state authority and resources to maintain economic competitiveness remained the principal goal permeating all levels of French urban planning during the 1980s and 1990s. From the late 1980s France was, of course, affected by the emergent ideas of sustainable development. But this was a distinctly secondary theme. Traditional commitment to high quality public transport and growing interest in investing in the declining areas of cities were at one with the new EU thinking. Yet, in general, France was not a leader in green urban planning compared to Germany, the Netherlands or Scandinavia. As already noted, though, the green movement began to gain in significance in Europe from the late 1980s, and some important innovations followed (www.verts.imaginet.fr). The principal stronghold of green thinking was in the region Nord-Pas de Calais, where a militant Green Party member became regional president in 1992. Green sentiments were also significant in the Ile de France. By the end of the century, there were wider signs of growing green influence, most notably when a Green politician became the French planning minister in 1997.

## DUNKIRK'S SUSTAINABLE INDUSTRIAL STRATEGY

In international terms, though, it was the heavy industrial city of Dunkirk in the Pas de Calais that became the main French centre of innovation (Beatley, 2000). Following serious decline in its steel and shipbuilding industries, in 1993 the city adopted policies to improve the environmental sensitivity of new industrial development, creating what were, in effect, sustainable industrial estates. The approach had an international resonance because it addressed one of the more difficult aspects of the green agenda. Local emission and pollution controls became much tighter. There was also protection of specific areas from industrial development (especially on the coast), regeneration of natural environments on former industrial sites and the use of surplus heat from steelmaking for district heating schemes. Overall, the concept fell some way short of the green ideal of truly ecological production, yet these were still notable steps for a heavy industrial area. In addition, the city adopted a compact-city planning strategy and planned important new public transport initiatives, including a cross-border connection to the Belgian tramway network.

## FRENCH PLANNING IN ITS INTERNATIONAL CONTEXT

France during the 1980s and 1990s was keener than ever to signal its international outlook, in Europe (as the popularity of Euro- or similar prefixes for major projects indicates) and the wider world. Within France, we have seen ample evidence of the eagerness with which foreign architects, planners and developers were embraced as part of this process. This was not new, but never before had it been pursued to this extent. Like Germany, though in a slightly different way, French urban leaders were showing that France could synthesise the world's best design expertise to create cities which, at their best, retained distinctive qualities even in an American-dominated global age. Nor was this internationalism confined just to design. The central planning ministry actively promoted learning from other countries, especially within the EU, as its website shows (www.urbanisme.equipement.gouv.fr). In turn, observers from other parts of the world, including France's European neighbours, found much to admire in French cities during these years. The confused state of London's planning and development, for example, caused many British planners to look wistfully at Paris' far more decisive and stylish interventions.

France also remained a very active exporter of planning ideas and practice. Thus the Paris regional planning agency, IAURIF, played the central role in founding the international Metropolis organisation in 1984 as an information network for big cities (www.metropolis.org). However, following the ambitious Cairo SDAU, which IAURIF prepared in the early 1980s, grand planning exercises on the model of the 1965 Paris regional plan were rare. Along with smaller planning exercises, IAURIF became a major source of managerial and technical advice and support for a wide range of cities, especially in the introduction of the new expertise of geographical information systems (www.iaurif.org). In 1997 and 1998, for example, it undertook several different kinds of work in various capacities in Manila, Santiago (Chile), Algiers, several Moroccan cities, Douala (Cameroon), Beirut, Bucharest and Guangzhou, and advised the Tunisian government.

The Paris city planning office meanwhile continued its own occasional international involvements (Lortie, 1995b). In 1994, for example, its staff prepared a conservation plan for Phnom Penh, Cambodia. In the 1990s the former Communist countries of Europe became an important new arena of French planning influence. Apart from IAURIF's work in Bucharest, French development bodies advised on creating an urban development company in Łódź in Poland, and assisted in the rehabilitation of a major housing complex in Ekaterinburg in Russia. In Hungary, the French SEM model was used to good effect in Budapest and Györ. This mixing of public and private enterprise promised a less abrupt transition for the ex-Communist states than the sudden exposure to the full rigours of American global capitalism that was their more general experience in the 1990s.

## THE UNITED STATES

The final confirmation that the 20th century really did belong to the United States came in 1991 when its main challenger for global hegemony, the Soviet Union, followed its former Communist satellites into collapse and disintegration (Patterson, 1999). After the unhappy 1970s, blighted by the Vietnam war and the Watergate scandal, the 1980s and 1990s saw a remarkable buoyancy in the American national outlook. To a large extent, the source of this general mood of satisfaction lay in the performance of the United States economy which moved on to undreamed planes of material success. Throughout the 1980s and 1990s, American economic (and population) growth rates comfortably exceeded those of western Europe. In the 1990s they also outperformed the Japanese economy which was experiencing unprecedented difficulties. Since 1945 the United States had led the global economy by virtue of its size. Now it was leading from the front, at least amongst the developed economies.

The reasons for these successes lay, at least partly, in governmental policies that vigorously promoted the doctrine of economic liberalisation. From 1980 to 1992, the right-wing Republican presidents Ronald Reagan and George Bush cut back public spending, reduced government regulation and generally asserted the hegemony of market principles. This approach was very similar to the policies simultaneously being pursued in Britain. The key difference was that the superpower status of the United States allowed these principles, which were especially favourable to American economic wellbeing, to become a global orthodoxy. Although many countries tried, scarcely any of them could entirely escape the new belief. This altered only slightly following the election of a Democrat president, Bill Clinton, in 1992. Though Clinton softened the domestic impacts of economic liberalisation he strengthened the global trend, largely because the collapse of Communism had removed the only serious obstacle to everyone on the planet being subsumed within the American dream of market capitalism. For many inhabitants of many poorer countries, of course, the dream could often seem more like a nightmare. Yet, in material terms, it served the vast majority of Americans across most of the income range (and most people in other rich and rapidly developing countries) very well.

In general, those parts of the world that benefited most from economic liberalisation – essentially the most developed countries – were also those with the most safeguards against its negative effects. So it was in the United States, where, despite the doctrine's general openness, economic liberalisation went only so far as was deemed consistent with the wider national interest. On the other hand, the logic of market economics was pursued relentlessly in the social sphere. The welfare system, for example, remained far less comprehensive than in Europe. As in Europe, however, environmental safeguards also grew in significance, particularly in those American states that had some tradition of action in this field. Overall though, both innovatory and typical practice in this area of planning normally fell short of continental European equivalents.

## THE MAKING OF THE BALTIMORE MODEL

The most influential American practice lay elsewhere, in the revitalisation of central city areas, especially waterfronts (Breen and Rigby, 1994; Garvin, 1996). The approach had begun earlier but came to fruition during the 1980s. In 1980, the Baltimore Harborplace, the second of developer James Rouse's 'festival marketplaces', opened (Frieden and Sagalyn, 1989). This marked the effective debut of Baltimore's inner harbour as a global prototype of waterfront regeneration. Along with the convention centre, opened in 1979, the aquarium, opened in 1981, and more development that followed during the 1980s and 1990s, Baltimore quickly drew world attention. By the late 1980s, the harbour was attracting 22 million visitors a year, seven million of them from outside the metropolitan area. These figures placed it in the Disneyland league as one of the country's top tourist draws. The numbers of international delegations with professional interest also grew very dramatically. They were there to observe the apparent success of this approach to urban regeneration (Breen and Rigby, 1996). Certainly the improvement rippled outwards to neighbourhoods immediately adjoining the harbour. But only a few blocks away there remained economic and social problems as bad as in any American city (Harvey, 1989). Baltimore became, in fact, one of the starkest models of the new dual urban economy, divided into haves and have-nots.

## WATERFRONT REGENERATION

Nevertheless, a large number of American cities, and many elsewhere, tried to emulate the Baltimore approach (Breen and Rigby, 1994; 1996). This was actually difficult, because of the long-term nature of the project. Preparatory public expenditure went back to the early 1960s and amounted to $625 million by the early 1990s. This was roughly a quarter of the total spend, much of it committed before private contributions were assured. In addition, the unusually close proximity of central business district and port in Baltimore conferred tremendous advantages that were difficult to replicate. Yet many tried. Alongside Baltimore, Boston, which had predated it in certain innovations, continued to be a reference point in the 1980s with important projects in different parts of its own extensive waterfront (Frieden and Sagalyn, 1989; Gordon, 1996). The most dramatic was at Rowe's Wharf, a spectacular mixed-use development which literally provided a gateway from the water to downtown Boston, completed in 1987. In north Boston, the redevelopment of the Charlestown Navy Yard became a major new project. It was begun in the late 1970s but only saw any significant development from the mid-1980s.

Other cities followed Baltimore and Boston. Thus Miami's Bayside Marketplace was a particularly successful example of Rouse's waterside festival marketplace concept, opened in 1987. The same developer's South Street Seaport had meanwhile taken the phenomenon to New York's East River in 1984 (Metzger, 2001). Simultaneously, however, a far more ambitious development fronting New York's other main river, the Hudson, was under way on a 37-hectare landfill site adjacent to the World Trade Center at Battery Park (Garvin, 1996; Gordon, 1996; Meyer, 1999). After much uncertainty during the 1970s, from 1982 development here proceeded rapidly under the leadership of a specific development authority. The involvement in a major office development of the Canadian developers, Olympia and York (later to play a comparable role in the development of London Docklands), was crucial to Battery Park's viability. High- and middle-income housing was, though, the dominant land use. Other features included high quality public spaces fronting the river and a new high school.

(As a postscript, we should note that after the terrorist attacks in September 2001, which destroyed the World Trade Center and severely damaged parts of the Battery Park development, this quarter of New York is now set for another major redevelopment.)

## DOWNTOWN MALLS

Although water seemed to be a magic ingredient for commercially successful regeneration, what happened in waterfront areas was symptomatic of a wider attempt to revitalise downtown or near-downtown areas. Shopping developments of various types were an important element in these strategies in many cities (Frieden and Sagalyn, 1989). The 1970s had seen the first moves in this direction, and the 1980s brought ever more imaginative attempts to create malls in downtown areas. The festival marketplace concept proliferated rapidly, not just in waterside locations. However, several failures, most notably in Minneapolis, Toledo (Ohio), Richmond (Virginia) and Flint (Michigan) were sufficient to check the trend by the late 1980s.

Despite the rather uncritical adoption of the concept during the 1980s there were some variations. Rouse and other shopping developers (most notably Ernest Hahn) sometimes combined elements of the festival market place, which largely attracted smaller retailers, with the suburban mall so beloved by the big chain stores. The Horton Plaza in San Diego, opened in 1985, was a seminal example (Garvin, 1996). It was a multiple-use (but primarily retailing) downtown district with large and smaller retailers, restaurants, a theatre, multiplex cinema and nightclub. The benign climate avoided the necessity for an air-conditioned mall that turned its back on the rest of the downtown area. Few other cities had the courage to follow this approach, especially in less comfortable climatic zones. Enclosed, often multistorey, malls of various kinds were therefore more usual. During the early 1980s developments of this type appeared in the downtown areas of, for example, Santa Monica (1980), Milwaukee (1982), Boston (1984) and St Louis (1985). Many others followed. Occasionally, historic structures, such as the Philadelphia Bourse (1982), were recycled as shopping malls. Increasingly common, too, were multiple-use developments, which variously combined offices, apartments, hotels, entertainment and other activities with major retailing activities.

## CONVENTION CITIES

As this last point suggests, other activities were also promoted to regenerate downtown areas (Frieden and Sagalyn, 1989; Garvin, 1996). None were exactly unknown but they became more widespread and much larger in scale. Thus, vast new or greatly enlarged convention centres appeared, learning from earlier examples such as the Renaissance Center in Detroit whose convention facilities were revamped and enlarged in the 1980s. (Baltimore's waterfront example has already been mentioned.) Other notable developments in the 1980s and 1990s included the Jacob K Javits Center in New York (opened in 1986), the Washington State Convention Center in Seattle (1988), the greatly extended Hynes Convention Center in Boston (1988) and the Pennsylvania Convention Center in Philadelphia (1993/4). The rationale was that these developments would increase the numbers of visitors and boost demand for hotel accommodation, restaurants, nightlife and other city services. By drawing business opinion-formers, they might also help to change investor perceptions of what were widely seen as economically troubled and crime-ridden cities.

## SPORTING CITIES

A further area of city policy that was particularly well developed in the United States was the creation of major sporting venues (Frieden and Sagalyn, 1989; Ward, 1998). The practice was led by Indianapolis, Baltimore and Atlanta, though there were few cities that did not engage in it to some extent. Reflecting an unusual degree of mobility amongst major American sports teams, such policies were a way of attracting or keeping them. The impact for tourism and other service industries was important, particularly in downtown areas where many of the sports stadiums were located. The sheer size of the sporting facilities also gave them a major significance in the wider development of these areas. Finally, of course, sports were extremely important for popular morale in declining cities.

Another dimension was the heightened international competition during the 1980s and 1990s to stage the Olympic Games or other international sporting events. The new era was opened by Los Angeles, which staged the games in 1984. Following the serious problems which had afflicted cities that had hosted the games in 1972, 1976 and 1980, Los Angeles secured huge economic returns for a relatively modest outlay, most of which went towards remodelling existing facilities. American cities therefore

*Figure 10.8* Urban problems were largely concentrated in the inner neighbourhoods of American cities. Large abandoned areas became more common, as here in the Northern Liberties district of Philadelphia, where an urban farm has replaced decayed housing.

became particularly aggressive competitors in the following years. Following extensive investment in major sporting facilities, Atlanta staged the games in 1996 (though with less impact on planning thought than had been the case with its predecessor, Barcelona).

## OTHER ASPECTS OF CITY ECONOMIC DEVELOPMENT

Sport was a metaphor for the whole ethos of intercity competition, which permeated urban policies during the 1980s. National policies which cut federal spending programmes and relied on market solutions encouraged a pragmatic and often reckless entrepreneurialism at city level. This was, as we have seen, part of a global process, though nowhere was it pursued quite so relentlessly as in the United States. American cities were obsessed with gaining a competitive edge over their rivals, often by offering new, ever more spectacular, attractions. The 1980s saw the age of aquaria dawning across the nation (again following the lead of Boston and Baltimore). Cultural districts with museums and galleries also played their part in many cities. It was, however, the festival marketplace, the convention centre, the sports arena and the aquarium, preferably located in close proximity to each other and a sheltered tract of water, that became the distinctively American contribution to global urban regeneration planning in the 1980s. The lessons were eagerly studied and, in varying degrees, copied across the world.

Yet the traffic in ideas was not all one-way. Within these American desires to restore the heart of the city as a vibrant entity there lingered a vague ideal of the European city. It was all done in a very American fashion, of course, with the intention of turning a good profit (Garvin, 1996). It was also expressed in terms of getting back to a more traditional idea of the American city. (The proliferation of brick-paved 'gas lamp' historic preservation districts was tangible proof of these sentiments.) But it was also a reference back to a time before the great exodus to the suburbs when the memories of the European way of living in cities were more vivid.

## THE ENTERPRISE/EMPOWERMENT ZONE

Alongside such vague references to Europe there were also occasional, more tangible, borrowings. A notable east-to-west Atlantic crossing, though one which took a long time to become established, was the enterprise zone, originated by the Thatcher administration in Britain in 1980 (Barnekov et al, 1989; B Cullingworth, 1997). Partly because it chimed in with the prevailing ethos of reducing big government, the concept soon found favour in the United States. Most notable (in part because it was his only urban policy) was President Reagan's abortive federal programme for enterprise zones, unveiled in early 1982. Despite several attempts, this never secured the backing of Congress. Less noticed, though they reflected the same influences, were state policies which were partly stimulated by what was believed to be the imminent possibility of federal support. By 1986, 32 states had designated 1,400 enterprise zones in 675 local jurisdictions. The planning deregulation content of the zones was, however, rather limited. As in Britain, the reduction of taxes was their most significant feature.

The federal initiative, meanwhile, did not succeed until 1993, under the Clinton administration (www.hud.gov). By this time, however, the concept had widened. Alongside the tax incentives there was direct and, for the chosen few, serious federal funding for social and physical improvements. These changes were signified by a new name, the 'empowerment zone'. By 1999, 24 such zones had been designated, mainly in cities. The first designations, in 1995, were in Atlanta, Baltimore, Chicago, Cleveland, Detroit, Los Angeles, New York and Philadelphia/Camden. The second round included Boston, Cincinnati, Gary (Indiana), Knoxville (Tennessee), Miami, Minneapolis, New Haven and St Louis. The same initiatives also created a much larger number of more modestly funded 'enterprise communities'.

## EDGE CITIES

Despite such innovations and the public resources devoted to urban revitalisation, the suburbs remained the most dynamic part of the typical urban metropolitan region. The time had long passed when the suburbs were largely residential or industrial phenomena. By the late 20th century they contained major concentrations of business, mainly office-based, retailing, administrative, hotel, leisure and cultural facilities (KT Jackson, 1985). Such suburban business nodes were overwhelmingly dependent on the car, with highways and parking often the biggest single land uses. Many of these areas, which had grown largely since 1960, were large enough 30 years later to rival the downtown areas of metropolitan core cities (Garreau, 1991). Outlets of major multiple retailers in these locations usually had higher sales turnovers than their equivalents in traditional downtowns. They were also increasingly likely to include the corporate headquarters of major companies which would formerly have preferred downtown locations.

In 1991, a journalist, Joel Garreau, published a book which coined a new name for these emergent suburban concentrations: *Edge City*. He identified about 200 such areas in the United States, around all the major metropolitan cities. The best-known example was roughly 20 kilometres west of downtown Washington at Tyson's Corner in Fairfax County, Virginia, and boasted a concentration of business activity greater than that in downtown Miami. However, it was around Los Angeles, the archetypal multicentred metropolis, that the grandest constellation of edge cities could be found. Apart from fairly permissive zoning regimes, planning (and especially strategic planning) nowhere played much part in the growth of these places. Some, admittedly, had arisen since the 1960s around the few more conscious attempts to create new communities, at Reston (Virginia), Columbia (Maryland) and Irvine (California). Yet these were very much the exceptions, a fact that partly accounted for the fragmented and rather raw quality of most edge cities.

## THE GENESIS OF THE MEGAMALL

This is not to say that public actions were irrelevant in the development of edge cities. Proximity to publicly provided facilities such as major highway intersections or airports was common. In some cases, public agencies were also important in site provision. The case of the Bloomington/Edina edge city, west of Minneapolis, is a case in point. In 1956 the suburban city of Edina had become the location of the world's first enclosed mall, at Southdale (Gruen and Smith, 1960). However, its complete emergence as a fully fledged edge city did not occur until the last two decades of the century (www.mallofamerica.com). These moves were related directly to Minneapolis's attempts at downtown revitalisation. Thus, in 1982, the city attracted the region's major baseball and football teams to a new sports facility in its heart, leaving a large unused site in Edina's neighbour, Bloomington. The Bloomington port authority bought the vacant site, which was less than 3 kilometres from Minneapolis international airport, with a view to promoting its development. They succeeded in attracting the Ghermezian brothers, the Canadian developers of the vast West Edmonton Mall (to be discussed more fully in the next chapter). With Melvyn Simon, a leading American retail developer, they embarked on a similar retailing and entertainment development called the Mall of America. Opened in 1992, it was the largest mall in the United States (though smaller than that in West Edmonton), with 520 stores open by 2000. It attracts more than a million visits per year (40 per cent from tourists), and employs over 12,000 people.

## THE NEW URBANISM

Not the least important of the debates triggered by Garreau's book was whether (and if so, how) edge cities could become real places comparable to traditional downtowns. In fact, a group of practitioners were already grappling with a variant of this problem: how to make new, largely suburban, developments into something that evoked a real (ie traditional) sense of place. Known as the new urbanism, these ideas spawned a formal organisation – the Congress for the New Urbanism – in 1993 (www.cnu.org). Seminal examples which demonstrated the principles of the movement were Seaside in Florida and Kentlands at Gaithersburg in Maryland, planned in 1981 and 1988 respectively by Andres Duany and Elizabeth Plater-Zyberk, and Laguna West in Sacramento County, California, planned in 1990 by Peter Calthorpe Associates (Calthorpe, 1993; Katz, 1994; Garvin 1996; RB Stephenson, 1997). All were fairly small, predominantly residential developments, the largest being Laguna West which was intended ultimately for some 3,600 dwellings.

The perceived virtues of these developments lay in their clear definition of space and compactness (compared to the very low densities and open layouts usual in American suburbia; by European standards even these higher densities were still low). They also used a connected street pattern (without culs-de-sac) and ensured that buildings fronted, and were closely related to, streets. Cars were not excluded, but there was a strong emphasis on pedestrian movement, hopefully in conjunction with public transit. The intention was also to create local services within walking distance, in a manner which evoked the classic American small town. It was assumed that these physical qualities would foster a strong sense of community and reduce crime.

The inspirations came from a variety of sources, especially the city beautiful tradition, the garden city movement and the ideas of urban community popularised from the 1960s by Jane Jacobs (Schuyler, 1997). The advocates of the new urbanism, particularly Calthorpe, tried to extrapolate it into a model for sustainable metropolitan development. There were to be development nodes along public transit routes, at the classic garden city density of about 12 houses per acre, and infill development at higher densities within existing urban areas. The reality was, however, that the new urbanism remained, in the United States at least, a way of giving a more urban character to the suburbs. By the later 1990s, direct connections to Garreau's ideas were apparent as new urbanist principles began to be applied directly to the planning of edge city areas. At Redmond in suburban Seattle, for example, the approach was used to convey the feel of a traditional downtown, with open public spaces that avoided the typical enclosed mall.

## GREEN URBANISM

The green movement in the United States was critical of the lack of any serious ecological content in the new urbanism (Beatley, 2000). This did not, though, prevent them recruiting its design principles into moves for a more sustainable pattern of urban development during the 1990s. Americans, like Europeans, were not immune to the new discourse of sustainability that emerged in the wake of the 1987 Brundtland report and the earth summits of the 1990s. The United States government certainly did not take a global lead on green matters. But at subnational level, the vocal and well-informed green movement had significant influence in some parts of America (www.greenparties.org). Compared to Germany and some other European countries, the green movement in the United States enjoyed little political success, and that mainly at the local level. However, the 1996 and 2000 presidential campaigns of their leader, the widely respected consumer activist Ralph Nader, raised the profile of green ideas.

## GROWTH MANAGEMENT

Even before the 1990s important moves towards sustainability were already well under way in a growing number of places. Most widespread was the growing commitment to urban growth management. As mentioned in Chapter 8 Oregon, particularly the cities of Portland and Eugene, and a few other states and individual cities, such as Boulder, Colorado, had given a lead in the 1970s (Beatley, 2000). These examples became better known in the 1980s and 1990s as more states and cities embraced these approaches.

The most dramatic turnaround came in Florida in 1985 when a large and extremely fast-growing state, traditionally dominated by developers, passed stringent growth management legislation (RB Stephenson, 1997). This reflected mounting concerns about deteriorating air and water quality, loss of natural environment and biodiversity, mounting traffic congestion and the infrastructure costs arising from rapid land development. The legislation provided strong powers to ensure that local plans complied with state intentions. It also prevented further development occurring where infrastructure and public facilities such as open space, recreation provision and mass transit could not cope. The whole policy was intended to encourage greater compactness in development. The new urbanist showpiece of Seaside was a timely, if controversial, exemplar of what might result from the new policies. More importantly, perhaps, major cities in Florida, such as St Petersburg, had already been experimenting with new approaches for some years.

Several other states adopted growth management during the 1980s and 1990s, including Rhode Island, Maine, New Jersey, Washington, Georgia and Maryland (B Cullingworth, 1997). In California a more varied pattern was evident with local examples of extremely stringent controls, usually where the local electorates were firmly anti-growth. Florida had, though, set a new benchmark for growth management, especially in its treatment of the infrastructure – a question to which even Oregon, the main early innovator, had given little attention. However, few states that adopted growth management principles ignored the question after Florida (though few went as far as it did). Infrastructure provision, of course, required public spending, so restrictions on growth also appealed to one of the major themes of political discourse in the Reagan era. The apparent denial of the market in the name of the new paradigm of sustainability was only partial.

## SMART GROWTH

In the last years of the century the narrow (and potentially rather negative and exclusionary) concept of growth management was supplemented by a more positive term – smart growth – which entered planning discourse from about 1996 (www.smartgrowth.org). In 1999 the federal Environmental Protection Agency sponsored the creation of the Smart Growth Network. An umbrella organisation, this brought together a wide range of existing organisations, including the Congress for the New Urbanism, the Growth Management Leadership Alliance and many other professional and pressure groups in the field of conservation and environmental protection.

The term 'smart growth' was a typically snappy American coinage that translated the global concept of sustainable development into everyday language. Like sustainable development, it was a compromise term which advocated sensible growth rather than being anti-growth. Its concerns were not, therefore, only with the environment. The familiar issues of air and water quality, the protection of natural environment and the promotion of biodiversity were, of course, important priorities. But there were also economic arguments about the public service costs of excessively low-density greenfield development and the virtues of infill and brownfield development. Social arguments, about promoting a sense of place and community, were also strongly advanced.

## EXAMPLES OF SMART GROWTH

Although it is too soon to judge the impact of smart growth, it appears to have enjoyed much early success as a unifying concept. It has evidently helped to push the idea of infill development beyond the older industrial cities to the more rapidly growing regions of the west and south. The idea has great potential in many American cities because of the relatively low densities of many inner suburban areas. It has, for example, been adopted by some of the traditional leaders in American green urbanism – for example, Seattle under its 1994 plan (Beatley, 2000). Yet the basis for action was widening beyond the usual innovators. A notable proponent was Austin, Texas, which in 1998 planned to encourage development in areas where it could readily be accommodated (including infill within existing neighbourhoods) while protecting more sensitive areas. Others included Chattanooga, Tennessee, which also encouraged infill and the conversion of a run-down shopping mall into a mixed-use district as a focus for increasing the density of an existing inner suburban neighbourhood. In 1999 Tucson, Arizona, launched a mixed residential, retailing and light industrial development, ultimately of about 2,600 dwellings, with a pedestrian-friendly design and advanced energy-conservation features. Other initiatives reflected the growing interest in transit-oriented development as advocated by Calthorpe and the new urbanists.

## OTHER ASPECTS OF GREEN URBANISM

Urban public transit improved significantly in the United States during the 1980s and the 1990s. New light-rail or metro systems of various types (excluding heritage tramways) opened in San Diego (1981), Buffalo (1984), Portland, Jacksonville, Miami (all 1986), Sacramento, Detroit and San José (all 1987), Los Angeles (1990), Baltimore (1992), St Louis (1993), Denver (1994) and Dallas in 1996 (www.lrta.org). These played important roles in supporting planning initiatives to boost downtowns and encourage more compact urbanisation.

There was, though, a greater reluctance to countenance any moves that would seriously restrict car use. Generally, Americans seem more likely to move to greener car use rather than to embark on widespread restrictions. California, in particular, has helped to encourage motor manufacturers to develop alternatives to the oil-based internal combustion engine. The most readily accepted urban planning restriction on the car has involved traffic calming in residential areas (Ewing, 1999). This gradually became more widespread with Portland, Austin and Bellevue (Washington), amongst others, beginning their first schemes in the 1980s. By the late 1990s, greater knowledge of European practice was apparent and, with federal encouragement, interest was poised to grow very rapidly. An innovation in one leading city, Portland, where demand was especially high, was to permit individual neighbourhoods deemed as low priorities to fund schemes directly without using city funds. The 1990s also saw experiments in using various financial and other means, including road pricing and freeway lane restrictions, to discourage car use. These occasionally met with local approval, for example in San Diego, but early large-scale action on this front is unlikely.

## THE INTERNATIONAL SIGNIFICANCE OF AMERICAN URBAN POLICIES

The two dominating agendas of urban planning during these years – economic competitiveness and sustainable development – had contrary effects on the flows of planning ideas and practice between the United States and other countries. While American planners were, by the 1990s, learning more about sustainable development from Europe than vice versa, on economic regeneration they were usually the innovators from whom other countries drew lessons. The Baltimore model of waterfront regeneration soon exerted a huge influence throughout the world. In some cases the references were direct, for example at the Darling Harbour in Sydney (Breen and Rigby, 1996). Others, such as Barcelona's old port, closely followed many aspects of the original without being quite so exact a copy (Meyer, 1999). Most of the (many) other waterfront regenerations also made at least some, often quite significant, reference to Baltimore. To varying degrees, other aspects of the dominant American approach to urban regeneration during the 1980s were also widely imitated. Convention centres, major spectator sports facilities, aquariums, festival marketplaces and cultural districts appeared in various combinations in cities across the world. City marketing became virtually universal.

In this shift towards the entrepreneurial city, the United States did not actually need to borrow very much from other traditions. Its leadership in areas such as waterfront regeneration did, though, encourage it to examine the efforts of other

*Figure 10.9 Baltimore's inner harbour became the most copied American effort at urban renewal. It managed to turn the city into a huge draw for tourists, though intractable social and economic problems remained.*

countries, to seek both confirmation and refinement of its domestic lessons. America's especial closeness to urban planning approaches in 1980s Britain stimulated interest in the hugely ambitious regeneration of London Docklands. There was also direct borrowing of the enterprise zone concept (itself, of course, partly inspired by the rapid growth in deregulated conditions in Hong Kong and other 'Asian tigers'). There was also, as we have seen, a rather vague general admiration of the vibrancy of European urbanity. It is significant, for example, that Boston was admired for its 'European' qualities.

## THE CHANGING INTERNATIONAL CONTEXT OF AMERICAN PLANNING IN THE 1990s

Far more specific were the more earnest attempts by some professionals to learn from European approaches to environmental planning. The burgeoning American interest in light rapid transit, for example, owed something to awareness of European success with modern tram systems. The encouragement of traffic calming in the United States during the later 1990s drew more directly on European countries and others that shared elements of the American outlook, such as Australia and Israel. By the end of the decade, there were also mounting expert arguments that American cities should draw more comprehensive lessons from the steps towards green urbanism taken by the more progressive European cities (Beatley, 2000).

This is not to say that any early adoption should be expected. A confident (and rather inward-looking) American nation that sees itself as beholden to no other country will not readily accept lessons from elsewhere, however much informed professionals may try to draw them (cf Rodgers, 1998). Compared with their counterparts in western Europe, proportionately more Americans also fear that environmental policies may damage national economic prowess and wellbeing. To a far greater extent than in the early 20th century, it will be necessary for European innovations to be successfully Americanised before any widespread interest can be expected. It is more likely that the United States will pursue technological 'fixes' to environmental problems (electric cars, for example), thereby shifting the terms of the whole sustainability debate.

Within the narrower realm of urban planning, the international salience of the American example in other advanced capitalist countries was reduced by the later 1990s. In Australia, where any proposals to urbanise the suburbs have special relevance, there has been strong interest in the new urbanism. There has also been some interest in other parts of the English-speaking world. The dominant association of new urbanism with greenfield development has, however, reduced its relevance in Britain. Moreover, the proposed densities have simply been too low to have much appeal as an approach to the compact city in a continental European context.

## AMERICAN PLANNING AND DEVELOPMENT AID

Western interest in American urban planning had therefore dwindled by the end of the 20th century. Development aid continued, though, to give it an important role elsewhere (www.usaid.gov). Urban planning as such has never been a major facet of American international aid (compared, for example, to the French). But agencies such as USAID (or international agencies strongly influenced by American thinking, such as the United Nations or the World Bank) funded a good deal of general advice on urban land-use planning in the 1980s and 1990s. Normally this was done through consultants, such as the Washington-based PADCO – Planning and Development Collaborative International (www.padcoinc.com).

Typically, by the 1990s the advice concerned systemic matters relating to the process of planning, rather than detailed planning proposals. The scale of operations was worldwide and included, for example, Egypt, Pakistan, Thailand and Indonesia as well as some of the smaller countries of central America. An especially important growth area in the 1990s was in the former Communist countries. It was hugely important for the wider establishment of market economies that their former system of urban planning was replaced by an approach that recognised the emergent realities of freer urban land markets. In such circumstances, western-style zoning was an instrument flexible enough to allow the pursuit of private profit to be reconciled with wider concerns. Thus PADCO was especially active in Russia, but also worked in other parts of the former Soviet Union, such as the Ukraine and Georgia, as well as eastern Europe.

## INTERIM CONCLUSIONS

In their different ways, therefore, the four major western traditions each made important contributions to the international planning discourse in the last decades of the 20th century. The United States and Britain essentially caused urban planning to find a place amongst the new imperatives of global competitiveness. Planners in both countries were, however, slower and less convincing in their embrace of the other main theme of the 1980s and 1990s – the promotion of environmental sustainability. By contrast, the more confident and credible development of a green approach to planning quickly became Germany's most distinctive contribution. Rather more than in Britain, German planners also aspired (without entirely succeeding) to fashion an approach that reconciled the urban pressures of globalisation with a more distinctively national and European identity. In France, too, similar contradictory tendencies were apparent. However, the most striking feature, compared to the Anglo-American approach, was the way the newly decentralised French state apparently allowed planners to maintain (partly, at least) a relatively interventionist role, even as they addressed the economic rigours of global competition.

As always, the experience of these four countries in the late 20th century lay at the very heart of western planning discourse. All, in varying degrees, added to a reservoir of thought and practice which economic, communications and other changes made more readily accessible to other parts of the west and the wider world. We will return to consider these more general themes about the acceleration of international diffusion at the end of the next chapter. Before that, however, we need to examine the contributions of other countries and cities, and their interplay with the wider body of planning ideas and practice.

# CHAPTER 11

# GLOBALISATION, COMPETITIVENESS AND SUSTAINABILITY II: THE OTHER TRADITIONS

For much of the 20th century the nation-state was the principal springboard for global significance in urban affairs. Put more simply, big nations largely shaped international planning discourse. Planners in a few smaller countries had, of course, sometimes been able to gain international recognition. Usually, though, this was because their work was admired or adopted by bigger nations. Much of the international resonance of Swedish and Dutch approaches to planning in the mid-20th century had, for example, rested largely on the interest of Anglo-American planners. By the end of the 20th century, however, the improved information flows associated with globalisation made it easier for the urban planning efforts of smaller nations to win international attention more actively, with less need for such 'sponsorship' by larger ones. In fact, the emphasis on the nation is itself a little misleading. More accurately, individual *cities* in these smaller countries projected an international profile, as did the regional cities in bigger nations. This general trend is especially important in this chapter, as it allowed urban planning in a larger number of smaller western countries to become widely known.

In Europe, the Netherlands and the Nordic countries renewed and strengthened their position in international planning discourse during the 1990s. Newly important, however, was Spain, dominated by the astonishing rise of Barcelona as a city that captured the imagination of western urban planners. Elsewhere, others such as Vancouver and Sydney achieved a genuinely international profile. There was also a growing interest in Japanese cities, though mainly from Japan's Asian neighbours. Despite the growing understanding throughout the world of Japanese industrial and consumer practices, western awareness of its urban planning remained rather modest. We begin, however, by examining the experiences of the smaller countries of Europe.

## THE NETHERLANDS

As in Britain, the economy in the Netherlands was particularly open to the various internationalising forces that constituted globalisation. This was most obvious amongst the Dutch population which, thanks to high immigration, grew by an eighth between 1980 and 2000, a very high rate of increase by north European standards. Meanwhile its dominant position in Europe's maritime trade and in the global market for oil were fundamental to the internationalising of its economy. During the 1980s the Dutch economy actually grew more slowly than those in the rest of western Europe, but it was more successful in the 1990s.

Politically, the Netherlands tended towards the right for most of these years. Reflecting both this and the growing social welfare costs during a period of high unemployment, there was partial adoption of some aspects of the Anglo-American market-led approach to public policy (Bolan, 1999). The extent of social welfare was curtailed and some key public services were privatised. This was echoed in urban policies, especially in the shift, from the mid-1980s, to a more entrepreneurial, urban marketing style with increasing emphasis on partnership with private investors. Yet, although the amount of public sector development declined, this did not seriously compromise traditionally strong Dutch commitments to urban planning (Tilman, 1997; Boelens, 1997). Government agencies also continued to be important in providing development land and affordable housing.

## WATERFRONT AND CULTURAL REGENERATION IN ROTTERDAM

Many significant exemplars of the changes in Dutch planning were in Rotterdam (Meyer, 1999; Hajer, 1993; McCarthy, 1999). Here, in what remained the world's busiest port, could be found the Netherlands' most ambitious attempts at regeneration and re-imaging. These were focused on the older maritime quarters of this essentially working-class city. In the 1970s a new social democratic administration had started to reassert the city as a model of urban planning. However, the first fruits did not appear until the early 1980s when a new group of younger urban designers began to dominate the city's urban development department. The shift became complete when, in 1986, a dynamic landscape architect, Riek Bakker, took charge.

A 1985 inner city plan had already identified areas close to the commercial centre where change would occur. These comprised a cultural zone and the historic Waterstad area around the city's oldest dock complex. Important museum and cultural developments, together with residential building, were already under way. Important and memorable new buildings were added alongside notable historic quarters that had survived wartime destruction. The bizarre 'pole dwellings' and pencil block at the Oude Haven appeared in the early 1980s. Many others followed, reviving the high modernism of Rotterdam's early postwar reputation. Bakker also improved the design of public spaces in the city. Most importantly, she also spearheaded the redevelopment of the Kop van Zuid. In the 1970s, this large but declining dock area had been scheduled for social housing. Now, under a plan prepared in 1987 by Teun Koolhaas (who prepared the original master plan for Almere new town), it was to include a 'Manhattan on the Maas' business district, with housing, leisure and cultural facilities. Bakker needed all her political skills to win business support and neutralise potentially damaging opposition. Development began in the early 1990s, greatly encouraged by the new Erasmus bridge link to central Rotterdam which was opened in 1995.

## SUSTAINABILITY AND DUTCH URBAN PLANNING

Amsterdam also had waterfront development plans, notably the eastern harbour area, where port use ended in the 1980s (DRO, 1994, 2000; www.dro.amsterdam.nl). The main replacement use was to be high-density housing, beginning with the Entrepôt

West development of the early 1990s (Breen and Rigby, 1996). But the fashion for waterfront development was only part of the influence of water on Dutch planning. An older national imperative reasserted itself as awareness grew of global climate change and rising sea levels. As the serious floods of 1995 showed, no other western country was as vulnerable as the Netherlands to global warming. This helped to make the country a world leader in environmental approaches to urban planning. There were also several pioneering initiatives in planning small ecological communities, such as Ecolonia at Alphen aan der Rijn, planned by the Belgian architect Lucien Kroll from 1989 (Beatley, 2000; www.arch.umanitoba.ca/la_www/sustainable).

## SUSTAINABLE TRANSPORT POLICIES

Of less qualitative significance, but far more influential, were the strategies adopted for the bigger cities. Following Amsterdam's adoption of the compact-city strategy in 1978, the Netherlands was in the vanguard of European Union initiatives to promote compact and sustainable urbanisation in the 1990s (DRO 1983, 1994; CEC, 1990a, 1990b). Its transport policies, which placed great reliance on bicycles and public

*Figure 11.1* Amsterdam's eastern harbour renewal began comparatively slowly. The earliest section was here at Entrepôt West, a stylish mixture of high density residential, entertainment and leisure facilities.

transport, were widely seen as exemplary. Particularly notable was the so-called A-B-C business location and transport policy. Introduced in the fourth national physical plan in 1993, its bold intention was to direct new employment investments to locations which exactly met their transport needs in order to reduce dependence on the car (Beatley, 2000). Undertakings which did not inherently rely on extensive motor vehicle use (for example major offices) could only choose 'A' locations. These had excellent public transport (and cycle) access and limits on car-parking provision would severely restrict car use by employees. The towering success of this policy was the new housing, planning and environment ministry building in The Hague. We should note, though, that in practice little else was achieved. The truth was that major international companies were not prepared to submit to these green strictures, however worthy. By 2001 the policy was in process of being diluted in favour of a more *laissez-faire* approach, though international perceptions have not yet registered this retreat.

## COMPACT GROWTH

Despite such setbacks Dutch cities still scored relatively highly on sustainability criteria, combining generally low-rise liveability with relatively high densities. No other western European country has been as successful in resisting the American-style outward movement of large-scale retailing and related activities (Bolan, 1999). Apart from carefully planned new centres of expansion, such as the new towns or around Amsterdam's Schiphol Airport, the 'edge city' phenomenon remains very underdeveloped.

All this reflects a long tradition of compact urbanisation. This has had the paradoxical result, however, that further growth quickly puts pressure on the urban fringe. The larger Dutch cities began to gain population in the later 1980s and 1990s. There was scope to intensify development in some areas (for example Amsterdam's western garden suburbs, built in the early post-1945 years) but infill development offered less scope in the Netherlands than, for example, in Britain or the United States. This has focused Dutch attention on achieving compact greenfield development, winning some international attention especially from environmental planners in the United States (Beatley, 2000). The trend was for predominantly low-rise, fairly high-density expansions. One of the most notable in the early to mid 1990s was at Nieuw Sloten, in Amsterdam (de Wit, 1998; DRO, 2000). This comprised some 5,000 dwellings (at a density of about 56 dwellings per hectare) together with some offices, shopping and local services.

*Figure 11.2 Nieuw Sloten was an example of Amsterdam's urban expansion in the 1990s. Its high but liveable densities, good local service facilities and good transport links stayed true to the admirable Dutch tradition of extending the city, rather than seeking to escape from it.*

## THE VINEX AREAS

By the mid-1990s, the compact-city approach was deeply embedded in national physical planning policy. One of the main concerns of the 1993 fourth national physical planning report was to meet the need for nearly two-thirds of a million new dwellings by 2005. Of these almost 0.3 million would be built in the seven largest urban areas, 100,000 in inner city areas. This left a major requirement for greenfield development. Areas to accommodate large housing expansions were identified around the bigger urban centres (www.archined.nl/vinexonsite; Beatley, 2000). Usually termed VINEX areas (a Dutch acronym derived from the name of the 1993 report), these were, ideally, to be mixed-use compact expansion areas with minimum net environmental impacts.

A good example is the Leidsche Rijn expansion at Utrecht. This is intended to accommodate some 20,000 new dwellings and many jobs by 2005 (van der Meijden, nd, c1996; Beatley, 2000). The overall housing density will be some 30 per hectare, a relatively high figure in a mixed-use setting. Tenure is also to be mixed, in familiar Dutch fashion, with 70 per cent private and 30 per cent public. Following approval of the overall plan in 1995, building began in 1997. Led by Riek Bakker, the former city planner of Rotterdam, the project has attracted international interest. Other notable areas include Nieuw-Oost Amsterdam, to be built at an unusually high VINEX density (about 60 dwellings per hectare) on the newly created island of IJburg, and Ypenburg in The Hague. Within some expansion areas, there have also been some important attempts to create leading edge ecological developments, on a larger scale than earlier pioneers. One such is the Oikos neighbourhood, some 600 dwellings within the Eschmarke VINEX site near Enschede, which is notable especially for its use of natural drainage (www.iclei.org/egpis). Overall though, there are fears that the broadly similar remit of the VINEX areas will fail to bring any distinctiveness. There are also fears that the mixed-use objectives will be difficult to achieve and that extensive car use will be inevitable.

## DUTCH PLANNING IN ITS INTERNATIONAL CONTEXT

As always, Dutch planners during the 1980s and 1990s combined a high degree of openness to international thinking with distinctive national approaches. Rotterdam's waterfront regeneration, of course, owed much to the American model (Hajer, 1993; Meyer, 1999). The partnership approach and marketing orientation that emerged during the 1980s was reminiscent of, and directly influenced by, the entrepreneurial regime of Baltimore and similar cities. Although the style of architecture was different, these buildings and spaces housed the same mix of activities. As well as major office developments, there was a strong emphasis on leisure, culture, tourism and attracting the more affluent to live in the heart of the city. There was also an awareness of British examples. Liverpool was an awful warning of what could happen to port cities that did not adapt and change. London's Docklands were a more important point of positive reference about how to stimulate the market. In Rotterdam, however, public planning was much stronger than in Docklands. At the Kop van Zuid, the lesson of ensuring good transport links in advance of development was well learnt. Another important influence was Barcelona, evident especially in the stylish approach to the design of public space. But both London and Barcelona were essentially variants of the American approach

The Dutch balance of trade in planning ideas was weighted more to export. Thus there was lesson-drawing from earlier innovations such as the management of vehicle traffic in residential areas (Hass-Klau, 1990; Ewing, 1999). As this was widely adopted throughout the world in the 1990s the seminal Dutch role was often recognised. Increasingly, though, a more comprehensive admiration was apparent. In the previous chapter, for example, we saw evidence of strong late 1990s British interest in many aspects of Dutch planning (Rogers, 1999). Meanwhile, the American advocates of green urbanism also saw Dutch cities as the epitome of what they were hoping, somewhat vainly, to achieve in their own country. There were many admiring reports from American environmental planners (Beatley, 2000). These, with the British Rogers report, have undoubtedly helped stimulate interest in Dutch innovations, in other parts of the Anglophone world. Dutch planning seemed, in fact, to offer a form of compact urbanisation that could realistically be adapted for an Anglo-American context (more so than the pattern of southern European cities). Yet interest in the Netherlands did not come solely from these sources. For example, the French planning ministry carefully examined the VINEX expansions, especially Leidsche Rijn (van der Meijden, nd, c1996). As we have seen, it was also notable that the EU forays into urban planning in the 1990s reflected many of the concerns and approaches the Dutch had pioneered.

## THE NORDIC COUNTRIES

Scandinavia and Finland were another part of Europe that was regarded as being at the leading edge of the new currents in sustainable urban planning. During the 1970s Sweden, the region's traditional leading nation in most things, began to falter (P Hall, 1998). The planning approach it had pioneered, based on state welfarism and massive commitment to planned public housing, ran into major problems as public dislike of the results grew and the national economy weakened. This broad pattern continued into the 1980s and the first half of the 1990s, as the economy continued to show serious problems. Older industries contracted and new sources of wealth developed only slowly. In the later 1990s, however, the economy showed strong growth, an improvement that coincided with Sweden's ties with the rest of Europe becoming closer after its entry into the EU in 1995.

Overall Sweden's neighbours, though certainly not immune to such problems, performed rather better, with important impacts on the course of their respective planning histories. Thus Finland's economy boomed during the 1980s, with an exceptionally high growth rate roughly twice that of Sweden. It fell back sharply in the early 1990s, particularly as the end of Communism brought disruption of trade with Russia. However, full membership of the EU from 1995 brought ample compensation and a resumption of strong growth. Norwegian growth was also high in the early and mid 1980s and for much of the 1990s (though it remained outside the EU). Denmark (the oldest Nordic member of the EU, but always sceptical of political moves towards ever closer union) also outperformed Sweden, though could not match the growth of Norway and Finland.

## ECONOMIC CHANGE AND SWEDISH PLANNING

It is not surprising, therefore, that Sweden tried the most extreme remedies. What had been one of the most state-led systems of any western capitalist country veered abruptly towards the free market in the 1980s (Newman and Thornley, 1996; P Hall, 1998). This continued in the 1990s as Swedish politics also moved rightward for the first time since the 1930s. Welfarism was weakened as governments of both political parties struggled to keep down the tax burden during a period of high unemployment. This also brought a marked reduction in the amount of social housing construction. Meanwhile, the deregulation of financial institutions encouraged major investment in property development, most obviously in the same proliferation of 'Eurosprawl' car-oriented retailing in suburban locations that could be found in many other parts of western Europe.

Increasingly, planning authorities tried to secure public facilities and amenities by negotiating with private developers, rather than relying on direct public provision. A related trend was the rise of urban marketing, triggered by the lurch towards the market and the pervasive sense of economic insecurity. Together, these changes signalled a very different style of urban planning to what had gone before. It was similar in some respects to the Anglo-American model though, as in many other European countries, Sweden did not travel as quickly, or as far, down this road.

## COMMUNITY PLANNING IN THE 1980s

Throughout the 1980s, therefore, high quality social housing provision remained quite common. There were no more large, monolithic satellites built by industrialised methods. The last Stockholm satellite suburb, Skarpnäck (1982–7), mimicked the more intimate character of the old inner city (Andersson, 1998; Hultin (ed), 1998). Its perimeter blocks with interior courtyards echoed traditional European cities, in similar vein to the Berlin IBA. Smaller scale designs, influenced particularly by Danish examples, also became more common. The British-born Swedish architect, Ralph Erskine, designed two particularly notable schemes in the Swedish capital during the decade. Myrstuguberget (1985–6) in the suburban district of Huddinge was reminiscent of his 1970s design for the Byker Wall in Newcastle in Britain, but on even more spectacular terrain. His later Ekerö (1985–90) is an outstanding example of how sensitive design and planning can transform cheap construction into some-thing of genuine quality. Another notable scheme was at Minneberg (1984–7). It was the first departure from functionalist design principles, with what was then seen as a daring orientation – to the waterfront rather than to maximise sunlight.

## GLOBEN AND SÖDERMALM

Far more dramatic, however, was the impact of the new developer-oriented negoti-ative planning approach that was taking shape at the same time. Its most visible impact on Stockholm was the Globen (Globe) arena, developed from 1986 to 1988

(Newman and Thornley, 1996). Here a public facility in the form of a sports arena was provided by developers on publicly owned land in return for the rights to create offices, shops and hotels in the adjoining area. Housed distinctively and unmistakably in the world's largest spherical building, the Globen arena embodied the new promotional approach to planning. Much play was also made of the Globen as a symbol of the new opening of Sweden to global forces.

A more appropriate symbol of Sweden's internationalism was the major urban renewal project at Södermalm, in inner Stockholm, on the site of the old South Station (T Hall, 1991a; Tonell, 1997; Andersson, 1998). The results of a 1981 ideas competition, it counterpoised visions of a 'Södra Manhattan' and a classic European city. Over the next few years it was the latter that dominated, much influenced by the philosophy of the Berlin IBA which was taking shape at the time. The master plan (by Jan Inghe of the city of Stockholm) was approved in 1984 and took shape from the late 1980s. Some 2,600 flats were provided in six- to eight-storey buildings, the high densities being offset by an urban park system. Most of the plan relied on a classic grid layout, though there was also a huge crescent, the Båge, designed by the Catalan architect Ricardo Bofill, and reminiscent of his work in Montpellier and Paris. A single 22-storey tower, which completed the development in 1997, was the one concession to the Manhattan vision.

## SUSTAINABLE URBAN DEVELOPMENT IN SWEDEN

Like most other European cities, Stockholm had moved by the 1990s to a strategy that sought to minimise greenfield development, and of which Södermalm was the first large-scale example. Even larger was the most important Stockholm waterfront project, Hammarby Sjöstad, begun in the early 1990s and set to continue into the early 21st century (Inghe, 1999; PHS, 1999). Developed largely on former industrial sites, the aim is a mixed-use district, with about 25,000 people ultimately living and working in the area. Again the Berlin IBA approach is favoured, creating a dense European city. Recent waterfront developments in Helsinki have also been a significant influence. To a greater extent than ever before in a large Swedish development, Hammarby Sjöstad shows advanced environmental features in energy production and use, water supply, waste treatment, construction materials and transport (www.hammarbysjostad.stockholm.se). Individual car use is to be discouraged and a new tramway is being provided.

By the late 1990s, therefore, Sweden's credentials in sustainable planning were becoming comparable with those of other leading edge European countries. Yet the advanced environmental 'friendliness' of Hammarby Sjöstad needs to be set against an unusually strong commitment to major road construction for much of the 1990s (Newman and Thornley, 1996). Thus, in 1992 the national government pushed through the Dennis Agreement (called after the banker who brokered the deal) to complete the hugely ambitious Stockholm inner ring road, long mired in political disagreement. The project involved extensive tunnelling, tolls and promised central environmental improvements. However, much of the scheme was aborted in 1998 following political changes in the city.

## COMPETITIVENESS AND SUSTAINABILITY IN SWEDISH PLANNING

Stockholm in 2000 fully reflects the planning tensions between competitiveness and sustainability. Even in an economic boom based on new electronic media, there is concern about the city's peripherality within Europe. The fall of Communism has seen a redrawing of the Baltic region in the 1990s which offers new trading possibilities. Yet, for the moment at least, these remain modest. The provincial cities of Göteborg and Malmö are best placed to connect with continental Europe and the EU heartlands. (This point, of course, has a significance for planning. We saw evidence of how, in the 1970s, both cities were quick to adopt planning innovations from Denmark, Germany and the Netherlands.) Stockholm's insecurities were greatly reinforced by the opening (in 2000) of the Öresund (Øresund in Danish) bridge and tunnel, giving direct road and rail links between Malmö and Copenhagen.

### ØRESTAD AND DANISH PLANNING

The real beneficiary of the links may turn out to be the region of the Danish capital because of its still closer proximity to the continent of Europe. (Another fixed link, to Germany via the Danish island of Lolland and the German island of Fehmarn, is being mooted. If built, it will further intensify these advantages.) Not surprisingly, the Copenhagen region has seen the most dramatic developments in Danish planning in recent years (Lemberg, 1997). In 1992 came the first steps to create Ørestad, a major internationally oriented project in the region (www.orestad.dk). Following a competition a Finnish design group, ARKKI, planned it in 1994/5. The concept is a linear development only 600 metres wide but stretching 5 kilometres southwards from Copenhagen university. A new elevated metro line (financed from sales at development value of what was formerly open land) services it. Developed in six districts, 60 per cent of the total floor space will be for commerce, providing up to 50,000 new jobs. A further 20 per cent is to be residential, for some 20,000 residents, with the remainder providing retailing and cultural facilities. Roughly a third of the 310-hectare area of Ørestad will be open space, or water in a lake or new canals. Many buildings will have a park or water frontage.

### THE ORIGINS OF SUSTAINABLE URBAN PLANNING IN DENMARK

Like many developments throughout the world since 1980, Ørestad is symptomatic of the growing internationalisation of business and cities. Yet it is rather untypical of the general course of recent Danish planning. A bit like the country itself, its planners have championed the small scale and have been wary of losing traditional identity. Not surprisingly, Denmark has been a leader in the way it both cherishes its urbanity

*Figure 11.3  The South Station development in Stockholm showed a Swedish openness to international design influences. Despite the tower, and Ricardo Bofill's great crescent (the end of which is just visible on the right), the main influences came from Berlin, reasserting the notion of a distinctively (north central) European city.*

and embraces the new paradigm of sustainability. The origins of this leadership go back, as we saw in Chapter 9, at least to the early pedestrianisation of the Strøget in Copenhagen in 1962, which was much extended over subsequent years (Gehl and Gemzøe, 1996). German cities had led the practice of pedestrianising existing central streets (Hass-Klau, 1990). Yet, more than any of the other pioneers, Danish planners realised that it was not enough simply to close streets: there had also to be a quantum leap in the quality of street life. Thus car-parking spaces were systematically reduced to allow more space for pedestrians. There were many changes in street furniture, and in the regulation of the space. Street entertainers and traders were encouraged. Shop windows had to be illuminated at night.

## LIFE BETWEEN BUILDINGS

The tireless champion of this approach (and the individual who, through this championing, probably did most to raise international awareness of Denmark's 'people friendly' planning approach) has been Jan Gehl. As noted earlier, he had in 1971 published a seminal book, *Livet mellum husene*, that drew on the early Danish experience with pedestrianised cities (Gehl, 2001). It became well known internationally during the 1980s, when it appeared in English as *Life between buildings* (with subsequent editions in 1996 and 2001). It has since been published in several other languages and a video film with the same title was made in 1999. Gehl's ideas continue to resonate with planners in many western (and, increasingly, former Communist) countries. They predated any conscious concept of sustainable planning but fitted easily into the emergent paradigm. His boundless enthusiasm for curbing the car in cities won him friends in green movements throughout the world. He also gave a human dimension to the evolving European model of the compact city, showing how a more traditional ideal of vibrant urbanity could also be reclaimed.

## ECOPLANNING IN DENMARK

There was, of course, little overt ecological content in what Gehl, an urban designer, was proposing. During the 1980s and 1990s, however, Denmark became a world leader in this field (Newman, nd, c1998; Beatley, 2000; www.arch.umanitoba.ca/la_www/ sustainable). There were many small initiatives, of which those at Slagelse and Kolding were the two best known. The former involved the ecological renewal of an area housing some 1,300 people, which adjoined the centre of this small town in southwest Sjælland. Building work began in 1989, though in most cases existing buildings were rehabilitated with many ecological features being incorporated. The district of Kolding, in south Jylland, was also adapted in the mid-1990s to create a green neighbourhood. Although it involved less than 150 (mainly existing) dwellings, its advanced ecological features have attracted widespread interest. By the time the Kolding scheme was finished, in 1996, there were many other, less individually notable, examples across the country including about 45 in Copenhagen.

Information about such developments was eagerly recycled in the flurry of texts and websites which, across the western world, sought to spread the ideas and practice of sustainable planning during the 1990s. As always in such exercises, examples that contradicted the stereotype of the country from which ideas were being borrowed were largely ignored. Across Europe, and in North America, Australia and elsewhere, Denmark was seen as a champion of sustainable 'small is beautiful' planning approaches. Yet, as many Danish planners acknowledge, the Øresund link (and the one being considered for Fehmarn), must surely test these priorities in the early 21st century.

## FINLAND AND THE NEW EUROPE

We have already begun to see something of the way traditional Swedish supremacy in Nordic planning matters was overturned. As noted, Denmark became more of a reference point. So too, in their different ways, did the other Nordic countries: Finland and Norway. In the case of the former, the use of Finnish designers for Ørestad, and the high regard in which Stockholm's planners held aspects of Helsinki's planning, especially its new waterfronts, reflected a wider ascendancy and self-confidence in Finnish planning and design. Finland's new-found economic prowess, heavily reliant on leading-edge communications technology and a new sense of being less on the periphery of Europe, was an important part of this self-confidence. Finland could at last aspire to become part of the mainstream of Europe. On a regional scale, the fall of Communism meant that it could look hopefully to the re-emergence of a Baltic region (Hedman, 1997).

## HELSINKI'S NEW PORT

These shifts were fully reflected in Helsinki's planning (ECFJS, 1997; HCPD, 2000). The most important provision was the development of a new international freight port at Vuosaari, in the northeastern suburbs. The site, on reclaimed land, could be closely integrated with road and rail links, especially those to the east, giving improved access to a huge hinterland in Russia. Close by the new port a new satellite suburb, planned for some 37,000 inhabitants by 2010, also took shape during the 1990s. Its basic concept followed the classic Scandinavian satellite pattern, with a shopping centre and higher density housing close to the metro station giving way to single-family houses at a greater distance. Especially notable, however, is the emphasis given to waterfront development, especially the Kallahti sub-area, the first large section of which was completed in 2000.

## WATERFRONT DEVELOPMENTS

Waterfront development was not traditionally favoured in the Nordic countries. Although Helsinki's peninsula setting created a very extensive shoreline, its planners had been especially wary of developing this, mainly because of the poor bearing capacity of the immediate waterside. Signs of a shift in thinking, reflecting international fashions and a growing interest in maximising the use of building land in the inner city, began to become apparent in the 1980s. The new high-density residential district of Pikku Huopolahti, developed from 1986 to 2000, showed signs of an increasing willingness to countenance waterside building.

It was, however, the decline of the traditional freight port facilities in the inner city that triggered extensive use. The first example was the west harbour area, where a new waterside district was planned for some 22,000 inhabitants and 12,000 jobs. Work began on Ruoholahti, the first part of this district, in 1991. It was this area that largely established the city's reputation as a Nordic leader in this type of development. The planning during the 1990s of the city's eastern waterfront, where port functions have remained active for longer, has also attracted much interest. In contrast to Anglo-American approaches, Helsinki has reflected the Finnish tradition of a strong public role in land acquisition and development.

## SUSTAINABLE PLANNING

The suburban municipalities surrounding Helsinki were less rigorous in using their ownership of development land as a planning tool, and left more scope to private

*Figure 11.4* Ruoholahti is Helsinki's major waterfront redevelopment area, combining superb housing design with pleasant waterside public spaces.

developers. Even there, however, the hand of planning remained relatively strong. As in other dynamic developed economies during the late 20th century, market capitalism assumed a greater role in some aspects of Finnish life. Yet urban planning was relatively untouched by these impulses. In turn, this helped Finnish planning to become an exemplar of the new paradigm of sustainable urban planning during the 1990s (Beatley, 2000). In common with the other northern European leaders, the commitment to public transport was extremely important (though Helsinki's pedestrians were given less dedicated space than their counterparts in the centres of other Nordic capitals). Helsinki was also an innovator in the international moves towards compact urbanisation, its high-density waterfront developments playing an important role in reurbanisation.

The main showpiece of sustainable urban development in Helsinki is Viikki, begun in 1995 (www.arch.umanitoba.ca/la_www/sustainable). It is the scale of the development that is especially impressive. It covers some 1132 hectares of open land in the geographical centre of the city, about 8 kilometres northeast of the central business area. Here a large university-related science park and residential and business premises are being developed, housing a population of about 13,000, with 6,000 jobs and 6,000 students. However, about three-quarters of the area will remain as open space or water. Throughout, leading-edge ecological principles are being applied in both construction and use, minimising harmful effects on nature and ecological systems and reducing pollution.

## BRUNDTLAND AND NORWAY

Europe's smallest Nordic country, Norway, claimed an even more central position than any of its neighbours in shaping the new discourse of sustainability. Thus it was the country's socialist prime minister, Gro Harlem Brundtland, who chaired the international commission which, in 1987, actually launched the term 'sustainable development' on the world (Brundtland, 1997). By the 1980s there was certainly an acute Norwegian awareness of environmental problems, though mainly in remoter rural areas. Acid rain (for which British coal-fired power stations were largely blamed) had an especially serious impact on Norwegian forests and freshwater fisheries. Yet early attempts at remediation were sometimes rather clumsily undertaken and worsened the situation. Moreover, the buoyant economy brought major growth in road traffic, with impacts in the bigger cities, particularly Oslo.

However, during the 1980s the most internationally significant development in Norwegian urban planning did not lie in the environmental field. Oslo's waterfront development at Aker Brygge was the first such project in the Nordic countries (Breen and Rigby, 1996). Though Norwegian-designed, the American influence was clear in its leisure/tourist focus. As in Baltimore, Aker Brygge benefited from a pedestrian-accessible location adjoining the city centre. The basic concept was defined in 1982, shortly after the shipyard on the site was closed and it was decided to remove most through traffic from the area by building a road tunnel. Construction of the development began in earnest in 1986. The result expressed the more cosmopolitan outlook of a Norway booming on oil revenues (Jensen, 1997).

## ROAD PRICING IN NORWAY

In the later 1980s and early 1990s it was Norway's adoption of urban road pricing that captured global, and not just European, attention (Beatley, 2000). In 1986 its second city, Bergen, introduced the first such system in Europe (and the second in the world after Singapore) – a toll ring around the central part of the city. It was followed by more sophisticated electronic systems in Oslo in 1990, and Trondheim in 1991 (eg www.iclei.org/egpis). Naturally, these were widely studied by planners and politicians in many other western countries as part of the quest for more sustainable cities. Actually, environmental considerations were only part of the intention of these schemes. Their main purpose was to raise funds for road building and, to a much lesser extent, public and other transport improvements. In a real sense, therefore, their role in traffic restraint was heavily compromised by their revenue-raising goal. Not surprisingly, traffic reductions have been modest, especially in Oslo.

## AN INTERNATIONAL PERSPECTIVE

Overall, therefore, the Nordic countries, despite their small size (and long-term tendency for low population growth), remained an important source of planning innovations, much admired by other countries, in the late 20th century. They were widely perceived as forming, with the Netherlands, and with Germany and its co-linguistic neighbours, the leading edge of action on sustainable urban planning as the century ended. The long-established and very extensive use of English by planners in all the Nordic countries helped, of course, to reinforce this international salience. It also did no harm that these countries were leaders in the information technology revolution of the 1990s. For their part, Nordic planners maintained a strong interest in planning developments elsewhere. We have already seen signs of how traditional links with German planning were reinvigorated during this period. Interest in Anglo-American developments also remained strong, especially in Denmark and Norway.

In some ways, however, the most interesting aspect of international lesson-drawing during this period lay within and between the Nordic countries themselves. The traditional dominance of Sweden, which was waning in the 1970s, was now comprehensively supplanted. What replaced it was not another single source of influence but a more complex interchange, to which each of its smaller neighbours contributed significantly.

## SPAIN

The Netherlands and the Nordic countries were, of course, largely embellishing their long-established reputations in international planning thought and practice. A far greater discontinuity was evident on the southern edge of western Europe. Here the (somewhat bumpy) transition from Franco's authoritarian regime to a less centralised, democratic Spanish state, from 1977 stimulated a remarkable flowering of local and regional governance, culture and design (McNeill, 1999). Spain also became part of the international community, most importantly with membership of the EU in 1986 and Barcelona's hosting of the Olympic Games in 1992. More than ever, its architects, planners and city leaders sought active links with ideas and practice in other western countries. Nor was this just a one-way learning process. The late 1980s and the 1990s saw a truly astonishing rise in the international reputation of Spanish urban design and planning.

Initially, at least, the real basis for this high regard was decidedly slim. There had been no shortage of expertise in the big cities, but under Franco planning had been marginalised. Successive plans were ignored. In a few cases, though, those prepared in the last years of the dictatorship (such as the Barcelona metropolitan plan of 1976) could now be applied with a new commitment (M Wynn, 1984a; Serratosa *et al*, 1996). The early 1980s also saw a flurry of new activity that produced major plans for many of Spain's cities, including Madrid and Seville. Yet, despite the high hopes and obvious technical competence invested in these exercises, the political salience of planning again diminished in the later 1980s, though certainly not to Francoist levels.

## THE BARCELONA MODEL

One very important city managed to buck this trend, and developed a blend of planning that combined obeisance to global capitalism with genuine popular appeal, local distinctiveness and real design quality. This was the Catalonian capital, Barcelona, under the inspired leadership of Pasqual Maragall, its socialist mayor from 1982 to 1997 (McNeill, 1999; T Marshall, 2000). With remarkable speed, Spain's second city (almost equal in size to Madrid) became one of the most potent international models of urban planning of the late 20th century. Influenced by the ideas of the radical sociologist Manuel Castells and the sociologist/geographer Jordi Borja (amongst others), Maragall articulated in Barcelona European socialism's most convincing response to globalisation and the right-wing pro-market philosophy that was otherwise dominating western urban policy discourse. His was essentially a middle way, accepting the competitive rigours of global capitalism but also nurturing the locality as a distinctive physical space that provided a setting for a specific social and cultural cohesion. Finally, and not least for our purposes, to architects, planners and designers everywhere Barcelona was a city where good design was pursued as a matter of consistent policy.

## PORT VELL AND AMERICAN INFLUENCES

Maragall showed wide awareness of the planning approaches of other western cities. His recognition of the dynamic resilience of capitalism may be traced back to his close encounters with the United States. He studied in New York during the early 1970s and returned to America to lecture in Baltimore in 1978 and 1979. Something of his awareness of the latter city appeared in the redevelopment of Port Vell (Barcelona's old port) during the mid-1980s (Meyer, 1999). There, prompted by the suggestions of James Rouse's Enterprise Development Company, the port authority created a mix of leisure/tourism-oriented activities that closely reproduced Rouse's Baltimore formula. As in Oslo, the engineering treatment of major roads, in this case by a combination of tunnel and cutting, has eased pedestrian links between the port and the historic centre. Overall Port Vell has attracted familiar criticisms (not least from David Harvey, Maragall's friend from his Baltimore days) for its favouring of the global over the local, or the 'American' over the 'European'.

Barcelona's wholehearted embrace of city marketing was another aspect of the Americanisation of urban policy and the acceptance of global competition (McNeill, 1999). During the 1980s the city began to target investors, tourists and residents. As in Glasgow, culture also became an important part of the marketing approach, with a proliferation of impressive new galleries, museums and other facilities. Everywhere in the city, efforts were made to use good design and high quality materials. Barcelona also made widespread use of public art. Traditional design assets, such as the buildings of Antoni Gaudí, added depth to the promoted image. All these efforts intensified in the years leading to 1992, when the Olympic Games became a tremendous global marketing opportunity (Chalkley and Essex, 1999). By this time, the city had effectively 'branded' itself as a distinctive product, an approach which became even more overt during the 1990s.

*Figure 11.5* Port Vell in Barcelona is a Baltimore-style waterfront redevelopment, albeit very stylishly designed and executed. The city proper's water frontage had already benefited by the taking of the traffic on the city's ring motorway below ground level. The towers of the Olympic Village area are just visible in the far right of this cable car view.

## PLANNING FOR LOCAL COMMUNITIES

Yet the many negative features of American cities were feared (McNeill, 1999). There were, for example, conscious attempts to avoid the flight to the suburbs. Barcelona was traditionally a very compact city of apartments, exactly what the evolving international discourse of sustainable urban development was promoting – and another reason for international attention. It was, however, acknowledged that this was a fragile pattern. Marseilles' experience showed that even high-density Mediterranean cities were not immune to serious outward migration, and the early signs were certainly present in Barcelona. The response was to improve the quality of life in the older neighbourhoods, to mitigate the worst aspects of high-density living and provide high quality urban facilities that made living in the city worthwhile.

All parts of the older and less well-endowed areas gained new parks, public spaces, public amenities and cultural facilities. One of the first (and biggest) parks was the Parc de l'Espanya Industrial in the Sants neighbourhood, created in response to strong neighbourhood pressures about the use of a former factory site. Other similar sites also provided opportunities to enhance amenities. Some spaces were created by selective demolition of housing in especially decrepit areas, such as the Raval district of the old city. Throughout, local civil society and activism played an important role in shaping what actually happened. From 1983, there was a decentralisation of power to the districts.

## PLANNING AN OLYMPIC CITY

Even when urban policy was decidedly 'top-down', the Barcelona approach showed distinctive features. An important difference between it and what might loosely be called the American approach has been that the spectacular architecture and individual, internationally oriented projects have not been pursued at the expense of wider planning considerations. This was most obvious in the changes made from 1986 to 1992 in preparation for the Olympic Games. In sharp contrast to the American Olympic cities of Los Angeles and Atlanta, Barcelona used the games to address the problems of the whole city (McNeill, 1999; Meyer, 1999; T Marshall, 2000). There were, for example, major investments in the road and transport infrastructure. The completion of the ring road system, begun tentatively in the 1970s, was extremely important and there was far greater sensitivity to the system's environmental effects on adjoining areas (especially along the coast).

Very large individual areas were also regenerated as part of the programme. The most significant changes came in the run-down and polluted coastal area in the northeast of the city between La Barceloneta and Poble Nou. There had long been a desire to reclaim this area, but little could be done until the award of the Olympics eased the financial constraints. An international team, headed by the local architect Oriol Bohigas (briefly the city's chief planner from 1982 to 1984), authored a major physical transformation. The proposals respected and extended Cerdà's famous 19th-century plan. A constellation of famous international architects realised different sections, giving visual diversity. The results included a stylish beach resort, and two seafront parks were created along with an Olympic Port and the Olympic Village itself (initially to accommodate the athletes, later a high-income residential area).

After the Olympic Games regeneration continued up to the city's eastern boundary in the delta of the Besòs river. Again, Cerdà provided the template, as his northwest-southeast diagonal highway (actually called the Diagonal) was extended to the sea. Several entirely new seafront blocks, developed for low- and middle-income housing, mimicked his distinctive grid. The first results of this post-Olympics phase began to appear in the late 1990s. Major new cultural facilities and high-speed rail links to France will eventually complete the development.

## GREEN BARCELONA?

There is much else that could be (and has been) said about Barcelona's planning. What should be stressed, though, is that it followed a different path to the northern European cities which pioneered environmentally aware forms of planning (T Marshall, 2000). Obviously the traditional compactness of the city, its good public transport and its commitment to brownfield development were all consistent with the new paradigm of sustainability. Yet the overt ecological content was low. Barcelona's reputation was based on its design credentials. In green matters it, like other Spanish cities, was a follower rather than a leader.

## OTHER SPANISH CITIES

For much of this period, the planning activities of other Spanish cities were in Barcelona's shadow. Madrid was comprehensively outshone by its Catalonian rival. This was despite much important activity in the national capital and its region, with great improvements in the transport infrastructure. It was symptomatic of the decentralisation of power, which was an integral part of the democratic transition, that it was other, regional, capitals that began to win international attention in the 1990s. As with the Barcelona Olympics, Seville's hosting of the Expo in 1992 occasioned a massive public investment in the city. The subsequent conversion of exhibition site into a high technology park was an important factor in Andalusian dreams of becoming the California of Europe (Castells and Hall, 1994). The Basque capital, Bilbao, clearly learnt from Barcelona, with ambitious regeneration plans, major investments in infrastructure and cultural facilities and outstanding design (www.bm30.es). The Guggenheim-Bilbao Museum, opened in 1997 as part of the waterfront regeneration, was a (literally) dazzling example of iconic design as international city marketing.

## THE INTERNATIONAL IMPACT

By 2000, therefore, Spanish urban planning enjoys a high reputation throughout the world. Reflecting its early successes, Barcelona has, to date, been the city that had the biggest impact on planning thought and practice, greatly reinforced by Maragall's active international role. In Europe, for example, he encouraged all regional (and smaller national capital) cities, showing that they really could slip the surly bonds of provincialism to become true global players. The Barcelona experience also demonstrated how socialist politics might be reconciled with global capital. This underlying message has had a particular impact in Britain. In 1999 the former mayor was directly enlisted by Richard Rogers to back his arguments for an urban renaissance (Rogers, 1999). The Blair government also used Maragall to bolster the case for strong city mayors (T Marshall, 2000). But important lessons have been drawn in cities as varied as Lisbon, Dublin, Sarajevo, Rome (the last where Maragall went to teach in 1997 and 1998) and many others. Architects and planners who are closely associated with the city, most notably Bofill and Bohigas, have worked extensively elsewhere, particularly in France.

Outside Europe, Barcelona has also been widely admired. In 1987 Harvard University honoured the city for its commitment to good design, and the close links with the Boston region remain. There have also been very specific attempts to promote connections with Latin America, reflecting both linguistic affinity and the experience of similar problems in the transition to democracy (Borja, 1996). Links have been especially close with Rio de Janeiro, Havana and Asunción (McNeill, 1999; Breen and Rigby, 1996). In Buenos Aires, meanwhile, the Puerto Madero waterfront project was inspired partly by Port Vell. There are currently no signs of the Barcelona bandwagon losing momentum.

# CANADA

Throughout Europe the 1980s and 1990s were characterised by low population growth. The American population grew substantially during this period, by some 21 per cent. Again, though, Canada and Australia were the fastest increasing western countries. Their populations – 31.3 million and 19.2 million respectively in 2000 – had grown by 27 per cent and 31 per cent since 1980. These trends reflected their prosperity and high immigration from nonwestern countries which changed them into increasingly multicultural societies. As well as new international pressures to enhance the competitiveness and sustainability of cities, this experience of growth was itself an important spur to urban change and planning in both countries.

The first of these, Canada, continued to show that it was possible, if not to perfect the large North American city, at least to mitigate its worst features. This was despite a political and economic climate that, with only minor variations, echoed that of the United States and Britain. Thus the 1980s were dominated by a pro-market, anti-intervention agenda. The 1990s brought a strengthening of market forces with the creation of a single North American free trade zone with the United States and Mexico (in 1994). Yet there was also a more overt government commitment to environmental protection and sustainability.

# WEST EDMONTON MALL

The place which most completely epitomised the market-led and essentially American side of the Canadian urban development process during the last two decades of the 20th century was the West Edmonton Mall or WEM (Smith, 1991; www.westedmontonmall.com). Here, in four phases completed in 1981, 1983, 1985 and 1998, the Canadian Ghermezian brothers created the world's biggest shopping mall (and car park). Ever since the opening of Victor Gruen's pioneering enclosed Southdale Mall in Edina, Minneapolis, in 1956 the harsh climate of the more northerly parts of the North American interior had made it ideal territory for innovations and refinements of the mall form. WEM was, though, a veritable quantum leap in mall design. This was not just on account of its immense size (by 1985 it covered 105 hectares), but also because from 1983 it linked shopping to extensive leisure development and hotel provision. The shopping mall was also therefore conceived of as a theme park and leisure resort. It was, of course, highly influential. Its developers subsequently played a central role in the creation of the similar (but slightly smaller) Mall of America discussed in Chapter 10. Its influence could also be detected in smaller European examples such as the Gateshead MetroCentre in Britain and CentrO in Oberhausen, Germany, also considered earlier.

It goes almost without saying that the role of public planning in the creation of WEM (and most of its offspring) was essentially passive and did not impede the creative aspirations of developers. This had always been, to some extent, the American way of planning, but the market-led model was in the 1980s achieving a wider international salience. Though it was to be a few years before Joel Garreau popularised the term 'edge city' in 1991, West Edmonton, located in the affluent suburbs of Alberta's largest city, was an essential building block of his concept. It was, at once, a monument to the passive Anglo-American planning of the 1980s and a challenge to the new paradigm of sustainable planning in the 1990s.

## TORONTO'S HARBOURFRONT AND SKY DOME

American influences and parallels were also apparent in other aspects of Canadian urban development during the 1980s and 1990s. In these, at least, there was a stronger role for urban planners than was usual in American cities. Thus we saw in Chapter 9 how Toronto had begun to transform itself architecturally into an exciting world city during the 1960s and 1970s (Sewell, 1993; Lemon, 1996). This process continued in the 1980s with the beginnings of the Harbourfront regeneration which, though overshadowed by Baltimore, was extremely influential (Breen and Rigby, 1996; Gordon, 1996). The adaptation of the massive Queen's Quay Terminal, undertaken from 1980 to 1983, for a mixture of retailing, office, residential and leisure activities was especially notable. It also marked one of the first internationally noticed developments of Olympia and York (soon to embark on even larger projects at Battery Park, New York, and Canary Wharf in London's Docklands). However, the larger Toronto waterfront regeneration, of which Queen's Quay was a flagship development, ran into major opposition during the mid to late 1980s when it seemed to be favouring profit over all else.

Toronto's other high-profile project of these years, built on the railway lands that had traditionally divided the city from the Lake Ontario waterfront, was the Sky Dome. This state-of-the-art sports stadium, adjoining the CN Tower and opened in

1989, added a second distinctive architectural signature on the Toronto skyline. Rather like the adjacent waterfront, it was simultaneously a symbol of American-isation, a massive boosterist gesture to assert the city's importance in a global era and something distinctively Canadian that could never have been built south of the border. American planners were awe-struck that any North American city could build a facility of this kind with so little car parking.

## WATERFRONT REGENERATION IN OTHER CITIES

Other Canadian cities also began to reclaim their waterfronts from industry and port activities during the 1980s and 1990s. These included the mixed-use conversion of the Stelco buildings along Montreal's Lachine Canal, and the waterfront at Trois Rivières in Quebec (Wolfe, 1994). But the example that was most expressive of 1980s Canada was at Pacific Place in Vancouver (North and Hardwick, 1992; Barnes *et al*, 1992). The 1970s waterfront venture at Granville Island spawned local imitations at New Westminster and Lonsdale Quay in North Vancouver. Pacific Place was, though, a far more internationally-oriented development than any of these. Opened to host the 1986 Expo, its concept and funding by Japan's Tokyu Corporation reflected Vancouver's belated (and, before the 1980s, reluctant) bid for global status. The city increasingly promoted itself as Canada's gateway to the Pacific Rim, a spatial construct barely recognised just a few years earlier (Olds, 2001).

## OTHER ASPECTS OF CANADIAN PLANNING IN THE 1980s

Behind these visible results lay the familiar Anglo-American weakening of the regulatory and state-led aspects of 1980s urban planning. This was particularly pronounced in British Columbia. The Greater Vancouver Regional District (GVRD, Vancouver's metropolitan authority), whose Livable Region Proposals (LRP) of 1976 had held such conceptual promise, now found itself divested of its explicit planning role. Yet, as we have noted in many European countries, the rhetoric and the reality did not always match up. Canadian cities, for example, kept their faith with public transit. Vancouver opened its Skytrain light rapid-transit line in 1986, though this did not prevent it being the most car dependent of Canada's big cities.

## HEALTHY CITIES

A notable initiative of genuinely international significance, which signalled the persistence of Canada's collective credentials, was the healthy cities movement (Wolfe, 1994). Its origins were in a 1984 symposium: Healthy Toronto 2000: Beyond Health Care. The underpinning ideas were developed by Len Duhl, a California academic, and Trevor Hancock, a Canadian health consultant. Basically the intention was look beyond the conventional parameters of health provision. Instead there would be a re-emphasising and updating of the approaches that had brought health improvement to 19th- and early 20th-century western cities. The emphasis was on

378

building strong and economically viable communities with high quality physical environments (including housing), good public services, respect for cultural traditions and diversity, and active grass roots community involvement. The level of health, in other words, was not a function of medical technology, hospitals or health centres alone. It derived from the nature of the places and societies in which people lived. The community, in other words, had to be healthy in all senses of the word.

The idea was applied with enthusiasm in Canada, with very active involvement by the Canadian Institute of Planners. It also formed the basis of an international movement when the World Health Organization (WHO) adopted its principles in 1986. Outside Canada, there was interest in some cities in the United States, parts of Europe and Asia. The country's leadership in this field obviously helped to promote contacts between Canadian planners and those elsewhere.

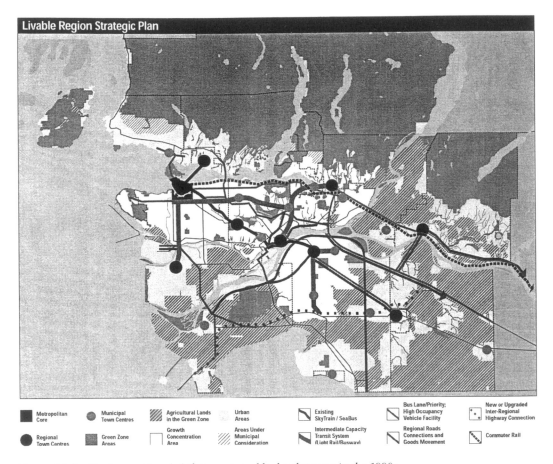

*Figure 11.6* *The international shift to sustainable development in the 1990s allowed Vancouver to revisit its pioneering 1970s concerns with liveable urban regions.*

## CANADIAN NEW URBANISM

The emphasis on healthy communities coincided with the emergence of the more overarching international discourse of sustainable development from 1987. There was, of course, a long-standing Canadian interest in protecting the natural environment. Yet Canada shared with the United States many lifestyle problems that contradicted the new thinking about the environment. Despite the success in maintaining the popularity of inner city living, many Canadians lived in low-density suburbs. And, despite generally good public transit and long-standing attempts to create nodal centres of employment and services in the suburbs, they also relied heavily on the automobile. In many ways, though, Canadian cities have proved more fertile territory than their American equivalents for the new urbanist project of urbanising the suburbs (Duffy, 1995; www.arch.umanitoba.ca/la_www/sustainable). The American leaders of the movement, Andres Duany and Elizabeth Plater-Zyberk, were in demand during the early and mid 1990s. During this period, for example, they produced master plans for major new suburban communities at McKenzie Towne in Calgary (for about 28,000 inhabitants) and Markham, a suburb of Toronto (for 36,000).

## TOWARDS SUSTAINABLE URBAN PLANNING

The suburban growth centres that were developed following Vancouver's LRP did not actually look like the transit-oriented developments that the new urbanists in the United States were now advocating. (Most obviously, they had too many tall buildings and favoured the enclosed mall form.) Yet their status as higher density transit hubs meant they fulfilled many of the American movement's broader objectives. In the late 1990s, for example, the planners of Seattle's northern suburbs found themselves citing the experience of their Canadian neighbour.

By this stage, though, the original LRP had been overtaken by a later (and stronger) version. From 1990, the emasculation of the metropolitan planning function of the GVRD began to be reversed. Its planners produced one of the first plans on the continent that explicitly embraced the new language of sustainable development. In 1993, for example, they ambitiously stated their intent to make Greater Vancouver the first urban region in the world to combine economic vitality with the highest standards of liveability and environmental quality (GVRD, 1993). By fulfilling this objective, it was claimed, their city would assume a historical significance comparable to that of Athens for the creation of democracy, or Vienna for music. Whether this will be so remains to be seen. In 1996, however, the Livable Region Strategic Plan was accepted (GVRD, 1999; www.gvrd.bc.ca). It promised protection of predominantly unbuilt areas; a compact-city strategy; more complete communities, focused on town centres throughout Greater Vancouver; and a widening of transport choices, with the promotion of car sharing as well as public transit.

## MAJOR URBAN PROJECTS IN THE LATE 1990s

By the end of the century Canadian cities were continuing to follow the two paths that led to global competitiveness and sustainability. The latter concern was more obvious in Vancouver (www.city.vancouver.nc.ca). The two main projects there were the revitalisation of problem-ridden downtown Eastside (which had drug-abuse problems as bad as any American city) and the development of the southeast False Creek area as a mixed-use sustainable community. Montreal, by contrast, was more economically troubled, and was also suffering from recurrent uncertainties as to whether Franco-phone Quebec would secede from the Canadian federation (Germain and Rose, 2000). Here the Quartier Internationale project, unveiled in 1997, was an essentially boost-erist regeneration (by a partnership of governmental and property interests) of an area adjoining the downtown business district and blighted by the Ville-Marie Expressway (www.ville.montreal.qc.ca; www.qimtl.qc.ca). The overall concept was of an internationally oriented mixed-use but essentially business district. It was inspired partly by Lyons' Cité Internationale, though its central proposal, the covering over of the expressway, also reflected the experiences of Boston and Barcelona.

Toronto, meanwhile, promises to outdo both its rivals after a substantial reorgan-isation of city government in 1998. The once innovative Metro authority (and six small cities that formed the lower tier of government) were replaced by a single, unitary city of Toronto. The new city government, now amongst the largest in North America, unveiled one of the world's most ambitious revitalisation projects in 1999 – to renew the entire 29-mile (46 kilometre) waterfront of the city (www.city.toronto.on.ca/waterfront). Central to the plan was the redevelopment of the port lands to the east of the downtown area, where most new construction would occur. Overall some 40,000 new dwellings are promised and 10 million square feet of business space. Amongst much else, there are also to be huge investments to clean water and beaches. The elevated Gardiner Expressway, long a major barrier between downtown Toronto and Lake Ontario, will finally be removed. There will also be a new public transit link along the entire waterfront, and major provision of new parks. If fully implemented, the development will undoubtedly become one of the international showpieces of western urban planning in the early 21st century.

## AUSTRALIA

Australia was also dramatically affected by the economic and human dimensions of globalisation (Bolton, 1996). There was a rapid internationalisation of inward and outward investment, especially in urban property development, and a comprehensive retreat from trade protectionism. By the 1980s the real economic achievements (and even greater potential) of its Asian neighbours, so long treated with a mixture of fear and condescension by Australia, were being widely seen as holding the key to its future. The very identity of the Australian nation also became more global as the earlier liberalisation of immigration policies began to create a noticeably more multi-ethnic (and increasingly Asian) population.

The political response of Australians to these larger global forces was, however, slightly different to that of the rest of the Anglophone west. This was a consequence of Labor's dominance of federal politics from 1983 to 1996. Rhetorically, at least, the sharp edges of the Anglo-American free market model, elsewhere made more jagged by evangelising right-wing governments, were perceptibly softer in Australia. Some lingering faith in interventionist government remained. In practice, however, the governments of the Labor prime ministers Bob Hawke and Paul Keating were far less radical than Gough Whitlam's in the 1970s. They saw cities (which by 1996 housed 86 per cent of Australians) first and foremost as economic engines in the emergent global market. Other considerations remained secondary. All of this was quite familiar, of course. Yet something of the Whitlam spirit lived on in the planning field (Lennon, 2000; Hamnett, 2000). Even though they produced little by way of practical action, newer ideas about urban form and sustainable development were quickly able to permeate the official discourse of Australian urban policy. The language, at least, was often radical, even if the results usually were not.

## WATERFRONT DEVELOPMENTS

In the event, therefore, the most obvious symptom of the impact of globalisation on Australian cities was the appearance of major internationally oriented developments. These were usually developed in a fairly opportunistic fashion that revealed a willingness to compromise the role of planning in order to garner investment. The most familiar type involved the redevelopment of former dock areas, very much on the Anglo-American pattern (Breen and Rigby, 1996). The first was Sydney's Darling Harbour, from 1984 (Young, 1988). This followed the Baltimore model very closely indeed (and was quite different to the more distinctive conservation-based approach adopted in Sydney's Rocks waterfront area during the 1970s). Thus James Rouse and his organisation's former chief planner were consultants and Harbourside, Darling Harbour's festival marketplace, was designed by Baltimore architects. In part, perhaps, the direct borrowing from this successful formula was to allow rapid completion in time for Australia's bicentennial celebrations in 1988. More ambitious (and less directly derivative) developments followed in the 1990s. In Sydney, for example, the City West renewal began from 1992 (CWDC, 1998). The Melbourne Docklands Authority was formed in 1991 to redevelop an area equal in size to the city's central business district (www.docklands.com.au). All were overseen by special purpose development agencies, modelled on Britain's urban development corporations.

## MULTI-FUNCTION POLIS

The 1980s also saw more Japanese-initiated developments in Australian cities. The multilevel Melbourne Central mall, anchored by the Japanese Daimaru department store, was one very visible example. Tourist developments, especially in Queensland, also reflected Japanese investment. In 1987, however, Japan's government proposed something that might have had much more direct implications for Australian planning thought and practice. This was a vision of a new science city of about 100,000 people in Australia, a utopian prototype of urban life, work and leisure for the 21st century (Castells and Hall, 1994; Hamnett, 1998). It is not entirely clear how far the Japanese intended the vision to be a practical basis for action, or whether they were merely floating an abstract idea that could combine Japan's technological capacity with Australia's physical space. The Australian government's initial reception was, though, nothing short of ecstatic.

382

However, the vagueness of the project soon raised many doubts. A site near Adelaide was eventually selected, but it seems unlikely that the project will ever be fulfilled in a form that comes close to the original vision. Political vacillation, a worsening economic situation in the early 1990s, a fading of active Japanese interest, and a general lack of private sector commitment saw the Multi-Function Polis (MFP) scaled down. By 1997 all its more ambitious features had been dropped. Some useful remediation of formerly polluted environments has occurred. But, at best, the MFP seems destined to become a medium-density suburb of Adelaide (and there are serious doubts even about this). What might have heralded a new synthesis of Japanese and Australian urban ideals ended as a farce. It was also symptomatic of the surprising lack of Asian influence on Australian planning.

## METROPOLITAN PLANNING

As in other western countries, most internationally oriented developments were, in varying degrees, products of developer pressures, political pipe dreams and flexible or

*Figure 11.7  Darling Harbour in Sydney was perhaps the most direct copy of Baltimore to be found anywhere in the world, reflecting the direct involvement of development and design expertise from that city.*

'fast track' planning regimes. Alongside these, however, there was also a revival in Australian metropolitan (and regional) planning (Lennon, 2000). From the later 1980s, the state-run metropolitan planning agencies issued a remarkable spate of plans that attempted to give some focus to growth and change in metropolitan Australia. Thus four plans were produced for Adelaide, in 1987, 1992, 1994 and 1998. Sydney also had four (1988, 1993, 1995, 1997), while Perth had three (1987, 1990 and 1996) and Melbourne also had three (1987, 1994 and 1995). In these efforts could be seen the Whitlam legacy, cherished by former members of the federal Urban and Regional Development Department who now found themselves in senior planning positions within the states. Ostensibly, the broad purpose of all these plans was to balance economic considerations, some long term but many very short term, against longer term social and environmental matters. In practice, the latter concerns received short shrift, especially as the economy weakened in the first half of the 1990s. But despite these important limitations, Australian planners in the early 1990s were working within a stronger strategic framework than their counterparts in North America.

**Figure 11.8** *Further American influence in recent Australian planning is evident here at the Perth new town of Joondalup, where new urbanist principles can been seen applied to the latest phase of commercial development, in contrast to the earlier mall style visible in the background.*

## URBAN CONSOLIDATION

Some specific ideas did stick. Even if they did not immediately bring dramatic changes, they became key parts of policy discourse. One of the most important was urban consolidation. This was the Australian term for creating cities that were more compact. In assessing the significance of this, it should be remembered that Australia's bungalow suburbs meant that its metropolitan densities were, with those of the most dispersed American cities, the lowest in the world. Such low densities raised major problems about the provision of public services, infrastructure, transport and, increasingly, actual housing costs.

The beginnings of the push for urban consolidation seems to have originated in Australia's largest city, Sydney, in 1980. It was quickly taken up throughout the country, encouraged by the Hawke government from 1983 and the federal Better Cities programme of the early 1990s, intended to support demonstration projects of good practice throughout the country (Hamnett, 2000). It was bolstered, too, by a parallel push for public transport improvements, the most impressive of which was Perth's suburban rail system, opened in 1992 (Newman, 1992). Also in Perth, the transport planners Peter Newman, Jeff Kenworthy and their associates undertook work of international significance on the relationship between transport and urban density (eg Newman and Kenworthy, 1989). It caused planners throughout the Anglophone world to revisit (if not always to reject) the axioms about the desirability of low urban densities that they had inherited from Raymond Unwin.

## URBAN CONSOLIDATION IN PRACTICE

Everywhere in Australia during the late 1980s and 1990s infill, brownfield developments and medium-density suburban developments were encouraged, involving apartments, town houses and smaller lot sizes (Hamnett, 2000). In New South Wales, for example, Landcom, the land development arm of the state's planning department, became an active force in promoting demonstration projects of urban consolidation. Expensive apartments in central or other prime locations could find ready buyers, especially in Sydney and Melbourne. Inner brownfield developments in cities such as Adelaide and Perth also did well during the 1990s. Yet there were problems. Even modest attempts at densification in suburban locations – though they were still very low density by Asian and European (even British) standards – could meet fierce resistance and fears of reduced property values. Despite Australia's growing multiculturalism, there remains a deep conservatism that sees low-density suburban living as synonymous with national identity. This will not readily be overcome, though the planning belief in the rectitude of urban consolidation remains robust.

## AUSTRALIAN NEW URBANISM

Given so much common ground between Australian and American suburbs, it was inevitable that the new urbanist philosophy would provide the design underpinning for urban consolidation. It was already known about in Australia by the mid-1990s when high-profile visits by Andres Duany in 1995 and Peter Katz in 1996 greatly strengthened interest in its ideas (Radio National, 1996). By 1996 early initiatives were already under way in Newcastle, New South Wales, and Subiaco in Perth. (The Adelaide MFP, referred to above, also followed many new urbanist principles.) A very large scheme was also under consideration at Mango Hill near Brisbane (finally approved in 1999). Lend Lease, the developer concerned, was the largest in Australia and therefore an important trendsetter. (In passing, it is worth noting that the company was fast becoming a major global operator, and was embarking at the same time on a regional shopping mall and satellite town development at Bluewater in southeast England.)

Lend Lease retained Duany himself to prepare the master plan for the largest of its new urbanist schemes, at St Mary's in western Sydney. Here some 10,000 dwellings were to be developed in four urban villages over a 20-year period. Increasingly, however, it was Australian architects and planners who actually applied new urbanist ideas, strongly supported by official agencies such as Landcom in New South Wales. Within a very short period new urbanism had established itself as the new orthodoxy.

## SUSTAINABLE URBAN DEVELOPMENT

As elsewhere, there were doubts as to whether the new urbanism was fundamentally different from conventional suburban development. By the end of the 1990s, however, real attempts were being made to add an ecological content. On a wider scale, the Sydney Olympic Games in 2000 provided an opportunity to showcase these principles (Chalkley and Essex, 1999). The Olympic site itself, at Homebush Bay, required remediation to remove extensive pollution and incorporated many advanced ecological features (and commendable public transport access). The adjoining Olympic Village at Newington (another Lend Lease development) also included many ecological features and was widely regarded as the Australian showpiece of new urbanism (though it was strikingly different from American examples).

After 1996 active governmental sponsorship of planning innovation had declined sharply, and the Better Cities programme, for example, was scrapped. But the combination of the new ideas that have been circulating since the mid-1980s and the wider international interest in sustainable development is likely to result in more lasting changes. Australia will not suddenly cease to be a suburban, car-dependent nation, but its planners and some of its developers now understand why it might be important to accept some limits.

## JAPAN

Although Japan remained the dominating economic force of east Asia, the last decade of the 20th century saw its economy far more troubled than at any time since 1945

(Allinson, 1997). Growth during the 1980s, though reduced from earlier decades, still comfortably exceeded that of any other advanced economy. By the late 1980s, however, economic optimism gave rise to a dangerous overconfidence, especially evident in the real-estate development industry (*CPIJ Newsletter*, 1993). This speculative bubble burst in 1992 and 1993 and growth plummeted. The malaise, largely reflecting weaknesses of management and in the financial sector, continued throughout the decade. Ever more ambitious attempts to kick-start the economy by major public works programmes (many with urban planning significance) did not succeed. One result was increased unemployment, a major trauma in a country that had traditionally offered jobs for life to loyal employees (Cybriwsky, 1999). Homelessness and other social problems increased, their results evident in streets and public spaces in some parts of Tokyo and other big cities. Longer term issues also lay in waiting (Zetter, 1994). Foremost were demographic changes. By 2000 increasing longevity, declining birth rates and very low immigration gave Japan the most rapidly ageing population of any advanced economy. Together all these problems cast a shadow over Japanese economic self-confidence. There was also a brutal reminder of a more ancient peril: the tectonic restlessness of the national terrain. The Great Hanshin-Awaji earthquake, which struck in January 1995, was the most serious to affect urban Japan since 1923 (*CPIJ Newsletter*, 1995). Combined with mounting international concerns about the global environment, these specifically national issues gave a growing importance to city planning in Japan in the late 20th century.

## WESTERN-STYLE WATERFRONT DEVELOPMENTS

Traditional Japanese interest in all aspects of western planning continued unabated. International examples were routinely studied with a rigour rarely reciprocated in the west. Not surprisingly, therefore, Japanese equivalents of waterfront development began to appear (though slowly) during the 1980s (*CPIJ Newsletter*, 1996a). The example that came closest to the western models was the Tempozan Harbour Village at Osaka, where construction began in 1988 (Breen and Rigby, 1996). Here dilapidated warehouses were replaced by a classic mix of waterfront activities – initially a major aquarium, closely followed by a festival marketplace and IMAX cinema. The overall concept was borrowed directly from Boston and Baltimore, with extensive use of American real-estate and architectural expertise.

The most spectacular of the Japanese waterfront developments currently under way is Minato Mirai 21 (MM21) in Yokohama, which covers some 180 hectares on reclaimed and former railway and dock land (Edgington, 1994). The concept of a mixed but primarily business district was unveiled in the 1980s and small early sections opened in the mid-1980s. But the individual developments that defined its scale and ambition did not appear until the mid-1990s. Like many western examples, there are several spectacular buildings, most notably in the flagship section known as Pacifico Yokohama. Here, for example, can be found Landmark Tower, Japan's tallest building. There is also an international hotel of very striking design, waterfront exhibition halls and a convention centre, the last created in partnership with American developers.

## WATERFRONT TELEPORT DEVELOPMENTS

Larger and more distinctively Japanese waterfront developments are also under way in Tokyo and Osaka (Edgington, 1994). The Tokyo teleport town, on a reclaimed island in Tokyo Bay, forms the most ambitious part of a large-scale waterfront transformation of the whole bay area, where over 40 separate projects were under way by 1997 (TMG, 1994). The teleport itself is envisaged primarily as a high-density business district based on an advanced telecommunications hub, though with a resident population of perhaps 60,000. Initiated in the boom years of the 1980s, and championed by Shun-ichi Suzuki, metropolitan Tokyo's governor from 1979 to 1995, its huge cost was supposed to be funded by developers (Cybriwsky, 1999). The recession stymied these plans, and opposition from voters caused the project to be scaled down. Improved road and rail links since 1993 have, however, encouraged a slow recovery of the prospects for development.

Despite its slightly different name, Technoport Osaka, also centred on reclaimed islands, is similar to the teleport (Edgington, 1994). (The advanced telecommunications aspects of both were spin-offs from the privatisation of the formerly state-owned telephone service, whereby some of the proceeds were invested in innovative urban projects.) At 775 hectares, it covers a larger area than the teleport, but is likely to have similar working and resident populations when completed in 2010. Early sections include the Cosmo Square, which mainly comprises an international trade mart.

## SCIENCE CITY AND TECHNOPOLIS DEVELOPMENTS

The teleport developments formed part of a national economic strategy to provide conditions conducive to future innovation. Osaka, especially, though it remained prosperous, had lost ground to the Tokyo-Yokohama region since 1945. With the strong encouragement of the national government, the Osaka region thus became the host to several major projects that were intended to boost its economy. The new 24-hour Kansai airport, built on a reclaimed island and opened in 1995, was one. However, the first of these projects had been mooted in the late 1970s and begun in earnest during the 1980s. This was Kansai Science City, very similar in its broad concept to the earlier Tsukuba (Castells and Hall, 1994). It was, though, planned on a multicentred basis, and implemented with much stronger private sector participation. The rich historical and cultural legacy of the area also required a more sensitive planning approach.

The 1980s also saw a much more ambitious national policy to launch a technopolis programme throughout the more peripheral regions of Japan. The idea, given legal form in 1983, was partly to provide a real alternative for the major Japanese firms that were investing in overseas branch plants in Taiwan, Korea and elsewhere in Asia. The hope was that technological innovation would be diffused to the lagging regions of Japan before going overseas. (There were potential contradictions between these objectives, since branch plants are often not effective in diffusing technical know-how.) Twenty-six of these technopolises were designated but success, particularly during the lean years of the 1990s, has at best been patchy.

## TECHNOLOGICAL VISIONS

The reality of these technologically led approaches to city planning helped to give a limited credibility to various Japanese dreams about an urban future built on the limitless possibilities of technology. At least before the economic problems of the 1990s, there remained an optimism about its application to cities (Obitsu and Nagase, 1998). One idea from the late 1980s, promoted by the Obayashi construction company, envisioned a gigantic two-level, kilometre-square platform city, with industry and functional activities (many fully automated) on the lower level and living areas above. The same company also recruited the British architect Norman Foster to develop the concept of an 800-metre, 150-storey Millennium Tower. It offered a mix of living, working and cultural and recreational areas, and its own public power and sewage-treatment infrastructure. There were also ideas for open high-rise blocks that provided suburban-style houses and gardens on each level. Although these projects stood little chance of realisation, they showed that 1980s Japan positively encouraged the technological visions that western planners (apart from a few architects) had largely rejected after 1970.

## PARTICIPATORY RECONSTRUCTION

Such fantasies were at odds with the hard realities that faced Japan in the 1990s. The hardest of these was the 1995 earthquake. This devastated the metropolitan area of Kobe and presented a more traditional task of physical reconstruction (*CPIJ Newsletter*, 1995; 1997b). Almost 5,500 people died and nearly 100,000 dwellings were completely destroyed (with a further 80,000 partially destroyed). Major public utilities and infrastructures were also devastated. All this needed (and got) decisive action. There was, though, an important difference to the reconstruction task in 1945. By the late 1990s Kobe's planners had to deal with a much more assertive civil society, which was far less willing to accept top-down planning. The first few weeks after the earthquake saw a rapid evolution from a proposed traditional land-readjustment approach to a more differentiated strategy that allowed active community involvement (Watanabe, 1996).

By coincidence Kobe, under a local 1981 ordinance, was already the Japanese leader in citizen participation, evidently influenced by western (especially American) thought and practice. But despite this promising start bureaucratic attitudes had been slow to change. The earthquake transformed the situation. In 1995 and 1996, for example, Kobe's *machizukuri kyogikai* (community building councils – the active neighbourhood bodies in the participation process) jumped from 11 to 115 in number. There was a corresponding rise in the number of advocate planners working for the councils (and funded by the city). One problem that cannot entirely be addressed by community involvement has, however, been population decline in the worst affected inner city areas. This reflects the fact that much of Kobe's permanent replacement housing, which was very rapidly provided, was not actually in the most devastated areas. In the latter, of course, infrastructure needed to be restored before any new

housing could be built. Though final judgements are premature, it therefore seems
unlikely that former communities can ever be entirely restored, however much participation there is.

## IMPROVING THE SMALL-SCALE URBAN ENVIRONMENT

This participatory dimension was, however, a sign of a widening concern for the 'fine
grain' of Japanese cities (TMG, 1994; *CPIJ Newsletter*, 1997a). In so far as Japanese
planning was admired in the other advanced capitalist countries, it was mainly for its
large-scale technology and infrastructure-based projects (Alden and Abe, 1994). Land-
use regulations and more detailed controls were generally seen as being inferior to
western practice (Hebbert, 1994). There were, however, definite Japanese moves
towards a small-scale planning emphasis during the 1980s and 1990s.

To some extent, the phenomenon was linked with international trends towards
creating liveable cities. Yet it occurred in a way that was distinctively Japanese. It was
a reaction to the insecurities of a country which had for so long changed at an
extraordinary pace. The relentless 'tear down and redevelop' syndrome began to be
challenged, in part by an ageing population that had learnt by experience how fragile
familiar urban scenes were. The 1980s saw the emergence, rather later than in the
west, of a strong movement for conservation. Traditional preindustrial structures had
long been respected. What was significant was that late 19th- and early 20th-century
buildings that reflected the westernisation of Japan were now being retained.

The rather belated trend towards shorter working hours and more leisure time was
another important factor that changed attitudes to cities as places to live and play in
rather than simply work in. Thus older neighbourhoods were increasingly cherished
with pocket parks, play areas and community spaces (Satoh, 1988c; TMG, 1994). In
Tokyo, streams that had long been culverted were opened providing one element in
the growing emphasis on urban landscape. There were a growing numbers of schemes
to enhance major streets and public spaces with stylish paving, lighting and street
furniture.

## DECENTRALISATION AND SUSTAINABLE DEVELOPMENT IN THE 1990s

These new directions of the 1980s blurred seamlessly into the new international
agendas of the 1990s (Watanabe, 1998). Longer term trends towards environmental
concerns were reinforced in the wake of the Brundtland report (1987) and the 1992
Earth Summit in Rio de Janeiro. By the end of the century, Japanese cities were at
least as concerned with urban air- and water-quality as their western equivalents
(Lainevuo, 1998). The small-scale in city planning was further enhanced by the
Decentralisation Act of 1995 (*CPIJ Newsletter*, 2000). This shifted the locus of
decision-making for planning further towards the lowest municipal tier, and further
strengthened the moves towards public participation. By the later 1990s, citizen
activism in Japanese planning was well developed. In some local governments, the
city planning divisions were renamed as the *machizukuri* divisions, signalling the new

emphasis on community involvement. Larger grass roots organisations, particularly the women's Seikatsu-sha Network, played a growing role in promoting citizen master plans for several local areas of Tokyo, beginning in 1994 in the western suburb of Chofu.

## LINKS WITH WESTERN PLANNING

As we have seen, Japanese planners continued their traditional interest in planning developments in the west. Some western architects (including a few with wider urbanistic interests, most prominently Norman Foster and Rem Koolhaas) showed a growing interest in Japanese cities as being the most highly developed of the Asian Pacific Rim. However, it would be wrong to imply that any very deep western understandings of the Japanese approach to city-making followed. The interest was mainly in large-scale projects in the (partly fulfilled) belief that this style of planning would spread to other Asian cities, giving many lucrative architectural opportunities.

From a quite different standpoint, growing Japanese investments in the west during the 1980s encouraged a wider trend towards a Japanisation of manufacturing practice. The admiration for Japanese economic prowess stimulated some western interest in its science and technology policies in relation to spatial planning and development. For example, the two large Japanese teleports became models for other countries (www.worldteleport.org). International lessons were similarly drawn from Kansai, Tsukuba and the technopolis policy (eg Castells and Hall, 1994). The serious problems of the Japanese economy in the 1990s rather weakened the western trend to economic Japanisation. However, some planners in the west continued to be bemused by the huge development projects funded by successive Japanese governments for macro-economic reasons. There were also a few signs of greater interest in the more detailed design and form of Japanese cities (Shelton, 1999).

## LINKS WITH ASIAN PLANNING

More significant was Japan's engagement with its Asian neighbours. During the 1980s these were becoming increasingly important as recipients of Japanese investment and, alongside this, professional expertise. In the planning field, at least, there was a growing desire to avoid the sense that Japanese approaches were being imposed or inappropriately transferred. The emphasis was increasingly, therefore, on two-way links, playing down the notion of a Japanisation of Asian planning. In 1989 the City Planning Institute of Japan (CPIJ) began an annual programme of international symposiums, the first of which was held in Seoul (Watanabe, 1990). From 1994 the meetings were held by rotation in Japan and its two former colonies, Korea and Taiwan, still the countries with which it had the closest economic links. Yet the aspiration of the symposia was more widely international. Proceedings were, remarkably, conducted in English and participants were actively solicited from all Asian countries. From 1989, the CPIJ also began publishing an international newsletter in English. It was partly aimed at a western audience, but it seems likely that its main readership came from within Asia. Meanwhile, Japanese planning education also became more open to foreign, mainly Asian, students (*CPIJ Newsletter*, 1990). In contrast to the American or British approaches, however, the emphasis was on comparing planning traditions rather than treating Japan as a universal model.

# THE DIFFUSION OF URBAN PLANNING INNOVATIONS IN A GLOBAL ERA

## ECONOMIC GLOBALISATION AND PLANNING

Throughout the affluent capitalist world of the 1980s and 1990s, national decision-makers have, then, sought to manage the tensions between the shorter term imperatives of global competitiveness and the longer term desires for sustainability. Everywhere, though, the pursuit of present economic growth has taken precedence over the protection of an uncertain future. The barriers to a global market in goods, investment capital (and increasingly services) have tumbled. Such changes have, in themselves, contributed to a more rapid diffusion of planning ideas and practices. Thus large-scale international real-estate development has become more common, helping to reproduce similar urban forms throughout (and beyond) the affluent world. It has also been associated with a globalisation of design and property services, particularly architecture, engineering and real estate management, but including urban planning. The use of internationally known professionals has become an integral part of assembling the finance to allow such developments to proceed.

## SUSTAINABLE DEVELOPMENT, GLOBALISATION AND URBAN PLANNING

None of the nations of the world's economic superleague have sought unilaterally to escape from the processes of economic globalisation. Even those with the very greenest credentials have not pursued the agenda of sustainable development to the detriment of global competitiveness. Some action has, though, been attempted on a global or multinational front. Yet such initiatives have disappointed progressive and radical opinion because they have not moved faster than the slowest. It has not helped that the United States, the world's most powerful economy and the ringmaster of globalisation, has been amongst the last to accept, and act decisively to achieve, sustainable development.

If national governments have been reluctant to take drastic action on an individual basis for fear of the economic damage that would result, cities have felt these pressures even more strongly. It is at this level, of course, that most urban planners, working for public agencies, have operated, directly interacting with (but not actually being part of) the most globalised sectors of economic activity. Their role has been to promote the global competitiveness of their cities, yet also to try and reconcile this with environmental concerns and social needs. They also have to do this in ways that their political masters (and, to a large extent, national and local electorates) are prepared to support.

## THE COMMUNICATIONS REVOLUTION

Less than ever, however, can these urban planners and their political masters plead ignorance of innovations or best practice elsewhere in the world. Quite apart from contacts with global developers and their professional experts, heightened international competitiveness itself encouraged constant vigilance as to what potential competitors were doing. And the means to be vigilant were close at hand. The trend to rapid improvements in international communications, apparent since before 1900, accelerated exponentially in the last decades of the 20th century. The volume of international travel grew rapidly as air travel became cheaper and, in western continental Europe at least, rail travel became more rapid. The easing of international border formalities was also important. Visa requirements, trade and currency regulations were eased and, in the case of the Schengen countries of the EU, practically all controls were eliminated.

Another hugely important development was the accelerating revolution in information technology. International telecommunications became cheaper, more reliable and capable of handling much higher traffic volumes. Combined with the tremendous improvements in computer hardware and software, this has facilitated the development of the Internet, which by the later 1990s was beginning to play an important role in the international dissemination of urban planning information. Finally, and certainly not least, English completed its long-term ascendancy to became the global language of the affluent world (something which international air travel and the Internet did a great deal to reinforce).

## COMMUNICATIONS AND THE DIFFUSION OF PLANNING KNOWLEDGE

All these developments had fairly direct implications for the diffusion of urban planning knowledge. The astonishingly rapid proliferation of conferences with an international dimension, for example, was hugely important. By such means, ever larger numbers of planning practitioners, researchers and educators were able to collect and disseminate information, and build close and potentially informative international contacts. The indirect effects for international consciousness amongst planners, as gathered knowledge was spread to fellow practitioners and students, was also important. The Internet was increasingly used to spread urban planning information. During the later 1990s major western urban planning agencies created websites (often available in English) that contained much information about their work. In some cases, for example the Parisian IAURIF website, there were links to many other cities (www.iaurif.org). National government agencies, such as the French infrastructure and planning ministry, or international organisations like the International Council for Local Environmental Initiatives (ICLEI), also used the World Wide Web to disseminate examples of good practice (www.iclei.org/egpis).

## INTERNATIONAL ORGANISATIONS IN PLANNING

Many of the conferences and websites that most actively promoted the international spread of planning information were those sponsored by international organisations. The 1980s and 1990s were notable for an increase in their number and activities. Several new bodies were created during these years, such as the Metropolis association of big city governments, founded in Paris in 1984 with the specific concern of securing the orderly development and management of big cities throughout the world (www.metropolis.org). By 2000 68 cities were members. As already implied, environmental concerns also encouraged several international organisations. We have already mentioned the most important, ICLEI. Founded in 1990, it had over 350 local governments throughout the world as members by 2000. Its most important early initiative was originating the Local Agenda 21 programme, which translated global environmental ideals into practical local actions.

International organisations with much wider remits also played an important role in supporting this strengthening global approach. The United Nations Centre for Human Settlements (Habitat) and other UN bodies were extremely important, though mainly in relation to the developing world, a dimension that was, of course, also important in the work of Metropolis and ICLEI (www.unchs.org). More specifically focused on the affluent world (though with an eye on spreading knowledge especially to transitional economies), was the Organization for Economic Cooperation and Development (OECD), created in 1961 (www.oecd.org). Urban planning was, of course, some way from being its core interest. Yet by the 1990s it was helping to spread best practice on issues relating to urban economic development, such as brownfield development and urban management.

## THE EUROPEAN UNION

The most important international body with significance for the diffusion of urban planning ideas and practice within the western world was, however, the European Union (RH Williams, 1996). This has featured in many of the national stories told in this and the previous chapter. Traditionally the EU, under its previous incarnations since the 1956 Treaty of Rome, had been obsessed with rural and agricultural matters to the exclusion of almost everything else. From the late 1980s, however, it began to focus more noticeably on a wider range of matters, including the urban environment. Its direct spending role in this (or indeed any other) field has remained small but the EU is extremely important, firstly in establishing a common discourse and, secondly, in facilitating the spread of information within its member countries.

On the first, the 1990 European Commission's Green Paper on the Urban Environment and its subsequent Expert Group on the Urban Environment were important stages in the emergent discourse (CEC, 1990a; 1990b). In particular, such initiatives helped to embed the compact-city ideal in European urban planning thought and practice. On the second, the various research projects and Internet or print publications it has produced or sponsored have also assisted the information flows. ICLEI's extensive web pages on European Good Practice in Local Sustainability were, for example, supported by the European Commission.

## INTERNATIONALISM IN WESTERN PLANNING DISCOURSE IN 2000

Self-evidently, the EU does not embrace the whole of the affluent capitalist world. Comparable trade groups in other world regions (such as the North American Free Trade Agreement in North America) have certainly not, to date, assumed the EU's wider, nontrade interests. Yet the EU can be seen, perhaps, as the most advanced expression of a trend towards internationalism and shared understanding in urban planning matters within the affluent capitalist world – one that has progressed remarkably since 1980. Truly, the internationalist spirit that helped to create modern urban planning when the 20th century opened was approaching some kind of maturity as the century came to a close.

# CHAPTER 12

# CONCLUSIONS

Urban planners are obliged to live in the present and do the best they can for the future. Yet they take most of their bearings from the past, and the 20th century has left them a mixed legacy. The ideas and practices of modern urban planning have embedded themselves, to varying extents, in the governance of every affluent capitalist nation. In 2000, certainly, belief in the potential of urban planning to improve the quality of human life was no longer as naively cherished as it once had been. A hundred years earlier the pioneers and advocates of urban planning genuinely thought it had the potential to transform the world. Over succeeding years, and especially after 1914, they came to see that there was more to creating the preconditions of human happiness than their original solutions. Urban planning, meaning essentially a regulated urban land market, good public infrastructure and good physical design, was not enough.

Yet, when combined with wider reforms, especially in housing and social welfare, urban planning could provide the physical basis for a better life. This, at least, came to be the assumption shared by all governments in the advanced capitalist world during the years after 1945. As we have seen, it was an assumption of state craft that reached its zenith in the third quarter of the 20th century. Since then, although urban planning was re-energised in the 1990s by the new imperatives of sustainable development, its salience has diminished. Certainly, it has become a routine function of city governments. Almost invariably, though, it now has less impact on the course of urban development than it had in the quarter-century after 1945.

This is adequate as a bald summary of 20th-century planning history, but it will be clear that it leaves much unsaid. As we have seen, urban planning has actually followed significantly different national courses within the affluent capitalist world. There has been a common international discourse, but with important variations in emphasis. Nor have the dynamics of how planning has changed and spread been a single uniform narrative. This final chapter brings together the major themes in the innovation and diffusion of urban planning in the affluent capitalist world over the last century. It also offers some thoughts about the century to come.

## THE ROOTS OF INNOVATION

### INDIVIDUAL CREATIVITY

Innovations begin, of course, with creative individuals. The vast majority of people in any activity are content to follow established patterns. A few, though, will make a difference and leave behind them something that was not there before. At this point, we should remind ourselves of the classic distinction between *invention*, meaning the generation of new concepts, and *innovation*, meaning their practical application. These two aspects of creativity have often been combined in urban planning, but the underlying distinction remains important. Broader economic, social and political circumstances must always play a significant part in establishing conditions conducive to urban planning innovation. But the requirements of the pure inventor might be very modest indeed, requiring no more than a small amount of leisure time, a vivid and reasonably methodical imagination and some problem on which it can work. This can give an apparently random quality to the individual creativity from which modern urban planning developed. There was, for example, no larger reason why an obscure London shorthand reporter and stenographer should have invented the garden city.

## THE CRITICAL CLUSTER OF INNOVATIONS

If we step back a little, however, certain patterns begin to emerge. The later 19th and the early 20th centuries saw many highly significant innovations, almost all of them directly identified, at least in historical narrative, with specific creative individuals. These included entirely practical figures such as Haussmann, a pure innovator, who resisted all temptation to conceptual exposition but still exerted a seminal influence. They also included a few visionaries, such as Howard, who may be seen as pure inventors. Most, however, such as Cerdà, Sitte, Stübben, Geddes, Unwin, Burnham, Garnier and Le Corbusier, spanned both empirical and theoretical realms. In many cases, lesser known figures were thinking along similar lines at roughly the same time. If Sitte had died before writing his book, then Buls's similar ideas would probably have become better known. Similarly, Poëte can be seen as a partial substitute for Geddes. Several possible substitutes for Le Corbusier can be suggested. The international history of urban planning would obviously not have followed exactly the same course without the names we remember, but its conceptual dimensions would not have been radically different.

## INDIVIDUAL CREATIVITY AFTER THE FORMATIVE PERIOD

No other period ever again experienced a chronological clustering of major innovations of comparable significance. Later ones usually took the form of refinements, of varying significance, of previous ideas. Of course, specific creative individuals sometimes stood out, such as van Eesteren, Abercrombie, Markelius, Gruen, Buchanan, Kleihues and Hall. In general, though, the 'heroic' narrative which tells only of lone inventors, and is often dubious even in the formative period of modern urban planning, has become progressively less appropriate. The creative individuals have still been there, but usually working in a more collective context, bouncing their own ideas around with others. There might still perhaps be a figurehead for the creative process, capable of lucid expression, but only rarely can such figures claim sole responsibility.

## REFORMIST AND PROFESSIONAL MILIEUS

This last observation broadens the understanding of creativity to embrace the milieus within which individual inventiveness was located. Even from the early (if not quite the earliest) stages, there were reformist and professional networks that provided a rich substrate on which individual creativity was able to feed and to which it contributed. At first, the networks were comparatively unfocused. The emergent ideas of urban planning were only a minor theme amongst many concerns of existing organisations such as the Musée Social, the Land Nationalisation Society, the Verband Deutscher Architekten und Ingenieurvereine and the Royal Institute of British Architects.

Yet, as we have seen, everywhere new organisations came into being – the Garden City Association (and its many equivalents in other countries), the Société Française des Urbanistes or the American City Planning Institute. While most have been national in form, international organisations such as the International Federation of Housing and Planning, the Congrès Internationaux d'Architecture Moderne or, more recently, the International Council for Local Environmental Initiatives, have exerted important influences. It has been within the increasingly formal settings provided by all these new organisations that urban planning discourse has developed, both in face-to-face encounters and through a growing volume of published material.

## INNOVATION AND THE ORGANISATIONAL NETWORKS OF URBAN PLANNING

The exact contribution of these networks to the innovation process has been subtle. Overall, there has certainly been a fairly direct correlation between their national strength, and the degree of adherence to them, and the extent of successful innovation in urban planning. In part, this is because individual inventors, however creative, need at the very least a sounding board for their efforts. Here we can point to the abject failure of Cerdà's extraordinary and early creativity, which predated any effective urban reformist networks in Spain. (There is a contrast here with the later Spanish innovator, Soria, who clearly understood the need to set new ideas into an organisational framework.)

Yet there was also a downside. The creation of specific organisations, particularly those of a more professional nature, defined urban planning as an area of knowledge. This concentrated, but also tended to constrain, the process of innovation more in the direction of technical refinement. It is interesting to speculate how the equivalent of a Howard or a Le Corbusier might today be received in such circles. Such radically new approaches as have appeared in recent years have come largely from outside the formal organisations that comprise the urban planning movement. It has been noticeable, for example, that the new directions planning has taken since the later 1980s, into sustainable urban development, drew their original momentum largely from the green movement. An increasingly large-scale urban development industry has generated important new forms of ordering urban space, with great influence for mainstream urban planning.

# The State and Planning Innovation

The state has been even more critical than individual creativity or organisational networks for the innovation process within western societies. As urban planning moved from the realm of autonomous reformist thought and action into actual urban governmental policy, the state, in various guises, began to become an important setting for planning innovation. The timing of this transition varied, of course, between different countries. It also varied between the different levels of government, so that some city authorities, such as those in Paris, Frankfurt or Birmingham, acquired early reputations as innovators. This tendency was well established by the 1930s, for example in Unwin's work on the planning of Greater London or van Eesteren and van Lohuizen's work on the extension of Amsterdam. After 1945, however, the trend had become a universal one. All levels of government in all countries became the principal arenas of planning action and, to a significant extent, of planning thought and innovation.

# The Preconditions of Innovative Government

What, then, have been the preconditions conducive to innovation in urban planning within a governmental framework? Obviously the nature of political control must always be important because it does much to shape the climate within which urban planning operates. There has to be, at the very least, passive political support for innovation. Often, this has meant political acceptance that a novel situation exists which depends upon finding innovative solutions. The reconstruction of destroyed cities or the building of entirely new settlements have been obvious examples, found in most western countries. Another was the widespread governmental recognition of the need to reconcile mass use of the car with urban planning. This triggered many important innovations, particularly in the wake of the British government's *Traffic in Towns* report. The politically contrived circumstances associated with a special, one-off spectacle in an individual city have also often been conducive to urban planning innovation. Two of the best known, amongst many other examples, were the 1893 World's Columbian Exposition in Chicago and the 1992 Barcelona Olympics.

# Transcending the Routine

It is also noticeable that innovation has tended to be greater in parts of government that stand outside the day-to-day administration of routine functions. Special official inquiries with a remit to consider new thinking, such as that headed by Buchanan, are the most obvious examples. But more modest versions of the same tendency litter the 20th-century history of urban planning innovation. Always the avoidance or minimisation of interests committed to the status quo has been an important prerequisite. It has been almost unknown, for example, for radical metropolitan plans (such as those for London in 1944 or Paris in 1965) to have been produced by local governments. Almost invariably some agency that is able, at least partially, to transcend existing positions has been necessary. Sometimes this has also meant insulation from close public accountability, but this is not always the case. The 1970s, for example, everywhere saw an upsurge of innovation built upon unusually close encounters between planner and planned.

## Public and private innovation

In general, recent Anglo-American rhetoric notwithstanding, governments obsessed with restricting their spending have not usually been good innovators. This may, though, sometimes be offset if, by this means, innovative private developers are given more freedom. Certainly, it can be argued that recent public-private partnership approaches, themselves an important innovation, have partly reflected a desire throughout all western countries to restrict state expenditure. In some cases, such as Baltimore Harbor, these arrangements have generated internationally important innovations. There, however, developer involvement certainly did not remove the need for very heavy city expenditure. Other partnership approaches associated with urban planning innovation, for example Euralille or some, at least, of the Dutch VINEX expansion areas, also show no abdication of the governmental role. Even London Docklands, the urban planning showpiece of Thatcherism, has absorbed huge quantities of public money.

## Specific mechanisms to promote innovation

Finally, we can note the specific devices some governments have used in more deliberate ways to foster urban planning innovation. Competitions, where planning and design rather than financial considerations have been the priority, remain very important. Even by 1900, it was clear that Germanic planning thought and practice had benefited a great deal from what was already a well-developed tradition of extension competitions. After 1900, French *urbanisme* was similarly enhanced by energetic participation in competitions throughout the world, offsetting what were rather dismal domestic opportunities for urban planning endeavour.

Recent years have seen the popularity of competitions soar, as cities have sought new ways to signal their international credentials with outstanding urban projects. One of the most interesting has been the German IBA tradition. This has involved the periodic identification of locations where many innovative developments of high design quality are deliberately fostered. Through both open competitions and direct invitations, architects, planners and related professionals from around the world have thus been drawn into what has often been a highly creative context. Governments of all western countries have, from time to time, encouraged demonstration projects of various kinds, though none seem to have been quite as systematic in promoting innovation as the IBA approach.

## Global power and planning innovation

Over and above the more specific factors that have a bearing on the innovation process there is the more general role of larger economic and geopolitical factors.

Have these determined, to any extent, the propensity to innovate in urban planning? The evidence is mixed. From the outset it was the four major nations of the capitalist world that led in the development of urban planning. All were large nations, with large cities, and by 1900 they were the hubs of major international flows of trade and investment and possessed military strength commensurate with their economic signi-ficance. They also presided over large overseas empires (or, in the case of the United States, exerted a growing international hegemony that stopped short of formal empire). Together, they represented the most complex and highly developed urban systems which then existed. Modern urban planning can therefore be seen, in some ways, as an activity generated to manage some of the tensions within these urban systems.

Of course, the 'big four' were not the only inventors of modern planning. The declining international powers Spain and Austria-Hungary contributed, as we have noted, to its conceptual repertoire. Yet their experiences also seem, in some ways, to confirm the importance of structural factors in understanding the distinction between individual inventiveness and innovation in a wider sense. Thus, the advanced thinking of some individuals in 19th-century Spain was certainly not matched by any wider national achievement. Austrian urban planning ideas, meanwhile, benefited because they quickly became part of German planning discourse.

## PROBLEMS WITH A STRUCTURAL EXPLANATION

During the course of the 20th century, the 'big four' have continued to be at, or near, the forefront of western planning discourse. Germany's standing has wavered, broadly in line with its troubled history, so its urban planning reputation fell sharply in the wake of its post-1945 defeat and shame. Yet it has certainly not been possible to 'read off' the contributions of different nations to urban planning in terms of their relative standing in the international pecking order. Over much of the 20th century Germany, Britain and France would probably show the closest correlation. But Japan, for example, has not (yet?) developed an innovative urban planning tradition that reflects its position as the world's second largest economy. Nor has the United States, always a powerful source of ideas about cities and, to a lesser extent, urban planning, ever assumed quite the dominating influence on international planning discourse that its superpower status would lead us to expect. Moreover, as we have seen, several smaller nations, particularly the Netherlands and the Nordic countries, have contributed much more than their size and importance would suggest. They benefited by the long eclipse of Germany during the Nazi period and its aftermath, but this certainly does not provide a complete understanding of their prominence.

## SUMMARISING INNOVATION

The explanation of innovation cannot, therefore, be found in any one of the major 'compartments' we have considered. Larger structural considerations certainly estab-lish, in general terms, some important and occasionally very powerful preconditions. But they have not determined the pattern of urban planning innovation in any very precise fashion. The specific institutional climate and, outside the state, the vigour of reformist and professional networks have always exerted a very large, and relatively autonomous, influence. Not least, of course, there remains the inventiveness of individuals. The most we can safely conclude is that their efforts have been much more likely to become successful innovations where wider circumstances have generated some need for them, and created a broadly sympathetic context for their reception. Even this, however, could be partly contradicted because of the speed at which promising new ideas were able to spread, provided they crossed the threshold of initial awareness.

## SOURCES AND PATTERNS OF DIFFUSION

### THE RISE OF GLOBAL INFORMATION

Even before the 20th century began, the steamship, the railway, the mechanised printing press and the postal service had transformed the international diffusion of information. Over the century they have given way to the telephone, the jet airliner, facsimile transmission, global television channels and the Internet. The general effect has been a speeding up of the flows of all kinds of information. There has also been a drastic reduction in the number of languages used in international communications. Wherever ideas originated, by 2000 it was increasingly likely that they would be expressed in English. If not, there was a strong likelihood that an English version would exist alongside the original. In 1900, French and German had been major international languages, widely used in the formation and spread of western planning discourse in the early part of the 20th century. Together with a few other western languages, such as Spanish and Swedish, both retain a 'regional' international significance. But no language remotely approaches the importance of English, whose success reflects the near consecutive global hegemonies of Britain until the early 20th century and, far more importantly, the United States since 1945. Today English, quite simply, is the language of globalisation.

### CONSTRAINTS ON INTERNATIONAL INFORMATION FLOWS

Not all the 20th-century changes have eased international communications, however. Even as transport improvements made international travel more practical, national governments introduced their own limitations, as passports, visas and currency controls replaced the older, largely informal, pattern after 1918. Wars also fractured, and caused longer term damage to, previous international linkages, especially the relationship of Germany to other western nations. Yet they also allowed more intense linkages to emerge amongst the western allies. Ultimately, though, it was the American-guaranteed reconstruction of western Europe and Japan after 1945 (and the equivalent role of the Soviet Union in eastern Europe) that created the west in its modern form, within which urban planning (and, of course, much other) information has flowed relatively freely.

## MAJOR ISSUES IN THE DIFFUSION OF URBAN PLANNING

Such considerations have obviously had a profound influence on the overall volume and dominant spatial patterns of international information flows, including those of urban planning. In addition, this specific field has benefited from the outset from its substantially visual nature, with illustrations, coloured plans, lantern slides, exhibitions and visits reducing dependence on language. Yet such observations about the means of transfer take us only part of the way to understanding the international diffusion of urban planning ideas and practice. Drawing together the many examples examined in this book, three key issues stand out. These are the active mechanisms of transfer; the degree of congruence between international flows of urban planning information and the larger economic, political and cultural relationships between the different national parties; and the relationship between international diffusion and innovation. These issues lead us to the defining elements of international diffusion and are critical to understanding the different types of diffusion we have identified.

## SYNTHETIC BORROWING

One of the most common types of diffusion, particularly amongst larger western countries, has been what can be called synthetic borrowing. This has involved urban planners in one country drawing lessons from the planning ideas and practices of other countries. Rather than simply copying them, however, they are 'unpacked' and disassembled into their constituent elements. Appropriate parts are then synthesised, together with other borrowings and indigenously generated elements, to make something new and distinctive. It is, in other words, a combination of diffusion and innovation. The spread of the garden city in many larger western countries was perhaps the fullest example of this kind of borrowing process. A more recent, and more specific, example would be the Dutch *woonerf* concept, itself derived in part from Buchanan's concept of the environmental area, and internationally influential in the development of traffic calming and home zones in Germany and other parts of northwest continental Europe.

Although the process of synthesis occurs to some extent unconsciously, it is not accidental and there are certain important preconditions. The most basic is that there has to be a relatively well-developed urban planning movement in the receiving country. This usually means reformist and professional networks, existing autonomously and within government. These urban planning milieus have the capacity to 'unpack' what are often complex packages of ideas and practices, and integrate them into planning discourse in a disassembled (sometimes also a dissembled) fashion. In turn, these circumstances tend to arise in the largest and most highly developed countries, that have no strong dependence on, or deference to, the one from which the lessons are being drawn. More typically, a tradition of indigenous innovation would coexist with a wide range of international contacts, allowing a rich pool of planning concepts to be created. In other words, the urban planners and decision-makers in the receiving country are the active agents in diffusion and exert a high degree of discretion over what is received and applied.

## SELECTIVE BORROWING

A slightly different situation was one where no identifiable innovation resulted from the borrowed ideas or practices. Although this could arise even in otherwise innovative countries, it was more characteristic of smaller western nations where the urban planning movement was both less highly developed and less innovatory. Generally the engagement with the imported planning models would be more shallow, with less 'unpacking'. The typical selective borrower would also show some cultural or technical deference to the countries from which lessons were being drawn. This deference might be reflected in, for example, linguistic affinity, tradition of technical training or a wider tendency to emulate innovations from the source countries. Belgium was a case in point, borrowing initially from France, Britain and Germany (and later the Netherlands). The smaller Nordic countries also showed similar tendencies. Most of them usually borrowed selectively, mainly from Anglo-American and German influences. Often such external lessons were drawn first in Sweden, which had the most innovative Nordic planning tradition for much of the 20th century. Its neighbours often received these ideas and practices through a Swedish filter.

## UNDILUTED BORROWING

Selective borrowing involved some degree of discretion being exercised in the borrowing process. In contrast, the final type of diffusion by borrowing involved a very uncritical receiving of external planning ideas and practices. Episodes of this form of borrowing could be occasionally found in otherwise innovatory or selective planning traditions. One thinks here of the way in which certain specific forms have occasionally appeared throughout the world in near identical form (for example, in the late 20th-century, Baltimore-style waterfront development). Yet this kind of borrowing was more characteristic of countries with rather undeveloped indigenous urban planning movements and without a tradition of significant home-grown innovation. Generally, the number of international contacts were much fewer than amongst countries that usually borrowed selectively or synthetically. Relations with the exporting nations would usually be strongly deferential, often with other clear signs of economic or geopolitical dependence. The borrowed aspects of planning would typically extend down to many detailed aspects, and often show a limited grasp of the underlying theory or concepts.

The most characteristic of the undiluted borrowers we have considered were Canada, Australia and Japan in the early to mid-20th century. In the first two, many detailed aspects of British and later American planning were directly borrowed, often with the direct participation of planners from the originating countries. Japan relied much more on indigenous agents to implement borrowed lessons, and also borrowed from all major western traditions. Even so, fairly direct copying was often apparent, at least until the 1950s, with a relatively slow synthesis of the imported ideas into a distinctive national approach. It follows from the experiences of all these countries that a heavy reliance on uncritical borrowing, especially from one or a small number of sources, would produce a clearly derivative planning tradition.

## Diffusion by imposition

Even in the most uncritical of borrowers, however, control of the process was firmly based in the receiving country. Fundamentally different were the types of diffusion that may be termed imposition, where the process was, to varying extents, controlled by the originator of the planning models. In most cases this situation arose in a colonial context, so it has not been a common feature within the countries examined in this book. On the contrary, many of these were themselves colonisers, imposing their own versions of planning in other continents. Of the exceptions, the white settler colonies of Australia became a self-governing nation at the start of the 20th century. Similarly Finland, although part of the Russian Empire until the 1917 revolution, had enjoyed a high degree of autonomy in urban planning matters.

## Authoritarian imposition

The most typical kinds of diffusion by imposition within the affluent capitalist world came in the wake of defeat in war. Where the winners seized or occupied the territory of the defeated power a new planning regime would, in some degree, be imposed. The exact nature of the imposition varied. Nazi Germany, for example, directly incorporated parts of adjoining countries into the German Reich in 1939 and 1940 and imposed a direct and authoritarian planning regime. The planners were invariably drawn from the winning side. Their plans would usually fulfil goals of the government of the victorious nation, while the property and democratic rights of the defeated peoples were routinely overridden. In extreme cases, deportations and the introduction of new settlers could change the ethnic composition of areas. In such circumstances, the imposed planning models might well be purer expressions of ideals that could only be achieved in a compromised form within the homeland of the victorious power.

## Negotiated and contested imposition

There were, of course, degrees of imposition. Western countries that were conquered but not directly annexed were left some degree of autonomy in urban planning matters, within certain limits. The imposition was, in other words, subject to some degree of negotiation and could sometimes be contested, albeit surreptitiously. (Wartime work on the replanning of Rotterdam was a case in point.) When the tables were turned after 1945, the western powers occupying Germany instituted a strict, externally imposed planning regime at the outset (particularly in the French zone). Yet, providing a basically democratic and capitalist framework was followed, they soon left most urban planning matters to the Germans themselves. A similar approach was followed in the other countries occupied by western powers, such as Japan.

Even lighter was the touch of the liberators in parts of western Europe other than Germany. Here American Marshall Aid bankrolled the reconstruction of capitalist democracy, but made no specific demands as to preferred forms of urban planning. Overall, therefore, diffusion by external imposition, especially the strictest kind, has been a rarity within western countries. In general, these nations have imposed their planning on the peoples of their empires, rather than their immediate neighbours. Eastern Europe, of course, followed a very different path, not directly examined in this book, after 1945. Even in the eastern zone of Germany, though, where the Soviet hand was heaviest, planning by German Communists who had been 'correctly' instructed in Moscow was preferred to direct Russian imposition.

## CONSENSUAL IMPOSITION

In complete contrast to the impositions that followed the wars of the first half of the 20th century, a rather different, partly rhetorical form of imposition by consent began to appear in its closing years. This arose where national governments in advanced capitalist countries voluntarily surrendered a little of their sovereignty in development patterns to some supranational authority or agreement. The most formalised example was the European Union seeking to impose common policy approaches on its member governments. Something of the same broad aspiration underlay the world environmental summits, beginning at Rio de Janeiro in 1992, if in a rather more dilute fashion (not least because of the less than wholehearted commitment of the United States). We should not, though, exaggerate the impacts of even the most successful of these moves, especially in relation to urban planning. Even in the EU, by 2000, they represented only a limited acceptance of fairly broad rhetorical principles about how urban development should proceed. (The EU was, of course, more significant in other policy areas, particularly agriculture.) What was more important, however, was that many of the moves towards supranational governance helped to promote a common planning discourse in relation to sustainable urban development and the compact city.

## A PREMATURE PLANNING HISTORY OF THE 21ST CENTURY

What, then, does the future hold for urban planning in the affluent capitalist world? The ending of one century and the starting of another does not, of itself, represent any momentous or meaningful historical transition. Nor is this any different when the new century also opens a new millennium. Yet these pivotal moments in our calibration of time acquire a certain significance because they encourage us to consider our destiny. They become times to take stock of what has gone before, to reflect on the processes and movements that have shaped our lives and, not least, to speculate on what is to come. Such tendencies are especially strong in the field of urban planning, in whose fertile soil during the 20th century has grown such an abundance of schemes and visions promising improvement in the way we live together in cities.

## 1900 AND 2000: A BALANCE SHEET

Of the four major western planning traditions that of Germany has consistently shown the strongest commitment, a continuity that can be traced back into the 19th century. The United States has, however, been at the other end of the spectrum: its dalliance with strong planning during the 1930s and 1940s proved very short-lived. Britain did not readily relinquish its late 19th-century traditions of regulating but not shaping urban development. Yet it evolved a relatively strong 20th-century urban planning tradition, only to marginalise it more completely than any other European country in the last quarter of the century. Finally France, despite important developments in the 19th century, was slower to acknowledge the new forms of urban planning in the early 20th century, though it recovered to become one of the stronger planning traditions after 1945.

Looking beyond the big four of 20th-century planning history, we see several smaller countries which have developed robust and disproportionately influential planning traditions. Foremost amongst these are the Netherlands and the Nordic countries which, throughout the 20th century, have shown strong governmental commitment to urban planning. (We could add here Switzerland and Austria, although these countries have figured only occasionally in the foregoing pages.) The patterns of southern Europe have been less consistent. There has been no shortage of high aspirations and moments of significant achievement, but these have coexisted with a tradition of generally laxer regulation than has been usual further north. Outside Europe, Canada and Australia have broadly followed the Anglo-American planning tradition, though with increasing, and significant, variations. Finally, Japan has borrowed extensively from all the major western ones to create a distinctive planning tradition that combines exceptionally strong commitment to large-scale infrastructural provision with rather weak mechanisms of detailed control.

## CONTINUITIES

The varying extents of national political commitment to urban planning in 2000 showed some interesting similarities to earlier patterns that go back to 1900, or even before. It was, for example, still possible to discern the traditionally much stronger Anglo-American belief in relatively unregulated free enterprise capitalism. Championed by Britain in the 19th century, and revisited by it in the late 20th, this attitude has dominated the thinking of American political leaders throughout the 20th century. It has also been an important moderating influence on governmental commitment to urban planning in other Anglophone countries. By contrast, Germany, France and many of the other countries of the European continent and Scandinavia betrayed definite overtones of an intrinsic belief in greater state initiative, control and regulation that echoed earlier, predemocratic, preindustrial phases of planning. In Japan, too, the debt owed by today's planners to the modernisers of the Meiji era remains clear. Throughout the affluent capitalist world, then, the new ideas and policies of 20th-century urban planning followed, at least to a large extent, broad national templates of statecraft that were already in place.

## ANOTHER AMERICAN CENTURY?

These continuities, which have already lasted for more than a century, are not readily going to disappear. If anything, the start of the 21st century suggests a United States that is even less willing to be drawn into commitments on sustainable development than it was in the late 20th century. Despite a small minority of ardent environmentalists (mainly on the Pacific coast) faith in uncontrolled market processes is being reasserted with a vengeance under the George W Bush presidency. And, of course, the policies of the United States, the world's only economic and military superpower, always have global significance. In the 1990s America led the pressure for world agreements to create a truly global market. As these agreements on trade and services are pressed, potentially large impacts for urban planning can be foreseen as national governments are obliged to relax planning controls which could be construed as restrictive. One impact, as retailing becomes increasingly globalised, might well be to force a relaxation of the planning constraints that, in most western countries outside North America, currently moderate or inhibit the trend to very large-scale, edge-of-city, car-based retailing. One wonders how far environmental pressures for compact, sustainable cities can withstand this countervailing manifestation of supranational governance.

## OTHER WESTERN LEADERS?

The countries of the EU are distinctly less enthusiastic about any strengthening of a global market approach over one based on sustainability. One wonders, however, whether, on this matter, it has sufficient political coherence and strength to press any line that is distinctively different to that of the United States. The signs are not good. In the foreseeable future, Europe's rather puny political energies (compared to the those of the United States) will probably be fully stretched by internal reform, the establishment of a single currency and enlargement. Although Europe, especially Germany and its continental and Nordic neighbours, can be seen as a leader in sustainable urban planning practice, the concept has a lower priority elsewhere. Britain, especially, clings to a semi-American agenda even as it tries to move towards its EU partners. Despite some promising aspects, Australia and Canada are even closer to the American line and, in any case, too small to give real global leadership. Japan could, but is too preoccupied with its own economic travails to assert a different line.

## THE ECLIPSE OF THE WEST?

It is obviously premature to assume that these early patterns will set a trend for the rest of the century. Short-term shocks can trigger longer term changes. Thus the appalling terrorist atrocities in New York in September 2001, which destroyed the World Trade Center and killed several thousand people, have, quite suddenly, made President Bush far more aware of his country's need for friends throughout the world. Whether this will herald any wider American commitments on issues such as the environment and development aid remains to be seen. But the possibility cannot be discounted (and would be widely welcomed).

Behind this specific point, though, lies a larger question: if the events of a few hours can shake the self-confidence of the world's only global superpower (and, significantly for our area of concern, topple one of its most potent urban symbols) surely much bigger changes are feasible by 2100? We may be on the brink of a new age of uncertainty. The balance of world economic and political power may shift. Important long-term demographic changes such as ageing populations may weaken the west, particularly if national opposition to mass immigration continues at current levels. A century on from now, when we are all dead, the world may look very different. Where then will stand the great inchoate cities of today's emergent economies – Shanghai, São Paulo, Mexico City, Mumbai, Jakarta, Lagos, Cairo? Already we can discern signs of planning innovation outside the west, bringing a neat and trim order to smaller cities such as Singapore or Curitiba. Perhaps such places are harbingers of a new wave of planning innovation, whose message will duly diffuse to what are at present intractable megacities, as the economic balance of the world shifts. The west too will learn from, and may even be overshadowed by, these new ascendants.

Ultimately, the wise historian should leave speculation about future grand narratives to others with larger imaginations. The most that can be said for certain is that we will continue to beat on towards an uncertain future but will, like boats against the current, be borne back ceaselessly into the past.

# BIBLIOGRAPHY

## A GENERAL NOTE ON SOURCES

This list consists of conventionally published works actually cited in the text, while including also the full citation of edited volumes within which part works directly cited are contained. Note that the in-text citations are largely intended as guidance on where readers of English can find further information. There is also a very large non-English literature which can only be alluded to here. Most of the non-English language material that is listed should be capable of being used, at least to some degree, by readers of English. Or at least it is important that English readers are aware of its existence.

Readers should also note that some of the source material used in researching this book is not cited here. In particular, very few actual plans are cited, nor standard statistical sources, nor background material drawn in particular from newspapers, nor material of a more ephemeral nature. Very many individuals also went to a great deal of trouble to explain aspects of the history and recent development of their country's urban planning. I have also been fortunate to be able to visit a very large number of the places referred to, enabling me to draw my own conclusions. If any readers require further information about sources, they are welcome to contact me at the School of Planning, Oxford Brookes University, Headington, Oxford OX3 OBP, UK <svward@brookes.ac.uk>.

Aalen, FHA 1992. English origins, in SV Ward (ed), *The Garden City: Past, Present and Future*, pp 28–51, London: Spon.

Aario, L 1986. The original garden cities in England and the garden city ideal in Finland, *Fennia*, vol 164, no 2, pp 157–209.

Abercrombie, P 1945. *The Greater London Plan 1944*, London: HMSO.

Adams, T 1929. The origin of the term 'town planning' in England, *Journal of the Town Planning Institute*, vol XV, no 11, pp 310–11.

Albers, G 1980. Town planning in Germany: change and continuity under conditions of political turbulence, in G E Cherry (ed), *Shaping an Urban World*, pp 145–160, London: Mansell.

Albers, G 1997. *Zur Entwicklung der Stadtplanung in Europa: Begegnungen, Einflusse, Verflechtungen*, Wiesbaden: Vieweg.

Albrecht, D (ed) 1995. *World War II and the American Dream: How Wartime Building Changed a Nation*, Washington DC/Cambridge MA: National Building Museum/MIT Press.

Alden, JD and Abe, H 1994. Some strengths and weaknesses of Japanese urban planning, in P Shapira, I Masser and DW Edgington (eds), *Planning for Cities and Regions in Japan* (a *Town Planning Review* special study), pp 12–24, Liverpool University Press.

Aldridge, HR 1915. *The Case for Town Planning: A Practical Manual for the Use of Councillors, Officers and Others Engaged in the Preparation of Town Planning Schemes*, London: National Housing and Town Planning Council.

Aldridge, M 1979. *British New Towns: A Programme Without a Policy*, London: Routledge and Kegan Paul.

Alexander, I 2000. The post-war city, in S Hamnett and R Freestone (eds), *The Australian Metropolis: A Planning History*, pp 98–112, London: Spon.

Allinson, GD 1997. *Japan's Postwar History*, Ithaca: Cornell University Press.

Altshuler, AA 1983. The intercity freeway, in DA Krueckeberg (ed), *An Introduction to Planning History in the United States*, pp 190–234, New Brunswick NJ: Center for Urban Policy Research.

Ambrose, P 1986. *Whatever Happened to Planning?*, London: Methuen.

Anderson, GM and Marr, W 1987. Immigration and social policy, in SA Yelaja (ed), *Canadian Social Policy* (second edition), pp 88–114, Waterloo: Wilfred Laurier University Press.

Anderson, C, Kaltenhalter, K and Luthardt, W (eds) 1993. *The Domestic Politics of German Unification*, Boulder: Lynne Rienner.

Andersson, M 1998. *Stockholm's Annual Rings: A Glimpse into the Development of the City*, Stockholm: Stockholmia Förlag.

Architecture et Maîtres d'Ouvrage (ed) 2000. *Les Bâtisseurs de la Modernité 1940–1945*, Paris: Le Moniteur.

Archives Nationales (ed) 1991. *Reconstruction et Modernisation: La France après les Ruines 1918 . . . 1945 . . .*, Paris: Archives Nationales.

Arnold, JL 1983. Greenbelt, Maryland, *Built Environment*, vol 9, nos 3 and 4, pp 198–209.

Artibise, AFJ and Stelter, G 1981. Conservation planning and urban planning: the Canadian Commission of Conservation in historical perspective, in R Kain (ed), *Planning for Conservation*, pp 17–36, London: Mansell.

Ascher, F 1997. The French metropolitan region: the new schéma directeur of the Ile-de-France region, in K Bosma and H Hellinga (eds), *Mastering the City: North-European City Planning 1900–2000* (2 volumes), vol 1, pp 48–55, Rotterdam: NAI Publishers/EFL Publications.

Ashton, NAW 1969. *The City of Stockholm and its Region*, Sydney: New South Wales Planning Commission.

Ashton, P 1993. *The Accidental City: Planning Sydney Since 1788*, Sydney: Hale and Iremonger.

Ashworth, W 1954. *The Genesis of Modern British Town Planning: A Study in Economic and Social History of the Nineteenth and Twentieth Centuries*, London: Routledge and Kegan Paul.

Åström, K 1967. *City Planning in Sweden*, Stockholm: The Swedish Institute.

Åström, SE 1979. Town planning in imperial Helsingfors 1810–1910, in I Hammarström and T Hall (eds), *Stockholm – Growth and Transformation of a City*, pp 59–68, Stockholm: Swedish Council for Building Research.

Aubry P and Bergeron, R 1994. Canada's urban planning contributions to developing countries, *Plan Canada Special Edition* (July), pp 160–8.

*Australian Planner, The* 1988; guest editors Robert Freestone and Alan Hutchins. Planning History Special Issue, vol 26, no 3 (September).

Bachofen, C and Picheral, JB nd. Dunkerque-Neptune: Transformation des Docks en Coeur de Ville, located at <www.urbanisme.equipement.gouv.fr/cdu/>

Bacon, EN 1974. *Design of Cities*, New York: Viking.

Banerjee, T and Southworth, M 1994. Kevin Lynch: his life and work, in DA Krueckeberg (ed), *The American Planner: Biographies and Recollections* (second edition), New Brunswick NJ: Center for Urban Policy Research, pp 439–68.

Banik-Schweitzer, R 1999. Urban visions, plans, and projects, 1890–1937, in E Blau and M Platzer (eds), *Shaping the Great City: Modern Architecture in Central Europe, 1890–1937*, pp 58–72, Munich: Prestel.

Bannon, MJ 1989. Irish planning from 1921–1945, in MJ Bannon (ed), *Planning: The Irish Experience 1920–1988*, pp 13–70, Dublin: Wolfhound Press.

Bannon, MJ (ed) 1989. *Planning: The Irish Experience 1920–1988*, Dublin: Wolfhound Press.

Barjot, D 1991. Les Entreprises du Bâtiment et des Travaux Publics et la Reconstruction (1918–1945), in Archives Nationales (ed), *op cit*, pp 231–44.

Barker, JM (ed) 1997. *Old Institutions – New Images*, Perth: John Curtin International Institute, Curtin University of Technology.

Barlow Commission (Royal Commission on the Distribution of the Industrial Population) 1940. *Report* (Cmd 6153), London: HMSO.

Barnekov, T, Boyle, R and Rich, M 1989. *Privatism and Urban Policy in Britain and the United States*, Oxford University Press.

Barnes, TJ, Edgington, DW, Denike, KG and McGee, TG 1992. Vancouver, the province and the Pacific rim, in G Wynn and T Oke (eds), *Vancouver and Its Region*, pp 171–99, Vancouver: UBC Press.

Bartholomew, H 1930. *A Plan for the City of Vancouver including Point Grey and South Vancouver and a General Plan of the Region 1929*, Vancouver: Town Planning Commission.

Barton, H (ed) 2000. *Sustainable Communities: The Potential for Eco-Neighbourhoods*, London: Earthscan.

Baudouï, R 1990a. Between regionalism and functionalism: French reconstruction from 1940 to 1945, in J Diefendorf (ed), *Rebuilding Europe's Blitzed Cities*, pp 31–47, Basingstoke: Macmillan.

Baudouï, R 1990b. L'Histoire dans la culture du projet à L'Institut d'Urbanisme de Université de Paris, 1919–1943, in J.-P. Gaudin (ed), *Villes Réfléchies: Histoire et Actualité des Cultures Professionelles dans l'Urbanisme*, Dossiers des Séminaires, Techniques, Territoires et Sociétés, no 11/12, pp 43–57, Paris: Délégation à la Recherche et à l'Innovation, Ministère de l'Equipement, du Logement, des Transports et de la Mer.

Baudouï, R 1991. La reconstruction de Tergnier, in Archives Nationales (ed), *op cit*, pp 245–9.

Baudouï, R 1993. From tradition to modernity: the reconstruction of France, *Rassegna*, no 54, pp 68–75.

Bauer, C 1934. *Modern Housing*, Boston: Houghton Mifflin; part reprinted in R LeGates and F Stout (eds), *Selected Essays*, London: Routledge/Thoemmes (1998), no pagination.

Bauman, JF 1983. Visions of a post-war city: a perspective on urban planning in Philadelphia and the nation 1942–1945, in DA Krueckeberg (ed), *An Introduction to Planning History in the United States*, pp 170–189, New Brunswick NJ: Center for Urban Policy Research.

Bauman, JF 1988. The paradox of post-war urban planning: downtown revitalization versus decent housing for all, in D Schaffer, *Two Centuries of American Planning*, pp 231–64, London: Mansell.

Baumeister, R 1876. Town Extensions: Their Links with Technical and Economic Concerns and with Building Regulations, translated into English in 1914 by F Koestler, reproduced in <www.library.cornell.edu/Reps/DOCS>.

Beatley, T 2000. *Green Urbanism: Learning from European Cities*, Washington DC: Island Press.

Beattie, S 1980. *A Revolution in London Housing: LCC Architects and Their Work 1893–1914*, Greater London Council/Architectural Press, London.

Becker, H-J and Schlote, W 1964. *New Housing in Finland*, London: Tiranti.

Bédarida, M 1990. La "renaissance des cités" et la mission de Geo B. Ford, in J-P. Gaudin (ed), *Villes Réfléchies: Histoire et Actualité des Cultures Professionelles dans l'Urbanisme*, Dossiers des Semiaires, Techniques, Territoires et Sociétés, no 11/12, pp 33–42, Paris: Délégation à la Recherche et à l'Innovation, Ministère de l'Equipement, du Logement, des Transports et de la Mer.

Bédarida, M 1991. 1918: Une modernisation urbaine frileuse, in Archives Nationales (ed), *op cit*, pp 262–6.

Beevers, R 1988. *The Garden City Utopia: A Critical Biography of Ebenezer Howard*, Basingstoke: Macmillan.

Bellamy, E 1888. *Looking Backward*, Boston: Ticknor.

Bendixson, T and Platt, J 1992. *Milton Keynes: Image and Reality*, Cambridge: Granta.

Benevolo, L 1980. *The History of the City*, London: Scolar.

Benton, T 1993. The housing question: the exemplary case of Roehampton, *Rassegna*, no 54, pp 28–33.

Berkelbach, C 1997. Randstad 1958: the development of the western part of the Netherlands, in K Bosma and H Hellinga (eds), *Mastering the City: North-European City Planning 1900–2000* (2 volumes), vol II, pp 298–303, Rotterdam: NAI Publishers/EFL Publications.

BFHH [Baubehörde der Freien und Hansestadt Hamburg] 1958. *Neu-Altona – Planung zum Aufbau und zur Sanierung eines Kriegszerstörten Stadtkerngebietes in der Freien und Hansestadt Hamburg*, Schriftenreihe der Baubehörde zum Bau-, Wohnungs- und Siedlungenswesen Heft nr 23, Hamburg: Freie und Hansestadt Hamburg.

BFHH 1963. *Handbuch für Siedlungsplanung*, Hamburger Schriften zum Bau-, Wohnungs- und Siedlungenswesen Heft nr 37, Hamburg: Freie und Hansestadt Hamburg.

Bianchetti, C 1993. Itineraries of the modernization: Milan 1943–1948, *Rassegna*, no 54, pp 34–41.

Bianchini F and Parkinson, M (eds) 1993. *Cultural Policy and Urban Regeneration: The West European Experience*, Manchester University Press.

Biles, R 1998. New towns for the Great Society: a case study in politics and planning, *Planning Perspectives*, vol 13, no 2, pp 113–32.

Birch, EL 1983. Radburn and the American planning movement: the persistence of an idea, in DA Krueckeberg (ed), *An Introduction to Planning History in the United States*, pp 122–51, New Brunswick NJ: Center for Urban Policy Research.

Birch, EL 1994a. An urban view: Catherine Bauer's five questions, in DA Krueckeberg (ed), *The American Planner: Biographies and Recollections* (second edition), pp 310–43, New Brunswick NJ: Center for Urban Policy Research.

Birch, EL 1994b. From civic worker to city planner: women and planning, 1890–1980, in DA Krueckeberg (ed), *The American Planner: Biographies and Recollections* (second edition), pp 469–506, New Brunswick NJ: Center for Urban Policy Research.

Birchall, J 1995. Co-partnership housing and the garden city movement, *Planning Perspectives*, vol 10, no 4, pp 329–58.

Birtles, T 1997. *Planning Australia's Capital City: Differing Ideas for Canberra* (fourth edition), Canberra: University of Canberra.

Blackmore, K 1988. A good idea at the time: the redevelopment of the rocks, in P Webber (ed), *The Design of Sydney: Three Decades of Change in the City Centre*, pp 120–39, Sydney: Law Book Co.

Blau, E 1999a. *The Architecture of Red Vienna 1919–1934*, Cambridge MA: MIT Press.

Blau, E 1999b. Vienna, 1919–1934, in E Blau and M. Platzer (eds), *Shaping the Great City: Modern Architecture in Central Europe, 1890–1937*, pp 205–14, Munich: Prestel.

Blau, E and Platzer, M (eds) 1999. *Shaping the Great City, Modern Architecture in Central Europe, 1890–1937*, Munich: Prestel.

Blowers, A (ed) 1993. *Planning for a Sustainable Environment: A Report by the Town and Country Planning Association*, London: Earthscan.

Blumenfeld, H 1987. *Life Begins at 65: The Not Entirely Candid Autobiography of a Drifter*, Montreal: Harvest House.

Boelens, L 1997. Government reports on physical planning: cartography and reality, in K Bosma and H Hellinga (eds), *Mastering the City: North-European City Planning 1900–2000* (2 volumes), vol I, pp 86–93, Rotterdam: NAI Publishers/EFL Publications.

Bohigas, O 1996. The facilities of the eighties, in M Palà and O Subirós (eds), *1856–1999 Contemporary Barcelona Contemporanea*, pp 210–13, Barcelona: Centre de Cultura Contemporània de Barcelona.

Bolan, R 1999. *The Dutch Retreat from the Welfare State and its Implications for Spatial Planning*, reproduced in <www.frw.uva.nl/ame/pub/bolan.dutch.htm>

Böll, T 1997. Essen, steel, cannons and workers' houses, *Rassegna*, no 70, pp 38–41.

Bollerey, F and Hartmann, K 1980. A patriarchal utopia: the garden city at the turn of the century, in A Sutcliffe (ed), *The Rise of Modern Urban Planning, 1800–1914*, pp 135–164, London: Mansell.

Bolton, G 1996. *The Middle Way, 1942–1995, The Oxford History of Australia, vol 5* (second edition), Melbourne: Oxford University Press.

Booth, P 1996. *Controlling Development: Certainty and Discretion in Europe, the USA and Hong Kong*, London: UCL Press.

Booth, P and Boyle, R 1993. See Glasgow, see culture, in Bianchini and Parkinson (eds), *op cit*: pp 21–47.

Borja, J 1996. *Barcelona: An Urban Transformation Model 1980–1995*, Urban Management Series vol 8, Quito: Urban Management Programme.

Bosma, JE 1990. Planning the impossible: history as the fundament of the future – the reconstruction of Middelburg, 1940–4, in J Diefendorf (ed), *Rebuilding Europe's Blitzed Cities*, pp 64–76, Basingstoke: Macmillan.

Bosma, K 1990. Town and regional planning in the Netherlands 1920–1945, *Planning Perspectives*, vol 5, no 2, pp 125–147.

Bosma, K 1997a. Zuider Zee project 1892: the arrangement of the IJsselmeer polders, in K Bosma and H Hellinga (eds), *Mastering the City: North-European City Planning 1900–2000* (2 volumes), vol II, pp 140–7, Rotterdam: NAI Publishers/EFL Publications.

Bosma, K 1997b. World centre of communication 1912, in K Bosma and H Hellinga (eds), *Mastering the City, op cit*, vol II, pp 176–83.

Bosma, K and Hellinga, H 1997a. Belgian urban planning: the whole country a garden city, in K Bosma and H Hellinga (eds), *Mastering the City: North-European City Planning 1900–2000* (2 volumes), vol II, pp 58–61, Rotterdam: NAI Publishers/EFL Publications.

Bosma, K and Hellinga, H 1997b. Dutch urban planning: between centralization and decentralization, in K Bosma and H Hellinga (eds), *Mastering the City, op cit*, vol II, pp 80–7.

Bosma, K and Hellinga, H 1997c. French urban planning: the problem of core and periphery, in K Bosma and H Hellinga (eds), *Mastering the City, op cit*, Vol II, pp 74–79.

Bosma, K and Hellinga, H (eds) 1997. *Mastering the City: North-European City Planning 1900–2000* (2 volumes), Rotterdam: NAI Publishers/EFL Publications.

Bossuat, G 1991a. L'Aide Américaine 1945–1955, in Archives Nationales, *op cit*, pp 291–300.

Bossuat, G 1991b. 9 Mai 1950, L'Invention de l'Europe?, in Archives Nationales, *op cit*, pp 301–7.

Boudeville, J-R. 1966. *Problems of Regional Economic Planning*, Edinburgh University Press.

Brechin, GA 1990. San Francisco: the city beautiful, in P Polledri (ed), *Visionary San Francisco*, pp 40–62, Munich: Prestel.

Breen, A and Rigby, D 1994. *Waterfronts: Cities Reclaim Their Edge*, New York: McGraw-Hill.

Breen, A and Rigby, D 1996. *The New Waterfront: A Worldwide Success Story*, London: Thames and Hudson.

Breitling, P 1980. The role of the competition in the genesis of urban planning: Germany and Austria in the nineteenth century, in A Sutcliffe (ed), *The Rise of Modern Urban Planning, 1800–1914*, pp 31–54, London: Mansell.

Briggs, A 1963. *Victorian Cities*, London: Odhams.

Brindley, T, Rydin, Y and Stoker, G 1988. *Remaking Planning: The Politics of Urban Change in the Thatcher Years*, London: Unwin Hyman.

Brine, J 1997. Canberra's post-Griffin planning: its theory and reality, in Barker (ed), *op cit*, pp 81–9.

*414*

Brouwer, P 1997a. Lelystad 1964: urban plan, in Bosma and Hellinga (eds), *op cit*, vol II, pp 316–23.

Brouwer, P 1997b. Almere 1977 provisional structure plan, in Bosma and Hellinga (eds), *op cit*, vol II, pp 338–45.

Brownill, S 1990. *Developing London's Docklands: Another Great Planning Disaster*, London: Paul Chapman.

Brundtland, GH 1987. *Our Common Future: Report of the World Commission on Environment and Development*, Oxford University Press.

Bruton, MJ 1975. *An Introduction to Transportation Planning*, London: Hutchinson.

Bruton, MJ 1981. Colin Buchanan 1907 –, in GE Cherry (ed), *Pioneers in British Planning*, pp 203–223, London: Architectural Press.

BSSUT/MUNRLB [Berlin Senatverstaltung für Stadtentwicklung, Umweltschutz und Technologie/Ministerium für Umwelt, Naturschutz und Raumordnung des Landes Brandenburg] 1998. *Joint Planning for Berlin and Brandenburg*, Berlin/Potsdam: Senatverstaltung für Stadtentwicklung, Umweltschutz und Technologie/Ministerium für Umwelt, Naturschutz und Raumordnung des Landes.

Buchanan, CD 1958. *Mixed Blessing: The Motor in Britain*, Leonard Hill, London.

Buder, S 1990. *Visionaries and Planners: The Garden City Movement and the Modern Community*, New York: Oxford University Press.

Bullock, N 1978. Housing in Frankfurt, 1925 to 1931 and the new Wohnkultur, *Architectural Review*, no 113, pp 335–42.

Bullock, N 1987. Plans for post-war housing in the UK: the case for mixed development and the flat, *Planning Perspectives*, vol 2, no 1, pp 71–98.

Bullock, N 1993. The Policies of the London County Council, 1945–1951, *Rassegna*, no 54, pp 50–7.

Bullock, N 1999. A short history of everyday Berlin, 1871–1989, in D Goodman and C Chant (eds), *European Cities and Technology: Industrial to Post-Industrial City*, pp 225–256, London: Routledge.

Bullock, N and Read, J 1985. *The Movement for Housing Reform in Germany and France, 1840–1914*, Cambridge University Press.

Burns, W 1963. *New Towns for Old: The Technique of Urban Renewal*, Leonard Hill, London.

Burns, W, Lane, L and Thomas, W 1962. Lessons from America, *Journal of the Town Planning Institute*, vol XLVIII, 192–8.

BVT [Bournville Village Trust] 1941. *When We Build Again: A Study Based on Research into Conditions of Living and Working in Birmingham*, London: Allen & Unwin.

Cadbury, G Jnr 1915. *Town Planning with Special Reference to the Birmingham Schemes*, London: Longmans Green.

Calabi, D 1980. The genesis and special characteristics of town-planning instruments in Italy, 1880–1914, in A Sutcliffe (ed), *The Rise of Modern Urban Planning, 1800–1914*, pp 55–70, London: Mansell.

Calabi, D 1984. Italy, in M Wynn (ed), *Planning and Urban Growth in Southern Europe*, pp 37–70, London: Mansell.

Calabi, D 1996. Marcel Poëte: pioneer of 'l'urbanisme' and defender of 'l'histoire des villes', *Planning Perspectives*, vol 11, no 4, pp 413–36.

Calabi, D 2000. *Storia dell'Urbanistica Europea: Questioni, Strumenti, Esemplari*, Torino: Paravia Scriptorum.

Calthorpe, P 1993. *The Next American Metropolis: Ecology, Community and the American Dream*, Princeton: Princeton Architectural Press.

Cardew, R 1998. Corridors of planning: recollections of the Sydney region outline Plan preparation, in R Freestone (ed), *The Twentieth Century Urban Planning Experience: Proceedings of the Eighth International Planning History Society Conference and the Fourth*

*Australian Planning/Urban History Conference*, pp 89–94. Sydney: Faculty of the Built Environment, University of New South Wales.

Caro, RA 1975. *The Power Broker: Robert Moses and the Fall of New York*, New York: Vintage.

Carr, D 1979. Metropolitan design, in J Gentilli (ed), *Western Landscapes*, pp 383–99, Nedlands: University of Western Australia Press.

Carver, H 1948. *Houses for Canadians*, Toronto University Press.

Carver, H 1962. *Cities in the Suburbs*, Toronto University Press.

Carver, H 1975. *Compassionate Landscape*, Toronto University Press.

Casciato, M 1996. *The Amsterdam School*, Rotterdam: 010 Publishers.

Casson, H 1946. *Homes by the Million: An Account of the Housing Methods of the U.S.A. 1940–1945*, Harmondworth: Penguin.

Castells, M 1977. *The Urban Question: A Marxist Approach*, London: Arnold.

Castells, M 1983. *The City and the Grassroots: A Cross-Cultural Theory of Urban Social Movements*, London: Arnold.

Castells, M and Hall, P 1994. *Technopoles of the World: The Making of 21st Century Industrial Complexes*, London: Routledge.

CEC [Commission of the European Communities] 1990a. *Green Paper on the Urban Environment* (EUR 12902 EN), Brussels: Commission of the European Communities.

CEC 1990b. *Green Paper on the Urban Environment: Expert Contributions* (EUR 13145 EN), Brussels: Commission of the European Communities.

Celis, J 1985. L'Architecture de la reconstruction entre le rond et la forme, in M Smets (ed), *Resurgam: La reconstruction en Belgique après 1914*, pp 131–152, Leuven: Crédit Communal.

*Central City*, Ann Arbor: UMI Research Press.

Chadwick, G 1971. *A Systems View of Planning*, Oxford: Pergamon.

Chaline, C 1985. *Le Villes Nouvelles dans le Monde*, Paris: Presses Universitaires de France.

Chalkley, B and Essex, S 1999. Urban development through hosting international events: a history of the Olympic Games, *Planning Perspectives*, vol 14, no 4, pp 369–94.

Chant, C (ed) 1999. *Pre-Industrial Cities and Technology Reader*, London: Routledge.

Chant, C and Goodman, D (eds) 1999. *Pre-Industrial Cities and Technology*, London: Routledge, 1999.

Charlesworth, G 1984. *A History of British Motorways*, London: Thomas Telford.

Cherry, GE 1974. *The Evolution of British Town Planning*, Leighton Buzzard: Leonard Hill.

Cherry, GE 1975. *Factors in the Origins of Town Planning in Britain: The Example of Birmingham 1905–1914*, Centre for Urban and Regional Studies Working Paper No. 36, University of Birmingham.

Cherry, GE 1981. George Pepler 1882–1959, in GE Cherry (ed), *Pioneers in British Planning*, pp 131–49, London: Architectural Press.

Cherry, GE 1988. *Cities and Plans: The Shaping of Urban Britain in the Nineteenth and Twentieth Centuries*, London: Arnold.

Cherry, GE 1990. Reconstruction: its place in planning history, in J Diefendorf (ed), *Rebuilding Europe's Blitzed Cities*, pp 209–20, Basingstoke: Macmillan.

Cherry, GE (ed) 1980. *Shaping an Urban World*, London: Mansell.

Cherry, GE (ed) 1981. *Pioneers in British Planning*, London: Architectural Press.

Cherry, GE and Penny, L 1986. *Holford: A Study in Architecture, Planning and Civic Design*, London: Mansell.

CHS [Commonwealth Housing Commission] 1944. *Final Report*, Canberra: Ministry of Post-War Reconstruction.

Churchill, H 1994. Henry Wright 1878–1936, in DA Krueckeberg (ed), *The American Planner: Biographies and Recollections* (second edition), pp 243–63, New Brunswick NJ: Center for Urban Policy Research.

416

Clapson, M 1999. Technology, social change and the planning of a post-industrial city: a case study of Milton Keynes, in D Goodman and C Chant (eds), *European Cities and Technology: Industrial to Post-Industrial City*, pp 279–300, London: Routledge.

Clapson, M, Dobbin, M and Waterman, P 1998. *The Best Laid Plans: Milton Keynes since 1967*, University of Luton Press.

Clark, M 1995. *A Short History of Australia*, Ringwood: Penguin.

Claude, V 1989. Sanitary engineering as a path to town planning: the singular role of the *Association générale des hygiénistes et techniciens muncipaux* in France and the French-speaking countries, 1900–1920, *Planning Perspectives*, vol 4, no 2, pp 153–66.

Clout, H 1999. The reconstruction of Upper Normandy: a tale of two cities, *Planning Perspectives*, vol 14, no 2, pp 183–207.

Cohen, J-L 1995. *Scenes of the World to Come: European Architecture and the American Challenge 1893–1960*, Paris: Flammarion/Canadian Centre for Architecture.

Cohen, J-L and Fortier, B (eds) 1992. *Paris: La Ville et Ses Projets/A City in the Making* (Édition Revue et Augmentée), Paris: Babylone/Pavillion de l'Arsenal.

Cohen, J-L and Lortie, A 1991. *Des Fortifs au Perif: Paris Les Seuils de la Ville*, Paris: Picard.

Cole, A 1998. *French Politics and Society*, London: Prentice Hall.

Collins, CC 1988. Hegemann and Peets: cartographers of an imaginary Atlas, in W Hegemann and E Peets, *American Vitruvius: An Architect's Handbook of Civic Art*, New York: Architectural Book Publishers; reprinted by Princeton Architectural Press, New York (1988), pp xii–xxii.

Collins, CC 1996. Werner Hegemann (1881–1936): formative years in America, *Planning Perspectives*, vol 11, no 1, pp 1–22.

Collins, GR and Collins, CC 1965. *Camillo Sitte and the Birth of Modern City Planning*, Columbia University Studies in Art History and Archaeology, no 3, London: Phaidon.

Colman, J 1993. The Liverpool connection and Australian planning and design practice 1945–1985, in R Freestone (ed), *The Australian Planner: Proceedings of the Planning History Conference held in the School of Town Planning*, University of New South Wales, Environmental Planning and Management Series, vol 93/1, pp 59–69, Sydney.

Comstock, WT (ed) 1919. *The Housing Book*, New York: William T Comstock.

Cooney, EW 1974. High flats in local authority housing in England and Wales since 1945, in A Sutcliffe (ed), *Multi-Storey Living: The British Working Class Experience*, pp 151–180, London: Croom Helm.

Copenhagen (City Engineer's Department) 1955. *Copenhagen: Town Planning Guide*, Copenhagen: Stadsingeniørens Direktorat.

Cornu, M 1990. Suresnes: La Modernité d'une École de Civisme, *Urbanisme et Architecture*, no 242, pp 63–5.

Couedelo, RA 1991. Aménagement et urbanisme: l'insertion des pouvoirs publics 1919–1950, in Archives Nationales (ed), *op cit*, pp 211–23.

CPIJ [City Planning Institute of Japan] (ed) 1988. *Centenary of Modern City Planning and Its Perspective*, Tokyo: City Planning Institute of Japan/Shokokusha.

*CPIJ Newsletter* 1990. No 4, Special Issue on Foreign Students and Japanese City Planning.

*CPIJ Newsletter* 1993. No 7, special issue on Land problems in Japan.

*CPIJ Newsletter* 1995. No 10, special issue on Great Hanshin-Awaji Earthquake.

*CPIJ Newsletter* 1996a. No 11, special issue on Postwar Restoration Planning in Japan.

*CPIJ Newsletter* 1996b. No 12, special issue on Waterfront Development Projects in Japan.

*CPIJ Newsletter* 1997a. No 14, special Issue on Urban Design in Japan.

*CPIJ Newsletter* 1997b. No 16, special Issue on the Third Year Since Great Hanshin-Awaji Earthquake.

*CPIJ Newsletter* 2000. No 18, special issue on Decentralization and Japanese City Planning.

Crawford, M 1994. *Building the Workingman's Paradise: The Design of American Company Towns*, London: Verso.

Crawford, M 1995. Daily life on the home front: women, blacks, and the struggle for public housing, in Albrecht (ed), *op cit*, pp 90–146.

Crawford, M 1997. John Nolen, the design of the company town, *Rassegna*, no 70, pp 46–53.

Creese, WL 1966. *The Search for Environment: The Garden City Before and After*, Cambridge MA: MIT Press.

Croizé, J-C 1991. Construire, reconstruire: elements de problematique (1940–1960), in Archives Nationales (ed), *op cit*, pp 253–61.

Cullen, G 1961. *Townscape*, London: The Architectural Press.

Cullingworth, B 1997. *Planning in the USA: Policies, Issues and Processes*, London: Routledge.

Cullingworth, JB 1975. *Environmental Planning 1939–1969, Vol I, Reconstruction and Land Use Planning 1939–1947*, London: HMSO.

Cullingworth, JB 1979. *Environmental Planning 1939–1969, Vol III, New Towns Policy*, London: HMSO.

Cullingworth, JB 1980. *Environmental Planning 1939–1969, Vol IV, Land Values, Compensation and Betterment*, London: HMSO.

Cullingworth, JB 1987. *Urban and Regional Planning in Canada*, New Brunswick NJ: Transaction.

Cullingworth, JB 1993. *The Political Culture of Planning*, London: Routledge.

Culpin, EG 1913. *The Garden City Movement Up to Date*, London: GCTPA.

Cuñat, F, Derville, A, Guignet, P and Maisonneuve, M-JL 1996. Lille, in J-L Pinol (ed), *Atlas Historiques des Villes de France*, pp 92–119, Paris/Barcelona: Hachette/Centre de Cultura Contemporània de Barcelona.

CWDC [City West Development Corporation] 1998. *City West Urban Renewal Six Years On*, Sydney: CWDC.

Cybriwsky, R 1999. *Tokyo: The Shogun's City at the Twenty-First Century* (second edition), Chichester: Wiley.

Davidoff, P 1965. Advocacy and pluralism in planning, *Journal of the American Institute of Planners*, vol 31, pp 186–97.

Davis, AF 1983. Playgrounds, housing and city planning, in DA Krueckeberg (ed), *An Introduction to Planning History in the United States*, pp 73–87, New Brunswick NJ: Center for Urban Policy Research.

Davison, G 1991. A brief history of the Australian heritage movement, in G Davison and C McConville (eds), *A Heritage Handbook*, pp 14–27, St Leonards NSW: Allen and Unwin.

De Meyer, R 1985. L'Architecte entre l'Image et la Réalité, in M Smets (ed), *Resurgam: La reconstruction en Belgique après 1914*, pp 153–167, Leuven: Crédit Communal.

De Soissons, M 1988. *Welwyn Garden City: A Town Designed for Healthy Living*, Cambridge: Publications for Business.

De Torres i Capell, M 1992. Barcelona: Planning Problems and Practices in the Jaussely Era, 1900–1930, *Planning Perspectives*, vol 7, no 2, pp 211–33.

De Wit, A 1998. *Nieuw Sloten: Van Tuin tot Stad*, Amsterdam: Dienst Ruimtelijke Ordening.

Deakin, D (ed) 1989. *Wythenshawe: The Story of a Garden City*, Chichester: Phillimore.

Deckker, T (ed) 2000. *The Modern City Revisited*, London: Spon.

DeGrace, W 1985. Canada's capital 1900–1950: five town planning visions, *Environments*, vol 17, no 2, pp 43–57.

Delafons, J 1997. *Politics and Preservation: A Policy History of the Built Heritage 1882–1996*, London: Spon.

Denby, E 1938. *Europe Rehoused*, London: Allen and Unwin.

Des Cars, J and Pinon, P (eds) 1991. *Paris-Haussmann, "le pari d'Haussmann"*, Paris: Pavillion de l'Arsenal/Picard.

*418*

Diefendorf, J (ed) 1990. *Rebuilding Europe's Blitzed Cities*, Basingstoke: Macmillan.

Diefendorf, JM 1993a. America and the rebuilding of urban Germany, in JM Diefendorf, A Frohn and H-J Repieper (eds) *American Policy and the Reconstruction of West Germany, 1945–1955*, New York: Cambridge University Press.

Diefendorf, JM 1993b. *In the Wake of War: The Reconstruction of German Cities after World War II*, New York: Oxford University Press.

Dix, G 1981. Patrick Abercrombie 1879–1957, in GE Cherry (ed), *op cit*, pp 103–30.

Docter, R 2000. Post-war town planning in its mid-life crisis: dilemmas in redevelopment from a policy point of view, in Deckker (ed), *op cit*, pp 197–213.

DOE [Department of the Environment] *et al* 1990. *This Common Inheritance: Britain's Environmental Strategy* (Cm 1200), London: HMSO.

Dosker, M 1997. Eindhoven 1930 general expansion plan, in Bosma and Hellinga (eds), *op cit*, vol II, pp 208–15.

Douglass, M and Friedmann, J (eds) 1998. *Cities for Citizens: Planning and the Rise of Civil Society in a Global Age*, Chichester: Wiley.

DRO [Dienst Ruimtelijke Ordening – Amsterdam Physical Planning Department] 1983. *Amsterdam: Planning and Development*, Amsterdam: Dienst Ruimtelijke Ordening.

DRO (L Bontje and A Jolles) 2000. *Amsterdam: The Major Projects*, Amsterdam: Dienst Ruimtelijke Ordening.

DRO (R Pistor, B Polak, M Riechelmann, P Rijnaarts, L Slot and J Smit eds) 1994. *A City in Progress: Physical Planning in Amsterdam*, Amsterdam: Dienst Ruimtelijke Ordening.

Dudley Report 1944. *The Design of Dwellings: Report of the Sub-Committee of the Central Housing Advisory Committee*, London: HMSO.

Duffy, H 1995. *Competitive Cities: Succeeding in the Global Economy*, London: Spon.

Dunleavy, P 1981. *The Politics of Mass Housing in Britain 1945–75: A Study of Corporate Power and Professional Influence in the Welfare State*, Oxford: Clarendon Press.

Düwel, J 1997a. Berlin in the cold war: confrontation of urban planning concepts, in Bosma and Hellinga (eds), *op cit*, vol II, pp 128–37.

Düwel, J 1997b. Berlin 1938: Generalbebauungsplan für die Reichshauptstadt, in Bosma and Hellinga (eds), *op cit*, vol II, pp 248–57.

Düwel, J (1997c), Berlin 1952: Stalinallee, in Bosma and Hellinga (eds), *op cit*, vol II, pp 282–9.

Dyos, HJ and Wolff, M (eds) 1973. *The Victorian City: Images and Realities* (2 volumes) London: Routledge and Kegan Paul.

Ebner, MH 1993. Prospects for the dual metropolis in the USA, *Planning History*, vol 15, no 3, 13–21.

ECFJS [Executive Committee of Finland-Japan Seminar] 1997. *Helsinki/City in the Forest*. Tokyo: Ichigaya.

Edgington, DW 1994. Planning for technology development and information systems in Japanese cities and regions, in P Shapira, I Masser, and DW Edgington (eds), *Planning for Cities and Regions in Japan* (a *Town Planning Review* special study), pp 126–7 Liverpool University Press.

Edwards, AM 1981. *The Design of Suburbia: A Critical Study in Environmental History*, London: Pembridge.

Edwards, AT 1914. A world centre of communication, *Town Planning Review*, vol 5, no 1, pp 14–30; reproduced in <www.library.cornell.edu/Reps/DOCS>.

Elkin, T, McLaren, D and Hillman, M 1991. *Reviving the City: Towards Sustainable Urban Development*, London: Policy Studies Institute/Friends of the Earth.

Elkins, TH with Hofmeister, B 1988. *Berlin: The Spatial Structure of a Divided City*, London: Methuen.

Ellis, C 1996. Professional conflict over urban form: the case of urban freeways, 1930–1970, in

MC Sies and C Silver (eds), *Planning the Twentieth Century American City*, pp 262–79, Baltimore: Johns Hopkins University Press.

Ellwood, DW 1993. The Marshall Plan, *Rassegna*, no 54, pp 84–9.

Elson, MJ 1986. *Green Belts: Conflict Mediation in the Urban Fringe*, London: Heinemann.

Ermers, M 1942. Planned housing in Vienna 1919–1934, in FJ Osborn (ed), *Planning and Reconstruction Year Book 1942*, pp 178–86, London: Todd.

Esher, L 1983. *A Broken Wave: The rebuilding of England 1940–1980*, Harmondsworth: Penguin.

Estapé, F 1996. Ildefons Cerdà I Sunyer, in M Palà and O Subirós, *1856–1999 Contemporary Barcelona Contemporanea*, pp 52–5, Barcelona: Centre de Cultura Contemporània de Barcelona.

Etienne-Steiner, C 1999. *Le Havre: Auguste Perret et la Reconstruction*, Inventaire Général des Monuments et des Richesses Artistiques de la France, Rouen: Inventaire Général.

Evenson, N 1979. *Paris: A Century of Change 1878–1978*, New Haven: Yale University Press.

Ewing, R 1999. *Traffic Calming: State of the Practice*, Washington DC: Institution of Transportation Engineers/Federal Highway Administration.

Faludi, A and van der Valk, A 1994. *Rule and Order: Dutch Planning Doctrine in the Twentieth Century*, Dordrecht: Kluwer.

Faludi, EG 1947–8. *Planning Progress in Canada*; reprinted from *Journal of the American Institute of Planners*, summer–fall and winter issues.

Faludi, EG 1950. *Designing New Canadian Communities in Theory and Practice*; reprinted from *Journal of the American Institute of Planners*, vol XVI, nos 2–3.

Fehl, G 1983. The Niddatal project: the unfinished satellite town on the outskirts of Frankfurt, *Built Environment*, vol 9, nos 3 and 4, pp 185–97.

Fehl, G 1992. The Nazi garden city, in SV Ward (ed), *The Garden City: Past, Present and Future*, pp 88–106, London: Spon.

Ferrer, A 1996a. The 1953 county plan and the codification of urban forms, in M Palà and O Subirós, *1856–1999 Contemporary Barcelona Contemporanea*, pp 132–3, Barcelona: Centre de Cultura Contemporània de Barcelona.

Ferrer, A 1996b. The undeserved discredit of the housing estate, in M. Palà and O. Subirós, *1856–1999 Contemporary Barcelona Contemporanea*, op cit, pp 150–5.

Filler, R 1986. *A History of Welwyn Garden City*, Chichester: Phillimore.

Findlay, JM 1992. *Magic Lands: Western Cityscapes and American Culture after 1940*, Berkeley: University of California Press.

Fischer, F 1990. German reconstruction as an international activity, in Diefendorf (ed), *op cit*, pp 131–44.

Fisher, ID 1994. Frederick Law Olmsted: The artist as social agent, in DA Krueckeberg (ed), *The American Planner: Biographies and Recollections* (second edition), pp 37–59, New Brunswick NJ: Center for Urban Policy Research.

Fishman, R 1977. *Urban Utopias in the Twentieth Century: Ebenezer Howard, Frank Lloyd Wright, Le Corbusier*, New York: Basic Books.

Fogelsong, RE 1986. *Planning the Capitalist City: The Colonial Era to the 1920s*, Princeton University Press.

Forshaw, JH and Abercrombie, P 1943. *County of London Plan*, London: Macmillan.

Forster, C 1995. *Australian Cities: Continuity and Change*, Melbourne: Oxford University Press.

Forster, C and McCaskill, M 1986. The modern period: managing metropolitan Adelaide, in A Hutchings and R Bunker (eds), *With Conscious Purpose: A History of Town Planning in South Australia*, pp 85–108, Netley SA: Wakefield/RAPI.

Fosler, RS and Berger, RA (eds) 1992. *Public-Private Partnership in American Cities: Seven Case Studies*, Lexington: Heath.

Fox, K 1985. *Metropolitan America: Urban Life and Urban Policy in the United States, 1940–1980*. New Brunswick NJ: Rutgers University Press.

Freestone, R 1983. John Sulman and 'the laying out of towns', *Planning History Bulletin*, vol 5, pp 18–24.

Freestone, R 1989. *Model Communities: The Garden City Movement in Australia*, Melbourne: Nelson.

Freestone, R 1995. Women in the Australian planning movement 1900–1950, *Planning Perspectives*, vol 10, no 3, pp 259–77.

Freestone, R 1996a. Sulman of Sydney: modern planning in theory and practice 1890–1930, *Town Planning Review*, vol 67, no 1, pp 45–63.

Freestone, R 1996b. The shattered dream: postwar modernism, urban planning, and the career of Walter Bunning, *Environment and Planning A*, vol 28, pp 731–52.

Freestone, R 1997. The British connection: convergence, divergence and cultural identity in Australian urban planning history, in Barker (ed), *op cit*, pp 61–70.

Freestone, R 2000a. From city improvement to the city beautiful, in S Hamnett and R Freestone (eds), *The Australian Metropolis: A Planning History*, pp 27–45, London: Spon.

Freestone, R 2000b. Master plans and planning commissions in the 1920s: the Australian experience, *Planning Perspectives*, vol 15, no 3, pp 301–22.

Freestone, R (ed) 1993. *The Australian Planner: Proceedings of the Planning History Conference held in the School of Town Planning*, University of New South Wales, Environmental Planning and Management Series, vol 93/1, Sydney.

Freestone, R (ed) 1998. *The Twentieth Century Urban Planning Experience: Proceedings of the Eighth International Planning History Society Conference and the Fourth Australian Planning/Urban History Conference*, Sydney: Faculty of the Built Environment, University of New South Wales.

Freestone, R (ed) 2000. *Urban Planning in a Changing World: The Twentieth Century Experience*, London: Spon.

Frei, N 1993. *National Socialist Rule in Germany: The Führer State 1933–1945*, Oxford: Blackwell.

Frick, D 1999. Berlin: a city without suburbs?, in M Ilmonen, M Johansson and H Stenius (eds), *Helsinki – Berlin – Stockholm I: 3 European Capitals Facing the Future*, pp 109–12, Espoo: Helsinki University of Technology, Centre for Urban and Regional Studies, Publication C53.

Fried, RC 1973. *Planning the Eternal City: Roman Politics and Planning since World War II*, New Haven: Yale University Press.

Frieden, BJ and Sagalyn, LB 1989. *Downtown, Inc.: How America Rebuilds Cities*, Cambridge MA: MIT Press.

Friedmann, J and Lehrer, U 1998. Urban policy responses to foreign in-migration: the case of Frankfurt-am-Main, in Douglass and Friedmann (eds), *op cit*, pp 67–90.

Friedrichs, J and Dangschat, JS 1993. Hamburg: culture and urban competition, in Bianchini and Parkinson (eds), *op cit*, pp 114–34.

Friend, JK and Jessop, JN 1969. *Local Government and Strategic Choice: an Operational Approach to the Processes of Public Planning*, London: Tavistock.

Fujimori, T 1988a. Ginza brick town, in CPIJ (ed), *op cit*, pp 32–3.

Fujimori, T 1988b. Replanning of Tokyo, in CPIJ (ed), *op cit*, pp 34–5.

Funigiello, PJ 1983. City planning in World War II: the experience of the national resources planning board, in DA Krueckeberg (ed), *An Introduction to Planning History in the United States*, pp 152–69, New Brunswick NJ: Center for Urban Policy Research.

Gans, HJ 1962. *The Urban Villagers: Group and Class in the Life of Italian-Americans*, New York: Free Press.

Gans, HJ 1967. *The Levittowners: Ways of Life and Politics in a New Suburban Community*, London: Allen Lane.

Garnaut, C 1999. *Colonel Light Gardens: Model Garden Suburb*, Darlinghurst, New South Wales: Crossing Press.

Garnaut, C 2000. Towards metropolitan organisation: town planning and the garden city idea, in S Hamnett and R Freestone (eds), *The Australian Metropolis: A Planning History*, pp 46–64, London: Spon.

Garpe, J 1964. Stockholm at the opening of the 1960s, in *Stockholm Regional and City Planning*, pp 23–36, Stockholm: Planning Commission of the City of Stockholm.

Garreau, J 1991. *Edge City: Life on The New Frontier*, New York: Doubleday.

Garvin, A 1996. *The American City: What Works, What Doesn't*, New York: McGraw-Hill.

Gaudin, JP 1992. The French garden city, in SV Ward (ed), *The Garden City: Past, Present and Future*, pp 52–68, London: Spon.

Gaudin, JP (ed) 1990. *Villes Réfléchies: Histoire et Actualité des Cultures Professionelles dans l'Urbanisme*, Dossiers des Semiaires, Techniques, Territoires et Sociétés, no 11/12, Paris: Délégation à la Recherche et à l'Innovation, Ministère de l'Equipement, du Logement, des Transports et de la Mer.

Gauldie, E 1974. *Cruel Habitations: a History of Working Class Housing*, London: Allen and Unwin.

Geddes, P 1968 [1915]. *Cities in Evolution: An Introduction to the Town Planning Movement and the Study of Civics*, London: Benn.

Gehl, J 2001. *Life between Buildings – Using Public Space* (fourth edition), Copenhagen: Arkitektens Forlag.

Gehl, J and Gemzøe, L 1996. *Public Spaces, Public Life*, Copenhagen: Danish Architectural Press and Danish Academy of Fine Arts School of Architecture.

Gentilli, J (ed) 1979. *Western Landscapes*, Nedlands: University of Western Australia Press.

George, H 1911 [1880]. *Poverty and Progress: An Inquiry into the Cause of Industrial Depression, and Increase of Want with Increase of Wealth: The Remedy*, London: Dent.

Georgiou, J 1979. The metropolitan region, in M Pitt-Morrison and J White (eds), *Western Towns and Buildings*, pp 247–65, Nedlands: University of Western Australia Press.

Germain, A and Rose, D 2000. *Montréal: The Quest for a Metropolis*, Chichester: Wiley.

Ghirardo, D 1989. *Building New Communities: New Deal America and Fascist Italy*, Princeton University Press.

Gimeno, E 1996. The birth of the Barcelona extension competition: the 1859 municipal competition for extension projects, in F Magrinyà and S Tarragó (eds), *Cerdà: Urbs i Territori [Planning Beyond the Urban]*, pp 155–66, Madrid: Electa.

Gimeno, E and Magrinyà, F 1996. Cerdà's part in the building of the extension, in F Magrinyà and S Tarragó (eds), *Cerda: Urbs i Territori [Planning Beyond the Urban]*, pp 167–87, Madrid: Electa.

Glendinning, M and Muthesius, S 1994. *Tower Block: Modern Public Housing in England, Scotland, Wales and Northern Ireland*, New Haven and London: Yale University Press for the Paul Mellon Centre for Studies in British Art.

Gobyn, R 1985. La crise de logement, in M Smets (ed), *Resurgam: La reconstruction en Belgique après 1914*, pp 169–88, Leuven: Crédit Communal.

Gold, JR 1997. *The Experience of Modernism: Modern Architects and the Future City 1928–1953*, London: Spon.

Goldberg, MA and Mercer, J 1986. *The Myth of the North American City: Continentalism Challenged*, Vancouver: University of British Columbia Press.

Goldfield, D 1979. Suburban development in Stockholm and the United States: a comparison of form and function, in I Hammarström and T Hall (eds), *Stockholm – Growth and Transformation of a City*, pp 139–56, Stockholm: Swedish Council for Building Research.

Goobey, AR 1992. *Bricks and Mortals – The Dreams of the 80s and the Nightmare of the 90s: The Inside Story of the Property World*, London: Century.

422

Goodman, D (ed) 1999. *The European Cities and Technology Reader: Industrial to Post-Industrial City*, London: Routledge.

Goodman, D and Chant, C (eds) 1999. *European Cities and Technology: Industrial to Post-Industrial City*, London: Routledge.

Gordon, DLA 1996. Planning, design and managing change in urban waterfront redevelopment, *Town Planning Review*, vol 67, no 3, pp 261–90.

Gordon, DLA 1998. A city beautiful plan for Canada's capital: Edward Bennett and the 1915 plan for Ottawa and Hull, *Planning Perspectives*, vol 13, no 3, pp 275–300.

Göteborg [City Planning and Housing Departments] 1960. *Göteborgbygger*, Göteborg: City Planning and Housing Departments.

Gould, P 1988. *Early Green Politics: Back to Nature, Back to the Land and Socialism in Britain 1880–1900*, Brighton: Harvester.

Gournay, I 1999. Le concours des architectes Américains, in F Cochet, M-C Genet-Delacroix and H Trocmé (eds), *Les Américains et la France 1917–1947*, pp 124–41, Paris: Maisonneuve et Larose.

Gournay, I 2001. Revisiting Jacques Gréber's *L'Architecture aux États-Unis*: from city beautiful to cité-jardin, *Urban History Review*, vol XXIX, no 2, pp 6–19.

Graham, J 1940. *Housing in Scandinavia: Urban and Rural*, Chapel Hill: University of North Carolina Press.

Grebler, L 1964. *Urban Renewal in European Countries: Its Emergence and Potentials*, Philadelphia: University of Pennsylvania Press.

Gruen, V 1964. *The Heart of Our Cities*, New York: Simon and Schuster.

Gruen, V and Smith, L 1960. *Shopping Towns USA: The Planning of Shopping Centers*, New York: Van Nostrand Reinhold.

Gutschow, N 1990. Hamburg: the 'catastrophe' of July 1943, in Diefendorf (ed), *op cit*, pp 114–30.

GVRD [Greater Vancouver Regional District] 1975. *The Livable Region 1976/1986: Proposals to Manage the Growth of Greater Vancouver Regional District*, Vancouver: GVRD.

GVRD 1993. *Creating Our Future: Steps to a More Livable Region*, Burnaby: GVRD.

GVRD 1999. *Livable Region Strategic Plan*, Burnaby: GVRD.

Hain, S 2001. Struggle for the inner city – a plan becomes a declaration of war, in WJV Neill and H-U Schwedler (eds), *Urban Planning and Cultural Inclusion: Lessons from Belfast and Berlin*, Basingstoke: Palgrave.

Hajdu, J 1983. Postwar development and planning of West German cities, in T Wild (ed), *Urban and Rural Change in West Germany*, London: Croom Helm.

Hajdu, J 1988. Pedestrian malls in West Germany, *Journal of the American Planning Association*, vol 54, pp 325–35.

Hajer, MA 1993. Rotterdam: redesigning the public domain, in Bianchini and Parkinson (eds), *op cit*, pp 48–72.

Hall, P 1988. *Cities of Tomorrow: An Intellectual History of Urban Planning and Design in the Twentieth Century*, Oxford: Blackwell.

Hall, P 1998. *Cities in Civilization: Culture, Technology and Urban Order*, London: Weidenfeld and Nicolson.

Hall, P and Ward, C 1998. *Sociable Cities: The Legacy of Ebenezer Howard*, Chichester: Wiley.

Hall, T 1979. The central business district: planning in Stockholm, 1928–1978, in I Hammarström and T Hall (eds), *Stockholm – Growth and Transformation of a City*, pp 181–232, Stockholm: Swedish Council for Building Research.

Hall, T 1986. *Planung Europäischer Haupstädte, Zur Entwicklung des Städtebaues im 19 Jahrhundert*, Stockholm: Almqvist and Wiksell.

Hall, T 1991a. Urban planning in Sweden, in T Hall (ed), *Planning and Urban Growth in the Nordic Countries*, pp 167–246, London: Spon.

Hall, T 1991b. Concluding remarks: is there a Nordic planning tradition?, in T Hall (ed), *Planning and Urban Growth in the Nordic Countries*, pp 247–59, London: Spon.

Hall, T 1997. *Planning Europe's Capital Cities: Aspects of Nineteenth Century Urban Development*, London: Spon.

Hall, T (ed) 1991. *Planning and Urban Growth in the Nordic Countries*, London: Spon.

Hall, T, Ponzio, M and Tonell, L 1994. Planning for future landscapes, in S Helmfrid (ed), *Landscape and Settlements*, pp 140–51, Stockholm: National Atlas of Sweden: Almqvist and Wiksell.

Hambleton, R 1995. Cross-national urban policy transfer – insights from the USA, in R Hambleton and H Thomas (eds), *Urban Policy Evaluation: Challenge and Change*, pp 224–38, London: Paul Chapman.

Hamnett, S 1998. The Adelaide Multi-function Polis: From Serendipity to Medium-Density Suburb; paper presented to the Eighth International Planning History Conference, Sydney.

Hamnett, S 2000. The late 1990s: competitive versus sustainable cities, in S Hamnett and R Freestone (eds), *The Australian Metropolis: A Planning History*, pp 168–88, London: Spon.

Hamnett, S and Freestone, R (eds) 2000. *The Australian Metropolis: A Planning History*, London: Spon.

Hancock, J 1988. The new deal and American planning: the 1930s, in D Schaffer, *Two Centuries of American Planning*, pp 197–230, London: Mansell.

Hancock, J 1994. John Nolen: the background of a pioneer planner, in DA Krueckeberg (ed), *The American Planner: Biographies and Recollections* (second edition), pp 60–84, New Brunswick NJ: Center for Urban Policy Research.

Hancock, J and Sotoike, H 1988. Japanese new town planning in the United States: the case of Mill Creek, Washington, in TIPHC, *The History of International Exchange of Planning Systems*, pp 113–134, Tokyo: City Planning Institute of Japan/Planning History Group.

Hancock, M 1994. Canadian Institute of Planners, *Plan Canada Special Edition* (July), pp 87–90.

Hansen, NM 1968. *French Regional Planning*, Edinburgh University Press.

Hardwick, WG 1974. *Vancouver*, Don Mills: Collier-Macmillan.

Hardwick, WG 1994. Responding to the 1960s: designing adaptable communities in Vancouver, *Environment and Behavior*, vol 26 (May), pp 338–62.

Hardy, D 1991a. *From Garden Cities to New Towns: Campaigning for Town and Country Planning, 1899–1946*, London: Spon.

Hardy, D 1991b. *From New Towns to Green Politics: Campaigning For Town and Country Planning, 1946–1990*, London: Spon.

Hardy, D 1992. The garden city campaign: an overview, in SV Ward (ed), *The Garden City: Past, Present and Future*, pp 187–209, London: Spon.

Hardy, D and Ward, C 1984. *Arcadia for All: The Legacy of a Makeshift Landscape*, London: Mansell.

Harms, H and Schubert, D 1989. *Wohnen in Hamburg – Ein Stadtführer*, Stadtplanung Geschichte nr 11, Hamburg: Christians.

Harris, CD 1991. Unification of Germany in 1990, *Geographical Review*, vol 81, pp 183–96.

Harrison, M 1991. Thomas Coglan Horsfall and 'The example of Germany', *Planning Perspectives*, vol 6, no 3, pp 297–314.

Harrison, M 1999. *Bournville: Model Village to Garden Suburb*, Chichester: Phillimore.

Harrison, P 1995; edited by R Freestone. *Walter Burley Griffin Landscape Architect*, Canberra: National Library of Australia.

Harvest, J 1978. Danish national planning policy, in G Golany (ed), *International Urban Growth Policies: New Town Contributions*, pp 105–14, New York: Wiley.

Harvey, D 1975. *Social Justice and the City*, London: Arnold.

*424*

Harvey, D 1989. *The Condition of Postmodernity: An Enquiry into the Origins of Cultural Change*, Oxford: Blackwell.

Hasegawa, J 1992. *Replanning the Blitzed City Centre*, Buckingham: Open University Press.

Hass-Klau, C 1990. *The Pedestrian and City Traffic*, London: Belhaven.

Hatano, N 1988. Association implemented land readjustment projects in Tokyo war-damage rehabilitation programme, in H Ishizuka and Y Ishida (eds), *Tokyo: Urban Growth and Planning 1868–1988*, pp 116–19, Tokyo: Center for Urban Studies, Tokyo Metropolitan University.

HCPD [Helsinki City Planning Department] 2000. *Urban Guide Helsinki*, Helsinki: City Planning Department.

HDCCS [Housing Development Committee of the Corporation of Sheffield] 1962. *Ten Years of Housing in Sheffield 1953–1963*, Sheffield: City Architect's Department.

HDL [Housing Department, Liverpool] 1937. *City of Liverpool Housing 1937*, Liverpool: Housing Committee.

Hebbert, M 1981. Frederic Osborn 1885–1978, in Cherry (ed), *op cit*, 177–202.

Hebbert, M 1983. The daring experiment – social scientists and land use planning in 1940s Britain, *Environment and Planning B*, vol 10, pp 3–17.

Hebbert, M 1994. Sen-biki amidst desakota: urban sprawl and urban planning in Japan, in P Shapira, I Masser and DW Edgington (eds), *Planning for Cities and Regions in Japan* (a *Town Planning Review* special study), pp 70–91, Liverpool University Press.

Hebbert, M 1998. *London: More by Fortune than Design*, Chichester: Wiley.

Hedgcock, D and Yiftachel, O (eds) 1992. *Urban and Regional Planning in Western Australia*, Perth: Paradigm Press.

Hedman, L 1997. Finnish Urban Planning: Suburbanization and Sustainability, in Bosma and Hellinga (eds), *op cit*, vol II, pp 50–5.

Hegemann, W and Peets, E 1922. *American Vitruvius: An Architect's Handbook of Civic Art*, New York: Architectural Book Publishers; reprinted by Princeton Architectural Press, New York (1988).

Hein, C 1998a. Japan and the transformation of planning ideas – some examples of colonial plans, in Freestone (ed), *op cit*, pp 352–7.

Hein, C 1998b. The Transformation of Planning Ideas in Japan and Its Colonies; paper presented at seminar on imported or exported urbanism, Beirut: American University/Cermoc.

Hein, C and Ishida, Y 1998. Japanische Stadtplanung und ihre deutsche Wurzeln, *Die Alte Stadt*, no 3, 1998, pp 189–211.

Hellinga, H 1997. Amsterdam 1934 general expansion plan, in Bosma and Hellinga (eds), *op cit*, vol II, pp 216–25.

Helmer, SD 1985. *Hitler's Berlin: The Speer Plans for Reshaping the Central City*, Ann Arbor: UMI Research Press.

Helmfrid, S (ed) 1994. *Landscape and Settlements*, Stockholm: National Atlas of Sweden: Almqvist and Wiksell.

*Helsinki Quarterly* 2000. Issue 2; special number on the history of Helsinki.

Hemmens, GC 1994. Tugwell in New York: the perils of liberal planning, in DA Krueckeberg (ed), *The American Planner: Biographies and Recollections* (second edition), pp 344–72, New Brunswick NJ: Center for Urban Policy Research.

Hénard, E 1910. The cities of the future, Royal Institute of British Architects, Town Planning Conference transactions, London: RIBA; reproduced in <www.library.cornell.edu/Reps/DOCS>

Henderson, SR 1995. A setting for mass culture: life and leisure in the Nidda Valley, *Planning Perspectives*, vol 10, no 2, pp 199–222.

Higgott, A 2000. Birmingham: building the modern city, in T Deckker (ed), *op cit*, pp 150–66.

Hines, TS 1974. *Burnham of Chicago: Architect and Planner*, New York: Oxford University Press.

Hiort, E 1952. *Housing in Denmark since 1930*, Copenhagen: Jul Gjellerups Forlag.

Hise, G 1995. The airplane and the garden city: regional transformations during World War II, in Albrecht (ed), *op cit*, pp 142–83.

Hise, G 1996. Homebuilding and industrial decentralization in Los Angeles: the roots of the post-World War II urban region, in MC Sies and C Silver (eds), *Planning the Twentieth Century American City*, pp 240–61, Baltimore: Johns Hopkins University Press.

Hodge, G 1991. *Planning Canadian Communities: An Introduction to the Principles, Practice, and Participants* (second edition), Scarborough: Nelson Canada.

Holm, P 1957. *Swedish Housing*, Stockholm: The Swedish Institute.

Home, R 1997. *Of Planting and Planning: The Making of British Colonial Cities*, London: Spon.

Horsfall, TC 1904. *The Improvement of the Dwellings and Surroundings of the People: The Example of Germany*, Manchester University Press.

Hötker, D 1988. The Ruhr region, in H van der Cammen (ed), *Four Metropolises in Western Europe: Development and Urban Planning of London, Paris, Randstad Holland and the Ruhr Region*, pp 178–238, Assen/Maastricht: Van Gorcum.

Howard, E 1898. *To-morrow: A Peaceful Path to Real Reform*, London: Swan Sonnenschein.

Howard, E 1902. *Garden Cities of To-morrow*, London: Swan Sonnenschein.

Howe, R 2000. A new paradigm: planning and reconstruction in the 1940s, in Hamnett and Freestone (eds), *op cit*, pp 80–97.

Hubbard, E and Shippobottom, M 1988. *A Guide to Port Sunlight Village*, Liverpool University Press.

Hughes, J and Sadler, S (eds) 2000. *Non-Plan: Essays on Freedom Participation and Change in Modern Architecture and Urbanism*, Oxford: Architectural Press.

Hughes, MR (ed) 1971. *The Letters of Lewis Mumford and Frederic J Osborn: A Transatlantic Dialogue*, Bath: Adams and Dart.

Hultin, O (ed) 1998. *The Complete Guide to Architecture in Stockholm*, Stockholm: Arkitektur Förlag.

HUPHA/IPHS [Hellenic Urban and Planning History Society] (eds) 1996. *The Planning of Capital Cities: Conference Proceedings* (2 volumes), Thessaloniki: School of Architecture, Aristotle University of Thessaloniki.

Hutchings, A 1986. Comprehensive planning comes to South Australia, in A Hutchings and R Bunker (eds), *With Conscious Purpose: A History of Town Planning in South Australia*, pp 61-83, Netley SA: Wakefield/RAPI.

Hutchings, A 2000. From theory to practice: the inter-war years, in Hamnett and Freestone (eds), *op cit*, pp 65–79.

Hutchings, A and Bunker, R (eds) 1986. *With Conscious Purpose: A History of Town Planning in South Australia*, Netley, SA: Wakefield/RAPI.

Huxley, J 1943. *TVA: Adventure in Planning*, Cheam: The Architectural Press.

Huxley, M 2000. Administrative co-ordination, urban management and strategic planning in the 1970s, in Hamnett and Freestone (eds), *op cit*, pp 131–48.

Huygen, P 1997. Emmen 1963: structure plan for the municipality of Emmen, in Bosma and Hellinga (eds), *op cit*, vol II, pp 310–15.

Hyder, J 1913. *The Case for Land Nationalisation*, London: Simpkin, Marshall, Hamilton, Kent.

IBA [Internationale Bauausstellung] Emscher Park 1999. *Katalog der Projekte*, np, Internationale Bauausstellung Emscher Park.

Ibelings, H 1997, La ville radieuse 1935, in Bosma and Hellinga (eds), *op cit*, vol II, pp 242–7.

Ilmonen, M, Johansson, M and Stenius, H (eds) 1999. *Helsinki – Berlin – Stockholm I: 3 European Capitals Facing the Future*, Espoo: Helsinki University of Technology, Centre for Urban and Regional Studies, Publication C53.

426

Imbert, M 1990. Les filières de formation à l'urbanisme à l'étranger et en France (aperçus rétrospectifs), in Gaudin (ed), *op cit*, pp 135–48.

Imrie, R and Thomas, H (eds) 1993. *British Urban Policy and the Urban Development Corporations*, London: Paul Chapman.

Inghe, J 1999. Stockholm – urban renewal policies, in Ilmonen, Johansson and Stenius (eds), *op cit*, pp 37–47.

Ishida, Y 1988a. Japan in the world history of modern city planning, in CPIJ (ed), *op cit*, pp 8–11.

Ishida, Y 1988b. Ougai Mori and Tokyo's building ordinance, in H Ishizuka and Y Ishida (eds), *Tokyo: Urban Growth and Planning 1868-1988*, pp 83–6, Tokyo: Center for Urban Studies, Tokyo Metropolitan University.

Ishida, Y 1988c. Some failures in the transference of western planning systems to Japan, in TIPHC, *The History of International Exchange of Planning Systems*, pp 543–55, Tokyo: City Planning Institute of Japan/Planning History Group.

Ishida, Y 1998. War, military affairs and urban planning, in Freestone (ed), *op cit*, pp 393–8.

Ishida, Y 2000. Eika Takayama: The Greatest Figure in Japanese Urban and Regional Planning in the 20th Century; paper delivered at the Ninth International Planning History Conference, Espoo-Helsinki, Finland.

Ishimaru, N 1996. On the original reconstruction planning in Tokyo ward area by means of the records of the city planning committee proceedings, in HUPHA/IPHS (ed), *op cit*, vol 2, pp 945–56.

Ishimaru, N 1998. On the progress and the present phase of policy for preserving atomic-bombed buildings in Hiroshima, in Freestone (ed), *op cit*, pp 405–10.

Ishizuka, H and Ishida, Y 1988. Tokyo, the metropolis of Japan and its urban development, in H Ishizuka and Y Ishida (eds), *Tokyo: Urban Growth and Planning 1868–1988*, pp 3–68, Tokyo: Center for Urban Studies, Tokyo Metropolitan University.

Ishizuka, H and Ishida, Y (eds) 1988. *Tokyo: Urban Growth and Planning 1868–1988*, Tokyo: Center for Urban Studies, Tokyo Metropolitan University.

ISMRH [Information Service of the Ministry of Reconstruction and Housing] 1947. *Holland's Reconstruction in Facts and Figures*, The Hague: Information Service of the Ministry of Reconstruction and Housing.

Ito, T 1988a. Imperial capital restoration project, in CPIJ (ed), *op cit*, pp 36–7.

Ito, T 1988b. Tokyo war-damage restoration plan, in CPIJ (ed), *op cit*, pp 38–9.

Itoh, T 1988. Design and layout of bridges and parks in the reconstruction project after the great Kanto earthquake – a comparative study of Tokyo and Yokohama, in H Ishizuka and Y Ishida (eds), *op cit*, pp 96–101.

Jackson, AA 1991. *Semi-Detached London: Suburban Development, Life and Transport 1900–1939* (second edition), Didcot: Wild Swan.

Jackson KT 1984. The capital of capitalism: the New York metropolitan region, 1890–1940, in A Sutcliffe (ed), *Metropolis 1890–1940*, pp 319–54, London: Mansell.

Jackson, KT 1985. *Crabgrass Frontier: The Suburbanization of the United States*, New York: Oxford University Press.

Jacobs, J 1964. *The Death and Life of Great American Cities: The Failure of Town Planning*, Harmondsworth: Penguin.

Jenks, M, Burton, E and Williams, K (eds) 1996. *The Compact City: A Sustainable Urban Form*, London: Spon.

Jensen, RH 1997. Norwegian city planning – Oslo: from provincial to cosmopolitan capital, in Bosma and Hellinga (eds), *op cit*, vol II, pp 32–41.

Johnson, DA 1988. Regional planning for the great American metropolis: New York between the world wars, in D Schaffer, *Two Centuries of American Planning*, pp 167–96, London: Mansell.

Johnson, DA 1996. *Planning the Great Metropolis: The 1929 Regional Plan of New York and Its Environs*, London: Spon.

Johnson-Marshall, P 1966. *Rebuilding Cities*, Edinburgh University Press.

Johnston, N 1994. Harland Bartholomew: precedent for the profession, in DA Krueckeberg (ed), *The American Planner: Biographies and Recollections* (2nd edition), pp 216–41, New Brunswick NJ: Center for Urban Policy Research.

Justement, L 1946. *New Cities for Old: City Building in Terms of Space, Time, and Money*, New York: McGraw-Hill.

Kain, R 1981. Conservation planning in France: policy and practice in the Marais, Paris, in R Kain (ed), *Planning for Conservation*, pp 199–233, London: Mansell.

Kain, R (ed) 1981. *Planning for Conservation*, op cit.

Kampffmeyer, H 1968. *Die Nordweststadt in Frankfurt am Main*, Frankfurt: Europäische Verlagsanstalt.

Kantor, HA 1994a. Benjamin C Marsh and the fight over population congestion, in D Krueckeberg (ed), *The American Planner: Biographies and Recollections* (2nd edition), pp 113–132, New Brunswick NJ: Center for Urban Policy Research.

Kantor, HA 1994b. Charles Dyer Norton and the origins of the regional plan of New York, in DA Krueckeberg (ed), *The American Planner: Biographies and Recollections* (2nd edition), pp 162–81, New Brunswick NJ: Center for Urban Policy Research.

Katoh, H 1988. Development of housing areas by Mitsui Trust Company, in Ishizuka and Ishida (eds), op cit, pp 106–11.

Katz, P 1994. *The New Urbanism: Toward an Architecture of Community*, New York: McGraw-Hill.

Kaulusche, B and Setzepfandt, W-C 1997. *Frankfurt am Main: Architekturführer* (second edition), Berlin: Dietrich Reimer.

Kennedy, D 1984. West Germany, in M Wynn (ed), *Housing in Europe*, pp 55–74, Beckenham: Croom Helm.

Kennedy, LW 1992. *Planning the City upon a Hill: Boston since 1630*, Amherst: University of Massachusetts Press.

Kenworthy, J 1992. Transport planning for Perth in the 1990s: a decade of healing?, in Hedgcock and Yiftachel (eds), op cit, pp 162–73.

King, AD 1980. Exporting planning: the colonial and neo-colonial experience, in Cherry (ed), op cit, pp 203–26.

King, AD 1990. *Urbanism, Colonialism and the World-Economy: Cultural and Spatial Foundations of the World Economic System*, London: Routledge.

King, R 1998. From guest-workers to immigrants: labour migration from the Mediterranean periphery, in D Pinder (ed), *The New Europe: Economy, Society and Environment*, Chichester: Wiley.

Kitchen, P 1975. *A Most Unsettling Person: An Introduction to the Ideas and Life of Patrick Geddes*, London: Gollancz.

Klinge, M and Kolbe, L 1999. *Helsinki: Daughter of the Baltic*, Helsinki: Otava.

Knudsen, T 1988. International influences and professional rivalry in early Danish planning, *Planning Perspectives*, vol 3, no 3, pp 297–310.

Kolb, E 1988. *The Weimar Republic*, London: Routledge.

Kolbe, L 1990. Garden suburb planners 1900–1914: a new middle class liberalism in conflict with the centrally governed town planning tradition in Finland, *Planning History*, vol 12, no 2, pp 10–16.

Kopp A 1970. *Towns and Revolution: Soviet Architecture and City Planning 1917–1935*, London: Thames and Hudson.

Korn, A 1953. *History Builds the Town*, London: Lund Humphries.

Korthals Altes, WK and Faludi, A 1995. Why the greening of red Vienna did not come to pass: an unknown chapter of the garden city movement 1919–1934, *European Planning Studies*, vol 3, no 2, pp 205–26.

Kropotkin, P 1974 [1899]. *Fields, Factories and Workshops Tomorrow*, London: Allen and Unwin.

Krueckeberg, DA (ed) 1983. *An Introduction to Planning History in the United States*, New Brunswick NJ: Center for Urban Policy Research.

Krueckeberg, DA (ed)1994. The American planner: a new introduction, in DA Krueckeberg (ed) *The American Planner: Biographies and Recollections* (second edition) pp 1–35, New Brunswick NJ: Center for Urban Policy Research.

Krueckeberg, DA (ed) 1994. *The American Planner: Biographies and Recollections* (second edition), New Brunswick NJ: Center for Urban Policy Research.

Krumholz, N 1983. A retrospective view of equity planning: Cleveland 1969–1979, in Krueckeberg (ed), *op cit*, pp 258–79.

Kudamatsu, Y 1988a. Tokyo Olympics and capital improvement, in CPIJ (ed), *op cit*, pp 40–1.

Kudamatsu, Y 1988b. Shinjuku subcenter, in CPIJ (ed), *op cit*, pp 42–3.

Kudamatsu, Y 1988c. New towns and their matured stage of development, in CPIJ (ed), *op cit*, pp 214–15.

KUKA [Kronsberg Umwelt Kommunikations Agentur] nd c1999. *Hannover Kronsberg: Model of a Sustainable New Urban Community*, Hannover: Kronsberg.

Kündiger, B 1997a. The German metropolitan region – Berlin: urban planning between history and modernity, in Bosma and Hellinga (eds), *op cit*, vol 1, pp 66–75.

Kündiger, B 1997b. Berlin 1910: gross-Berlin, in Bosma and Hellinga (eds), *op cit*, vol II, pp 160–7.

Kunzmann, K 1997. The future of the city region in Europe, in Bosma and Hellinga (eds), *op cit*, vol I, pp 16–29.

Kurokawa, K 1978. The concept and method of new town planning in Japan, in G Golany (ed), *International Urban Growth Policies: New Town Contributions*, pp 191–215, New York: Wiley.

Ladd, B 1990. *Urban Planning and Civic Order in Germany, 1860–1914*, Cambridge MA: Harvard University Press.

Lafrenz, J 1999. The Foundation of Abuja – the New Capital City of Nigeria – as Synthesis of Planning Principles from Europe and America; paper presented at the Eighth Conference of the Society for American City and Regional Planning History, Washington DC.

Lainevuo, A 1998. Visions of Japanese ecocities, in J Päivänen, and K Lapintie, *After All These Years*, pp 69–80, Helsinki: Helsinki University of Technology, Centre for Urban and Regional Studies.

Lampugnagi, VM 1996. Cerdà's plan or progressive urbanism, in M. Palà and O. Subirós, *1856–1999 Contemporary Barcelona Contemporanea*, pp 56–65, Barcelona: Centre de Cultura Contemporània de Barcelona.

Landau, B 1995. Techniciens Parisiens et Échanges Internationaux, in A Lortie (ed), *Paris S'Exporte: Architecture Modèle ou Modèles d'Architecture*, pp 205–15, Paris: Picard/Pavillion de l'Arsenal.

Lane, BM 1968. *Architecture and Politics in Germany, 1918–1945*, Cambridge MA: Harvard University Press.

Lang, MH 1996. The design of Yorkship garden village: product of the progressive planning, architecture and housing reform movements, in MC Sies and C Silver (eds), *Planning the Twentieth Century American City*, pp 120–44, Baltimore: Johns Hopkins University Press.

Lang, MH 2001. Town planning and radicalism in the progressive era: the legacy of FL Ackerman, *Planning Perspectives*, vol 16, no 2, pp 143–68.

Larsson, B and Thomassen, T 1991. Urban planning in Denmark, in T Hall (ed), *op cit*, pp 6–59.

Larsson, LO 1984. Metropolis architecture, in A Sutcliffe (ed), *Metropolis 1890–1940*, London: Mansell.

Larsson, Y 1964. Building a city and a metropolis, in Stockholm [Planning Commission of the City of Stockholm] (ed), *Stockholm Regional and City Planning*, pp 8–22, Stockholm: Planning Commission of the City of Stockholm.

Lash, H 1976. *Planning in a Human Way: Personal Reflections on the Regional Planning Experience in Vancouver*, Ottawa: Macmillan for Ministry of State for Urban Affairs.

LCC [London County Council] 1937. *London Housing*, London: LCC.

LCC 1961. *The Planning of a New Town*, London: LCC.

Le Corbusier 1922. Une ville contemporaine, in Le Corbusier and P Jeanneret (eds), *Oeuvre Complete de 1910–1929* (1964), Zurich: Les Editions d'Architecture.

Le Corbusier 1925. Plan Voisin (de Paris), in Le Corbusier and Jeanneret (eds), *Oeuvre Complete, op cit*.

Le Corbusier 1946 [1927]. *Towards a New Architecture*, trans F Etchells, London: Architectural Press; originally published as *Vers Une Architecture* (1923), Editions Cres, Paris.

Leblicq, Y 1995. La Belgique et le Modèle Haussmannien, in A Lortie (ed), *Paris S'Exporte: Architecture Modèle ou Modèles d'Architecture*, pp 73–81, Paris: Picard/Pavillion de l'Arsenal.

Lecoin, JP 1988. Paris and the Ile de France region, in H van der Cammen (ed), *Four Metropolises in Western Europe: Development and Urban Planning of London, Paris, Randstad Holland and the Ruhr Region*, pp 63–115, Assen/Maastricht: Van Gorcum.

Lefebvre, H 1968. *Le Droit à la Ville*, Paris: Anthropos.

LeGates, R and Stout, F (eds) 1998. *Selected Essays*, London: Routledge/Thoemmes.

Lemberg, K 1997. Danish urban planning: urban developments in the Copenhagen region, in Bosma and Hellinga (eds), *op cit*. vol II, pp 20–31.

Lemon, JT 1996. *Liberal Dreams and Nature's Limits: Great Cities of North America since 1600*, Toronto: Oxford University Press.

Lennon, M 2000. The revival of metropolitan planning, in Hamnett and Freestone (eds), *op cit*, pp 149–67.

Lewis, D and McKenzie, JRP (eds) 1995. *The New Germany: Social, Political and Cultural Challenges to Unification*, University of Exeter Press.

Lewis, RA 1952. *Edwin Chadwick and the Public Health Movement 1832–1854*, London: Longmans Green.

Ley, D, Heibert, D and Pratt, G 1992. Time to grow up? From urban village to world city, in G Wynn and T Oke (eds), *Vancouver and Its Region*, pp 234–66, Vancouver: UBC Press.

Lind, O and Lund, A 1996. *Copenhagen Architecture Guide*, Copenhagen: Arkitektens Forlag.

Loach, J 2000. QT8: a neglected chapter in the history of modern town planning, in Deckker (ed), *op cit*, pp 125–49.

Lock, M 1946. *The Middlesbrough Survey and Plan*, Middlesbrough Corporation.

Lock, M 1947. *Reconstruction in the Netherlands: An Account of a Visit to Post-War Holland by Members of the Town Planning Institute*, London: Jason.

Lorange, E and Myhre, JE (1991). Urban planning in Norway, in Hall (ed), *op cit*, pp 116–66.

Lortie, A 1995a. La ville métropole: entre image et organisation, in A Lortie (ed), *Paris S'Exporte: Architecture Modèle ou Modèles*, pp 49–55, Paris: Picard/Pavillion de l'Arsenal.

Lortie, A 1995b. Des exportations à géométrie variable, in A Lortie (ed), *Paris S'Exporte, op cit*, pp 218–32.

Lortie, A (ed) 1995. *Paris S'Exporte: Architecture Modèle ou Modèles*, Paris: Picard/ Pavillion de l'Arsenel.

Lovelace, E 1993. *Harland Bartholomew: His Contributions to American Urban Planning*, Urbana: University of Illinois Press.

Lubove, R 1963. *Community Planning in the 1920s: The Contribution of the Regional Planning Association of America*, University of Pittsburgh Press.

Lundén, T 1994. Stockholm, in Helmfrid (ed), *op cit*, pp 110–15.

Lyon Confluence 1998. *Projet Urbain/Strategy for Urban Renewal*, Lyons: Les Cahiers Lyon Confluence.

Mäding, H 1999. Planning in Berlin, in Ilmonen, Johansson and Stenius (eds), *op cit*, pp 92–108.

Maes, J 1985. L'Expérience des cités-jardins dans le contexte de la reconstruction de la Belgique après 1918, in M Smets (ed), *Resurgam: La reconstruction en Belgique après 1914*, pp 189–213, Leuven: Crédit Communal.

Magrinyà, F and Tarragó, S (eds) 1996. *Cerdà: Urbs i Territori/Planning Beyond the Urban*, Madrid: Electa.

Manzoni, HJB 1939. *The Building of 50,000 Municipal Houses*, City of Birmingham.

Marconis, R 1996. Toulouse, in J-L Pinol (ed), *Atlas Historiques des Villes de France*, pp 230–54, Paris/Barcelona: Hachette/Centre de Cultura Contemporània de Barcelona.

Marcuse, P 1980. Housing policy and city planning: a puzzling split in the United States, 1893–1921, in Cherry (ed), *op cit*, pp 23–58.

Margarit, I 1996. Biography: Ildefons Cerdà, in Magrinyà, and Tarragó (eds), *op cit*, pp 141–53.

Marley Committee 1935. *Report of the Departmental Committee on Garden Cities and Satellite Towns*, London: HMSO.

Marmot, AF 1982. The legacy of Le Corbusier and high rise housing, *Built Environment*, vol 7, no 2, pp 82–95.

Marriott, O 1969. *The Property Boom*, London: Pan.

Marshall, RJ and Masser, I (1982). British planning methodology: three historical perspectives, *Built Environment*, vol 7, no 2, pp 121–9.

Marshall, T 2000. Urban planning and governance: is there a Barcelona model?, *International Planning Studies*, vol 5, no 3, pp 299–319.

Marwick, A 1964. Middle opinion in the thirties: planning, progress and political agreement, *English Historical Review*, vol LXXIX, no 311, pp 285–98.

Mason, T and Tiratsoo, N 1990. People, politics and planning: the reconstruction of Coventry's city centre, 1940–53, in Diefendorf (ed), *op cit*, pp 90–113.

Masser, I and Yorisaki, T 1994. The institutional context of Japanese planning: professional associations and planning education, in P Shapira, I Masser, and DW Edgington (eds), *Planning for Cities and Regions in Japan* (a *Town Planning Review* special study), pp 113–25, Liverpool University Press.

Matzerath, H 1984. Berlin 1890–1940, in A Sutcliffe (ed), *Metropolis 1890–1940*, pp 289–318, London: Mansell.

Mawson, TH 1927. *The Life and Work of an English Landscape Architect*, London: Richards.

McCann, L and Smith, PJ 1991. Canada becomes urban: cities and urbanization in historical perspective, in T Bunting and P Filion (eds), *Canadian Cities in Transition*, pp 69–99, Toronto: Oxford University Press.

McCarthy, J 1999. The redevelopment of Rotterdam since 1945, *Planning Perspectives*, vol 14, no 3, pp 291–309.

McDougall, G 1979. The state, capital and land: the history of town planning revisited, *International Journal of Urban and Regional Research*, vol 3, no 3, pp 361–80.

McKay, DH and Cox, AW 1979. *The Politics of Urban Change*, Beckenham: Croom Helm.

McKelvey, B 1963. *The Urbanization of America 1860–1915*, New Brunswick NJ: Rutgers University Press.

McKelvey, B 1968. *The Emergence of Metropolitan America 1915–1966*, New Brunswick NJ: Rutgers University Press.

McLoughlin, JB 1969. *Urban and Regional Planning: A Systems Approach*, London: Faber.

McLoughlin, JB 1992. *Shaping Melbourne's Future?: Town Planning, the State, and Civil Society*, Cambridge University Press.

McMillan, JF 1992. *Twentieth Century France: Politics and Society 1898–1991*, London: Arnold.

McNeill, D 1999. *Urban Change and the European Left: Tales from the New Barcelona*, London: Routledge.

Meller, H 1990. *Patrick Geddes: Social Evolutionist and City Planner*, London: Routledge.

Meller, H 1995. Philanthropy and public enterprise: international exhibitions and the modern town planning movement, 1889–1913, *Planning Perspectives*, vol 10, no 3, pp 295–310.

Meller, H 2001. *European Cities 1890–1930s: History, Culture and the Built Environment*, Chichester: Wiley.

Melotte, B 1993. Margaret Anne Feilman: An Australian Planning Pioneer, in Freestone (ed), *op cit*, 162–7.

Mens, N 1997. Rotterdam 1928 general expansion plan, in Bosma and Hellinga (eds), *op cit*, vol II, pp 200–7.

Merlin, P 1971. *New Towns: Regional Planning and Development*, London: Methuen; originally published as *Les Villes Nouvelles* (1969), Presses Universitaires de France, Paris.

Metzger, JT 1994. Rebuilding Harlem: public housing and urban renewal, 1920–1960, *Planning Perspectives*, vol 9, no 3, pp 255–96.

Metzger, JT 2001. The failed promise of a festival market place: South Street Seaport in lower Manhattan, *Planning Perspectives*, vol 16, no 1, pp 25–46.

Meyer, H 1999. *City and Port: Transformation of Port Cities London, Barcelona, New York, Rotterdam*, Utrecht: International Books.

MHPPN [Ministry of Housing and Physical Planning, Netherlands] 1970. *The "Randstad": The Urbanized Zone of the Netherlands*, The Hague: Information Service.

Middleton, M 1991. *Cities in Transition: The Regeneration of Britain's Inner Cities*, London: Michael Joseph.

Miliutin, NA 1974. *Sotsgorod: the Problem of Building Socialist Cities*, Cambridge MA: MIT Press.

Miller, M 1989. *Letchworth: The First Garden City*, Chichester: Phillimore.

Miller M 1992. *Raymond Unwin: Garden Cities and Town Planning*, Leicester University Press.

Miller, M and Gray, AS 1992. *Hampstead Garden Suburb*, Chichester: Phillimore.

MLCERG [Max Lock Centre Exhibition Research Group] 1996. *Max Lock 1909–1988: An Exhibition of his Life and Work*, London: University of Westminster.

Molema, J 1996. *The New Movement in the Netherlands 1924–1936*, Rotterdam: 010 Publishers.

Monclús, FJ 1996. Barcelona: urban discourse and planning strategies 1897–1923, in HUPHA/ IPHS (ed), *op cit*, vol 1, pp 295–310.

Morgan, EP 1991. *The 60s Experience: Hard lessons about Modern America*, Philadelphia: Temple University Press.

Morison, I 2000. The corridor city: planning for growth in the 1960s, in Hamnett and Freestone (eds), *op cit*, pp 113–30.

MT [Ministry of Transport] 1963. *Traffic in Towns: A Study of the Long Term Problems of Traffic in Urban Areas: Reports of the Steering Group and Working Group appointed by the Minister of Transport*, London: HMSO.

Mulder, S 1997. Cologne 1923: Generalsiedlungsplan, in Bosma and Hellinga (eds), *op cit*, vol II, pp 192–9.

Mullin, JR 1978. German new towns: perspectives and overview, in G Golany (ed), *International Urban Growth Policies: New Town Contributions*, pp 129–46, New York: Wiley.

Mumford, E 1995. The "tower in a park" in America: theory and practice, 1920–1960, *Planning Perspectives*, vol 10, no 1, pp 17–41.

Mumford, E 2000. *The CIAM Discourse on Urbanism, 1928–1960*, Cambridge MA: MIT Press.

Mumford, L 1961. *The City in History: Its Origins, its Transformations and its Prospects*, New York: Harcourt Brace.

National Board of Housing, Building and Planning 1995. *Sweden 2009 – A Spatial Vision: Comprehensive Summary*, Karlskrona: National Board of Housing, Building and Planning.

Negrier, E 1993. Montpellier: international competition and community access, in Bianchini and Parkinson (eds), *op cit*, pp 135–54.

Neill, WJV, Fitzsimmons, DS and Murtagh, B 1995. *Reimaging the Pariah City: Urban Development in Belfast and Detroit*, Aldershot: Avebury.

Neill, WJV and Schwedler, H-U (eds) 2001. *Urban Planning and Cultural Inclusion: Lessons from Belfast and Berlin*, Basingstoke: Palgrave.

Nettlefold, JS 1908. *Practical Housing*, Letchworth: Garden City Press.

Nettlefold, JS 1914. *Practical Town Planning*, London: St Catherine Press.

Newman, P 1992. The re-birth of Perth's suburban railways, in Hedgcock and Yiftachel (eds), *op cit*, pp 174–87.

Newman, P nd c1998. *From Symbolic Gesture to the Mainstream: Next Steps in Local Sustainability*, reproduced in <wwwistp.murdoch.edu.au/community/spn/spn_pap1.html >

Newman, P and Kenworthy, J 1989. Gasoline dependence and cities: a comparison of US cities with a global survey, *Journal of the American Planning Association*, vol 55, pp 24–37.

Newman, P and Thornley, A 1996. *Urban Planning in Europe: International Competition, National Systems and Planning Projects*, London: Routledge.

Niitani, Y 1992. Town planning in Nagoya – reconstruction plan and projects for war-damaged areas, *CPIJ Newsletter*, no 6.

Nishiyama, Y 1992. Land adjustment and Japanese town planning, *CPIJ Newsletter*, no 6.

Noguchi, K 1988. Construction of Ginza Brick Street and conditions of house owners, in Ishizuka and Ishida (eds), *op cit*, pp 76–82.

Noin, D and White, P 1997. *Paris*, Chichester: Wiley.

North, RN and Hardwick, WG 1992. Vancouver since the Second World War: an economic geography, in G Wynn and T Oke (eds), *Vancouver and Its Region*, pp 200–33, Vancouver: UBC Press.

Nowlan, KI 1989. The evolution of Irish planning, 1934–1964, in Bannon (ed), *op cit*, pp 71–85.

Nuti, LP 1988. Public and private interest in new town planning: the case of Italy 1922–1942, *Planning Perspectives*, vol 3, no 1, pp 81–98.

Nyström, L 1996. *Living in Sweden – Between Tradition and Vision*, Karlskrona: National Board of Housing, Building and Planning, Urban Environment Council.

O'Connor, TH 1993. *Building a New Boston: Politics and Urban Renewal 1950–1970*, Boston: Northeastern University Press.

Obitsu, H and Nagase, I 1998. Japan's urban environment: the potential of technology in future city concepts, in GS Golany, K Hanake and O Koide (eds), *Japanese Urban Environment*, pp 324–36, Oxford: Pergamon.

Olds, K 2001. *Globalization and Urban Change: Capital, Culture and Pacific Rim Mega-Projects*, Oxford University Press.

Olmsted, FL 1870. Public parks and the enlargement of towns, Boston: American Social Science Association; reprinted in LeGates and Stout (eds), *op cit*, no pagination.

Olmsted, FL 1997; edited by SB Sutton. *Civilizing American Cities: Writings on City Landscapes*, New York: Da Capo.

Omura, K 1988a. Nazi city planning, in CPIJ (ed), *op cit*, 126–7.

Omura, K 1988b. New trends in city planning – West Berlin, in CPIJ (ed), *op cit*, pp 250–3.

Osborn, FJ and Whittick, A 1977. *The New Towns: Their Origins, Achievements and Progress*, London: Leonard Hill.

Pace, S 1993. Solidarity on easy terms: the INA-Casa plan 1948–1949, *Rassegna*, no 54, pp 20–7.

PAG [Planning Advisory Group] 1965. *The Future of Development Plans*, London: HMSO.

Pahl-Weber, E and Schubert, D 1991. Myth and reality in National Socialist town planning and architecture: housing and urban development in Hamburg, 1933–45, *Planning Perspectives*, vol 6, no 2, pp 161–88.

Palà, M and Subirós, O (eds) 1996. *1856–1999 Contemporary Barcelona Contemporanea*, Barcelona: Centre de Cultura Contemporània de Barcelona.

Parkinson, M, Foley, B and Judd, D (eds) 1988: *Regenerating the Cities: The UK Crisis and the US Experience*, Fulbright Papers no 4, Manchester University Press/Fulbright Commission.

Park Lee, S 2001. Conflicting élites and changing values: designing to historic districts in downtown Seattle, 1958–73, *Planning Perspectives*, vol 16, no 3, pp 243–68.

Parsons, DW 1986. *The Political Economy of British Regional Policy*, London: Croom Helm.

Parsons, KC 1992a. American influence on Stockholm's post World War II suburban expansion, *Planning History*, vol 14, no 1, pp 3–14.

Parsons, KC 1992b. British and American community design: Clarence Stein's Manhattan transfer, 1924–1974, *Planning Perspectives*, vol 7, no 2, pp 211–33.

Parsons, KC (ed) 1998. *The Writings of Clarence S Stein, Architect of the Planned Community*, Baltimore: Johns Hopkins University Press.

Pass, D 1973. *Vällingby and Farsta – From Idea to Reality: The New Community Development Process in Stockholm*, Cambridge MA: MIT Press.

Paterson, AB 1995. *The Works of 'Banjo' Paterson*, Ware: Wordsworth Editions.

Patterson, J 1998. *Grand Expectations: The United States 1945–1974*, New York: Oxford University Press.

Patterson, J 1999. *America in the Twentieth Century: A History* (fifth edition), Fort Worth: Harcourt.

Paul, J 1990. Reconstruction of the city centre of Dresden: planning and building during the 1950s, in Diefendorf (ed), *op cit*, pp 170–89.

Pawlowski, CF 1993. *Tony Garnier: pionnier de l'urbanisme du XXe, siècle* (second edition), Lyon: Les Créations du Pelican.

Peel, M 1995. *Good Times, Hard Times: The past and the future in Elizabeth*, Melbourne: Melbourne University Press.

Perks, WT 1985. Idealism, orchestration and science in early Canadian planning: Calgary and Vancouver re-visited 1914/1928, *Environments*, vol 17, no 2, pp 1–27.

Perry, CA 1929. The Neighborhood Unit, in Regional Survey of New York and its Environs, vol VII, *Neighborhood and Community Planning*, New York: Committee on Regional Plan of New York and its Environs, pp 22–140.

Perry, CA 1939. *Housing for the Machine Age*, New York: Russell Sage Foundation.

Peterson, JA 1983a. The city beautiful movement: forgotten origins and lost meanings, in Krueckeberg (ed), *op cit*, pp 40–57.

Peterson, JA 1983b. The impact of sanitary reform upon American urban planning, 1840–1890, in Krueckeberg (ed), *op cit*, pp 13–39.

Peterson, JA 1996. Frederick Law Olmsted Sr and Frederick Law Olmsted Jr: the visionary and the professional, in MC Sies and C Silver (eds), *Planning the Twentieth Century American City*, pp 37–54, Baltimore: Johns Hopkins University Press.

Phillips, WRF 1996. The 'German example' and the professionalization of American and British city planning at the turn of the century, *Planning Perspectives*, vol 11, no 2, pp 167–84.

PHS [Project Hammarby Sjöstad] 1999. *Hammarby Sjöstad: Architecture*, Stockholm: Project Hammarby Sjöstad.

Pinkney, J 1958. *Napoleon III and the Rebuilding of Paris*, Princeton University Press.

Pinol, J-L (ed) 1996. *Atlas Historiques des Villes de France*, Paris/Barcelona: Hachette/Centre de Cultura Contemporània de Barcelona.

Pinon, P 1995. L'Haussmanisation: réalité et perception en Europe, in Lortie (ed), *op cit*, pp 43–8.

Piron, O 1994. 1943–1993: Un anniversaire oublié, *Études Foncières*, no 62, pp 34–6.

Pitt-Morrison, M and White, J (eds) 1979. *Western Towns and Buildings*, Nedlands: University of Western Australia Press.

434

Plunz, R 1990. *A History of Housing in New York City: Dwelling Type and Social Change in the American Metropolis*, New York: Columbia University Press.

Polledri, P (ed) 1990. *Visionary San Francisco*, Munich: Prestel.

Poole, M 1979. Town planning, in Pitt-Morrison and White (eds), *op cit*, pp 220–32.

Porritt, J and Winner, D 1988. *The Coming of the Greens*, pp 203–23, London: Fontana.

Pouvreau, B 2000. Claudius-Petit, maire de Firminy, in Architecture et Maîtres d'Ouvrage (ed), *op cit*, pp 68–74.

Proudfoot, H 2000. Founding cities in nineteenth century Australia, in Hamnett and Freestone (eds), *op cit*, pp 11–26.

Pulzer, P 1995. *German Politics 1945–1995*, Oxford University Press.

Purdom, CB 1925. *The Building of Satellite Towns: A Contribution to the Study of Town Development and Regional Planning*, London: Dent.

Purdy, S 1997. Industrial efficiency, social order and moral purity: housing reform thought in English Canada, 1900–1950, *Urban History Review*, vol XXV, no 2, pp 30–40.

Rabinow, P 1995. *French Modern: Norms and Forms of the Built Environment*, University of Chicago Press.

Rådberg, J 1994. *Den Svenska Trädgårdsstaden*, Stockholm: Byggforskningsrådet.

Radford, G 1996. *Modern Housing for America: Policy Struggles in the New Deal Era*, University of Chicago Press.

Radio National 1996. *New Urban Myths*; transcript of broadcast, 10 November 1996, reproduced in <www.abc.net.au/talks/bbing/stories/s10622.htm>

Rasmussen, SE 1948. *London: The Unique City* (revised edition), London: Cape.

Ravetllat, PJ 1996. Future Barcelona, in Palà and Subirós, *op cit*, pp 86–97.

Ravetz, A 1974a. *Model Estate: Planned Housing at Quarry Hill*, London: Croom Helm.

Ravetz, A 1974b. From working class tenement to modern flat: local authorities and multi-storey housing between the wars, in A Sutcliffe (ed), *Multi-Storey Living: The British Working Class Experience*, pp 122–50, London: Croom Helm.

Read, J 1978. The garden city and the growth of Paris, *Architectural Review*, no 113, pp 345–52.

Reid, A 2000. *Brentham: A History of the Pioneer Garden Suburb 1901–2001*, Ealing: Brentham Heritage Society.

Reps, JW 1965. *The Making of Urban America*, Princeton University Press.

Reps, JW 1991. *Washington on View: The Nation's Capital since 1790*, Chapel Hill: University of North Carolina Press.

Reps, JW 1997. *Canberra 1912: Plans and Planners of the Australian Capital Competition*, Melbourne University Press.

Reulecke, J 1984. The Ruhr: centralization versus decentralization in a region of cities, in A Sutcliffe (ed), *Metropolis 1890–1940*, pp 381–402, London: Mansell.

Rey, H 1996. *La Peur des Banlieues*, Paris: Presses de la Fondation Nationale des Science Politiques.

Reynolds, J 1983. *The Great Paternalist: Titus Salt and the Growth of Nineteenth Century Bradford*, London: Temple Smith.

Reynolds, JP 1952. Thomas Coglan Horsfall and the town planning movement in England, *Town Planning Review*, vol XXII, no 1, pp 52–66.

Richardson, BW 1876. *Hygeia: A City of Health*, London: Macmillan; reprinted in LeGates and Stout (eds), *op cit*, no pagination.

Roberts, GK (ed) 1999. *The American Cities and Technology Reader: Wilderness to Wired City*, London: Routledge.

Roberts, GK and Steadman, P 1999. *American Cities and Technology: Wilderness to Wired City*, London: Routledge.

Roberts, J 1992. *Changed Travel – Better World? A Study of Travel Patterns in Milton Keynes and Almere*, London: TEST.

Robertson, KA 1997. Downtown retail revitalization: a review of American downtown strategies, *Planning Perspectives*, vol 12, no 4, pp 383–402.

Robson, B 1988. *Those Inner Cities: Reconciling the Economic and Social Aims of Urban Policy*, Oxford: Clarendon Press.

Rodgers, DT 1998. *Atlantic Crossings: Social Politics in a Progressive Age*, Cambridge MA: Harvard University Press.

Rogers [Lord Rogers of Riverside] 1999. *Towards an Urban Renaissance: Final Report of the Urban Task Force Chaired by Lord Rogers of Riverside*, London: Spon.

Rogers, R 1997; edited by P Gumuchdjian. *Cities for a Small Planet*, London: Faber.

RPA [Regional Plan Association] 1936. *Information Bulletin no 33: The Freeway, a Modern Highway for General Traffic in Metropolitan Areas*, New York: Regional Plan Association.

RPA 1937. *Information Bulletin no 35: Great Progress on Regional Highway System Revealed in Region-Wide Survey*, New York: Regional Plan Association.

RPA 1938. *From Plan to Reality Two: Eight Years of Progress on the Regional Development of New York and its Environ, with a Detailed Report of Those Projects That Have Realized or Officially Adopted in the Four Years, 1933–1936, Inclusive*, New York: Regional Plan Association.

RPFPTD [Regional Planning Federation of the Philadelphia Tri-State District] 1932. *The Regional Plan of the Philadelphia Tri-State District*, Philadelphia: Regional Planning Federation.

Rubenstein, JM 1978. *The French New Towns*, Baltimore: Johns Hopkins University Press.

Rudberg, E 1999. *The Stockholm Exhibition 1930: Modernism's Breakthrough in Swedish Architecture*, Stockholm: Stockholmia Förlag.

Russell, B 1981. *Building Systems, Industrialization and Architecture*, London: Wiley.

Salvadó, T and Miró, JM 1996. The appendages of the city of the kidneys, in Palà and Subirós, *op cit*, pp 134–49.

Sandercock, L 1975. *Cities for Sale*, Melbourne University Press.

Sandercock, L 1998. The death of modernist planning: radical praxis for post-modern age, in Douglass and Friedmann (eds), *op cit*, pp 163–84.

Satoh, S 1988a. Den-en Toshi, Inc. and Dojunkai, in CPIJ (ed), *op cit*, pp 46–7.

Satoh, S 1988b. National capital region development plan, in CPIJ (ed), *op cit*, pp 44–5.

Satoh, S 1988c. Development with citizen participation, in CPIJ (ed), *op cit*, pp 212–13.

Saunier, P-Y 1999. Changing the city: urban international information and the Lyon municipality, *Planning Perspectives*, vol 14, no 1, pp 19–48.

Schaffer, D 1988. *Two Centuries of American Planning*, London: Mansell.

Schlereth, TJ 1994. Burnham's *plan* and Moody's *manual*: city planning as progressive reform, in Krueckeberg (ed), *op cit*, pp 133–61.

Schlusche, G 1997. Berlin – strategies for a changing city, *Urban Design Quarterly*, issue 63 (July); reproduced in <www.rudi.net>.

Schnaidt, C 1965. *Hannes Meyer: Bauten, Projekte und Schriften*, London: Tiranti.

Schubert, D 1995. Origins of the neighbourhood units idea in Great Britain and Germany: examples from London and Hamburg, *Planning History*, vol 17, no 3, 32–40.

Schubert, D 1997. *Stadterneuerung in London und Hamburg: Eine Stadtebaugeschichte zwischen Modernisierung und Disziplinierung*, Wiesbaden: Vieweg.

Schubert, D 2000. The neighbourhood paradigm: from garden cities to gated communities, in Freestone (ed), *op cit*, 118–38.

Schumpeter, JA 1939. *Business Cycles: A Theoretical, Historical and Statistical Account of the Capitalist Process* (2 volumes), New York: McGraw-Hill.

Schuyler, D 1997. The new urbanism and the modern metropolis, *Urban History*, vol 24, no 3, pp 344–58.

Schwagenscheidt, W 1964. *Die Nordweststadt: Idee und Gestaltung [The Nordweststadt: Conception and Design]*, Stuttgart: Karl Krämer Verlag.

*436*

Scott, M 1969. *American City Planning Since 1890.* Berkeley: University of California Press.

Sellier, H and Bruggeman, A 1927. *Le Problème du Logement: Son Influence sur les Conditions de l'Habitation et d'Aménagement des Villes,* Paris: Universitaire de Paris/Carnegie Foundation.

Serratosa, A, Solans, J A and Pié, R 1996. The general metropolitan plan of Barcelona, in Palà and Subirós (eds), *op cit,* pp 201–9.

Sewell, J 1993. *The Shape of the City: Toronto Struggles With Modern Town Planning,* Toronto University Press.

Shanks, M 1977. *Planning and Politics: The British Experience, 1960–1976,* London: Political and Economic Planning/Allen and Unwin.

Shapira, P, Masser, I and Edgington, DW (eds) 1994. *Planning for Cities and Regions in Japan* (a *Town Planning Review* special study) Liverpool University Press.

Sharp, T 1940. *Town Planning,* Harmondsworth: Penguin.

Shelton, B 1999. *Learning from the Japanese City,* London: Spon.

Sherwood, DH 1994. Canadian Institute of Planners, *Plan Canada Special Edition* (July), pp 20–1.

Shoji, S 1988. Enzo Ohta and reconstruction work after the great Kanto earthquake, in Ishizuka and Ishida (eds), *op cit,* pp 92–5.

Sidenbladh, G 1964. Planning problems in Stockholm, in *Stockholm Regional and City Planning,* pp 55–64, Stockholm: Planning Commission of the City of Stockholm.

Sies, MC and Silver, C (eds) 1996. *Planning the Twentieth Century American City,* Baltimore: Johns Hopkins University Press.

Simkhovitch, MK 1994; introduction by SM Wirka. Housing, in Krueckeberg (ed), *op cit,* pp 85–111.

Simon, ED 1937. *Moscow in the Making,* London: Longmans.

Simpson, M 1985. *Thomas Adams and the Modern Planning Movement: Britain, Canada and the United States,* London: Mansell.

Sitte, C 1965 [1889]; trans GR Collins and CC Collins. *City Planning According to Artistic Principles,* London: Phaidon Press.

Skeffington Committee 1969. *People and Planning: Report of the Committee on Public Participation in Planning,* London: HMSO.

Skilleter, KJ 1993. The role of public utility societies in early British town planning and housing reform, 1901–36, *Planning Perspectives,* vol 8, no 2, pp 125–65.

Smales, L and Whitney, D 1996. Inventing a better place: urban design in Leeds in the post-war era, in G Haughton and CG Williams (eds), *Corporate city? Partnership, participation and partition in urban development in Leeds,* pp 199–218, Aldershot: Avebury.

Smets, M 1977. *L'Avènement de la Cité-Jardin en Belgique: Histoire de l'Habitat Social en Belgique de 1830 à 1930,* Bruxelles: Pierre Mardaga.

Smets, M 1987. Belgian reconstruction after World War I: a transition from civic art to urban planning, *Planning Perspectives,* vol 2, no 1, pp 1–26.

Smets, M 1995. *Charles Buls: Les Principes de l'Art Urbain,* Liège: Pierre Mardaga.

Smets, M (ed) 1985. *Resurgam: La reconstruction en Belgique après 1914,* Leuven: Crédit Communal.

Smith, PJ 1986. American influences and local needs: adaptations to the Alberta planning system in 1928–1929, in AFJ Artibise and GA Stelter (eds), *Power and Place: Canadian Urban Development in the North American Context,* pp 109–32, Vancouver: University of British Columbia Press.

Smith, PJ 1991. Coping with mega-mall development: an urban planning perspective on West Edmonton Mall, *The Canadian Geographer,* vol 35, no 3, pp 295–305.

Smyth, H 1994. *Marketing the City: Flagship Developments in Urban Regeneration,* London: Spon.

Soane, J 1999. Dresden: its destruction and rebuilding 1945–1985, in A Clayton and A Russell (eds), *Dresden: A City Reborn*, Oxford: Berg.

Soria y Mata, A 1996; trans MD Gonzalez. *The Linear City*, Stanford: Stanford University Program on Urban Studies; reprinted in LeGates and Stout (eds), *op cit*, no pagination.

Soria y Puig, A 1995. Ildefonso Cerdá's general theory of urbanización, *Town Planning Review*, vol 66, no 1, pp 15–40.

Spann, EK 1996. *Designing Modern America: The Regional Planning Association of America and Its Members*, Columbus: Ohio State University Press.

Spence-Sales, H 1956. Urban growth and its problems, in Canadian Federation of Mayors and Municipalities (CFMM), *Forecast of Urban Growth Problems and Requirements 1956–1980: A Brief Submitted to the Royal Commission on Canada's Economic Prospects*, Montreal: CFMM, Section M.

*Stadtforum* 1999. Number 36, special issue: Future of the City – Berlin in the 21st Century.

Stannage, T 1996. *Lakeside City: The Dreaming of Joondalup*, Nedlands: University of Western Australia Press.

Stansfield, K 1981. Thomas Sharp 1901–1978, in Cherry (ed), *op cit*, 150–176.

Starkie, DA 1982. *The Motorway Age: Roads and Traffic Policies in Post-War Britain*, Oxford: Pergamon.

Steenhuis, M 1997. Paris 1934 plan d'aménagement de la région Parisienne, in Bosma and Hellinga (eds), *op cit*, vol II, pp 226–33.

Stein, CS 1958. *Toward New Towns for America* (second edition), Liverpool University Press.

Stephenson, G 1992; edited by C de Marco. *On a Human Scale: A Life in City Design*, Fremantle Arts Centre/Liverpool University Press.

Stephenson, G and Hepburn, JA 1955. *Plan for the Metropolitan Region Perth and Fremantle*, Perth: Western Australian Government Printing Office.

Stephenson, RB 1997. *Visions of Eden: Environmentalism, Urban Planning and City Building in St Petersburg, Florida, 1900–1995*, Columbus: Ohio State University Press.

Stieber, N 1998. *Housing Design and Society in Amsterdam: Reconfiguring Urban Order and Identity, 1900–1920*, Chicago: University of Chicago Press.

*Stockholm Regional and City Planning* 1964. Stockholm: Planning Commission of the City of Stockholm.

Stokes, R and Hill, R 1992. The evolution of metropolitan planning in Western Australia, in Hedgecock and Yiftachel (eds), *op cit*, pp 111–30.

Strobel, RW 1998. Socialist Realism in East Germany: The Importation of Stalin's Urban Design; paper delivered at the seminar 'Imported or Exported Urbanism', Beirut, Lebanon.

Stroschein, C 1994. *Metropole Berlin*, Berlin: Land Berlin.

Stübben, J 1885; trans by WH Searles, 1893. Practical and aesthetic principles for the laying-out of cities; reproduced in <www.library.cornell.edu/Reps/DOCS>

Stynen H 1985. Le rôle des institutions, in Smets (ed), *op cit*, pp 99–127.

Subias, X 1996. Urban planning of 1953–1970, in Palà and Subirós (eds), *op cit*, pp 180–1.

Süchting, W and Weiss, P 2001. A new plan for Berlin's inner city: planwerk innenstadt, in Neill and Schwedler (eds), *op cit*, pp 69–84.

Sundman, M 1991. Urban planning in Finland after 1850, in Hall (ed), *op cit*, pp 60–115.

Sureshha, B 1998. Urban waterfront development patterns: an integrated design structure, in Freestone (ed), *op cit*, pp 836–41.

Sutcliffe, A 1970. *The Autumn of Central Paris, The Defeat of Town Planning 1850–1970*, London: Arnold.

Sutcliffe, A 1981. *Towards the Planned City: Germany, Britain, the United States and France 1780–1914*, Oxford: Blackwell.

Sutcliffe, A 1988. Britain's first town planning act: a review of the 1909 achievement, *Town Planning Review*, vol 59, no 3, pp 289–303.

438

Sutcliffe, A 1993. *Paris: An Architectural History*, New Haven CT: Yale University Press.

Sutcliffe, A (ed) 1974. *Multi-Storey Living: The British Working Class Experience*, London: Croom Helm.

Sutcliffe, A 1980 (ed). *The Rise of Modern Urban Planning, 1800–1914*, London: Mansell.

Sutcliffe, A (ed) 1981. *British Town Planning: The Formative Years*, Leicester University Press.

Sutcliffe, A (ed) 1984. *Metropolis 1890–1940*, London: Mansell.

Suzuki, S 1988. Urban planning in Tokyo during the 1960s, in Ishizuka and Ishida (eds), *op cit*, pp 120–4.

Swenarton, M 1981. *Homes Fit For Heroes: The Politics and Architecture of Early State Housing in Britain*, London: Heinemann.

Swenarton, M 1985. Sellier and Unwin, *Planning History Bulletin*, vol 7, no 2, pp 50–7.

Tarn, JN 1973. *Five Per Cent Philanthropy: An Account of Housing in Urban Areas Between 1840 and 1914*, Cambridge University Press.

Taverne, ERM 1990. The Lijnbaan (Rotterdam): a prototype of a postwar urban shopping centre, in Diefendorf (ed), *op cit*, pp 145–54.

Taylor, J 1996. Whose plan? Planning in Canada's capital after 1945, in HUPHA/IPHS (ed), *op cit*, vol 2, pp 781–94.

Tetlow, JD 1959. Sources of the neighbourhood idea, *Journal of the Town Planning Institute*, vol XLV, no 5, pp 113–15.

Thomas, JL 1994. Lewis Mumford, Benton MacKaye and the regional vision, in Krueckeberg (ed), *op cit*, pp 265–309.

Thompson-Fawcett, M 1998. Leon Krier and the organic revival within urban policy and practice, *Planning Perspectives*, vol 13, no 2, pp 167–94.

Thornley, A 1991. *Urban Planning Under Thatcherism: The Challenge of the Market*, London: Routledge.

Tilman, H 1997. The Dutch metropolitan region: the Randstad, in Bosma and Hellinga (eds), *op cit*, vol 1, pp 76–85.

TIPHC [Third International Planning History Conference] 1988. *The History of International Exchange of Planning Systems*, Tokyo: City Planning Institute of Japan/Planning History Group.

Tisdall, C and Bozzolla, A 1977. *Futurism*, London: Thames and Hudson.

TMG [Tokyo Metropolitan Government] 1994. *A Hundred Years of Tokyo City Planning*, TMG Municipal Library no 28, Tokyo: TMG.

Todd, K 1988. A history of roundabouts in the United States and France, *Transportation Quarterly*, vol 42, no 4, pp 599–623.

Tonell, L 1997. Swedish urban planning – Stockholm: transformation and decentralization, in Bosma and Hellinga (eds), *op cit*, vol II, pp 42–9.

Toulier, B 1999. *Architecture et Patrimoine du XXe Siècle en France*, Paris: Éditions du Patrimoine.

TPI [Town Planning Institute] 1956. *The British Planner Abroad*, London: Town Planning Institute.

Tregenza, J 1986. Charles Reade: town planning missionary, in Hutchings and Bunker (eds), *op cit*, pp 45–59.

Tripp, HA 1942. *Town Planning and Road Traffic*, London: Arnold.

Tudor-Walters Committee 1918. *Report of the Committee to Consider Questions of Building Construction in Connection with the Provision of Dwellings for the Working Classes in England and Wales, and Scotland* (Cd 9191), London: HMSO.

Unwin, R 1909. *Town Planning in Practice: An Introduction to the Art of Designing Cities and Suburbs*, London: Fisher Unwin.

Unwin, R 1912. *Nothing Gained by Overcrowding: How the Garden City Type of Development May Benefit Both Owner and Occupier*, London: GCTPA.

*Urbanisme* 1999. Number 309, Special Issue: Le XXe Siècle: De la Ville à L'Urbain – Chronique Urbanistique et Architecture de 1900–1999.

Uthwatt Committee 1942. *Final Report of the Expert Committee on Compensation and Betterment* (Cmd 6386), London: HMSO.

UVG [Urban Villages Group] 1992. *Urban Villages: A Concept for Creating Mixed Use Urban Development on a Sustainable Scale*, London: Urban Villages Group.

Uyttenhove, P 1985. Les efforts internationaux pour une Belgique moderne, in Smets (ed), *op cit*, pp 32–68.

Uyttenhove, P 1990a. Continuities in Belgian wartime reconstruction planning, in Diefendorf (ed), *op cit*, pp 48–63.

Uyttenhove, P 1990b. L'Entente Franco-Belge et le premier enseignement d'urbanisme en France, in Gaudin (ed), *op cit*, pp 21–31.

Uyttenhove, P 1990c. The garden city education of Belgian planners around the First World War, *Planning Perspectives*, vol 5, no 4, pp 271–93.

Vale, B 1995. *Prefabs : A History of the UK Temporary Housing*, London: Spon.

van der Cammen, H 1988. Randstad Holland: growth and planning of a ring of cities, in H van der Cammen (ed), *Four Metropolises in Western Europe: Development and Urban Planning of London, Paris, Randstad Holland and the Ruhr Region*, pp 118–175, Assen/Maastricht: Van Gorcum.

van der Cammen, H (ed) 1988. *Four Metropolises in Western Europe*, op cit.

van der Heiden, CN 1988. Foreign influence on Dutch planning doctrine, in TIPHC, *op cit*, pp 89–112.

van der Kruit, C 1997. Lyon 1904: cité industrielle, in Bosma and Hellinga (eds), *op cit*, vol II, pp 154–9.

van der Meijden, J nd c1996. *Pays-Bas, le projets vinex: Le cas d'Utrecht et Vleuten-de-Meern*, reproduced in <www.urbanisme.equipement.gouv.fr/cdu/accueil/elabproj/vinex.htm>

van der Wal, C 1997. *In Praise of Common Sense: Planning the Ordinary. A physical planning history of the new towns in the Ijsselmeerpolders*, Rotterdam: 010 Publishers.

van Es, E 1997. Milton Keynes 1970: plan for Milton Keynes, in Bosma and Hellinga (eds), *op cit*, vol II, pp 330–7.

van Hoogstraten, D 1997. Paris 1965: schéma directeur d'aménagement et d'urbanisme de la région de Paris, in Bosma and Hellinga (eds), *op cit*, vol II, pp 324–9.

van Rooijen, M 1989. The garden city ideology in the Netherlands: the political debates on garden cities and green towns 1910–1935, *Planning History*, vol 11, no 3, pp 8–12.

van Roosmalen, P 1997. Le Havre 1946: plan for the reconstruction, in Bosma and Hellinga (eds), *op cit*, vol II, pp 266–73.

Vaysierre, B 2000. Les hommes du MRU, in Architecture et Maîtres d'Ouvrage (ed), *op cit*, pp 21–3.

Venturi, R, Brown, DS and Izenour, S 1972. *Learning from Las Vegas*, Cambridge MA: MIT Press.

Vlassenrood, L 1997. Stockholm 1952: generalplan för Stockholm, in Bosma and Hellinga (eds), *op cit*, vol II, pp 290–97.

Voldman, D 1989. Urban reconstruction in France after World War II, *Planning History*, vol 11, no 2, pp 13–17.

Voldman, D 1990. Reconstructors' tales: an example of the use of oral sources in the history of reconstruction after the Second World War, in Diefendorf (ed), *op cit*, pp 16–30.

Voldman, D 1991a. Reconstruire sous le bombes (1940–1944), in Archives Nationales (ed), *op cit*, pp 225–9.

Voldman, D 1991b. 1945: Reconstruire des villes en Béton ou en Grès Rose des Vosges?, in Archives Nationales (ed), *op cit*, pp 267–76.

440

Voldman, D 2000. Le Ministère de la Reconstruction et de l'Urbanisme, in Architecture et Maîtres d'Ouvrage (ed), *op cit*, pp 19–20.

Volle, J-P and Lacave, M 1996. Montpellier, in J-L Pinol (ed), *op cit*, pp 204–29.

Vollerin, A 1999. *Histoire de l'Architecture et de l'Urbanisme à Lyon au XXe Siècle*, Lyon: Editions Mémoire des Arts.

von Beyme, K 1990. Reconstruction in the German Democratic Republic, in Diefendorf (ed), *op cit*, pp 190–208.

von Hertzen and Speiregen, PD 1973. *Building a New Town: Finland's New Garden City – Tapiola* (revised edition), Cambridge MA: MIT Press.

von Petz, U 1990a. Margarethenhöhe, Essen: garden city, worker's colony or satellite town?, *Planning History*, vol 12, no 2, pp 3–9.

von Petz, U 1990b. Urban renewal under National Socialism, practical policy and political objectives in Hitler's Germany, *Planning Perspectives*, vol 5, no 2, pp 169–187.

von Petz, U 1996. Berlin after 1989: the renewal of a capital, in HUPHA/IPHS (ed), *op cit*, vol 2, pp 540–9.

von Petz, U 1997a. The German metropolitan region – the Ruhr basin: toward a new spatial policy, in Bosma and Hellinga (eds), *op cit*, vol I, pp 56–65.

von Petz, U 1997b. Ruhr basin 1920: Wirtschaftsplan für den Ruhrkohlenbezirk, in Bosma and Hellinga (eds), *op cit*, vol II, pp 184–91.

von Petz, U 1999. Robert Schmidt and the public park policy in the Ruhr district, 1900–1930, *Planning Perspectives*, vol 14, no 2, pp 163–82.

Wagenaar, C 1993. Rotterdam and the model of the welfare city, *Rassegna*, no 54, pp 42–9.

Walker, M, Kabos, A and Weirick, J 1994. *Building for Nature: Walter Burley Griffin and Castlecrag*, Castlecrag NSW: Walter Burley Griffin Society Incorporated.

Ward, SV 1986. Planmaking versus implementation: the example of list Q and the depressed areas 1922–1939, *Planning Perspectives*, vol 1, no 1, pp 3–26.

Ward, SV 1988. *The Geography of Interwar Britain: The State and Uneven Development*, London: Routledge.

Ward, SV 1992. The garden city introduced, in SV Ward (ed), *The Garden City: Past, Present and Future*, pp 1–27, London: Spon.

Ward, SV 1994. *Planning and Urban Change*, London: Paul Chapman.

Ward, SV 1997. A paradoxical persistence? British influences on Canadian and Australian urban planning, in Barker (ed), *op cit*, pp 51–60.

Ward, SV 1998. *Selling Places: The Marketing and Promotion of Towns and Cities 1850–2000*, London: Spon.

Ward, SV 1999. The international diffusion of planning: a review and a Canadian case study, *International Planning Studies*, vol 4, no 1, pp 53–77.

Ward, SV (ed) 1992. *The Garden City: Past, Present and Future*, London: Spon.

Watanabe, SJ 1980. Garden city Japanese style: the Case of Den-en Toshi Company Ltd, 1918–1928, in Cherry (ed), *op cit*, 129–143.

Watanabe, SJ 1984. Metropolitanism as a way of life: the case of Tokyo, 1868–1930, in Sutcliffe (ed), *op cit*, pp 403–30.

Watanabe, SJ 1988. Japanese vs western urban images: western influences on the Japanese architectural profession 1910s–1920s, *Proceedings of the Third International Planning History Conference*, pp 568–84, Tokyo.

Watanabe, SJ 1990. Toward fruitful international co-operation, *CPIJ Newsletter*, no 3 (April), p 1.

Watanabe, SJ 1992. The Japanese garden city, in Ward (ed), *op cit*, pp 69–87.

Watanabe, SJ 1996. The 1995 Kobe earthquake and its reconstruction planning: a historical analysis, in HUPHA/IPHS (ed), *op cit*, vol 2, pp 723–35.

Watanabe, SJ 1998. Changing paradigm of the Japanese urban planning system, in Freestone (ed), *op cit*, pp 947–52.

Weaver, J 1979. The property industry and land-use controls: the Vancouver experience, 1910–1945, *Plan Canada*, vol 19, no 3, pp 211–25.

Webb, MJ 1979. Urban expansion, town improvement and the beginning of town planning in metropolitan Perth, in Gentilli (ed), *op cit*, pp 359–82.

Webber, P (ed) 1988. *The Design of Sydney: Three Decades of Change in the City Centre*, Sydney: Law Book Co.

Werquin, A-C and Demangeon, A 1995. Chicago et Daniel Burnham, l'inconditionnel d'Haussmann, in Lortie (ed), *op cit*, pp 168–76.

White, DA 1988. Frederick Law Olmsted, the placemaker, in Schaffer, *op cit*, pp 87–112.

White, RB 1971. *Prefabrication: A History of its Development in Great Britain*, London: HMSO.

Whitham, D 1994. Drancy revisited, *Planning History*, vol 16, no 1, pp 29–34.

Whittick, A (ed) 1980. *Encyclopaedia of Urban Planning*, Huntingdon NY: Krieger.

Wiebenson, D 1970. *Tony Garnier: The Cité Industrielle*, London: Studio Vista.

Wilks, J 1993. The (incomplete) professionalization of planning in Victoria 1940–1985, in Freestone (ed), *op cit*, pp 84–93.

Williams, K, Burton, E and Jenks, M (eds) 2000. *Achieving Sustainable Urban Form*, London: Spon.

Williams, RH 1996. *European Union Spatial Policy and Planning*, London: Paul Chapman.

Williamson, ML (ed) 1997. *Greenbelt: History of a New Town 1937–1987 New 1997 Edition Including the Sixth Decade 1987–1997*, Virginia Beach: Donning.

Wilson, WH 1980. The ideology, aesthetics and politics of the city beautiful movement, in Sutcliffe (ed), *op cit*, pp 166–98.

Wilson, WH 1983. Moles and skylarks, in Krueckeberg (ed), *op cit*, pp 88–121.

Wilson, WH 1988. The Seattle park system and the ideal of the city beautiful, in Schaffer, *op cit*, pp 113–37.

Wilson, WH 1989. *The City Beautiful Movement*, Baltimore: Johns Hopkins University Press.

Winston, D 1957. *Sydney's Great Experiment*, Sydney: Angus and Robertson.

Wirka, SM 1996. The city social movement: progressive women reformers and early social planning, in Sies and Silver (eds), *op cit*, pp 55–74.

Wohl, AS 1974. *The Eternal Slum: Housing and Social Policy in Victorian London*, London: Arnold.

Wohl, AS 1983. *Endangered Lives: Public Health in Victorian London*, London: Dent.

Wojtowicz, R 1996. *Lewis Mumford and American Modernism: Eutopian Theories for Architecture and Urban Planning*, New York: Cambridge University Press.

Wolfe, JM 1994. Our common past: an interpretation of Canadian planning history, *Plan Canada* Special Edition (July), pp 12–34.

Woodbridge, SB 1990. Visions of renewal and growth: 1945 to the present, in Polledri (ed), *op cit*, pp 119–51.

Woods, S 1975. *The Man in the Street: A Polemic on Urbanism*, Harmondsworth: Penguin.

Wright, G 1983. *Building the Dream: A Social History of Housing in America*, Cambridge MA: MIT Press.

Wright, G 1991. *The Politics of Design in French Colonial Urbanism*, Chicago University Press.

Wright, M 1982. *Lord Leverhulme's Unknown Venture*, London: Hutchinson.

Wrigley, RL 1983. The plan of Chicago, in DA Krueckeberg (ed), *op cit*, pp 58–72.

Wynn, G and Oke, T (eds) 1992. *Vancouver and Its Region*, Vancouver: UBC Press.

Wynn, M 1984a. Spain, in M. Wynn (ed) *Planning and Urban Growth in Southern Europe*, pp 111–64, London: Mansell.

Wynn, M 1984b. Spain, in M Wynn (ed), *Housing in Europe*, pp 121–54, Beckenham: Croom Helm.

Wynn, M (ed) 1984. *Planning and Urban Growth in Southern Europe*, London: Mansell.

*442*

Yasuda, T and Terauchi, M 1996. Dai Osaka (Greater Osaka) movement and planning as a capital of economic activities in inter-war period Japan, in HUPHA/IPHS (ed), *op cit*, vol 1, pp 150–9.

Yelling, JA 1986. *Slums and Slum Clearance in Victorian London*, London: Allen and Unwin.

Yelling, JA 1992. *Slums and Redevelopment: Policy and Practice in England, 1918–45*, London: UCL Press.

Young, B 1988. Darling harbour: a new city precinct, in Webber (ed), *op cit*, pp 190–213.

Zetter, J 1994. Challenges for Japanese urban policy, in Shapira, Masser and Edgington (eds), *op cit*, pp 25–32.

# WEBSITES

This list consists only of websites actually cited in the text (or containing material cited in the bibliography). A cautionary note is necessary because websites are not fixed entities. The ones listed here were visited during the period 1999–2001, and checked in June 2001 shortly before the book was delivered. In general, I have given the minimum information consistent with finding the reference cited. As noted at the head of the bibliography, readers requiring further information are welcome to contact the author.

<www.abc.net.au/rn/talks/bbing/stories/s10622.htm> Australian Broadcasting Corporation, transcript of New Urban Myths, broadcast 10 November 1996.

<www.arch.umanitoba.ca/la_www/sustainable> Sustainable community design, Faculty of Architecture, University of Manitoba, Canada.

<www.archined.nl/vinexonsite> VINEX Onsite, located on the website of the Architectural Institute of the Netherlands.

<www.bm30.es> Bilbao Metropoli-30: Association for the Revitalisation of Metropolitan Bilbao, Spain.

<www.centro.life.de> CentrO shopping and leisure complex, Oberhausen, Germany.

<www.city.toronto.on.ca/waterfront> City of Toronto, Canada, waterfront renewal plan.

<www.city.vancouver.nc.ca> City of Vancouver, Canada.

<www.cnu.org> Congress for the New Urbanism, USA.

<www.docklands.com.au> Melbourne Docklands Authority, Australia.

<www.dro.amsterdam.nl> Amsterdam physical planning department, the Netherlands.

<www.feedmag.com/re/re114.2.html> Feed magazine, interview with Rem Koolhaas on Berlin's reconstruction.

<www.frw.uva.nl/ame/pub/bolan.dutch.htm> Amsterdam Centre for the Study of the Metropolitan Environment, University of Amsterdam, paper by Richard Bolan.

<www.greenparties.org> Green Parties of the United States.

<www.gruene.de> Germany Green Party.

<www.gvrd.bc.ca> Greater Vancouver Regional District, Canada.

<www.hafencity.com> Hamburg Hafen City (harbour redevelopment) agency, Germany.

<www.hammarbysjostad.stockholm.se> Project Hammarby Sjöstad, Stockholm, Sweden.

<www.hud.gov> United States Government Department of Housing and Urban Development.

<www.iaurif.org> Paris regional planning agency (IAURIF), France.

<www.iclei.org/egpis> International Council for Local Environmental Initiatives, examples of good practice.

<www.info.tsukuba.org> Tsukuba Science City, Japan.

<www.library.cornell.edu/Reps/DOCS> Urban Planning, 1794–1918: An international anthology of articles, conference papers and reports, selected by Professor John W Reps, Cornell University, USA.

<www.lrta.org> Light Rail Transit Association, UK.

<www.mallofamerica.com> Mall of America, Bloomington, Minnesota, USA.

<www.marseilles.com> Marseilles official website, France.

<www.metropolis.org> Metropolis organisation.

<www.oecd.org> Organization for Economic Co-operation and Development.

<www.orestad.dk> Ørestad, Copenhagen, Denmark.

<www.padcoinc.com> Planning and Development Collaborative International Incorporated, USA.

<www.qimtl.qc.ca> Quartier Internationale, Montreal, Canada.

<www.rudi.net> Resource for Urban Design Information, UK.

<www.smartgrowth.org> Smart Growth network, USA.

<www.stadtentwicklung.berlin.de> Berlin Senat Department of Urban Development, Germany.

<www.worldteleport.org> World Teleport Association.

<www.unchs.org> United Nations Centre for Human Settlements (Habitat).

<www.urbanisme.equipement.gouv.fr> French planning ministry.

<www.usaid.gov> United States Agency for International Development.

<www.urbanistes.com> Société Française des Urbanistes (SFU), France.

<www.verts.imaginet.fr> French Green Party.

<www.ville.montreal.qc.ca> City of Montreal, Canada.

<www.westedmontonmall.com> West Edmonton Mall, Edmonton, Alberta, Canada.

<wwwistp.murdoch.edu.au> Institute for Sustainability and Technology, Murdoch University, Perth, Australia.

# INDEX

470